Depictio

viewing (A) is to find a blue letter of an B. The task

find a green *T*.

Brooks/Cole Publishing Company
Pacific Grove, California

Brooks/Cole Publishing Company

A Division of Wadsworth, Inc., Belmont, California 94002.

© 1994 by Wadsworth, Inc., Belmont, California 94002. A̲l̲l̲ ̲r̲i̲g̲h̲t̲s̲ ̲r̲e̲s̲e̲r̲v̲e̲d̲. No part of this book may be reproduced, stored in a retrieval system, or transcribed, in any form or by any means—electronic, mechanical, photocopying, recording, or otherwise—without the prior written permission of the publisher, Brooks/Cole Publishing Company, Pacific Grove, California 93950.

Printed in the United States of America

10 9 8 7 6 5 4 3 2

Library of Congress Cataloging-in-Publication Data

Galotti, Kathleen M., [date]
  Cognitive psychology in and out of the laboratory / Kathleen M. Galotti.
    p. cm.
  Includes bibliographical references and index.
  ISBN 0-534-21054-6
  1. Cognitive psychology. 2. Cognition. I. Title.
BF201.G35 1994
153—dc20   93-26748
                                                                  CIP

Sponsoring Editor: Vicki Knight
Editorial Assistant: Lauri Banks Ataide
Production Editor: Laurel Jackson
Production Assistant: Tessa A. McGlasson
Manuscript Editor: Lynne Fletcher/Betty Seaver
Permissions Editor: Lillian Campobasso
Interior and Cover Design: Katherine Minerva
Cover Illustration:Morris Louis, Beta Cappa, Gift of Marcella Louis Brenner, © 1993 National Gallery of Art,
  Washington
Art Coordinator: Susan Haberkorn
Interior Illustration: Matrix Communications Inc.
Photo Editor: Diana Mara Henry
Typesetting: University Graphics, Inc.
Cover Printing: Southeastern Color Graphics
Printing and Binding: Arcata Graphics/Fairfield

Credits continue on p. 525

THIS BOOK IS PRINTED ON
ACID-FREE RECYCLED PAPER

For Lloyd, for all the adventures;

For Timothy, for the biggest one yet;

and

For Tandy, Bussey, and Eskie, for sharing in it all

Kathleen M. Galotti holds a B.A. in psychology and economics from Wellesley College, as well as an M.A. and Ph.D. in psychology and an M.S.E. in computer and information sciences from the University of Pennsylvania. At Carleton College, she is an associate professor of psychology and currently serves as chair of the Psychology Department. She also helped to establish, and served as the first coordinator of, an interdisciplinary program in cognitive studies.

Dr. Galotti is the author or coauthor of numerous studies in cognitive and developmental psychology. Her research centers on the development of reasoning and decision-making skills from the preschool period through adulthood.

In her spare time, Dr. Galotti, with her husband's help, raises and trains Bernese Mountain Dogs and shows them in competition in licensed obedience trials.

BRIEF CONTENTS

CONTENTS

PREFACE

Cognitive psychology is a challenging area in which to do research. The subject matter is exciting: it raises questions about how the mind works—how we perceive people, events, and things; how and what we remember; how we mentally organize information; how we call on our mental information and resources to make important decisions. These questions have fascinated me for years.

For me, even more of a challenge than doing research is teaching cognitive psychology to undergraduate students while conveying to them my own excitement about the field. Although cognitive psychologists find topics within the area deeply puzzling, important, and stimulating to think about, some students regard these topics as boring or mechanical. My primary goals in writing this book were to address this perceptual gap and to show the relationships between elegant, sophisticated theoretical models and everyday cognitive experiences. To attain these goals, I have used many examples drawn from personal experience.

A textbook author can choose either to be comprehensive and strive for encyclopedic coverage or to be selective and omit many worthwhile topics and studies. I hope to have struck a balance between these extremes but must confess to a preference for the latter. Again, this reflects my own teaching goals; I like to supplement textbook chapters with primary literature from journals. I have tried to keep chapters relatively short in the hope that instructors will supplement the text with other readings. My firm belief is that the best courses are those in which instructors are enthusiastic about the material; the relative brevity of the text is intended to encourage instructors to supplement and customize it with added coverage on topics they find especially interesting.

Finally, I hope to encourage instructors and students alike to consider cognitive phenomena as having contexts that both foster and constrain their occurrence. Too often, topics in cognitive psychology are presented as absolute, unchanging aspects of everyone's experience. Recent work in developmental psychology, cross-cultural psychology, and individual differences strongly suggests that this presentation is at best, oversimplification; at worst, fiction. I hope newer work in cognitive psychology can retain its rigor and elegance but can frame questions and issues more inclusively, reflecting a recognition of the ways in which people and situations differ, as well as share similarities.

This book is intended for a one-semester or one-term course for students who have already completed an introductory psychology course. The book is organized into five parts. The first, containing the introductory chapter, locates the field historically, theoretically, and methodologically. In Part I, I introduce the major schools of thought that underlie the field of cognitive psychology. Part II is a review of topics that would generally be regarded as core aspects of cognition: perception, attention, and memory. The emphasis in these chapters is to review both the "classic" studies that define the field and the newer approaches that challenge long-standing assumptions. The focus of Part III is on knowledge representation and organization. These chapters focus on questions of how we mentally represent and store the vast amounts of information we acquire throughout our lives. Part IV covers topics such as reasoning and decision-making perhaps more extensively than in other books, probably due to my own research interests. In these chapters, I have tried to draw several connections between laboratory-based models and real-world problems.

Part V is the one that departs most from a "prototypical" cognitive psychology textbook. The last two chapters, on individual differences and cross-cultural approaches, include material not often covered in cognitive psychology courses. I feel strongly that these topics belong with a thorough examination of cognitive phenomena. Although it is true that traditional cognitive psychologists don't always consider these issues in their work, I believe they ought to and, in the future, will.

Acknowledgments

The actual writing of this book has been a 5-year project. However, the groundwork for the book evolved over 15 years, stretching back to my own undergraduate and graduate education. I was fortunate to have benefited from the rigorous and dynamic teaching of Blythe Clinchy at Wellesley College and of Jonathan Baron, John Sabini, and Henry and Lila Gleitman at the University of Pennsylvania. My education and thinking about cognitive and developmental issues continues to profit from interactions with colleagues at Carleton College, particularly Lloyd Komatsu, Steve Kozberg, and Peter Guthrie.

One of the real joys of working at Carleton has been the privilege of teaching some incredibly talented, motivated, and energetic students. Many of them volunteered to read parts of this book and provide me with feedback from a student's point of view. For doing so, and especially for resisting the temptation to gloat over their prof's spelling errors and grammatical or logical lapses, I thank Alex Boyer, Sara Brose, Terri Huston, Andrea Matchett, Dan Simons, and James Whitney. Melissa Mark read every chapter and prepared extensive commentary on each one, and therefore deserves special mention and gratitude. Other current and former Carleton students helped me with the mundane but necessary tasks of checking references or writing for permissions, including Stephanie Aubry, Julie Greene, Simin Ho, Kitty Nolan, Scott Staupe, Jennifer Tourjé, Elizabeth White, and James Whitney. My two secretaries, Ruby Hagberg and Marianne Elofson, and their student assistants—Karen Dawson, Ruby Eddie-Quartey, Lareina Ho, and Aimee Mayer—helped me with the author index.

Carleton College has supported this project through a sabbatical and two summer faculty development grants. Dean Roy Elveton enthusiastically endorsed this endeavor from the start and found ways to fund it. He has returned from the "dark side" of administrative duties to become a most trusted mentor and colleague in the Cognitive Studies Program and Philosophy Department at Carleton. Much of the early work on the book was completed during a sabbatical leave spent at the Claremont Graduate School and Pomona College. Colleagues there, including Bill Banks, Dale Berger, Mary Gauvain, and Kathy Pezdek, provided a stimulating and productive environment in which to write.

I owe a special debt to Vicki Knight, my editor at Brooks/Cole. Her wise counsel, sharp sense of humor, love of animals, and excellent taste in restaurants has made this project one I've looked forward to working on. Her knowledge of psychology and its pedagogy never ceases to astound me. Vicki took over this project from Phil Curson and thus was "stuck with" it, but she never made me feel like a burden and never stinted on her time and encouragement. I am extremely grateful to have had the chance to work so closely with such a gifted individual. Lauri Banks Ataide, Susan Haberkorn, Carline Haga, Diana Mara Henry, Laurie Jackson, Tessa A. McGlassum, and Katherine Minerva have all displayed much graciousness and patience in working with a novice author. Nancy Ashmore, publications director at St. Olaf College and a close friend, provided almost all the photographs. She found ways of putting on film ideas that I could only describe imprecisely—and did it all without ever losing her characteristic calm demeanor! Thanks, Nancy.

The following reviewers all provided useful commentary and feedback on portions of the book at various stages of completion: Sharon Armstrong, Central College (Pella, IA); Terry Au, University of California, Los Angeles; Ira Fischler, University of Florida; John H. Flowers, University of Nebraska–Lincoln; Margery Lucas, Wellesley College; Robert Seibel; Steven M. Smith, Texas A & M University; and Margaret Thomas, University of Central Florida. Other colleagues, including Jonathan Baron, Michael Flynn, and Kenneth Schweller also provided extensive comments on one or more chapters. The remaining gaps and shortcomings in the book reflect my own stubbornness.

The most important source of professional and personal support throughout this project remains to be thanked. Lloyd Komatsu, my husband, colleague, collaborator, coach, cheerleader, and fellow dog-lover, has made innumerable contributions throughout the project. He has read and commented on several chapters, argued numerous points, brainstormed, and celebrated each milestone of the book's progress. His professional and personal integrity, commitment to teaching, broad background in the field, and general cleverness have helped me focus my energy, develop a sound professional philosophy, and keep the project in perspective. I am both humbled and grateful to have so much of his energy and support.

—*Kathleen M. Galotti*

PART

I

Overview

CHAPTER 1

Traditions Within Cognitive Psychology

This book is about cognitive psychology—that branch of psychology concerned with how people acquire, store, transform, use, and communicate information. Put differently, cognitive psychology deals with our mental life—what goes on inside our heads when we perceive, attend, remember, think, categorize, reason, decide, and so forth. To get a better feel for the domain of cognitive psychology, let's consider a few examples of cognitive activity.

You're walking along a dark, unfamiliar city street. It's raining and foggy, and you are cold and a bit apprehensive. As you walk past a small alley, you catch some movement out of the corner of your eye. You turn to look down the alley and start to make out a shape coming toward you. As the shape draws nearer, you are able to make out more and more features and you suddenly realize that it's . . .

What cognitive processes are going on in this admittedly melodramatic example? In general, this example illustrates the initial acquisition and processing of information. In particular, the cognitive processes depicted include **attention,** mentally focusing on some stimulus (the mysterious shape); **perception,** interpreting sensory information to yield meaningful information; and **pattern recognition,** classifying a stimulus into a known category. In recognizing the shape as something familiar, you no doubt called on **memory,** the storage facilities and retrieval processes of cognition. All of this processing occurred rapidly, probably within a few seconds or less. Most of the cognitive processing in this example appears so effortless and automatic that we usually take it for granted.

An ordinary activity, such as reading a map, involves a great deal of cognitive processing.

Here's another example.

You're in a crowded, public place, such as a shopping mall during the holiday season. Throngs of people push past you, and you're hot and tired. You head for a nearby bench, aiming to combine some rest with some people-watching. As you make your way, a young woman about your age jostles up against you. You both offer polite apologies ("Oh, excuse me!" "Sorry!"), glancing at each other as you do. She immediately exclaims, "Oh, it's you! How *are* you? I never thought I'd run into anyone I know here—can you believe it?" You immediately paste a friendly but vague smile on your face, to cover your frantic mental search: Who *is* this woman? She looks familiar, but why? Is she a former classmate? Did you and she attend camp together? Is she saying anything you can use as a clue to place her?

This example illustrates your use of memory processes, including **recognition** (you see the woman as familiar) and **recall** (you try to determine where you know her from). Other cognitive processes are involved here, too, although they play a lesser role. For instance, you perceive the entity talking to you as a person, specifically a woman, more specifically a vaguely familiar woman. You pay attention to her. You may be using various **reasoning** and **problem-solving** strategies or techniques to try to figure out who she is. Your success or failure at this task may also depend on your mental organization of the knowledge you have accumulated in your lifetime—your **knowledge representation.** To communicate with her, you use **language** as well as nonverbal cues or signals. Eventually, you'll have to decide how to deal with the situation—will you admit your forgetfulness, or will you try to cover it up?

As these two examples demonstrate, our everyday lives involve a great deal of cognition. Furthermore, this everyday cognition is complex, often involving several cognitive processes. We tend to remain unaware of this complexity, however, because much of our cognitive processing occurs so often, so rapidly, and with so little effort that we may not even know that it is taking place.

In both of the preceding examples, several cognitive processes were occurring either simultaneously or very closely in time. In fact, specifying in either of these examples exactly how many cognitive processes occurred or in what sequence is hard. This uncertainty typifies everyday situations—so much is going on so quickly that we can't be sure of even what information is being received or used.

How, then, can cognition be studied with any precision? This kind of problem is one all scientists face—how to study a naturally occurring phenomenon with sufficient experimental rigor to draw firm conclusions. The answer, for many, is to try to isolate the phenomenon and bring it (or some stripped-down version of it) into the laboratory. The challenge, then, is to decide what is essential and what is inessential about the phenomenon under study.

For example, in studying how memory works, psychologists have often used experiments in which people are presented with lists of words or nonsense syllables while variables such as the complexity, length, frequency, meaningfulness, relatedness, and rate of presentation of items on the list, along with the state of alertness, expertise, practice, and interest of the research subjects are controlled or systematically varied. The experimenters' assumption is that though in everyday life people do not encounter material to be remembered in this manner, the processes of memory work in essentially the same ways in laboratory experiments as in everyday life.

A corollary assumption is that factors that increase or decrease performance in the laboratory will also increase or decrease performance under less-controlled conditions. So, if increasing the number of items to be remembered decreases memory performance in a laboratory, then having to remember more information in an everyday situation would also be expected to be more difficult than remembering less under the same circumstances.

The key challenge for all scientists, however, is to make sure that the laboratory tasks they develop really do preserve the essential workings of the processes under study. The most rigorously controlled experiment is of at best limited value if the phenomenon being studied does not occur or occurs in significantly different ways outside the laboratory. Unfortunately, there is no simple or guaranteed way to ensure that laboratory tasks model everyday tasks. Therefore, students and other "consumers" of science must take a critical stance when considering how experimental situations apply to everyday ones. Throughout this book, we will be looking at how laboratory models do or don't accurately describe, explain, and predict cognitive processing in real life. We will also consider how situational and personal factors, such as people's level of development, personality variables, degree of expertise, gender, and cultural background, affect cognitive processing.

Before we discuss specific cognitive processes, however, an overview of the field of cognitive psychology will provide a useful framework within which to consider specific topics, experiments, and findings in the field. We will first examine the historical roots of cognitive psychology to see how the field has developed. Next, we'll look at traditional and common research methods used in cognitive psychology. Finally, we'll consider three **paradigms,** or schools of thought, that represent the current streams of thought in the field.

A Brief History of the Study of Cognition

A complete treatise on how modern cognitive psychology has evolved over the course of human history could fill several volumes, and would obviously be beyond our scope. Worth noting, however, is that several ideas about certain mental abilities date back to at least the Greek philosophers Aristotle and Plato (Murray, 1988). For example, both of these philosophers wrote extensively on the nature of memory. Plato, for instance, likened storing something in memory to writing on a wax tablet. In other writings, he compared the mind to an aviary in which many birds are flying, and memory retrieval to trying to catch a specific bird: sometimes you can, but other times you can grab only a nearby bird. Similarly, when I try to recall the name of the girl who sat behind me in third grade, I have trouble latching onto exactly the right one (was it Joan? Joanne? Anne?), but my choices are probably pretty close.

Other historians of psychology trace the field's roots to the philosophers of the 17th to 19th centuries, including John Locke, David Hume, John Stuart Mill, René Descartes, and Immanuel Kant. These philosophers also debated the nature of mind and knowledge, with Locke, Hume, and Mill following Aristotle and a more empiricist position, and Descartes and Kant aligning with Plato and a nativist position.

Briefly, **empiricism** rests on the tenet that knowledge comes from an individual's own experience. Empiricists recognize individual differences in genetics but emphasize human nature's malleable, or changeable, aspects. Empiricists believe that people are the way they are, and have the capabilities they have, largely because of previous learning. One mechanism by which such learning is thought to take place is through the mental **association** of two ideas. Locke (1964/1690) argued that two distinct ideas or experiences, having nothing to do with each other, could become joined in the mind simply because they happened to occur or to be presented to the individual at the same time. Empiricists accordingly believe that the environment plays a powerful role in determining one's intellectual (and other) abilities.

Nativism, by contrast, emphasizes the role of genetics over the role of learning in the acquisition of abilities and tendencies. Nativists attribute differences in individuals' abilities less to differences in learning than to differences in their original, biologically endowed capacities and abilities. Nativism is an important idea in cognitive psychology, as we will see in the chapters to come. "Hard-wired" functions such as short-term memory, for example, are attributed to innate structures of the human mind that are present in at least rudimentary form at birth and are not learned, formed, or created as a result of experience.

Interestingly, only in the last 120 years have central cognitive issues such as the nature of mind and the nature of information in the mind been seen as amenable to scientific psychological investigation. Indeed, until the 1870s, no one really thought to ask whether actual data could help resolve any of these questions. When people began doing so, experimental psychology was born. We will look next at different schools of experimental psychology that laid the foundations for cognitive psychology today.

Structuralism

Many students are surprised to find out that psychology as a formal discipline has been around for little more than a century. Historians often date the "founding" of the actual field of psychology back to 1879, when Wilhelm Wundt converted a laboratory to the first institute for research in experimental psychology (Fancher, 1979).

Wundt wanted to establish a "science of mind," to discover the laws and principles that explained our immediate conscious experience. In particular, Wundt wanted to identify the simplest essential units of the mind. In essence, he wanted to create a table of "mental elements," much like a chemist's periodic chart. Once the set of elements was identified, Wundt believed, psychologists could determine how these units combine to produce complex mental phenomena. Wundt foresaw an entire field devoted to the study of how systematically varying stimuli would affect or produce different mental states; he described this field in a volume entitled *Principles of Physiological Psychology* (Fancher, 1979).

Wundt and his students carried out hundreds of studies, many involving a technique of investigation called **introspection.** Although this term today connotes "soul-searching," Wundt's technique was much more focused. It consisted of presenting highly trained observers (usually graduate students) with various stimuli and asking them to describe their conscious experiences. Wundt assumed that the raw materials of consciousness were sensory in nature, and thus "below" the level of meaning. In particular, Wundt thought that any conscious thought or idea was the result of a combination of sensations that could be defined in terms of exactly four properties: *mode* (for example, visual, auditory, tactile, olfactory), *quality* (for example, color, shape, texture), *intensity,* and *duration.* Wundt's goal was to "cut through the learned categories and concepts that define our everyday experience of the world" (Fancher, 1979, p 140). Wundt believed strongly that with proper training, people could detect and report the workings of their own minds.

A student of Wundt, Edward B. Titchener, applied the term **structuralism** to his own endeavors as well as to Wundt's (Hillner, 1984). The term was meant to convey Wundt's focus on the content and structure of the mind rather than its function—how the mind works as opposed to why.

The method, unfortunately, proved problematic, as we'll see shortly. Nonetheless, modern cognitive psychologists owe Wundt more than a historical debt. A pioneer in the study of many cognitive phenomena, he was the first to approach cognitive questions scientifically, and the first to try to design experiments to test cognitive theories.

Functionalism

While Wundt was working in Leipzig, an American named William James was working to establish the new discipline of psychology in the United States. In many ways, Wundt and James were opposites. A prolific researcher who personally carried out or supervised hundreds of rigorous experiments, Wundt was not known for his interpersonal style. James (the brother of the writer Henry James), in contrast, carried out little original research but wrote eloquently of psychological findings and their relevance to everyday life (Fancher, 1979). His textbook *The Principles of Psychology* (1983/1890) is still highly regarded and widely cited today.

James regarded psychology's mission to be to explain our experience. Like Wundt, James was interested in conscious experience. Unlike Wundt, however, James was not interested in how the mind works—that is, its structure or content. Instead, he asked *why* the mind works the way it does. His assumption was that the way the mind works has a great deal to do with its *function:* the purposes of its various operations. Hence came the term **functionalism.**

James's writings, which introduced psychological questions to American academics, still offer food for thought to students and teachers of psychology, perhaps because they address so directly everyday life. Consider one of the best known chapters in his textbook, on "Habit." James saw habit as the "fly-wheel of society," a mechanism basic to keeping our behavior within bounds. James saw habits as inevitable and powerful, and drew from this a practical conclusion:

> Every smallest stroke of virtue or of vice leaves its never so little scar. The drunken Rip Van Winkle, in Jefferson's play, excuses himself for every fresh dereliction by saying, "I won't count this time!" Well! he may not count it, and a kind Heaven may not count it; but it is being counted none the less. Down among his nerve-cells and fibres the molecules are counting it, registering and storing it up to be used against him when the next temptation comes. (James, 1983/1890, Vol. 1, p. 131)

James's point, of course, is that people should take great care to avoid bad habits and establish good ones. He offered advice about how to do this, urging people to never allow an exception when trying to establish a good habit, to seize opportunities to act on resolutions, and to engage in a "little gratuitous effort" every day to keep the "faculty of effort" alive (James, 1983/1890, Vol. 1, p. 130).

Other American psychologists shared James's assumptions and approaches. Fellow functionalists such as John Dewey and Edward L. Thorndike, for example, shared James's conviction that the most important thing the mind did was to allow the individual to adapt to her or his environment. Functionalists drew heavily on Darwinian evolutionary theory and tried to extend biological conceptions of adaptation to psychological phenomena (Hillner, 1984).

Structuralists and functionalists differed in their methods as well as their focus. The structuralists were convinced that the proper setting for experimental psychology was the laboratory, where experimental stimuli could be stripped of their everyday meanings to determine the true nature of mind. Functionalists disagreed sharply with this approach, attempting instead to study mental phenomena in real-life situations. Their basic belief was that psychologists should study whole organisms in whole, real-life tasks (Hillner, 1984).

Behaviorism

You probably learned the terms *classical conditioning* and *instrumental conditioning* in your introductory psychology class. The Russian psychologist Ivan Pavlov used the first, and psychologists such as Edward Thorndike, the second, to explain psychological phenomena strictly in terms of observable stimuli and responses. In the United States, a school of psychology known as **behaviorism** took root in the 1930s, dominating academic psychology until well into the 1960s. Many regard it as a branch of functionalism (Amsel, 1989).

One of the general doctrines of behaviorism is that references to unobservable, subjective, mental states (such as consciousness) as well as to unobservable, subjective processes (such as expecting, believing, understanding, remembering, hoping for, deciding, perceiving) were to be banished from psychology proper, which behaviorists took to be the scientific study of behavior. Behaviorists rejected such techniques of study as introspection, which they found in principle to be untestable. John Watson described his view of what psychology was and wasn't most directly in an article published in 1913:

> Psychology as the behaviorist views it is a purely objective natural science. Its theoretical goal is the prediction and control of behavior. Introspection forms no essential part of its methods, nor is the scientific value of its data dependent upon the readiness with which they lend themselves to interpretation in terms of consciousness. The behaviorist, in his efforts to get a unitary scheme of animal response, recognizes no dividing line between man and brute. The behavior of man, with all of its refinement and complexity, forms only a part of the behaviorist's total scheme of investigation. (Watson, 1913, p. 158)

Why did behaviorists so disdain the technique of introspection? Mainly, because of its obviously subjective nature and its inability to resolve theoretical disagreements. Suppose of two observers presented with the same stimulus that one reports an experience of "greenness"; the other, an experience of "green-yellowness." Which one is correct? Is one misrepresenting or misinterpreting her experience? If no physiological cause (for example, color-blindness) explains the different reports, then the scientist is left with an unresolvable dispute. Titchener restricted his research subjects to graduate students trained to introspect "properly" (advising those who couldn't learn to do this to find another career). This, however, created more problems than it solved. The reasoning here is circular: How do we know that a particular sensation is a true building block of cognition? Because trained observers report it to be so. How do we know that the observers are trained? Because they consistently report that certain sensations and not others are the true elements of consciousness.

Watson, in fact, regarded all "mental" phenomena as reducible to behavioral and physiological responses. Such things as "images" and "thoughts," he believed, were the result of low-level activity of the glands or small muscles. In his first textbook, Watson cited evidence showing that when people report that they are "thinking," muscles in the tongue and larynx are actually moving slightly. Thought, for Watson, simply amounted to the perception of these muscle movements (Fancher, 1979).

Watson's contribution to cognitive psychology—the banishment of all "mental language" from use—was largely negative in character, insofar as he believed that the scientific study of mental phenomena was simply not possible. Watson and his followers did, however, encourage psychologists to think in terms of measures and research methods that moved beyond subjective introspection, thereby challenging later psychologists to develop more-rigorous and more-testable hypotheses and theories, as well as stricter research protocols.

B. F. Skinner (1984), psychology's best known behaviorist, took a different tack with regard to mental events and the issue of mental representations, arguing that such "mentalistic" entities as images, sensations, and thoughts should *not* be excluded simply because they are difficult to study. Skinner believed in the existence of images, thoughts, and the like and agreed that they were proper objects of study but objected to treating mental events and activities as fundamentally different from behavioral events and activities. In particular, he objected to hypothesizing the existence of **mental representations** (internal depictions of information), which he took to be internal copies of external stimuli. Skinner believed that such hypotheses would be of little help in explaining the causes of action and experience.

Other behaviorists were more accepting of the idea of mental representations. Edward Tolman, for example, believed that even rats have some goals and expectations. As he explained it, a rat learning to run a maze must have the goal of attaining food and must acquire an internal representation—some cognitive map or other means of depicting information "in the head" about the maze—to locate the food at the maze's end. (Tolman's specific terminology was "means-end-expectations as to the general spatial direction of the goal box" [Tolman, 1932, p. 118].) Tolman's work centered around demonstrating that animals had both expectations and internal representations that guided their behavior.

Gestalt Psychology

The school of **Gestalt psychology** began in 1911 in Frankfurt, Germany, at a meeting of three psychologists: Max Wertheimer, Kurt Koffka, and Wolfgang Köhler (Murray, 1988). As the name *Gestalt* (a German word that loosely translates to "configuration" or "shape") might suggest, their central assumption was that psychological phenomena could not be reduced to simple elements but, rather, had to be analyzed and studied in their entirety. Gestalt psychologists, who studied mainly perception and problem solving, believed that an observer did not construct a coherent perception from simple, elementary sensory aspects of an experience but instead apprehended the total structure of an experience as a whole.

As a concrete example, consider Figure 1-1. You will notice that (a), (b), and (c) contain the same elements—namely, eight equal lines. However, most people experience the three arrays quite differently, seeing (a) as four pairs of lines, (b) as eight unrelated lines, and (c) as a circle made up of eight line segments. The arrangement of lines, the relationships among the elements as a whole, plays an important role in determining our experience.

(A)

(B)

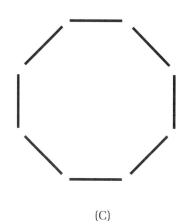

(C)

FIGURE 1-1.   Examples of Gestalt figures

The Gestalt psychologists thus rejected structuralism, functionalism, and behaviorism as offering incomplete accounts of psychological,
and, in particular, cognitive, experiences. The Gestalt psychologists chose
to study people's subjective experience of stimuli and to focus on how people use or impose structure and order on their experiences. They believed
that the mind imposes its own structure and organization on stimuli and, in

particular, that the mind organizes perceptions into *wholes* rather than discrete parts. These wholes tend to simplify stimuli. Thus, when we hear a melody, we experience not a collection of individual sounds but larger, more organized units—melodic lines.

Genetic Epistemology

Jean Piaget, a Genevan scientist known as a naturalist, philosopher, logician, educator, and developmental psychologist (Flavell, 1963) conducted studies of the cognitive development of infants, children, and adolescents that have also helped to shape modern cognitive psychology. Piaget's work was largely sympathetic to the Gestalt idea that the relationship between parts and wholes is a complex one. Piaget sought to describe the intellectual structures underlying cognitive experience at different developmental points, through an approach he called "genetic epistemology."

Piaget's observations of infants and children convinced him that a child's intellectual structures differ qualitatively from those of a mature adult. As he watched young children, for example, Piaget noticed that their assumptions about the numerosity of objects seemed to differ from those of an older child or adult. Specifically, young children seemed to believe that a row of, say, five buttons becomes more numerous if the row is simply spread out—an assumption that a 6- or 7-year-old will find laughable:

> Char [aged 4 years, 4 months] also began by making a compact row of 11 buttons to equal the 6 spaced out buttons of the model, then as his row was longer than the other he removed 3 from the end, thus obtaining the same length: "Are they the same?—*Yes.*—Exactly?—*Yes.*—(The 6 elements of the model were then put further apart, and the 8 in his copy were put closer together.) And now?—*There are more there* (the 6)." (Piaget, 1965, p. 75)

We will cover Piaget's work and theory in much more detail in Chapter 12.

The Study of Individual Differences

Yet another strand of the history of psychology is important to mention here, even though no particular "school" is associated with it: the investigations into **individual differences** in human cognitive abilities by Sir Francis Galton and his followers.

Galton, a half-cousin of Charles Darwin, inherited a substantial sum in his early twenties that afforded him the time and resources to pursue his interests. A child prodigy himself (he read and wrote by the age of 2 1/2, Galton trained in medicine and mathematics at Cambridge University, England. Like many of his fellow students (and many of today's college students), Galton felt a great deal of academic pressure and competitiveness and "was constantly preoccupied with his standing relative to his fellow students" (Fancher, 1979, p. 257). This strong preoccupation (which may have contributed to a breakdown he suffered at Cambridge) turned into a lifelong interest in the measurement of intellectual ability.

Galton's interest in intellectual differences among people stemmed in part from his reading of his cousin Charles Darwin's writings on evolution. Darwin believed that animals (including humans) evolved through a process he called natural selection, by which certain inherited traits are perpetuated because individuals possessing those traits are more likely to survive. Galton wondered whether intellectual talents could also be inherited.

Galton noticed that "intelligence" or "smartness" or "eminence" seemed to run in families; that is, smart parents appeared to produce smart children. Of course, this could be explained in terms of either genetics or environment (for example, intelligent parents may have greater resources to spend on their children's education). Thus, Galton's question of how large a role genetics plays in intelligence was a difficult one to answer. To address it, Galton put his mathematical training to use analyzing data (usually family trees of "eminent" men) and, later, inventing statistical tests, some of which are still in use today.

Galton (1907/1883) studied a variety of cognitive abilities, in each case focusing on ways of measuring the ability and then noting its variation among different individuals. Among the abilities he studied (in both laboratory and "naturalistic" settings) was mental imagery. He developed a questionnaire, instructing respondents to "think of some definite object—suppose it is your breakfast-table as you sat down this morning—and consider carefully the picture that rises before your mind's eye" (p. 58). He then asked: Is the image dim or clear? Are all of the objects in the image well defined? Does part of the image seem to be better defined? Are the colors of the objects in the image distinct and natural? Galton was surprised to discover much variability in this capacity: some subjects reported almost no imagery; others experienced images so vividly that they could hardly tell that they were images!

Galton left a large legacy to psychology, and to cognitive psychology in particular. His invention of tests and questionnaires to assess mental abilities inspired later cognitive psychologists to develop similar measures. His statistical analyses, later refined by other statisticians, allowed hypotheses to be rigorously tested. His work on mental imagery is still cited by current investigators. Most broadly, Galton's work challenged psychologists—both those who believed in the importance of genetic influences and those strongly opposed to the idea—to think about the nature of mental—that is, cognitive—abilities and capacities.

The "Cognitive Revolution"

Despite the early attempts to define and study mental life, psychology, especially American psychology, came to embrace the behaviorist tradition in the early to mid-1900s. A number of historical trends, both within and outside of academia, came together in the years during the following World War II to produce what many psychologists think of as a "revolution" in the field of cognitive psychology. The revolution was mainly a rejection of the behaviorist assumption that mental events and states were beyond the realm of scientific study or that mental representations did not exist.

One of the first of these historical trends was a product of the war itself: the establishment of the field of **human factors engineering.** During the war, military personnel had to be trained to operate complicated pieces of equipment. Engineers quickly found that they needed to design equipment (such as instrument operating panels, radar screens, communication devices) to suit the capacities of the people operating it.

Lachman, Lachman, and Butterfield (1979) offer an anecdote about why such problems were important to solve:

> One type of plane often crashed while landing. It turned out that the lever that the pilot had to use for braking was near the lever that retracted the landing gear. During landing, the pilot could not take his eyes off the runway: He had to work by touch alone. Sometimes pilots retracted their landing gear instead of putting on their brakes; they touched the ground with the belly of the plane at top speed. The best way to keep them from crashing was not to exhort them to be careful; they were already highly motivated to avoid crashing and getting killed. Improving training procedures was also an inefficient approach; pilots with many safe landings behind them committed this error as well as rookie pilots. The most reasonable approach was to redesign the craft's controls so that completely different arm movements were required for braking and for retracting the landing gear. (p. 57)[1]

Psychologists and engineers thus developed the concept of the man-machine system, now more accurately referred to as the person-machine system: the idea that machinery operated by a person must be designed to interact with the operator's physical, cognitive, and motivational capacities and limitations.

Psychologists in World War II also borrowed concepts, terminology, and analogies from communications engineering. Engineers concerned with the design of such things as telephones and telegraph systems talked about the exchange of information through various "channels" (such as telegraph wires and telephone lines). Different kinds of channels differ in how much information they can transmit per unit of time and how accurately. Psychologists learning of this work started to describe human beings as "communication channels," examining their capacities for receiving, sending, and processing information, and the circumstances under which they distort the information they receive. Humans were quickly seen to share properties with better known, inanimate communications channels and came to be described as **limited-capacity processors** of information.

---

[1]From *Cognitive Psychology and Information Processing: An Introduction,* by Lachman/Lachman/Butterfield. Copyright © 1974 by Lawrence Erlbaum Associates, Inc., Publishers. Reprinted by permission.

What does it mean to be a limited-capacity processor? As the name suggests, it means that people can do only so many things at once. When I'm typing, I find it difficult (actually, impossible) to simultaneously keep up my end of a conversation or read an editorial or follow a television news broadcast. Similarly, when I concentrate on balancing my checkbook, I can't also recite multiplication tables or remember all of the teachers I've had from kindergarten on. Although I can do some tasks at the same time (I can fold the laundry while I watch television), the number and kinds of things I can do at the same time are limited.

Many of the landmark studies of cognitive psychology—those that cognitive psychologists regard as "classics"—date from just after World War II and clearly focus on exploring the nature of our capacity limitations. George Miller, in his 1956 paper *"The Magical Number Seven, Plus or Minus Two,"* for instance, observed that (1) the number of unrelated things we can perceive distinctly without counting, (2) the number of unrelated things on a list we can immediately remember, and (3) the number of stimuli we can make absolute discriminations among is for most normal adults between five and nine. Miller's work thus exemplified how the limits of people's cognitive capacities could be measured and tested.

At about the same time, developments in the field of **linguistics,** the study of language, made clear that people sometimes had to process enormously complex information. Work by Noam Chomsky revolutionized the field of linguistics, and both linguists and psychologists began to see the study of how people acquire, understand, and produce language as of central importance to both fields. In addition, Chomsky's early work (1957, 1959, 1965) showed that behaviorism could not adequately explain language.

Consider the question of how language is acquired. A behaviorist might explain language acquisition as a result of a child's parents' reinforcing grammatical utterances and punishing (or at least not reinforcing) ungrammatical utterances. However, both linguists and psychologists soon realized that such an account had to be wrong. For one thing, psychologists and linguists who observed young children with their parents found that parents typically respond to the *content* rather than the *form* of the child's language utterances (Brown & Hanlon, 1970). For another, even when parents (or teachers) explicitly tried to correct children's grammar, they could not. Children seemed simply not to "hear" the problems, as is evident in the following dialogue:[2]

>**Child:** Nobody don't like me.
>**Mother:** No, say, "Nobody likes me."
>[eight repetitions of this dialogue]
>**Mother:** No, now listen carefully; say, *"Nobody likes me."*
>**Child:** Oh! Nobody don't likes me. (McNeill, 1966, p. 69)

[2]From "Developmental Psycholinguistics," by D. McNeill. In F. Smith and G. A. Miller (Eds.), *The Genesis of Language: A Psycholinguistic Approach,* pp. 15–84. Copyright © 1966 by The MIT Press. Reprinted by permission.

Chomsky's work thus posed a fundamental challenge to psychologists: here were human beings, already shown to be limited-capacity processors, acquiring what seemed to be an enormously complicated body of knowledge—language—quickly and using it easily. The evidence seemed to indicate that, however our minds are structured and whatever cognitive processes we use, these structures and processes must be capable of the complications of language. Reversing engineers' arguments that machines must be designed to fit people's capabilities, many linguists argued that the mind must have structures complex enough to process language.

Chomsky (1957, 1965) argued that underlying people's language abilities is an implicit system of rules, collectively known as a *generative grammar.* These rules allow speakers to construct, and listeners to understand, sentences that are "legal" in the language. For example, the sentence "Did you eat all the oat bran cereal?" is a legal, well-formed sentence, but "Bran the did all oat eat you cereal?" is not. Our generative grammar, a mentally represented system of rules, tells us this, because it can produce (generate) the first sentence but not the second.

Chomsky (1957, 1965) did not believe that all the rules of a language are consciously accessible to speakers of that language. Instead, he believed that the rules operate implicitly—we don't know exactly what the rules are, but we use them rather easily to produce understandable sentences and to avoid producing gobbledygook.

There is yet one more thread to the cognitive revolution to consider, also dating from about World War II: the development of computers and artificially intelligent systems. In 1936, a mathematician named Alan Turing wrote a paper describing universal machines—mathematical entities that were simple in nature but capable in principle of solving logical or mathematical problems. This paper ultimately led to what some psychologists and computer scientists call the computer metaphor—the comparison of people's cognitive activities to an operating computer.

Just as computers have to be fed data, people have to acquire information. Both computers and people often store information and must therefore have structures and processes that allow for such storage. People and computers often need to recode information—that is, change the way it is recorded or presented. People and computers must also otherwise manipulate information—transform it in some way, for example, by rearranging it, adding to or subtracting from it, deducing from it, and so on. Computer scientists working on the problem of **artificial intelligence** now study how to make computers that can solve the same kinds of problems humans can, and whether computers can use the same methods people apparently use to solve them.

Current Trends in the Study of Cognition

During the 1970s, researchers in different fields started to notice that they were investigating common questions: the nature of mind and of cognition; how information is acquired, processed, stored, and transmitted; how knowledge is represented. Scholars from fields such as cognitive psychology, computer science, philosophy, linguistics, neuroscience, and anthropology, recognizing their mutual interests, came together to found an interdisciplinary field known as **cognitive science.** Gardner (1985) even gives this field a birth date: September 11, 1956, when several of the founders of the field attended a symposium on information theory at MIT.

Gardner (1985) points out that the field of cognitive science rests on certain common assumptions. Most important among these is the assumption that cognition must be analyzed at what is called the level of representation. This means that cognitive scientists agree that cognitive theories will incorporate such constructs as symbols, rules, images, or ideas—in Gardner's words, "the stuff . . . found between input and output" (1985, p. 38). Thus, cognitive scientists focus on representations of information rather than on how nerve cells in the brain work or on historical or cultural influences.

A second school of thought has arisen in recent years. Practitioners of **cognitive neuropsychology** (Ellis & Young, 1988) study cognitive deficits in certain brain-damaged individuals. Ellis and Young (1988) describe, for example, a 19-year-old who lost his right arm in a motorcycle accident and sustained a severe head injury that left him in a coma for almost two weeks. Four years after his accident, P.H. appeared to have normal language abilities, including reading, and he tested normal in many short- and long-term memory tests. His IQ (91) also seemed normal. His head injury appeared to have caused at least one cognitive deficit, however:

> One of PH's problems was most resistant to rehabilitation; he could not recognize people's faces. As soon as a familiar person spoke he would know who it was but, to PH, all faces seemed unfamiliar. He could tell if a face belonged to a man or a woman, an old or a young person, and he could describe the general appearance and facial features reasonably accurately. But PH had no sense of recognising people who had previously been very familiar to him. In neuropsychological terms, his accident had left PH *prosopagnosic*—able to see, but unable to recognise once familiar faces. (Ellis & Young, 1988, pp. 1–2)

Cognitive neuropsychologists proceed by identifying individuals with certain patterns of brain damage and examining their cognitive performance. What cognitive processes can these individuals no longer perform? What cognitive activities have been spared? By finding answers to such questions, cognitive neuropsychologists might not only help certain individuals but they might better understand how everyone's cognitive processes operate.

General Points

Each of the schools of psychology described above has left a visible legacy to modern cognitive psychology. Structuralism set the question: what are the elementary units and processes of the mind? Functionalists reminded psychologists to focus on the larger purposes and contexts that cognitive processes serve. Behaviorists challenged psychologists to develop testable hypotheses and to avoid unresolvable debates. The Gestalt psychologists pointed out that an understanding of individual units would not automatically lead to an understanding of whole processes and systems. Piaget reminded cognitive psychologists to consider how cognition develops and evolves, while Galton demonstrated that individuals can differ in their cognitive processing. Developments in engineering, computer science, and linguistics have uncovered processes by which information can be efficiently represented, stored, and transformed, providing analogies and metaphors for cognitive psychologists to use in constructing and testing models of cognition. Work in cognitive neuropsychology has focused psychologists on the question of how cognitive processes are carried out in the brain. As we take up particular topics, we will see more of how cognitive psychology's different roots have shaped the field.

Keep in mind that cognitive psychology shares in the discoveries made in other fields, just as other fields share in the discoveries made by cognitive psychology. This sharing and borrowing of research methods, terminology, and analyses gives many investigators a sense of common purpose. It also all but requires that cognitive psychologists keep abreast of new developments in fields related to cognition.

Research Methods in Cognitive Psychology

Throughout this book, we will be reviewing different empirical studies of cognition. Before we plunge into those studies, however, we will look at some of the different kinds of studies cognitive psychologists conduct. The following descriptions do not exhaust all the studies a cognitive psychologist *could* conduct but should aquaint you with the major methodological approaches to cognitive psychology.

Naturalistic Observation

As the name suggests, **naturalistic observation** consists of an observer watching people in familiar, everyday contexts going about their cognitive business. For example, an investigator might watch as people try to figure out how to work a new automated teller machine (ATM) at an airport. Ideally, the observer remains as unobtrusive as possible, so as to disrupt or alter the behaviors being observed as little as possible. In the example above, for instance, the investigator might stand near the ATM and surreptitiously note what people who use it do and say. Being unobtrusive is much harder than it might sound. The observer needs to be sure that the people being observed are comfortable and do not feel as though they are "under a microscope." At the same time, the observer wants to avoid causing the people being observed to "perform" for the observer. In any case, the observer can hardly fully assess her or his own effects on the observation: after all, how can one know what people would have done had they not been observed?

Observational studies have the advantage that the things studied really do occur in the real world, and not just in an experimental laboratory. Psychologists call this property of studies **ecological validity.** Furthermore, the observer has a chance to see just how cognitive processes work in natural settings—how flexible they are, how they are affected by environmental changes, how rich and complex actual behavior is.

The disadvantage of naturalistic observation is a lack of **experimental control.** The observer therefore has no means of isolating the causes of different behaviors or reactions. All she can do is collect observations and try to discover relationships among them. However plausible different hypotheses may seem, the observer has no way of verifying them.

A second problem, one all scientists face, is that an observer's recordings are only as good as her initial plan for what is important to record. The settings and people she chooses to observe, the behaviors and reactions she chooses to record, the manner of recording, and the duration and frequency of observation—all influence the results and conclusions she can later draw.

Introspection

We have already seen one special kind of observation, dating back to the laboratory of Wilhelm Wundt. In the technique of introspection, as we have already seen, the observer observes his own mental processes. For example, subjects might be asked to solve complicated arithmetic problems without paper or pencil, and to "think aloud" as they do so. Introspection has all the benefits and drawbacks of other observational studies, plus a few more. One additional benefit is that observing one's own reactions and behavior might give one better insight into an experience and the factors that influenced it, yielding a richer, more complete picture than an outsider could observe.

But observing yourself is a double-edged sword. Though perhaps a better observer in some ways, you might also be more biased in regard to your own cognition. People observing their own mental processes might be more concerned with their level of performance and be motivated to subtly and unconsciously distort their observations. They might tend to try to make their mental processes appear more organized, logical, thorough, and so forth, than they actually are. They might be unwilling to admit when their cognitive processes seem flawed or random. Moreover, with some cognitive tasks (especially demanding ones), observers might have few resources left with which to observe and record.

Controlled Observation and Clinical Interviews

As the term **controlled observation** suggests, this method gives researchers a little more influence over the setting in which observations are conducted. Investigators using this research method try to standardize the setting for all participants, in many cases, manipulating specific conditions to see how participants will be affected. In the ATM machine example, for instance, the investigator might arrange for the ATM machine to display different instructions to different people. The study would still be observational in character (because the researcher would not control who uses the machine or when), but the researcher would be trying to direct the behavior in certain ways.

 Clinical interviews are to introspection what controlled observations are to naturalistic observations: the investigator again tries to direct the process more. In a clinical interview, the investigator begins by asking each participant a series of open-ended questions. Using the introspection example cited above, for instance, the interviewer might again ask the subject to think about the problem and describe his approaches to it. With this method, however, instead of allowing the subject to respond freely, the interviewer follows up with another set of questions. Depending on the subject's responses, the interviewer may pursue one or another of many possible lines of questioning, trying to follow each subject's own thinking and experience while focusing on specific issues or questions.

Experiments and Quasi-Experiments

The major distinction between experiments and observational methods is the investigator's degree of experimental control. Having experimental control means that the experimenter can assign subjects to different experimental conditions so as to minimize pre-existing differences between them. Ideally, the experimenter can control all variables that might affect the performance of research participants *other than* the variables that are the focus of the study. A true experiment is one in which the experimenter manipulates one or more independent variables (the experimental conditions) and observes how the recorded measures (dependent variables) change as a result. For example, an experiment in cognitive psychology might proceed as follows: an experimenter recruits a number of people for a study of memory; randomly assigns them to one of two groups; presents each group with exactly the same stimuli using exactly the same procedures and settings, varying only the instructions (the independent variable) for the two groups of participants; and observes the overall performance of the participants on a later memory test (the dependent variable).

 This example illustrates a **between-subjects design,** wherein different experimental subjects participate in different experimental conditions. In contrast, a **within-subjects design** exposes experimental subjects to more than one condition. For example, subjects might perform several memory tasks but receive a different set of instructions for each task.

Some independent variables preclude random assignment. For example, experimenters cannot reassign subjects to a different gender, ethnicity, age, or educational background. Studies that appear in other ways to be experiments but have one or more of these factors as independent variables (or fail to become true experiments in other ways) are called **quasi-experiments** (Campbell & Stanley, 1963).

Scientists value experiments and quasi-experiments because they enable researchers to isolate causal factors and make better supported claims about causality than possible using observational methods alone. However, many experiments fail to fully capture real-world phenomena in the experimental task or research design. The laboratory setting or the artificiality or formality of the task may prevent research participants from behaving normally, for example. Further, the kinds of tasks that are amenable to experimental study may not be those that are most important or most common in everyday life. As a result, experimenters risk studying phenomena that relate only weakly to people's real-world experience.

This brief outline of different research designs barely scratches the surface of all the important things we could look at. There are a few general points to note, however. First, cognitive psychologists use a variety of approaches to study cognitive phenomena. In part, these reflect philosophical differences among psychologists over what is important to study and how certain drawbacks and benefits should be traded off. In part, they reflect the intellectual framework that researchers find themselves working in. They may also reflect how amenable different areas of cognition are to different research approaches.

Second, no research design is perfect. Each one has certain potential benefits and limits that researchers must weigh in designing studies. Students, professors, and other researchers must also examine the design of studies both critically and appreciatively, thinking carefully about how well the research design answers the research question posed. I hope you'll keep these thoughts in mind as you read in the rest of the book examples of the wide variety of research studies cognitive psychologists have carried out.

Paradigms of Cognitive Psychology

Having looked at cognitive psychology's historical roots and research methods, we can focus on cognitive psychology today. In this section, we will examine the three major paradigms that cognitive psychologists use in planning and executing their research.

First of all, what is a paradigm? The word has several related meanings, but you can think of it as a body of knowledge structured according to what its proponents consider important and what they do not. Paradigms include the assumptions investigators make in studying a phenomenon. Paradigms also specify what kinds of experimental methods and measures are appropriate to use in an investigation. Paradigms are thus intellectual frameworks that guide investigators in studying and understanding phenomena.

In this section, we'll review three paradigms used by cognitive psychologists today. In learning about each one, you should ask yourself the following questions: What assumptions underlie the paradigm? What questions or issues does the paradigm emphasize? What analogies (for example, the computer-mind) does the paradigm use? What research methods and measures are favored in the paradigm?

The Information-Processing Approach

The **information-processing** approach dominated cognitive psychology in the 1960s and 1970s, and remains strong and influential today. As its name implies, the information-processing approach draws an analogy between human cognition and computerized processing of information.

Central to the information-processing approach is the idea that cognition can be thought of as information (what we see, hear, read about, think about) passing through a system (us, or more specifically, our minds). Those following an information-processing approach often assume that information is processed (that is, received, stored, recoded, transformed, retrieved, transmitted) in stages and that it is stored in specific places while being processed. One goal within this framework, then, is to determine what these stages and storage places are and how they work.

Other assumptions underlie the information-processing approach as well. One is that people's cognitive abilities can be thought of as "systems" of interrelated capacities. We know that different individuals have different cognitive capacities—different attention spans, memory capacities, and language skills, to name a few. Information-processing theorists try to find the relationships between these capacities to explain how individuals go about performing specific cognitive tasks.

In accordance with the computer metaphor, information-processing theorists assume that people, like computers, are general-purpose symbol manipulators. This means that, like computers, people can perform astonishing cognitive feats applying only a few mental operations to symbols (such as letters, numbers, propositions, scenes). Information is then stored symbolically, and the way it is coded and stored greatly affects how easy it is to use it later (for example, when we want to recall information or manipulate it in some way).

A general-purpose information-processing system is shown in Figure 1-2. Note the various memory stores where information is held for possible later use, and the different processes that operate on the information at

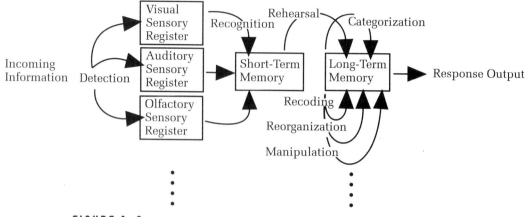

FIGURE 1-2.   A typical information-processing model

different points or that transfer it from store to store. Certain processes, such as detection and recognition, are used at the beginning of information processing; others, such as recoding or retrieval, have to do with memory storage; still others, such as reasoning or concept formation, have to do with ways in which information can be put together in new ways. In this model, boxes represent stores, and arrows, processes (leading some to refer to information-processing models as "boxes-and-arrows" models of cognition). Altogether, the model is depicted best by something computer scientists call flowcharts.

The information-processing tradition is rooted in structuralism, in that its followers attempt to identify the basic capacities and processes we use in cognition. The computer metaphor used in this approach also shows an indebtedness to the fields of engineering and communications. Psychologists working in the information-processing tradition are interested in relating individual and developmental differences to differences in basic capacities and processes. Typically, information-processing psychologists use experimental and quasi-experimental techniques in their investigations.

The Connectionist Approach

Early in the 1980s, researchers from a variety of disciplines began to explore alternatives to the information-processing approach that could explain cognition. The framework they established is known as **connectionism** (sometimes also called parallel distributed processing, or PDP). Its name is derived from models depicting cognition as a network of connections among simple (and usually numerous) processing units (McClelland, 1988). Because these units are sometimes compared to *neurons,* the cells that transmit electrical impulses and underlie all sensation and muscle movement, connectionist models are sometimes called **neural networks** (technically speaking, there are distinctions between connectionist and neural network models, but we will not review them here).

Each unit is connected to other units in a large network. Each unit has some level of activation at any particular moment in time. The exact level of activation depends on the input to that unit from both the environment and other units to which it is connected. Connections between two units have weights, which can be positive or negative. A positively weighted connection will cause one unit to excite, or raise the level of activation of units to which it is connected; a negatively weighted connection will have the opposite effect, inhibiting or lowering the activation of connected units.

Figure 1-3 depicts a connectionist network, showing both units and their connections. In this example, the units are the circles at the center of the figure, with all the arrows pointing to them. These units (sometimes called *nodes*) each depict a certain individual. Each unit is connected to other units that depict certain information about individuals, for example, their names, cars, professions. The arrows between units depict excitatory, or positively weighted, connections. When any unit reaches a certain level of activation, it activates all the other units to which it has positively

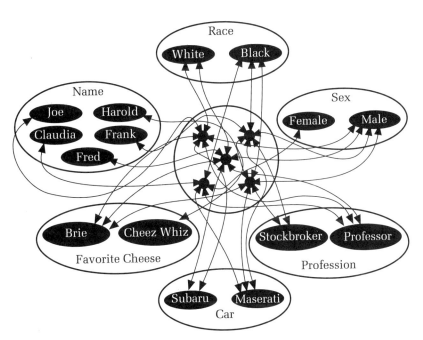

FIGURE 1-3.   A typical connectionist model. From Martindale, 1991. SOURCE: From *Cognitive Psychology: A Neural Network Approach,* by C. Martindale. Copyright © 1991 by Wadsworth, Inc. Reprinted by permission of Brooks/Cole Publishing Company, Pacific Grove, CA 93950.

weighted connections. In this example, all units within the same circle have negatively weighted, or inhibitory, connections. Thus, if the node for "Joe" is activated, it inhibits activation of the nodes "Claudia," "Fred," "Frank," and "Harold." At the same time, the "Joe" node activates the top right-hand node in the center circle, which in turn activates the nodes "male," "professor," "Subaru," and "brie." The activation of these nodes will inhibit, or lower the activation of all other nodes in their respective circles.

One major difference between the information-processing and the connectionist approaches is the manner in which cognitive processes are assumed to occur. In information-processing models, cognition is typically assumed to occur *serially*—that is, in discrete stages (first one process occurs, feeding information into the next process, which feeds information into the next process, and so on). In contrast, most (but not all) connectionist models assume that cognitive processes occur in *parallel,* many at the same time.

The connectionist framework allows for a wide variety of models that can vary in the number of units hypothesized, the number and pattern of connections among units, and the connection of units to the environment. All connectionist models share the assumption, however, that there is no need to hypothesize a central processor that directs the flow of information from one process or storage area to another. Instead, different patterns of activation account for the various cognitive processes (McClelland, 1988). Knowledge is not stored in various storehouses but within connections between units. Learning occurs when new connective patterns are established that change the weights of connections between units.

Feldman and Ballard (1982), in an early description of connectionism, argue that this approach is more consistent with the way the brain functions than an information-processing approach. The brain, they argue, is made up of many neurons that are connected to one another in various complex ways. The authors assert that "the fundamental premise of connectionism is that individual neurons *do not transmit large amounts of symbolic information.* Instead they compute by being *appropriately connected* to large numbers of similar units. This is in sharp contrast to the conventional computer model of intelligence prevalent in computer science and cognitive psychology" (p. 208). Rumelhart puts the issue more simply: connectionism seeks to replace the computer metaphor of the information-processing framework with a brain metaphor (1989, p. 134).

Like the information-processing approach, connectionism draws from structuralism an interest in the elements of cognitive functioning. However, whereas information processors look to computer science, connectionists look to cognitive neuropsychology for information to help them construct their theories and models. Connectionism, being much newer than information-processing, is just beginning to map out explanations for individual and developmental differences. Most connectionist work seeks to replicate the findings of experimental and quasi-experimental research using computer programs based on a neural network model.

The Ecological Approach

A third major approach to the study of cognition comes from both psychologists and anthropologists, who share a set of beliefs opposite in many ways to those held by investigators in the information-processing and connectionism traditions. The most important is that cognition does not occur in isolation from larger cultural contexts; that is, all cognitive activities are shaped by the culture and by the context in which they occur.

Jean Lave, a current theorist in this tradition, has conducted some fascinating work that can illustrate the **ecological approach.** In a recent work Lave described the results of the Adult Math Project, "an observational and experimental investigation of everyday arithmetic practices" (1988, p. 1). Lave, Murtaugh, and de la Rocha (1984) studied how people used arithmetic in their everyday lives. In one study, they followed people on grocery shopping trips to analyze how and when people calculate "best buys."

What they found was that people's methods of calculation varied with the context. This was somewhat surprising, since students in our culture are taught to use the same specified formulas on all problems of a given type to yield one definite numerical answer. To illustrate, compare a typical third-grade arithmetic problem, presented by teachers to students—"Brandi had eight seashells. Nikki had five more. How many seashells did the two of them have together?"—with the following problem, posed and solved by one of the "shopping" subjects, regarding the number of apples she should purchase for her family for the week:

> There's only about three or four [apples] at home, and I have four kids, so you figure at least two apiece in the next three days. These are the kinds of things I have to resupply. I only have a certain amount of storage space in the refrigerator, so I can't load it up totally . . . . Now that I'm home in the summertime, this is a good snack food. And I like an apple sometimes at lunchtime when I come home. (Murtaugh, 1985, p. 188)

Lave (1988) points out a number of contrasts between this arithmetic problem solving and the kind used in solving school problems. First, the second example has several possible answers (for example, 5, 6, 9), unlike the first problem, which has one (13). Second, the first problem is given to the problem solver to solve; the second is constructed by the problem solver herself. Third, the first problem is somewhat disconnected from personal experience, goals, and interests, while the second comes out of practical daily living.

Although there has been much recent interest in the ecological approach, the idea of studying cognition in everyday contexts actually began several years earlier. A major proponent of this point of view was J. J. Gibson, whose work on perception we will discuss at length in Chapter 2. Ulric Neisser, a friend and colleague of Gibson, wrote a book in 1976 aimed

Research following the ecological approach examines the cognitive processing of people in everyday situations.

at redirecting the field of psychology toward studying more "realistic" cognitive phenomena.

We can see the influences of both the functionalist and the Gestalt schools on the ecological approach. The functionalists focused on the purposes served by cognitive processes, certainly an ecological question. Gestalt psychology's emphasis on the context surrounding any experience is likewise compatible with the ecological approach. The ecological approach would deny the usefulness (and perhaps even the possibility) of studying cognitive phenomena in artificial circumstances divorced from larger contexts. Thus, this tradition relies less on laboratory experiments or computer simulations and more on natural observation and field studies to explore cognition.

General Points

Each of these three paradigms makes an important contribution to cognitive psychology, and in some ways, the three offer complementary perspectives on how the underlying principles of cognition ought to be investigated and understood. The information-processing paradigm, for example, focuses researchers on the functional aspects of cognition—what kinds of processes are used, toward what end. The connectionist approach, in contrast, focuses on the underlying "hardware"—how the global cognitive processes described by an information-processing model are implemented in the human brain. The ecological approach stresses the need to consider the context of any cognitive process to understand more completely how that process functions in the real world.

Not all cognitive research fits neatly into one of these three paradigms. Some research incorporates parts of different paradigms; some fits no paradigm neatly. I hope, however, that these three paradigms will provide a useful backdrop against which to consider individual studies.

Summary

We've seen so far that cognition plays a large role in our everyday existence. We take much of our cognitive experience for granted, because the ways in which we function cognitively are so routine that we simply don't pay attention to them. Nonetheless, cognitive activities are seen to be astonishingly complex upon closer inspection.

We've examined different traditions in the study of cognition, tracing the history of study back at least as far as Wundt's Leipzig laboratory. We've seen how different major schools of thought—structuralism, functionalism, behaviorism, and Gestalt approaches—have framed cognitive questions. We've also seen how the present study of cognitive psychology grows out of, and contributes to, innovations in other fields, such as computer science, communications engineering, linguistics, and anthropology. Finally, we've reviewed three major approaches to the modern study of cognitive phenomena—the information-processing, connectionist, and ecological paradigms—and research methods commonly used in cognitive research.

This framework ought to provide you with a sense of where we're headed in the rest of the book, as we take up specific cognitive topics in more detail. Throughout, you should examine how the research studies discussed bear on cognitive activities in your everyday life. Are the questions posed, and the research approaches used to answer them, appropriate? How do the theoretical assumptions shape the way the questions are posed? What do the research findings mean, and what new questions do they raise?

Cognitive psychology is my field. Not surprisingly, I've found it to be full of fascinating, deeply rooted questions; complex as well as elegant; and relevant to many real-world issues. I hope, after reading this book, that you too will find this field an important one, one worth knowing about.

Recommended Readings

General works on the history of psychology include Fancher (1979), Heidbreder (1933), and Murray (1988). Rieber (1980) edited a volume of writings on Wilhelm Wundt that explores his contributions, shortcomings, and relationships to other philosophers and psychologists. William James's writings (1983/1890) speak for themselves eloquently, and still provide a clear introduction to his ideas. Watson's (1913) paper lays out clearly his criticisms of introspection as a technique and consciousness as an object of study, and Skinner's (1984/1963) paper (and the replies it generated, which immediately follow) speak directly to behaviorism's view of cognitive psychology. Amsel (1989) offers historical perspectives on behaviorism and its relationship to cognition. Köhler's (1929/1947) work introduces Gestalt psychological principles. Flavell (1963) offers a good introduction to Piagetian theory. Gardner (1985) provides a good overview of the "cognitive revolution" and the beginning of cognitive science. Simon (1992) reflects on the cognitive revolution's redefinition of what it means to explain behavior. A collection of papers on topics in cognitive science has been edited in three volumes by Osherson and Lasnik (1990); Osherson, Kosslyn, and Hollerbach (1990); and Osherson and Smith (1990). Ellis and Young (1988) present a good introduction to the field of human cognitive neuropsychology.

Good sources on research design include Kerlinger (1986), Martin (1991), and Rosenthal and Rosnow (1984).

Lachman, Lachman, and Butterfield (1979) present a good introduction to the information-processing framework. A corresponding (yet more technical) introduction to connectionism can be found in a two-volume work edited by Rumelhart and McClelland (1986; McClelland & Rumelhart, 1986). Neisser (1976), Lave (1988), and Rogoff (1990) provide good introductions to the ecological approach.

REVIEW QUESTIONS

1. What roles do laboratory experiments and naturalistic observation play in cognitive research?

2. What similarities and differences exist among the following three "schools" of psychology: structuralism, functionalism, behaviorism?

3. What is a *mental representation,* and how is this concept viewed by: Gestalt psychologists, information-processing psychologists, behaviorist psychologists, and connectionists?

4. Describe how research on cognitive development and individual differences might bear on cognitive psychology.

5. What was the "cognitive revolution"? What resulted from it?

6. Describe and critique the major research methods of cognitive psychology.

7. Compare and contrast the three major paradigms of cognitive psychology reviewed in this chapter (information-processing, connectionism, the ecological approach).

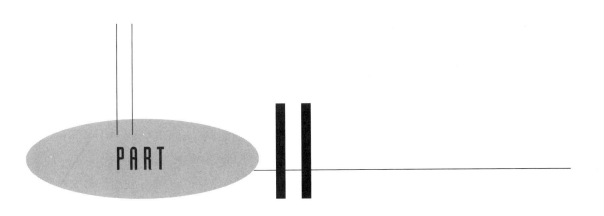

PART II

Basic Processes

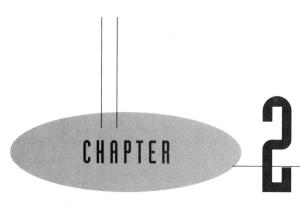

CHAPTER 2

Perception and
Pattern Recognition

s I write this chapter, I'm looking out toward the entrance to my office, and I can see my office door as well as another door leading to a hallway. My recognition of these two objects as doors is almost instantaneous and takes little effort. How do I do this, and what makes the process so rapid and effortless?

The central problem of perception is explaining how we attach meaning to sensory information we receive. In this example, I received and somehow interpreted, a great deal of sensory information—I "saw" certain objects as doors, hallways, and so forth. I recognized certain objects—that is, saw them as things that I had seen before. The question for cognitive psychologists is how we manage to accomplish these feats, and do so so rapidly and (usually) errorlessly.

The vast topic of perception can be subdivided into visual perception, auditory perception (the two best studied forms), olfactory perception, and so forth. For the purposes of this chapter, we will concentrate on visual perception—in part to keep our discussion manageable and in part because visual perception is the kind psychologists study most. From time to time, we will also look at examples of other kinds of perception to illustrate different points.

Notice that when we look at an object, we acquire specific bits of information about it, including its location, shape, texture, size, and (for familiar objects) name. Some psychologists, namely those working in the tradition of James Gibson (1979), would argue that we also immediately acquire information about the object's function. Cognitive psychologists attempt to describe how we acquire such information and what we then do to it in processing it.

Several related questions immediately arise. How much of the information that we acquire through perception draws on past learning? How much of our perception do we infer and how much do we receive directly? What specific cognitive processes enable us to perceive objects (and events and states and so on)? Where can the line be drawn between perception and sensation, the first reception of information in a specific sensory modality—vision, hearing, olfaction? Where can the line be drawn between perception and other kinds of cognition, such as reasoning or categorization?

Clearly, even defining perception so as to answer these questions is a challenge. For the present, we will adopt what might be called the "classic" approach to defining perception. Figure 2-1 illustrates this approach for visual perception. Out in the real world are objects and events—things to be perceived—a book or, as in my earlier example, doors and a hallway. Each such object is a distal stimulus. For a living organism to process information about these stimuli, it must first receive the information through one or more sensory systems—in this example, the visual system. The reception of information and its registration by a sense organ make up the proximal stimulus. In our earlier example, light waves reflect from the doors and

Distal Stimulus
(book)

Proximal Stimulus
(retinal image of book)

Percept
(recognition of
object as a book)

FIGURE 2-1.   Distal stimuli, proximal stimuli, and percepts hallway to my eyes, in particular to a surface at the back of each eye known as the retina. There, an image of the doors and hallway, called the **retinal image,** is formed. This image is two-dimensional, and its size depends on my distance from the doors and hallway (the closer I am, the larger the image). In addition, the image is upside-down, and reversed with respect to left and right.

The meaningful interpretation of the proximal stimulus is the **per-cept**—my interpretation that the stimuli are doors and a hallway. From the upside-down, backward, two-dimensional image, I quickly (almost instan-taneously) "saw" a set of objects that I recognized—two doors and a hall-way. I also "recognized" that the second door led to the hallway, and that the hallway appeared to recede in depth away from me. This information was not part of the proximal stimulus. Somehow, I had to interpret the proximal stimulus to know it.

Although researchers studying perception disagree about much, this much they do agree on: percepts are not the same things as proximal stimuli. Consider a simple demonstration of **size constancy.** Extend your arm away from your body, and look at the back of your hand. Now, keeping the back of your hand facing you, slowly bring it toward you a few inches, then away from you. Does your hand appear to be changing size as it moves? Probably not, although the size of the hand in the retinal image is most certainly changing. The point here is that perception involves some-thing different than the formation of retinal images.

Related to perception is a process called **pattern recognition.** This is the **recognition** of a particular object, event, and so on, as belonging to a class of objects, events, and so on. My recognition of the object I'm looking at as belonging to the class of things called doors is an instance of pattern recognition. Because the formation of most percepts involves some classification and recognition, most, if not all, instances of perception involve pattern recognition.

Psychologists studying perception distinguish between **bottom-up** and **top-down processes.** The term *bottom-up* (or *data-driven*) essentially means that the perceiver starts with small bits of information from the envi-ronment, that he combines in various ways to form a percept. A bottom-up model of my example might describe my seeing edges, rectangular and other shapes, and certain lighted regions, and putting this information together to "conclude" that I'm seeing doors and a hallway.

In top-down processing (also called *theory-driven* or *conceptually-driven processing*), in contrast, the perceiver's expectations, theories, or concepts guide the selection and combination of the information in the pat-tern recognition process. For example, a "top-down" description of my example might go something like this: I knew that I was in my office and knew from past experience approximately where the door was. When I looked in that direction, I expected to see a door and the hallway beyond. These expectations guided where I looked, what I looked at, and how I put information together.

We will begin by looking at models that are purely bottom-up. Next, we will examine phenomena that have led many cognitive psychologists to argue that some top-down processes must occur in perception. We will then examine recent work inspired by J. J. Gibson (1979) on "direct perception." Gibson's view departs from most other theories of perception in that he claims that perceivers actually do little "processing" of information, either bottom-up or top-down. Instead, he believes that the information available in the world is sufficiently rich that all the perceiver needs to do is detect or "pick up on" that information.

Bottom-Up Processes

To say that a process works from the bottom up means that the process starts with some input that through manipulation yields a more richly specified output (that is, a meaningful interpretation of the object or event). The idea here is that the system works in one direction, starting from the input and proceeding to a final interpretation. Whatever happens at a given point is unaffected by later processing; the system has no way of going back to an earlier point to make adjustments. To picture bottom-up processing, imagine a row of students seated at desks. The student in the last seat of the row starts the process by writing a word down on a piece of paper and handing the paper to the student in front of her. That student adds some information (maybe another word, maybe an illustration) and, in turn, hands the paper to the student in front of him, and so on until the paper reaches the student at the front of the row. Students at the front of the row have no opportunity to ask students behind them for any clarification or additional information.

When psychologists speak of bottom-up perceptual processes, they typically have in mind something that takes information about a stimulus (by definition a "lower" level of processing) as input. Bottom-up processes are relatively uninfluenced by expectations or previous learning (the so-called higher-level processes). We will consider in this section three distinct examples of bottom-up models of perception.

Template Matching

Figure 2-2 shows a copy of a check. Notice the numbers at the bottom of the check. These numbers encode certain information about a checking account—the account number, the bank that manages it, and so forth. These numbers may look funny to you, but they wouldn't look at all funny to machines known as check sorters, such as those the Federal Reserve banks, use to sort checks and deliver them to the correct banks for payment. These

9000

_____ 19 ____   99-0000/9999

PAY TO THE
ORDER OF _____ | $ [   ]

_____ DOLLARS

MEMO _____   _____

⑈:999000000⑈: 999999000 00⑈' 9999

FIGURE 2-2.   A sample bank check. Note the numbers at the bottom.

machines "read" the numbers and compare them to previously stored patterns, called **templates.** The machines "decide" which number is represented by comparing the pattern they read to these templates, as shown in Figure 2-3. A tour of your local Federal Reserve bank will convince you that this system works most impressively.

You can think of a template as a kind of stencil—one of the art supplies you probably owned as a child. If you remember, those stencils let you trace as many copies as you wanted of the same thing. Templates work like stencils in reverse. An unknown incoming pattern is compared to all of the templates (stencils) on hand and identified by the template that best matches it.

As a model of perception, template matching works this way: Every object, event, or other stimulus that we encounter and want to derive meaning from is compared to some previously stored pattern, or template. The

FIGURE 2-3.   Illustration of template matching. The input (4) is compared either serially or simultaneously with all of the available templates. The match to "4" is the best.

I like cog. psych.

I like cog. psych.

I like cog psych.

I like cog. psych.

I like cog psych

I like cog psych

I like cog. psych.

I like cog. Psych.

FIGURE 2-4.   Handwriting samples

process of perception thus involves comparing our incoming information to the templates we have stored, looking for a match. If a number of templates match or come close, we need to engage in further processing to sort out which template is most appropriate. Notice that this model implies that, somewhere in our knowledge base, we've stored millions of different templates—one for every distinct object or pattern we can recognize.

As may already be apparent to you, template-matching models have several theoretical holes. First, for such a model to be true, we would need to have stored an impossibly large number of templates. Second, as technology develops and our experiences change, we become capable of recognizing new objects—VCRs, a Ford Probe, a laptop computer, a Hacky Sack®. Template-matching models thus have to explain how and when templates are created, and how we keep track of an ever-growing number of templates.

A third problem is that people recognize many patterns as more or less the same thing, even when the stimulus patterns differ greatly. Figure 2-4 illustrates this point. I constructed this figure by having eight people write the sentence "I like cog. psych." in their own handwriting. You should be able to read each sentence despite the wide variation in the size, shape, orientation, and spacing of letters. How can a template-matching model explain your recognition that all eight people have written the "same" sentence? In everyday life, much of the stimulus information we perceive is far from regular, whether because of degradation, an unfamiliar orientation (compare an overturned cup or bicycle with one that is rightside up), or deliberate alteration. Is a separate template needed for each variation? And how is the perceiver to know whether an object should be rotated or otherwise adjusted before she tries to match it to a template? Remember, matching information to templates is supposed to tell the perceiver what the object is. The perceiver can't know ahead of time whether or not an input pattern should be adjusted before trying to match it to different templates, because presumably the perceiver does not yet know what the object is!

So, although there are examples of template matching, we probably don't rely heavily on such a process. Template matching works only with relatively clean stimuli, for which we know ahead of time what templates might be relevant. It does not adequately explain how we perceive as effectively as we typically do the "noisy" patterns and objects—blurred or faint letters, objects that are partially blocked, sounds against a background of other sounds—we encounter every day.

Featural Analysis

I'm once again staring at the object I perceive to be my office door. As I do, I'm able to recognize not only the whole door but also certain parts—the narrow edge facing me, the inside and outside doorknobs, the latch, the metal plate on the bottom of the outside of the door to protect it from scuffing. Some psychologists believe that such analysis of a whole into its parts underlies the basic processes used in perception.

Instead of processing stimuli as whole units, we might instead break them down into their component parts, using our recognition of those parts to infer what the whole represents. The parts that are searched for and

TABLE 2-1.   Features of capital letters

Features	A	E	F	H	I	L	T	K	M	N	V	W	X	Y	Z	B	C	D	G	J	O	P	R	Q	S	U
Straight																										
horizontal	+	+	+	+		+	+								+				+							
vertical		+	+	+	+	+	+	+	+	+				+		+		+				+	+			
diagonal /	+							+	+		+	+	+	+	+											
diagonal \	+							+	+	+	+	+	+	+									+	+		
Curve																										
closed																+		+			+	+	+	+		
open V														+												+
open H																	+		+	+					+	
Intersection	+	+	+	+			+	+					+			+						+	+	+		
Redundancy																										
cyclic change		+						+	+							+							+			
symmetry	+	+		+	+		+	+	+		+	+	+	+		+	+	+			+					+
Discontinuity																										
vertical	+		+	+	+		+	+	+	+				+								+	+			
horizontal		+	+			+	+								+											

SOURCE: From Eleanor J. Gibson, *Principles of Perceptual Learning and Development,* © 1969, p. 88. Reprinted by permission of Prentice Hall, Englewood Cliffs, New Jersey.

recognized are called **features**. Recognition of a whole object, in this model, thus depends on recognition of its features.

Such a model of perception—called **featural analysis**—fits nicely with some neurophysiological evidence. Some studies of the retinas of frogs (Lettvin, Maturana, McCullogh, & Pitts, 1959) involved implanting microelectrodes in individual cells of the retina. Lettvin et al. found that specific kinds of stimuli could cause these cells to fire more frequently. Certain cells responded strongly to borders between light and dark, and were called "edge detectors." Others responded selectively to moving edges, and others, jokingly called "bug detectors," responded most vigorously when a small, dark dot (much like an insect) moved across the field of vision. Hubel and Wiesel (1962, 1968) later discovered fields in the visual cortexes of cats and monkeys that responded selectively to moving edges or contours in the visual field that had a particular orientation. In other words, they found evidence of separate "horizontal line detectors" and "vertical line detectors," as well as other distinct detectors.

How does this evidence support featural analysis? Certain detectors appear to scan input patterns, looking for the presence of a particular fea-

E I M V W X   C D G O R U

X M Z W V I   R D Q O C G

V I E X W M   G R D C O U

W V X Q I E   D C U R Z G

(A)   (B)

FIGURE 2-5.   Visual search stimuli. Notice how long it takes to find a Z or a Q in the two different arrays.

ture. If that feature is present, the detectors respond rapidly. If that feature is not present, the detectors do not respond as strongly. Each detector, then, appears to be designed to detect the presence of just one kind of feature in an input pattern. That such detectors exist, in the form of either retinal or cortical cells, confirms the applicability of the featural analysis model.

Other research has provided evidence that people process features, too. For example, flashing letters on a **tachistiscope** (a machine that allows experimenters to display images for a set, brief amount of time) typically results in certain predictable errors. For example, subjects are much more likely to confuse a *G* with a *C,* than they are with an *F*. Presumably, this is because the letters *C* and *G* share many features: a curved line, an opening to the right. Eleanor Gibson (1969) has tabulated the features of capital letters for the Roman alphabet we use, and this is shown in Table 2-1.

Studies by Neisser (1963) confirm that people use features to recognize letters. Neisser had his subjects perform a **visual search task,** in which they were presented with arrays of letters, such as those shown in Figure 2-5. They were asked to respond if they detected the presence of a particular target, such as the letter *Q* or *Z*. Shown an array like Figure 2-5(a), subjects took much longer to find a *Z* than they did to find a *Q*, with the reverse true for arrays similar to Figure 2-5(b). The nontarget letters in array (a) all share features like straight and angular lines, whereas those in array (b) share features like roundness. Similarity between the target letter (*Z* or *Q*) and the nontarget letters can make the search much harder.

Similar findings have been reported for auditory perception of syllables that share many articulatory features. For example, *da* and *ta* are more likely to be confused with each other than are two syllables that share fewer similarities, such as *da* and *sa* (Miller & Nicely, 1955). Examples of articulatory features (for consonants) include voicing, vibration of the vocal cords (*b,* is voiced, for example, but *p* is not); nasality, whether the air is directed into the nasal passages (*n*) or not (*l*); duration, how long the (consonant) sound lasts (compare *s* with *t*); and place of articulation, where in the mouth the sound is formed (compare *p* and *b,* formed in the front; *t* and *d,* formed in the middle; and *k* and *g,* formed in the back).

Selfridge (1959) developed a model for the perception of letters that was based on featural analysis. The model was called "Pandemonium," for reasons that will soon become clear. It consists of a number of different kinds of "demons" (you can think of them as kinds of detectors). Demons at the bottom (first) level of processing scan the input, while demons at higher levels scan the output from lower-level demons. In response to what they find, the demons scream. The first kind of demons are image demons, who convert the proximal stimulus into representations, or internal depictions of information, that higher-level demons can work with. Each representation is scanned by several feature demons, each looking for a different particular feature (such as a curved or a vertical line). If it finds such a feature, the demon looking for it screams. Feature demons communicate their confidence that the feature is present by screaming softer or louder. Letter demons cannot look at the stimulus itself but can only listen to the feature demons. The letter demons pay particular attention to the demons associated with their particular letter. The *A* demon, for instance, listens especially hard to the feature demons for "slanted line" and "vertical line." Letter demons scream when the output from the feature demons convinces them that their letter is in the representation, again, louder or softer depending on their confidence. A single decision demon listens to all this screaming and decides what letter is being presented. Figure 2-6 illustrates the structure governing the screaming chaos of the demons.

Although Pandemonium was named with a sense of humor, it illustrates a number of important aspects of featural analysis. First, demons can scream louder or softer, depending on the clarity and quality of the input. This allows for the fact that real-life stimuli are often degraded or incomplete, yet objects and patterns can still be recognized. Second, feature demons can be linked to letter demons in such a way that more important features carry greater weight. This takes into account the fact that some features matter more than others in pattern recognition. Take the case of the letter *A.* In writing this letter, some people are sloppy about their slanted vertical lines (sometimes the lines are almost parallel), and yet the *A* is still often recognizable. Without the horizontal line, however, the pattern seems to cease to be an *A.* Lastly, the weights of the various features can be changed over time, allowing for learning. So, a demon model can learn to recognize my husband's handwritten *A*'s, even though he makes his capital *A*'s with no slanted lines, only two very curved lines. With practice, this model could learn to read even my husband's handwriting—something even I have trouble with!

Featural analysis models are not without problems, however. To begin with, there are at present no good definitions of what can be a feature and what cannot. Consider the perception of a face. Are there general fea-

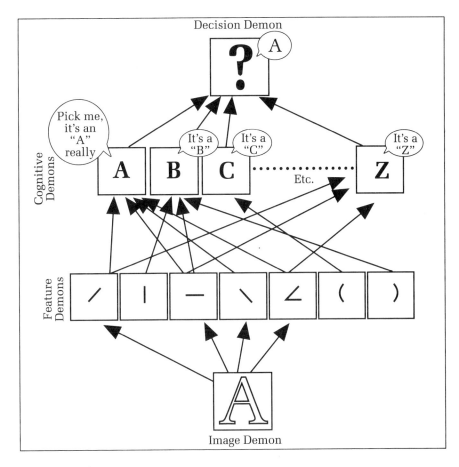

FIGURE 2-6.   A depiction of Selfridge's (1959) Pandemonium model

tures for eyes, nose, mouth? Are there specific features for right nostril, left eyebrow, lower lip? Just how many features can there be? Do different kinds of objects have different sets of features? Consider a vertical line. While this feature is no doubt important for perceiving the letter *A,* how does it relate to perceiving a real human face? A beach ball? A wave crashing on shore? If there are different sets of features for different objects, how does the perceiver know which ones to use to perceive an object (remember, this has to be decided *before* the perceiver knows what the object is)? If the same set of features applies to all objects, the list of possible features would appear to be huge. How does the perceiver perceive objects so fast, then?

Prototype Matching

Another kind of perceptual model, one that attempted to correct some of the shortcomings of both template matching and featural analysis models, is known as *prototype matching.* Such models also explain perception in terms of a process of matching an input to a stored representation of information. In this case, however, the stored representation, instead of being a whole pattern that must be matched exactly or closely (as in template-matching models), is, rather, an abstraction, a **prototype,** an idealized representation of some class of objects or events—the letter *M,* a cup, a VCR, a collie, and so forth. You can think of a prototype as an idealization of the thing it represents. The prototypical dog, for instance, would be a depiction of a very, very typical dog. There may or may not be in existence any particular dog that looks exactly like the prototype. Figure 2-7 shows variations of the letter *M.* Most readers of English judge those toward the center to be more prototypical.

Prototype-matching models describe perceptual processes as follows: When a sensory device registers a new stimulus, it compares it with previously stored prototypes. An exact match is not required; in fact, only an approximate match is expected. Prototype matching models thus allow for discrepancies between the input and the prototype. An object is "perceived," when a match is found.

Prototype models differ from template and featural analysis models in that they do not require that an object contain any one specific feature or set of features to be recognized. Instead, the more features a particular object shares with a prototype, the higher the probability of a match. Moreover, prototype models take into account not only an object's features or parts but also the relationships among them.

FIGURE 2-7.   Examples of the letter *M*

Where, though, do prototypes come from? Posner and Keele (1968) demonstrated that people can form prototypes surprisingly quickly. They showed subjects a series of dot patterns created by arranging nine dots in a 30-by-30 grid to form a letter, a triangle, or a random pattern. The dots were then moved slightly to different positions in the grid (Posner, Goldsmith, & Welton, 1967). The original patterns were designated prototypes, and the others (which were really variations on the same basic patterns), distortions. Some examples are shown in Figure 2-8. Subjects viewed the various distortions but not the prototypes and were not told that the distortions were in fact distortions. Subjects learned to classify the distortions into

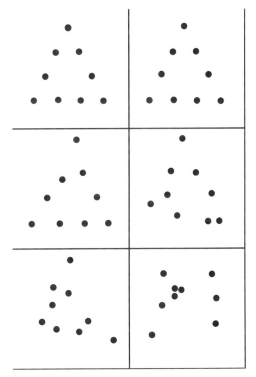

FIGURE 2-8.   Stimuli used by Posner and Keele (1968). The top left-hand box shows the prototype; other boxes show distortions. SOURCE: From "Perceived Distance and the Classification of Distorted Patterns," by M. I. Posner, R. Goldsmith, and K. E. Welton, Jr., 1967, *Journal of Experimental Psychology, 73*, 30. Copyright © 1967 by the American Psychological Association. Reprinted by permission.

75%

50%

25%

P
100%

0%

FIGURE 2-9.   An example of stimuli used by
Solso and McCarthy (1981). SOURCE: From "Prototype
Formation of Faces: A Case of Pseudo-memory," by
R. L. Solso and J. E. McCarthy, 1981, *British Journal
of Psychology, 72,* 499–503. Copyright © 1981 by The
British Psychological Society. Reprinted by permis-
sion.

groups, based (unbeknownst to the subjects) on the original pattern from which the distortion was derived. After subjects could perform this classification without errors, they were shown another series of dot patterns and asked to classify them in some way. The dot patterns shown in this part of the experiment were of three types: *old*—that is, distortions that subjects had seen before—*new,* distortions that subjects had not previously encountered—and *prototypes,* which subjects had also not previously seen.

Subjects correctly classified about 87% of the old stimuli, about 67% of new stimuli (still better than chance), and 85% of the prototypes. Given that subjects had never seen the prototypes before, their accuracy in classifying them is truly surprising. How can it be explained? Posner and Keele (1968) argued that during the initial classification task, people formed an abstract representation of each class of items. These abstract representations might be mental images or pictures. Some subjects described verbal rules for where dots were clustered and in what kinds of configurations. In any event, subjects used these representations when classifying new patterns.

In a related study, Solso and McCarthy (1981) used faces drawn with police Identikits as stimuli. Some examples are shown in Figure 2-9. These investigators found that subjects falsely "recognize" prototypes as previously seen figures and do so with greater confidence than when they recognize a face they have actually seen.

This work lends credence to the idea that we form and use prototypes in our everyday perception. Indeed, we will encounter the idea of prototypes again in Chapter 8, when we talk about concepts and categorization. The challenge, then, is to figure out when and how we form and use prototypes, what kind of processing is involved in matching, and how we know what prototypes to try to match inputs to. Note that many of these issues, including the number and origins of the stored representations, also came up for template matching models. This set of problems has led other psychologists to develop models that work in very different ways.

Top-Down Processes

All of the bottom-up models described so far also share some other problems. Two of the biggest are **context effects** and expectation effects. Consider the display in Figure 2-10. Notice that the second character of both words is identical. Despite this, you probably read the two words as "they bake," perceiving the character in question unambiguously as an *h* the first time and then, milliseconds later, as an *a.* The context surrounding the character, *t* and *ey* the first time and *b* and *ke* the second time, obviously influenced what you perceived. The context in which a pattern or object appears apparently sets up certain expectations in the perceiver as to what objects will occur. Similar context effects have been demonstrated with per-

THEY
BHKE

FIGURE 2-10.   An example of context effects in perception

ceivers looking to identify objects in real-world scenes: both accuracy and
the length of time needed to recognize objects vary with the context (Biederman, Glass, & Stacy, 1973; Palmer, 1975). For example, people recognize
objects such as food or utensils faster in a scene depicting a kitchen than
they do in the same scene jumbled up.

These effects have led many psychologists to argue that any model

The context surrounding an object can make perceiving it easy or hard. If we were
to measure reaction time, we might find it takes people longer to recognize the
toaster in the photo on the left than to recognize the same toaster in the photo on
the right. The coherent kitchen scene sets up a context that aids perception of
objects we expect to see in kitchens. The jumbled version of the scene destroys this
context.

of perception must incorporate context and expectations. We will look next at further demonstrations of the need to include top-down processes in theories and models of perception and pattern recognition.

Top-down, or conceptually driven, processes, are those that are directed by expectations derived from context or past learning or both. If someone were to tell you that there is a fly in the room you are in right now, where would you look? Notice how this looking would change if you were to look for a spider or a cockroach. Your past experience with such creatures guides where you look first—whether to the walls, the floor, or the ceiling. You can think of the processing you do when you look for different insects as being top-down, in that your expectations and knowledge guide where you look.

Top-down processes have to interact with bottom-up processes, of course. Otherwise, you would never be able to perceive anything that you were not expecting, and you would always perceive what you expected to perceive—clearly not true. In the next section, we will review evidence that complete models of perception require both top-down and bottom-up processing.

Perceptual Learning

That perception changes with practice has been well documented (E. J. Gibson, 1969). A classic study by James and Eleanor Gibson (1955) illustrates this. Subjects (both children and adults) were first shown the card in the center of Figure 2-11, by itself, for about five seconds. Next, subjects were shown other cards, randomly mixed in with which were four copies of the original card. The subject's task was to identify these exact copies. Subjects received no feedback, but after seeing all of the cards, they were shown the original card again for five seconds, then shown the other cards in a new order. This procedure continued until each subject correctly identified all and only the four copies of the original card.

When Gibson and Gibson (1955) analyzed the errors subjects made on this task, they found that these errors were not random. Rather, the number of errors appeared to depend most on the number of similarities a stimulus shared with the original. Subjects were more likely to falsely recognize a stimulus that had the same number of coils and was oriented in the same direction as the original than they were to falsely recognize a stimulus that only had the same number of coils.

What seemed to be occurring was that, over time, subjects noticed more about the figures, responding to features of the stimuli that they previously appeared not to notice. This explanation accords with other, everyday

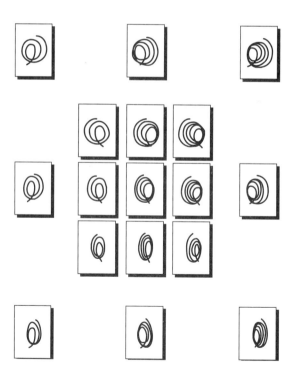

FIGURE 2-11.   Stimuli used by Gibson and Gibson (1955). SOURCE: From "Perceptual Learning: Differentiation or Enrichment?" by J. J. Gibson and E. J. Gibson, 1955, *Psychological Review, 62,* 36. Copyright © 1955 by the American Psychological Association. Reprinted by permission.

Perceptual learning is demonstrated at American Kennel Club licensed dog shows. Here, the judge is examining all the Old English Sheepdogs to determine which one best approaches an ideal standard. It takes years of practice to develop an eye to distinguish among dogs that, to the novice, might all look the same.

examples of perceptual learning. Take wine tasting as an example. Experienced wine tasters will tell you that one needs much practice to really taste subtle differences. Novice wine tasters might be able to distinguish (by taste!) between a red and a white wine, or even between a fruity and a dry white wine. Experts, by contrast, might even be able to identify the vineyard that bottled a wine in a particular year. Novices simply miss this information—their taste buds might work exactly like those of experts, but some information seems to be simply overlooked.

What exactly is going on? Apparently, perceptually practiced individuals learn what aspects of the stimulus to attend to, and try harder to consciously distinguish between different kinds of stimuli. With regard to top-down processes, a perceiver's experience appears to help guide what aspects of the stimulus to attend to, and also facilitates the "pick-up" of more information.

The Word Superiority Effect

A study by Reicher (1969) illustrates a related phenomenon—the effects of context on perception in practiced perceivers. The basic task was simple: Subjects were asked to identify which of two letters (for instance,

D or *K*) was presented on a tachistiscope. Later, they were presented with two alternatives for what the letter might have been, displayed directly above the letter's original position. Figure 2-12 depicts the experimental procedure.

The experiment contained an interesting twist, however. Sometimes, a single letter was presented. Other times, the letter appeared in the context of a word (such as *WORD* or *WORK;* notice that either *D* or *K* forms a common English word in combination with the same three letters). Still at other times, the letter was presented with three other letters in a combination that did not form a word (*OWRD* or *OWRK,* for instance). In each case, the stimuli were then masked, and the subject was asked merely to say which letter, *D* or *K,* had been presented.

Surprisingly, subjects could much more accurately identify letters that had been presented in the context of words than they could the same letters presented alone or in the context of nonwords. This result, called the **word superiority effect** or the word advantage, has been replicated several times (Massaro, 1979). Letters are apparently easier to perceive in a familiar

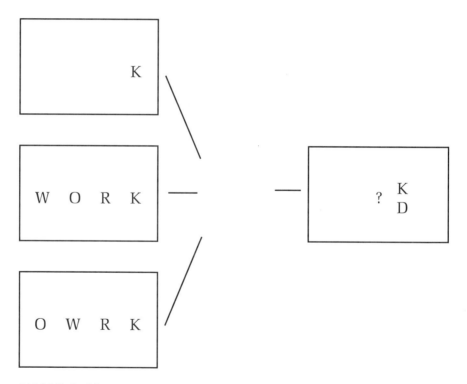

FIGURE 2-12.   Stimulus displays and procedures used by Reicher (1969). SOURCE: From "Perceptual Recognition as a Function of Meaningfulness of Stimulus Material," by G. M. Reicher, 1969, *Journal of Experimental Psychology, 81,* 277. Copyright © 1969 by the American Psychological Association. Reprinted by permission.

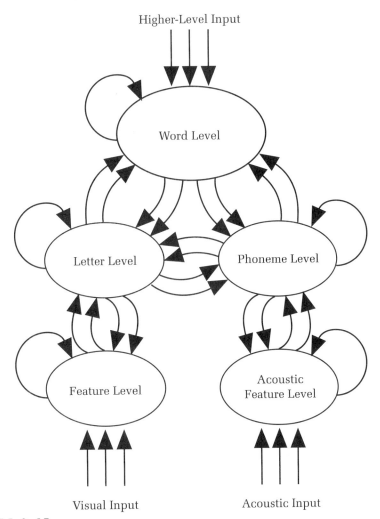

FIGURE 2-13.   McClelland and Rumelhart's (1981) model of letter perception. SOURCE: From "An Interactive Model of Context Effects in Letter Perception: Part 1. An Account of Basic Findings," by J. L. McClelland and D. E. Rumelhart, 1981, *Psychological Review, 88,* 378. Copyright © 1981 by the American Psychological Association. Reprinted by permission.

context (a word) than in an unfamiliar context or in no context at all. Theoretical explanations of this effect are still debated (Massaro, 1979; Papp, Newsome, McDonald, & Schvaneveldt, 1982). Not clear, for instance, is whether people detect more features in the letter when it occurs in a word or whether people make inferences about—guess at—the letter that would best complete the word. The point for our present purposes is that, once again, context and perceptual experience (for instance, at reading words)

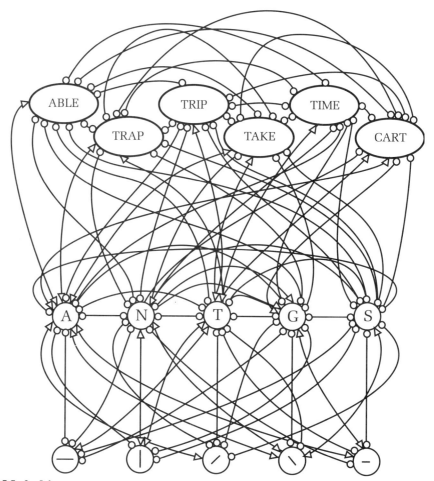

FIGURE 2-14.   Nodes and connections in McClelland and Rumelhart's (1981) model of letter perception. SOURCE: From "An Interactive Model of Context Effects in Letter Perception: Part 1. An Account of Basic Findings," by J. L. McClelland and D. E. Rumelhart, 1981, *Psychological Review, 88,* 380. Copyright © 1981 by the American Psychological Association. Reprinted by permission.

influence even as straightforward a task as perceiving a single letter. This insight has led to the creation of detailed models of letter perception that incorporate context-guided—that is, top-down—processes with bottom-up processes such as feature detection (McClelland & Rumelhart, 1981; Rumelhart & McClelland, 1982).

One of these is a connectionist model of letter perception, presented by McClelland and Rumelhart (1981). Figure 2-13 illustrates some of the processing levels assumed in the model. Note that input (whether written—visual—or spoken—acoustic—or of a higher level, such as arising from the context or the observer's expectations) is assumed to be processed at several different levels—whether in terms of features, letters, phonemes (sounds), or words. Notice, too, the several arrows in the diagram, depicting the assumption that the different levels of processing feed into one another. Each level of processing is assumed to be forming a representation of the information at a different level of abstraction—with features considered less abstract than letters, and letters less abstract than words.

The model is presented in more detail in Figure 2-14. Each circle and oval in this figure depicts a node of processing in the model. The model assumes a different node for each distinct word, letter, and feature. Nodes have a certain level of activity at any given point in time. When a node reaches a given level of activity, we can say that the feature, letter, or word associated with it is perceived.

Note all the lines between nodes. These represent connections, which can be either excitatory or inhibitory. When an excitatory connection links two nodes, the two nodes suggest each other. Consider the nodes for the word *TRAP* and the letter *T,* for example. Imagine seeing a stimulus such as "___RAP"—a crossword puzzle with four blanks, the last three of which are filled in with *R, A,* and *P,* for example. Wouldn't this suggest the word *TRAP* to you? If so, a connectionist would say that your node for *TRAP* had been activated.

Once a node is activated, that activation spreads along that node's excitatory connections to other nodes. If the *TRAP* node has an excitatory connection to the *T* node, then the *T* node will become more active when the *TRAP* node becomes more active, and vice versa. Excitatory connections are depicted in Figure 2-14 by arrows ending with points.

Connections can also be inhibitory, as that shown between the *TRAP* node and the *ABLE* node in Figure 2-14. That means that if the *TRAP* node is active, the *ABLE* node becomes less active. If you perceive the word *TRAP,* you are less likely to perceive the word *ABLE* at the same instant. The assumption is that you can perceive only one word at any given instant.

More could be said about this model, but our focus here is how a connectionist model can be used to explain the word superiority effect. Why might a letter be easier to perceive in the context of a word? According to this model, perception of a word—that is, activation of the relevant node for the word—also activates the nodes corresponding to all of the letters within the word, thereby facilitating their perception. Without the word context, the node for the individual letter is less active, so perception of the letter takes longer.

Gestalt Approaches to Perception

One of the most important aspects of visual perception has to do with how we interpret stimulus arrays as consisting of objects and backgrounds. Con-

FIGURE 2-15.   Goblet/silhouetted faces

sider, for instance, Figure 2-15. This stimulus pattern can be seen in two distinct ways: as a white vase against a black background or as two silhouetted faces against a white background. This segregation of the whole display into objects (also called the *figure*) and the background (also called the *ground*) is an important process known to cognitive psychologists as form perception.

This segregation has many consequences. That part of the display seen as figure is seen as having a definite shape, as being some sort of "thing," and will be better remembered than that part of the display interpreted as ground, which will be seen as more shapeless, unformed, and further away in space (Brown & Deffenbacher, 1979). Form perception is a cognitive task that most of us perform quickly and easily, and thus take for granted. We assume, intuitively, that we perceive objects and backgrounds because there really are objects and backgrounds; all we do is see them.

But consider Figure 2-16. Almost everyone will see this figure as consisting of two triangles, overlaid so as to form a six-pointed star. The corners of the top triangle are typically seen as resting on three black circles. Now look closely at the figure, in particular at the top triangle. Recall that a triangle is defined as a closed geometric figure that has three sides. Notice that in the figure itself, there are no sides. There is only white space that you, the viewer, interpret as a triangle. You, the viewer, are somehow adding the three sides or contours. Gregory (1972), who studies this phenomenon (called illusory, or subjective, contours), believes this relatively complex display is subject to a simplifying interpretation: a triangle is lying atop other parts of the figure and blocking them from view. The point here

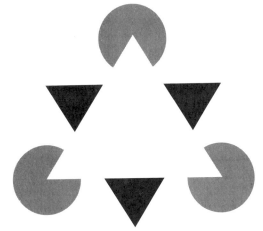

FIGURE 2-16.   Subjective, or illusory, contours

is that this perception is not completely determined by the stimulus display—it requires the perceiver's active participation.

A number of individuals in the early part of this century—among them Max Wertheimer, Kurt Koffka, and Wolfgang Köhler—were deeply interested in how perceivers come to recognize objects or forms. These researchers, who formed the Gestalt school of psychology, were particularly concerned with how people apprehended *whole* objects, concepts, or units. The Gestalt psychologists believed that perceivers follow certain laws or principles of organization in coming to the interpretations they do. They first and foremost asserted that the whole, or Gestalt, is not the same as the sum of its parts. Put another way, Gestalt psychologists rejected the claim that we recognize objects by identifying individual features or parts; instead, we see and recognize each object or unit as a whole.

What are the principles of organization that allow us to see these wholes? The complete list is too long to describe (see Koffka, 1935), so we will here examine only five major principles. The first is the principle of proximity, or nearness. Look at Figure 2-17(a). Notice that you tend to perceive this as a set of rows, rather than as a set of columns. The reason for this is that the elements within rows are closer than the elements within columns. Following the principle of proximity, we group together things that are nearer to each other.

Figure 2-17(b) illustrates the principle of similarity. Notice that you perceive this display as formed in columns (rather than rows), grouping together those elements that are similar. A third principle, the principle of good continuation, depicted in Figure 2-17(c), states that we group together objects whose contours form a continuous straight or curved line. Thus, we typically perceive Figure 2-17(c) as two intersecting curved lines and not as other logically possible elements (for example, Figure 2-17(d)).

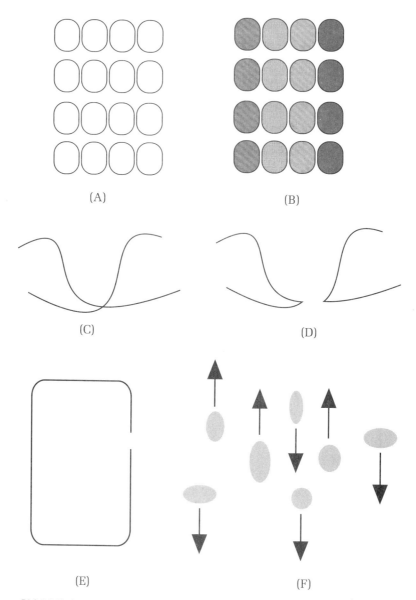

(A)   (B)

(C)   (D)

(E)   (F)

FIGURE 2-17.   Gestalt principles of perceptual organization

We encountered the fourth principle, the principle of closure, when we looked at subjective contours. Figure 2-17(e) illustrates this principle more exactly. Note that we perceive this display as a rectangle, mentally filling in the gap to see a closed, complete, whole figure. The fifth principle, the principle of common fate, is difficult to illustrate in a static drawing. The idea is that elements that move together will be grouped together, as depicted in Figure 2-17(f). You can construct a better demonstration of this principle yourselves (Matlin, 1988). Take two pieces of transparent plastic (such as report covers, cut in half). Glue some scraps of paper on each. Lay one sheet upside down on top of the other, and you will have a hard time telling which sheet of plastic any particular scrap is on. Now, move one sheet, holding the other still. You will suddenly see two distinct groups of scraps.

Most of the Gestalt principles are subsumed under a more general law, the law of Prägnanz (Koffka, 1935). This law states that, of all the possible ways of interpreting a display, we will tend to select that organization that yields the simplest and most stable shape or form. Thus simple and symmetrical forms are seen more easily than more-complicated and asymmetrical forms. This law may help to explain our experience of Figure 2–16, with subjective contours. Because the phantom "triangle" forms a simple, symmetrical form, we "prefer" to interpret the pattern as if the triangle were there.

Despite its intuitive appeal, the Gestalt approach to form perception leaves a number of questions unanswered (Pomerantz & Kubovy, 1981). We don't know, for instance, just how these principles are translated into cognitive or physiological processes. Moreover, without further specification, the law of Prägnanz can be seen as circular. (Why do we see two triangles in Figure 2-16? Because this interpretation makes for a simple, stable figure. How do we know that this figure is simple and stable? Because we so readily see it.)

Many cognitive psychologists studying perception acknowledge their debt to the Gestalt psychologists. The challenge for current researchers is to blend the rich observations of Gestalt psychology with research techniques designed to tell us just how the processes used in form perception operate.

Direct Perception

The models of perception we have looked at so far all share a common assumption. Recall that, as shown in Figure 2-1, the perceiver has to acquire information about a distal stimulus, presumably by interpreting the proximal stimuli (retinal images, in the case of visual perception). The common assumption underlying the models of perception we have examined (especially the top-down models) is that the perceiver does something to the proximal stimulus. Presumably, because the proximal stimulus doesn't contain all of the information we need to identify the object (for instance, because retinal images are two-dimensional instead of three-dimensional or because objects might be blurred or blocked by other objects), we as observers have to use our knowledge to fill in gaps.

Put more simply, these models describe the act of perception as the construction of mental representations of objects. From the information we are perceiving we somehow construct a depiction that may or may not physically resemble the object or event being perceived but that our cognitive and physiological processes can recognize as corresponding to the information to be perceived. We use both the information in the proximal stimulus and information from our long-term memory to construct these mental representations.

This idea is called the constructivist approach to perception (J. E. Hochberg, 1978), for obvious reasons. It describes people as adding to and distorting the information in the proximal stimulus to obtain a percept, a meaningful interpretation of incoming information. People are not seen as passively taking in all the available information—instead, they are seen as active selectors, integrators, and constructors of information.

James J. Gibson and his followers (Gibson, 1979; Michaels & Carello, 1981) adopted an opposite stance. Gibson rejected the idea that perceivers construct mental representations from memories of past encounters with similar objects and events. Instead, Gibson believed that the perceiver does very little work—mainly because the world offers so much information, leaving little need to construct representations and draw inferences. Gibson believed, in contrast, that perception consists of the direct acquisition of information from the environment.

According to this view, the light that hits the retina contains highly organized information that requires little or no interpretation. In the world we live in, certain aspects of stimuli remain invariant (or unchanging), despite changes over time or in our physical relationship to them. You may already be familiar with the idea of invariance. For example, consider a melody played on a piano in the key of C. Now, imagine that same melody transposed to the key of G. Though all of the individual notes in the melody have been changed, the melody is still easily recognized. Many listeners might not even recognize the key change, if sufficient time lapses between renditions. The elements (notes) have changed, but the relationships between the notes have remained constant or invariant.

A visual example of perceptual invariance was demonstrated in a study by Johansson (1973). Light bulbs were attached to the shoulders, elbows, wrists, hips, knees, and ankles of a model who wore black clothing and was photographed in the dark, so that only the lights could be seen, as shown in Figure 2-18. Subjects shown a still photograph of the model reported seeing only a random group of lights. Subjects who saw a videotape of the model engaged in familiar activities—walking, dancing, climbing and so forth—immediately recognized a person carrying out a particular activity. Later work (Koslowski & Cutting, 1977) even showed that subjects could tell the difference between a male and a female model, just by the movement of the lights!

Apparently, the motion of the light bulbs relative to one another provides an observer enough information to detect a human being in motion. Note that in this example the observer does not get to see the shape

FIGURE 2-18.   A depiction of Johansson's (1973) experimental stimuli. SOURCE: From "Visual Perception of Biological Motion and a Model for Its Analysis," by G. Johansson, 1973, *Perception and Psychophysics, 14,* 202. Reprinted by permission of Psychonomic Society, Inc.

of the person, or any individual features such as hair, eyes, hands, feet. If a human form can be quickly recognized under these limited viewing conditions, imagine how much more information is available under normal circumstances.

Gibson (1950) became convinced that motion—in particular, patterns of motion—provides a great deal of information to the perceiver. His work selecting and training pilots in World War II led him to thinking about the information available to pilots as they landed their planes. He developed the idea of optic flow, depicted in Figure 2-19 as the visual array presented to a pilot approaching a runway for landing. The arrows represent perceived movement—that is, the apparent movement of the ground, clouds, and other objects relative to the pilot. There is a texture to this

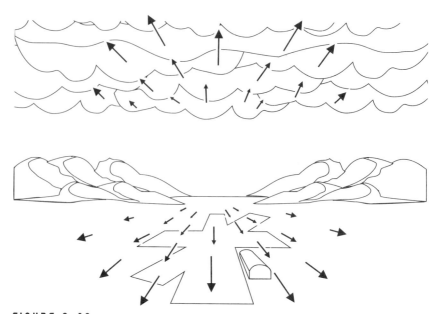

FIGURE 2-19.   A depiction of optic flow. SOURCE: From Gibson, James J., *The Perception of the Visual World.* Copyright © 1971, 1950 by Houghton Mifflin Company. Used with permission.

motion: nearer things appear to move faster than things farther away, and the direction an object seems to move depends on the angle of the plane's movement in relation to it. The pilot can use all of this information to navigate the plane to the runway.

Turvey, Shaw, Reed, and Mace (1981) argue that whereas non-Gibsonian models of perception try to explain how people come to perceptual beliefs and judgments, Gibson tries to explain how people "adjust," physically and otherwise, to the environment. For Gibson, the central question of perception is not how we look at and interpret a stimulus array but rather how we see and navigate among real things in the world. How is it that we don't normally walk into walls, for instance, or that we flinch from a perceived impending collision?

Another important idea in Gibson's theory is that the information available to an organism exists not merely in the environment but in an animal-environment ecosystem (Michaels & Carello, 1981). As animals move about, they continuously experience their environments. Different biological organisms will have different perceptual experiences, because (among other things) different organisms have different environments, different relationships to their environments, or both.

According to Gibson, organisms directly perceive not only shapes and whole objects, but also each object's **affordances**—the "acts or behaviors permitted by objects, places, and events" (Michaels & Carello, 1981, p.

42)—in other words, the things offered by the environment to the organism. Thus, for human beings, chairs afford sitting, a handle or knob affords grasping, a glass window affords looking through. Gibson (1979) claims that the affordances of an object are also directly perceived—that is, we "see" that a chair is for sitting, just as easily as we "see" that a chair is two feet away or made of wood.

According to Gibson, then, we avoid crashing into walls and closed doors because such surfaces do *not* afford passing through, and we perceive this as we move toward them. We sit on chairs or tables or floors but not on top of bodies of water, because the former objects afford sitting while the latter does not. By virtue of our activity with and around different objects, we pick up on these affordances and act accordingly. Perception and action, for Gibson, are intimately bound.

Gibsonian theory has been both staunchly admired and sharply criticized. Fodor and Pylyshyn (1981), for example, argue that Gibson's proposals, while intriguing, are not well defined. Without sharp definitions of what an affordance is, they argue, the theory is not helpful in explaining perception. They charge that Gibson failed to specify just what kinds of things are invariant, and what kinds are not. Without this specification, the following kinds of circular explanations can result:

> So, for example, we can give the following disarmingly simple answer to the question: how do people perceive that something is a shoe? There is a certain (invariant) property that all and only shoes have—namely, the property of being a shoe. Perceiving that something *is* a shoe consists in the pickup of this property. (Fodor & Pylyshyn, 1981, p. 142)

How much of a challenge do Gibsonian views pose to constructivist views of perception? Put another way, can the constructivist and the direct perception views be reconciled? Cognitive psychologists have not yet resolved the issue. One proposal tried to incorporate aspects of both approaches. Neisser (1976) describes what he calls the perceptual cycle, depicted in Figure 2-20. Cognitive structures called schemata (singular: **schema**), derived from the knowledge base and containing expectations derived from context, guide the perceiver to explore the environment in particular ways. The environment, in turn, supplies certain information that confirms some expectations but not others. This helps the perceiver modify her expectations, and, perhaps, bring other schemata to bear in the next cycle of perception. We will discuss the idea of schemata in much greater depth in Chapter 6. Note, for the present, that Neisser's model again assumes an active perceiver.

However the debate between supporters and critics of Gibson is resolved, he has reminded everyone in cognitive psychology of the need to pay attention to the way cognition operates outside of the laboratory, and of the relationship between the way information is processed and the goals and needs of the organism doing the processing. We will return to these themes throughout the book.

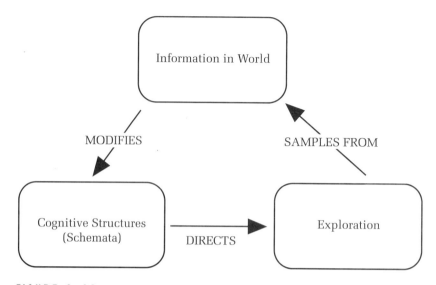

FIGURE 2-20.   Neisser's (1976) perceptual cycle. SOURCE: From *Cognition and Reality,* by Ulric Neisser. Copyright © 1976 by W. H. Freeman and Company. Reprinted by permission.

Summary

We have seen a number of distinct approaches to the study of perception. Despite differences in the theoretical assumptions made and the experimental methods used in each approach, researchers would agree on at least three general principles.

The first is that perception is more than the sum of static, individual sensory inputs. Perception clearly involves some integration and, perhaps, some interpretation of the sensations we receive. Perception is *not* a matter of simply taking in information from the world and creating from it a duplicate internal representation. Perception sometimes involves "seeing" things that are not there (as in the case of subjective contours) or distorting things that are (as in the case of other context effects).

Second, perception involves the acquisition of a great deal of information. The fact that we perceive most things quickly and easily hides the fact that the process of perception is complicated indeed. The connectionist model of letter perception illustrates just how complex the task of recognizing single letters (all typewritten in a single, simple font) can be. Imagine, then, how difficult perceiving objects and events in the real world can be.

Finally, perception involves a great deal of activity on the part of the perceiver. We do more than simply record the visual world around us; we are not cameras. In both the constructivist and the direct-perception approaches to perception, perception is assumed to be the result of activity, either mental or physical. We navigate through the world, gathering information as we go, seeking more information about objects of interest as a matter of course. Any theory of perception must ultimately take into account our own activity in our everyday perception.

The topic of perception is fundamental to the study of cognition and will relate to many of the topics discussed later in this book. Perception relates directly to attention, for example, the subject of Chapter 3, in that often our level of attention affects whether or not we perceive and remember something. When we talk about imagery, in Chapter 7, we will look again at how people process visual information. Moreover, what is perceived often constrains what else the perceiver can do with the information, in terms of recording and storing it, thinking about it, and drawing inferences from it. We will thus continue to encounter perceptual issues in the chapters ahead.

Recommended Readings

Good general introductions to the topic of perception can be found in J. E. Hochberg (1978) and Rock (1983). Recent reviews of literature relating to perception include Cutting (1987), J. Hochberg (1988), and Banks and Krajicek (1991). Pinker (1984) offers a particularly good bridge between topics covered under "bottom-up" models in this book, and current research problems. Diehl (1981) critiques the feature-detection approach to speech perception, and Biederman (1987) offers an account of how we recognize objects by the detection of primitive units called *geons,* that can be thought of as configurations of features. A recent article by Robertson and Lamb (1991) reports on neuropsychological work on the perception of whole objects versus the perception of parts of objects.

Classic works in Gestalt psychology include those by Koffka (1935) and Köhler (1929/1947), and chapters in Kubovy and Pomerantz (1981) provide an update on research relating to many of the Gestalt proposals. Arnheim (1986) corrects some modern misconceptions of Gestalt theory.

Gordon (1989) covers all of the major schools of perception, including chapters on psychophysics, neuropsychology, Gestalt psychology, and direct perception. A volume edited by Beck (1982) contains a number of relevant chapters, including ones by Kaniza and Gerbino on subjective contours, James Gibson on direct perception, and Eleanor J. Gibson on a comparison between Gibsonian and Gestalt approaches to perception.

Computer scientists interested in artificial intelligence face many of the problems confronting perceptual psychologists as they try to build computer systems that can perceive real objects and scenes. A textbook by Charniak and McDermott (1985) provides an introduction to some of this work. The interested student might also look at the work of David Marr (1982), a researcher who tried to bring together work in neuropsychology, artificial intelligence, and cognitive psychology to develop a "computational" approach to vision. Gordon (1989) provides a good introduction to his work; Marr's own book is quite technical.

REVIEW QUESTIONS

1. Describe the differences in assumptions about perception made by researchers working in the (a) information-processing, (b) connectionist, and (c) Gibsonian ecological paradigms.

2. Distinguish between bottom-up and top-down perceptual processes.

3. In what ways are featural analysis and prototype-matching models an improvement over template-matching models? In what ways are they not?

4. Describe some real-life examples of context effects in perception.

5. Describe two of the Gestalt laws of perceptual organization, illustrating each with a specific example.

6. Consider McClelland and Rumelhart's connectionist model of letter perception. How might a Gestalt psychologist regard this model—what would she or he see as the model's strengths and weaknesses?

7. Discuss the following: "Part of the reason that Gibson's supporters and detractors have such spirited debates is that they are talking past each other. Gibson doesn't just present a different model of perception—he redefines what the task of perception is."

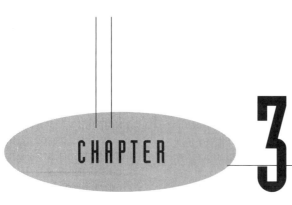

CHAPTER 3

Attention and Automaticity

Consider the task of driving a car. Besides involving many physical skills—such as steering, braking, and shifting, if you're driving a car with a manual transmission—driving also involves many cognitive processes. Perception is obviously one of them—you need quickly to recognize relevant objects, such as stop signs, pedestrians, or oncoming cars.

Driving also requires mental effort or concentration—what cognitive psychologists call **attention.** The amount of attention required at any given time depends partly on the complexity of the situation around you— driving on wide side streets with no traffic is usually easier than driving during rush hour on crowded freeways. Your level of concentration also depends on your level of expertise at driving.

Recall your first driving experiences. Most people, behind the wheel of a car for the first time, wear a look of extreme concentration. Gripping the wheel tightly, eyes darting at the street or parking lot ahead, the novice driver has great difficulty carrying on a conversation, tuning the car radio to a favorite station, or eating a hamburger. Six months later, given both sufficient driving experience and normal conditions, the same driver may well be able to converse, fiddle with knobs, eat, and drive—all at the same time.

Cognitive psychologists studying attention are concerned primarily with cognitive resources and their limitations. At any given time, they believe, people have only a certain amount of mental energy to devote to all the possible tasks confronting them. If they devote some portion of those resources to one task, less is available for others. The more complex and unfamiliar the task, the more mental resources must be allocated to that task to perform it successfully.

Consider again the example of driving. The novice driver faces a complicated task indeed. She must learn to operate many mechanisms—gas pedal, brake, gear shift, clutch, lights, high-beam switch, turn signal, and so on. At the same time, while the car is in motion, the driver must scan ahead to see what's in front of the car (the road, trees, brick walls, and the like) and should also occasionally check the speedometer and the rearview mirrors. That's a lot to master and, unsurprisingly, presents such a complicated set of demands that few cognitive resources are left for other kinds of cognitive tasks—talking, tuning the radio, fishing out a stick of gum from a purse or backpack.

However, with practice, the driver knows exactly where all the mechanisms are and how to operate them. An experienced driver can "find" the break pedal with little effort, for example. The practiced driver has learned how to operate the car, scan the road, check relevant instruments—all more or less simultaneously. With many more cognitive resources available to devote to other tasks, experienced drivers do all sorts of other things while they drive—listen to the radio, talk on car phones, plan their day, rehearse speeches, and so on.

Anyone who has to operate complicated equipment or monitor many instruments simultaneously faces similar challenges. Air traffic controllers, medical personnel working in hospital intensive-care wards, and commercial pilots must all process a great deal of information from different monitors and instruments—much of it arriving simultaneously—and respond quickly and appropriately. Mistakes in any of these jobs can be costly.

The following example, quoted in a recent study of the design of auditory warning sounds in airplane cockpits (Patterson, 1990), illustrates how too much incoming information can lead to a breakdown in task performance.

> "I was flying in a Jetstream at night when my peaceful reverie was shattered by the stall audio warning, the stick shaker, and several warning lights. The effect was exactly what was *not* intended; I was frightened numb for several seconds and drawn off instruments trying to work out how to cancel the audio/visual assault rather than taking what should be instinctive actions.
>
> "The combined assault is so loud and bright that it is impossible to talk to the other crew member, and action is invariably taken to cancel the cacophony before getting on with the actual problem." (p. 485)

Clearly, people who design equipment and instruments should know how people process large amounts of information and how much information we can process at one time. System designers often consult human factors psychologists, who study just these sorts of issues (C. D. Wickens, 1987).

Our goal in this chapter is to explain what is going on, cognitively speaking, in the preceding examples. More specifically, we will examine

An operator working with this instrument panel has a great deal of information to monitor simultaneously.

the issue of mental resources and how they are assigned to various cognitive tasks. We'll first explore the notion of mental concentration; in particular, we will try to explain what "paying attention" to someone or something means. We will see that at least part of "paying attention" is concentrating—shutting out other activities or information to devote more mental resources to the object on which you want to focus.

Second, we'll examine how a person's concentration level changes with practice. For many tasks, extensive practice can result in the task's becoming so easy and effortless that performing it requires little attention. When this happens, performance is said to be automatic. An example of automatic performance from my own experience again relates to driving. I alternate between driving two cars—a Plymouth Voyager and a Honda Civic. The Voyager has the gear shift on the wheel; the Civic's gear shift is on the floor. If I've been driving the Civic for a while and then start driving the Voyager, I find that I automatically reach for a gear shift on the floor—much to the surprise and consternation of any passengers. I do this quickly and effortlessly, without thinking about it. In fact, it takes more effort to *stop* myself from doing this than to simply do it.

By contrast, however, I can do certain kinds of tasks simultaneously with other tasks. For example, I can read the newspaper while listening to music; I wrote a version of this sentence while listening to an old episode of *Dragnet*. To be sure, the number and kinds of things I can do simultaneously is limited. Cognitive psychologists are interested in when and how people divide their attention among different tasks. We'll explore these issues toward the end of this chapter.

Selective Attention

The term *selective attention* refers to the fact that we usually focus our attention on one or a few tasks or events rather than on many. To say that we mentally focus our resources implies that we shut out (or at least process less information from) other, competing tasks. Presumably, we process information about things we are not now paying attention to differently (if at all) from information about those things we are focusing on.

How do cognitive psychologists study what information people process about things to which they are not paying attention? If you think about it, this is a tough challenge: how do you present people with information while making sure that they do not pay attention to it? Simply instructing them to not pay attention is almost guaranteed to have the opposite effect.

It turns out that there is a solution well known to cognitive psychologists, known as the **dichotic listening task,** depicted in Figure 3-1. It works like this: A person listens to an audiotape over a set of headphones. On the tape are different messages, recorded so as to be heard simultaneously in opposite ears or simultaneously in both ears. Subjects in a dichotic listening task typically are played two or more different messages (often texts borrowed from literature, newspaper stories, or speeches) and asked to "shadow"—that is, to repeat aloud—one of them. Information is typically presented at a rapid rate (150 words per minute), so the shadowing task is a demanding one. At the end of the shadowing task, subjects are asked what information they remember from either message—the attended message or the unattended message.

The logic of this experimental setup is as follows: The subject must concentrate on the message to be shadowed. Because the rate of presentation of information is so fast, the shadowing task is difficult and requires a

At long last they came to a fork in the road . . .

Many linguists make a distinction between the logical form . . .

FIGURE 3-1.   Depiction of a dichotic listening task. The listener hears two messages and is asked to repeat ("shadow") one of them.

great deal of mental resources. Therefore, fewer resources are available to process information from the nonshadowed, nonattended message.

Cherry (1953) demonstrated in a classic study that people are capable of shadowing a message spoken at a normal to rapid rate with few errors. When these subjects were later questioned about the material in the unattended message, they were nearly always able to report accurately whether the message contained speech or noise and, if speech, whether the voice of the speaker belonged to a man or to a woman. When the unattended message consisted of speech played backward, subjects reported noticing that some aspect of the message, which they assumed to be normal speech, was vaguely odd. Subjects were unable to recall the content of the unattended message or the language it was spoken in. In one variation of the procedure, the language of the unattended message was changed from English to German, but subjects apparently did not notice the switch.

Subjects in another experiment (Moray, 1959) heard prose in the attended message and a short list of simple words in the unattended message. Subjects failed to recognize the occurrence of most of the words in the unattended message, even though the list had been repeated 35 times!

Filter Theory

To explain these findings, Broadbent (1958) proposed a **filter theory** of attention, which states that the amount of information that can be attended to at any given time is limited. Therefore, if the amount of information available at any given time exceeds capacity, an attentional filter is used to let some information through and block the rest. The filter (see Figure 3-2) is based on some physical aspect of the attended message: the location of its source or its typical pitch, for instance. Only material that gets past the filter can be analyzed later for meaning. This theory explains why so little of the meaning of the unattended message can be recalled: the meaning from an unattended message is simply not processed.

Does this mean that people can never pay attention to two messages at once? Broadbent (1958) thought not, believing instead that what is limited is the amount of information we can process at any given time. Two messages that contain little information or that present information slowly can be processed simultaneously. For example, a subject might be able to attend simultaneously to more than one message (if one repeated the same word over and over again because it would contain little information). In contrast, messages that present a great deal of information quickly take up more mental capacity; fewer can be attended to at once. The filter thus serves to protect us from "information overload" by shutting out messages when there is too much information to process all at once.

Other investigators soon reported results that contradicted filter theory. Moray (1959) discovered one of the most famous, called the cocktail party effect: Subjects' shadowing performance is disrupted when their own

Incoming Messages

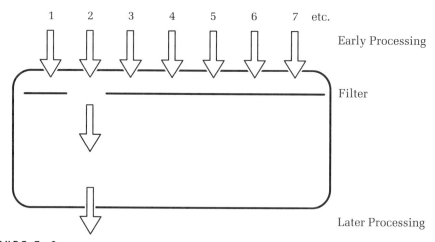

FIGURE 3-2.   Depiction of a filter model of attention. Different incoming messages, shown as arrows, all arrive at the same time. The filter (black line) blocks all but Message 2, which goes on for more cognitive processing.

name is embedded in either the attended or the unattended message. Moreover, subjects hear and remember hearing their names. You may have had a similar experience at a crowded social gathering: While engaged in conversation with one or more people, you hear someone behind you say your name. Until your name was spoken, you "heard" nothing that that speaker was saying; the sound of your name, in contrast, seems to reach out and grab your attention.

Why does the cocktail party effect pose a problem for filter theory? Filter theory predicts that all unattended messages will be filtered out—that is, not processed for recognition or meaning—which is why subjects in dichotic listening tasks can recall little information about such messages. The cocktail party effect shows something completely different: people *do* hear their own names in an unattended message or conversation, and hearing their names will cause them to switch their attention to the previously unattended message.

Moray (1959) concluded that only "important" material can penetrate the filter set up to block unattended messages. Presumably, messages such as those containing a subject's name are important enough to get through the filter and be analyzed for meaning. Left to be explained, then, is how the filter "knows" which messages are important enough to let pass.

Treisman (1960) discovered a related problem. She played subjects two messages, each presented to a different ear, and asked the subjects to shadow one of them. At a certain point in the middle of the messages, the

FIGURE 3-3.   Depiction of Treisman's (1960) experimental paradigm. The two messages "switch ears" at the point indicated by the slash mark.

content of the first message and the second message was switched, so that the second continued the first and vice versa (see Figure 3-3).

Immediately after the two messages "switched ears," many subjects repeated one or two words from the "unattended ear." In the example shown, for instance, a subject shadowing Message 1 might say, "At long last they came to a fork in the road but did not know which way to go. The trees on the left *side of* refers to the relationships . . .," with the italicized words following the meaning of the first part of Message 1 but coming from the unattended channel (because they come after the switch point).

To explain this result, Treisman reasoned that subjects must be basing their selection of which message to attend to at least in part on the meaning of the message, a possibility that filter theory does not allow for. Interestingly, most subjects had no idea that the passages had been switched, or that they had repeated words from the "wrong ear." Again, this poses a problem for filter theory, because it predicts that information from the unattended channel would be shut out.

Attenuation Theory

In response, Treisman (1960) proposed a modified filter theory, one she called attenuation theory. Instead of considering unattended messages to be completely blocked before they can be processed for meaning (as in filter theory), Treisman argued that their "volume" was "turned down"—in other words, that some meaningful information in unattended messages might still be available, even if it were hard to recover. She explained this idea as follows: Incoming messages are subjected to three kinds of analysis. In the first, the message's physical properties, such as pitch or loudness, are analyzed. The second analysis is linguistic in nature, a process of parsing the message into syllables and words. The third kind of analysis is semantic, processing the meaning of the message.

Some meaningful units (such as words or phrases) tend to be processed quite easily. Words that have subjective importance (such as your name) or that signal danger ("Fire!" "Watch out!") have permanently lowered thresholds; that is, they are recognizable even at low volumes. You might have noticed yourself that it is hard to hear something whispered behind you, though you might recognize your name in whatever is being whispered. Words or phrases with permanently lowered thresholds require little mental effort by the hearer to be recognized. Thus, according to Treisman's theory, the subjects in Moray's experiments heard their names because recognizing their names required little mental effort.

Only a few words have permanently lowered thresholds. However, the context of a word in a message can temporarily lower its threshold. If a subject hears, "The dog chased the . . .," the word *cat* is **primed**—that is, especially ready to be recognized. Even if the word *cat* were to occur in the unattended channel, little effort would be needed to hear and process it. This explains why subjects in Treisman's experiment "switched ears": hearing the previous words in a sentence primed the subjects to detect and recognize the words that followed, even when those words occurred in the unattended message.

Similarly, MacKay (1973) showed that the presence of a word in the unattended message (for instance, *river*) helps "disambiguate" (clarify) the meaning of an ambiguous sentence in the attended message (for instance, "They threw stones toward the bank yesterday"). The sample sentence is ambiguous because the word *bank* could refer to the shores of a river or to a financial institution. If the unattended message contains the word *river,* however, the subject will understand the sentence to be referring to the shores of a river. To explain this result, we must assume that at least some meaningful aspects of the unattended message are processed. Here, as we saw in Chapter 2, perceiving and attending to information we are expecting is easier than perceiving and attending to unexpected information.

According to Treisman (1964), people process only as much as is necessary to separate the attended from the unattended message. If the two messages differ in physical characteristics, then we process both messages only to this level and easily reject the unattended message. If the two messages differ only semantically, we process both through the level of meaning and select which message to attend to based on this analysis. Processing for meaning takes more effort, however, so we only do this kind of analysis when necessary.

Messages that are not attended to are not completely blocked but, rather, weakened in much the way that turning down the volume weakens an audio signal from a stereo. Parts of the message with permanently lowered thresholds ("significant" stimuli) can still be recovered, even from an unattended message. Note the contrasts here between attenuation theory and filter theory: Attenuation theory allows for many different kinds of analyses of all messages, while filter theory allows for only one. Filter theory holds that unattended messages, once processed for physical characteristics, are discarded and fully blocked; attenuation theory holds that unattended messages are weakened but the information they contain is still available.

Late Selection Theory

Broadbent's (1958) filter theory held that no information about the meaning of an unattended message gets through the filter to be retained for future use. Treisman's (1964) attenuation theory allows for some information about meaning getting through to conscious awareness. Deutsch and Deutsch (1963) proposed a theory, called the *late-selection theory,* that goes even further. Later elaborated and extended by Norman (1968), this theory holds that *all* messages are routinely processed for meaning—that selection of which message to respond to thus happens "late" in processing.

Note that filter theory hypothesizes a *bottleneck*—a point at which the processes a person can bring to bear on information is greatly limited—at the filter. Late-selection theory also describes a bottleneck but locates it later in the processing, after the meaning has been extracted. All material is processed up to this point, and that information judged to be most "important" is elaborated more fully. This elaborated material is more likely to be retained; unelaborated material is forgotten.

A message's "importance" depends on many factors, including its context and the personal significance of certain kinds of content (such as your name). Also relevant is the observer's level of alertness: at low levels of alertness (as when we are asleep) only very important messages (such as the sound of our newborn's cry) will capture attention. At higher levels of alertness, less important messages (such as the sound of a television program) can be processed. Generally, the attentional system functions to determine which of the incoming messages is the most important; this message is the one to which the observer will respond.

Multimode Theory

Strictly interpreted, filter theory doesn't quite explain why some messages (or some parts of messages) in the unattended channel become noticed. On the other hand, a strict late-selection theory encounters problems in explaining why, if many messages can be simultaneously processed for meaning, any messages ever get shut out. Though each model appears to explain different aspects of attention, some broader model, which incorporates both other models, seems needed.

Johnston and Heinz (1978) proposed such a model, called the *multimode theory.* In their view, attention is a flexible system that allows selection of one message over others at several different points. They describe three stages of processing: Stage 1, during which sensory representations of stimuli are constructed; Stage 2, during which semantic representations are constructed; and Stage 3, during which sensory and semantic representations enter consciousness. (For purposes of comparison, Johnston and Heinz associate Broadbent's filter theory with Stage 1 selection, and Deutsch and Deutsch's late-selection model with Stage 3 processing). More processing requires more capacity and thus more mental effort. When messages are selected on the basis of Stage 1 processing ("early selection"), less capacity is required than if selection is based on Stage 3 processing ("late selection"). Thus, the later the selection, the harder the task.

Johnston and Heinz (1978) tested this proposal in a clever experiment. Subjects were asked to perform two tasks simultaneously. The first was a standard dichotic listening task. The sex of the speaker presenting the messages sometimes differed, thus facilitating early selection. At other times, the same speaker presented both messages, which differed only in meaning, thus requiring late selection.

The second task involved detecting and responding as quickly as possible to randomly presented lights by pressing a key. Johnston and Heinz (1978) reasoned that the more attention required by the listening task, the less processing capacity would be available for other tasks. Hence, they predicted that with fewer resources available subjects would react slower in pressing the keys. The results supported their predictions. Selecting a message on the basis of sound (the speaker's sex) was easy, as shown by the quickness with which subjects responded to the light. Presumably, relatively little capacity was needed for the listening task, leaving more mental resources available for detecting the light. On the other hand, selecting a message on the basis of meaning is hard, and subjects required to do so responded much more slowly to the light.

Interestingly, a later experiment by Johnston and Heinz (1978) showed that reaction times were similar whether subjects had to select a message from among two or three messages. This finding implies that processing unattended messages does not require many mental resources (if it had, then selecting one message out of three ought to have been harder than selecting one message out of two). What appears to take mental effort is the selection of one message from among two or more.

Attention, Capacity, and Mental Effort

Broadbent (1958) originally described attention as a bottleneck that squeezed some information out of the processing area. To understand the analogy, think about the shape of a bottle. The smaller diameter of the bottle's neck relative to the diameter of the bottom of the bottle reduces the rate of spillage. The wider the neck, the faster the contents can spill. Applying this analogy to cognitive processes, the wider the bottleneck, the more information can "spill through" to be processed at any point in time.

Work such as that by Johnston and Heinz (1978) has led many to use new metaphors when talking about attention. For example, some compare attention to a spotlight that highlights whatever information the system is currently focused on (Johnston & Dark, 1986). Accordingly, psychologists are concerned less with determining what information *can't* be processed than with studying what kinds of information people choose to *focus* on (as a spotlight, aimed at one spot, also more or less lights surrounding areas, depending on the size and intensity of the spotlight).

Some cognitive psychologists, such as Daniel Kahneman (1973), view attention as a set of cognitive processes for categorizing and recognizing stimuli. The more complex the stimulus, the harder the processing, and therefore the more resources are engaged. However, people have some control over where they direct their mental resources—they can often choose what to focus on and devote their mental effort to.

Figure 3-4 presents Kahneman's (1973) model of attention, based on the capacity theory. Essentially, this model depicts the allocation of mental resources to various cognitive tasks. Many factors influence this allocation, which itself depends on the extent and type of mental resources available. The availability of mental resources, in turn, is affected by the overall level of *arousal,* or state of alertness. Kahneman (1973) argues that one of the effects of being aroused is that more cognitive resources are available to devote to various tasks. Paradoxically, however, the level of arousal also depends on the difficulty of a task. This means that we are less aroused while performing easy tasks, such as adding 2 + 2, than we are when performing more difficult tasks, such as multiplying our social security number by pi. We therefore bring fewer cognitive resources to easy tasks, which, fortunately, require fewer resources to complete.

Arousal thus affects our **capacity** (the sum total of our mental resources) for tasks. But the model still needs to specify how we allocate our resources to all the cognitive tasks that confront us. Look again at Figure 3-4, this time at the region labeled "allocation policy." Note that this policy is affected by an individual's enduring dispositions (for example, your preference for certain kinds of tasks over others), momentary intentions (your vow that you will find your meal card right now before doing anything else!), and evaluation of the demands on one's capacity (the knowledge that a task you need to do right now will require a certain amount of your attention). Essentially, this model predicts that we pay more attention to things that we are interested in, are in the mood for, or have judged to be important. For example, opera lovers listen carefully during an operatic performance, concentrating on nuances of the performance. People less interested in opera may sometimes have a hard time even staying awake.

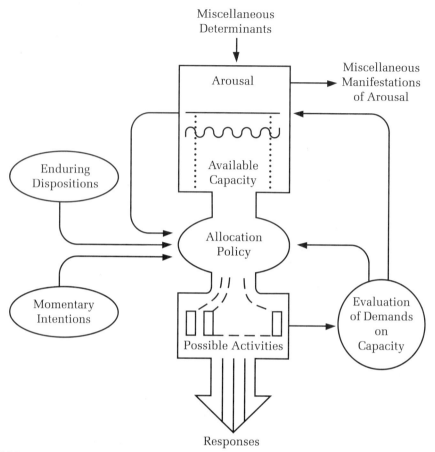

FIGURE 3-4.   Kahneman's (1973) model of attention and effort. SOURCE: From Daniel Kahneman, ATTENTION AND EFFORT, © 1973, p. 10. Adapted by permission of Prentice Hall, Englewood Cliffs, New Jersey. Reprinted by permission.

In Kahneman's (1973) view, attention is part of what the layperson would call mental effort. The more effort expended, the more attention we are using. This view raises the question of what limits our ability to do several things at once. We've already discussed arousal. A related factor is alertness as a function of the time of day, the hours of sleep obtained the night before, and so forth. At certain times we are able to attend to more tasks with greater concentration. At other times, as when we are tired and drowsy, focusing is hard. Everyday examples come readily to mind. Most people find that the time to engage in highly demanding mental activities, such as playing chess or balancing a checkbook, is not when they are tired. Such tasks are best left for times when we are well rested and seem to have more mental energy available to devote to them.

Effort is only one factor that influences performance on a task. Greater effort or concentration results in better performance of some tasks—

those that require resource-limited processing, performance of which is constrained by the mental resources or capacity allocated to it (Norman & Bobrow, 1975). Taking a midterm is one such task. Other tasks are such that one cannot do better no matter how hard one tries. An example might be trying to detect a dim light or a soft sound in a bright and noisy room. Even if you concentrate as hard as you can on such a task, your vigilance may still not help you detect the stimulus. Performance on this task is said to be data limited, meaning that it depends entirely on the quality of the incoming data, not on mental effort or concentration. Norman and Bobrow point out that both kinds of limitations affect our ability to perform any cognitive task.

Automaticity and the Effects of Practice

Another important variable that governs the number of things we can do simultaneously is the capacity consumed by a given task. Adding 2 + 3 consumes little of my capacity, leaving some left over for other tasks (such as planning what to have for dinner tonight and wondering if I have all the necessary ingredients at home).

What affects the capacity any given task requires? One factor is obviously the difficulty of the task. Another is the individual's familiarity with the task. Though easy for me, adding 2 + 3 still represents something of a challenge to a 5-year-old. The difference between us with respect to this task is practice—I've added 2 + 3 many more times than any 5-year-old has.

Practice is thought to decrease the amount of mental effort required to perform a task. Recall the earlier example of a novice automobile driver. The unpracticed task of controlling a car in motion requires so much mental effort that little capacity is available for other tasks, such as turning on a radio or responding to a conversation. Even coordinating driving with looking at the relevant instruments on the dashboard may be difficult, so intently focused may a novice driver's mental energy be. With just a few months' practice, however, a driver needs much less effort for the driving task itself. Mental capacity is available for other tasks, and the driver can now steer and talk at the same time. However, a complicated situation (such as a traffic accident during rush hour) will require even the most practiced driver to pay additional attention, temporarily diminishing his or her ability to converse or sing along with the radio.

The Stroop Task

A famous demonstration of the effects of practice on the performance of cognitive tasks was given by John Ridley Stroop (1935). Stroop presented

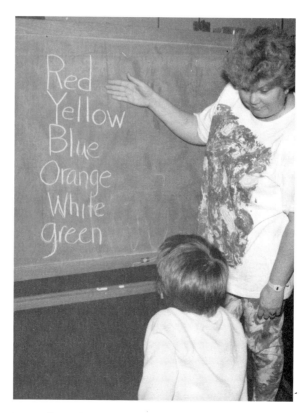

Extensive practice with reading will improve reading skills but will cause greater interference in the Stroop task.

subjects with a series of color bars (red, blue, green, brown, purple) or color words (red, blue, green, brown, purple) printed in conflicting colors (the word *red,* for example, might be printed in green ink), as shown in the left-hand figure on the inside front cover of this book. Subjects were asked to name, as quickly as possible, the ink color of each item in the series. When shown bars, subjects were able to do so quickly, with few errors and apparently little effort. Things changed dramatically when the items consisted of words that named colors other than that of the ink in which the item was printed. Subjects stumbled through these lists, finding it difficult to not read the word formed by the letters.

According to Stroop (1935), the difficulty stems from the following: Adult, literate subjects have had so much practice reading that the task requires little attention and is performed rapidly. In fact, according to Stroop, literate adults read so quickly and effortlessly that *not* reading is hard. Thus, when confronted with items that consisted of words, subjects couldn't help but read them. We call this kind of response—one that takes little attention and effort and is hard to inhibit—an *automatic* one.

The task actually given subjects, to *name* colors, was one they had practiced much less. Subjects in one of Stroop's (1935) subsequent experiments, given eight days of practice at the naming task, in fact showed less interference in performing the so-called **Stroop task** and became faster at naming colors with all stimuli. Moreover, a summary of the literature on the Stroop effect suggests that Stroop interference begins when children learn to read, peaking at around second or third grade (when reading skills develop), then declining over the adult years until about age 60 (MacLeod, 1991). The implication here is that the more practice an individual has reading words, the more interference will be observed in the color-naming task. Conversely, extensive practice at color naming facilitates performance.

Automatic Versus Attentional (Controlled) Processing

Posner and Snyder (1975) offered three criteria for cognitive processing to be called "automatic": (1) it must occur without intention, (2) it must occur without involving conscious awareness, and (3) it must not interfere with other mental activity.

Let's consider our driving example once again. A practiced driver driving a familiar route under normal, nonstressful conditions may well be operating the car automatically. Driving home, for example, I've often found myself in the middle of making a turn without actually intending to—my hand seems to hit the turn signal and my arms to turn the steering wheel without my consciously deciding to do so. Indeed, sometimes I follow my usual route home even when I've previously intended to go a different way. For example, I will intend to go to the dry cleaners but start thinking of something else, and then to my surprise and embarrassment will find myself in my own driveway, simply because I forgot to change my automatic routine!

Schneider and Shiffrin (1977) examined automatic processing of information under well-controlled laboratory conditions. They asked subjects to search for certain targets, either letters or numbers, in different arrays of letters or numbers, called *frames.* Previous work had suggested that when people search for targets of one type (such as numbers) in an array of a different type (such as letters), the task is easy. Numbers against a background of letters seem to "pop out" automatically. In fact, the number of nontarget characters in an array, called distractors, makes little difference *if* the distractors are a different type than the targets. Finding a specific letter against a background of other letters seems much harder. When the target and the distractors are of the same type, the number of distractors does make a difference. Try these searches for yourself in the two frames presented in Figure 3-5.

Schneider and Shiffrin (1977) had two conditions in their experiment. In the *varied-mapping* condition, the set of letters or numbers to be

QSKPL

GJWXT

NZU8R

VDBCY

TQPRY

BMZXC

SLDKJ

WNJTF

FIGURE 3-5.   Example of visual search displays. Try searching for an *8* in the top panel, and compare that to searching for an *X* in the bottom panel.

searched for, called the memory set, consisted of one or more letters or numbers; the stimuli in each frame were also letters or numbers. Targets in one trial could become distractors in subsequent trials. The task was expected to be hard in this condition and to require concentration and effort. In the *consistent-mapping* condition, the memory set consisted of numbers, and the frame, of letters, or vice versa. Stimuli that were targets in one trial were never distractors in other trials. The task was expected to require less capacity to carry out in this condition. Figure 3-6 depicts the Schneider and Shiffrin task.

In addition, Schneider and Shiffrin (1977) varied three other factors to manipulate the attentional demands of the task. The first was the *frame size*—that is, the number of letters and numbers presented in each display. This number was always between one and four. Slots not occupied by a letter or number contained a random dot pattern.

Also manipulated was the *frame time*—that is, the length of time each array was displayed. This varied from approximately 20 milliseconds

FIGURE 3-6.   Depiction of stimuli presented in the Schneider and Shiffrin (1977) task. Their caption reads: "Two examples of a positive trial in the multiple-frame search paradigm of Experiment 1: (A) varied mapping with memory set = (J, D), and (B) consistent mapping with memory set = (4, 7, 8, 1). (1: presentation of memory set; a: fixation dot goes on for .5 sec when subject starts trial; b: three dummy frames that never contain target; c: distractor frames; d: target frame; e: distractor frames; f: dummy frames that never contain target. Frame time is varied across conditions.)" SOURCE: From "Controlled and Automatic Human Information Processing: I. Detection, Search and Attention," by W. Schneider and R. M. Shriffin, 1977, *Psychological Review, 88,* 11. Copyright © 1977 by the American Psychological Association. Reprinted by permission.

to 800 milliseconds. The last variable manipulated was the *memory set*— that is, the number of targets the subject was asked to find in each trial.

Though a bit complicated, Schneider and Shiffrin's results are depicted in Figure 3-7. In the consistent-mapping condition, argued to require only automatic processing, subjects' performance varied only with the frame time, not with the memory set or frame size. This means that subjects were just as accurate searching for one as for four targets, and searching among one, two, or four items in a frame. Accuracy depended only on the length of time the frames were displayed. In the varied-mapping condition, thought to require more than automatic processing, subjects' performance in detecting the target depended on all three variables.

Schneider and Shiffrin (1977) explained these results by distinguishing between two kinds of processing. **Automatic processing** is used for easy tasks and with familiar items. It operates in parallel (meaning that it can operate simultaneously with other processes) and does not strain capacity limitations. This is the kind of processing done in the consistent-mapping condition: because the targets "popped out" from the background, little effort or concentration was required. The fact that searching for four targets was as easy as searching for one illustrates the parallel nature of this kind of processing: several searches can be conducted simultaneously.

FIGURE 3-7.   Results of Schneider and Shiffrin's (1977) experiments. Notice that for subjects in the *consistent mapping* condition, only the variable of frame time affects reaction time. Subjects in the *varied mapping* condition are also affected by frame size, and memory set size. SOURCE: From "Controlled and Automatic Human Information Processing: I. Detection, Search and Attention," by W. Schneider and R. M. Shiffrin, 1977, *Psychological Review, 88,* 12. Copyright © 1977 by the American Psychological Association. Reprinted by permission.

Schneider and Shiffrin (1977) dubbed the second kind **controlled processing.** Controlled processing is used for difficult tasks and ones that involve unfamiliar processes. It usually operates serially (with one set of information processed at a time), requires attention, is capacity limited, and is under conscious control. Controlled processing occurred in the varied-mapping condition. More generally, controlled processing is what we use with nonroutine or unfamiliar tasks.

Can we learn to use automatic processing in place of controlled processing for a task? Much work suggests that we can, with massive amounts of practice in a task. Bryan and Harter (1899) first made this point in an early study of the development of the ability to receive and send telegraph messages. They found, first, that with practice, people got better at both sending and receiving telegraphed messages. Second, their subjects reported that as they became accustomed to the task, they shifted the focus of their attention. At first, they struggled to simply send or receive individual letters. After a few months, they concentrated on words rather than on individual letters. Still later, their focus shifted again, this time from words to phrases or groups of words. Practice apparently had the effect of making individual responses (such as the detection of a letter) automatic, or "habits," as Bryan and Harter called them, thus freeing attention for higher-level responses (words instead of letters, phrases instead of words).

If you play video games, you may have noticed a similar kind of learning effect. When you first play a new game, learning how to operate the controls to move your video figure across the screen probably takes awhile. (My first game of Mario Brothers, for instance, lasted approximately 15 seconds.) At first, you need full concentration to figure out when, where, and how to move your figure about the screen. You have little capacity left to notice impending danger. With practice, playing the game takes much less effort. I know "expert" Mario Brothers players who can play 30-minute games and still have enough cognitive resources left to carry on an extended discussion with me! My processing of information in playing Mario Brothers is still of the controlled sort. My friends, because of their extensive practice, now process much of the information automatically.

Feature Integration Theory

By now you might be wondering about the role attention and automaticity play in perception, and vice versa, because many of the experiments we've talked about in this chapter certainly involve the perception and recognition of familiar stimuli.

Anne Treisman, inspired by the work of Schneider and Shiffrin, investigated just this question, developing what has come to be called *feature integration theory*. Her general idea is that we perceive objects in two distinct stages. In the first stage, which is preattentive, or automatic, we register features of objects, such as their color or shape. In the second stage, attention allows us to "glue" the features together into a unified object (Tsal, 1989a).

Treisman reported several experimental results that support feature integration theory. In one experiment (Treisman & Gelade, 1980), subjects were presented with a series of simple objects (such as letters) that differed in several features (such as color or shape). An example of such a display is presented in part A of the right-hand figure on the inside front cover of this book. Subjects were asked to search for a particular object—for example, a pink letter or the letter *T*. If the item being searched for differed from the background items in the critical feature (for example, a pink item among green and brown items, or a *T* among *O*'s), the target item seemed to pop out of the display, and the number of background items did not affect subjects' reaction times. Treisman and Gelade (1980) interpreted this pattern of results as evidence that the detection of individual features is automatic—that is, requiring little attention or concentration and occurring in parallel. As a result, detecting a circle or the color blue or any other single feature is relatively easy.

In another condition, subjects were asked to search for an object with a combination of features—such as a pink *T*—against a background of objects that had one or the other feature—in this example, both pink items that were not *T*'s and *T*'s that were not pink (see part B of the figure on the inside front cover of this book). In this condition, subjects' reaction times varied with the number of background items. Treisman and Gelade (1980) argued that searching for a conjunction, or combination, of features requires controlled, nonautomatic processing.

Interestingly, in a later study (Treisman & Schmidt, 1982), Treisman showed that when attention is diverted or "overloaded," subjects make integration errors, resulting in what Treisman calls *illusory conjunctions.* Consider the example of glancing quickly and without much attention out the window at a red Honda Civic and a blue Cadillac. Later, when asked to report what you saw, you might say, "A blue Honda Civic." Such combining of two stimuli is erroneous; the conjunction reported, illusory.

In the experimental demonstration of this phenomenon (Treisman & Schmidt, 1982), subjects saw displayed two black digits on either side of a row of three larger colored letters, presented briefly (for 200 milliseconds). They were asked to pay attention to and recite the black digits, with the experimenter emphasizing the importance of accuracy. Subjects were also asked, after they had reported the digits, to report the positions (left, right, or middle), colors, and names of any letters they had seen. They were asked to report only information about which they were highly confident. Subjects were able to provide correct information on letters 52% of the time but reported illusory conjunctions (such as a red X instead of either a blue X or a red T) in 39% of the trials. In other words, when mentally taxed, people mistakenly combined features in illusory conjunctions.

Putting these ideas together, we can say that individual features can be recognized automatically, with little mental effort. What apparently requires mental capacity is the integration of features, the putting together of pieces of information to recognize more complicated objects. Thus, according to Treisman, the perception of individual features takes little effort or attention, whereas "gluing" features together into coherent objects requires more. Many researchers (Tsal, 1989a, 1989b; Briand & Klein, 1989) are currently testing the theory's predictions and offering refinements and critiques.

Divided Attention

If attention is a flexible system for allocating resources, and if tasks differ in the amount of attention they require, then people should be able to learn to perform two tasks at once. Indeed, a practiced driver's ability to converse while driving is a familiar instance of our capacity to learn to do two things together. Parents of teenagers often marvel over how their children seem to be able to listen to music, talk on the phone to their friends, and study all at the same time. The question that arises next is, "How difficult is doing two or more tasks at once, and on what factors does this ability depend?"

Spelke, Hirst, and Neisser (1976) examined this question in a clever laboratory study. Two Cornell University students were recruited as subjects in this demanding study. Five days a week, for 17 weeks, working in one-hour sessions, these students learned to write words dictated while they read short stories. Their reading comprehension was periodically tested. After 6 weeks of practice, their reading rates approached their normal speeds, as shown in Figure 3-8. Also by the end of 6 weeks, their scores

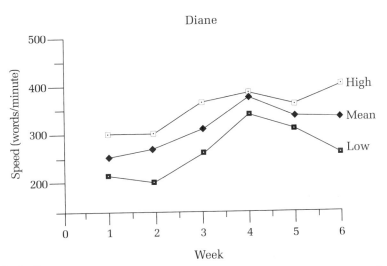

FIGURE 3-8.   Reading speeds during practice phase of learning to do two things at once. Weekly means and interquartile ranges of reading speeds, plotted for each week of practice, for two subjects, John and Diane. Adapted from Spelke, Hirst, and Neisser (1976).

on the reading comprehension tests were comparable, whether they were only reading stories (and thus presumably giving the reading task their full attention) or reading stories while writing down dictated words. Further investigation revealed that the subjects were also able to categorize the dictated words by meaning and to discover relations among the words without sacrificing reading speed or comprehension.

Many psychologists were surprised that the subjects in this study could process information about meaning without conscious attention, and some offered alternative explanations for the findings. One hypothesis is that the subjects alternated their attention between the two tasks, attending first to the story, then to the dictation, then back to the story, and so on. Although this possibility was not directly tested, the authors argue that the fact that the subjects' reading speeds were comparable whether they were taking dictation or not suggests that if they were alternating their attention, they were doing so without any measurable lag.

Hirst, Spelke, Reaves, Caharack, and Neisser (1980) found evidence against this hypothesis. Their subjects were trained in ways similar to those used by Spelke, Hirst, and Neisser (1976). All subjects copied dictated words while reading. Some subjects read short stories, presumably containing some redundant material and therefore requiring relatively little attention. Other subjects read encyclopedia articles, thought to contain less redundant material and thus to require more concentration. After they reached normal reading speeds and reading comprehension during dictation, the subjects' tasks were switched—those who had been reading short stories were now given encyclopedia articles, and those trained using encyclopedia articles now read short stories. Six of the seven subjects performed comparably with the new reading material, indicating that the subjects were probably not alternating their attention between the two tasks. If they were, then learning to take dictation while reading short stories should not transfer well to doing so while reading encyclopedia articles.

A second explanation for subjects' ability to learn to do two tasks at once is that one of the two tasks (for example, the dictation task) is being performed automatically. According to one of Posner and Snyder's (1975) criteria for automaticity—that processing not interfere with other mental activity—taking dictation in this study might be considered automatic. However, subjects were clearly aware that words were being dictated, and they typically recognized about 80% of the dictated words on tests immediately following trials. Moreover, subjects clearly intended to copy the dictated words. Therefore, taking dictation does not meet Posner and Snyder's last two criteria—occurrence without intention and occurrence without involving conscious awareness.

Hirst et al. (1980) also offered evidence against the possibility that one task becomes automatized. Subjects trained to copy complete sentences while reading were able to comprehend and recall those sentences, suggesting that the subjects had processed the dictation task for meaning. This in turn suggests that they paid at least some attention to the dictation task, as most psychologists believe that automatic processing occurs without comprehension.

A third explanation for how subjects came to perform two tasks at once, one that Hirst et al. (1980) favor, is that the subjects learned to combine two specific tasks: reading and taking dictation. That is, specific practice with the two tasks caused the tasks to be done differently than they were when the subjects did them at first. This implies that if either one of these tasks was to be combined with a third (such as shadowing prose), additional practice would be needed before the two tasks could be done together efficiently.

Practice thus appears to play an enormous role in performance, and is one important determiner of how much attention any task will require. As Hirst et al. (1980) put it:

> A skilled individual has learned to detect new stimulus constellations and execute new patterns of action, not just to do old things intermittently or unconsciously. The experienced birdwatcher who scans tree tops for a woodpecker is not automatically processing the same features that she once examined in a conscious way; the commands that a skilled typist issues automatically to his fingers are not the same as those that governed his behavior as a novice. (pp. 115–116)

We now know little about the limits, if there are any, on the effects of practice on attention and performance. Studies such as those by Hirst et al. are not without critics (see Shiffrin, 1988). However, this and related work are beginning to change our understanding of the role practice plays in cognitive tasks.

On the basis of studies such as these, Ulric Neisser (1976) offered a schema-based conceptualization of attention. Neisser argues that we don't filter, attenuate, or forget unwanted material. Instead, he argues, we never acquire it in the first place. Neisser compares attention to apple picking: The material we attend to is akin to apples we pick off a tree—we grasp it. Unattended material is analogous to the apples we don't pick. To assume that the unpicked apples were "filtered out" of our grasp would be ridiculous; a better description is that they simply were left on the tree. So it is, Neisser believes, with unattended information—it is simply left out of our cognitive processing.

Neisser and Becklen (1975) performed a relevant study of visual attention. They created a "selective looking" task, by having subjects watch one of two visually superimposed films. Figure 3-9 shows an example of what subjects in this study saw. One of the films showed a "hand game," two pairs of hands playing the familiar hand-slapping game many of us played as children. The second film showed three people passing or bouncing a basketball, or both. Subjects in the study were asked to "shadow" (attend to) one or the other of the films, and to press a key whenever a target event (such as a hand slap in the first film or a pass in the second game) occurred.

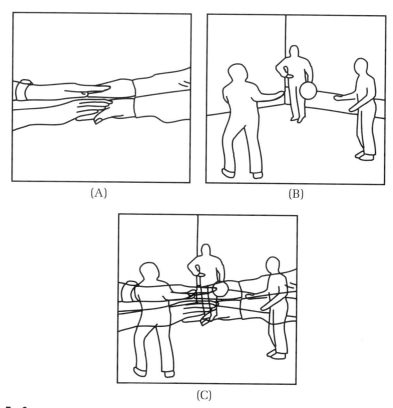

(A)   (B)

(C)

FIGURE 3-9.   Outline tracings of typical video images used in the Neisser and Becklen (1975) study. A shows the handgame alone; B, the ballgame alone; C, the handgame and ballgame superimposed. SOURCE: From "Selective Looking: Attending to Visually Specified Events," by U. Neisser and R. Becklen, 1975, *Cognitive Psychology,* 7, 485. Copyright © 1975 by Academic Press. Reprinted by permission.

Neisser and Becklen (1975) found, first, that subjects were able to follow the correct film rather easily, even when the target event occurred at a rate of 40 per minute in the attended film. Subjects ignored occurrences of the target event in the unattended film. Subjects also failed to notice unexpected events in the unattended film. For example, subjects monitoring the ballgame failed to notice that in the handgame film, one of the players stopped hand slapping and began to throw a ball to the other player.

Neisser (1976) believes that skilled perceiving rather than filtered attention explains this pattern of performance. Neisser and Becklen (1975) argue that

once picked up, the continuous and coherent motions of the ballgame (or of the handgame) guide further pickup; what is seen guides further seeing. It is implausible to suppose that special 'filters' or 'gates,' designed on the spot for this novel situation, block the irrelevant material from penetrating deeply into the 'processing system.' The ordinary perceptual skills of following visually-given events . . . are simply applied to the attended episode and not to the other. (pp. 491–492)

Summary

The different theoretical approaches to attention surveyed here suggest that psychologists are far from agreed on how to explain attentional phenomena. Nonetheless, some general themes have emerged. Attention has been shown to be a flexible aspect of cognition. We see that attention, rather than being rigidly and mechanically limited, as first described, is instead a more flexible system, affected by things such as practice, the kinds of tasks being performed, and intention of the subject. Whereas once attention was compared to a bottleneck, today the appropriate metaphor seems to be a spotlight. Just as a spotlight's focal point can be moved from one area of a stage to another, so can attention be directed and redirected to various kinds of incoming information. Just as a spotlight illuminates best what is at its center, so too is cognitive processing usually enhanced when attention is directed toward a task. Attention, like a spotlight, has fuzzy boundaries. Spotlights can highlight more than one object at a time, depending on the size of the objects. Attention, too, can be directed at more than one task at a time, depending on the capacity demands of each task.

Like many topics in psychology, attention captured the interest of William James in the late 1800s. James (1983/1890) anticipated the recent writings of investigators studying attention when he argued that only one system or process of conception can go on at a time very easily; to do two or more things at once, he believed, required that the processes be habitual.

James's (1983/1890) description of attention, as clear today as it was a hundred years ago, ably sums up the phenomenon psychologists study when they investigate attention:

Everyone knows what attention is. It is the taking possession by the mind, in clear and vivid form, of one out of what seem several simultaneously possible objects or trains of thought. Focalization, concentration, of consciousness are of its essence. It implies withdrawal from some things in order to deal effectively with others, and is a condition which has a real opposite in the confused, dazed, scatterbrained state which in French is called *distraction* and *Zerstreutheit* in German. (pp. 381–382)

Recommended Readings

Classic readings on attention and automaticity include Broadbent (1958), Deutsch and Deutsch (1963), Cherry (1953), Kahneman (1973), Moray

(1959), Norman (1968), Schneider and Shiffrin (1977), Shiffrin and Schneider (1977), Stroop (1935), and Treisman (1960, 1964). Recent reviews include Broadbent (1982), Johnston and Dark (1986), and Shiffrin (1988). Navon and Gopher (1979) have updated and extended Kahneman's model, and Fisher (1984) and Schneider and Fisk (1982) have followed up on the work of Schneider and Shiffrin.

MacLeod (1991) presents an extensive review of the literature on the Stroop effect, offering some new proposals. Cohen, Dunbar, and McClelland (1990) present a connectionist model of the Stroop task, and Chen and Ho (1988) present work on the Stroop effect with bilingual speakers of Chinese and English.

Treisman (1986) provides an overview of feature integration theory. Critiques of feature integration theory can be found in Tsal (1989a, 1989b), Briand and Klein (1989), and Cave and Wolfe (1990).

Hirst and Kalman (1987) and Navon and Miller (1987) present additional work on divided attention and have analyzed factors that interfere with performing two tasks simultaneously. Phaf, Van der Heijen, and Hudson (1990) present a detailed connectionist model of performance in a selective attention task that, though somewhat technical, offers interested readers a concrete example.

REVIEW QUESTIONS

1. Cognitive psychologists have offered several different definitions of the term *attention*. Which one seems to you the most useful? Describe and defend your criteria.

2. Describe the dichotic listening task, and explain why cognitive psychologists find it a useful way to study attention.

3. Describe the differences and similarities among the following: filter theory, attenuation theory, late-selection theory.

4. Describe and evaluate Kahneman's capacity model of attention.

5. Evaluate Posner and Snyder's criteria for what makes a cognitive process automatic. Which criterion is the strongest, and why?

6. Consider the studies on divided attention. Can these findings be used in training workers who need to process a great deal of information from different sources simultaneously? Why or why not?

CHAPTER 4

Memory

Coming up with examples to illustrate the topic of memory is fairly easy. We rely on memory whenever we think back to a personal event—when we remember, for example, our first day of school, our tenth birthday, or a trip to Disneyland. Memory is also obviously involved when we remember information about historical events, such as the Challenger explosion, the Chernobyl disaster, the Persian Gulf War.

All of these cases illustrate **retrieval,** the calling to mind of information that has been previously stored. The processes by which we do so are the focus of this chapter.

In one way or another, **memory** enters into almost every cognitive activity. Clearly, activities such as taking an exam or remembering the name of your third-grade teacher require memory. But other activities, such as balancing a checkbook or comprehending a sentence, also involve some aspect of memory. While doing the calculations necessary to balance a checkbook, we have to keep some numbers in mind, at least momentarily. Similarly, when we hear or read a sentence, we have to keep the beginning of the sentence in mind while we process its middle and end.

We use memory so frequently that, as with other cognitive processes, we tend to take it for granted. Try, for example, to recall your first day at college. What do you remember about that day? Now ask yourself how you are able to recall any of these memories (if in fact you can). If you drew a total blank, why? What exactly goes on when you try to recall? What makes some information memorable and other information hard to recall? (For example, can you describe what your cognitive psychology professor wore two lectures ago?)

Sometimes, we fail to notice how extraordinary a particular ability is until we encounter someone who lacks it. Baddeley (1990) has described the tragic case of Clive Wearing, a musician and broadcaster who, because of brain damage caused by encephalitis, has been left with severe amnesia. Although many people suffer from amnesia, Wearing's case is one of the most devastating on record. As Baddeley describes it,

> his amnesia was so dense that he could remember nothing from more than a few minutes before, a state that he attributed to having just recovered consciousness. Left to his own devices, he would often be found writing down a time, for example, 3.10, and the note, 'I have just recovered consciousness,' only to cross out the 3.10 and add 3.15, followed by 3.20, etc. If his wife left the room for a few minutes, when she returned he would greet her with great joy declaring that he had not seen her for months and asking how long he had been unconscious. Experienced once, such an event could be intriguing and touching, but when it happens repeatedly, day in, day out, it rapidly loses its charm. (pp. 4–5)

It is interesting that a few of Wearing's memorial abilities appear to have been spared. He has apparently conducted a choir through a complex piece of music and can still play the harpsichord and piano. These abilities are the exception rather than the rule, however. Wearing cannot go out alone because he will quickly become lost and unable to find his way back. He cannot recognize much in photographs of familiar places, and his memories of his own life are quite sketchy.

In this chapter, we will try to explain these phenomena. To do so, we will look in detail at the processes we use to store and retrieve information. We will examine theoretical approaches to the study of memory, considering memory that lasts only briefly, as well as memory that appears to endure for hours, weeks, and even years.

Much of the research described in this chapter comes from the laboratory, where experimental subjects, often college-student volunteers, are presented with lists or series of words, syllables, or pictures under highly controlled conditions. Later in the chapter, we will consider how well laboratory-based models apply to memory phenomena that occur outside the laboratory.

A brief review of terminology is in order before we begin. We say that **encoding** occurs when information is first translated into a form that can be used by other cognitive processes. It is held in storage in some form or another for later retrieval. We say we are **forgetting** information that we cannot retrieve.

The Modal Approach

One theoretical approach to studying memory, which dominated cognitive psychology throughout the 1960s and 1970s, distinguishes among kinds of memory according to length of time information is stored. In this approach, called the **modal approach,** information is assumed to be received, processed, and stored differently for each kind of memory (Atkinson & Shiffrin, 1968; Waugh & Norman, 1965). Information presented very quickly and not attended to is stored only briefly in **sensory memory.** Information attended to is held in **short-term memory (STM)** for periods up to 20 to 30 seconds. (Synonyms for STM include *primary memory* and *short-term storage* [STS].) Information needed for longer periods of time—what you ate at your last meal, for example, or the name of your fourth-grade teacher—is transferred to **long-term memory** (**LTM**), sometimes called *secondary memory* and *long-term storage* (LTS). Figure 4-1 depicts an overview of the modal view of memory.

Many empirical findings seem to support the idea of different memory systems. One well-known finding comes from *free-recall* experiments, in which people are given a list of words to remember, such as that shown in Figure 4-2(a), and asked to recall the words in any order. Next, the experimenter, using data from all the subjects, computes the probability of recall of each word as a function of the word's *serial position* in the original list. In our example, *table* would have serial position 1, because it is the first word on the list; *candle,* serial position 2, and so forth. Figure 4-2(b) shows an idealized version of typical results (Murdock, 1962).

Notice that the two ends of the curve are higher than the middle. This indicates that people recall more words at either the beginning or the end of the list than they do words in the middle. This is known as the **serial position effect.** The improved recall of words at the beginning of the list is called the **primacy effect;** that at the end of the list, the **recency effect.**

What accounts for these two effects? Subjects typically report subvocalizing to themselves as follows when they first start the experiment:

Experimenter *(E; reading list at a fixed rate):* Table.
Subject *(S; to self):* Table-table-table-table.
E: Candle.
S *(a little faster):* Table-candle-table-candle.
E: Maple.
S *(very rapidly):* Table-candle-maple-table-candle.
E: Subway.
S *(giving up on rehearsing earlier words):* Subway.

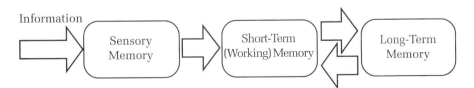

FIGURE 4-1.   The modal view of memory. Each box depicts a memory storage system. The arrows represent the transfer of information between systems.

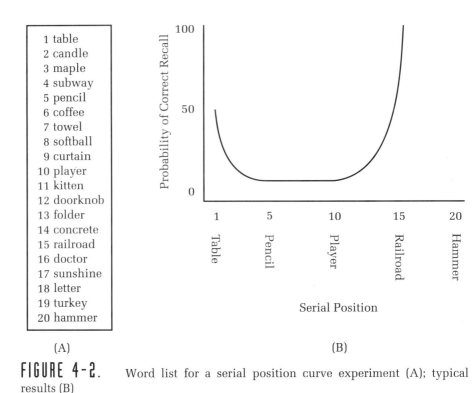

1 table
2 candle
3 maple
4 subway
5 pencil
6 coffee
7 towel
8 softball
9 curtain
10 player
11 kitten
12 doorknob
13 folder
14 concrete
15 railroad
16 doctor
17 sunshine
18 letter
19 turkey
20 hammer

(A)   (B)

FIGURE 4-2.   Word list for a serial position curve experiment (A); typical results (B)

We'll see below that the subject's repetition of items, or **rehearsal,** is thought to help the items enter long-term storage. In fact, if the experimenter reads the list rapidly enough to prevent the subject from having enough time to rehearse, the primacy effect disappears, although the recency effect stays intact (Murdock, 1962).

The recency effect is thought to result from subjects' using either sensory memory or short-term memory. Subjects often report that they can still "sort of" hear the last few words, and they often report these first and quickly. If the experimenter prevents the subject from reporting words right away by having him or her first perform an unrelated counting task, the recency effect (but not the primacy effect) disappears (Postman & Phillips, 1965).

The fact that the primacy and recency effects can be independently affected suggests that they reflect two kinds of memory. In addition, some psychologists argue for a third kind of memory, sensory memory, which is thought to work differently than both of the other systems. Those who endorse the idea of sensory memory believe that incoming information first passes through this rapidly decaying storage system. If attended to, the information next moves to short-term memory. To be held for longer than a minute or two requires yet another transfer, this time to long-term memory.

Sensory Memory

This kind of "memory" is closely connected to what we call "perception." Sensory memory has been described as a record of our percepts (Baddeley, 1990) because it refers to the initial brief storage of sensory information—what you might retain, for example, if you glance up quickly at a billboard and then glance quickly away.

Sperling (1960) conducted an elegant experiment, now considered a classic, to measure this capacity. He presented subjects with displays containing letters, such as that shown in Figure 4-3, and asked them to recall the letters they saw. The displays were presented only briefly—for only 50 milliseconds. Sperling found that, on average, people could report only 4 or 5 of the 12 letters presented. Extending the display time—even to 500 milliseconds—did not improve performance. The problem wasn't a perceptual one—500 milliseconds, or half a second, is plenty of time to perceive something about all the letters (Klatzky, 1980).

Sperling (1960) did find a way to improve subjects' performance, however, inventing what has come to be known as the *partial-report technique*. It worked like this: After seeing the display, subjects heard a low-, medium-, or high-pitched tone. A low pitch indicated that they were to report only the letters in the bottom row of the display; a high pitch, those in the top row; and a medium pitch, those in the middle row. Regardless of which tone was sounded, subjects were almost always completely accurate in their reporting. This finding suggests that subjects must have stored the whole display, because they did not know ahead of time which tone would be sounded. If their accuracy on a randomly chosen row was, say, 90%, we can infer that their accuracy for any row would have been 90%. In fact, Sperling found that with the partial-report technique, subjects accurately recalled an average of about 3 out of 4 letters in any given row, suggesting an average total recall of about 75% or more.

What caused the better performance? Sperling believed that in the

S D F G

P W H J

X C V N

FIGURE 4-3.   Example of the kind of stimulus display used by Sperling (1960). SOURCE: From "The Information Available in Brief Visual Presentations," by G. Sperling, 1960, *Psychological Monographs,* *74*(11), 3. Copyright © 1960 by the American Psychological Association.

original condition (called the *whole-report condition* because subjects had to report the whole display) subjects lost the information in their memory during the time they took to report the first few letters. Put another way, even as subjects were recalling the display, the information was fading from wherever it was being stored. This implies that information lasts only briefly in this memory system. In fact, Sperling found that if the tone was delayed one second, subjects giving partial reports did no better than subjects giving whole reports.

Neisser (1967) called this kind of memory the *icon.* The icon is a sensory memory storage system for visual material, holding information for up to about one second. The information it holds is in a relatively unprocessed form, as another of Sperling's (1960) experiments showed: if the displays contained both consonants and vowels, and two different tones cued the subject to report either all the vowels or all the consonants, subjects' performance roughly matched their performance giving whole reports. From this, Sperling inferred that the icon holds information that has not yet been categorized as to type of letter (vowel or consonant).

Averbach and Coriell (1961) showed that the icon can be "erased" by other stimuli presented immediately after the icon, a phenomenon known as *masking.* For instance, if the display with letters was followed by a display with circles, and the subject was to report which letters had been in the locations of the circles, the circles appeared to "erase" the memory trace of the letters originally shown.

Other work investigated how many ways subjects could be cued to give partial reports (see Coltheart, 1980, for a review). Different investigators showed that such things as the color or brightness of the letters can be used to cue partial reports. It is interesting that cueing partial reports by category or phonological sound (for instance, "Report all the letters that rhyme with *B*") is all but impossible. This suggests that the information available in the icon is visual only—not auditory or related to the type of thing a stimulus is.

There is also a sensory memory for auditory material, which Neisser (1967) called the *echo.* Moray, Bates, and Barnett (1965) offered a clever demonstration of the echo. Their subjects were given a "four-eared" listening task, similar to a dichotic listening task (see Chapter 3 if you've forgotten what this is), hearing, over headphones, four channels of incoming information, each apparently coming from a different location, consisting of a string of random letters. (The four channels were created by stereophonic mixing.) In one condition, similar to Sperling's (1960) whole-report condition, subjects were asked to report all the letters they had heard. In another condition, each subject held a board with four lights on it, each light corresponding to one of the channels, cueing the subject to report only the letters from a particular channel. Like Sperling, Moray and his associates found that subjects giving partial reports could report proportionately more letters. This suggests that the echo, like the icon, stores information only briefly.

Darwin, Turvey, and Crowder (1972) later replicated this result, using better experimental controls. They also found that recall could be cued by category, at least to some degree, suggesting that the echo works somewhat differently than the icon. Crowder (1976), reviewing the literature on echoic memory, proposed also that echoic memory has a larger capacity than iconic memory. Recent investigations (Watkins & Watkins, 1980) also provide evidence that echos can last longer than icons, perhaps even as long as 20 seconds.

Although research continues to refine our understanding, sensory memory can currently best be described by a number of properties. First, sensory memories are *modality specific;* that is, the visual sensory memory contains visual information; the auditory sensory memory, auditory information; and so forth. Second, sensory memory capacities appear relatively large, but the length of time that information can be stored is quite short. Third, the information that can be stored appears to be relatively unprocessed, meaning that most of it has to do with physical aspects of the stimuli, rather than meaningful ones.

Recent proposals (Haber, 1983; Neisser, 1983) have disputed the idea that the icon and echo play a necessary role in perception or memory. Although no one disputes the findings reported by Sperling (1960) and others, some argue that there are problems with the interpretations of the findings. In particular, some assert that the tachistoscopic presentation of stimuli created an artificial task for subjects, one unlike anything people would need or want to do outside the laboratory. The debate over the usefulness of the icon in theories of memory is very much alive, however.

Short-Term Memory

Most of the time when people think about memory, they think about holding onto information for longer than a second or two. In the next two sections, we'll talk about the kinds of memory that are more familiar to the nonpsychologist. We'll first look at what has been called short-term memory (STM). This kind of memory system is the one that you use when you look up a phone number, walk across a room to a telephone, and dial the number. Suppose I asked you to call one of my colleagues, whose phone number is 555-4375. Suppose further that you couldn't take this book with you but had to remember the number until you could dial it on a nearby phone. How would you accomplish this task? Chances are, you'd begin by rehearsing the number aloud several times as you walked across the room. You'd dial the number, but as soon as the conversation started, you'd be likely to have forgotten the number you dialed. This example illustrates one aspect of short-term memory: it lasts only a short while.

Is there any other distinguishing characteristic that separates short- from long-term memory, other than length of time information is stored? Psychologists who make the distinction believe there are a number of such characteristics, including how much information can be stored (capacity), the form in which the information is stored (coding), the ways in which information is retained or forgotten, and the ways in which information is retrieved.

Capacity

If you are going to store information for only a short period of time (as in the phone-number example), how much room do you have to do so? In other words, how much information can you remember for only a brief period of time?

A classic paper by George Miller (1956) begins with the following rather unusual confession addressing these questions:

> My problem is that I have been persecuted by an integer. For seven years this number has followed me around, has intruded in my most private data, and has assaulted me from the pages of our most public journals. This number assumes a variety of disguises, being sometimes a little larger and sometimes a little smaller than usual, but never changing so much as to be unrecognizable. The persistence with which this number plagues me is far more than a random accident. There is, to quote a famous senator, a design behind it, some pattern governing its appearances. Either there really is something unusual about the number or else I am suffering from delusions of persecution. (p. 81)

The integer plaguing Miller was 7 (plus or minus 2). Among other things, 7 (plus or minus 2, depending on the individual, the material, and other situational factors) seems to be the maximum number of independent units we can hold in short-term memory. We call this the **capacity** of short-term memory.

Miller (1956) reviewed evidence demonstrating that if you are presented with a string of random digits, you'll be able to recall them only if the string contains about seven or fewer. The same is true if you are presented with random strings of any kinds of units: letters, words, abbreviations, and so on. The only way to overcome this limitation is by somehow **chunking** the individual units into larger units. For instance, consider the following string of letters: N F L C B S I R A M T V. This twelve-letter string would normally exceed almost everyone's short-term memory capacity. But if you look closely at the letters, you'll see that they really form four sets of abbreviations for well-known entities: NFL (the National Football League), CBS (one of the three major television networks currently operating in the United States), IRA (an individual retirement account), and MTV (the rock video cable television station). If you notice that the twelve letters are really four organized sets, you'll be more likely to recall the entire string. In recognizing that the three letters really "go together" and forming them into a single unit, you are said to be chunking them.

Chunking depends on knowledge. Someone not familiar with our culture might regard MTV as merely three randomly presented letters.

Miller regarded the process of forming chunks (he called it "recoding") as a fundamental process of memory—a very powerful means of increasing the amount of information we could process at any given time, and one that is used constantly in our daily lives. The process of chunking can be seen as an important strategy in overcoming the severe limitation of having only seven or so slots in which to temporarily store information.

Coding

The term **coding** refers to the way in which information is mentally represented, that is, the form in which the information is held. When you try to remember a phone number, as in the example above, how do you represent it? A study by Conrad (1964) addresses this question. He presented subjects with lists of consonants for later recall. Despite the fact that the letters were presented visually, subjects were likely to make errors that were similar in *sound* to the original stimuli. So, if a *B* had been presented, and subjects later misrecalled this stimulus, they were much more likely to report a letter that sounded like *B*, (for example, *G* or *C)* than they were to report a letter than looked like *B* (for example, *F*). Remember, the original presentation was visual, but subjects apparently were confused by the sound. Subjects were apparently forming a mental representation of the stimuli by the acoustic rather than the visual properties. Later work by Baddeley (1966a, 1966b) confirmed this effect even when the stimuli were words rather than letters: similar-sounding words make for poor immediate recall although similar-meaning words don't, and the reverse is true for delayed recall.

Retention Duration and Forgetting

We regard short-term memory as the storage of information for short periods of time. But how short is short? Brown (1958) and Peterson and Peterson (1959), working independently, came to the same conclusion: if not rehearsed, information is lost from STM in as little as 20 seconds.

The *Brown-Peterson task* works like this: Subjects are presented with a three-consonant trigram, for example, BKG. They are also given a number, for example, 347, and asked to count backward out loud by threes, at the rate of two counts per second, in time to a metronome. The purpose of the counting task is to prevent the subject from rehearsing the trigram. The length of time a subject has to count varies. If asked to count backward for only three seconds, roughly 80% of subjects can recall the trigram. If asked to count for 18 seconds, the percentage drops to about 7. The interpretation offered for this finding by both Brown and the Petersons was that the **memory trace**—that is, the encoded mental representation of the to-be-remembered information in STM that is not rehearsed—**decays,** or breaks apart, within about 20 seconds.

Putting this interpretation into our phone-number example above gives us the following: If I tell you my phone number, and you fail to do something to remember it (say, by rehearsing it or writing it down), you'll be able to remember it only for a maximum of about 20 seconds. After that time the memory trace will simply decay and the information will be lost.

It wasn't long before other cognitive psychologists began to challenge this explanation of forgetting. They proposed a different mechanism, called **interference,** that worked as follows: some information can "displace" other information, making the former hard to retrieve. You can think of the interference explanation as being akin to finding a piece of paper on my desk. At the start of each academic term, my desk is (relatively) free of clutter. Any piece of paper placed on the desktop is trivially easy to find. However, as the term goes on and my time grows short, I tend to allow all kinds of memos, papers, journals, and the like to accumulate. Papers placed on my desk at the beginning of the term become buried—they're there, all right, but can be very difficult to find at any given moment. The late-arriving papers have "displaced" the early papers.

How then, could one explain the Brown-Peterson task results in terms of interference? Think once again about the counting task. Notice that it supposedly has very little purpose other than to distract the subject from rehearsing the trigram. Yet, it may be that the counting task does more than prevent subjects from rehearsing; it may actually interfere with their short-term storage of the trigram. As the subject counts aloud, she computes and announces the values. As she computes and announces the values, she puts them into STM. Thus, the counted values might actually be displacing the original information.

A study by Waugh and Norman (1965) demonstrates the role of interference in STM. They invented the *probe digit task,* which works as follows: Subjects are given a 16-digit number, for example, 1596234789024815. The last digit in the number is a cue for the subject to report the number that first came after the first occurrence of the cue in the number. (It's a little complicated to follow that instruction, but it can be done.) In our example the cue is 5 (it's the last digit of the number), and the first occurrence of 5 in the number is followed by a 9, so the response should be 9.

Waugh and Norman (1965) presented the numbers either quickly, at the rate of four digits per second, or slowly, at the rate of one digit per second. Their reasoning was that if decay caused forgetting from STM, then subjects receiving a slow rate of presentation should be less good at recalling digits from early in the number. This is because more time would have elapsed on trials with the slow presentation, causing more decay from the beginning of the number. Figure 4-4 shows, however, that this is not what happened. Subjects showed equivalent performance on recalling digits throughout the number regardless of rate of presentation. On all trials, subjects were not as good at recalling digits from early in the number than from later in the number, implicating interference rather than decay in forgetting information in STM.

Other evidence also supported the view that interference, not

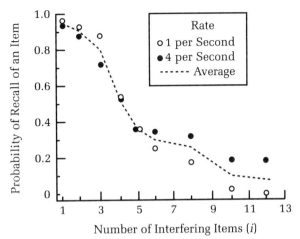

FIGURE 4-4.   Results from Waugh and Norman's (1965) probe digit task study. SOURCE: From "Primary Memory," by N. C. Waugh and D. A. Norman, 1965, *Psychological Review, 72,* 91. Copyright © 1965 by the American Psychological Association. Reprinted by permission.

decay, accounts for forgetting from STM. Keppel and Underwood (1962), for instance, found that forgetting in the Brown-Peterson task doesn't happen until after a few trials have occurred. They suggest that over time, **proactive interference** builds up. The term refers to a phenomenon that material learned first can disrupt later learning. (We'll discuss this phenomenon in greater detail, below.) Keppel and Underwood showed that even one trial's worth of practice recalling a three-letter trigram was enough to hurt subsequent memory for other trigrams.

Wickens, Born, and Allen (1963) extended the idea one more step. They reasoned as follows: if STM, like LTM, is subject to proactive interference, then STM, like LTM, should also be subject to a related phenomenon, *release from proactive interference.* The idea is that if you learn a number of pieces of similar information, after a while any new learning becomes more difficult because the old learning interferes with the new (because of proactive interference). The greater the similarity among the pieces of information, the greater the interference. This implies that if a new and very distinct piece of information were to be presented, the degree of interference would be sharply reduced.

Wickens and colleagues (1963) demonstrated this idea in a clever experiment. They gave subjects a series of either three-digit strings (for example, 179) or three-letter strings (for example, DKQ). There were ten trials in all. Some subjects received ten trials of the same type (that is, all-letter strings or all-digit strings). Other subjects saw a "switch" in the stimuli part way through the ten trials. For example, a subject might see three trials with letters but then be switched to seeing digits on all subsequent trials. Figure 4-5 shows the results. Subjects getting a "switch" performed almost

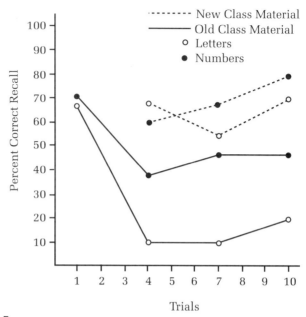

FIGURE 4-5.   Results from the Wickens, Born, and Allen (1963) study on release from proactive interference in short-term memory. SOURCE: From "Proactive Inhibition and Item Similarity in Short-term Memory," by D. D. Wickens, D. Born, and C. Allen, 1963, *Journal of Verbal Learning and Verbal Behavior, 2,* 442. Copyright © 1963 by Academic Press. Reprinted by permission.

as well immediately after the switch as they did on the first trial. Their memory is said to have been released, or freed, from the clutches of proactive interference!

All this evidence might lead you to think that all cognitive psychologists are agreed that only interference causes forgetting from STM. The picture, however, is not that neat. Reitman (1971, 1974) initially offered evidence supporting an interference explanation of forgetting from STM. Her subjects performed a Brown-Peterson task while simultaneously working on what was supposed to be an interfering task: detecting a syllable like "doh" in a spoken stream of repetitions of a similar syllable ("toh"). The auditory-detection task was supposed to prevent subjects from rehearsing the trigram but not to interfere with material stored in STM. An interference account of forgetting from STM would predict no loss of the trigrams over the retention periods, and this is indeed what Reitman (1971) found. However, in an important follow-up, Reitman (1974) found that her subjects were "cheating" a bit: surreptitiously rehearsing the letters while they performed the detection task. When Reitman looked only at the performance of the subjects who hadn't been rehearsing, she found clear effects of decay: only 65% of the trigrams were retained after a 15-second interval. From this, Reitman concluded that information really could decay if not rehearsed in STM.

This leaves us with an unresolved issue: Is it trace decay or interference that causes forgetting from STM? It is impossible to rule one of these out, at least for now. One problem is that it is hard to think of a task in which no interference can occur. Thus, designing a definitive experiment (or series of definitive experiments) is beyond our current capabilities.

It may also be that the question "Is it decay or is it interference?" is a poor one because it rules out the possibility that it may be both. That is, that there may be more than one mechanism by which information is lost from STM. Either-or questions omit this possibility. Baddeley (1990) makes the argument that some (although very little) trace decay does occur in STM along with interference.

Retrieval of Information

We've talked about the ways in which we hold onto information for brief periods of time—how we encode it, how much we can encode, and how long we can retain it. That brings us to the question "How do we retrieve this information from STM when we need it again?

Saul Sternberg (1966, 1969), through a clever series of experiments, found some surprising things about how we retrieve information from short-term memory. Before turning to his experiment, let's consider various possibilities of how retrieval of information from STM might work.

Sternberg's first question was whether the way we search for information held in STM is *parallel* or *serial*. Imagine, for example, that STM is full of some (small) number of movie titles. Let's say STM holds a list of your all-time favorite movies. Let's call the *number* of movie titles the *memory set size*. Now suppose that someone asks you if "Silence of the Lambs" is on your list, and that to answer the question, you mentally search the list.

If you compare "Silence of the Lambs" simultaneously to all of the titles on your list, you are said to be performing a *parallel* search. That essentially means that no matter the number of titles, you examine them at the same time, and it takes you no more time to compare "Silence of the Lambs" to one title than to all the titles. Figure 4-6(a) depicts how the data would look if you used parallel search, plotting time to search against memory-set size.

Suppose, instead, that you use *serial* search. In our movie titles example, this would mean comparing "Silence of the Lambs" to the first movie title on your list, *then* to the second title on your list, and so on until you come to the last title. The comparisons are done one at a time. In this model, it should take longer to decide if "Silence of the Lambs" matches a title on your list the longer your list is.

In addition to the question of whether the mental search is parallel or serial, we can also ask whether the search is *self-terminating* or *exhaustive*. A self-terminating search stops when a match is found. Suppose your list of movie titles is "Terms of Endearment," "Wayne's World," "Silence of the Lambs," and "Gone with the Wind." If you do a self-terminating search,

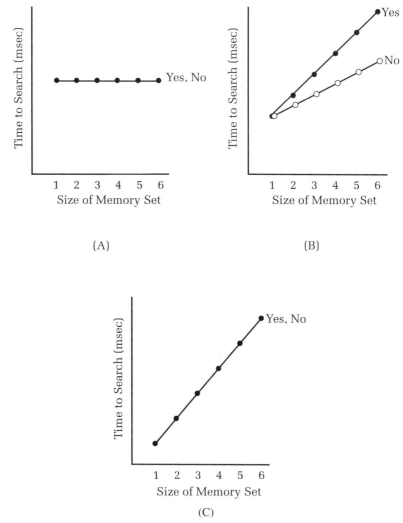

FIGURE 4-6.   Theoretically predicted results from the Sternberg (1966) short-term memory-scanning experiment. "Yes" and "No" refer to whether the subject will report finding the probe letter in the memory set. A depicts a parallel search; B, a serial, self-terminating search; C, a serial, exhaustive search. The data Sternberg reported looked most like those in C.

you will stop after the third comparison because you've found a match. On average, then, successful searches take less time (because you don't continue searching after you've found the match) then unsuccessful searches (where you have to search through everything). Figure 4-6(b) depicts the results we should see if retrieval from memory uses serial, self-terminating search.

The other kind of serial search is exhaustive, meaning that even if a match is found, you continue looking through every other item in the set. In our example, this would mean that even after you find "Silence of the Lambs," you check the remaining titles on the list. With this kind of search, it takes just as long for successful as for unsuccessful searches. Figure 4-6(c) shows this possibility.

Sternberg's (1966) experimental task was the following: First, subjects were presented with a set of seven or fewer letters. These were to be encoded and held in short-term memory, and hence can be called the "memory set." After the subject had the set in memory, she or he indicated readiness for an upcoming trial. A single letter, called a probe, was presented, and the subject's task was to decide, as quickly as possible, whether the probe was in the memory set. For example, the memory set might be *B K F Q*, and probes might be *K* (yes, in the memory set) and *D* (no, not in the memory set).

As counterintuitive as it sounds, Sternberg's (1966) results argue for serial, exhaustive search as the way we retrieve information from STM. Sternberg's explanation is that the search process itself may be so rapid and have such momentum that it is hard to stop it once it starts. It may be more efficient from a processing point of view just to let the search process finish, then make one decision at the end, instead of several decisions, one after each item in the memory set. A review by Hunt (1978) showed that people of all sorts (college students, senior citizens, people with exceptionally good memories, retarded people) all showed results consistent with the idea that retrieval from STM uses serial, exhaustive search, although the rate of searching changes with the group, being fastest for people with exceptional memories, and lower for senior citizens.

As with just about any scientific proposal, later work by other investigators turned up problems with Sternberg's (1966, 1969) proposal of serial exhaustive search. Baddeley (1976) provides a review of some of the problems and alternative explanations of Sternberg's findings. An intriguing twist on the Sternberg study comes from DeRosa and Tkacz (1976), who demonstrated that with certain kinds of stimuli, such as those shown in Figure 4-7, people apparently search STM in a parallel way.

Note that the stimuli De Rosa and Tkacz used consisted of ordered sequences of pictures, for example, a golfer executing a golf swing. If the memory set consisted of some randomly selected subset of the nine pictures, for example, pictures 1, 4, 6, 8, and 9, from any of the sets, then the results looked like the typical Sternberg results. On the other hand, if the memory set consisted of an ordered subset of the original sequence, for instance pictures 2, 3, 4, 5, and 6, then it took subjects no longer to search through five items than it did through two. It was interesting that it didn't matter whether the ordered subset was presented in order (for example, picture 2, then picture 3, then picture 4, and so on) or not (for example, picture 5, then picture 2, then picture 6, and so on); subjects still apparently performed a parallel search. This work suggests that STM does treat ordered, organized material differently than unorganized material. Just as the chunk-

Stimulus Type   Ordinal Position

FIGURE 4-7.   Stimuli used by DeRosa and Tkacz (1976). SOURCE: From "Memory Scanning of Organized Visual Material," by D. V. DeRosa and D. Tkacz, 1976, *Journal of Experimental Psychology: Human Learning and Memory, 2,* 690. Copyright © 1976 by the American Psychological Association. Reprinted by permission.

ing of digits or letters into more coherent patterns changes the apparent capacity of STM, so using organized material apparently affects the way it is processed.

  This study makes an important point: memory processes apparently work differently as a function of the material (stimuli) to be remembered. Therefore, generalizing results from the laboratory to everyday life cannot be done automatically. Instead, we need to consider what kinds of information are processed in what ways, in order to know which laboratory models bear on which kinds of phenomena.

  Let's summarize our review of the short-term memory system so far. The general picture that emerges is that STM is a short-term, limited-capacity storehouse, where information is coded acoustically and maintained through rehearsal. Information can be retrieved from this storage using high-speed, serial, exhaustive search. The nature of the information in STM, however, can help to change the capacity and the processing of the information stored.

Long-Term Memory

Long-term memory is thought to differ from short-term memory in many ways. You can think of long-term memory as a place for storing large amounts of information for indefinite periods of time. In other words, long-term memory is commonly thought to be a sort of mental "treasure chest" or "scrapbook"—the material you have cognitively collected in your lifetime is stored there in some form.

Capacity

What is the capacity of LTM? The question cannot be answered with a single number. Think about the information you have stored in your long-term memory. It would have to include your memory of all the word meanings that you know (probably at least 50,000), all the arithmetic facts, all the historical, geographical, political, and other kinds of information you've learned. You also probably stored in long-term memory at one time or another the names and faces of all sorts of people: family members, significant teachers, neighbors, friends, enemies, and others. You also surely have stored various pieces of other information about each of them: physical attributes, birthdays, favorite color or musical group, and so on. All of your information about various ways of doing familiar things—getting a transcript from the registrar's office; checking out a book from the library; asking for, accepting, or turning down a date; finding a phone number, addressing a letter—must also be in long-term memory. Indeed, a complete list of all information that you have at one time or another put into long-term storage would be very long. This intuition has led most psychologists to estimate that the capacity of long-term memory is virtually unlimited.

This is not to assert that all the information in LTM is retrievable. Indeed, there are many everyday examples of failures to retrieve information. You meet someone you *know* you know but can't place, or you're thinking of a word but can't name it. The information probably is in your long-term storage somewhere, but you somehow can't get to it.

Coding

Many studies of recall from long-term memory report a common finding: errors made while recalling information from long-term memory are likely to be semantic confusions. Thus, words or phrases that mean similar things to the words or phrases that were actually presented are likely to be "recalled" in error, if errors are made. Baddeley (1966b) demonstrated this phenomenon experimentally. He presented subjects with lists of words that sounded similar (for example, mad, map, man) or were matched to the first list but did not sound alike (for example, pen, day, rig). Other subjects also saw a list of words with similar meanings (for example, huge, big, great;

these are called *semantically similar*) and another list of control words matched to the third list, but that did not share meaning (for example, foul, old, deep). Recall was tested after a 20-minute interval, during which subjects worked on another task to prevent rehearsal and to ensure that the material would be drawn from long-term rather than short-term storage. The results showed that acoustic similarity produced little effect on performance, but the list of semantically similar words was harder to learn. Baddeley (1976), reviewing this and other work, concludes that the following generalization, although not absolute, is roughly true: acoustic similarity affects STM; semantic similarity affects LTM.

Retention Duration

How long can information be stored in long-term memory? Although most laboratory experiments test recall after several hours or days, there is also abundant evidence that at least some information can last decades or even a lifetime. Harry Bahrick (1983, 1984) has studied people's memory for material learned to varying degrees at varying times, including memory for the faces of college classmates 20 or 30 or even 50 years after graduation.

In one study, Bahrick (1984) tested 733 adults who had taken or were taking a high school or college course in Spanish. The subjects who were not currently enrolled in a Spanish course had not studied Spanish for

Bahrick's (1984) work suggests that some material from high school or college foreign language classes can be retained for over 50 years.

periods ranging from one to fifty years. They also varied in their original degree of learning of Spanish. Bahrick plotted "forgetting curves" for different aspects of knowledge of Spanish, for example, grammar recall, idiom recognition. Although forgetting differed slightly as a function of the measure, the pattern of results was remarkably consistent. For the first three to six years after completing Spanish study, subjects' recall declined. But, for the next three decades or so, the forgetting curve was flat, suggesting no further loss of information. Retention showed a final decline after about 30 to 35 years.

Bahrick (1984) interpreted the findings as follows:

Large portions of the originally acquired information remain accessible for over 50 years in spite of the fact the information is not used or rehearsed. This portion of the information in a "permastore state" is a function of the level of original training, the grades received in Spanish courses, and the method of testing (recall vs. recognition), but it appears to be unaffected by ordinary conditions of interference. (p. 1)

So you thought you'd forget everything about cognitive psychology after the final exam? If your professor contacts you in 20 years or so, you can surprise both of you—you'll probably remember at least some of the course material!

If information can last indefinitely in LTM, why is it that so much of it doesn't seem to be available, even a week later? There are several familiar examples: "knowing" you know the answer to an exam question but being unable to quite remember it; meeting someone on the street who is extremely familiar but you don't know from where. What has happened to your memory in these instances? Has it been erased somehow?

Forgetting

Forgetting or even "misremembering" is a topic that dates back to the early days of experimental psychology. Hermann Ebbinghaus, a Prussian psychologist, pioneered the empirical study of memory under controlled conditions (Hoffman, Bamberg, Bringmann, & Klein, 1987). His master work (Ebbinghaus, 1885/1913) reports on 19 of his studies using himself as a subject. Ebbinghaus created stimuli he thought were carefully controlled and free from any contamination from prior learning; he called them nonsense syllables ("rur," "hal," or "beis"). He carefully and precisely presented, at a controlled rate, hundreds of lists of these syllables, to a single and dedicated subject: himself. Day after day, Ebbinghaus memorized, tested himself, recorded the results, and prepared new stimuli. All together, he spent about 830 hours memorizing 85,000 syllables in 6,600 lists (Hoffman et al., 1987). The primary questions he asked had to do with the number of repetitions of material needed for perfect recall, the nature of forgetting, the effects of fatigue on learning, and the effects of widely versus closely spaced practice.

One of Ebbinghaus's many findings is presented in Figure 4-8. Depicting a "forgetting curve," the graph plots the amount of time it took him to relearn a list of nonsense syllables after initial learning followed by a retention interval of varying amounts of time (retention interval is plotted on the x-axis). Ebbinghaus's assumption was that the more forgetting, the more effort it would take to relearn a list; conversely, the less forgetting, the less effort in relearning. The forgetting curve suggests that forgetting is not a simple linear function of time. Instead, forgetting is rapid at first and then levels off. Notice how well this laboratory finding anticipates the real-world memory studies of Bahrick, reported above.

As with short-term memory, many psychologists believe that interference, not decay, accounts for "forgetting" from long-term memory (McGeoch, 1932). They believe that material that can't be retrieved successfully from LTM is there but "buried" or in some other way unavailable.

Much of the literature on interference has used a task called **paired associate learning.** Subjects hear lists of pairs of words, for example, flag-spoon, drawer-switch. After one or more presentations of a list, the experimenter presents subjects with the first word in each pair, for example, "flag," and the subject is asked to recall the word that was originally paired with it, "spoon." Interference has been studied experimentally with this task in two basic ways (see Table 4-1).

The first way is through **proactive interference (PI),** the phenomenon described above in the section on short-term memory. PI refers to the fact that previous learning can make subsequent learning more difficult. Thus, if a group of subjects learns a list of paired associates, and then learns a second list with the same set of first terms but new second ones, learning will be harder.

FIGURE 4-8.   Ebbinghaus's (1885/1913) forgetting curve. SOURCE: From *Memory: A Contribution to Experimental Psychology*, by H. Ebbinghaus in 1913. Copyright © 1964 by Dover Publications, Inc. Reprinted by permission.

TABLE 4-1.   Experimental paradigms for creating proactive and retroactive interference

Phase	Experimental Group	Control Group
	Proactive Interference	
I	Learn List A-B	(Unrelated activity)
II	Learn List A-C	Learn List A-C
Test	List A-C	List A-C
	Retroactive Interference	
I	Learn List A-B	Learn List A-B
II	Learn List A-C	(Unrelated activity)
Test	List A-B	List A-B

A more familiar example might come from foreign-language vocabulary learning. Imagine you are taking beginning courses in French and in German at the same time, and for some perverse reason you decide to study their vocabularies sequentially. You first learn a list of French words by pairing them with their English alternatives, for example, dog–*chien,* and so forth. Next, you learn the German equivalents for the English words, again by pairing, for example, dog–*hund,* and so forth. If we compare how long it takes you to learn the second list to how long it takes your roommate (who is not studying French), we'll generally find, all other things being equal, that you need more time for the task. We call the kind of interference you experience *proactive,* to indicate earlier material is interfering with subsequent material.

The other kind of interference is called **retroactive interference.** Imagine that you and another friend both study a list of English words and their French equivalents. Your friend now works on a physics problem set while you work on a list of the same English words with their German equivalents. The next day, you and your friend take a quiz in French class. All other things being equal, your recall of French will be worse than your friend's because of retroactive (or backward) interference.

It has been argued that interference plays a role in most, if not all, forgetting of material from the long-term storage system (Briggs, 1954; Barnes & Underwood, 1959; Postman and Stark, 1969). Of course, it is impossible to rule out the idea that decay occurs, because it is impossible to design a task where interference cannot occur. Leaving this unresolvable issue aside, however, we can ask what happens to information that is retained instead of forgotten? Let's look now at how successful retrievals of information from long-term memory are made.

Retrieval of Information

Suppose you want to be able to improve the chances of recalling information at a later date (for example, to study for an upcoming midterm in cognitive psychology). What do we know about retrieval that can help? We'll discuss in Chapter 7 a number of **mnemonics,** techniques to improve memory, many of them having to do with imagery. For the present, we will consider a few principles of retrieval that can be used to aid recall.

The first is the principle of **categorization.** This states that material organized into categories or other units is more easily recalled than information with no apparent organization. This effect happens even when organized material is initially presented in a random order. Bousfield (1953) presented subjects with a list of 60 words. The words were presented in scrambled order but came from one of four categories: animals, names, professions, and vegetables. Despite this, subjects tended to recall the words in clusters—for example, a number of animals together, then a group of vegetables, and so on. It turns out that even if the material doesn't have apparent organization, asking people to organize them into their own subjective categories improves recall (Mandler, 1967).

A second principle of retrieval, discovered by Thomson and Tulving (1970), is called **encoding specificity.** The idea here is that at the time material is first put into LTM, it is encoded in a particular way, depending on the context present at the time. The manner in which information is encoded is specific to that context. At the time of recall, the person is at a great advantage if the same information available at encoding is also available. Aspects of the information function as cues to the retrieval.

Tulving and Thomson (1973) demonstrated the encoding-specificity principle in the following way: Subjects saw lists of words, with the to-be-remembered words in capital letters. Some subjects saw these "target" words paired with other words that were printed in small letters. Subjects were then told that the words in small letters were cues or hints. Cues were either highly related to the target (for example, hot–COLD) or not very related (for example, ground–COLD). At recall, subjects who hadn't seen any cues were aided by the highly related cues. Subjects who had seen the not-very-related cues could in fact use them to help their recall, and these cues were even better than the highly related cues in aiding recall. Thomson and Tulving believe that even a weakly related word can become a retrieval cue if it is presented at the time of encoding.

To help your understanding of encoding specificity, you might think of material stored in LTM as a series of bubbles with hooks attached, as shown in Figure 4-9. The bubbles contain the material to be stored. The hooks represent information associated to the material. Apparently, many of these associations are formed at the time the to-be-remembered material is first encoded. If these hooks are created at encoding, and presented again at the time of attempted retrieval, the target material in the bubble is retrieved easily, by a process akin to mentally grabbing one of the hooks.

Apparently, even information unrelated to the material—such as the environmental stimuli present at the time of encoding—can become a hook. One of my favorite studies is that of Godden and Baddeley (1975), who presented lists of 40 unrelated words to 16 scuba divers, all wearing scuba gear. Divers learned some of the lists on the shore, and the others, 20 feet under water. They were later asked to recall the words either in the

FIGURE 4-9.   Abstract depiction of long-term memory storage. Circles represent units of information. "Hooks" that are attached to the information at the initial encoding depict associations to the information and attach one unit of information to another.

same environment where they were learned or in the other environment. Results showed that recall was best when the environment was the same as the learning environment. Lists learned underwater were best recalled underwater, and lists learned on the shore were recalled best on the shore. This finding, that recall is best when performed in the original environment, is called a **context effect.** It is interesting that recognition memory was later shown not to evidence the same context effect (Godden & Baddeley, 1980), suggesting that recognition and recall work differently.

Bower (1981) also showed that even your mood at the time you learn something will serve as a hook. If you hear a biology lecture while in a "blue funk," you will actually recall more of it if you can reinstate that emotional frame of mind. Other studies have demonstrated similar effects (called **state-dependent learning**) with pharmacological states: material learned while in a chemically intoxicated state is usually recalled better when the person recreates that state (Eich, 1980).

Further support for the model of memory depicted in Figure 4-9 comes from a phenomenon known as the **spacing effect** (Ross & Landauer, 1978). You may already be familiar with this effect because probably many of your teachers are. Simply, if you repeatedly study the same material, you are much better off with a number of short study sessions spaced some time apart than you are with one long session. Ross and Landauer note: "In most cases, two immediately successive presentations [of a piece of information] are hardly more effective than a single presentation, while two well-spaced presentations are about twice as effective as one" (p. 669). In other words, cognitive psychology supports your instructors' exhortations that cramming for exams really isn't very useful.

A variety of theories attempt to explain the spacing effect (Glenberg, 1977; Ross & Landauer, 1978). Among the most common is one called *encoding variability*. In terms of the model in Figure 4-9, the idea is that spacing allows the context of encoding to change, and hence a wider variety of hooks are able to be attached to the material. The greater the number of hooks, the greater the chances of getting hold of one or more of them at the time of retrieval.

Other Approaches to the Study of Memory

The modal approach to memory, summarized above, makes a distinction between different kinds of memory: for example, sensory, short-term, and long-term memory stores. These components are thought to process information differently, store information differently, and retain information for different lengths of time. The component being used at any given time depends primarily on the length of time information is stored.

The modal approach is not universally endorsed, however. Some psychologists argue that there is only one *kind* of memory storage (Melton, 1963), but different kinds of processing of information held within that store. Others take issue with the modal-approach description of certain kinds of memory stores, such as STM. In this section, we'll review two alternate proposals to explain the nature of memory.

Working Memory

The idea that memory comprises a number of information-processing stores was most completely described by Atkinson and Shiffrin (1968). These authors distinguished between the information being stored, calling this "memory" (for example, STM, LTM) and the structure that did the storing, which they termed a "store" (for example, STS, LTS). Their conception of STS was that it does more than merely hold onto seven or fewer pieces of information for a few seconds. In addition, they thought, information in STS somehow activates relevant information from LTS, the long-term store, and gathers some of that information into STS. They equated STS with consciousness, and saw it as the location of various *control processes* that govern the flow of information, such as rehearsal, coding, integration, decision making. STS is involved in transferring information to LTS, in integrating various pieces of information, and in keeping certain information available.

Baddeley and Hitch (1974) performed a series of experiments to test this model. The general design was to have subjects temporarily store a number of digits (thus absorbing some of the storage capacity of STS) while simultaneously performing another task, such as reasoning or language comprehension. These tasks were also thought to require resources from STS—specifically, the control processes mentioned above. The hypothesis was that if the capacity of STS is taken up by the storage of digits, fewer resources are available for other tasks, and therefore performance on other tasks suffers.

We'll look at one of these studies in detail. Subjects saw a sentence that described the order of appearance of two letters, for example, "*A* is preceded by *B*," together with two letters in a particular order, for example, "*B–A*." The task was to decide, as quickly as possible, if the sentence correctly described the two letters. Subjects were given from one to six digits to hold in memory while they verified the sentences. Subjects were able to verify the sentences while holding one or two digits in memory about as well as they could without holding any digits in memory. However, a six-digit memory load did hurt performance: it took longer to verify the sentence. The effect was especially pronounced if the sentence was negative and passive (for example, "The *B* is not preceded by the *A*"), both of which are known to be harder to process. Although performance was hurt by storing six digits, the effects were not catastrophic (Baddeley, 1990). That is, it took people much longer to reason while rehearsing six digits, but they still could perform the task. According to the predictions derived from Atkinson and Shiffrin's (1968) model, they should not have been able to do so.

Related experiments showed that storing digits in memory also interfered with reading comprehension and the recall of recently learned material. Baddeley and Hitch (1974; Baddeley, 1981) interpreted the findings from the various studies in the following way. First, there does seem to be a common system that contributes to cognitive processes such as temporarily storing information, reasoning, or comprehending language. Filling up short-term memory with six digits does hurt performance on a variety of cognitive tasks, suggesting that this system is used in these tasks. However, the memory loads used, thought to be near the limit of STM capacity, do not totally disrupt performance. Because STM is thought to have a capacity of about 7 ± 2 items, the six-digit memory load should have essentially stopped any other cognitive activity. Baddeley and Hitch (1974) therefore argued for the existence of what they called **working memory.** Working memory is seen as consisting of a limited-capacity "work space" that can be divided between storage and control processing.

Baddeley (1981, 1986, 1990) conceives of working memory as consisting of three components, as depicted in Figure 4-10. The first is the *central executive.* This component is responsible for directing the flow of information, choosing which information will be operated on when and how. It is assumed to have a limited amount of resources and capacity to carry out its tasks. Some of this capacity can be used to store information. The central executive is thought to function more as an attentional system than a mem-

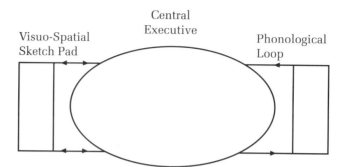

FIGURE 4-10. Baddeley's (1990) model of working memory. SOURCE: From *Human Memory: Theory and Practice*, by A. Baddeley. Copyright © 1990 by Allyn and Bacon. Reprinted by permission.

ory store (Baddeley, 1990), meaning that rather than dealing with the storage and retrieval of information, the central executive deals with the way resources are allocated to cognitive tasks.

The two other components are concerned with the storage and temporary maintenance of information: the *phonological loop,* used to carry out subvocal rehearsal to maintain verbal material, and the *visuo-spatial scratch pad,* used to maintain visual material through visualization. The phonological loop is thought to play an important role in such tasks as learning to read, comprehending language, and acquiring a vocabulary. The visuo-spatial scratch pad involves the creation and use of mental images, a topic we postpone discussion of until Chapter 7.

Notice that postulating the existence of a separate phonological loop explains *why* having a subject remember digits (which presumably loads the phonological loop) does *not* totally devastate performance on other tasks requiring working memory. It is thought that this is so because the tasks that have been spared are drawing on another part of working memory.

Thus, there has been an evolution in the way psychologists regard memory for material being held in the "here and now." From a view of short-term memory as a passive, temporary, limited-capacity storehouse, psychologists now are investigating the active role played by the processing system that is actively operating on current information, and separating this function from the temporary storage of information. Working memory is thought to be involved in the translation of visual information into an acoustic code, the formation of chunks, rehearsal to keep attention focused on the material to be remembered (as in the phone number example, earlier), and sometimes, the elaboration of information, calling up from long-term memory knowledge relevant to incoming information. Thus, the term *working memory,* or WM, is meant to convey more than a temporary storehouse but, instead, a place where active mental effort to attend to, and often to transform, the material, takes place.

In terms of the diagram in Figure 4-1, we can describe the development of the concept of working memory as the articulation of different components of short-term memory. Instead of regarding short-term memory as a single entity, then, we are beginning to conceptualize it in a new way, and give it a new name, to indicate that it includes several components and is involved in a variety of cognitive processing.

Levels of Processing

Another alternative to the modal view of memory is the **levels of processing** approach. In this model, memory is thought to depend not on the length of storage of material but on the initial level of processing of the to-be-remembered information (Craik & Lockhart, 1972). The fundamental assumption is that retention and coding of information depend on the kind of perceptual analysis done on the material at encoding. Some kinds of processing done at a superficial or "shallow" level do not lead to very good retention. Other kinds of "deeper" (more meaningful or semantic) processing improve retention. According to the levels-of-processing view, improvement in memory comes not from rehearsal and repetition but from greater depth of analysis of the material.

A typical levels-of-processing investigation was performed by Craik and Tulving (1975). Subjects were presented with a series of questions about particular words. Each word was preceded by a question, and subjects were asked to respond to the questions as quickly as possible; no mention was made of memory or learning. Any learning that occurs that is not in accord with the subject's purpose is called **incidental learning.**

In one experiment, three kinds of questions were used. One kind asked the subject whether the word was printed in capital letters. Another asked if the word rhymed with another word. The third kind asked if the word fit into a particular sentence (for example, "The girl placed the ——— on the table."). The three kinds of questions were meant to induce different kinds of processing. To answer the first question, you need look only at the typeface (physical processing). To answer the second, you need to read the word and think about what it sounds like (acoustic processing). To answer the third, you need to retrieve and evaluate the word's meaning (semantic processing). Presumably, the "depth" of the processing needed is greatest for the third and least for the first kind of question.

As predicted, Craik and Tulving (1975) found that on a subsequent surprise memory test, words processed semantically were remembered best, followed by words processed acoustically. However, the experiment gave rise to an alternative explanation: subjects spent more time answering questions about sentences than they did questions about capital letters. To respond to this explanation, in subsequent experiments the authors showed that even if the physical processing were slowed down (by asking subjects, "Does this word follow a consonant-vowel-consonant-vowel-consonant-vowel pattern?"), memory is still best for more deeply processed information.

Craik and Tulving (1975) initially equated depth of processing with degree of semantic processing. Bower and Karlin (1974), studying memory for faces, found similar results with nonverbal stimuli: subjects who rated faces for "honesty" showed better memory than subjects who rated the faces according to gender. One problem with this approach, though, was pinning down the definition of what defined a level, and what made for "depth" (Baddeley, 1978).

Craik and Tulving (1975) found, for instance, that the "meaningfulness" of the initial task was not the only factor that could account for better retention. Subjects asked to determine if words fit into sentences showed poorer recall for simple sentences (for example, "She cooked the ———.") than they did for more complex sentences (for example, "The great bird swooped down and carried off the struggling ———."). Levels-of-processing theory as initially formulated would argue that both words were processed semantically, so that could not account for the difference in recall. Craik and Tulving therefore extended the levels-of-processing idea, arguing that the elaboration of material could also aid recall. Presumably, the second, more complicated sentence calls to mind a richer idea—the sentence itself has more underlying propositions (There was a bird. The bird was very large. The bird swooped down. The bird carried something off.) than the first sentence (There is a female. She is baking something.). Sentences that specified the relation of the target word to the context more precisely were found to be especially likely to increase the probability of recall of the target word (Stein & Bransford, 1979).

Craik and Lockhart (1972) viewed memory as a continuum of processes, from the "transient products of sensory analyses to the highly durable products of semantic . . . operations." This view ties memory in with other cognitive systems quite neatly. For example, recall the work on dichotic listening tasks, reviewed in Chapter 3. Recall that material from the unattended channel is typically not remembered after the task is completed. The levels of processing approach can account for this finding, holding that material that is not analyzed for meaning receives only "shallow" processing, and this results in poor retention.

Baddeley (1978) presented a thorough critique of the levels of processing approach. He argued that without a more precise and independent definition of *depth of processing,* the usefulness of the theory was very limited. Second, he reviewed studies that showed greater recall of information processed acoustically than semantically, under certain conditions. Finally, he described ways in which the modal view of memory could explain the typical levels-of-processing findings.

Nonetheless, the levels of processing approach does help to reorganize the thinking of memory researchers, making them pay more attention to the importance of the way material is encoded. The approach has helped cognitive psychologists think about the ways in which people approach learning tasks. It has reinforced the idea that the more "connections" an item has to other pieces of information (for example, retrieval cues), the easier it will be to remember, a point that fits nicely with the idea of encoding specificity, discussed earlier.

Recent memory research has also encouraged psychologists to pay attention to how encoding changes with the type of material presented. Some aspects of information, for instance, appear to be encoded seemingly without much effort, or even intention. Frequency of occurrence is one such aspect (Hasher & Zacks, 1984). For example, if you are a movie fan, you see lots of movies, and you may even see some more than once. Although you probably have no reason to keep track of how many times you saw a particular movie, you may have a clear sense that you've seen one a few more times than you've seen another. Chances are quite good that your sense is correct. If so, Hasher and Zacks would explain your impression as an instance of *automatic encoding:* Certain aspects of experience, such as frequency of occurrence, have a special representation, and are kept track of in memory without effort or even intention.

Everyday Memory

Thus far, we have concentrated on laboratory studies of memory. This tradition dates back at least to Ebbinghaus, who worked with nonsense-syllable stimuli in an effort to avoid contaminating his findings with his own personal associations to words. One can't help but admire Ebbinghaus's dedication and feel gratitude for the many insights about memory he described. However, a similarly common reaction is to find his efforts somewhat amusing. After all, what relevance do his heroic studies have to memory in "real life?" Does the study of memory for nonsense syllables really tell us very much about how to study for an upcoming midterm, or how to remember where we left our house key, or how we recall our first day of kindergarten (if in fact we remember anything about it)?

Another pioneer in the study of memory, Frederick Bartlett, rejected the emphasis on laboratory studies of memory. Bartlett (1932) believed that much of the way memory worked in the real world (as opposed to the laboratory) was to make use of world knowledge and *schemata,* organizations of past experiences, to *reconstruct* the material at the time of retrieval. Bartlett tested both friends and students, first presenting them with stories such as the one shown in Box 4-1.

Bartlett used the method of *serial reproduction,* meaning that subjects were asked to recall the stories on more than one occasion, with varying retention intervals, some as long as years. Bartlett was interested in what information was remembered and what information was "misremembered"—distorted or reordered in the subjects' recollection. Box 4-2 provides examples of repeated recollections of the "War of the Ghosts" story of one of his subjects. It shows concretely that over time, the same subject's recall is progressively more distorted. Bartlett used this evidence to argue for a *constructive* view of long-term memory. He believed that subjects unintentionally introduced the distortions to make the material more rational and more coherent from their own point of view. Bartlett thus rejected the idea of long-term memory as a warehouse where material is stored unchanged until retrieval. Rather, he saw memory as an active and often inaccurate process that encodes and retrieves information in such a way as to make it all "make sense."

Neisser (1982a) offered related arguments regarding studying memory in natural settings. Neisser was skeptical of the possibility that laboratory studies of memory will inevitably be relevant to memory in natural set-

---

BOX 4-1   "The War of The Ghosts": A story used by Bartlett (1932) to investigate long-term memory

One night two young men from Egulac went down to the river to hunt seals, and while they were there it became foggy and calm. Then they heard war-cries, and they thought: "Maybe this is a war-party." They escaped to the shore, and hid behind a log. Now canoes came up, and they heard the noise of paddles, and saw one canoe coming up to them. There were five men in the canoe, and they said:

"What do you think? We wish to take you along. We are going up the river to make war on the people."

One of the young men said: "I have no arrows."

"Arrows are in the canoe," they said.

"I will not go along. I might be killed. My relatives do not know where I have gone. But you," he said, turning to the other, "may go with them."

So one of the young men went, but the other returned home.

And the warriors went on up the river to a town on the other side of Kalama. The people came down to the water, and they began to fight, and many were killed. But presently the young man heard one of the warriors say: "Quick, let us go home: that Indian has been hit." Now he thought: "Oh, they are ghosts." He did not feel sick, but they said he had been shot.

So the canoes went back to Egulac, and the young man went ashore to his house, and made a fire. And he told everybody and said: "Behold I accompanied the ghosts, and we went to fight. Many of our fellows were killed, and many of those who attacked us were killed. They said I was hit, and I did not feel sick."

He told it all, and then he became quiet. When the sun rose he fell down. Something black came out of his mouth. His face became contorted. The people jumped up and cried.

He was dead.

SOURCE: *From* Remembering: A Study in Experimental and Social Psychology, *by F. C. Bartlett. Copyright © 1932 by Cambridge University Press. Reprinted by permission.*

tings, and therefore believed that laboratory studies are not enough to understand the use of memory in everyday life. Neisser called for the study of how people construct and use memories of their own past experiences, how they remember events of historical significance, how we use memory to plan and carry out everyday errands, and so on. In this section, we will take up some of these questions.

B O X   4 - 2   One Subject's Recall of "The War of the Ghosts"

Recalled 15 minutes after hearing story: The Ghosts

There were two men on the banks of the river near Egulac. They heard the sound of paddles, and a canoe with five men in it appeared, who called to them, saying: "We are going to fight the people. Will you come with us?"

One of the two men answered, saying: "Our relations do not know where we are, and we have not got any arrows."

They answered: "There are arrows in the canoe."

So the man went, and they fought the people, and then he heard them saying: An Indian is killed, let us return."

So he returned to Egulac, and told them he knew they were ghosts.

He spoke to the people of Egulac, and told them that he had fought with the Ghosts, and many men were killed on both sides, and that he was wounded, but felt nothing. He lay down and became calmer, and in the night he was convulsed, and something black came out of his mouth.

The people said:

"He is dead."

Recalled two weeks later: The Ghosts

There were two men on the banks of a river near the village of Etishu (?). They heard the sound of paddles coming from the up-stream, and shortly a canoe appeared. The men in the canoe spoke, saying: "We are going to fight the people: will you come with us?"

One of the young men answered, saying: "Our relations do not know where we are; but my companion may go with you. Besides, we have no arrows."

So the young man went with them, and they fought the people, and many were killed on both sides. And then he heard shouting: "The Indian is wounded; let us return." And he heard the people say: "They are the Ghosts." He did not know he was wounded, and returned to Etishu (?). The people collected round him and bathed his wounds, and he said he had fought with the Ghosts. Then he became quiet. But in the night he was convulsed, and something black came out of his mouth.

And the people cried:

"He is dead."

SOURCE: *From* Remembering: A Study in Experimental and Social Psychology, *by F. C. Bartlett. Copyright © 1932 by Cambridge University Press. Reprinted by permission.*

Eyewitness Testimony

Imagine yourself a juror assigned to a robbery/murder case. The defendant, a young man, is alleged to have robbed and killed a 7-11 store clerk at gunpoint around 11:00 P.M. No physical evidence (for example, fingerprints, fiber samples) linking the defendant to the crime has been produced. Instead, the case hinges on the sworn testimony of a 7-11 patron who swears the defendant is the man she saw on the night in question. The defense attorney, in cross-examination, gets the witness to agree that the lighting was poor, the robber was wearing a stocking cap over his face, she was nervous and paying more attention to the gun than to the face of the robber, and so on. Despite these admissions, the witness remains convinced of one thing: the defendant is the man she saw that night rob and murder the store clerk.

How much would the eyewitness testimony convince you of the defendant's guilt? Elizabeth Loftus, a cognitive psychologist specializing in the study of eyewitness testimony, would argue that the testimony would have a disproportionate effect on your behavior. She says that "eyewitness testimony is likely to be believed by jurors, especially when it is offered with a high level of confidence," even when the confident witness is inaccurate. Indeed, she believes that "all the evidence points rather strikingly to the conclusion that there is almost nothing more convincing than a live human being who takes the stand, points a finger at the defendant, and says 'That's the one!'" (Loftus, 1979, p. 19).

Several studies reviewed by Loftus (1979), however, suggest that confidence in eyewitness testimony may be far too strong. In one study, for example, subjects viewed a series of slides that depicted a (simulated) automobile accident (see photos for examples). The automobile, a red Datsun, came to either a stop sign (for half the subjects) or a yield sign (for the other half) before becoming involved in an accident with a pedestrian.

The experimental manipulation came in the questioning following the viewing of slides. About half of the subjects (half of whom had seen a stop sign; the other half, a yield sign) were asked, "Did another car pass the red Datsun while it was stopped at the stop sign?" The other half of the subjects were asked, "Did another car pass the red Datsun while it was stopped at the yield sign?" After answering these and other apparently routine questions, subjects worked on an unrelated activity for 20 minutes. Then, they were given a recognition test of several slides.

Included in the test was a critical test pair, depicting a red Datsun stopped either at a stop sign or at a yield sign. Subjects were to decide which of the two slides they had originally seen. Subjects who received a question *consistent* with the slide originally seen (that is, a question about the stop sign when the slide they had previously seen contained a stop sign, not a yield sign) correctly recognized the slide 75% of the time. Subjects who received an *inconsistent* question, however, had an overall accuracy rate of 41%, a dramatic decrease when guessing alone would have produced an overall accuracy rate of 50%.

Stimuli from the Loftus, Miller, and Burns (1978) study

Other studies by Loftus (1975) have demonstrated that people's memories can apparently be altered by presenting misleading questions. For example, some subjects viewed a film and were then asked, "How fast was the white sports car going when it passed the barn while traveling along the country road?" Other subjects were merely asked, "How fast was the white sports car going while traveling along the country road?" Actually, there was no barn presented in the film. One week later, all subjects were asked whether they had seen a barn. Fewer than 3% of the subjects in the second condition reported having seen a barn whereas 17% of the subjects asked the misleading question so reported.

"Memorial malleability" fits well with some laboratory studies of sentence recall; both support Bartlett's conception of memory as a *constructive* process. A classic study by Bransford and Franks (1971) illustrates this idea. They gave subjects a list of sentences, all of which were derived from four basic sentences, such as "The ants were in the kitchen," "The jelly was on the table," "The jelly was sweet," and "The ants ate the jelly." The sentences the subjects saw included two of the above sentences, two combinations of the simple sentences (for example, "The sweet jelly was on the table,") and combinations of three of the simple sentences (for example, "The ants ate the sweet jelly on the table.") On a later recognition test, the subjects were asked to decide, for each sentence presented, if they had seen that exact sentence before and to rate their confidence in their judgment. They were most confident in "recognizing" the sentence that combined all four of the simple sentences, "The ants in the kitchen ate the sweet jelly that was on the table," even though it had never been presented.

Bransford and Franks (1971) explained that the subjects had not stored a copy of the actually presented sentences in memory. Instead, they had abstracted and reorganized the information in the sentences, integrating the ideas and storing the integration. The subjects were later unable to distinguish between the sentences that had been presented and their own integration. One might argue that this is just what Loftus's subjects were doing: integrating the original memories with later questions. If the later questions were misleading, that incorrect information became integrated with the original memory to produce a distorted memory.

Flashbulb Memories

Where were you when you learned of the explosion of the space shuttle Challenger on January 29, 1986? Many of us recall information not only about the tragic disaster itself but about where we were, who we were with, and what we were doing at the time we first heard about it. Brown and Kulick (1977) coined the term **flashbulb memory** to describe this phenomenon. Other examples of it might be found in your parents' or older siblings' recollections of where they were when they heard about the assassinations of John F. Kennedy, Martin Luther King, Robert F. Kennedy, and John Lennon. Other events that have led to the flashbulb-memory phenomenon include the attempted assassination of President Ronald Reagan (Pillemer, 1984), and the 1989 San Francisco earthquake (Neisser, Winograd, & Weldon, 1991).

Given the historical importance and surprising nature of these events, it may be small wonder that most of us old enough to have experienced them remember them. Why, though, do we remember details about our own circumstances when we first heard the news? Some have argued that part of the explanation involves a physiological response that happens to us when we hear this kind of news: parts of the brain that are involved in emotional responses become activated, and the cognitive effects of this activation result in the storage of a great deal of information that is related to the main information only indirectly (Brown & Kulik, 1977). Pillemer (1984) found, for example, that his subjects who reported a stronger emotional reaction to the news of the assassination attempt on President Reagan also had stronger and more detailed flashbulb memories.

Neisser (1982b) offered a different explanation for the origin of flashbulb memories: people are finding a way to link themselves to history; flashbulb memories come about because the strong emotions produced by the news prompt people to repeat their own stories of where they were when they heard the news. Flashbulb memories, then, result from the retellings of stories. Over time, flashbulb memories can become distorted, in much the same ways that Bartlett's (1932) subjects distorted the recollections of the "War of the Ghosts" story; people elaborate and fill in gaps in their stories, making them approximate a standard story format.

Bonhannon (1988) studied 686 undergraduate students' flashbulb memories of the Challenger disaster. Either two weeks or eight months after the explosion, subjects were asked to recall the circumstances surrounding their first discovery of the news, including when they heard, what the weather was like that day, what they were doing, what they were wearing, where they were, and from whom they received the news. Subjects were also asked to estimate the strength of their emotional reaction to the news and to estimate the number of times they had retold their "Space Shuttle stories" to anyone else.

Results provided support for both the physiological activation and the story-retelling explanations for flashbulb memories. Subjects who reported stronger emotional reactions once again recalled more details, were more confident about their memories, and had more complete recollections than subjects who reported being less upset. At the same time, subjects who reported more retellings also showed higher confidence and more remembered details than did subjects reporting fewer retellings.

The question of whether flashbulb memories differ *in kind* from other types of memories is being actively debated (see, for example, McCloskey, Wible, & Cohen, 1988; Pillemer, 1990; Cohen, McCloskey, & Wible, 1990). McCloskey and colleagues (1988), for example, found evidence that some flashbulb memories are quite inaccurate, and that the kinds of forgetting and distortion evident in flashbulb memories are predictable from traditional studies of ordinary memory. The area promises great opportunities for research activity.

Summary

We've seen in this chapter that cognitive psychologists approach the study of memory in a variety of ways, and that this diversity dates back at least to "founding" cognitive psychologists such as Ebbinghaus and Bartlett. Some of the diversity arises in theoretical orientations—some psychologists seek evidence for the proposition that there are different memory *stores* (for example, sensory memory, short-term memory, long-term memory); others focus on the kind of processing that is done with to-be-remembered information.

From the thousands of memory studies reported since those of Ebbinghaus and Bartlett, a few general principles have emerged. The first is that the more active and meaningful the original processing of information, the more memorable the information will be. This idea has obvious and practical relevance for students: if you want to improve your recall of material for later testing (in midterms and finals), it behooves you to organize it and to think about its meaning rather than merely reading, underlining, or highlighting the words. Memory is also seen to be an active, constructive process. This means that the information does not "sit still" in the storehouse, waiting to be retrieved. Instead, it appears that some further processing of the information occurs, either during storage or at the time of retrieval, such that we can "remember" events that never actually occurred. We have also seen that a number of contextual factors affect recall, suggesting that the more similar the recall environment is to the initial encoding environment, the higher the probability of recall.

We have seen, as well, a controversy in the explanations proposed for why we forget information. The question is whether information in a memory store ever decays or "disintegrates," or whether all supposedly "forgotten" information is actually buried information that has been displaced by interference from other information. Although these two possibilities are quite distinct, it is very difficult as a practical matter to design critical experiments that would rule one out. It may also be that both kinds of processes play some role in forgetting.

We have also seen a tension between psychologists who insist on rigorous laboratory controls and those who want to be sure that the memory phenomena studied occur in everyday life. Recent work in eyewitness testimony and flashbulb memories does examine real-world phenomena. Some of the findings that have emerged in this field—for example, the constructive nature of recall—fit well with laboratory findings. It remains to be seen whether study of memory outside the laboratory will yield findings that call for new principles and theories to be developed.

Throughout this chapter, we've been focusing on memory for specific events (for example, witnessing a crime or hearing a list of stimuli read to you). Often, however, our memories of a particular event call upon our memories of general knowledge. For example, if I were to recall my previous lecture, I might use my general knowledge about lectures (where students sit, the kinds of equipment, such as chalk or overhead projectors, I typically use) to reconstruct my memory of that particular class. In the next chapter, we will examine more closely the ways in which our general knowledge is stored and organized.

We will see in other chapters to come that memory plays a significant role in almost every instance of cognitive processing. Thus, as developments occur within this field to change our conceptions of how memory works, we can expect new developments in almost every other area of cognition.

Recommended Readings

Classic studies on memory include Atkinson and Shiffrin (1968), Bartlett (1932), Craik and Lockhart (1972), Ebbinghaus (1885/1913), Miller (1956), Sperling (1960), Sternberg (1966), and Waugh and Norman (1965). Some comprehensive textbooks on memory include Baddeley (1990) and Ellis and Hunt (1993). Recent review articles relevant to the topics presented in this chapter, especially those having to do with long-term memory and levels of processing, are Estes (1988) and Horton and Mills (1984). Haber (1983) presents a critique of the concept of the icon, and there are numerous replies to his proposal immediately following. This lively exchange by psychologists interested in visual memory is published together with Haber's (1983) proposal, and shows that opinion is very much divided on the idea of how much of a role sensory memory plays in ordinary cognitive processing of information.

Baddeley (1986, 1990) describes his emerging ideas about working memory, and reviews investigations of both the phonological loop and the visuo-spatial scratchpad in detail. Reisberg, Rappaport, and O'Shaughnessey (1984) describe a particularly clever series of experiments testing ways of increasing immediate-memory capacity, and the implications of an increase for the nature of working memory. Dempster (1981) reviews studies of individual and developmental differences in memory span. Anderson (1983) and Cowan (1988) offer new and similar conceptions of relations between STM and LTM. Mandler (1980) reviews the literature on recognition, and argues for a new model of how that process works. A recent study of recall of television shows that lasted for only one season is reported by Squire (1989), who uses the findings to investigate the nature of recall from very-long-term memory. Estes (1980) presents an interesting comparison of human and computer memory.

Loftus's (1979) book provides an excellent introduction to studies of eyewitness testimony. A later exchange between Loftus (1983) and some of her critics (McCloskey & Egeth, 1983) and a recent paper by Kassin, Ellsworth, and Smith (1989) present a debate over the proper role of cognitive psychologists as expert witnesses in legal trials testifying about psychological research on eyewitness testimony. Finally, a spirited exchange between Banaji and Crowder (1989) and Neisser (1991) debates the usefulness of "everyday" versus laboratory studies of memory in developing general theories and principles.

An emerging field, cognitive neuroscience, studies the physiological underpinnings of cognitive processes, such as memory. The literature on the neurological study of memory is reviewed by Thompson, Donegan, and Lavond (1988) and by Woody (1986).

REVIEW QUESTIONS

1. Review the evidence that has led some psychologists to assume that different memory stores (for example, sensory memory, short-term memory, long-term memory) exist.

2. Psychologists have posited two distinct mechanisms for forgetting: decay and interference. Describe each of these, briefly review the experimental evidence supporting each, and describe the problem in distinguishing between them.

3. Describe the methods used in Saul Sternberg's memory-scanning experiment. What do the results tell us about retrieval of information from STM?

4. Describe and evaluate the concept of *encoding variability* as a principle of retrieval of information.

5. How does Baddeley's conception of *working memory* differ from traditional descriptions of STM?

6. How do findings from the eyewitness testimony and the flashbulb memory literature fit with laboratory-based findings reported earlier? What are the differences, if any?

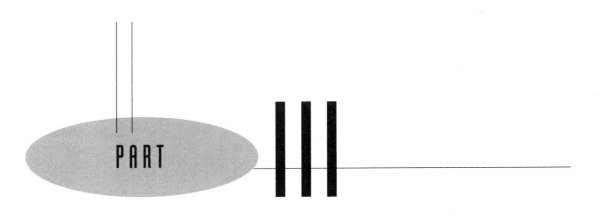

PART **III**

The Representation and Organization of Knowledge

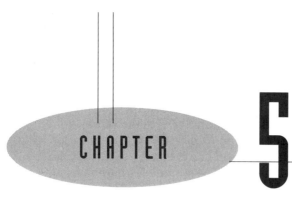

CHAPTER 5

Knowledge Representation

As a psychologist, teacher, and amateur dog trainer, I have a great deal of knowledge about different topics mentally stored. Often, I surprise my students (and sometimes myself) by remembering the approximate title, author, journal, and year of an article that would complement their independent study problems. Less often, when I teach dog-obedience classes and am stumped by a dog who just can't seem to learn a simple task, I am able to call up from memory an idea that I heard about years ago at a dog-training seminar.

The question that cognitive psychology needs to answer is, how do I hold onto information in such a way that I'm able to access it sometimes years after I've stored it?

Consider the vast range of information that everyone must have stored in permanent memory. In addition to information regarding events in your life (your sixth birthday party, the time you broke your arm, going to the circus, your first day of junior high), you also have stored a great deal of knowledge: definitions of the words you know, arithmetic facts and procedures, historical, scientific, and geographical knowledge, and (I hope) even some knowledge of principles of cognitive psychology. In this chapter, we will take a more detailed look at this second kind of permanent memory—memory for knowledge.

One of the questions that will concern us is how stored knowledge is organized. There are several distinct ways of arranging and storing information, and each has different implications for ease of access and retrieval.

An analogy to your bookshelves might help. Think about your books and how they are arranged. You might have a section for textbooks, a section for nonfiction, a section for mysteries, and a section for trashy romances. Or you might have all the books arranged alphabetically by author. Or you might have tall books on one shelf, paperbacks on another. Each possibility represents a different way of organizing. Each possibility has different implications for how you look for a particular book, and how easy it is to find it. Suppose you want to find *Gone with the Wind* but you've forgotten the author's name. If you've arranged your books alphabetically by author, you'll have a much more difficult time than if you've arranged them by title or by category.

We'll see in this chapter a similar conclusion with regard to models of knowledge representation. A variety of models have been proposed for how our knowledge is mentally represented and organized. Each makes different predictions about how you search for particular pieces of information.

To start, do your memories of specific events (say, your sixth birthday party) differ in important ways from your memories of general knowledge (for example, that 2 + 2 = 4). Endel Tulving (1972, 1983) draws a distinction between memories for events and memories for general knowledge. Tulving argues that long-term memory consists of two separate and distinct yet interacting systems. One system, **episodic memory,** holds memories of specific events that you yourself somehow participated in. The other system, **semantic memory,** holds information that has entered your general knowledge base—you can recall parts of that base, but the information recalled is generic in nature, it doesn't have much to do with your personal experience. For example, your memory of the fact that Sigmund Freud was a founding practitioner of psychoanalysis is presumably in your general knowledge base but divorced from your personal memories of what happened to you at a certain time. It's likely, actually, that you can't even remember when the fact about Freud entered your memory. Contrast this situation with when information about your first date or the Challenger explosion entered your memory. You might recall for those instances not only the information itself but the circumstances surrounding your acquisition of the information (where, when, why, how, and from whom you heard, saw, or otherwise acquired it).

After reviewing arguments and evidence for the episodic/semantic distinction, we'll go on to concentrate on semantic memory. Specifically, we'll look at a number of proposals for how our knowledge bases are organized, and the implications organization has for the ways we access this information.

Finally, we'll review some recent work suggesting that some of our memories are not accessible to our conscious recollection. Some psychologists use the term **implicit memory** as a description of phenomena that show that some experiences leave memory traces without your being aware of them; we know that these traces exist, however, when they are shown to influence your behavior later. Work with **amnesic** patients—those who have apparently lost the ability to recollect information from their past experience—will be discussed. We will see that much of the work on implicit memory is carried out within a semantic memory framework.

The Semantic/Episodic Distinction

Tulving (1972, 1983) proposed a classification of long-term memories into two kinds: episodic and semantic. Episodic memory is memory for information that is temporally dated; the information stored has with it some sort of marker for when it was originally encountered. Any of your memories that you can trace to a single time are considered to be in episodic memory. If you recall your high school graduation, or your first meeting with your freshman-year roommate, or the time you first learned of an important event (for example, the start of the Persian Gulf war), you are recalling episodic memories. Even if you don't recall the exact date or even the year, you know that the information was first presented at a particular time and place, and you have a memory of that presentation.

Semantic memory, in contrast, is thought to store general information about language and world knowledge. When you recall arithmetic facts (for example, 3 × 6 is 18), historical dates ("In 1492, Columbus sailed the ocean blue"), the past tense forms of various verbs (run, ran; walk, walked; am, was), you are calling on semantic memory. Notice in these examples, that in recalling "2 + 2 = 4," you aren't tracing back to a particular moment when you learned the fact, as you might do with the Challenger explosion. Instead of "remembering" that 2 + 2 = 4, most people speaking of "knowing" that 2 + 2 = 4. It is this distinction between memories of specific moments and recall from general knowledge that marks the major difference between semantic and episodic memory.

Why make such a distinction? Doing so captures our intuitions that the recall of some things is different from the recall of others. Recalling your graduation simply has a different "feel" to it than does recalling the sum of 2 and 2. Tulving (1983) provides another argument, comparing the topic of "memory" to the topic of "locomotion":

> Seeking for general theories of memory is like seeking for a general theory of, say, locomotion. Memory has to do with the after-effects of stimulation at one time that manifest themselves subsequently at another time; locomotion is concerned with the change of position of a living creature from one location to some other location. Consider now the problem facing the theorist of locomotion when he contemplates the variety of forms of locomotion that this theory has to handle. A very small sample would include an amoeba moving by changing the shape of its entire protoplasmic mass, an earthworm literally eating itself through the ground, a protozoan drawing itself through water by beating its flagella, a mollusk gliding along a track of slime that it itself secretes, a Portuguese man-of-war relying on its gas-filled float to propel itself across water like a sailboat, and many different insects

that swim, run, jump, burrow, or fly from one place to another, not to mention spiders, snakes, monkeys, and human infants. . . . What do all these forms of locomotion—the swimmings, crawlings, walkings, runnings, flyings, jumpings, wigglings, glidings, slidings, and jet propulsions—have in common, other than the fact that they get the creature from one point to another under its own steam, and that it spends energy in doing so?

What do the almost equally endless variety of forms of memory in the broad sense have in common, other than that they can be subsumed under the definition, and that they manifest one of the basic characteristics of intelligent matter? (p. 7)[1]

Tulving (1972, 1983) went on to describe episodic and semantic memory as **memory systems** that operate on different principles and hold onto different kinds of information. Tulving (1983) pointed to a number of differences in the ways episodic and semantic memory seem to work. The differences are summarized in Table 5-1. A full explanation of every entry in the table is given in Tulving (1983), so only a few will be explored here.

As we have just discovered, the nature of the information held in the two memory systems is different. In episodic memory, we hold onto information about events and episodes that have happened to us directly. In semantic memory, we store knowledge: facts, concepts, and ideas. With episodic memory, the memories are encoded in terms of personal experience, and show great effects of context. Recalling memories from the episodic system takes the form of "Remember when. . . ." With semantic memory, the information is encoded as general knowledge, context effects are less pronounced, and retrieval of information consists of answering questions from our general knowledge base in the form of "Remember what. . . ." Organization of episodic memory is temporal, that is, one event will be recorded as having occurred before, after, or at the same time as another. Organization of semantic memory is arranged more on the basis of meanings and meaning relationships among different pieces of information.

Tulving's (1972, 1983) proposals have provoked strong controversy within the field of cognitive psychology. McKoon, Ratcliff, and Dell (1986) present a series of arguments centering on the usefulness of considering episodic and semantic memories to be two separate memory *systems,* and the kind of evidence needed to support the distinction. Many psychologists find it hard to draw sharp lines between knowledge that includes information about the time it was first learned, and knowledge that is more "generic" in character. Others, such as Baddeley (1984), draws an analogy to looking down on a forest from an airplane:

Out of the window, the forest beneath looked like a grey-green carpet, totally different from what its appearance would have been had I been standing in the forest. I could easily produce a long list of perceptual differences in terms of sight, sound, and even smell between the forest as experi-

[1]From *Elements of Episodic Memory,* by E. Tulving. Copyright © 1983 by Oxford University Press. Reprinted by permission of Oxford University Press.

TABLE 5-1.   Differences between episodic and semantic memory

Diagnostic Feature	Episodic	Semantic
Information		
Source	Sensation	Comprehension
Units	Events; episodes	Facts; ideas; concepts
Organization	Temporal	Conceptual
Reference	Self	Universe
Veridicality	Personal belief	Social agreement
Operations		
Registration	Experiential	Symbolic
Temporal coding	Present; direct	Absent; indirect
Affect	More important	Less important
Inferential capability	Limited	Rich
Context dependency	More pronounced	Less pronounced
Vulnerability	Great	Small
Access	Deliberate	Automatic
Retrieval queries	Time? Place?	What?
Retrieval consequences	Change system	System unchanged
Retrieval mechanisms	Synergy	Unfolding
Recollective experience	Remembered past	Actualized knowledge
Retrieval report	Remember	Know
Developmental sequence	Late	Early
Childhood amnesia	Affected	Unaffected
Applications		
Education	Irrelevant	Relevant
General utility	Less useful	More useful
Artificial intelligence	Questionable	Excellent
Human intelligence	Unrelated	Related
Empirical evidence	Forgetting	Analysis of language
Laboratory tasks	Particular episodes	General knowledge
Legal testimony	Admissible; eyewitness	Inadmissible; expert
Amnesia	Involved	Not involved
Bicameral men	No	Yes

SOURCE: From *Elements of Episodic Memory,* by E. Tulving. Copyright © 1983 by Oxford University Press. Reprinted by permission of Oxford University Press.

> enced from the plane and as experienced from within. Would I therefore be entitled to conclude that they were quite separate forests? Clearly not. By analogy, one can reasonably argue that the semantic and episodic memory emphasize different aspects of the same system. (p. 238)

However, almost everyone agrees that at the very least there seem to be two kinds of memories—semantic and episodic—even if they are stored within a single system.

Most of the topics covered in Chapter 4 had to do with episodic memory. After all, when subjects in an experiment are given a list of words to remember, they subsequently are asked to recall *those* words, which they memorized at a particular time, not just any words they happen to know. In this chapter we will concentrate on semantic memory, considering the way this kind of information is stored, processed, and retrieved.

Semantic memory is thought to have enormous capacity, hence it is important to know how it is organized. We've already discussed the library analogy for semantic memory. If a library contains only a handful of books, it makes little difference how they are arranged or stored; it would be an easy matter for a patron looking for a particular book simply to browse through the entire collection. As the number of books grows, however, the need for some sort of organizational system becomes pressing. One might say that our knowledge bases are comparable to a large library; therefore, understanding their organization is crucial for understanding how we retrieve and use information.

Semantic Memory Models

Many of the semantic memory models in existence came about because psychologists and computer scientists interested in the field of artificial intelligence wanted to build a system having what most people refer to as "commonsense knowledge." The premise was that associated with your knowledge of an explicit fact is a great deal of implicit knowledge, information that you know but take for granted.

An example of implicit knowledge in our understanding of everyday routines is the following. Consider the directions typically found on a shampoo bottle: "Wet hair. Apply shampoo. Lather. Rinse. Repeat." If you slavishly followed these directions, you would emerge from the shower only when the bottle was empty! However, most of us do manage a shampoo, even before our first cup of coffee. What we rely on is not just the directions but our world knowledge or common sense that one or two repetitions of the lather-rinse cycle is sufficient (Galotti & Ganong, 1985).

Our vast knowledge of language and concepts also appears to have associated with it a great deal of implicit knowledge. For instance, if I asked you, "Does a Bernese mountain dog have a liver?" you would very likely answer (correctly), "Yes." Your answer comes (I assume) not from your extensive study of Bernese mountain dogs but from your knowledge that Bernese mountain dogs are dogs, dogs are mammals, mammals have livers. In this section, we will consider models of how knowledge is represented in semantic memory such that we can make these inferences and demonstrate our common sense.

To build such models, we need to make a number of inferences about our mental representations of information from our performance on specific tasks. For example, if we can retrieve some information very quickly (say, think of words beginning with the letter L) relative to other information (say, think of words with L as the fourth letter), that suggests something about the organization of knowledge. In this example, for instance, we can infer that our **lexicons,** or mental dictionaries, are organized by the first letter, not the fourth, in a word. In the specific models presented next, you'll see that the tasks invented were meant to answer very specific questions about the nature of the mental organization of information.

The Hierarchical Semantic Network Model

Because our world and language knowledge is so great, the storage-space requirements to represent it are large. One way to conserve space would be to try to avoid storing redundant information wherever possible. Therefore, rather than storing the information "has live young" with the node for Bernese mountain dog, and again with the nodes for human, lion, tiger, and bear, it makes more sense to store it once at the higher-level node for mammal. This illustrates the principle of **cognitive economy:** properties and facts are stored at the highest level possible. To recover information, you use inference, much as you did to answer the earlier question about Bernese mountain dogs' having livers.

A landmark study on semantic memory was performed by Collins and Quillian (1969). They tested the idea that semantic memory is analogous to a network of connected ideas. As in later connectionist networks, this one consists of nodes, which in this case correspond roughly to words or concepts. Each node is connected to related nodes by means of *pointers,* or links that go from one node to another. Thus, the node that corresponds to a given word or concept together with the pointers to other nodes to which the first node is connected constitute the semantic memory for that word or concept. The collection of nodes associated with all the words and concepts one knows about is called a **semantic network.** Figure 5-1 depicts a portion of such a network for a person (like me) who knows a good deal about Bernese mountain dogs. (The photograph on page 147 shows three Bernese mountain dogs.) Readers familiar with computer science might be reminded of linked lists and pointers, a metaphor that was intended by Collins and Quillian.

Collins and Quillian (1969) also tested the principle of cognitive economy, described above. They reasoned that if semantic memory is analogous to a network of nodes and pointers, and if semantic memory honors the cognitive economy principle, the closer in a network a fact or property is stored to a particular node, the less time it should take to verify the fact and property. Collins and Quillian's reasoning led to the following prediction: if a person's knowledge of Bernese mountain dogs is organized along the lines of Figure 5-1, she or he should be able to verify the sentence "A Bernese mountain dog has an exuberant disposition" more quickly than to verify "A Bernese mountain dog has live young." Note that the property "has exuberant disposition" is stored right with the node for Bernese mountain dog, indicating that this property is specific to that kind of animal. The property "has live young" is not specific to Bernese mountain dogs, and so is stored a number of levels higher in the hierarchy.

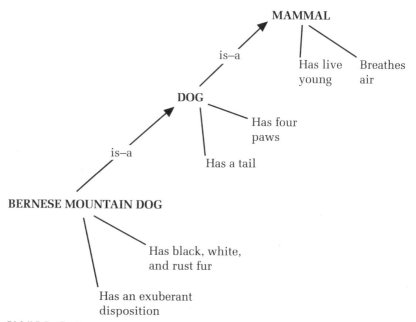

FIGURE 5-1.   Partial semantic network representation for *Bernese mountain dog*

In their study (see Figure 5-2), Collins and Quillian (1969) presented people with a number of similar sentences, finding as predicted that it took people less time to respond to sentences whose representations should span two levels (for example, "A canary is a bird") than they did to sentences whose representations should span three (for example, "A canary is an animal").

The model was called a hierarchical semantic network because the nodes were thought to be organized in terms of hierarchies. Most nodes were thought to have superordinate and subordinate nodes. Superordinate nodes would correspond to the category name for which the thing corresponding to the subordinate node was a member. So, for example, a node for CAT would have the superordinate node of ANIMAL and perhaps several subordinate nodes, such as PERSIAN, TABBY, CALICO, and so on.

Meyer and Schvaneveldt (1971) performed a series of experiments that elaborated the semantic network proposal. They reasoned that if related words are stored close by one another and connected to one another in a semantic network, then whenever one node was activated or energized, energy would spread to the related nodes, as depicted in Figure 5-3. They demonstrated this in a series of **lexical decison task** experiments. In this kind of experiment, subjects see a series of letter strings and are to decide, as quickly as possible, if the letter strings form real words. Thus, they respond "yes" to strings such as BREAD, and "no" to strings such as RENCLE.

Meyer and Schvaneveldt (1971) discovered an interesting phenomenon. In their study, subjects saw two words at a time, one above the other,

Three actual Bernese mountain dogs

and had to decide if both strings were words or not. If one of the strings was a real word (for example, BREAD), subjects were faster to respond if the other string was a semantically associated word (for example, BUTTER) than if it was an unrelated word (for example, CHAIR) or a nonword (for example, RENCLE). One interpretation of this finding invokes the concept of **spreading activation,** the idea that excitation spreads along the connections of nodes in a semantic network. Presumably, when the subject read the word BREAD, he or she activated the corresponding node in semantic memory. This activity **primed,** or changed the activation level, of the nodes corresponding to words related to BREAD. Thus, when processing of the word BUTTER began, the node corresponding to it was already excited, and thus, processing was faster. This priming effect, originally discovered by Meyer and Schvaneveldt, has been widely replicated in the years since (Neely, 1990).

You might note here a connection to the research on the word-superiority effect described in Chapter 2. Recall that people are generally faster to recognize a particular letter (for example, *D* or *K*) in the context of a word (for example, WOR_) than they are to recognize it with no context or in the context of a nonword (for example, OWR_). The explanations offered went roughly along the following lines: the word context helps letter recognition

(A)

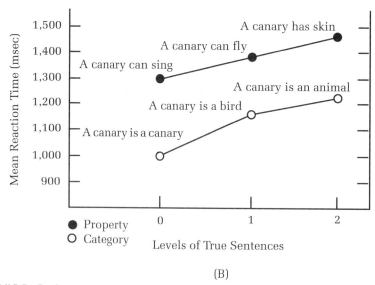

(B)

FIGURE 5-2.   Illustration of the Collins and Quillian (1969) experiment. Panel A shows the hypothesized underlying semantic network, and Panel B shows reaction times to verify sentences about information in the semantic network. SOURCE: From "Retrieval Time from Semantic Memory," by A. M. Collins and M. R. Quillian, 1969, *Journal of Verbal Learning and Verbal Behavior, 8,* 241. Copyright © 1969 by Academic Press. Reprinted by permission.

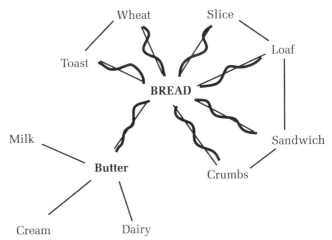

FIGURE 5-3.   Depiction of spreading activation. Once the node for bread is excited, the activation travels to related nodes, reaching butter first because it is the closest node in the network.

because a node corresponding to a word is activated in the former case. This automatic activation facilitates the recognition of all parts of the word, thus facilitating letter recognition. The Meyer and Schvaneveldt (1971) results extend this idea a little more: individual nodes can be activated not just directly, from external stimuli, but indirectly, through spreading activation from related nodes.

Soon after Collins and Quillian (1969) presented their model, others found evidence that contradicted the model's predictions. One line of evidence was related to the prediction of cognitive economy, the principle that properties and facts would be stored with the highest and most general node possible. Conrad (1972) found evidence that contradicted this assumption. Subjects in her sentence-verification experiments were no faster to respond to sentences such as "A shark can move" than to "A fish can move" or "An animal can move." However, the principle of cognitive economy would predict that the property "can move" would be stored closest to the node for "animal," and thus that the three sentences above should have required decreasing amounts of time to verify. Conrad argued that the property "can move" is one frequently associated with "animal," "shark," and "fish," and that frequency of association rather than cognitive economy predicts reaction time.

A second prediction of Collins and Quillian's (1969) model had to do with the hierarchical structure. Presumably, if the network represents such words (that in turn represent concepts) as *animals, mammals,* and *pigs,* then it should do so by storing the node for mammal under the node for animal, and the node for pig under the node for mammal. However, Rips, Shoben, and Smith (1973) showed that subjects were faster to verify

"A pig is an animal" than to verify "A pig is a mammal," thus demonstrating a violation of predicted hierarchical structure.

A third problem for the hierarchical network model was that it failed to explain why certain other findings kept appearing. One such finding is called a **typicality effect.** Rips and associates (1973) found that responses to sentences such as "A robin is a bird" were faster than responses to "A turkey is a bird," even though these sentences should have taken an equivalent amount of time to verify. In general, typical instances of a concept are responded to more quickly than atypical instances; robins are typical birds, and turkeys are not. The hierarchical network model did not predict typicality effects, instead predicting that all instances of a concept should be processed similarly.

These, among other problems, led to some reformulations, as well as to other proposals regarding the structure of semantic memory. Some investigators abandoned the idea of networks altogether; others tried to extend and revise them. We'll consider each of these approaches in turn.

Set Theoretic Models

A number of models were developed in the 1970s in response to the short-comings of semantic network models. These models regarded the representation of a concept as a set of attributes or features. You may recall our discussion of physical features when we reviewed topics in perception (Chapter 2). Here, the features are aspects of meaning rather than physical attributes, but the meaning of the term is otherwise the same. As an example, Bernese mountain dogs are described as sharing a certain set of features (black, white, and rust fur; moderately wavy coat; brown eyes; broad chest; working breed; exuberant disposition), and collies are described as sharing others (long coat; herding breed; narrow head; moderate chest; reserved disposition). Accessing the node corresponding to a concept would then involve accessing and processing these features or attributes.

Meyer (1970) developed one such model, called the *predicate intersection* model. Its intent was to explain performance on tasks such as the sentence verification of logical statements, such as "Some S are P" or "All S have P," where the S and P terms would be replaced with familiar nouns. The model, depicted in Figure 5-4, involved two processing stages. The first stage was exclusively used if the sentence to be verified was quantified with the word "Some." Therefore, if a subject had to verify sentences such as "Some poodles are dogs" or "Some animals have wings," he or she would use only Stage 1.

Stage 1 required the retrieval of the names of all categories that intersect with the predicate (second) term of the sentence. As an example, if given the sentence "Some poodles are dogs," people presumably bring to mind all the kinds of dogs that they know—cocker spaniels, golden-retrievers, German shepherds, Doberman pinschers, Lhasa apsos, poodles,

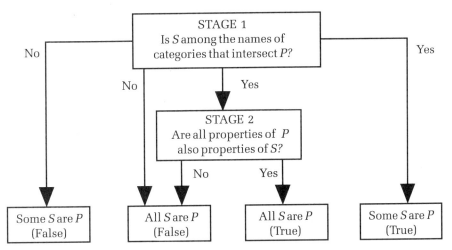

FIGURE 5-4. Depiction of the predicate intersection model, from Chang (1986). SOURCE: From "Semantic Memory: Facts and Models," by T. M. Chang, 1986, *Psychological Bulletin, 99*, 211. Copyright © 1986 by the American Psychological Association. Reprinted by permission.

Bernese mountain dogs, and any other kinds of dogs they can think of. They also put on the list—the intersection file—any category that includes dogs, such as animals, living beings, pets.

People next search through the intersection file for the name of the first term (called the subject or *S* term) of the sentence, in our example, poodle. The search time varies with the size of the difference between the *S* category and the intersection file. If the difference is small (that is, there are few nonpoodle choices in the intersection file), the search time will be short, and the response made quickly. Also, if the *S* term and the *P* term share no members, then the subject can immediately respond "false" to the sentence. This explains the finding that subjects very quickly respond "false" to a sentence such as "Some gorillas are spatulas"—the *S* term (gorilla) and the *P* term (spatulas) have no members in common. Thus, the predicate intersection model does explain, as the Collins and Quillian (1969) model does not, how people can respond "false" very quickly.

Sentences quantified by the word *all* require additional processing, as depicted by Stage 2 in Figure 5-4. Here, the relationship between the *S* category and the intersection file must be considered more carefully. If all of the properties of items in the intersection file are also properties of *S*, then the person will eventually respond "true." If this is not the case, the person will respond "false." Thus, sentences beginning with *All* ought to take longer to process, all other things being equal, a finding Meyer (1970) reported but Rips (1975) later found evidence against.

The predicate intersection model also appeared to offer an explanation for a finding known as the *category size effect* (Landauer & Meyer, 1972). This refers to the fact that if one *P* term is a subcategory of another *P* term, subjects will generally be faster to verify the sentence with the smaller category. Accordingly, people are faster to verify "A collie is a dog," than to verify "A collie is an animal." Notice how the predicate intersection model would explain this: small differences between the *S* category and the intersection file result in less time to search through both. A smaller *P* category results in a smaller intersection file, which decreases the search time.

However, the predicate intersection model, like Collins and Quillian's (1969) model, cannot explain typicality effects: faster evaluations of sentences about typical members of the predicate. The model also has difficulty handling "hedges," statements like "A bat is sort of like a bird." People in fact can verify such a sentence quite quickly, but this model cannot explain how.

Thus, although Meyer's (1970) model was able to explain some things that Collins and Quillian's (1969) was not, there were still a number of findings it could not account for. Other researchers tried to extend the approach Meyer took in order to develop a more complete version. Smith, Shoben, and Rips (1974) proposed one such model, called a *feature comparison model*. The assumption behind the model is that the meaning of any word or concept consists of a set of elements called features. (We encountered the idea of features earlier, when we reviewed models of perception.) Features come in two types: *defining*, meaning that the feature must be present in every example of the concept, and *characteristic*, meaning that the feature is usually, but not necessarily, present.

For instance, think about the concept "bachelor." The defining features here would include "male," "unmarried," and "adult." It is not possible for a 2-year-old to be a bachelor (in our common use of the term), nor for a woman, nor for a married man. Features such as "is young" or "lives in own apartment" are also typically associated with bachelors, though not absolutely necessarily in the way that "male" or "unmarried" are—these are the characteristic features. Below are feature list representations of three other concepts.

Bachelor	Bernese Mountain Dog	Chair
Male	Dog	Furniture
Adult	Black, white, rust fur	Has a seat
Unmarried	Brown eyes	Has a black
Human	Large size	Has legs
	Bred for draft	
	Exuberant disposition	

Assuming that semantic memory is organized in terms of feature lists, how is its knowledge retrieved and used? In particular, how can performance on a sentence-verification task be explained? In the Smith and associates (1974) model, the verification of sentences such as "A robin is a bird" is again carried out in two stages, as depicted in Figure 5-5. In the first stage, the feature lists (containing both the defining and the characteristic features) for the two terms are accessed, and a quick scan and comparison

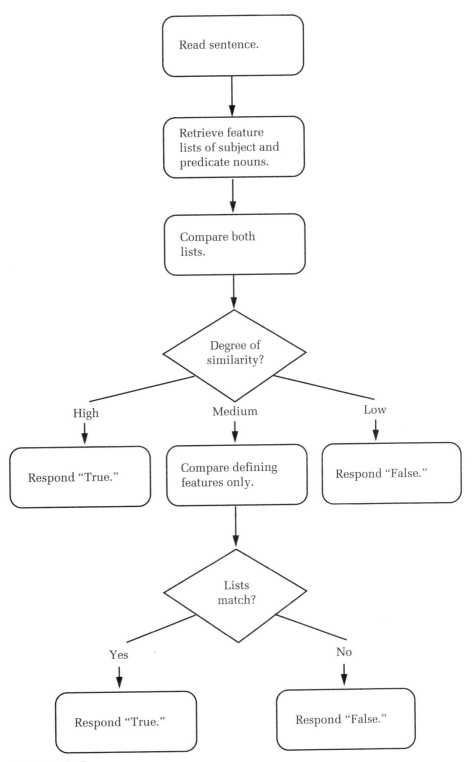

FIGURE 5-5.   Depiction of the Smith, Shoben, and Rips (1974) feature comparison model. SOURCE: From "Structure and Process in Semantic Memory: A Featural Model for Semantic Decisions," 1974, *Psychological Review, 81*, 22. Copyright © 1974 by the American Psychological Association. Reprinted by permission.

are performed. If the two lists show a great deal of overlap, the response "true" is made very quickly. If the overlap is very small, then the response "false" is made, also very quickly. If the degree of overlap in the two feature lists is neither extremely high or extremely low, then a second stage of processing occurs. In this stage, a comparison is made between the sets of defining features only. If the lists match, the person responds "true"; if the lists do not match, the person responds "false."

The feature-comparison model can explain many findings that previously developed models could not. One finding it explains is the typicality effect: sentences such as "A robin is a bird" are verified more quickly than sentences such as "A turkey is a bird" because robins, being more typical examples of birds, are thought to share more characteristic features with "bird" than do turkeys. The feature-comparison model also explains fast rejections of false sentences, such as "A table is a fruit." In this case, the list of features for "table" and the list for "fruit" presumably share very few entries.

The feature-comparison model handles the category-size effect in a similar way. It assumes that as categories grow larger (for example, from robin, to bird, to animal, to living thing), they also become more abstract. With increased abstractness, there are fewer defining features. Thus, in the first stage of processing, there is less overlap between the feature list of a term and the feature list of an abstract category.

The model is also able to explain how hedges such as "A bat is sort of like a bird" are processed. Most of us know that even though bats fly and eat insects, they are really mammals. The feature-comparison model explains that the processing of hedges consists of a comparison of the characteristic but not the defining features. Because bats share some characteristic features with birds (namely, flying and eating insects), we agree that they are "sort of like" birds. We recognize, however, that bats aren't really birds—presumably because they don't share the same defining features.

In spite of the successes of the feature-comparison model, evidence and arguments began to mount against its being taken as a complete model of how knowledge is represented. Among the most fundamental criticisms is one that rejects the very existence of defining features. Consider a concept such as bird. Most people would initially agree that "has wings" is a defining feature. But suppose through genetic or environmental accident a bird's wings are removed. Can we say that it is no longer a bird? Other arguments challenge the view that all, or even some, concepts have defining features (Rosch & Mervis, 1975). We will look at these assertions more carefully in Chapter 6 when we examine concepts in more detail.

Other Network Models

Collins and Loftus (1975) presented an elaboration of the Collins and Quillian (1969) hierarchical network model, which they called the **spreading**

activation theory. In general, these authors attempted both to clarify and extend the assumptions made about the manner in which people process semantic information. They again conceived of semantic memory as a network, with nodes in the network corresponding to concepts. They also saw related concepts as connected by paths in the network. They further asserted that when one node was activated, the excitation of that node spreads down the paths or links to related nodes. They believed that as activation spreads outward, it decreases in strength, thus activating very related concepts a great deal but activating distantly related nodes only a little bit.

Figure 5-6 shows a representation of part of a semantic network, as Collins and Loftus (1975) conceived it. Notice that in this model, very similar concepts, for example, car and truck, have many connecting links, and

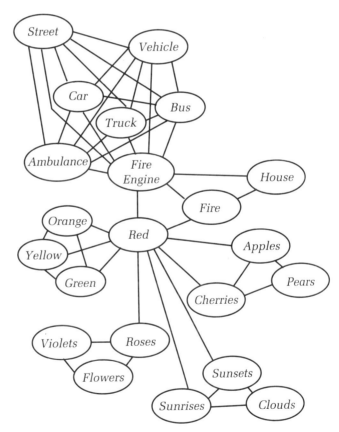

FIGURE 5-6.   Partial network representation of related concepts. Length of line segments indicates the degree of relatedness or connection between two concepts. SOURCE: From "A Spreading-activation Theory of Semantic Processing," by A. M. Collins and E. F. Loftus, 1975, *Psychological Review, 82,* 412. Copyright © 1975 by the American Psychological Association. Reprinted by permission.

are placed close by each other. Less similar concepts, such as house and sunset (both are red, at least sometimes), have no direct connections and are therefore spaced far apart. Each link or connection between two concepts is thought to have a certain weight or set of weights associated with it. The weights indicate how important one concept is to the meaning of a concept it is connected to. Weights may vary for different directions along these connections. Thus, it may be very important to the meaning of *truck* that it is a type of vehicle, but not so very important to the meaning of *vehicle* that *truck* is an example.

Collins and Loftus (1975) describe a number of other assumptions made by this model, together with explanations of how the model accounts for data from many other experiments. They dispense with the assumptions of cognitive economy and hierarchical organization, helping their model to avoid the trouble that the Collins and Quillian (1969) model experienced. However, many psychologists find the breadth of this model, which is its major strength, to be its major shortcoming as well because it is difficult to make clear and strong predictions from the model regarding empirical findings. This means that although the model is consistent with a number of findings, such as the typicality effect, the category-size effect, and others, it is pretty hard to think of data that would falsify the model. Thus, the proposal is regarded more as a descriptive framework than as a specific model.

Another network theory of memory has been developed and refined over several years by John Anderson (1976, 1983). The latest version, called ACT* ("act-star") will be the one described here. ACT stands for "Adaptive Control of Thought"; the star indicates that it is a revision of the previous model, ACT. ACT* is based on analogies to computers, and it has given rise to several computer simulations of cognitive processing of different tasks.

ACT* does not make the semantic/episodic distinction described earlier but distinguishes among three kinds of memory systems. The first is *working memory,* thought to contain information that the system is currently using. The other two kinds are **declarative memory** and **procedural memory.** Declarative memory contains knowledge, facts, information, ideas—basically, anything that can be recalled and described in words, pictures, or symbols. In contrast, procedural memory holds information concerning action and sequences of actions. For example, when you ride a bicycle, swim, or swing a golf club, you are thought to be drawing on your procedural memory. The distinction between declarative and procedural memory should help to explain the intuition that your memory of who is currently president of the United States has a qualitatively different feel than your memory of how to execute a particular dance step.

Anderson (1983) believes that declarative memory stores information in networks that contain nodes. There are different types of nodes, including those corresponding to spatial images or to abstract propositions. As with other network models, ACT* allows for both the activation of any of the nodes, and for spreading activation to connected nodes. Anderson uses features of his ACT* framework, too numerous to describe here, to explain phenomena in pattern recognition, the acquisition of skills and language, and problem solving, along with phenomena in semantic memory.

Anderson's (1983) proposal is not merely meant to address the question of knowledge representation. Instead, his aim was to create a theory of *cognitive architecture,* a "theory of the basic principles of operation" built into human cognition. Interestingly, this broad goal led him to develop proposals about knowledge representation that fit well with those of researchers whose aims were more focused.

We have seen several proposals for how knowledge is represented. The debate continues over the relative merits of network versus feature models to describe semantic memory. (For reviews, see Chang, 1986; Johnson & Hasher, 1987; Rumelhart & Norman, 1988.) Still, the discovery of semantic priming, the idea of spreading activation, and the experimental innovations designed to test models of semantic memory have all contributed to our understanding of the principles by which knowledge is stored and retrieved. The work reviewed here so far relates directly to another topic in cognitive psychology, the formation and use of concepts to classify information. We will examine this area in more detail in Chapter 6, looking there at other proposals for conceptual representation.

Implicit versus Explicit Memory

We have already seen that some psychologists favor making a distinction between two types of memory: episodic and semantic. Many argue that these two kinds of memory form different systems; that is, they operate on different principles, store different kinds of information, and so on. Others disagree, declaring that there is no compelling reason to believe that more than one *type* of memory exists.

Recently, some cognitive psychologists have proposed another distinction between kinds of memory: implicit and explicit (Roediger, 1990; Schacter, 1987). **Explicit memories** are things that are consciously recollected. For example, in recalling your last vacation, you explicitly refer to a specific time (say, last summer) and a specific event or series of events. Your recall is something you are aware of, and may even be something deliberate. **Implicit memory,** by contrast, is memory that is not deliberate or conscious but shows evidence of prior learning and storage.

Laboratory work on implicit memory has been mainly concerned with a phenomenon known as *repetition priming.* We've already reviewed the phenomenon of *semantic priming,* where exposure to one word (for example, NURSE) facilitates the recognition or other cognitive processing of a semantically related word (for example, DOCTOR). Repetition priming is priming of a somewhat different sort: facilitation in the cognitive processing of information after a recent exposure to that same information (Schacter, 1987, p. 506). For example, subjects might be given a very brief exposure (of

30 milliseconds or less) to a word (for example, BUTTON), and soon after-ward be given a new, word-completion task (for example, fill in the blanks to create the English word that comes to mind: _U _T O_). The repetition-priming effect is demonstrated by an increased probability of responding BUTTON to the stimulus given in the word-completion task, relative to the performance of subjects not shown the word BUTTON. (Note that there are other possible ways to complete the word, such as MUTTON, SUITOR).

This work has yielded several findings relevant to the topic of knowledge representation. The first is that nonwords typically show no or little repetition priming, relative to real words. Thus, exposing a subject to a stimulus such as DAXTON will probably not prime the subject to recognize or remember it later. Presumably, this is because DAXTON is not a word and therefore has no associated node in semantic memory that can be acti-vated.

A second finding is that priming is greatest for words that share the same morphology, or roots of meaning, relative to words that are visually or aurally similar. Thus, a stimulus such as SEES can prime responses to SEEN (a word that shares meaning with SEES) but not to SEED (a visually similar stimulus) or SEIZE (a similar-sounding stimulus).

Do laboratory demonstrations of implicit memory have any real-world relevance? Investigators who study implicit memory believe so. One real-world example of implicit memory was reported by Sergei Korsakoff, who in 1889 described patients with amnesic symptoms that have come to be known as Korsakoff's syndrome. One patient to whom he had adminis-tered an electric shock professed not to remember the shock, but upon see-ing the case containing the shock generator, told Korsakoff that he feared Korsakoff had probably come to electrify him (Schacter, 1987, pp. 503–504).

Other work with amnesic patients demonstrated findings to support the idea of a dissociation between implicit and explicit memory. For exam-ple, Warrington and Weiskrantz (1970) conducted a more controlled inves-tigation: they presented a variety of memory tasks to four amnesic patients, as well as to eight patients without brain damage who served as a control group.

In one experiment (Experiment 2), subjects received two "explicit-memory" tasks (the quotation marks indicate that the authors did not use this term to describe them), a free-recall task and a recognition task, similar to those described in Chapter 4. Subjects also worked on two "implicit-memory" tasks. One was a word-completion task, similar to the one just described. The other presented subjects with words in which the letters were visually degraded; subjects were asked to guess the word being dis-played.

All four tasks involved a prior presentation of various words. In the two "explicit" tasks, subjects were asked to recall consciously or recognize the words previously presented. In the two "implicit" tasks, subjects were *not* reminded of the prior presentation of words but merely asked to guess what the word being presented (that is, in degraded letters or partially, by a word stem), was. Figure 5-7 presents the results. It shows quite clearly that

Explicit Tests

Implicit Tests

FIGURE 5-7.   Results from the Warrington and Weiskrantz (1970) study; figure created by Roediger (1990). SOURCE: From "Amnesic Syndrome: Consolidation or Retrieval?" by E. K. Warrington and L. Weiskrantz, 1970, *Nature, 228*, 630. Copyright © 1970 by Macmillan Magazines Limited.

amnesic subjects perform noticeably more poorly on the explicit memory tasks but quite comparably to nonamnesic subjects on the implicit memory tasks. In other words, their amnesia seemed to hurt performance on explicit memory tasks selectively. The results have been replicated several times, and on a variety of tasks (Shimura, 1986).

Dissociative phenomena do not by any means occur only with amnesic subjects. Many studies (reviewed by Roediger, 1990) have demonstrated striking differences in performance on implicit and explicit memory tasks with normal subjects. How are such dissociation phenomena best explained? Roediger (1990) presents two distinct possibilities. One is to postulate two memory *systems*, such as declarative and procedural memory, and to assert that explicit memory tasks rely on the former, and implicit memory tasks rely on the latter. The dissociation in performance on the two tasks is then assumed to reflect the fact that two memory systems that operate in different ways, are at work.

The second possibility is that the two kinds of memory tasks require different cognitive procedures, although they both tap into a common memory system (Roediger, 1990). One idea consistent with this proposal is that most implicit memory tasks require *perceptual* processing, and that explicit memory tasks require *conceptual* processing. In this view, it is the type of processing required in the two types of tasks that explains the dissociation phenomena. Much current debate focuses on the question of whether the two approaches can be reconciled (Schacter, 1989).

Taken as a whole, work on implicit memory suggests that our permanent knowledge is organized on the basis of meaning rather than on other possible bases, for example, alphabetically or chronologically. The organization makes certain kinds of accessing (for example, by meaning) easy relative to other kinds of accessing (for example, by sound). Further, whenever information is accessed, other, related information is "primed" or made easier to process. Moreover, accessing information can be deliberate and conscious (as in the case where we try to remember something), or automatic (as defined in Chapter 3, for example, when some information automatically becomes activated as a result of presentation of other information).

Summary

We have surveyed a number of different theoretical frameworks and empirical tests of the ways in which information in permanent memory is stored and organized. We have also seen three distinct proposals for dividing memory into systems that function quite differently. Tulving's proposal divorces episodic memory from semantic memory, seeing the latter as a storage of permanent knowledge. In this framework, knowledge is deemed to consist of a number of interrelated ideas, each comprising, typically, smaller units that correspond to the basic "packets" of meaning. The various models—hierarchical networks, feature lists, propositional networks—differ on the exact structure of the mental representation but generally agree that the "basic" unit of information represented is at the level of the individual word or concept.

A second proposal for separate memory systems distinguishes between declarative (knowing that X) and procedural (knowing how to do X) memory. In this proposal, general knowledge is stored in declarative memory. Theorists often assert that declarative memory is organized as something analogous to a propositional network.

A third proposed division of memory distinguishes between explicit and implicit memory: the former refers to conscious recollections; the latter, to facilitation in performance as a function of past learning without awareness of that past learning. In this proposal, implicit memory phenomena have been seen as ways of determining how general knowledge is organized.

How well these three proposals fit together is a matter of some debate (Schacter, 1987). For instance, semantic memory can be mapped onto declarative memory. One might propose that explicit memory relies on this declarative-semantic base. Procedural memory might be the one involved in implicit memory phenomena. Alternatively, one could argue that episodic memory is the basis for explicit memory of autobiographical events, and that semantic memory is involved in many implicit memory tasks. It is also possible to reject the proposals for distinct memory systems, as does Baddeley (1984).

It is clear that despite the existence of a number of complex, logically crafted models of knowledge representation and organization, we are apparently a long way from a satisfying account of how these processes work. The bulk of the work done to date makes a compelling case for using networks to model our knowledge representation and organization; however, no single network model has been proposed that accounts for all of the data.

We can expect much research in this area in the coming years. Questions such as, What is the nature of the mental representation? What inferences are easy to make using simply general knowledge and what inferences are harder? and How does knowledge representation change as a function of practice and expertise? must all be answered.

Knowledge representation and organization are critically important to cognitive psychologists. For one thing, the issue of how knowledge is mentally represented underlies the important question, What is common sense? Workers in artificial intelligence are discovering over and over again that a truly intelligent program or system must have a wide and deep knowledge base, and must be able to store and retrieve a great deal of information about the world. The knowledge base must be organized efficiently. So far, the only creatures who have demonstrated efficient organization of such vast knowledge bases are human beings. The challenge now is to find out just how we accomplish this marvelous feat.

Recommended Readings

Discussion of the semantic/episodic distinction originated in a paper written by Tulving (1972). The volume containing the Tulving paper, edited by Tulving and Donaldson (1972), contains a number of other important papers on the topic of the organization of memory. In recent years, Tulving surveyed the status of the distinction and offered some modifications (1983, 1984); his 1984 paper drew a great deal of commentary (published together with the paper). A more recent exchange by McKoon and associates (1986) and Tulving (1986) speaks to the idea that the debate is very much alive.

Recent reviews of topics pertaining to semantic memory can be found in Chang (1986), Horton and Mills (1984), Johnson and Hasher (1987), and Rumelhart and Norman (1988). The last also describes some recently developed artificially intelligent systems and their mechanisms for representing knowledge. Neely (1990) reviews the growing literature on priming effects. Johnson-Laird, Herrmann, and Chaffin (1984) critique existing semantic network models.

Both Schacter (1987) and Roediger (1990) provide good reviews of the implicit memory literature. Some work on implicit memory phenomena in amnesic patients has been reported in classic papers and a recent article by Warrington and Weiskrantz (1968, 1970, 1982).

REVIEW QUESTIONS

1. Describe the semantic/episodic memory distinction, and discuss the reasons that some psychologists make the distinction and others don't.

2. Contrast the following models of semantic memory, noting which experimental findings each is able to explain and which findings each is less able to explain: hierarchical semantic network (Collins & Quillian); predicate intersection (Meyer); feature comparison (Rips, Shoben, & Smith).

3. Explain the concept of spreading activation, and review the evidence that leads some psychologists to maintain that it is a property of memory.

4. The research on knowledge representation typically involves laboratory research with people working on somewhat artificial tasks (for example, lexical decision, sentence verification). Does such research have much bearing on cognition in real life? Defend your answer, and use specific examples to illustrate your points.

5. Describe the distinction between declarative and procedural memory and that between implicit and explicit memory. Do these two distinctions fit together well? How and how not?

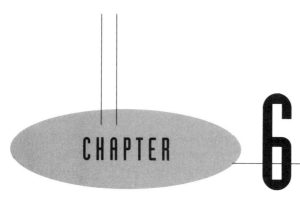

CHAPTER 6

Concepts and Categorization

I like popular, entertaining, not-necessarily-with-a-message movies. I saw the first three Superman movies, often on the day they opened. A few years later, I queued up to be one of the first to see "Batman."

Still later, I went to the opening of *Dick Tracy*. I watched a movie-review program of *Dick Tracy* a few nights ago, and the critic talked about "cartoon superhero" movies, comparing all of the movies I just mentioned. Only later did I realize that the critic had formed or discovered a new category ("cartoon superhero movie") and classified the above-mentioned films into it. Presumably, the critic had a mental representation of this category, something a cognitive psychologist would call a **concept**.

We have encountered the idea of mental representations several times before. We have seen that many cognitive psychologists believe that such representations guide our cognitive processing and, often, our behavior. How you regard something may often be influenced by what type of thing you believe it to be. For example, you would probably react and behave one way if told that a severe thunderstorm was taking place outside, and another way if you were told it was a hurricane. Your classification of storms into two categories suggests, first, that you see distinctions between them. Presumably, such distinctions cause your reactions to storms to be classification-dependent.

A related, real-life example comes from medical diagnosis. Suppose you wake up one day feeling achy, lethargic, congested, and feverish. Your symptoms could indicate nothing more serious than influenza. Or your symptoms could be the harbinger of a much more serious illness. It is the job of your doctor to make the diagnosis, which essentially is to assign your pattern of symptoms to a category corresponding to known diseases or medical problems. The categorization allows the physician to determine appropriate treatment and to predict the time course of recovery. To make the diagnosis, your physician must have a concept of the various categories (possible medical problems) to be considered.

In this chapter, we'll look at concepts, and how they are formed. We'll examine different theoretical descriptions of how concepts are structured, and the implications they have for how we assume our mental representations work. We'll then focus on how concepts are accessed and used in categorizing new objects, patterns, or events. Many of the ideas discussed in the early part of the chapter will extend and elaborate on proposals presented in Chapter 2, "Perception and Pattern Recognition" (pattern recognition and classification have many similarities, as we shall see) and in Chapter 5, "Knowledge Representation." Similarly, our examination of categorization will anticipate some of the discussions in Chapter 8, "Language"; Chapter 9, "Thinking, Problem Solving, and Creativity"; and Chapter 10, "Reasoning." You can probably already see that an understanding of how people form and use concepts is relevant to several other cognitive processes and abilities. Medin (1989) has in fact argued that "concepts and categories serve as building blocks for human thought and behavior" (p. 1469).

What are concepts and categories, and what are the differences between them? The distinction turns out to be a little blurry but can still be made. Medin (1989, p. 1469) defines a concept as "an idea that includes all that is characteristically associated with it." In other words, a concept is a mental representation, of some object, event, or pattern, that has stored in it much of the knowledge that is typically thought to be relevant to that object, event, or pattern. Most people's concept of dog, for example, would include information to the effect that it is an animal, has four legs and a tail, has a reputation as "man's best friend," is a common pet, and so on.

A **category** can be defined as a class of similar things. Usually when a psychologist thinks about categories, she thinks about several different ones, into which various things get sorted. In the game "20 Questions," a common opener is "Is it an animal, mineral, or vegetable?" This question seeks to categorize, or sort, the to-be-guessed item into one of three things. Sometimes, categories are described as things that exist objectively in the world, and concepts are described as mental representations of categories (Medin, 1989).

Concepts help us to establish order over our knowledge base (Medin & Smith, 1984). Concepts also allow us to categorize, giving us "mental buckets," as it were, in which to sort the things we encounter, thereby allowing us to treat new, never-before-encountered things in the same way that we treat familiar things we perceive to be in the same set (Neisser, 1987a). Categorization also allows us to make predictions and to act accordingly. If I see a four-legged creature with a tail coming toward me, my classification of it as either a dog or a wolf has implications for whether

I'll want to call to it, run away, pet it, or call for help. Smith and Medin (1981) elaborate on the important role concepts play in our mental life:

> Without concepts, mental life would be chaotic. If we perceived each entity as unique, we would be overwhelmed by the sheer diversity of what we experience and unable to remember more than a minute fraction of what we encounter. And if each individual entity needed a distinct name, our language would be staggeringly complex and communication virtually impossible. Fortunately, though, we do not perceive, remember, and talk about each object and event as unique, but rather as an instance of a class or concept that we already know something about. (p. 1)

We will first examine different theoretical accounts about the nature and structure of concepts. Next, we'll look at how concepts are formed or acquired. Finally, we'll examine how people actually use concepts through the process of categorization. Throughout this chapter, we'll be focusing on concepts of objects and nouns, because they are the most commonly studied at present in cognitive psychology. We will see, however, that the *kind* of concept studied may affect the theories of concepts that are subsequently created. So, it will be useful to keep in mind that psychologists have yet to explore fully the entire range of people's concepts.

Theoretical Descriptions of the Nature of Concepts

In Chapter 5 we reviewed proposals for how our knowledge bases are represented and organized. Models of semantic memory (for example, Collins & Quillian's [1969] semantic network model) described the ways in which representations of different concepts were interrelated. Here, we will concentrate on the representation and organization of individual concepts.

In this section, we will explore five distinct proposals on how concepts are represented and structured. Each one provides a different answer to the question, What information do we have when we have a particular concept? Each proposal will therefore have different implications for the question of how concepts are formed, acquired, or learned.

The Classical View

The classical view was the dominant view in psychology up until the 1970s, and dates back to Aristotle (Smith & Medin, 1981). This proposal is organized around the belief that all examples or instances of a concept share fundamental characteristics, or **features** (Medin, 1989). In particular, the classical view holds that the features represented are individually *necessary* and collectively *sufficient* (Medin, 1989). To say that a feature is individually necessary is to say that each example must have the feature if it is to be regarded as a member of the concept. For example, "has three sides" is a necessary feature of the concept of triangle; things that do not have three sides are automatically disqualified from being triangles. To say that a set of features is collectively sufficient is to say that anything that has each feature in the set is automatically an instance of the concept. For example, the set of features "has three sides" and "closed, geometric figure" is sufficient to specify a triangle; anything that has both of these is a triangle. Other examples of sets of features or of concepts that are individually necessary and collectively sufficient include the following:

Bachelor	Triangle	Uncle	Prime Number
Male	Geometric figure	Male	Integer
Adult	Three-sided	Sibling	Divisible only by
Unmarried	Planar	One or more	two numbers:
Human		siblings has	itself and 1
		a child	

The classical view of concepts has several implications. First, it assumes that concepts mentally represent lists of features. That is to say, concepts are not representations of specific examples but, rather, abstractions that contain information about properties and characteristics that all examples must have. Second, it assumes that membership in a category is clear-cut: either something has all of the necessary and sufficient features (in which case it is a member of the category) or it lacks one or more of the features (in which case it is not a member). Third, it implies that all members within a category are created equal: there is no such thing as a "better" or "worse" triangle.

Work by Eleanor Rosch (1973; Rosch & Mervis, 1975) confronted and severely weakened the attraction of the classical view. Rosch found that people judged that different members of a category vary in "goodness." For instance, most people in North America consider a robin or a sparrow a very good example of a bird but find other examples, such as chickens, penguins, and ostriches, not as good. Notice the problem that this result presents for the classical view of concepts. That view holds that membership in a category is all-or-none; either an instance (such as robin or ostrich) belongs to a category or it doesn't. The classical view has no way to explain peoples' intuitions that some birds are "birdier" than others.

People's judgments of *typicality,* the "goodness" of the instance in the category, was later shown to predict several aspects of their performance on different tasks. For example, subjects in a sentence-verification task were faster to respond (true or false) to a sentence such as "A robin is a bird" than they were to a sentence such as "A chicken is a bird" (McCloskey & Glucksberg, 1979; Rosch, 1973; Smith, Shoben, & Rips, 1974). When asked to list instances of a concept, people are more likely to list typical than atypical instances (Mervis, Catlin, & Rosch, 1976). In semantic priming studies (see Chapter 5 for review), highly typical instances often lead to better priming (Rosch, 1975; Rosch, Simpson, & Miller, 1976).

All of these results are not easily explained within a classical framework. In addition, other studies cast doubt on the idea that people typically store and refer to a list of necessary features when judging category membership. McCloskey and Glucksberg (1978) gave subjects a list of items and asked them to judge whether the items belonged to certain categories (for example, Does "chair" belong to the category "furniture"?). The classical view would predict very strong agreement across people, but McCloskey and Glucksberg's subjects in fact showed considerable disagreement on atypical instances (for example, Do "bookends" belong to the category "furniture"?). Subjects were often inconsistent in their own responses in different sessions. This result argued especially strongly against the classical view assumption that categories have clearly defined boundaries. Finally, even when given specific instructions to do so, most people are unable to generate lists of features that are individually necessary and collectively sufficient to specify membership in a category (Ashcraft, 1978; Rosch & Mervis, 1975).

The Prototype View

A second theoretical view of the nature of concepts, known as the prototype view, was proposed in the 1970s. It denied the existence of necessary-and-sufficient feature lists, instead regarding concepts as a different sort of abstraction (Medin & Smith, 1984). The abstractions included features or aspects that were *characteristic*—that is, typical—of members of the category rather than necessary and sufficient. No individual feature or aspect had to be present in the instance in order for it to count as a member of the category, but the more characteristic features or aspects an instance had, the more likely it was to be regarded as a member of the category.

This view of concepts and categories often refers to the **family-resemblance** structure of concepts (Wittgenstein, 1953), a structure in which each member has a number of features, sharing different features with different members. Few, if any, features are shared by every single member of the category; however, the more features a member possesses, the more typical it is.

Figure 6-1 provides an example of family resemblance. Note that the Smith brothers (modeled after the men on Smith Bros. cough drop boxes) have several shared features: light hair, bushy mustache, large ears, and eyeglasses. Not every Smith brother has every feature, but the brother in the middle, having them all, would likely be judged by Smith friends to be the most typical Smith of the bunch. Note that he shares big ears, eyeglasses and light hair with the brother in the "nine o'clock" position, and a mustache and big ears with the "seven o'clock" brother. Indeed, different pairs of brothers share different features.

FIGURE 6-1.   An example of family resemblance.
SOURCE: From "What Some Concepts Might Not Be," by S.
Armstrong, L. R. Gleitman, and H. Gleitman, 1983, *Cognition, 13*, 269. Copyright © 1983 by Elsevier Science Publishers BV. Reprinted by permission.

The prototype view of concepts explains typicality effects by reference to family resemblance. The idea is that the more features an instance
of a concept has, the stronger the family resemblance to other instances,
and therefore, the more typical an instance it is. Presumably, then, a robin
is thought of as a more typical bird than a penguin because the robin possesses more bird-characteristic features, for example, "is small," "flies,"
"eats worms," "lives in a tree."

A **prototype,** in this sense, is some sort of abstraction that includes
all of the characteristic features of a category. The prototype may or may not
be an actual instance of the category. Prototypes are often thought of as
mental "summaries" or "averages" of all the instances, although there are
some problems with this view (Barsalou, 1985). The general idea of the prototype view, then, is that concepts have one or more "core" representations
(that is, the prototypes) but no rigid boundaries.

Rosch and her colleagues (Rosch, Mervis, Gray, Johnson, & Boyes-
Braem, 1976) made another important discovery about concepts. Although
concepts exist at many different levels of a hierarchy (for example, Bernese
mountain dog, dog, canine, mammal, animal), there is one level of abstrac-

tion that appears to be psychologically fundamental. They called this the "basic" level, and demonstrated that basic level is the best compromise between carrying the most information, including more physically similar instances, and being the most differentiated from other concepts. "Piano" and "guitar" are examples of two basic-level categories. Such categories include members who are maximally similar to one another, unlike superordinate levels of categories (for example, "musical instruments"), which contain members (for example, pianos and guitars) that are dissimilar in several respects. At the same time, basic level categories are most differentiated from one another, especially relative to subordinate categories. "Grand piano" and "upright piano" are two categories at the subordinate level; these categories are less distinct than are two basic level categories, for example, "piano" and "guitar." The list below presents examples of basic level categories, along with related superordinate and subordinate categories.

Superordinate	Basic level	Subordinates	
Musical instrument	Guitar	Folk guitar	Classical guitar
	Piano	Grand piano	Upright piano
	Drum	Kettle drum	Bass drum
Fruit	Apple	Delicious apple	McIntosh apple
	Peach	Freestone peach	Cling peach
	Grapes	Concord grapes	Green seedless grapes
Tool	Hammer	Ball-peen hammer	Claw hammer
	Saw	Hack handsaw	Cross-cutting handsaw
	Screwdriver	Phillips screwdriver	Regular screwdriver
Clothing	Pants	Levis	Double-knit pants
	Socks	Knee socks	Ankle socks
	Shirt	Dress shirt	Knit shirt
Furniture	Table	Kitchen table	Dining-room table
	Lamp	Floor lamp	Desk lamp
	Chair	Kitchen chair	Living-room chair
Vehicle	Car	Sports car	Four-door sedan car
	Bus	City bus	Cross-country bus
	Truck	Pickup truck	Tractor-Trailer truck

SOURCE: From "Basic Objects in Natural Categories, " by E. Rosch, et al., 1976, *Cognitive Psychology, 8*, 388. Copyright © 1976 by Academic Press. Reprinted by permission.

Rosch and colleagues (1976) believe that much of the reason that people form the concepts that they do results from the regularities built into the world around them, where certain attributes or features are more likely to co-occur with some features than with others. For example, "barks" and "has a tail" go together more often than "barks" and "has wings" do. Basic level categories incorporate information about which sets of features naturally go together. These categories divide the world of objects into groups that follow the differentiation already conveniently provided by nature.

The prototype view does a very good job at explaining why certain members of a category are seen as more typical than others. It also explains why people have a hard time providing strict definitions of their concepts: strict definitions do not exist. Finally, the prototype view can explain why some classifications are especially easy to make and others are unclear. Take tomatoes, which some people classify as a vegetable and others classify as a fruit. Tomatoes are often eaten with other vegetables instead of with other fruits, and they share some similarities with other vegetables. However, to a biologist, tomatoes are a fruit because they develop from the flower of the plant (technically, the pistil). Vegetables, in contrast, are any nonreproductive parts of a plant, for example, the stem or root. The prototype view explains the ambiguity of tomatoes: they share features both with vegetables (thus leading to classification as a vegetable) and with fruits (thus leading to classification as a fruit).

The prototype view is not wholly free of problems. For one thing, it fails to capture people's knowledge about the limits of conceptual boundaries. To illustrate, even though a Pomeranian seems in many ways more similar to a Siamese cat than to a Great Dane, the Pomeranian and Great Dane are classified together, as dogs (Komatsu, 1992). The prototype view has a hard time telling us why. Unlike the classical view, which sets *constraints* or boundaries around which things can and can't belong to a category, the prototype view does not specify clear constraints.

Rosch (1978; Rosch & Mervis, 1975; Rosch et al., 1976) has argued that some part of the constraints around different categories comes from the environment itself. Having wings and being able to fly, for example, tend to co-occur, often in those things we call birds (but also in airplanes, butterflies, and insects). Boundaries between categories, then, come not from us as cognitive processors of information but from the way the world works: certain patterns of attributes or features occur in the world and others don't (Komatsu, 1992; Neisser, 1987a). People's main job in categorizing, then, is to pick up information about the world's regularities, not to impose arbitrary groupings, as the classical view might imply. (The idea of "picking up information" about the world might remind the alert student of Gibsonian theories of perception, discussed in Chapter 2).

A second problem for the prototype view has to do with typicality ratings. Barsalou (1985, 1987) and Roth and Shoben (1983) showed that the typicality of an instance depends to some extent on context. So, although a robin might be seen as a very typical bird in the context of birds you see in the neighborhood, it is very atypical in the context of birds you see in a barnyard. These findings contrast with the idea that a member of a category has a certain level of typicality. Instead, typicality apparently varies with the way the concept itself is being thought about.

Studies by Armstrong, Gleitman, and Gleitman (1983) demonstrated additional problems with typicality ratings. In these studies, the investigators asked subjects to rate the typicality of instances of both natural concepts (for example, vehicle, fruit) previously studied by Rosch and her colleagues, and of well-defined concepts (for example, even number, female, geometric figure). Armstrong and associates found that subjects happily rated the typicality of members of well-defined categories, generally agreeing that 3 is a more typical odd number than is 57, for example. The same subjects also agreed, however, that the category "odd number" was well defined, and that it makes little sense to talk about degree of membership in the category—numbers either are or are not odd. The investigators concluded that the typicality-ratings task is a flawed one, at least for discovering the underlying representation of concepts.

The Exemplar View

The previous two views of concepts both hold that concepts are some sort of mental abstraction or summary. In other words, individual instances are not specifically stored or mentally represented but, instead, are averaged into some sort of composite representation. The exemplar view makes just the opposite assumption: it asserts that concepts include representations of at least some actual individual instances.

The approach assumes that people categorize new instances by comparing them to representations of previously stored instances, called *exemplars.* Like the prototype view, it thus explains peoples' inability to state necessary and defining features: there are none to be stated. It also explains why people might have difficulty categorizing unclear, atypical instances: are similar to exemplars from different categories (for example, tomato is similar to both fruit exemplars, such as oranges or apples, and to vegetable exemplars, such as beets or squash) or not similar enough to any known exemplars (Medin & Smith, 1984). Typical instances are thought to be more likely to be stored than less typical ones (Mervis, 1980), more similar to stored exemplars, or both. This accounts for why people are faster to process information about typical instances. So, in trying to retrieve information about a typical instance, it is faster to find very similar stored exemplars. Atypical instances, on the other hand, being rather dissimilar from stored exemplars, take longer to process.

The biggest problem with the exemplar view is that like the prototype view, it is too unconstrained. It fails to specify, for instance, which instances will eventually be stored as exemplars and which will not. It also does not explain how different exemplars are "called to mind" at the time of categorization. However, many psychologists believe that people often store information about some specific category members in their conceptual representations, as we will see below.

The Schemas/Scripts View

We have already briefly touched on the concept of a **schema,** or organized framework for representing knowledge, in talking about Bartlett's (1932) work on people's memories for stories. The term *schema* is usually meant to refer to something larger than an individual concept. *Schemata* (the plural of *schema*) are thought to be somewhat like scripts of plays: they have characters, plots, and settings. Schemata incorporate both general knowledge about the world and information about particular events.

Bartlett (1932) defined a schema as an "active organization of past reactions, or of past experiences, which must always be supposed to be operating in any well-adapted organic response" (p. 201). The key term here is "organization." A schema is thought to be a large unit of organized information used for representing concepts, situations, events, and actions in memory (Rumelhart & Norman, 1988).

Rumelhart and Ortony (1977) viewed schemata as the fundamental building blocks of cognition, units of organized knowledge analogous to theories. Generally, they saw schemata as "packets of information" that contain variables, along with a fixed part. Consider a schema for dog. The fixed part would include the information that a dog is a mammal, has (typically) four legs, is domesticated, and the variables would be things like breed (poodle, cocker spaniel, Bernese mountain dog), size (toy, medium, extra large), color (white, brown, black, tricolored), temperament (friendly, aloof, vicious), name (Spot, Rover, Tandy), and so on.

Schemata exist for things bigger than individual concepts, however. For example, consider meeting a new college roommate for the first time. Your knowledge of such an event can be said to be guided by a schema. Included in this schema would be the fixed part (the setting: a dormitory room; the characters: two students), and the variables (the opening conversation: "Hi. I'm Jane. Are you Susan?"; the sex of the students; the type of room; whether the students have previously talked or corresponded; whether parents are present). Schemata fill in *default values* for certain aspects of the situation, which let us make certain assumptions. For instance, student ages were not given. Lacking such specification, many readers would assume that the two students were first-year students. This assumption would be the default value for the variable. Notice, however, that the default can be overridden, simply by mentioning other values in the description of the situation.

Schemata can embed themselves in one another hierarchically. Thus, any schema can have subschemata and/or superschemata. The "meeting a college roommate for the first time" schema can be a subschema of an "orientation to college" schema, which may be embedded in an "attending college" schema, and so on. Similarly, the "meeting a college roommate for the first time" schema might contain subschemata of "dorm room," "meeting new person," and "roommate" embedded within it. The schema for "dog" might be a part of the schemata for "mammal" or "pet" or "animal" or "living thing"; it might contain subschemata such as "fur," "paws," or "wagging tail." Schemata are assumed to exist at all levels of abstraction, and thus, schemas can exist for small parts of knowledge (what letter does a particular configuration of ink form?) to very large parts (what is the theory of relativity?).

Schemata are thought of as active processes rather than as passive units of knowledge. They are not simply called up from memory and passively processed. Instead, people are thought to be constantly assessing and evaluating the fit between their current situation and a number of relevant schemata and subschemata.

Schemata are thought to be used in just about every aspect of cognition. They are deemed to play an important role in perception and pattern matching as we try to identify the objects we see before us, in memory and as we call to mind relevant information to help us interpret current information and make decisions about what to do next; and in text and discourse comprehension, as we try to follow the meaning of a conversation, story, or textbook.

The notion of schemata as underlying organizational units of memory has had significant impact on cognitive psychologists' thinking about how memory is organized and concepts represented. Some (Komatsu, 1992) have seen the schema view as sharing features with both the prototype view (in that both schemata and prototypes store information that is abstracted across instances) and with the exemplar view (in that both schemata and exemplars store information about actual instances).

The schema view also shares some of the problems of the prototype and exemplar views. It does not specify clear enough boundaries among individual schemata. Moreover, some psychologists argue that in its current state, the schema framework is not sufficiently delineated to be empirically testable (Horton & Mills, 1984). Answers need to be found for the following questions: What kinds of experiences lead to the formation of new schemata? How are schemata modified with experience? How do people know which schemata to call up in different situations—that is, what sorts of environmental cues are used?

The Knowledge-Based View

Recently, a number of cognitive psychologists (Keil, 1989; Murphy & Medin, 1985) have argued that concepts have much more to do with people's knowledge and worldviews than has been previously recognized. Murphy and Medin (1985) suggested that the relationship between a concept and examples of the concept are analogous to the relationship between a theory and data supporting that theory. The idea here is that a person classifying objects and events doesn't just compare features or physical aspects of the objects and events to features or aspects of stored representations.

Instead, the person uses her or his knowledge of how the concept is organized to justify the classification, and to explain *why* certain instances happen to go together in the same category.

The knowledge-based view helps to explain how some apparently disparate collection of objects can form a coherent category in particular circumstances. To take an example from Barsalou (1983), consider the category comprising children, pets, photo albums, family heirlooms, and cash. On the face of it, these things don't seem to go together very well, but in the context of the scenario of a fire about to envelop a house, these things fall neatly into the category "things to salvage." We know that each of the objects mentioned is precious to its owner or parent, and also irreplaceable. Notice, however, that the category becomes coherent only when we have knowledge about the purpose of the category.

Recall that the prototype, exemplar, and schema approaches to concepts and categories fail to provide much of an answer to the question, How do things in the same category go together? The knowledge-based view proposes that people's theories or mental explanations about the world are intertwined with their concepts and provide the basis for categorization. The view allows people to explain to themselves and to others the instances that go together and why, the features or aspects or instances that are important and why, and the features or aspects that are irrelevant and why.

Until now, we have looked at different proposals for what concepts are—their nature and structure. In the next section, we will examine empirical studies looking at how concepts are actually formed and used. Presumably, understanding something about the ways in which people classify new instances can shed light on what the nature of concepts is. The studies we'll review below will help us think more carefully about the five approaches just discussed.

Forming New Concepts and Classifying New Instances

To have a concept of something is to group similar things together, treating members of the category the concept includes in more or less similar ways. To form a concept, people must have some basis for generalization, for grouping certain things but not others together. When you think about it, the formation of a concept is a remarkable cognitive achievement. It requires that we figure out which attributes or features of things are relevant and which should be ignored. Often, we have to carry out the task with very little feedback. In this section, we'll explore some investigations of how people manage this complex undertaking. Throughout, we'll see that psychologists' assumptions about *how* concepts are mentally represented have influenced their views on how people acquire or form new concepts.

Concept-Attainment Strategies

Bruner, Goodnow, and Austin (1956) conducted some of the earliest work on how people form (or in their terminology, "attain") concepts. They saw several components in the process: acquiring the information necessary to isolate and learn a concept, retaining the information for use later, and transforming the information to make it usable when testing ideas about new possible instances.

Bruner and colleagues (1956) studied the ways in which people attained concepts, using cards depicting differing geometric figures, as shown in Figure 6-2. Note that each card has one of three shapes (circle, square, or cross); one of three colors (here, black, white, or striped); different numbers of shapes (one, two, or three); and different numbers of borders around the shapes (one, two, or three). The experimenter first placed before each subject all of the cards appearing in Figure 6-2. Subjects were told that the experimenter had in mind a certain concept, such as "the black circles," "all cards containing two borders and striped figures," or the like. Subjects were then shown one of the cards that illustrated the concept, in other words, a positive instance. Their subsequent task was to test the other cards, one at a time, for inclusion in the category. The experimenter pro-

FIGURE 6-2.   Stimuli used by Bruner, Goodnow, and Austin (1956). SOURCE: From *A Study of Thinking*, by J. S. Bruner, J. J. Goodnow, and G. A. Austin. Copyright © 1956 by John Wiley & Sons, Inc. Reprinted by permission.

vided feedback after each card was considered. The subject was asked to determine the nature of the concept as efficiently as possible, choosing cards in any order, and offering hypotheses whenever he or she felt comfortable to do so. From the subjects' choices, Bruner and colleagues tried to determine the strategies being used.

Bruner and colleagues (1956) described four distinct strategies that could be used to perform the task. The first they called *simultaneous scanning*. Subjects who pursue this strategy use each card to test and rule out multiple hypotheses. The strategy requires that subjects figure out ahead of time to which hypothesis each card is relevant, and consider carefully how to eliminate the maximum number of hypotheses by choosing the optimal card at each point in the process. As you might expect, this strategy is a difficult one to use, and makes heavy demands on working memory.

A second strategy, *successive scanning,* appeared to be more manageable. Here, a subject tests one hypothesis at a time, for example, first tries to see if the concept is "black figures" by choosing appropriate cards; if she becomes convinced that this is the wrong concept, next tests another idea, and so on, until amassing enough evidence that the correct concept has been attained. The contrast between simultaneous and successive scanning is that the former involves testing a number of ideas at the same time; the latter involves testing ideas one at a time. Successive scanning is therefore less efficient but more cognitively manageable.

A third strategy is *conservative focusing,* which consists of finding a card that is a positive instance of the concept (called the "focus card"), then choosing other cards that vary in only one aspect from the focus card. For instance, if the focus card has two black crosses and one border, the subject might next select one of the following cards: a card with two black circles and one border; a card with one black cross and one border; a card with two black crosses and two borders; or a card with two white crosses and one border. If any of these cards is also a member of the category, then the subject can logically eliminate the changed attribute as being relevant to the concept. For example, if the card with two white crosses and one border is also a member of the category, then the subject knows that a single color does not define the concept. This strategy is interesting because it is both efficient and relatively easy, but unless the cards are laid out in an orderly fashion so that a particular one can be easily located, it may be difficult to carry out.

The final strategy Bruner and colleagues (1956) described is called *focus gambling.* Again, it involves a focus card, which has been established as a positive instance of the concept. The subject then chooses other cards that differ in many aspects from the focus card—in other words, varying as many things as possible, all at the same time. In our example above, the focus card was one with two black crosses and one border. A subject using focus gambling might next choose a card with one white circle and two borders, or a card with three striped squares and two borders. If the gamble is a lucky one, she can discover the concept in very few trials. If the gamble doesn't pay off, it will take her much longer to attain the concept than it would if she used conservative focusing.

Bruner and colleagues (1956) found that the effectiveness of each of their strategies depended to some extent on the conditions of the task. For instance, when subjects had to do the problem "in their heads," without the cards' being displayed, subjects had more trouble using scanning strategies than using focus strategies. The strategy subjects adopted also depended to some extent on the task. When cards were arranged in an orderly way, subjects were more likely to adopt conservative focusing, relative to other subjects who saw the same cards randomly arranged.

Aficionados of the game Mastermind might recognize that, at base, it has many similarities to the Bruner and colleagues (1956) concept-attainment task. Laughlin, Lange, and Adamopoulos (1982) studied college students playing a simplified version of the game and found that the two dominant strategies that emerged were similar to Bruner and colleagues' conservative focusing and simultaneous scanning. Subjects who used these strategies had more success at playing the game relative to subjects who did not, with the conservative focusing strategy being the most successful.

Notice the kind of concept being learned in these tasks. In all the tasks, valid instances of the category share necessary and sufficient features. In fact, the concepts involved in these experiments were what philosophers and psychologists might call *nominal*—concepts that have precise definitions (Schwartz, 1980). The results of the Bruner and colleagues (1956) studies suggest that when concepts are defined with necessary and sufficient features, subjects will form representations that include necessary and sufficient features. We will see below that when people acquire other kinds of concepts, especially those that do not have clear-cut definitions, their acquisition strategies vary.

Acquiring Prototypes

You may remember that in Chapter 2, we reviewed experiments performed by Posner and Keele (1968) on people's ability to classify dot patterns. Their study suggested that, at least in some circumstances, people are able and find it natural to form prototypes, and that they are better able to classify actual prototypes than previously encountered instances.

In part of the study, the experimenters began with four specific dot patterns: a triangle, the letters *M* and *F,* and a random pattern. Next, they created distortions of these patterns (prototypes) by varying the position of the dots. They also varied the number of dots moved as well as the amount of distortion, sometimes moving each dot very slightly, other times, by a great distance. Undergraduates learned to classify correctly either low-distortion or moderate-distortion stimuli but were never shown the original prototypes. The assumption was that students who saw the low-distortion stimuli ought to have had a better conception of the prototypes than those who saw the moderate-distortion stimuli. Conversely, the moderate-distortion subjects ought to have had a better sense of how much variation there could be from the prototype. Both groups of subjects were later shown some novel, high-distortion stimuli. Subjects in the moderate-distortion group were significantly better able to classify these patterns. Further, all subjects found it easier to classify novel patterns that were similar to prototypes.

These results suggest two things. First, people do form and use prototypes, even when given highly distorted instances during the learning phase. Second, learning about category variability may be at least as important as learning about prototypes, especially if categorizations are to be made later of new instances that vary a great deal from the prototype.

A related study by Reed (1972) presented subjects with two categories of faces, shown in Figure 6-3. After subjects studied the five faces in each of two categories, they were given 20 or so novel faces to classify. Reed's question was, how did subjects perform this task?

Reed (1972) believed there were at least four distinct strategies that could have been used. The first, the *prototype strategy,* was to form some sort of abstract image (prototype) for each category, and then compare each novel face to each prototype, classifying it in the category with the best match. A second strategy might be called the *exemplar strategy.* It involved looking at all ten original faces, classifying the novel face in the category with the one original face that most closely matched it. The *feature-frequency strategy* required the subject to compare the features in the novel face (for example, long or short nose; high or low forehead) and the features in the original faces, counting only exact matches, and then to classify the novel face in the category that had the highest number of matches. Finally, the *average distance strategy* involved comparing the novel face to each of the ten original faces, computing the average similarity between the novel face and all of the faces in a given category, and matching the novel face with the category with the highest overall similarity.

Classification of the novel face varied in accord with the strategy subjects followed. This allowed Reed (1972) to examine the pattern of classification to determine which strategy subjects had adopted; most had adopted the prototype strategy. Indeed, when subjects were given descriptions of the four strategies and asked to describe the one they had used, 58% chose the prototype description; 28%, feature frequency; 10%, exemplar; and 4%, average distance. Other studies have showed, however, that different stimuli might make subjects more likely to adopt the latter two strategies (Hayes-Roth & Hayes-Roth, 1977; Medin, Altom, Edelson, & Freko, 1982).

The results of Reed (1972) and of Posner and Keele (1968) appear very different from those of Bruner and colleagues (1956). What might account for this? Two important differences are apparently the type of stimuli being used and the type of concepts being acquired. Notice that the Bruner and colleagues task involved concepts with clear-cut definitions; the tasks of Reed and of Posner and Keele did not. The latter tasks, in contrast, involved the learning of concepts defined by similarity to previous exam-

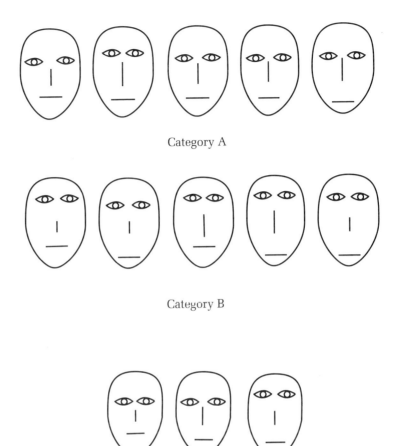

Category A

Category B

Test Stimuli

FIGURE 6-3.   Stimuli used by Reed (1972). SOURCE: From "Pattern Recognition and Categorization," by S. K. Reed, 1972, *Cognitive Psychology, 3*, 383–384. Copyright © 1972 by Academic Press. Reprinted by permission.

ples. When categories are defined in this way, people apparently learn to classify by forming and using mental representations of prototypes. Taken as a whole, the results from all of these studies reinforce the idea that the way people form and learn concepts depends critically on the instances and the categories they must work with.

Implicit Concept Learning

The results just described imply that people can and do form and use prototypes, at least under certain conditions and with certain stimuli. This raises the question of whether subjects ever retain and make use of information about specific exemplars.

Arthur Reber (1967, 1969, 1976) conducted a series of studies bearing on this issue. In his experiments, subjects were given strings of letters to learn, such as the ones shown in Figure 6-4(a). Unbeknownst to subjects in some of the experimental groups, the letters were not randomly chosen but were generated by a structure sharing similarities with certain kinds of language grammars. Figure 6-4(b) depicts one such grammar. To generate a "legal" letter string—that is, in accord with the grammar—imagine yourself starting at the path marked "In" and moving to the path marked "Out," following the directional arrows as you go. As you take each path, you add the letter of that path to your string. So, the first letter of a "legal" string will always be either a *T* or a *V*. Notice two loops in the grammar: one labeled "P" and one "X." These loops can be followed any number of times (each time adding either a *P* or *X* to the letter string), thereby allowing letter strings that are infinitely long.

Reber (1967, 1976) found, first, that subjects learning letter strings

(A)

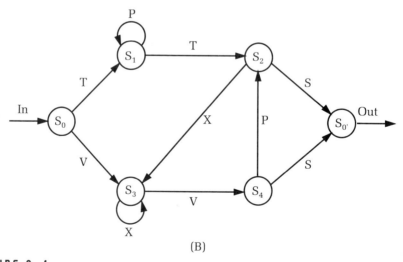

(B)

FIGURE 6-4.   Possible stimuli (A) and their underlying "grammar" (B) used by Reber (1967). SOURCE: From "Implicit Learning of Artificial Grammar," by A. S. Reber, 1967, *Journal of Verbal Learning and Verbal Behavior, 6,* 856. Copyright © 1967 by Academic Press. Reprinted by permission.

following the grammar made fewer errors than did control subjects learning random letter strings. More surprisingly, subjects who were told ahead of time that letter strings followed certain complex rules remembered strings *less* well than subjects who were simply asked to memorize particular letter strings but were not told anything about the strings' following of a structure. Reber concluded that when complex underlying structures existed (such as his grammar), people are better off memorizing exemplars than they are trying to figure out what the structure is, primarily because subjects who try to guess the structure often induce or invent incorrect rules or structures.

Brooks (1978, 1987) believes that the processes Reber (1967) discovered are at work much of the time in ordinary cognition. Brooks calls these processes *nonanalytic concept formation,* drawing a contrast to analytic (logical, scientific, focused) concept formation. Nonanalytic concept formation requires that people pay attention to individual exemplars, storing information about and representations of them in memory. Later classification is done by comparing new instances to the representations, drawing analogies between new and old.

In one study, Brooks (1978) had subjects perform a paired-associates learning task, learning to associate hieroglyphic symbol strings with English words. Figure 6-5(a) presents examples of his stimuli. Each symbol in the string had a certain meaning, as shown in Figure 6-5(b), but subjects were not alerted to this fact. Later, subjects unexpectedly were given new strings, such as those in Figure 6-5(c), and asked four questions: Does it fly? Is it big? Is it alive? Does it attack? Most of the subjects reported that they answered the questions by thinking of a previously memorized exemplar and drawing an analogy to it. Further, subjects were generally unable to point to any particular symbol in the string as a basis for their response.

These results pose a puzzle for cognitive psychologists. Apparently, subjects sometimes test specific hypotheses when forming concepts (as in the Bruner and colleagues [1956] experiments); sometimes form prototypes (as in the Posner and Keele [1968] and Reed [1972] experiments); and sometimes memorize exemplars (as in the Reber [1967, 1976] and Brooks [1978] experiments). The question is, when and why do people adopt such different approaches?

Brooks (1978) believes that the answer has to do with the concept-formation task itself. Some simple laboratory tasks, such as the one used by Bruner and colleagues (1956) seem to lead subjects to adopt an analytical, hypothesis-testing framework. Other, more complex stimuli lead people to abandon this approach for another. Brooks goes on to describe five factors that encourage people to store information about individual exemplars.

The first factor involves task requirements to learn information that distinguishes among individual instances. Brooks (1978) reminds us that in natural situations, different individuals in the same category must sometimes be treated differently. It is all very well to recognize that Rover, the lovable family mutt, and Killer, the attack dog for the company down the

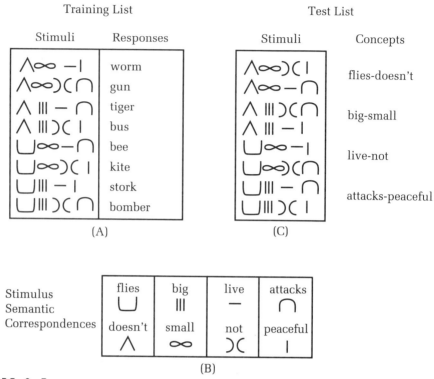

Training List

Test List

FIGURE 6-5.   Stimuli from Brooks's (1978) semantabit experiments. SOURCE: From "Nonanalytic Concept Formation and Memory for Instances," by L. Brooks in *Cognition and Categorization,* edited by E. Rosch and B. B. Lloyd. Copyright © 1978 by Lawrence Erlbaum Associates, Inc. Reprinted by permission.

street, are both dogs, but the child or adult who treats them as interchangeable could be in for a painful surprise. A second factor involves the original learning situation. In many real-life situations, instances are not presented one at a time in rapid succession (as they are in many laboratory experiments). Instead, the same instance may repeatedly appear, affording the individual a chance to get to know certain instances very well. Third, some stimuli lend themselves to hypothesis testing more than others do. Notice that in the Bruner and colleagues (1956) stimuli, instances vary on only four dimensions. In real life, things vary in many complicated ways. Often, the relevant dimensions of variation will not be apparent to the novice, an idea we discussed in the section on perceptual learning. A fourth factor is that in real-life concept learning, instances may belong to a number of categories, all at the same time. Rover might belong to any of the following categories: "dog," "family pet," "partner to take to obedience classes," "source of mud on rainy days," or even "incurrer of large food bills." Finally, Brooks points out that in natural settings, we learn about instances without knowing how we will be called on to use the information later.

Kemler-Nelson (1984) also argues that much of our real-life conceptual knowledge is acquired nonanalytically rather than analytically. Her research has shown that children are especially likely to use this mode of concept learning, as are adults when not allowed to devote many cognitive resources to the task, for example, when forced to process information more rapidly than they might otherwise do (Smith & Kemler, 1984).

Furthermore, Kemler Nelson (1984) believes that nonanalytic concept formation is especially likely with materials that have strong family-resemblance structures. Subjects in one of her experiments were presented with artificial faces, such as those in Figure 6-6. The faces varied in four attributes: curliness of hair, length of nose, size of ears, and breadth of mustache, with each attribute having three values (for example slightly curly mustache, medium curly mustache, and very curly mustache). Subjects learned which faces belonged to the category "doctors" and which to the category "policemen." Faces presented during the learning phase were carefully chosen, such that there was one attribute that distinguished between the two categories (in this example, length of nose—doctors have long noses; policemen, short ones). At the same time, the two categories differed in their family-resemblance structure, although the difference is not absolute. In this example, doctors tend to have slightly curly mustaches, large ears, and broad

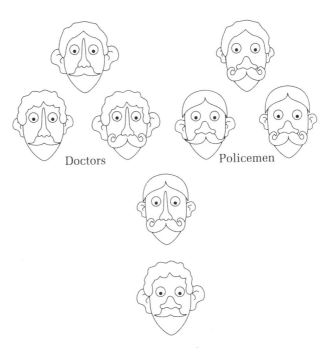

Doctors   Policemen

Test Stimuli

FIGURE 6-6.   Stimuli used by Kemler Nelson (1984).
SOURCE: From "The Effect of Intention on What Concepts are Acquired," by D. G. Kemler Nelson, 1984, *Journal of Verbal Learning and Verbal Behavior, 23,* 742. Copyright © 1984 by Academic Press. Reprinted by permission.

mustaches; policemen, very curly mustaches, small ears, and thinner mustaches, although not every instance shared all of these features.

In the subsequent test phase, subjects were presented with a number of test faces, including two "critical" test faces, and asked to classify each one. These faces pitted the criterial feature (for example, length of nose) against the family-resemblance structure. The way subjects classified these faces revealed the basis of their classification: if they used a criterial feature, they classified them one way; if they used family-resemblance structure, they were more likely to make a different classification. In this example (see Figure 6-6 again), note that the top face has a long nose, suggesting it belongs to the "doctor" category, but has more overall similarity to faces in the "policemen" category; the reverse is true for the second face.

Some of Kemler-Nelson's (1984) subjects were explicitly told to search for a means of distinguishing between doctors and policemen, others were simply asked to learn to recognize the pictures. Kemler-Nelson found that the latter group was especially likely to use family-resemblance structure as a basis for classification; approximately 60% did so. Of subjects in the former group, only 46% used that approach. She concluded that both the kinds of concepts being learned and the instructions about the task influence the concept-acquisition strategy people adopt.

Using and Forming Scripts

We've seen so far how people can form or acquire concepts according to the classical, prototype, and exemplar approaches. This brings us to the question, how does the schema view explain how people form or acquire new schemata? In this section, we'll look at one specific proposal.

One kind of schema, a schema for routine events, has been called a **script** (Schank & Abelson, 1977). Consider the most well known example of scripts: that for going to a restaurant. Think for a moment (and even better, before reading further, make a few notes) about what happens when you go to a restaurant. Now, do the same thing for these other events: attending a lecture, getting up in the morning, grocery shopping, visiting a doctor. Schank and Abelson (1977) noticed that people's knowledge of what is involved in going to a restaurant was widely shared, and structured in very similar ways. They explained this similarity by saying that people share scripts.

Scripts are thought to be used in a variety of situations. For instance, if you go to a new restaurant, one in a city you've never visited before, you can call on a script to tell you what to expect. In general, you should expect on entry to be greeted by a host or hostess, shown to a table when one is available, given menus, and so on. This knowledge cues you for how to behave appropriately. So, if you enter a restaurant but don't see a host or hostess, it is normally a good idea to wait (at least a little while) before sitting down—your script tells you this.

Scripts also allow us to make a number of inferences (Rumelhart &

Norman, 1988). Consider this story: "Lloyd really wanted some Japanese food. So he went to a restaurant and ordered udon. Finally, he asked for the check, paid it, and left." Other, apparently omitted information can be inferred, by use of the script. For instance, we can infer that Lloyd entered the restaurant and was seated, that someone took and delivered his order, that someone cooked his udon, that he had money before entering the restaurant, and so on. The story didn't need to say all of this because it gave enough information for us to be able to call up the appropriate script ("going to a restaurant"), and that script filled in the rest.

Bower, Black, and Turner (1979) investigated how much people typically use scripts. They first asked subjects to write their scripts for the events listed above (going to a restaurant, attending a lecture, getting up in the morning, grocery shopping, visiting a doctor). They compared the notes generated by all of their subjects, and found a high degree of overlap in what people mentioned. The subjects generally agreed about which characters to describe, which props and actions to mention, and the order in which different actions would occur. Box 6-1 shows part of their results. The investigators also found a high degree of agreement in the level of description. Thus, most people would mention "eating the food" instead of "picking up a spoon, dipping it into soup, raising the spoon to lips, and sipping."

In another study, Bower and associates (1979) showed that if information from a story was presented in scrambled order, people tended to recall it in the scripted order. In a further experiment, the investigators presented stories that mentioned only some of the events in a typical script. They found that in a later recall task, subjects would often "recall" information that wasn't in the story but was in the relevant script.

The preceding finding was replicated in a study by Owens, Bower, and Black (1979). They presented subjects with stories about a character's doing such things as making coffee, visiting a doctor, going to a lecture, and other routine events. Subjects in the experimental condition read a three-line description of a problem, such as "Nancy woke up feeling sick again and she wondered if she really were pregnant. How would she tell the professor she had been seeing? And the money was another problem." Subjects were later asked to recall the stories as close to verbatim as possible. Subjects who read the problem description recalled more of the story episodes than control subjects, but also "recalled" more than was in the stories. These intrusions appeared to come from the underlying scripts, and became more frequent with longer retention intervals. The authors suggested that although scripts play an important role in helping us organize recall, they force us to pay a price: the price of other, script-related information intruding into our memory.

Psychological Essentialism

A recent proposal by Medin (1989), drawing on work by the philosopher Hilary Putnam (1975), has examined people's reliance on underlying nature

BOX 6-1   Script Norms for Five Events

Going to a restaurant	Attending a lecture	Getting up	Grocery shopping	Visiting a doctor
Open door	Open door	*Wake up*	ENTER STORE	*Enter office*
Enter	ENTER ROOM	Turn off alarm	GET CART	CHECK IN WITH
Give reservation	*Look for friends*	Lie in bed	Take out list	RECEPTIONIST
name	FIND SEAT	Stretch	Look at list	SIT DOWN
Wait to be seated	SIT DOWN	GET UP	Go to first aisle	Wait
Go to table	Settle belongings	Make bed	*Go up and down*	Look at other people
BE SEATED	TAKE OUT	*Go to bathroom*	*aisles*	READ MAGAZINE
Order drinks	NOTEBOOK	Use toilet	PICK OUT ITEMS	*Name called*
Put napkins on	*Look at other*	*Take shower*	Compare prices	Follow nurse
lap	*students*	*Wash face*	Put items in cart	*Enter exam room*
LOOK AT	*Talk*	Shave	Get meat	Undress
MENU	Look at professor	DRESS	Look for items	*Sit on table*
Discuss menu	LISTEN TO	Go to kitchen	forgotten	Talk to nurse
ORDER MEAL	PROFESSOR	Fix breakfast	Talk to other	NURSE TESTS
Talk	TAKE NOTES	EAT BREAKFAST	shoppers	Wait
Drink water	CHECK TIME	BRUSH TEETH	Go to checkout	Doctor enters
Eat salad or	Ask questions	Read paper	counters	Doctor greets
soup	Change position	*Comb hair*	*Find fastest line*	Talk to doctor about
Meal arrives	in seat	*Get books*	WAIT IN LINE	problem
EAT FOOD	Daydream	Look in mirror	*Put food on belt*	Doctor asks questions
Finish meal	Look at other students	Get coat	Read magazines	DOCTOR EXAMINES
Order dessert	Take more notes	LEAVE HOUSE	WATCH CASHIER	Get dressed
Eat dessert	*Close notebook*		RING UP	Get medicine
Ask for bill	*Gather belongings*		PAY CASHIER	Make another
Bill arrives	Stand up		*Watch bag boy*	appointment
PAY BILL	Talk		Cart bags out	LEAVE OFFICE
Leave tip	LEAVE		Load bags into car	
Get coats			LEAVE STORE	
LEAVE				

Uppercase items were mentioned by the most subjects; italic items by fewer subjects; and lowercase items by the fewest subjects. SOURCE: *From "Scripts in Memory for Text," by G. H. Bower, J. B. Black, and T. J. Turner, 1979,* Cognitive Psychology, 11, *179. Copyright © 1979 by Academic Press. Reprinted by permission.*

as a basis for many concepts. Medin proposes a new framework he calls psychological essentialism, and describes several assumptions. The first is that people generally act as if objects, people, or events have certain *essences* or underlying natures that make them what they are. Presumably, for instance, a human being is a human being by virtue of having a certain molecular structure. That essence constrains or limits the kinds of variation different instances of a category can show. So, for instance, people can vary in height, weight, hair color, eye color, bone structure, and the like but must have certain other properties in common by virtue of the underlying essence they share. People's theories about the essences of various categories help them to connect deeper properties (for example, the structure of DNA) to more superficial properties (for example, eye color, hair color). As an example, Medin (1989) points out that although the categories "male" and "female" are believed by most of us to be genetically determined, most of us look at characteristics such as hair length, facial hair, and so on rather than conducting genetic tests when classifying a new person as a woman or a man. We may make errors in using superficial characteristics, but we probably won't often be led astray.

People's knowledge of the essence of a category varies by level of expertise. Biologists, in general, know a lot more about the genetic structure of a human being than do lay persons. For this reason, experts can generally be expected to make different and more accurate classifications, especially if the bases for the classifications are subtle. Medin's (1989) idea is that classifying on the basis of perceptual or other superficial similarity may be a strategy that can be pretty effective much of the time. Still, when the situation calls for it and if the expertise is possessed, people will classify on the basis of deeper principles. This suggestion implies, then, that people's classification of instances will change as they become more experienced and knowledgeable, an idea that fits well with our discussion of perceptual learning, as well as with the current available data.

It may also be that the way people acquire and mentally represent concepts varies as a function of what the concepts are. Some psychologists have adopted the perspective of philosophers in distinguishing among kinds of concepts. *Nominal-kind* concepts include concepts that have clear definitions. *Natural-kind* concepts, such as of gold or tiger, are of things that are naturally occurring in some environment (Putnam, 1975). A third kind of concept, *artifacts,* are things that have been constructed to serve some function or accomplish some task (see Keil, 1989; Schwartz, 1978, 1979, 1980).

Different information may be represented in different kinds of concepts. For instance, nominal-kind concepts may include information about necessary and sufficient features because these things exist as part of the definition of the concept. Natural-kind concepts might include more information about definitional or essential features, especially about molecular or chromosomal structure. Natural-kind concepts may also be more likely to have a family resemblance structure but can be equally well explained within a knowledge-based approach. Artifact concepts, on the other hand, might highlight information about the object's purpose or function, and may be adequately described only within the knowledge-based approach.

In a recent study, Barton and Komatsu (1989) presented subjects with five natural kind concepts (for example, goat, water, gold) and five artifacts (for example, TV, pencil, mirror). With each concept, they asked the subjects to imagine different transformations. Some of the transformations were in terms of function or purpose, (for example, a female goat that did not give milk; a TV with no visible picture); others were in terms of physical features, (for example, gold that was red in color; a pencil that was not cylindrical). A third type of change was molecular, such as water that did not consist of the formula H_2O, or a mirror not made out of glass. The investigators found that although subjects were sensitive to molecular transformations with natural kind terms, they were also sensitive to functional changes with artifact terms. Apparently, then, all concepts are *not* treated equally, and under at least some conditions, people use their knowledge about why instances of a category should be grouped together in their representation of the related concept.

Summary

We have looked so far at a number of proposals for how concepts are mentally represented and structured, and what information they contain. We have also reviewed a number of investigations of how concepts are acquired. We have seen that different experiments have provided different answers to the questions, what is learned and how?

The five approaches to conceptual structure reviewed above have been themselves categorized into two major types: similarity-based and explanation-based (Komatsu, 1992). The similarity-based category, comprising the classical, prototype, and exemplar views (and some parts of the schema view), includes the approaches where categorization is assumed to be done on the basis of the similarity of an instance to some abstract specification of the category (for example, a definition or a prototype) or to one or more stored exemplars. The explanation-based category, comprising both some of the schema view and the knowledge-based view, instead sees people as classifying instances on the basis of meaningful relationships among instances and categories.

The five approaches to concepts differ on several dimensions. The first of these is the *cognitive economy* of the mental representation. If you recall our discussion of cognitive economy from Chapter 5, you'll remember that the idea is to save on mental resources (for example, storage space, processing time) by limiting the amount of information we have to store. If we treated every single object or event as completely unique, thereby forming a unique mental representation for each, we would not be using our cognitive resources very economically. On the other hand, if we categorized all objects into one category (called "things"), the category itself wouldn't be very informative. So, any theory of concepts and categorization has to strike a balance between cognitive economy and informativeness (Komatsu, 1992).

Finally, any theory of concepts must explain a concept or category's *coherence*—what holds the class of things together into a natural grouping. Some approaches, such as the classical approach, do this very directly; others have more fuzzy boundaries around and between concepts.

We have also seen that the ways in which people approach a concept-learning task influence the nature of the concept finally acquired. When people are explicitly asked to form concepts and to search for underlying rules or features, they seem to acquire and use different kinds of information than they do when left to their own exploration. This raises the question of applicability of very traditional laboratory-based investigations of concept formation to the processes people use outside the laboratory. What gets learned depends, it seems, on the original learning materials, the task instructions, and the learner's anticipation of how the learned information will be used in the future. As in other areas of cognition, then, the way people process information is flexible, and varies with the situation and purpose of the task.

Recommended Readings

Classic works on concepts, categorization, and the nature of meaning are Bruner, Goodnow, and Austin (1956), Bourne (1970), Rosch and Mervis (1975), and Rosch, Mervis, Gray, Johnson, and Boyes-Braem (1976). Reviews of work in this field have been conducted by Komatsu (1992), Medin (1989), Medin and Smith (1984), and Smith (1990). Edited volumes containing a variety of perspectives on concepts and categorization are Neisser (1987b), Rosch and Lloyd (1978), and Vosniadou and Ortony (1989).

Katz (1972) presents the arguments for the classical view of concepts, and Mervis and Rosch (1981) and Rosch and Mervis (1975) do the same for the prototype view. Recent work has assessed the fit of a family-resemblance structure for other kinds of concepts, such as situations and emotions (Cantor, Mischel, & Schwartz, 1982; Fehr, 1988). Armstrong, Gleitman, and Gleitman (1983), Lakoff (1987), and Osherson and Smith (1981) present important critiques of the methodology and reinterpretations of the conclusions drawn from some of the prototype studies. Landau (1982) and Rosch (1983) propose "hybrid" models combining some of the features of the classical and prototype approach. Reber (1989) provides an overview of literature on implicit learning. Brooks (1987) summarizes evidence and arguments supporting the exemplar approach, and presents an extension of this work to real-life medical diagnosis (Brooks, Norman, & Allen, 1991). Homa, Sterling, and Trepel (1981) propose a combined exemplar-prototype approach.

Ward and Scott (1987) take issue with Kemler-Nelson's view of how people learn concepts, and present evidence that people *can* use criterial features in learning concepts with a family-resemblance structure. They debate this question in a series of exchanges: Ward, Vela, and Hass (1990); Kemler-Nelson (1990); and Ward (1990).

Proposals for the knowledge-based view include those of S. Gelman (1988); Keil (1989), Murphy and Medin (1985); and Schank, Collins, and Hunter (1986). Recent studies by Medin, Wattenmaker, and Hampson (1987) and Smith and Shapiro (1989) investigate the bases of classification people use when given different instructions, procedures, and stimulus materials.

REVIEW QUESTIONS

1. Describe the distinction many cognitive psychologists make between *concepts* and *categories*. What are the cognitive benefits of having concepts? Explain.

2. Contrast the classical, prototype, and exemplar proposals for how concepts are mentally represented. What kinds of arguments and/or empirical findings support each? What kinds of arguments and/or empirical data are troublesome for each?

3. Describe what a *family-resemblance* structure is and how it relates to the prototype approach to concepts.

4. Compare and contrast the schema view and the knowledge-based view of concepts. Are the two compatible? How or how not?

5. Briefly review Reber's work on implicit learning and its implications for concept formation.

6. Give some new examples of *scripts*, and justify your examples.

7. Discuss: "Any approach to concepts must strike some balance between cognitive economy and informativeness."

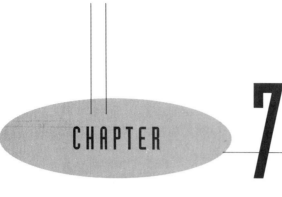

CHAPTER 7

Visual Imagery

Think of the house or apartment you consider your permanent residence. In particular, think about its kitchen. How many cabinet doors does it have?

Obviously, this question draws on your memory. Most people are able to answer it after some amount of mental work. What sort of work is required? In the process I used, I first recognized that I don't have the information needed already stored—that is, I didn't know the answer "off the top of my head." So, I had to determine the answer in another way. I mentally pictured my kitchen by drawing on memory. Then, starting at one end of the room, I scanned my mental picture, counting cabinet doors. My procedure is neither difficult nor original (Shepard, 1966) but seemingly one that is commonly used.

The nature of these "mental pictures," or **visual images,** is the focus of this chapter. We will look at the role of images in memory, and how images are used in techniques called **mnemonics,** designed to aid or improve memory. Later, we will consider recent experiments investigating the ways in which people construct and use visual images, and what these findings suggest about cognition. Finally, we will turn our attention to the nature of visual images, considering the kind of mental representation(s) used to create and store them.

Throughout the chapter, we will confine ourselves to discussion of visual images. We must recognize, however, that other kinds of mental images exist. Examples include auditory images (for example, the imagined sound of your dog's barking), olfactory images (for example, the imagined smell of fresh-baked bread), and cutaneous images (for example, the imagined feel of your toe's being stubbed into the wall). Visual images, like visual perception, have received the most attention within cognitive psychology. Thus, as we did in our examination of perception (Chapter 2), where we focused on visual perception, we will here focus on visual imagery.

The study of visual imagery has had a controversial history within psychology (Paivio, 1971). Although occasional references to imagery were made at the turn of the century, the rise of behaviorism essentially dictated that even the concept of an image be rejected. Visual images are problematic as objects of scientific inquiry. After all, the experience of a visual image is just about as private an experience as one can have. If I assert that I am forming a visual image of my kitchen, no one but me can tell if I really have the image or am just pretending. Visual images, unlike behaviors, cannot be seen, counted, or controlled by others. Because visual images can be reported by only the person who asserts he or she is experiencing them, they can be distorted or biased by that person, either consciously or inadvertently. Proponents of behaviorism argued that imagery is not the sort of topic that can be investigated with sufficient scientific rigor or control.

Nonetheless, interest in visual imagery never completely vanished (Paivio, 1971), and in fact became stronger after the popularity of behaviorism waned in the 1960's. It is difficult to explain how people perfom certain cognitive tasks, such as the one described earlier, without talking about visual images. Moreover, research in memory suggested that people who reported using imagery were better able to recall information than people who didn't. Psychologists recognized that to eliminate imagery as a subject of discussion and investigation is to overlook a potentially fundamental aspect of cognition. Hence, visual imagery has regained credibility as a worthwhile topic among most cognitive psychologists.

Mnemonics and Memory Codes

If you want to increase your chances of remembering (and especially recalling) information, there are several techniques available, collectively called mnemonics. We will see that many (although not all) involve the construction of mental pictures or images. We'll begin by looking at a number of the most well known mnemonics, examining two theoretical explanations for why they work.

Mnemonics

Around 500 B.C., the Greek poet Simonides was called out from entertaining diners at a banquet. While he was out of the hall, the roof caved in, crushing the guests so badly that they could not be identified by members of their families. Simonides, by recalling where each guest sat, was able to help relatives find the remains of their family members (Paivio, 1971). Thus was invented one of the first mnemonic techniques, often called the *method of loci*.

The method of loci, as the name might suggest, requires the learner to imagine a series of places (loci or locations) that have some sort of order to them. For example, I might use a series of landmarks I pass on my way from my office to the campus snack bar. I then divide the material I want to remember, mentally picturing the different pieces at the different landmarks.

Suppose, for instance, I need to remember to bring certain things to a meeting—for instance, a tablet, a pen, certain computer printouts, a book, and a calculator. I could use the method of loci to remember this material in the following way. First, I imagine myself walking through my office doorway (first locus), and these propping the first object (the tablet) against the door as a doorstop. Next, I see myself walking by my secretary's desk, leaving my pen on the desk atop a letter or note. Then I see myself walking into the hall and down the nearby stairwell, draping the printouts over the railing at the top of the stairs. I mentally exit the building, pass a big oak tree to my left, and place the book on one of its branches. Finally, as I enter the student union, I picture the calculator hung from the front door.

When I need to remember these five items, all I need do is mentally "take a walk" over the same route, noticing the objects I pass. Essentially, I take the same path again, this time looking around in my image as I do so. Bower (1970a) provided a list of principles that improve the workings of the method-of-loci technique (see Box 7-1). Figure 7-1 shows how the method of loci might work in remembering items from a shopping list. Ross and Lawrence (1968) showed that college students trained in using the method of loci could recall up to 38 of 40 words after one presentation; by any account, this level of performance is exceptional.

BOX 7-1   Principles of Use of the Method of Loci

1. Use list of cues that you know well. You can't retrieve any associations if the cue images aren't available at both presentation and recall.
2. The cues must be memory images of geographic locations.
3. Associations must be formed between the items to be remembered and the cue locations at the time you originally encounter the items.
4. The associations between cue locations and the items must be one-to-one.
5. Use imagery, especially visual imagery, to form associative links.
6. Use interactive images to link the item and its cue location.
7. If you study the items more than once, the same cue location should be used for a given memory item.
8. During recall, cue your own memory by using the list of locations.
9. Use the same recall cues (locations) that you used during the study.

SOURCE: *From "Spatial and Verbal Components of the Art of Recall," by Lee Brooks, 1968,* Canadian Journal of Psychology, 22, *350–351. Copyright © 1968 by the Canadian Psychological Association. Reprinted by permission.*

FIGURE 7-1.   Illustration of the method of loci. Items to be remembered: hot dogs, cat food, tomatoes, bananas, whiskey. Locations: driveway, garage, front door, closet, kitchen sink. (After Bower, 1970a). SOURCE: From "Analysis of a Mnemonic Device," by Gordon H. Bower, 1970, *American Scientist, 58*, 497–499. Copyright © 1970 Sigma Xi Science Research Society. Reprinted by permission.

Another technique for improving memory could be called the technique of *interacting images.* A study reported in 1894 anticipated the usefulness of this technique. The results indicated that recall of concrete nouns on a list was improved when subjects were told to form images of the words, in comparison to when they were not given such instructions (Kirkpatrick, 1894). Bower (1970b) found similar results in experiments of paired-associates learning (review Chapter 4 if you've forgotten what this is). In other words, if subjects were given pairs such as "goat–pipe," subjects who formed images of, say, a goat smoking a pipe, recalled almost twice as many paired associates as control subjects who were not instructed to use imagery. (These figures may underestimate the effect because some control subjects may have spontaneously used imagery.)

Bower's (1970b) research showed in particular that for images to be maximally effective in paired associates, subjects should try to form images that interacted—for example, a goat *smoking* a pipe rather than simply a picture of a goat next to a picture of a pipe, with the two pictures separated in space. The principle of interactive imagery applies equally to the method of loci technique: the images should depict the to-be-remembered items interacting in some way with items at the various loci (see principle 6 in the list on the preceding page). Notice that in Figure 7-1, which depicts the use of the method of loci, all of the images involve interaction between the to-be-remembered items and other aspects of the different locations.

A third mnemonic technique, one that also involves imagery, is called the *pegword method.* Like the method of loci, it involves picturing the items with another set of ordered "cues." In this case, the cues are not locations but, rather, nouns that come from a memorized rhyming list: "One is a bun, two is a shoe, three is a tree, four is a door, five is a hive, six is sticks, seven is heaven, eight is a gate, nine is wine, and ten is a hen." The method calls for the subject to picture the first item interacting with a bun, the second with a shoe, the third with a tree, and so forth (notice that the method works for lists of only ten items or fewer). Bugelski, Kidd, and Segmen (1968) showed that the method also improves recall in paired-associates tasks, as long as subjects are given four seconds or more per item to form the images.

Not all mnemonic techniques have to do with imagery. One set of techniques that does not involve visual imagery per se involves *recoding* the material to be recalled, adding extra words or sentences to *mediate,* or go between, your memory and the material. One example, familiar to most schoolchildren, involves taking the first letter of each word that you want to remember, and forming a word or sentence from these letters. This technique can be used to recall the names of the Great Lakes (HOMES = Huron, Ontario, Michigan, Erie, Superior), or to recall the names of the notes on the lines of a musical staff ("Every good boy deserves fudge"). Research investigating the usefulness of this technique reports mixed results, although the technique is a popular one (Carlson, Zimmer, & Glover, 1981). Notice, by the way, that the words and sentences serve functions similar to those of the images in the techniques described previously. Both are *mediators:* internal codes that intervene between the items to be remembered and your (later) overt responses (Klatzky, 1980).

Finally, as mentioned in Chapter 4, various types of categorization and organization of material also improve recall. Arranging material into categories helps to organize the material, and this in turn raises its probability of recall. As discussed in Chapter 4, organization presumably adds to the number of "hooks" attached to the material to be remembered, and the greater the number of hooks, the greater the probability of recall.

Why is it that so many of the mnemonic techniques involve the use of visual imagery? How differently do imagery-based mnemonics function than non-imagery-based mnemonics? Is there something about visual images per se that makes them especially memorable? We will consider two opposing views on this matter.

The Dual-Coding Hypothesis

Allan Paivio (1969, 1971, 1983) originated the **dual-coding hypothesis** of memory to explain the workings of various mnemonics. According to Paivio, long-term memory contains two distinct coding systems (or codes) for representing information to be stored. One is verbal, containing information about an item's abstract, linguistic meaning. The other involves imagery, mental pictures of some sort that represent what the item looks like. Items to be remembered can be coded by either verbal labels or visual images, and in some cases, by both. Paivio's idea is that pictures and concrete words give rise to both verbal labels and visual images—that is, they have two possible internal codes or mental representations. Abstract words, on the other hand, typically have only one kind of code or representation: a verbal label.

One study by Paivio (1965) provided evidence to support the hypothesis. Subjects were asked to learn one of four lists of noun pairs. The first list (CC) included pairs in which both referred to concrete objects (for example book–table). The second list (CA) included pairs in which the first noun was concrete and the second abstract (for example, chair–justice). The third list (AC) was the converse of the second (for example, freedom–dress). The fourth (AA) contained pairs of abstract nouns (beauty–truth). Of a possible 16 correct responses, subjects averaged 11.41, 10.01, 7.36, and 6.05 for the CC, CA, AC, and AA lists, respectively.

Paivio (1965) explained the results as follows: whenever possible, subjects spontaneously formed visual images of the noun pairs. The formation was easiest with concrete nouns. Paivio (1969) assumed that visual imagery, unlike verbal labeling, increases as a function of concreteness. The more concrete the noun, the richer the image and the more elaborated the internal code. This helps explain why pictures (very concrete) are often remembered better than words (for example, Kirkpatrick, 1894; Shepard, 1967).

When items are coded by both images and verbal labels (as concrete nouns can be), the chances of the learner's retrieving them are obviously better. If the learner forgets the verbal label, he might still access the visual image, or vice versa. Items coded only by verbal labels are disadvantaged; if the verbal label is forgotten or "misplaced," the learner has less to go on.

Further, Paivio (1969) believed that the first noun in a pair (called the "stimulus" noun) serves as a *conceptual peg* on which the second, "response" noun is hooked. In this sense, the stimulus noun serves as a "mental anchor," a place to which the representation of the response noun can be attached. Thus, the imaginability of the first noun is particularly important in improving memorability, explaining why recall in the CA condition is significantly higher than in the AC condition.

The Relational-Organizational Hypothesis

Bower (1970b) proposed an alternative to the dual-coding hypothesis that he called the *relational-organizational* hypothesis. He believed that the reason imagery improved memory was not because images are necessarily richer than verbal labels but because imagery produces more associations between the items to be recalled. Forming an image (say, between two words in a pair, or between a word and a location, as in the method of loci) typically requires the subject to create a number of links or hooks between the information to be remembered and other information. Recall, from Chapter 4, that the more "hooks" a piece of information in memory has to other information, the greater the chances of recalling it. Bower's argument, then, is that imagery works by facilitating the creation of a greater number of hooks.

Bower (1970b) performed an experiment to distinguish between the dual-coding and the relational-organizational hypotheses. Subjects were divided into three groups, each given different instructions for a paired-associates learning task. One group was told to use "overt rote repetition" (that is, rehearse aloud); the second, to construct two images that did not interact and were "separated in imaginal space"; the third, to construct an interactive scene of the two words in a pair (p. 530). Results showed that all subjects recognized about 85% of the previously seen words. However, recall of those words differed greatly. Subjects who used rote memorization recalled about 30% of the paired associates; subjects using noninteractive imagery, 27%; and subjects who formed interacting images, about 53%.

The prediction was that if imagery simply leads to more elaborated coding of the paired associates, as the dual-coding hypothesis predicts, then subjects in the two-imagery-instructions conditions ought to have performed similarly. In fact, only subjects who formed interacting images showed an improvement over the rote memorizers. Apparently, it is not imagery per se that helps memory but, rather, the way in which imagery is used. Interacting images presumably create or suggest more links between the target information and other information, making the target information easier to retrieve.

Although the dual-coding hypothesis continues to attract proponents (see Yuille, 1983), still unresolved are how well it explains the workings of imagery mnemonics and what kind of explanations it provides for nonimagery mnemonics. However imagery mnemonics work, there is at least little doubt that many do aid memory. To understand how these mnemonics work, it will be necessary to explore further what imagery is and how it works, topics we turn to next.

Empirical Investigations of Imagery

A series of studies by Lee Brooks (1968) is widely regarded as yielding some of the best evidence that images are distinct from verbal materials or at least use different processes than verbal materials do. Figure 7-2 depicts different conditions of Brooks's primary experiment. In one condition, subjects were asked to imagine a letter (such as the outlined capital *F* in part A of Figure 7-2) Then to move clockwise mentally from a particular corner (marked in Figure 7-2 with an asterisk) and indicate, for each corner, whether it was at the extreme top or extreme bottom of the letter. In this example, the correct responses are "yes, yes, yes, no, no, no, no, no, no, yes."

Subjects indicated their responses in different ways. One mode of response was verbal: subjects said "yes" or "no," as above. Another

(A) Start at the corner marked with an asterisk, and indicate whether or not each corner is at the extreme top or bottom.

A BIRD IN THE HAND IS NOT IN THE BUSH.

(B) For each word in the sentence above, indicate whether or not each word is a noun.

FIGURE 7-2.   Stimuli from the Brooks (1968) study. SOURCE: From "Spatial and Verbal Components of the Art of Recall," by Lee Brooks, 1968, *Canadian Journal of Psychology, 22*, 350–351. Copyright © 1968 by the Canadian Psychological Association. Reprinted by permission.

response mode was spatial; subjects were given a response sheet, on which the letters *Y* and *N* were printed in an irregular pattern, and pointed to either a *Y* or an *N* in each row to indicate their responses. Brooks (1968) found that subjects took almost two and a half times longer when they responded by pointing than they did by responding verbally.

On a second task, subjects were asked to remember a sentence, such as "A bird in the hand is not in the bush," and, for each word, to indicate whether it was a concrete noun. In this example, the correct responses are "no, yes, no, no, yes, no, no, no, no, yes." As with the previous task, sometimes subjects responded verbally, and other times they pointed to *Y* or *N* on a response sheet. With this task, however, subjects were faster to respond by pointing than they were to respond verbally (although the difference in response times were not as great).

One explanation for these results goes as follows. The first task requires the formation of a visual image of an *F*. The visual image probably has at least some picture-like qualities (spatial or visual), so that a spatial or visually guided response (pointing) would be interfered with to a greater extent than a verbal response. In other words, the visual image is more disruptive of, and disrupted by, another spatial or visual type of task (pointing) than by a verbal kind of task (talking). The converse is also true: holding a sentence in memory (a verbal task) is easier to do with a concurrent visual/spatial task (such as pointing) than with another verbal task. Notice that pointing or talking do not differ in difficulty overall but vary in difficulty as a function of the task they are being performed with. Brooks's (1968) work supports the idea that images and words make use of different kinds of internal codes (as the dual-coding hypothesis suggests).

Brooks's (1968) task is not the only one that apparently requires people to form visual images. Here is another one. Answer the following question: Which is larger, a pineapple or a coconut? (Finke, 1989). To answer the question, you most likely constructed a visual image of a coconut next to a pineapple and "read" the answer from your image.

Moyer (1973) asked subjects similar questions, and found that people were faster to respond when the two objects (in his study, animals) differed greatly. This effect, called the *symbolic-distance effect,* works as follows. Other things being equal, you'd be faster to answer the question "Which is bigger, an whale or a roach?" than the question "Which is bigger, a hog or a cat?" Interestingly, the same pattern of response times is also obtained when people look at actual objects (Paivio, 1975). In other words, you'd be faster to answer the first question even if, instead of consulting visual images, you looked at the actual animals or at photographs of the animals. This result suggests that images seem to function, at least in some ways, like pictures. If people merely retrieved verbal information (for example, from a semantic network such as those described in Chapter 5), it would be difficult to explain this pattern of results.

Mental Rotation of Images

The studies above suggest that people create and use visual images to answer certain questions and perform certain tasks. They also suggest that the images created are in some ways picture-like (although this conclusion is energetically debated, as we'll see below). At the same time these findings were reported, other studies were described that showed that people could do more than simply create images; they could also, apparently, mentally transform them.

One of the most famous studies of this type was performed by Shepard and Metzler (1971). They showed subjects perspective line drawings of three-dimensional objects; Figure 7-3 presents examples. On each trial, sub-

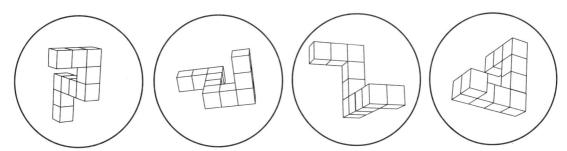

FIGURE 7-3.   Stimuli from the Shepard and Metzler (1971) study. SOURCE: From "Mental Rotation of Three-Dimensional Objects," by Roger N. Shepard and J. Metzler, 1971, *Science, 171,* 701. Copyright © 1971 by the American Association for the Advancement of Science. Reprinted by permission.

jects would see two drawings. In some cases, the two drawings depicted the same object but with one rotated by some degree. In the other cases, the drawings depicted mirror images reversals—in other words, the objects were similar but not identical. The mirror images were also sometimes rotated. The kinds of rotations used were either in the picture plane (that is, as if the drawing were rotated on the page) or in depth (that is, if the object were coming toward or away from the viewer).

Shepard and Metzler (1971) found that the amount of time it took subjects to decide if the two drawings depicted the same object or a mirror image reversal was directly proportional to the angle of rotation between the drawings. Figure 7-4 shows their results. This close correspondence between the angle of rotation of the two drawings and the subjects' reaction

Angle of Rotation (deg)

FIGURE 7-4.   Results from the Shepard and Metzler (1971) study. SOURCE: From "Mental Rotation of Three-Dimensional Objects," by Roger N. Shepard and J. Metzler, 1971, *Science, 171,* 701. Copyright © 1971 by the American Association for the Advancement of Science. Reprinted by permission.

The popular computer game Tetris involves rotating block designs in ways similar to the tasks presented to subjects in mental-rotation experiments.

times strongly suggests that the way subjects performed the task was by mentally rotating one of the drawings. Moreover, the time it took subjects to come to a decision was the same for rotations in the picture plane and in depth. This suggests that subjects were mentally rotating three-dimensional images, not just the two-dimensional drawings. Had subjects been rotating only the latter, their performance would have differed as a function of whether the rotation was in the picture plane or in depth.

Later studies by Cooper and Shepard (1973, 1975) showed that subjects also mentally rotated more recognizable stimuli, such as alphabetic letters or drawings of hands. In one study (Cooper and Shepard, 1973), subjects were sometimes given a drawing of the letter to be used on a trial, followed by a cue showing the orientation the test stimulus would be rotated to, before the test stimulus appeared. If these two cues were presented early enough (for example, 1,000 milliseconds before the

ADVANCE INFORMATION   TEST

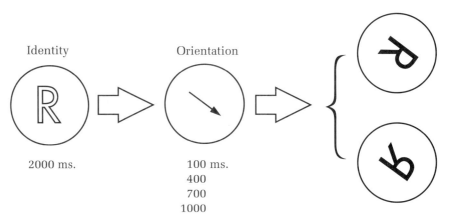

FIGURE 7-5.   Cooper and Shepard's (1973) experimental design. SOURCE: From "The Time Required to Prepare for a Rotated Stimulus, " by L. A. Cooper and R. N. Shepard, 1973, *Memory and Cognition, 1,* 247. Reprinted by permission of Psychonomic Society, Inc.

test stimulus appeared), then the subjects' performances were the same for all angles of rotation. Figure 7-5 depicts the experimental conditions of the experiment, and Figure 7-6 shows the results. Note the shape of the curves in Figure 7-6, which suggests that subjects were able mentally to rotate their images either clockwise or counterclockwise, depending on which direction leads to a lesser angle. These results differ from those of Shepard and Metzler (1971), presumably because alphanumeric characters have a known "upright" position, whereas the line drawings of Shepard and Metzler's did not. By the way, one reason for the "peaks" in reaction times at 180 degrees might be that subjects were uncertain about which direction to rotate the figure, and the uncertainty contributed to some hesitance.

Are subjects in these experiments mentally rotating the whole stimulus or are they looking only at certain parts? To answer this question, Lynn Cooper (1975) performed studies presenting subjects with irregular polygons, such as those shown in Figure 7-7. The polygons were formed by connecting a randomly scattered number of points, with more complex polygons resulting from a greater number of points. Subjects were first trained to discriminate between original and mirror image reflections of the polygons. Next, they were shown either the original polygons or the reflections at different angles of rotation and asked to determine whether the object depicted was the original or a reflection of the original.

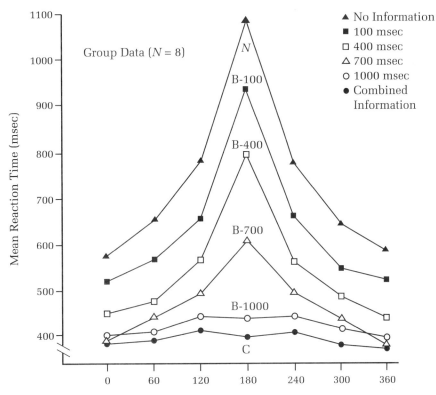

FIGURE 7-6.   Results from the Cooper and Shepard (1973) study. SOURCE: From "The Time Required to Prepare for a Rotated Stimulus," by L. A. Cooper and R. N. Shepard, 1973, *Memory and Cognition, 1,* 248. Reprinted by permission of Psychonomic Society, Inc.

Cooper (1975) found that the reaction times once again increased linearly with the angle of rotation, and that the rate of rotation was the same for all the polygons, regardless of their complexity. If subjects were attending only to parts of the polygons, then performance ought to have differed as a function of the polygon complexity. Instead, it appears that subjects mentally rotated entire polygons, treating the very simple polygons in exactly the same manner as they did the very complex ones.

In another study, Cooper (1976) showed that mental rotations, like physical rotations, are continuous in nature. Her demonstration worked as follows: she determined, for each subject, his or her rate of mental rotation. To do this, subjects were shown a polygon at a particular orientation. The polygon was removed, and subjects were asked to start mentally rotating it in a clockwise direction. As subjects were doing this, a test shape (the polygon, or its mirror image reflection) was presented in some orientation. If the test shape was presented at the ori-

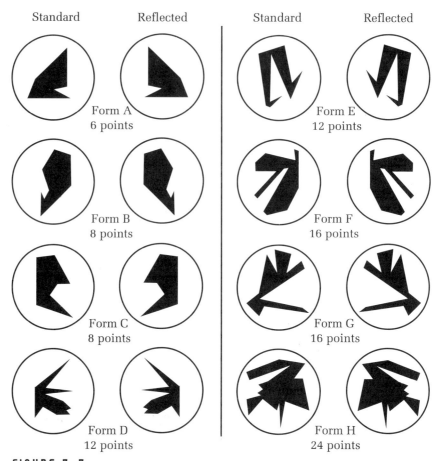

Standard   Reflected   Standard   Reflected

Form A
6 points

Form B
8 points

Form C
8 points

Form D
12 points

Form E
12 points

Form F
16 points

Form G
16 points

Form H
24 points

FIGURE 7-7.   Stimuli from the Cooper (1975) study. SOURCE: From "Mental Rotation of Random Two-Dimensional Shapes," by L. A. Cooper, 1975, *Cognitive Psychology, 7,* 23. Copyright © 1975 by Academic Press. Reprinted by permission.

entation corresponding to the orientation the subjects' visual images would be expected to be at, their reaction times were always fast. As the disparity between the actual orientation of the test shape and the expected orientation of the visual image grew, the reaction times to respond grew longer.

These results in particular suggest that mental rotation works like physical rotation. If you draw a shape on a piece of paper and slowly rotate the paper 180 degrees, the drawing will pass through intermediate orientations: 10 degrees, 20 degrees, and so on. Similarly, it appears from Cooper's (1976) work, rotating images pass through intermediate angles of orientation.

Scanning Images

The research reviewed so far suggests that people can construct and transform their visual images. This evidence seems also to suggest that images are in many ways like pictures: they contain visual information, and the kinds of transformations performed on them seem to correspond to similar transformations on pictures. Another series of studies, carried out by Stephen Kosslyn, investigated the spatial properties of images. The series typically required subjects to first form a visual image, and then to scan it, moving from one location to another in their image. The idea is that the time it takes subjects to scan reveals something about the ways spatial properties such as location and distance are represented in images (Finke, 1989).

In one study, Kosslyn (1973) had subjects study drawings of objects such as those shown in Figure 7-8. Notice that these drawings are elongated either vertically or horizontally, and each has three easily describable parts—each end, and the middle. After the initial learning phase, subjects were told to form an image of one of the drawings, and then to "look for" a particular part (for example, the petals of the flower). Some subjects were told to focus first on one part of the image (for example, the top or the left), and then to scan, looking for the designated part. Kosslyn's results showed that it took people longer to say whether the part they were looking for was in the drawing, the longer the distance from the designated end to the location of the part. So, for example, subjects told to image the flower, and to start scanning at the bottom, took longer to "find" the petals (at the top of the drawing) than they did to "find" the leaves (in the middle of the drawing). Presumably, this is because the visual image formed preserves many of the spatial characteristics of the drawings: Parts of the drawings that are separated in space will also be separated in the image.

FIGURE 7-8.   Stimuli from the Kosslyn (1973) study. SOURCE: From "Scanning Visual Images: Some Structural Implications," by S. M. Kosslyn, 1973, *Perception and Psychophysics, 14,* 91. Reprinted by permission of Psychonomic Society, Inc.

The results of the study were not entirely clear, however. Lea (1975), for instance, argued that perhaps the increase in reaction times came about *not* because of increased distance in the image but because of the number of items in the image that had to be scanned over. Notice in the flower example that starting from the bottom, one would scan over the roots and the leaves on the way to the petals, but only over the roots to get to the leaves. Lea reported results supporting this interpretation.

In reply, Kosslyn, Ball, and Reiser (1978) performed another series of studies of image scanning. In one, they first created a map of a fictional island, and had subjects memorize the locations of seven objects shown on the map, reproduced in Figure 7-9. Notice that the seven objects allow for the construction of 21 distinct paths, for example, from the tree to the lake, the tree to the hut, and so on. The paths vary in length, from 2 cm to 19 cm, and none contains any intervening objects.

Subjects were instructed to focus mentally on one object. A few seconds later, the experimenter named another object on the island, and subjects were then asked to imagine scanning to this second object, by imagining a small black speck moving across the map in a straight line. They were instructed to push a button when they "arrived" at the second object, and

FIGURE 7-9.   Stimuli from the Kosslyn, Ball, and Reiser (1978) study. SOURCE: From "Visual Images Preserve Metric Spatial Information: Evidence from Studies of Image Scanning," by S. M. Kosslyn, T. M. Ball, and B. J. Reiser, 1978, *Journal of Experimental Psychology: Human Perception and Performance, 4,* 51. Copyright © 1978 by the American Psychological Association. Reprinted by permission.

their reaction times were recorded. The reaction times to scan between objects were correlated with the distance between objects (Kosslyn et al., 1978), so that subjects took more time to scan between two distant objects than they did two nearby ones. This reinforced the idea that images preserve spatial relations. Related studies by Pinker (1980) show similar results when the stimulus is a three-dimensional array of objects (toys suspended inside an open box).

Kosslyn's work suggests that people's scanning of their visual images is in some ways similar to their scanning of actual pictures: The greater the distance between two parts, the longer it takes to scan between them. Images apparently depict at least some spatial information, and people can retrieve this information from their images. These conclusions have strengthened the metaphor of images as kinds of "mental pictures" (Kosslyn, 1980).

The Nature of Mental Imagery

All of the results reviewed so far suggest that images share some properties with pictures. People typically report their experience of images as looking at mental pictures, and the kinds of mental transformations done on images look to be very similar to transformations done on pictures. This leads directly to the question, just what are images? What kinds of properties do images have, and how are these like and unlike the properties that real pictures have?

Presumably, answers to such questions have implications for the way information is stored, retrieved, and used. Research on visual imagery, then, can potentially tell us a great deal about how information is mentally represented and organized. Our coverage of knowledge representation (Chapter 5) and concepts (Chapter 6) focused primarily on verbal information. Research on visual imagery suggests that there may be another kind of information that is stored and used.

Debate over the nature of visual images has been intense in cognitive psychology. We will review highlights of the debate here, taking a close look at the image-as-mental-picture metaphor. To organize this discussion, we will first review Ronald Finke's (1989) principles of visual imagery. Then we will examine critiques of this research and of the image–mental picture metaphor.

Principles of Visual Imagery

Finke's (1989) principles of visual imagery, taken together, are meant to describe the fundamental nature and properties of visual images. There are five principles, and each covers a different aspect or characteristic of imagery.

Implicit Encoding

Finke's first principle of visual imagery states:

> Mental imagery is instrumental in retrieving information about the physical properties of objects, or about physical relationships among objects, that was not explicitly encoded at any previous time. (Finke, 1989, p. 7)

This principle implies that images are places from which some information can be obtained, even if that information was never intentionally stored. Imagery can thus be used to answer questions that you probably don't have a directly stored answer for. The task at the beginning of this chapter—you were asked about the number of cabinet doors in the kitchen of your permanent residence—is a case in point. My guess is that if you are like most people, you've never had much reason to count kitchen-cabinet doors. So, this information was probably not represented directly in long-term memory. However, the information was *implicitly* stored, meaning that it was stored unintentionally along with other information that allows you to construct a visual image of your kitchen. To answer the question, then, all you need to do is to form the visual image, scan it, and count cabinets.

Brooks's (1968) task, in which subjects had to answer questions about an outlined capital *F* provides another illustration. Presumably, most people have never bothered to check whether each corner of an outlined capital *F* is at the top or bottom of the letter. Yet, people are able to perform this task, presumably because the required information has been implicitly encoded together with the information that allows for the formation of a visual image of an *F*.

Perceptual Equivalence

Finke's second principle of visual imagery has to do with the similarities between the construction of visual images and the perception of real objects and events. It states:

> Imagery is functionally equivalent to perception to the extent that similar mechanisms in the visual system are activated when objects or events are imagined as when the same objects or events are actually perceived. (Finke, 1989, p. 41)

In other words, many of the same kinds of internal processes used in mental visualization are used in visual perception as well.

An early study by Perky (1910) bears on this principle. Perky had subjects imagine they were looking at an object (for example, a tomato, a banana, an orange, a leaf) while staring at a blank screen. After subjects reported having formed the image, they were briefly distracted by one experimenter while another two experimenters operated an apparatus that projected faint pictures of the objects the subjects were imagining. Perky found that many of the subjects were unable to distinguish between their own images and the faint pictures. Presumably, this is because images share many similarities with faint pictures.

A related group of studies, including many more experimental controls, was reported by Martha Farah (1985). Subjects were asked to form an image of a certain letter, for example, an *H* or a *T*. Very soon after, they were sometimes presented with one of these letters, but at a low level of contrast, making the letters very difficult to see. Subjects who imagined a letter first were more accurate at detecting the actually presented letter than they were at detecting another letter. These results suggest that imagery can "prime" the visual pathway used in detecting an actual stimulus (Finke, 1989). Some authors even regard visual imagery as perceptual "anticipation": the visual system "getting ready" actually to see something (Neisser, 1976).

Farah (1988) also reports on the work of a number of investigators examining neuropsychological aspects of visual imagery. Some work has examined the pattern of blood flow in the brain. Cerebral blood flow is thought to provide a fairly precise measure of brain activity in a particular region. Roland and Friberg (1985) asked subjects to perform three cognitive tasks while their cerebral blood flows were being monitored. The tasks were mental arithmetic, memory scanning of an auditory stimulus, and visual imagery (visualizing a walk through a familiar neighborhood). The experimenters made sure that the tasks were approximately equal in difficulty. They found that each subject tested showed massive activation in the parts of the brain important for visual processing of information (mostly in the occipital lobe and other posterior regions) during the imagery task. During the other two tasks, however, there were no such increases in cerebral blood flow to those parts. Farah and her colleagues have replicated these results, using other neuropsychological measures, such as *event-related potentials* (ERPs) measuring electrical activity in the brain (Farah, Péronnet, Gonon, & Giard, 1988).

Spatial Equivalence

Finke's third principle of visual imagery has to do with the way spatial information, such as location, distance, and size, are represented in visual imagery. The principle states:

> The spatial arrangement of the elements of a mental image corresponds to the way objects or their parts are arranged on actual physical surfaces or in an actual physical space. (Finke, 1989, p. 61)

Much of the evidence for this principle comes from the scanning studies by Kosslyn and associates, reviewed above. The general finding is that the amount of time it takes subjects to scan from one element on a visual image to another corresponds to the distance between the elements in a physical representation. Thus, the spatial relationships among elements of a drawing or object (for example, relative locations, distances, sizes) all seem to be preserved in the visual image of the drawing or object.

Separating the visual characteristics from the spatial characteristics of an image (or object, drawing, and so on) is quite difficult. But an ingenious series of studies by Nancy Kerr (1983) has apparently succeeded at this task. Hers was a map-scanning study, very similar to that of Kosslyn, Ball, and Reiser (1978), described earlier. However, in this case, some of the subjects were congenitally blind, and learned the "map" by feeling objects (each of which had a distinct shape) placed on a flat surface. Once subjects had learned the locations, they heard the experimenter name a pair of objects, and were asked to focus mentally on one, and imagine moving a raised dot from that object to the second. Kerr found that both blind and sighted subjects took longer to scan, the greater the distance between objects. Results of this study echoed those of Kosslyn and associates, suggesting that visual imagery has spatial properties. The spatial properties are similar to visual representations but need not be visual, because congenitally blind subjects—without vision—apparently are able to make use of visual images.

Transformational Equivalence

Finke's fourth principle of visual imagery has to do with the way images are mentally transformed. It states:

> Imagined transformations and physical transformations exhibit corresponding dynamic characteristics and are governed by the same laws of motion. (Finke, 1989, p. 93)

The best evidence for this principle comes from the studies of mental rotation. Recall that the findings from those studies suggest that mental rotation apparently works in the same way that physical rotation does: it is continuous, with rotating objects moving through intermediate orientations on their way to their final orientation. The time it takes to perform mental rotation depends on how much rotation is to be done, as with physical rotation. And, as with physical rotation of an object, the whole object, and not just parts of it, are rotated. The principle of transformation equivalence extends beyond mental rotation, however, in asserting that other kinds of transformations will work with images in much the same way that they work with real objects.

Structural Equivalence

Finke's fifth principle of visual imagery has to do with the ways images are organized and assembled. It states:

> The structure of mental images corresponds to that of actual perceived objects, in the sense that the structure is coherent, well organized, and can be reorganized and reinterpreted. (Finke, 1989, p. 120)

Imagine that you need to draw a picture of an object or (if your artistic skills and inclinations are as poor as mine) that you need to look carefully at an object. How would you do this, and what properties of the object would influence the difficulty of your task? Generally speaking, the larger the object, the more time it would take to look it over or to draw it. Also, the more complicated the object—that is, the more different parts it has—the harder it would be (and the longer it would take) to look at it carefully or to draw it.

Apparently, the construction of visual images works the same way. Visual images are not formed all at once but in pieces that are assembled into a final rendition (Finke, 1989). Kosslyn, Reiser, Farah, and Fliegel (1983) studied image generation as it relates to the complexity of the object to be imagined. Subjects were asked to form images of pictures that differed in amount of detail, such as those in Figure 7-10(a). It took subjects about one and a third times as long to form an image of the detailed pictures as it did other subjects to form images of outline drawings. In a related study, the authors used geometric forms such as those shown in Figure 7-10(b) as stimuli, all of which allowed for different descriptions. For instance, Figure 7-10(b) can be described either as "five squares in the shape of a cross" or as "two overlapping rectangles." Subjects first read a description, then saw the corresponding figure, then covered it up and formed a visual image of the figure. Kosslyn and associates showed that subjects given the first description took longer to form the image than did subjects given the second description, even though the physical pattern was the same. Notice, by the way, that it would probably be faster to draw or look over Figure 7-10(b) if you conceived of it as two rectangles than as five squares. Apparently, with images, the greater the complexity of the *conceived* structure of the object, the longer it takes to assemble an image of it.

Critiques of Mental-Imagery Research and Theory

In the introduction to this chapter, I noted that the study of imagery has been controversial in psychology, and it is time now to examine the controversy. Although almost every imagery study has been subject to some debate (Finke, 1989, provides several examples), we will here focus on three general and interrelated themes. The first concerns criticism of imagery research. In particular, the criticism is that the experiments themselves give enough "hints," either explicitly or implicitly, for subjects to rely on their beliefs and knowledge rather than relying strictly on visual imagery to perform. A second critique questions the metaphor between images and pictures. A third kind of criticism is more theoretical in nature, questioning the need to talk about imagery as a distinct kind of internal code. We will consider each critique in turn.

Tacit Knowledge and Demand Characteristics

Pylyshyn (1981) argues that the results from many imagery studies reflect subjects' underlying and implicit, tacit knowledge and beliefs about the task rather than their construction and manipulation of visual images. He pays special attention to image-scanning experiments. Subjects' scanning time is proportional to distance scanned, Pylyshyn asserts, because subjects know that the amount of time it takes to physically scan between two

(A)

(B)

FIGURE 7-10.   Stimuli from the Kosslyn, Reiser, Farah, and Fliegel (1983) study. SOURCE: From "Generating Visual Images: Units and Relations," by S. M. Kosslyn, B. J. Reiser, M. J. Farah, and S. L. Fliegel, 1983, *Journal of Experimental Psychology: General, 112,* 280–287. Copyright © 1978 by the American Psychological Association. Reprinted by permission.

points in a visual display depends on distance, *and* because they expect the experiment demands this kind of performance.

Finke (1989) explains how this knowledge and expectation could distort results. Imagine that you want to move an object (say, your coffee cup) from one location (the right side of your desk) to another (the left side of your desk). You could (à la movie scenes in western bars) try to slide the cup across the desk, but it would probably be safer to pick up your cup and place it in the new location. Suppose, however, you believed or expected that the amount of time it took to move the coffee cup to the new location should depend on the total distance from the old to the new location. You could adjust your time by pausing and holding the cup over the new location for some amount of time before you placed it down on the desk. Then your reaction time in moving the cup would be proportional to the distance the cup moved, although the time is depending arbitrarily on the time you choose to pause.

Pylyshyn's (1981) argument is that people may be "mentally pausing" in image-scanning experiments because of their beliefs and expectations about what the experimenters want them to do. Tasks that are affected by subjects' beliefs and expectations are termed by Pylyshyn to be *cognitively penetrable.* Some tasks make it obvious to subjects how they ought to perform; the instructions, the tasks themselves, or something else about the situation cues the subject how to behave. Such a task is said to have **demand characteristics** (Orne, 1962). In other words, the task "demands" somehow that the subject behave in a certain way. Typically, subjects in psychology experiments try to please, and may behave artificially, just to perform in ways they believe will satisfy the experimenter.

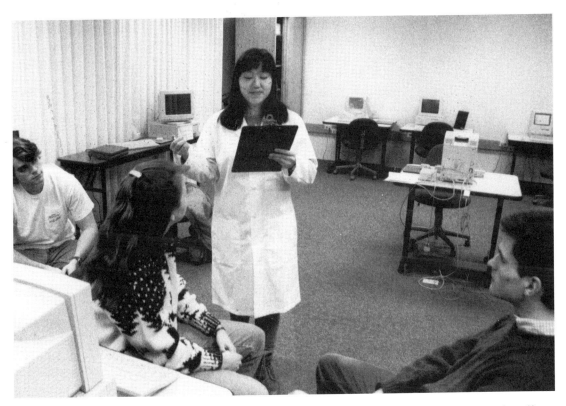

Research on visual images has been shown to be especially sensitive to the effects of experimenter expectations.

Moreover, sometimes experimenters unconsciously give subtle cues to subjects. Intons-Peterson (1983) has argued that these **experimenter expectations** have influenced at least some of the investigations of imagery. In various studies, she had undergraduate experimenters conduct a number of imagery studies. Some of the experimenters were led to believe the results would turn out one way; the other experimenters were led to believe the opposite. In all of the studies, subjects performed as experimenters expected them to.

In one study, Intons-Peterson (1983) had four undergraduate experimenters, all known "for their intelligence, dependability, good judgment, and maturity" (p. 396). None was familiar with the imagery literature. Each experimenter was assigned to run a total of 18 subjects in three different conditions in a mental rotation study. Some subjects were "primed" by either seeing or imagining a stimulus before each trial; subjects in a control condition received no primes. Two of the four experimenters were told to expect that imaginal primes (that is, primes that subjects were asked to imagine) would be more effective than perceptual primes (that is, primes that were actually presented to subjects). The other two experimenters were told the opposite: perceptual primes would be more effective than imaginal primes. Although all stimuli were presented by microcomputer, and although experimenters were not in the same room with the subjects, except initially when they read instructions, the results mirrored the experimenters' beliefs. Those subjects run by experimenters who believed imaginal primes would be more effective than perceptual primes produced data to support the belief; subjects run by the other experimenters produced data that went in the opposite direction.

Intons-Peterson (1983) found similar results in imaginal-scanning experiments. She concluded that subjects in imagery experiments were sensitive to subtle, unintentional cues given by experimenters, including slight differences in intonation or pauses when reading instructions. Intons-Peterson further argued that imagery research, by virtue of the subjective nature of the phenomenon, may be especially vulnerable to demand characteristics and experimenter expectations. Although she does *not* assert that results from all visual-imagery experiments are the result of experimenter effects and demand characteristics, she does warn that special care must be taken by visual-imagery researchers to minimize these effects.

Neuropsychological work by Farah (1985) is particularly effective in addressing the issues of demand characteristics. Farah argues that the data from her laboratory, showing that visual imagery involves activation of the same parts of the brain used in vision, are not susceptible to a demand-characteristics explanation, unless certain questionable assumptions are made:

> A tacit knowledge account of the electrophysiological and blood flow data, implicating the use of cortical visual areas during visual imagery activity, would need to include the following two assumptions: (a) that subjects know what parts of their brains are normally active during vision and (b) that subjects can voluntarily alter their brain electrical activity, or modulate

or increase regional blood flow to specific areas of their brains. (Farah, 1985, p. 314)

Thus, at least some data from visual-imagery experiments exist that seem to escape the demand-characteristics or experimenter-expectancies type of criticism.

The Picture Metaphor

Much of the discussion so far has suggested an analogy between pictures and images. Some psychologists speak casually of visual images as "mental pictures." The question is, how far does the analogy go? As Pylyshyn (1973) pointed out, there are several ways in which pictures and images differ. Perhaps the most important difference is this: you can physically look at a picture without first knowing what it's a picture of (say, if someone word-lessly hands you a photograph, and you ask, "What's this?"), but it is impossible to "look" at an image unless you first know what it is. After all, images are internal constructions that are formed with some intention in mind. You don't just spontaneously create random images; rather, you form images of particular things.

Second, pictures and images are disrupted, and disruptable, in different ways. You can cut a photograph in half, with the result that arbitrary parts of the objects depicted disappear. Images are organized more meaningfully, and when they fade, it is only the meaningful parts that disappear (Finke, 1989).

Last, images seem to be more easily distorted by the viewer's interpretations than are pictures or photographs. Remember Bartlett's work on story recall? (See Chapter 4 if you need to review.) We saw how people's memory for stories changed over time, and often depended on their initial or subsequent interpretations. So it is with images. Carmichael, Hogan, and Walter (1932) presented to subjects patterns such as those in Figure 7-11 with one of two labels (different subjects were given different labels). Subjects' later reproductions of the patterns (presumably based on imagery) were distorted in accordance with the label initially provided, as shown in the figure. Similarly, Nickerson and Adams (1979) have shown that people make many errors when trying to reproduce their images of familiar objects. Try drawing a picture of a penny without looking at one, and then compare it to a real penny. Is Lincoln facing the right way? Is the right motto in the right place? How about the date? Notice in this case that your image probably has far less information in it than would a clear picture or photograph of a penny.

What's the significance of finding differences between images and pictures? Visual images are thought to be one means of internal coding and representation of information. Although many cognitive psychologists believe in the existence of visual imagery as a distinct mental code, and although they believe that the code has many visual and/or spatial qualities, the evidence to date suggests that the "visual image = picture" analogy works only roughly.

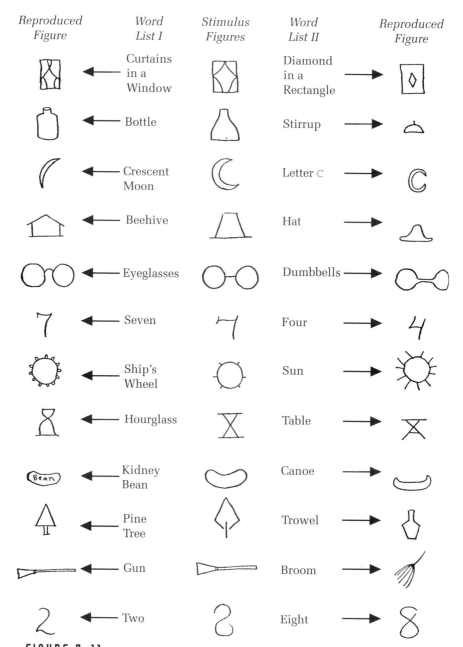

FIGURE 7-11.   Materials from the Carmichael, Hogan, and Walter (1932) study.
SOURCE: From "An Experimental Study of the Effect of Language on the Reproduction of Visually Perceived Form," by L. Carmichael, H. P. Hogan, and A. A. Walter, 1932, *Journal of Experimental Psychology, 15,* 80.

Propositional Theory

A broader criticism of work on imagery is a theoretical one, and is aimed at the very premise behind the field. Proponents of *propositional theory* reject the idea that images serve as a distinct mental code for representing information. Instead, propositional theorists believe that there is a single code, neither visual nor verbal but propositional in nature (Anderson & Bower, 1973), that is used to store and mentally represent all information. As we saw in Chapter 5, propositions are a means of specifying relationships between different concepts. For example, the idea that New York is a city located to the west of Boston might be represented by the following propositions: CITY (New York); WEST-OF (Boston, New York). Propositions can be linked together in networks, with two very related ideas joined by virtue of sharing a number of propositions.

Pylyshyn (1973) asserted that propositional theory could explain the results of imagery experiments. His idea was that all information is mentally represented and stored by propositions. Subjects in visual-imagery experiments might *look* as though they are consulting or manipulating internal visual representations, but they are actually using internal propositional representations, the same kind of representations that underlie their processing of verbal material, such as sentences or stories.

Two studies by Kosslyn (1976) attempted to test this assertion. Kosslyn first tested the *association strength* between animals and their physical attributes. For instance, for most people, "claws" are more strongly associated with "cat" than is "head," although cats, of course, have both. Kosslyn found that when people did *not* use imagery, they were faster to verify that cats had claws (high association value, small visual part of a cat) than that cats had heads (low association value, large visual part of a cat). Propositional theory would predict that the higher the association value, the more propositions relating the two items, and thus the faster the verification time (Finke, 1989). However, when subjects reported having used imagery to do the task, their reaction times went in the opposite direction. Here, they were faster to verify visually larger parts with low association values than visually smaller parts with higher association values. Apparently, using imagery results in performance that propositional theory does not predict.

Summary

Despite the theoretical possibility that only one propositional code is used to perform all of the tasks described above, many cognitive psychologists are persuaded by the evidence of the existence of some sort of a distinct visual-spatial code. We have reviewed evidence in this chapter suggesting that this code can aid memory, and is in fact used in a number of mnemonic techniques.

Other work on visual imagery has suggested that images function in some ways like internal pictures, undergoing certain kinds of mental operations and transformations. These mental operations and transformations appear to function in ways similar to those of corresponding physical operations and transformations. However, other researchers and theoreticians have pointed out limitations in the image-as-picture metaphor. There are a number of ways in which images work differently than pictures do. Some investigators such as Farah (1988), have therefore concluded that "imagery is not *visual* in the sense of necessarily representing information acquired through visual sensory channels. Rather, it is visual in the sense of using some of the same neural representational machinery as vision" (p. 315).

Resolving the imagery debate will be difficult, if not impossible. Images are necessarily a private mental experience. However, for this reason alone, many researchers in cognitive psychology and other allied cognitive disciplines (neurology, artificial intelligence, philosophy, linguistics) consider the empirical investigations of imagery a major victory in the larger task of understanding how cognition, a collection of private mental experiences, functions.

Recommended Readings

Paivio's (1971) book outlines the early evidence for the dual-coding hypothesis. An edited volume by Yuille (1983) surveys more recent work in that tradition. Yates (1966) provides an overview of different mnemonic techniques, and Luria (1968) describes the abilities of S, a person with remarkable memorial abilities, known as a *mnemonist*. Herrmann (1992) presents some of the latest research on different mnemonics.

Many of the classic papers on imagery by Shepard and Cooper are reprinted in a volume they co-edited (1982). Kosslyn's work is summarized in his (1980) volume. An excellent and up-to-date review of the imagery literature is contained in Finke's (1989) very readable volume.

Critiques of imagery research and theory come from Pylyshyn (1973, 1979a, 1979b, 1981), Banks (1981), and Intons-Peterson (1983). Block's edited volume (1981) contains articles from psychologists and other cognitive scientists debating these issues. Anderson's (1978) paper also contributes to the debate, and has elicited replies from Hayes-Roth (1979) and Pylyshyn (1979b).

Recent studies by Intons-Peterson and Roskos-Ewoldsen (1989); Kosslyn, Cave, Provost, and von Gierke (1988); and Roth and Kosslyn (1988) examine how people construct visual images. Farah, Hammond, Levine, and Calvanio (1988) report a fascinating case study of the imagery abilities of a brain-damaged patient who shows severe impairment in visual recognition. Farah's (1985) review article describes visual-imagery research using neuropsychological methods, and Tippett (1992) presents a very recent review of this literature.

REVIEW QUESTIONS

1. Describe four mnemonics, two that rely on visual imagery and two that don't, and contrast the underlying mechanisms thought to account for their effectiveness.

2. Describe and contrast the dual-coding hypothesis and the relational-organizational hypothesis, and describe experimental means of distinguishing between them.

3. What interpretations have cognitive psychologists performing mental rotation studies (for example, Shepard, Metzler, Cooper) drawn from their findings? In what ways are such interpretations consistent with those drawn by Kosslyn from his image-scanning experiments?

4. Describe and discuss Finke's five principles of imagery.

5. Pylyshyn asserts that many of the results from visual-imagery experiments are attributable to tacit knowledge and demand characteristics. Describe and critique his arguments.

6. What are the objections Intons-Peterson raises to some of the findings from visual-imagery experiments? In your view, how strong are such objections? Defend your view.

7. In what ways are visual images like pictures? In what ways are they different?

PART **IV**

The Use and Manipulation of Information

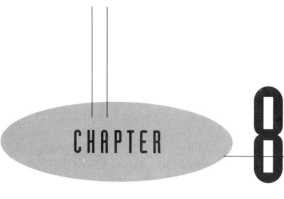

CHAPTER 8

Language

Right now, as you read this sentence, you are engaged in the process of language comprehension. As I write this sentence, I am engaged in language production. Probably, neither of us finds our behavior remarkable.

We comprehend and produce language all day long—when we read or speak, listen to dialogue or conversations, struggle to write a term paper (or a textbook chapter), or even when we compose the most mundane pieces of prose ("Gone to the library. Meet me at 5 at the car."). In short, we take our language abilities for granted.

Evidence is abundant, however, that language use and abilities are not so straightforward. Researchers studying artificial intelligence have found it extremely difficult to build computer systems that can understand language (spoken or written) as easily as a four-year-old child can. Parents of toddlers can attest that although language acquisition is rapid, it takes several years for a person to become proficient. Many high school and college students come to appreciate fully the complexities of language only when they try to master a second one.

Language use is intimately connected to cognition. Much of the information we receive comes from spoken or written language, and we use language to ask questions, explain conclusions, clarify problems, and so on. Like perception or memory, then, language seems to be a crucial cognitive ability so easily used that we typically overlook its complexity.

In this chapter, we will first look at the structural elements of a language—the pieces or aspects that go into the elaborated, rule-governed, and creative communication systems that we recognize as different human languages. We will then examine models of language comprehension and production—how we understand and create spoken discourse and written material. Finally, we will consider the relationship between language and other cognitive processes. In particular, we will evaluate assertions that the language one speaks shapes the ways in which one thinks.

It is important to define language precisely and, in particular, to distinguish between *language* and *communication.* Although language is often used as a communication system, there are other communications systems that do not form true languages. Many bees, for example, use elaborate dances to tell other bees about a newfound source of food. Birds have songs and calls to broadcast territorial boundaries or to attract mates (Demers, 1988). How do these systems of communication differ from language? To decide, we must first have a definition of what a language is.

A natural language (as opposed to an artificial language, such as a computer language) has two necessary characteristics: it is *regular* (governed by a system of rules, called a **grammar**) and it is *productive,* meaning that infinite combinations of things can be expressed in it. Other characteristics of human languages include *arbitrariness* (the lack of a necessary resemblance between a word or sentence and what it refers to), *discreteness* (the system can be subdivided into recognizable parts, for example, sentences into words, words into sounds), and some others (see Demers, 1988, or Hockett, 1960).

Using these criteria, we can conclude that bees do not have a language because the physical motions in the dance carry information about the honey source (lack of arbitrariness). Further, the dances are restricted to communicating about food sources, thus failing on the grounds of productivity. Bird songs and calls also cannot be classified as a language, primarily

Although these animals are clearly commmunicating, there is little evidence that their communication system forms a true language.

on the grounds of productivity because the songs and calls communicate only about certain topics (mostly mates, predators, and territories; Demers, 1988). These illustrations help to clarify the relationship between language and communication systems: all human languages are communication systems, but not all communication systems share the necessary criteria to be classified as natural languages.

In recent work, investigators have attempted to teach various language and communication systems to chimpanzees (Gardner & Gardner, 1971; Premack, 1976; Terrace, 1979; Savage-Rumbaugh, McDonald, Sevcik, Hopkins, & Rubert, 1986). Some investigators have taught their subjects to use sign language; others have relied on systems of plastic tokens or geometric symbols. Most agree that chimpanzees can be taught to use symbols or signs to make requests or label objects (for example, "Kanzi chase Sue," "Me more eat," or "Orange juice"). A recent study by Sue Savage-Rumbaugh and her collaborators (1986) suggests that pygmy chimpanzees can even learn to show spontaneous use of symbols to communicate—learning to use symbols simply by watching others (people or chimpanzees) use them, and learning to understand spoken English words.

Despite these impressive findings, most researchers in this field would agree that there are substantial differences in the language that even the brightest and most linguistically sophisticated chimpanzees have acquired to date and the language of most three-year-old children. Most would agree, too, that although chimpanzees can acquire many vocabulary items and some rudimentary language structure, their communication system still falls far short of any known human language. To explain why, we will need to review the structure of human language in detail.

The Structure of Language

As with any complex ability, language comprises a number of systems working together. We will illustrate some of the ways in which the systems work together through the example of conversation.

When you have a conversation, you first have to listen to and perceive the sounds directed at you by the speaker. Different languages have different sounds (called **phonemes**). The ways in which phonemes can be combined in any given language constitutes the study of **phonology.** Next, you have to put the sounds together in some coherent way, identifying the meaningful units of language, an aspect known as *morphology.* Word endings, prefixes, tense markers, and the like are critical parts of each sentence. Some of the **morphemes** (smallest meaningful units of language) are words, and you also need to identify these and to determine the role each word plays in a sentence. To do this, you need to determine the **syntax,** or structure, of each sentence. We will come back to the topic of sentence structure very shortly.

A syntactically correct sentence does not by itself make for a good conversation. The sentence must also mean something to the listener. **Semantics** is the branch of linguistics and psycholinguistics devoted to the study of meaning. Finally, there needs to be some flow or give-and-take in the conversation for it to work. Listeners must pay attention and make certain assumptions, and speakers must craft their contributions in ways that will make the listener's job feasible. This aspect of language, **pragmatics,** will conclude our discussion of the structure of language. Keep in mind throughout that although the various aspects of language will be discussed separately, they must work together in actual conversation.

We will repeatedly encounter the idea of different linguistic rules (for example, phonological rules, syntactic rules) in this section. These rules make up the *grammar* of the language and, taken together, define the way a language works. It is important that linguists and psychologists use the term *grammar,* in a very restricted sense here, meaning "the set of rules for a language." In particular, *grammatical* in this context has nothing to do with the "rules" of "good English" such as "Don't use *ain't*" or "Don't split infinitives." To a linguist or a psycholinguist, the sentence "I ain't going to happily do it" is perfectly meaningful and "legal" (that is, it follows the "rules" of English that native speakers observe)—and therefore grammatical. (You understand it perfectly well, right?) Grammar here refers not to polite ways of speaking but to ways of speaking that form intelligible phrases or utterances recognizable as examples of language a native speaker of the language might produce.

Linguists and psychologists distinguish between people's explicit and implicit knowledge of linguistic rules. It is doubtful, for instance, that any of us could state with precision or accuracy just what the rules for English syntax are. (If it were easy, many linguists would be out of a job!) Still, most of us can easily and almost immediately detect violations of the rules—for example, syntactically ill-formed sentences, such as "Ran the dog street down cat after yellow the very." Moreover, not only would we recognize the example as ungrammatical, we would never produce gross violations like it (although we frequently produce sentences with minor grammatical violations). Our knowledge of the rules is therefore not explicit (we cannot articulate what all the rules are, nor are we consciously aware of all of them) but implicit (whatever the rules are, we somehow follow them). We can often articulate the so-called *prescriptive* rules (such as "Don't say *ain't*"), which tell us how we *should* talk or write, even though we may violate them (for instance, whenever we actually say *ain't*). In contrast, we find it hard to articulate the descriptive rules of English, which characterize which sentences are legal and which are not.

Linguists and psychologists also distinguish linguistic **competence** from linguistic **performance.** *Competence* refers to the underlying linguistic knowledge that allows people to produce and comprehend their language. Competence is not always fully evident in actual use or performance of language. Lapses of attention or memory, nervousness or tiredness, environmental changes, shifts in interest, and random error can all interfere with our use of language, causing us to produce ungrammatical sentences or to comprehend a sentence incorrectly. Linguistic performance would reflect linguistic competence only under completely ideal conditions (Chomsky, 1965). In real life, such ideal conditions are never achieved. So, if you over-hear an ungrammatical utterance, it is probably not that the speaker's linguistic knowledge (competence) is faulty (especially if she is speaking in her native language) but, rather, that various other factors and pressures in her life at the time she spoke (performance) caused the error or errors.

Phonology

To me, French sounds musical and German sounds harsh. No doubt, you too would describe various languages with various adjectives. Part of what distinguishes languages are their idiosyncratic sounds. Here, we will consider the sounds of language (in our case, English), and how they are combined. We will draw upon findings from two disciplines: **phonetics,** the study of speech sounds and how they are produced, and *phonology,* the study of the systematic ways in which speech sounds are combined and altered in language.

The English language has about 41 phonetic segments (sometimes called phones). Although a language may have a large number of phones, only certain ones are "meaningful" to it. Linguists use the term *phoneme* to refer to the smallest unit of sound that makes a meaningful difference in a given language. That means that if one phoneme in a word is exchanged for another, the word itself is changed. So, the word *duck* becomes *tuck* if the phoneme \d\ is replaced with the phoneme \t\. In English, we make a distinction between the \l\ and the \r\ sound; other languages, such as the Cantonese dialect of Chinese, do not. Some of the dialect jokes about a Chinese speaker's saying "flied lice" instead of "fried rice" are based on the fact that a native speaker of Cantonese dialect simply wouldn't hear the differences (Fromkin & Rodman, 1974). Of course, there are sound distinctions that other languages make that English doesn't, and native English speakers learning those languages can make errors that are just as ridiculed by the native speakers.

Linguists and phoneticians make a distinction between consonants and vowels. Vowels work without obstructing the airflow, simply depending on the shape and position of the tongue and lips (Halle, 1990). Try articulating vowel sounds, and observe how your mouth changes configurations as you do.

Consonants are more complicated. In general, they are phonemes made by closing, or at least almost closing, part of the mouth. They differ first in what linguists call "place of articulation," meaning where the obstruction of the airflow occurs. For example, the \b\ and \p\ sounds are made by closing the lips, and the \s\ and \z\ sounds are made by placing the tongue against the hard palate of the roof of the mouth, just behind the ridge of gums. Consonants differ also in "manner of articulation," the mechanics of how the airflow is obstructed. The \m\ sound, for example, is made by closing the mouth while opening the nasal cavity; the \f\ sound is made through an obstruction of the airflow, producing a hissing sound. A third distinction between groups of consonants is known as *voicing*. Compare the \s\ in the syllable "sa" with the \z\ in "za." The \s\ does not require the vocal cords to be vibrated as the \z\ does; therefore, the \z\ is said to be voiced and the \s\, unvoiced.

Features of phonemes, such as those just reviewed, are involved in certain *phonological rules* that govern the ways in which phonemes can be combined. For example, if two "true" consonants (that is, all of the consonants except \h\, \w\, or \y\, plus certain other sounds, such as the \th\ in "thy," the \th\ in "thigh," the \ch\ in "chip") are at the beginning of an English word, then the first must be an \s\ (Clark & Clark, 1977). This rule prevents word strings such as "dtop" or "mkeech" from being "legal" words in our language (although they might be so in other languages), whereas *stop* and *speech* are. These phonological rules also explain how to pronounce new words, and how to pronounce prefixes and suffixes to words, such as in plural or past tense endings. To illustrate, the way to form a plural for an English word depends on the phoneme the singular form of the word ends with. From work in phonetics, we can state the following rule (after Halle, 1990):

The Plural Ending of a Word Is:	If the Word Ends With:	Examples:
\z\	\s z c j s z\	places, porches, cabbages
\s\	\p t k f\	lips, lists, telegraphs
\z\	anything else	clubs, herds, phonemes

Different languages have different phonological rules, hence there are two answers to the question Why do different languages sound different? One answer: because they contain different sounds (phonemes). A second answer: because they have different rules for combining those sounds (phonology).

Syntax

Syntax refers to the arrangement of words within sentences or, more broadly, to the *structure* of sentences, their parts and the way the parts are put together. Syntactic rules, similar to phonological rules, govern the ways in which different words or larger phrases can be combined to form "legal" sentences in the language. Thus, sentences such as "The book fell off the table" are clearly acceptable to English speakers, and word strings such as "Chair the on sits man" are not. The aim of syntactic rules is twofold: They should be able to describe every "legal" sentence, and should never be able to describe an "illegal" sentence (Chomsky, 1957).

What does it mean to say that sentences have structure? Consider the sentence

(1)   The poodle will chase the red ball.

If you were to try to divide the words of this sentence into groups (linguists call these *constituents*), you might proceed as follows. Certainly the word "poodle" goes with the word "The." Similarly, "red" appears to modify "ball," and "the" forms another constituent with "red ball." "Chase" could also form a constituent with "the red ball," and "will" seems to modify this larger grouping. Notice that there are various levels of groupings or constituents, as depicted in Figure 8-1(a). This diagram is called a *tree diagram*, and the small black circles, called *nodes*, depict the various constitutents of

(A)

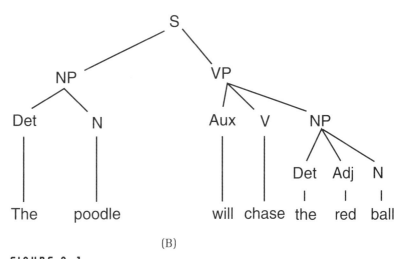

(B)

FIGURE 8-1.   Tree diagrams of Sentence 1

the sentence. Notice also that each word is a constituent by itself but that there are higher-level constituents as well, made out of different word groupings. So, the word "ball" is a member of four constituents: [ball]; [the red ball]; [chase the red ball]; and [The poodle will chase the red ball].

Figure 8-1(b) shows a similar diagram of the sentence, but here labels that tell us the type, or category, of each constituent have replaced the black dots. At the very bottom level in the tree, you'll see labels for familiar terms; V for verb, N for noun, ADJ for adjective, and so forth. The labels give us some idea of the role each word plays in the sentence and allow us to see that generally speaking, if we replace a noun with another noun, we will still have a syntactically grammatical sentence. So, substituting "shoe" for "ball" gives us "The poodle will chase the red shoe." Higher up in the tree, other labels categorize the larger constituents. Thus, the constituents "The poodle," and "the red ball" are both noun phrases. The labeling is meant to capture our intuition that these constituents are similar to other constituents, such as "The angry fireman," "Her grandfather's birthday," or "My first tooth." Figure 8-1(b) is called a *labeled tree diagram,* and it depicts what is called the *categorical constituent structure* of the sentence.

Notice that one NP can be substituted for another in a sentence, yielding a sentence that is semantically anomalous (its meaning, if any, is hard to determine) but syntactically grammatical. So, we could substitute the NP "my first tooth" for "poodle" in the sentence (1) and get "My first tooth chased the red ball," an odd but certainly "legal" sentence.

What's the point of such diagrams? For one thing, they help to explain why certain kinds of changes can be made in a sentence and others can't. One illustration comes from a change called "preposing," taking a certain part of a sentence and moving it to the front, usually for emphasis (Radford, 1988). In the following examples, the italicized material has been preposed:

(2)   *My naughty dog,* I'm mad at.
(3)   *That inflated price,* I will not pay.
(4)   *Up the mountain,* the hikers climbed furiously.

Preposing works (results in a grammatical or legal sentence) only when certain kinds of whole phrases or constituents are moved to the front. Thus, it isn't legal to say, "Naughty dog, I'm mad at my," "Price, I will not pay the inflated"; or "Mountain, the hikers climbed furiously up the." Tree diagrams such as the ones in Figure 8-1 provide answers to which parts of the sentence form constituents and are therefore candidates for preposing.

It is interesting that this kind of analysis of sentences explains an apparent paradox: the following four sentences are all "legal":

(5)   Susan rang up Jodie.
(6)   Martha stood up her blind date.
(7)   Adrian looked up the number.

(8)   Aristophanes ran up the mountain.

Although preposing the phrase "up the mountain" can result in a legal sentence,

(8a)   Up the mountain, Aristophanes ran.

none of the other sentences can undergo preposing in this way, as the illegal sentences (marked with asterisks) below show:

(5a)   *Up Jodie, Susan rang.
(6a)   *Up her blind date, Martha stood.
(7a)   *Up the number, Adrian looked.

Figure 8-2 provides tree diagrams of sentences 5 through 8, and shows that in sentences 5 through 7, the word "up" is part of the constituent involving the verb, and hence has to "stay with" the verb in the sentence. However, in sentence 8, the word "up" is a part of the constituent "Up the mountain," so it is perfectly acceptable to prepose it, as long as the entire constituent gets moved.

How can we concisely summarize this discussion of what can and can't be legally preposed? Linguists do so by formulating constraints on syntactic rules like this: only constituents labeled as being whole phrases (for example, nodes marked as NP or VP) can undergo movement from one position in a sentence to another. Such rules describe the ways in which parts of sentences are formed and work together.

A variety of syntactic rules are proposed by various linguists, as well as a variety of *kinds* of syntactic rules. For example, Chomsky (1965) proposed one set of rules, called *phrase-structure rules,* that functioned to generate the structures depicted in tree diagrams such as Figures 8-1 and 8-2. These rules, sometimes called "rewrite rules," describe the ways in which certain symbols can be rewritten as other symbols. The rule S→NP VP is a phrase-structure rule that says that a symbol S (which stands for "sentence") consists of different constituents, and can be rewritten as the symbol NP (the symbol for the constituent "noun phrase") followed by the symbol VP (the symbol for the constituent "verb phrase"). The point is that phrase-structure rules allow certain symbols to be rewritten as other symbols. To rewrite a symbol with an actual word in the English language (for example, N→poodle) requires a different type of syntactic rule, a *lexical-insertion rule,* which allows for the insertion of words (linguists call these "lexical items") into the structures generated by the phrase-structure rules.

Another type of syntactic rule is a *transformational rule.* Transformational rules turn structures such as those depicted in tree diagrams into other structures. Preposing phrasal constituents, for example, might be allowed through a transformational rule.

Even a brief explanation of these or other syntactic rules, or other proposals for what the rules could be would take us far afield (interested readers are referred to an introductory linguistics course, or to Cowper [1992]). The point here is to show that just as the sounds of a language are

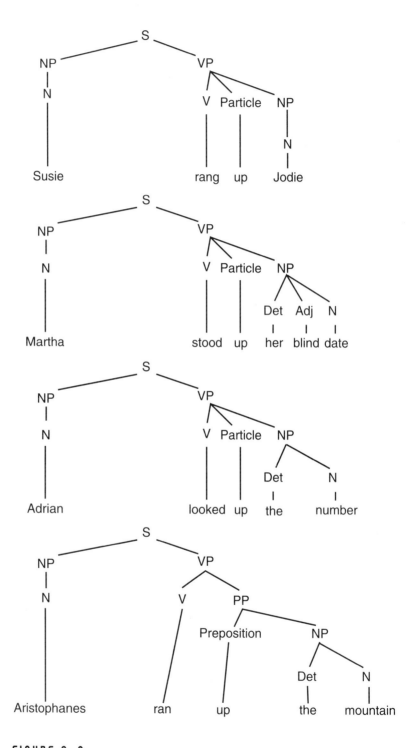

FIGURE 8-2. Tree diagrams of sentences 5 through 8

organized and rule-governed in the way that they are combined, so too are phrases and sentences. Again, rules of syntax, like rules of phonology, are probably not rules that you are consciously aware of. However, the evidence accumulated by linguists and psycholinguists strongly suggests that you have some access to these rules because your language behavior indicates a great deal of compliance with them, and your judgments of grammaticality (under reasonable conditions) are remarkably consistent.

Semantics

Semantics, the study of meaning, also plays an important role in our language use. After all, the sounds we produce are meant to communicate ideas, and for communication to take place, the listener (or audience) must somehow receive the speaker's (or sender's) meaning. The task of creating a complete theory of meaning is daunting and currently unfinished.

Theories of meaning have to explain several things, at a minimum (Bierwisch, 1970):

- Anomaly (Why one can't really say things like "Coffee ice cream can take dictation.")
- Self-contradiction (Why it is contradictory to say, "My dog is not an animal.")
- Ambiguity (Why it isn't clear where I intend to go in "I need to go to the bank"—to a financial institution or to the side of a river.)
- Synonymy (Why does "The rabbit is not old enough" mean the same thing as "The rabbit is too young"?)
- Entailment (Why does "Pat is my uncle" mean that Pat is male?)

Such theories should also explain how we use word meanings to process whole sentences and discourses. Much of cognitive psychologists' interest in semantics has to do with how knowledge is organized and stored, and theories of how people form concepts and categorize things accordingly, topics we discussed in Chapters 5 and 6, respectively.

Let's examine, with the following example, how semantics enters into our understanding of a sentence. Consider "Sara exchanged a dress for a suit." Generally, we interpret this to mean that Sara brought her dress somewhere (most likely, to the store from which she bought it), gave it to someone (probably a salesperson), and in return, that person gave Sara a suit. Exchanging thus seems to have something to do with two people, each giving something to the other, although *mutual giving* and *exchanging* are not defined as precisely the same thing (Miller & Johnson-Laird, 1976). What exactly does *exchanging* mean? Miller and Johnson-Laird (1976, p. 577) offer the following definition: Someone, x, "exchanges" something, w, for something, z, with someone, y, if two conditions are met: (1) x gives w to *y* and (2) this obligates *y* to give *z* to *x*. Notice that this analysis explains why exchanging and mutual giving are similar but not identical: Exchanging creates an *obligation* for *y* to give something back to *x*, although *y* might renege on the deal; in mutual giving, *x* and *y* must give something to the other.

When listeners figure out the meaning of a sentence, they need to pay attention to more than just the meanings of individual words. Syntax also gives clues as to what a sentence means. Were this not the case, the two sentences below, because they make use of the same words, would mean exactly the same thing:

(9)   The professor failed the student.
(10)   The student failed the professor.

Clearly, the meaning of "failed" in the two sentences is not identical. Something in the way that words are arranged, then, must cue the listener or reader about who the actor of the sentence is, what the action is, and to whom or what the action is done.

The study of semantics also involves the study of *truth conditions* of sentences, and of the relationships between sentences. As the term itself suggests, truth conditions are simply the circumstances that make something true. Refer to our earlier example sentence: "Sara exchanged a dress for a suit." Under what circumstances would this sentence be true?

First of all, Sara has to be the person either actually carrying out the exchange or causing the exchange to happen (perhaps she sends Jane, her personal assistant, to the store). Second, Sara must at the beginning of the transaction have a dress to give, and must give it to someone who gives her back a suit. If Sara gets back a hat instead of a suit, or gives a skirt rather than a dress, then the sentence is false. The point here is that our understanding the meaning of this sentence requires (1) an understanding of the meaning of each word in the sentence; (2) an understanding of the syntax of the sentence; and (3) an understanding of the truth conditions of the sentence.

Pragmatics

To communicate verbally with another speaker of the English language, the utterances you produce will have to follow rules of phonology, syntax, and semantics. In addition, a fourth set of rules has to be honored if you want to communicate successfully. This set of *pragmatic* rules has to do with the social rules of language, which include certain etiquette conventions, such as not interrupting another speaker and beginning conversations with certain conventional greetings (for example, "Hi. How are you?").

Searle (1979) points out that in listening to another person, we must understand not only the sounds, words, and structure of the utterances but the kind of utterances being spoken. Different kinds of utterances demand different responses from us. For instance, *assertives* are speech acts in which the speaker asserts her or his belief in some proposition, for example, "It's hot in here" or "I'm a Libra." These require little overt response from the listener, who is assumed to add the information asserted by the speaker into her or his own model of the world. *Directives,* another kind of speech act, are instructions from the speaker to the listener, for example, "Close the door" or "Don't believe everything you hear." *Commissives* are utterances that commit the speaker to some later action, for example, "I promise to clean my room" or "I guarantee this will work." *Expressives* describe psychological states of the speaker, for example, "I apologize for eating the last piece of pie" or "I thank you for the favor you did for me." Finally, *declarations* are speech acts in which the utterance is itself the action. Examples include "I now pronounce you husband and wife" or "You're fired." According to Searle's *speech act theory,* part of our job as listeners is to figure out which of the five types a particular utterance is and to respond appropriately.

Moreover, there are usually a number of distinct ways of stating or asking something. Imagine, for instance, that you are sitting in a room, and that a cold breeze is blowing through an open window. You want the window closed, but for one reason or another do not wish to close it yourself. What could you say to someone else to get him or her to close the window? Here are a few possibilities (all of which would be classified as "directives" in Searle's [1979] classification): (a) "Close the window." (b) "Could you close the window, please?" (c) "Hey, would you mind if we closed the window?" (d) "I'm getting cold." (e) "Gee, there's quite a breeze today, no?" How are you to choose among these (or other) options?

Note that in this example, how you choose to make your request will no doubt depend on to whom you are talking and where the conversation takes place (say, to your child in your house versus to your host in his house). Option (e), for instance, might be too subtle to communicate your intention if you are speaking to a preschooler (who might take it as a general and rather uninteresting comment on the weather). On the other hand, (a) might communicate clearly but mark you as an overbearing and rude guest if you were to say this to your host while dining at his house.

Gibbs (1986) studied the way in which adult subjects choose to frame requests. His data suggest that speakers anticipate the potential obstacles their listeners face in fulfilling a request and formulate it accordingly. For instance, imagine that you are working in the library when your pen runs out of ink. You don't have a backup, so you look around for someone from whom to borrow a pen. You don't know the student at the next table, and he is engrossed, but he is the only person in sight, and he has two extra pens next to his books and papers. Would you say (a) "I need a pen," (b) Please give me a pen," (c) "Excuse me, would you mind lending me a pen?" or (d) "Do you have an extra pen?" Gibbs's subjects, given similar scenarios, chose (c), responding to the biggest perceived obstacle of imposing on a stranger. A less-good choice would be (d), if you can see the extra pens, but it might be appropriate if you didn't know whether or not the student had extra pens with him.

So far, we've seen that our language is structured and rule-governed at several different but interacting levels. Although there is much more to be said about each of these levels (each of which gives rise to several linguistics courses), we need to turn our attention to how the structure of language directs and is influenced by other kinds of cognitive processing. We'll look first at how speakers of a language process incoming utterances or written sentences in order to comprehend the meaning.

Language Comprehension and Production

Like other information, language has to be transformed from raw input to meaningful representations. One of the first stages of this transformation is perceptual. In this section, we'll examine the perception of speech, noticing the special ways that speech input is initially processed. We will then turn our attention to further stages of processing, in particular comprehension and the processing of discourse, such as conversations. Finally, we will examine the processing of written language through reading.

Speech Perception

One of the ways we encounter and use language is in the form of speech. Understanding the speech of someone talking to you is usually quite easy, unless it is in a foreign language or the speaker has a very marked speech impediment. We can almost always understand the speech of children, adults, fluent speakers, and those with strong foreign or regional accents. As we will see, this ability is pretty remarkable.

It might seem reasonable to suppose that we perceive speech in the way (we think) we perceive written text: one sound at a time, using the pauses between sounds (like the white space between letters) to identify letters, and the pauses between words to identify when one word ends and another begins. (Actually, evidence suggests that we really don't process written text letter by letter, either). Unfortunately, this tidy explanation does not work.

Miller (1990) describes two fundamental problems in speech perception. First, speech is continuous. Rarely are there pauses around each sound; different sounds from the same word blend into one another. This is shown most clearly in Figure 8-3, which displays a spectrogram of a spoken sentence. A spectrogram is a graphic representation of speech, showing the frequencies of sound in hertz (cycles per second) along the y-axis, plotted against time on the x-axis. Darker regions in the figure indicate the loudness of each sound at each frequency. Note that the boundaries (white

Th i   s   is   a   p   e   n

FIGURE 8-3.   Spectrogram of a person pronouncing the indicated sentence

spaces) do not correspond to word or syllable boundaries. Indeed, there is nothing in the physical stimulus itself to indicate where these boundaries are. In other words, although when you listen to someone talk it sounds as though there are pauses in between syllables and words, many of those pauses are illusory!

A second problem in speech perception is that a single phoneme sounds different, depending on context. Although it sounds as if the same sound starts *baby, boondoggle,* and *bunny,* this is not the case. Figure 8-4 presents a spectrogram of my pronouncing the three words, and examination of the spectrogram reveals few if any properties present for all three words. Add to this the facts that men and women generally speak with different pitches (women's voices generally having higher pitch, or frequencies); that different people have different accents; and that speakers talk differently when shouting, coaxing, whispering, or lecturing, and you'll realize just how complicated it is to ascertain which phoneme is being produced simply from the physical properties of the acoustic stimulus.

Given these problems, how is it that most of us manage to perceive speech rather easily? In part, the answer is that we appear to come specially equipped to perceive speech in efficient ways. Although the actual acoustic stimulus can vary infinitely in its phonetic properties, it turns out that our perception of speech sounds is *categorical.* This means that in processing speech sounds, we automatically, without awareness or intention, force the sounds into discrete categories.

ba   by   b oon   dogg   le   b u n n y

FIGURE 8-4.   Spectrogram of the words *baby, boondoggle,* and *bunny*

Lisker and Abramson (1970) demonstrated the categorical perception of speech sounds. They used a computer to generate artificial speech sounds consisting of a bilabial stop consonant (which sounds like either a \b\ or a \p\ sound) followed by an "ah" sound. The \b\ and \p\ sounds have the same consonantal features and differ only in voice onset time. (Voice onset time, or VOT, has to do with how quickly after the consonant sound is released the vocal folds begin to vibrate; negative values of VOT indicate that the vocal cords begin to vibrate *before* the sound is released.) Lisker and Abramson varied the VOT, by computer, from −.15 seconds to +.15 seconds, thereby generating 31 syllables. When they presented the syllables to listeners, the listeners "heard" only two sounds: a "ba" and a "pa." Any syllable with a VOT of +.03 seconds or less was heard as a "ba," and any syllable with a VOT of more than +.03 seconds was heard as a "pa." Subjects did not report differences in the sounds of the syllables that were on the same side of the boundary. To them, a syllable with a voice onset time of −.10 seconds was indistinguishable from a syllable with a voice onset time of −.08 seconds. However, two syllables that were just as close in VOTs, but fell on opposite sides of the boundary (for example, +.02 and +.04) were identified by 100% of the subjects as being different sounds: a "ba" sound and a "pa" sound, respectively.

Apparently, then, we pay attention to certain acoustic properties of speech (those that make a meaningful difference in our language) but ignore others. This might explain why we can understand the speech of a stranger (who speaks our language) quickly and effortlessly: we ignore the differences in his speech (pitch of voice, accent) that don't make meaningful differences. Incidentally, categorical perception has also been demonstrated for some nonspeech sounds, such as tones, buzzes, and musical notes played on different instruments (Harnad, 1987).

A clever study by Massaro and Cohen (1983) demonstrated that we also make use of visual information in the perception of speech. These investigators examined the categorical perception of the stop consonants \b\ and \d\, two sounds that differ only in the place of articulation. Subjects heard nine computer-synthesized syllables that ranged in their acoustic properties from a clear "ba" sound to a clear "da" sound. In the "neutral" condition, subjects heard the syllables with no visual information. In two other conditions, subjects heard the syllables while watching a silent but synchronized videotape of a speaker who was pronouncing either "ba" or "da." One question was whether subjects would notice a discrepancy when the auditory information presented was "ba" but the videotaped speaker was saying "da." The subjects did not. It is interesting, however, that what the speaker appeared to be saying influenced what was heard: syllables in the middle of the "ba–da" continuum were perceived slightly differently as a function of what the speaker appeared to be saying relative to the perception reported in the neutral condition.

Apparently, then, visual cues affect how sounds are perceived. One might describe this as a kind of **context effect,** first described in Chapter 2. A number of other studies have demonstrated that speech perception is subject to a number of other context effects.

Studies by Warren and his collaborators (Warren, 1970; Warren & Obusek, 1971) have demonstrated that in some cases, people "hear" phonemes that are not there! In the 1970 study, Warren presented subjects with a recording of the sentence "The state governors met with their respective legi*latures convening in the capital city," in which a 120-millisecond portion had been replaced with a coughing sound (indicated by the asterisk). Only one of 20 listeners reported detecting a missing sound covered by a cough, and the one who did misreported its location. The other 19 demonstrated *phoneme restoration effect,* so called because listeners apparently "restore" the missing phonemes predicted by other linguistic information in the speech during the course of perception.

People are capable of using a great deal of information to "predict" what the correct sound of a missing segment should be. Warren and Warren (1970) demonstrated this by presenting people with one of four sentences. Each was the same recording, with the exception of the final word that had been spliced on, and each contained a missing segment, as indicated by an asterisk:

(11)   It was found that the *eel was on the *axle.*
(12)   It was found that the *eel was on the *shoe.*
(13)   It was found that the *eel was on the *orange.*
(14)   It was found that the *eel was on the *table.*

Depending on the sentence (which provided a context for the missing sound), subjects reported hearing *wheel, heel, peel,* or *meal.* Here again, we see that the context directs the listener's perception of a sound—typically without the listener's even being aware of this influence.

Other studies also suggest that people use context to help them perceive speech. One study by Marslen-Wilson and Welsh (1978) required subjects to "shadow" speech, that is, to repeat it aloud. (We encountered shadowing tasks in Chapter 3, as you may recall.) The investigators introduced some distortions into the speech presented to subjects (for example, the pseudoword "cigaresh"). They found that subjects were often likely to restore the distortion to the proper pronunciation ("cigarette"), especially if the word was highly predictable from the preceding context (for example, "Still, he wanted to smoke a ———"). This result suggests that readers and listeners typically use the context of the previous words in a sentence to predict the next word, and even can "mishear" or "misread" that word if it is presented in a distorted fashion. You might note here a parallel to context effects in visual perception, a topic we reviewed in Chapter 2.

Speech Errors in Production

So far, we have examined the ways in which we perceive language, specifically spoken sounds, but this is only part of the story regarding the ways in which we process speech. As native speakers of a language, we do more than comprehend and process it—we also produce speech for others to comprehend and process.

One kind of study of speech production focuses on *speech errors,* defined as instances where what the speaker intended to say is quite clear, but the speaker makes some substitution or reorders the elements. Some examples of speech errors are the following (from Garrett, 1990):

(15)   Sue keeps food in her *v*esk. [Substitution of "v" for "d"]
(16)   Keep you cotton-pickin' hands off my weet *s*peas. [Shift of "s"]
(17)   . . . got a lot of po*ns* and pa*ts* to wash. [Exchange of sounds]
(18)   We'll sit around the *song* and sing *fires.* [Exchange of words]

Much of the data from speech-error studies is observational rather than experimental, for the simple reason that it seems difficult to control experimentally the ways in which people produce speech. Because of the observational nature of the studies, assertions about causation are problematic. However, one can look at the relative frequency of occurrence of different kinds of errors and make inferences regarding the underlying mechanisms. Garrett (1990) advocates this approach.

In studying one kind of speech error, word substitution, Garrett (1988) found two broad classes: errors that showed meaning relations (for example, using "finger" in place of "toe" or "walk" instead of run"), and errors that showed form relations (for example, "guest" instead of "goat," "mushroom" for "mustache"). Garrett argued that the two kinds of errors were very distinct: those that showed similarities of meaning rarely involved similarities of form and vice versa. Although such errors are possible (for example, "head" for "hair," "lobster" for "oyster"), they seldom occur.

According to Garrett (1990), the relative infrequency of word-substitution errors showing both meaning and form similarities indicates that the language-production system processes information about meaning and information about form at different points in sentence construction. His reasoning: If meaning and form processes operate simultaneously, then sentences in which both kinds of similarity are present ought to produce the most errors because there is greater opportunity for error to come about. That this doesn't happen suggests that the two kinds of processing are separate and operate at different points.

Sentence Comprehension

How is it that people understand or recover the meaning from sentences? It is a complicated task and, as we have seen, requires retrieving not only the meaning of individual words but also syntactic structure. Much evidence suggests that people pay attention to syntactic constituents, such as those described earlier. In a series of studies, Jarvella (1971) had subjects listen to long passages of speech. Interruptions during the passages were cues to the subjects to recall, as precisely as possible, whatever they could from the sentence just heard. Jarvella created passages that contained identical phrases, except that the phrases "belonged" to different clausal constituents. Consider passages 19 and 20 below, and notice that the middle clauses in each are the same, although they belong to different sentences:

(19)   With this possibility, Taylor left the capital. After he had returned to Manhattan, he explained the offer to his wife.

(20)   Taylor did not reach a decision until after he had returned to Manhattan. He explained the offer to his wife.

Subjects' recall for the initial clauses (the ones that differ in the two passages above) was similar, and averaged around 16% verbatim recall. Recall for the third clause ("he explained the offer to his wife") was similar for both groups of subjects, averaging 85%, presumably because subjects were still actively processing this part of the sentence, and were therefore still holding it in working memory. A more interesting result concerned the middle clause ("after he had returned to Manhattan"). It contained the same words and sounds, but was part of the first sentence in passage 19, and of the second sentence in passage 20. Subjects listening to passages such as 19 showed overall accuracy of about 54%, but those listening to passage 20, only 20%, for the clause at issue. Jarvella argued that in 19, the second clause is still being processed because the sentence is not yet finished; therefore, the clause is still in working memory. However, in 20, the second clause belongs to a sentence for which processing is finished. (Work by Just and Carpenter [1987], described below, suggests that we don't always process sentences clause by clause.) Ordinarily, it seems, when we finish the processing of a sentence, we "discard" the exact wording and store only a representation of its gist (Sachs, 1967).

Apparently, then, some of the syntactic rules described in the section above are similar to those people ordinarily rely on as they interpret speech. Although people might never consciously think about the function of a word or phrase in a sentence, the evidence overwhelmingly suggests that they are sensitive to it and make use of information about syntax as they understand.

Comprehending a sentence often involves resolving its possible ambiguities. Box 8-1 offers examples of phonological, lexical (that is, word-level), and syntactic ambiguities present in different sentences. The interesting thing about the sentences is that we would ordinarily not notice the ambiguities; our processing would result in one unambiguous representation. It is only rarely, and with certain kinds of sentences, that we even notice ambiguities. Consider the following sentences (Garrett, 1990, p. 137):

(21)   Fatty weighed three hundred and fifty pounds of grapes.
(22)   The cotton shirts are made from comes from Arizona.
(23)   The horse raced past the barn fell.

These sentences are sometimes called *garden path sentences* because they lead the listener or reader down one path, to one interpretation, until some-

---

BOX 8-1   Examples of Ambiguous Sentences

Phonetic ambiguity
Remember, a spoken sentence often contains many words not intended
Ream ember us poke can cent tense off in contains *men knee* words *knot in ten did*
to be heard.
tube bee herd.

Lexical ambiguity
I've got to go to the bank this morning.
I've got to go to First National this morning.
or
I've got to go to the river's edge this morning.

Syntactic ambiguity
Have the missionaries eaten.
(Spoken by the bishop as a question or spoken by a cannibal chief as an order)

SOURCE: *From "Sentence Processing," by M. F. Garrett, in* An Invitation to Cognitive Science, Volume 1: Language, *edited by D. N. Osherson and H. Lasnik. Copyright © 1990 by The MIT Press. Reprinted by permission.*

where in the middle or the end of processing, the listener or reader realizes that the interpretation is incorrect and that the sentence processing needs to be redone. Whatever the normal sentence processing is, it somehow goes astray with these examples.

The three sentences above have initial fragments (for example, "The cotton shirts are made from") that are *syntactically ambiguous,* which is to say they are consistent with at least two different parses. In this sentence the word "cotton" could be treated as an adjective, modifying "shirts" (as in "The cotton shirts are made from dyed fibers") or as a noun (as in "The cotton shirts are made from comes from Arizona"). Some have argued that we have a preference for parsing the fragment in certain ways. By this line of thinking, we come to the second interpretation only when forced to because the first parse does not work. We notice that the first parse does not work only when we get to the fragment "comes from Arizona" and don't know what to do with it (Altmann, 1987).

There are other ambiguities a sentence processor encounters as well. One type is called *lexical ambiguity.* It occurs with words that have two meanings, such as *bank,* which could refer either to a financial institution or an edge of a river. How are lexical ambiguities normally resolved? A study by Swinney (1979) offers some insights.

Swinney presented subjects with spoken passages. Some of these contained ambiguous words and other, similar passages did not. In each case the unambiguous version included a word synonymous with one of the meanings of the ambiguous word. An example of such a passage (with the ambiguous/unambiguous words italicized):

(24)   Rumor had it that, for years, the government building had been plagued with problems. The man was not surprised when he found several roaches, spiders, and other *(bugs/insects)* ‡ in the corner of his room.

Simultaneously, subjects participated in a visual lexical-decision task (we discussed such tasks in Chapter 5), where they were presented with a string of letters and asked to decide, as quickly as possible, whether the string formed an English word. The letter strings were presented at the point marked with a double dagger ‡ in the above example. Previous work by Swinney and others had demonstrated the existence of priming across the modalities (that is, a spoken word can prime a visually presented word). Swinney's question here was, Would all of the meanings (for example, "insect," "recording device") of an ambiguous word (for example, "bug") be subject to priming, or would priming occur only for the meaning activated by the context?

Swinney's results suggested that even in highly biasing contexts such as the one above *both* meanings of an ambiguous word (in this case, "bug") were able to prime performance in the lexical-decision task, if the visual presentation happened immediately after the auditory presentation of the ambiguous word. So, for example, passage 24 primed both *spy* and *ant,* which are semantically related to different meanings of the word *bug,* when they were presented immediately after the subjects heard "bug." If the visual presentation of letter strings was delayed even for as little as four syllables after the auditory presentation of the ambiguous word, however, priming occurred for only the contextually appropriate meaning of the ambiguous word. So, with a delayed presentation of words visually, the spoken word "bug" would prime *ant* but not *spy*, in the context of passage 24.

These results have several implications. First, when we process ambiguous sentences, all of the meanings of an ambiguous word are temporarily available. This means that however context effects operate, they do not operate immediately to restrict the listener or reader to the most appropriate "reading" of the words. Instead, for a period of time, all meanings are accessible; however, the period is very short. Three syllables after presentation of the ambiguous word (for most people, this is about 750–1,000 milliseconds), only one meaning remains active, suggesting that people resolve the ambiguity of a sentence fairly quickly.

Garrett (1990), reviewing these and other results, concludes that sentence comprehension normally occurs with left-to-right processing (that is, each word in the sentence is processed sequentially), with each word normally processed once and normally one interpretation assigned. Processing results in each sentence's being assigned a "logical structure," so that the reader knows the role each word has in the sentence and how the sentence fits with preceding sentences. The existence of garden path sentences, however, serves to demonstrate that normal processing can sometimes fail. Still, the rarity of garden path sentences suggests that most of the time, we are able to process sentences very rapidly and efficiently.

Comprehending Text Passages

We've just examined some evidence of how we process individual sentences. One question we can now ask is how processing of individual sentences works when they are bundled together into connected passages, such as paragraphs or stories. Much of the time, when we encounter text passages they are in written form. Thus, to examine text processing, we will first need to review briefly some findings on how people read.

Marcel Just and Patricia Carpenter (1987) have conducted a number of studies on how people read. They often use computer-driven instruments to measure and record eye *fixations* on parts of the written text. Fixations are brief pauses that everyone makes as eyes scan text. Reading consists of a series of fixations and jumps between fixations. The average fixation lasts about 250 milliseconds (about a quarter of a second); the average jump, 10 to 20 milliseconds (Just & Carpenter, 1987).

Just and Carpenter's model of reading assumes that as soon as readers encounter a new word, they try to interpret it and assign it a role. They call this the *immediacy assumption.* In addition, Just and Carpenter (1987)

The language comprehension processes used in reading are complex but are often taken for granted.

make what they call the *eye-mind hypothesis,* which holds that the interpretation of each word occurs during the time it is fixated. Therefore, the time spent on each fixation provides information about ease of interpretation.

Just and Carpenter (1987) believe that a number of variables influence fixation duration and, therefore, ease of interpretation. Among the factors that increase fixation duration are word length, word infrequency, and syntactically or semantically anomalous words. Just and Carpenter (1980; Carpenter & Just, 1983) presented college-student subjects with passages from such magazines as *Newsweek* or *Time* describing scientific inventions, technical innovations, or biological mechanisms.

Box 8-2 shows sample results for one subject. Numbers above each word indicate the fixation time for that word (measured in milliseconds). Note that content words, such as *flywheels, engine,* or *devices,* almost always receive longer fixations than function words, such as *the, on,* or *a,* which often are not fixated at all. Although not every word is fixated, the content words almost always are. These results suggest that more time is spent on the meaningful or semantically rich parts of the text, as would be expected, given the reader's goal of understanding meaning.

Other work in reading also suggests that semantic factors influence the reading task. Kintsch and Keenan (1973) showed that two sentences of equal length might be differentially difficult to process. The source of the difficulty, they believe, lies in the *propositional complexity* of the sentences, the number of basic ideas conveyed. The two sentences in Figure 8-5 are approximately equal in length, although they differ greatly in the number of underlying propositions, or basic ideas. This model predicts that the second sentence, having the same number of words but more propositions than the first, will be more difficult to process, and indeed this is what Kintsch and Keenan found.

Subjects were asked to press a button after reading a sentence (or passage) silently, and then to immediately recall as much of the sentence as they could. The more propositions a sentence contained, the longer it took for the subjects to read and comprehend it. Further, the subjects were much more likely to recall the more "central" propositions, those critical to the meaning of the sentence, than the more peripheral ones that merely elaborated on the central ideas. This result suggests that propositions are mentally represented in some sort of hierarchy, with more central propositions at the top of the hierarchy, as shown in Figure 8-5. The peripheral, lower-

---

BOX 8-2 Gaze Durations of a Typical Reader

Eye fixations of a college student reading a scientific passage. Gazes within each sentence are sequentially numbered above the fixated words with the durations (in msec) indicated below the sequence number.

1	2	3	4	5	6	7	8		9	1
1566	267	400	83	267	617	767	450		450	400
Flywheels	are	one	of the	oldest	mechanical	devices	known	to	man.	Every

2	3		5	4	6	7	8		9		10
616	517		684	250	317	617	1116		367		467
internal	combustion		engine	contains		a small	flywheel	that	converts	the	jerky

11	12	13	14	15	16	17		18	19	20	21
483	450	383	284	383	317	283		533	50	366	566
motion	of the pistons	into	the	smooth	flow	of	energy that	powers	the	drive	shaft.

SOURCE: *From "A Theory of Reading: From Eye Fixations to Comprehension," by J. Just and P. Carpenter, 1980,* Psychological Review, *87, 4, 329–354. Copyright © 1980 by the American Psychological Association. Reprinted by permission.*

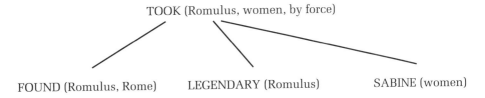

TOOK (Romulus, women, by force)

FOUND (Romulus, Rome)   LEGENDARY (Romulus)   SABINE (women)

"Romulus, the legendary founder of Rome, took the women of the Sabine by force."

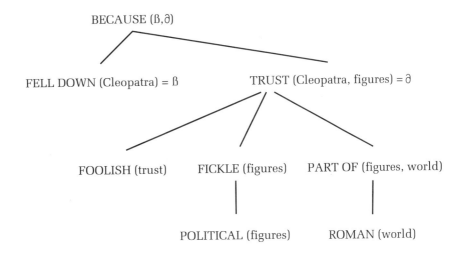

BECAUSE (ß,∂)

FELL DOWN (Cleopatra) = ß   TRUST (Cleopatra, figures) = ∂

FOOLISH (trust)   FICKLE (figures)   PART OF (figures, world)

POLITICAL (figures)   ROMAN (world)

"Cleopatra's downfall lay in her foolish trust in the fickle political figures
of the Roman world."

FIGURE 8-5.   Propositional structure of two sentences. SOURCE: From "Reading Rate and Retention as a Function of the Number of Propositions in the Base Structure of Sentences," by W. Kintsch and J. Keenan, 1974, *Cognitive Psychology, 5*, 259. Copyright © 1977 by Academic Press. Reprinted by permission.

level propositions apparently serve the function of elaborating the more central propositions and so are less important to remember.

Another factor influencing the processing of text has to do with the relationships among sentences. How is it that people integrate related ideas that may come from different sentences? Haviland and Clark (1974) describe what they call the *given-new* strategy, a pragmatic approach to processing sentences whereby listeners and readers divide sentences into two parts: the given and the new. The given part of a sentence contains information that is (or should be) familiar from the context, the preceding information (including other sentences just presented), or background knowledge.

The new part, as the term implies, contains unfamiliar information. Listeners first search memory for information corresponding to the given information, and then update memory by incorporating the new information, often as an elaboration of the given.

The given-new strategy can work only if the information in the given part of the sentence corresponds to some information in the listener's memory, called the *antecedent*. One way to help the listener make this connection is to use the same description in the given part of the sentence as is in memory. However, as a practical matter, it is often easier to use slightly different ways of referring to things, and to expect the listener to make some connections—the obvious ones—on her or his own. Making the connections, called *bridging inferences,* will naturally take some time. In one experiment, Haviland and Clark (1974) presented subjects with passages consisting of context followed by target sentences. Sometimes (as in 25, below) the target sentence had given information that exactly matched the antecedent information (from the context); other times, subjects had to draw a bridging inference (as in 26).

(25)   We got some beer out of the car. The beer was warm.
(26)   We checked the picnic supplies. The beer was warm.

As predicted, it took subjects longer to read and comprehend the target sentence in (26) than it did subjects who read the same target sentence in (25), presumably because those subjects reading (25) had to draw the bridging inference, "The picnic supplies included beer."

The role of context in processing language has been extensively documented by John Bransford and Marcia Johnson. Read the passage in Box 8-3, then cover it and try to recall as much as you can. If you are like

---

BOX 8-3   An Ambiguous Story

If the balloons popped, the sound wouldn't be able to carry since everything would be too far away from the correct floor. A closed window would also prevent the sound from carrying, since most buildings tend to be well insulated. Since the whole operation depends on a steady flow of electricity, a break in the middle of the wire would also cause problems. Of course, the fellow could shout, but the human voice is not loud enough to carry that far. An additional problem is that the string could break on the instrument. Then there could be no accompaniment to the message. It is clear that the best situation would involve less distance. Then there would be fewer potential problems. With face to face contact, the least number of things could go wrong.

SOURCE: *From "Contextual Prerequisites for Understanding: Some Investigations of Comprehension and Recall," by J. D. Bransford and M. K. Johnson, 1972,* Journal of Verbal Learning and Verbal Behavior, 11, *718. Copyright © 1972 by Academic Press. Reprinted by permission.*

FIGURE 8-6.   Context for story in Box 8-3. SOURCE: From "Contextual Prerequisites for Understanding: Some Investigations of Comprehension and Recall," by J. D. Bransford and M. K. Johnson, 1972, *Journal of Verbal Learning and Verbal Behavior, 11,* 717. Copyright © 1972 by Academic Press. Reprinted by permission.

Bransford and Johnson's (1972) subjects, you might find the task very difficult, and your recall might include only a few of the ideas. However, if you were first provided with a context for the passage, such as the one depicted in Figure 8-6, your recall would be much more complete. Bransford and Johnson showed that with the context provided before the passage, subjects recalled an average of 8.0 out of 14.0 distinct ideas. Without any context, or even with the context provided after the passage, subjects only recalled about 3.6 ideas.

You may note a connection here to the idea of schemata, discussed in Chapter 6. Recall that schemata are organized frameworks for representing knowledge that often function like scripts of a play, with characters, plots, and settings. You might think of the contexts Bransford and Johnson (1972) provided some of their subjects as schemata. Their experimental results, then, show that schemata aid in the comprehension, and therefore the recall, of text passages.

Story Grammars

In Chapter 6, we also encountered the idea of scripts, defined as schemata for routine events. Earlier in this chapter, we discussed the idea of grammars—systems of rules that result in legal entities, such as sentences. Some cognitive psychologists have put these two ideas together, forming the concept of a **story grammar** to describe the way people comprehend large, integrated pieces of text.

Story grammars are similar to scripts in that both have variables or slots that are filled in differently for different stories. For example, different stories have different protagonists, settings, plots, conflicts, and resolutions. Story grammars are also similar to syntactic grammars in that they help to identify the units (constituents) and the role each unit plays in the story (Just & Carpenter, 1987). Like syntactic grammars, story grammars attempt to describe the hierarchical structure of the story, specifying how each part of the story relates to the other parts. Story grammars produce a division (or parse) of the story into parts or constituents. Text passages that cannot be parsed by a grammar are then seen as "illegal" or "ungrammatical" stories, just as strings of words that cannot be parsed by a syntactic grammar are identified as "ungrammatical." Like other schemata, story grammars provide the listener or reader with a framework with which to expect certain elements and sequences, and to fill in with "default values" things that are not explicitly stated. For example, young children expect stories to begin with some sort of setting, say, "Once upon a time" or "A long time ago."

One example of a story grammar is shown in Table 8-1 (Thorndyke, 1977). It divides a story into several constituents: settings, themes, plots, resolutions, and so forth. Each of these parts may also have subparts. For example, settings might have location, characters, and time. Some parts may also have a number of different instances of certain subparts, for example, the plot may have several episodes. The asterisk indicates that certain subparts (for example, "episode," in rule 4) can be repeated an indefinite number of times. Parentheses around a subpart indicate that the subpart is optional.

Mandler and Johnson (1977) found that stories conforming to the structure of a story grammar were better recalled than were stories that conformed less well. In fact, subjects were more likely to "misremember" details that made for a better fit with the story grammar. Interestingly, when these authors analyzed Bartlett's "War of the Ghosts" story (see Chapter 4), they found that it contained several violations of their story grammar. Some of the recall attempts Bartlett (1932) reported showed errors of recall at precisely these points. We can analyze the problem in a story grammar framework as follows: at least part of the reason Bartlett's subjects had so much trouble

TABLE 8-1.   Example of a story grammar

Rule Number	Rule
(1)	STORY → SETTING + THEME + PLOT + RESOLUTION
(2)	SETTING → CHARACTERS + LOCATION + TIME
(3)	THEME → (EVENT)* + GOAL
(4)	PLOT → EPISODE*
(5)	EPISODE → SUBGOAL + ATTEMPT* + OUTCOME
(6)	ATTEMPT → { EVENT* / EPISODE }
(7)	OUTCOME → { EVENT* / STATE }
(8)	RESOLUTION → { EVENT / STATE }
(9)	{ SUBGOAL / GOAL } → DESIRED STATE
(10)	{ CHARACTERS / LOCATION / TIME } → STATE

SOURCE: From "Cognitive Structures in Comprehension and Memory of Narrative Discourse" by P. W. Thorndyke, 1977, *Cognitive Psychology, 9,* 79. Copyright © 1977 by Academic Press. Reprinted by permission.

remembering the story was that it did not fit the structure they were expecting. They tried to make the story fit the expected structure a little more, and in the process, inadvertently distorted their representation of the story.

Thorndyke (1977) has argued that people use story grammars to guide their reading and their interpretation. One way he tested this idea was to ask people to read and recall various stories that he had previously analyzed according to a story grammar. Box 8-4 depicts an example of one of his stories. He predicted that the higher up in the levels of the story hierarchy a part of the story occurred, the better it would be recalled, and results confirmed this prediction. Notice that this result is similar to those reported in studies by Kintsch and Keenan (1973), discussed earlier, on which parts of sentences people typically remember.

Other cognitive psychologists have criticized the idea of story grammars, arguing that the analogy between sentence and story grammars is "ill conceived" (Wilensky, 1983). At the heart of the analogy is the comparison of sentences (linguistic entities that are either "legal" or "illegal" in a language by virtue of their syntax) with stories (conceptual entities that include goals, events, and other mental objects that are neither "legal" nor "illegal." Current work in both cognitive psychology and artificial intelligence is reassessing the usefulness of story grammars as a way of understanding how people process connected text.

BOX 8-4   Example Story and Its Structure

(1) Circle Island is located in the middle of the Atlantic Ocean, (2) north of Ronald Island. (3) The main occupations on the island are farming and ranching. (4) Circle Island has good soil, (5) but few rivers and (6) hence a shortage of water. (7) The island is run democratically. (8) All issues are decided by a majority vote of the islanders. (9) The governing body is a senate, (10) whose job is to carry out the will of the majority. (11) Recently, an island scientist discovered a cheap method (12) of converting salt water into fresh water. (13) As a result, the island farmers wanted (14) to build a canal across the island, (15) so that they could use water from the canal (16) to cultivate the island's central region. (17) Therefore, the farmers formed a procanal association (18) and persuaded a few senators (19) to join. (20) The procanal association brought the construction idea to a vote. (21) All the islanders voted. (22) The majority voted in favor of construction. (23) The senate, however, decided that (24) the farmers' proposed canal was ecologically unsound. (25) The senators agreed (26) to build a smaller canal (27) that was 2 feet wide and 1 foot deep. (28) After starting construction on the smaller canal, (29) the islanders discovered that (30) no water would flow into it. (31) Thus the project was abandoned. (32) The farmers were angry (33) because of the failure of the canal project. (34) Civil war appeared inevitable.

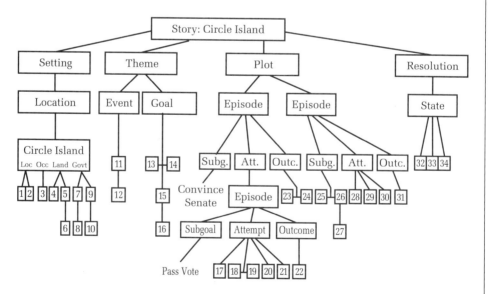

SOURCE: *From "Cognitive Structures in Comprehension and Memory of Narrative Discourse," by P. W. Thorndyke, 1977, Cognitive Psychology, 9, 80–82. Copyright © 1977 by Academic Press. Reprinted by permission.*

Gricean Maxims of Conversation

Not all of the connected text that people have to process occurs in written form. We can think of ordinary conversations as examples of spoken connected text. Conversations are interesting things to study because they occur so frequently, and because (unlike with written text) a participant normally produces a great deal of language with little time for planning and revision.

We've already seen a number of examples of linguistic rules people follow in producing or comprehending language. Some of these have to do with ways of combining sounds to produce words, combining words to produce sentences, or even combining ideas to produce meanings. Many researchers believe, however, that yet another set of rules is necessary for people to use language appropriately or effectively, especially in conversations: pragmatic rules.

Here, we will examine some pragmatic rules specific to conversations called the *Gricean maxims of cooperative conversation* (Grice, 1975).

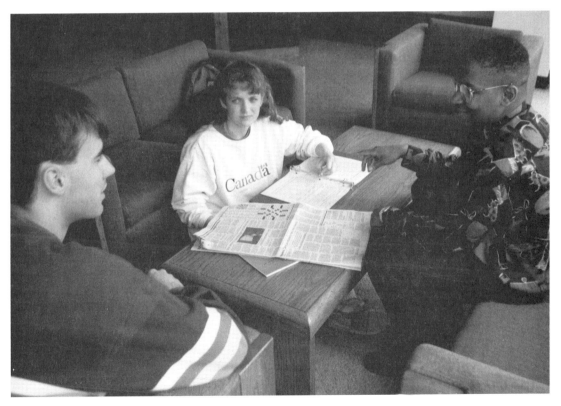

Grice proposed four maxims, or rules, people must follow to have a successful conversation.

Grice believed that for people to converse, each had to do more than produce utterances that are phonologically, syntactically, and semantically appropriate. Consider the following "conversation":

Speaker A: I just heard that Joe got promoted today. Isn't that great?
Speaker B: Salt Lake City is located in Utah.
Speaker C: No, Charles Darwin is the father of modern evolutionary theory.
Speaker A: What's the square root of 34?
Speaker B: Chocolate ice cream is sweet.

What is wrong with this conversation? Notice that all of the sentences the speakers have produced are "legal," and at several levels. Each obeys the phonological rules of English. Each is syntactically well formed. Each is meaningful. Yet, all together, they don't add up to a conversation. In part, what is going on is a lack of connection between anything one speaker says and anything else another speaker says. Normally in conversation, each of a person's contributions or utterances bears some relationship to what others have already said, or what the speaker plans to say later. In this sense, speakers could be said to be providing a context for one another's contributions.

Grice (1975) argued that for a conversation to take place, all the speakers have to cooperate with one another. Although speakers in a conversation have many choices to make concerning what they will say, as well as when and how they will say it, there are still constraints, or general rules, that they must obey (Miller & Glucksberg, 1988). Grice described speakers in a conversation as all following a general "cooperative principle." Speakers do this, Grice believed, by following four specific conversational *maxims* or rules (Grice, 1975):

- **Maxim of Quantity.** Make your contribution as informative as required. Do not make your contribution more informative than is required.
- **Maxim of Quality.** Try to make your contribution one that is true. Do not say what you believe to be false. Do not say that for which you have no evidence.
- **Maxim of Relation.** Be relevant.
- **Maxim of Manner.** Be perspicuous. Avoid obscurity of expression. Avoid ambiguity. Be brief. Be orderly.

Violations of the maxims produce conversations that are noticeably odd. For instance, if someone asks, "Do you have a watch?" and you respond, "Yes, I do," you are violating the first maxim of quantity; you are being less informative than is required. Your conversational partner is not, in all likelihood, taking a census for Timex or Rolex; he or she probably wants to know the time. As a member of the language community you live in, you are expected to know that the question asked is really a request for the time and to respond appropriately.

It is also possible to violate the first maxim by being too informative. For example, some of my students occasionally invite me to eat with them in the campus dining halls. When we arrange a luncheon date, they often ask something like "Where should we meet?" My response ought to be something on the order of "How about if you come to my office?" rather than something much more detailed like "Please come to my office door, and I will be standing 27 centimeters inside of it." The latter is bizarre, presumably by virtue of being overly specific.

The second maxim has to do with truthfulness. Generally, conversational partners assume the other is telling the truth, or at least what each believes to be the truth. On some occasions, it is permissible to violate this maxim—for example, to be ironic. Imagine that a friend who's missed a lecture in a class in which you are both enrolled asks, "How was class today?" You can respond, "Utterly fascinating!" even if it really was dry as toast, *if* you somehow signal that your answer isn't to be taken literally. Rolled eyes, exaggerated intonation, winks, and the like help to communicate that your violation of the maxim of quality is itself meant to communicate something—in this case, ironic humor. If you simply utter an untruthful response without letting your listener know you aren't being candid, then your conversation will not be successful, and your conversational partner could legitimately complain about your conversational skills.

Someone who consistently violates the maxims of quantity or quality might well be perceived as uncooperative or obnoxious, and after a while, may find it difficult to attract conversational partners. Someone who consistently violates the third maxim of relation by responding with irrelevant utterances will have a bigger problem: he or she will simply be regarded as, at best, very bizarre. To illustrate, imagine a conversation between Tom and Joe, two college roommates: Tom [looking around] "Hey, Joe, have you seen my sweater?" Joe [looking at Tom, and smiling] "Lo, a flaming squirrel!" If Joe persists in violating the maxim of relation, he will likely find himself at a complete loss for conversational partners, if not roommates and friends.

The fourth maxim, the maxim of manner, generally governs the way you choose to construct your conversational contributions. The general idea is that you should speak as clearly and as briefly as possible, using language appropriate to your listener and the context. Among other things, this maxim forbids you to answer your professors in pig Latin or your younger siblings in "academese." It also prevents you from holding a filibuster (unless you are a congressperson), and requires that you at least try to organize what you say before you begin speaking.

Gricean maxims are not always obeyed, but the assumption is that people try to obey them most of the time. When they are violated, the speaker apparently either wishes to end the conversation, avoid the conversation, or expects the listener to understand that the violation is occurring and why (Miller & Glucksberg, 1988). Again, though, it is doubtful that the average person is consciously aware of the rules. As with most linguistic rules, maxims are implicitly understood, even if they can't be precisely stated.

Language and Cognition

Language is used in ways other than social conversation. Lecturers use language to get ideas across to students; authors, to readers; newscasters, to audiences, and so on. It should be evident by now that language is used in a number of cognitive processes. When we perceive a familiar object and name it (either aloud or to ourselves), we use language; when we follow one conversation rather than another, we are processing language; when we repeat information aloud or take notes to organize it, we are using language. Similarly, when we reason, make plans, or brainstorm new ideas, we rely heavily on language, as we will see in the next three chapters.

Our use of language in a wide variety of cognitive tasks raises the following important question: What influences does language have over other cognitive processes? Two extreme positions exist: (1) language and other cognitive processes operate completely independently, and (2) language and other cognitive processes are completely related, with one determining the other. Between the extremes is a broad middle ground, where language and other cognitive processes are seen as related in some ways but independent in others.

The relationship between language and thought has been heavily debated. In the early days of American psychology, John B. Watson (1930) asserted that thought was language and nothing more. In particular, he rejected the idea that there could be thought (that is, internal mental representation or other cognitive activity) without some sort of conditioned language responses occurring. Watson believed that all apparent instances of thinking (for example, computing sums in one's head; daydreaming about a vacation; weighing the pros and cons of a plan) were really the results of subvocal speech. Thinking was equated with talking to yourself, even if so quietly and covertly that no one (including you) knew you were using language.

Smith, Brown, Toman, and Goodman (1947) conducted a heroic experiment to test Watson's theory. Smith served as the subject, and allowed himself to be injected with a curare derivative, which acted to paralyze all of his muscles, necessitating the use of an artificial respirator for the duration of the experiment. Because he could not move any muscles, he could not engage in subvocal speech. The question was, Would this also prevent him from other kinds of cognitive activity? The answer was a decisive *no*. Smith reported remembering and thinking about events that took place while under curare. Apparently, then, subvocal speech and thought are not equivalent.

The Modularity Hypothesis

A recent proposal from the philosopher Jerry Fodor (1983, 1985) has made a quite different argument about the relationship of language to other aspects of cognition. Fodor argues that some cognitive processes, in particular perception and language, are *modular.* What does it mean for a process to be a module? First, it means that the process is *domain-specific:* it operates specifically with certain kinds of input and not others. With regard to language, for example, Fodor argues that sentence parsing involves processes that are specific to the division of phrases and words into constituents. Such processes are meant only for parsing, and are of little use in other cognitive tasks.

Modularity of a process also implies that the process is *informationally encapsulated:* it operates independent of the beliefs and the other information available to the processor. Another way of explaining this is to say that an informationally encapsulated process operates relatively independent of other processes. Fodor compares informationally encapsulated processes to reflexes:

> Suppose that you and I have known each other for many a long year . . . and you have come fully to appreciate the excellence of my character. In particular, you have come to know perfectly well that under no conceivable circumstances would I stick my finger in your eye. Suppose that this belief of yours is both explicit and deeply felt. You would, in fact, go to the wall for it. Still, if I jab my finger near enough to your eyes, and fast enough, you'll blink. . . . [The blink reflex] has no access to what you know about my character or, for that matter, to any other of your beliefs, utilities, and expectations. For this reason the blink reflex is often produced when sober reflection would show it to be uncalled for. (Fodor, 1983, p. 71)

The modularity hypothesis, then, argues that certain perceptual and language processes (in the case of language, one such process is that which parses input utterances) are modules. These processes are thought to be set apart from other cognitive processes, such as memory, attention, thinking, and problem solving, that are thought to be nonmodular. Modular processes operate reflexively, and independent (at least at the first stages of processing) of other cognitive processes, such as thought. Modular processes are domain-specific, which means that they are specialized to work with only certain kinds of input. The syntactic parsing aspects of language, then, are not used in other kinds of cognitive processing. In this sense, then, language really is a special and very independent cognitive process.

Is there evidence for the modularity hypothesis? The experiment by Swinney (1979) on lexical ambiguity resolution offers findings that support the modularity hypothesis. Recall that Swinney found that when presented with an ambiguous word (even in a context that should disambiguate the meaning of the word), all possible meanings are triggered for a fraction of a second. This triggering appears to be automatic and reflexive. That all the meanings are activated independent of the context demonstrates some informational encapsulation.

The Whorfian Hypothesis

The modularity hypothesis can be taken as a proposal for treating language (or at least certain aspects of language) as quite independent of any other cognitive process. Other investigators have argued for a different proposal: strong relations exist between language and other cognitive processes. One hypothesis, called the *Whorfian hypothesis of linguistic relativity,* was originated by Benjamin Whorf, a chemical engineer whose hobby was studying Native American languages of North America. It states that language both directs and constrains thought and perception. Whorf (1956) stated the hypothesis as follows (pp. 213–214):

> We dissect nature along lines laid down by our native languages. The categories and types that we isolate from the world of phenomena we do not find there because they stare every observer in the face; on the contrary, the world is presented in a kaleidoscopic flux of impressions which has to be organized by our minds—and this means largely by the linguistic systems in our minds. We cut nature up, organize it into concepts, and ascribe significance as we do, largely because we are parties to an agreement to organize it in this way—an agreement that holds through our speech community and is codified in the patterns of our language. The agreement is, of course, an unstated one, but its terms are absolutely obligatory.

Whorf believed that the language (or languages) one grows up learning and speaking thus organizes and directs the way one perceives the world, organizes information about the world, and thinks.

Whorf (1956) based his hypothesis on the observation that each language differs in the way it emphasizes various aspects of the world. For example, he observed that the Eskimo language has several words for snow, whereas English has one. (Pullum [1991] offers evidence and arguments to refute this belief about Eskimos and snow in a very amusing essay.) English has a number of words to describe basic colors; the language of the Dani, an Indonesian agricultural group, has only two: *mili* for dark or black, and *mola* for white or light (Heider, 1972). Whorf's hypothesis predicts that these language differences could limit the information available to speakers of different languages: as English speakers, we might fail to make distinctions between kinds of snow that Eskimos are thought to make routinely. Similarly, the Dani might process information about colors in very different ways than we do because of differences in language about color terms.

Eleanor Rosch (formerly Heider) conducted a series of studies that directly tested the Whorfian hypothesis. If Whorf is correct, then the Dani should have great difficulty perceiving or remembering colors that are not named in their language (for example, green versus yellow), relative to speakers of English, whose language names each color. Dani-speaking and English-speaking subjects were shown various color chips. Some depicted basic or *focal* colors—chips considered to be the best examples of basic color terms (say, a very green green, as opposed to a blue green). Others depicted nonfocal colors, those that English speakers would describe as a combination of focal colors or as a shade of a focal color (for example, light pink, scarlet, olive green, aquamarine).

Heider (1972) presented subjects with a chip of either a focal or a nonfocal color, typically for five seconds. Thirty seconds later, subjects were shown 160 color chips and asked to point to which one matched the chip they had just seen. Like English speakers, and contrary to Whorf's hypothesis, Dani speakers performed much better if the initial chip showed a focal rather than a nonfocal color. In another experiment, Rosch (1973) asked subjects to learn new, arbitrary names for colors. Once again, Rosch found that Dani speakers, like English speakers, performed better when the colors shown were focal rather than nonfocal.

Apparently, then, even if a language does not mark particular differences, it does not always prevent its speakers from either perceiving those differences or from learning them, contrary to Whorf's hypothesis. Indeed, work by anthropologists Berlin and Kay (1969) suggests that all languages observe certain rules about the way colors are named. They found that in every language, no more than eleven basic color terms (that is, not derived from other color terms) are recognized. Moreover, the way that colors are recognized is hierarchical. The hierarchy is depicted in Table 8-2. It shows that if a language has only two color terms, they will always be something corresponding to "black" (or "dark") and "white (or "light"). If a language has three color terms, then a term meaning "red" will be added to this list. Languages with four color terms will also have either a term for "green" or one for "yellow," but not both, and so on. English, which recognizes all eleven terms as names for focal colors, includes words for all the colors in the hierarchy. No other language recognizes more colors as basic. The implication here is that color terms and concepts are in an important way universal. It should be noted, however, that some have argued that because Rosch's task depended so heavily on color perception (which might in turn

TABLE 8-2. Hierarchy of color terms in different languages

Number of Color Terms	Names of Color Terms
2	White, black
3	White, black, red
4	White, black, red + yellow or green
5	White, black, red, yellow, green
6	White, black, red, yellow, green, blue
7	White, black, red, yellow, green, blue, brown
8 through 11	White, black, red, yellow, green, blue, brown plus some combination of one or more of the following: pink, purple, orange, gray

After Berlin and Kay (1969).

have physiological determinants), it is not as crucial a test of Whorf's hypothesis as it was claimed to be (Hunt & Agnoli, 1991).

A more recent controversy regarding linguistic relativity comes from a proposal of Alfred Bloom (1981), who proposed to study a weaker form of the Whorfian hypothesis: the presence of certain linguistic markers makes some kinds of comprehension and thinking easier or more natural. Specifically, Bloom noticed that the Chinese language lacks a structure equivalent to those in Indo-European languages that marks a *counterfactual inference,* such as "If your grandmother had been elected president, there would be no taxation." Counterfactuals require inferences to be drawn based on a premise known to be false. English marks the fact that the premise is false by using the past tense of the verb, or by the phrase "were to" in the first clause. In contrast, Chinese has no direct marker of a counterfactual, although there are various indirect ways of getting the idea across.

Based on anecdotal evidence from Chinese-speaking associates, Bloom (1981) hypothesized that Chinese speakers would have a more difficult time drawing counterfactual inferences than would speakers of English, especially when text passages containing counterfactual inferences are difficult. In a series of studies, Bloom gave both Chinese-speaking and English-speaking subjects different stories to read in their native languages. He reported that only 7% of the Chinese-speaking subjects offered counterfactual interpretations of the story, whereas 98% of the English-speaking subjects did so. At first blush, these findings offered nearly perfect confirmation of Bloom's predictions (and thus, predictions derived from the Whorf hypothesis).

Later investigations by native Chinese speakers, however, disputed Bloom's findings. They maintained that various *artifacts,* or unrelated aspects of the way he conducted the studies, accounted for his results. Au (1983, 1984), for instance, argued that Bloom's Chinese versions of his story were unidiomatic—that is, they were awkwardly phrased. When she provided new and more idiomatic stories to her Chinese-speaking subjects, they showed very little difficulty responding idiomatically. Liu (1985) replicated Au's findings on counterfactual interpretations with Chinese-speaking subjects who had minimal or no exposure to the English language.

It seems, then, that there is little evidence that language constrains or even has large influences on either perception (as demonstrated in the color-naming studies) or higher-level forms of thinking (as demonstrated in the counterfactual reasoning studies). Cognitive psychologists and linguists generally agree that to date little empirical support for the Whorf hypothesis has been found.

Nonetheless, it is true that language at least reflects thought in many instances. For example, although most of us have only a single word for snow, those interested in the white stuff (for example, skiers) have developed a more extensive vocabulary, presumably to communicate better about conditions on the slope. In general, experts or connoisseurs in given areas do tend to develop their own specialized vocabularies that reflect distinctions and differences that novices might have difficulty (at first) seeing or labeling. Presumably, this is because the experts need to communicate about the subtle differences, and so they develop the enabling vocabulary. Novices, who have little need to discuss the differences, don't develop the vocabulary (nor, by the way, do they develop the perceptual differentiation skills, as we saw in Chapter 2).

Summary

We have seen that language is structured on several levels: the phonological (sound), syntactic (ordering and structuring of words and phrases in sentences), semantic (meaning), and pragmatic (the ways in which language is actually used), to name a few. We have seen examples of the kinds of rules linguists propose and study. We have also discussed what it means to say that people "follow" the rules of a language, drawing a distinction between conscious awareness of a rule (which neither psychologists nor linguistics believe in when it comes to most linguistic rules) and implicit access to a rule (where a person follows a rule even though perhaps unaware of its existence, and completely unable to articulate just what the rule is).

We have seen that people make use of different linguistic rules both when they produce and when they comprehend language. The ways in which a number of our perceptual systems are set up help us to master the very complicated task of processing language relatively easily. Despite the existence of ambiguity in many of the utterances we encounter, we are able to use the context of the utterance as well as other strategies to settle on the most likely intended meaning.

We have noted the existence of perceptual context effects at many levels. We have seen that context can affect even the perception of individual sounds. The phoneme restoration effect demonstrates that people effortlessly "fill in" experimentally created gaps in a stream of speech. Context affects the ways in which individual words are interpreted, although Swinney's (1979) study suggests that context effects do not operate instantaneously but after a brief (fraction-of-a-second) period.

Finally, we have reviewed two very distinct proposals regarding the relation of language to other cognitive processes. The modularity hypothesis proposes that some aspects of language, especially syntactic processes, function autonomously, independent of any other cognitive process. This proposal, being relatively recent, awaits rigorous empirical testing, although there is some evidence consistent with it. The Whorfian hypothesis of linguistic relativity, despite its intriguing nature, has so far failed to receive strong or lasting empirical support. It remains for future research to determine how language and other cognitive processes interact, as indeed they must.

Recommended Readings

General overviews of the psychology of language can be found in a text by Carroll (1986). Volumes edited by Newmeyer (1988) and Osherson and Lasnik (1990) contain chapters on different aspects of the psychology of language. Savage-Rumbaugh and colleagues (1986) provide a good review of the chimpanzee language literature, plus a detailed report on her work with two pygmy chimpanzees.

Ladefoged (1975) is a classic work on phonetics; Kaye (1989) introduces the field of phonology (although the treatment is somewhat advanced); and Cowper (1992) provides a comprehensive introduction to syntax. Miller and Glucksberg (1988) and Larson (1990) review recent work on psychological aspects of semantics and pragmatics.

Miller (1990) provides a review of speech perception. Samuel (1981) describes his investigations of the phoneme restoration effect, and the journal *Cognition* has a special issue (vol. 25, nos. 1–2) devoted to spoken-word recognition in speech perception.

Garrett's (1990) article reviews both sentence comprehension and production. Ferreira and Clifton (1986), and Altmann and Steedman (1988) describe investigations of people's processing of sentences. Bock (1986) and Hupet and Tilmant (1986) describe their investigations of how people produce different sentences. Just and Carpenter (1987) provide an introductory overview of topics relating to language comprehension and reading, and a book edited by Lesgold and Perfetti (1981) contains chapters that discuss cognitive processing of information during reading. Wilensky (1983) reviews and critiques the idea of story grammars. Isaacs and Clark (1987) describe how experts (in this case, New Yorkers) talk to novices (here, non–New Yorkers) about familiar information (postcards of New York scenes).

Fodor's (1983) book lays out the modularity hypothesis and its implications. A shorter version of the book was published in 1984 in *Behavioral and Brain Sciences,* along with several replies (all published as part of the article). A volume edited by Garfield (1987) presents essays describing arguments and empirical evidence relative to the modularity hypothesis.

Classic works in the language-and-thought debate are Whorf (1956), Heider (1972), and Rosch (1973). Lucy and Shweder (1979) critique Heider's studies, and offer a different interpretation of the Whorfian hypothesis. Takano (1989) discusses common methodological problems in conducting studies of linguistic relativity, and Hunt and Agnoli (1991) provide a more sympathetic review of the literature pertaining to the Whorfian hypothesis.

REVIEW QUESTIONS

1. Describe and evaluate the criteria linguists and psychologists use to distinguish between (human) languages and communication systems.
2. What does the term *grammar* mean to linguists and psychologists? How does their understanding of the term differ from that of a layperson?
3. Explain the competence/performance distinction and the arguments linguists and psychologists have for making it.
4. What does it mean to say that our knowledge of linguistic rules is implicit rather than explicit? Discuss the implications of this statement.
5. Contrast the Gricean maxims of conversation with syntactic and phonological rules.
6. Describe the modularity hypothesis and its implications for the study of language as part of cognitive psychology.
7. What is the Whorfian hypothesis of linguistic relativity? Evaluate the empirical evidence bearing on it.

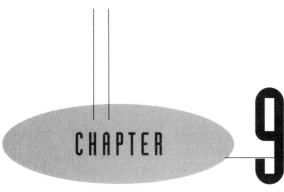

CHAPTER 9

Thinking and Problem Solving

Т

his chapter is about different kinds of thinking and problem solving, the kind of mental work you do in each of the following tasks: Think of your favorite restaurant. What is its name? Where is it?

What are its best dishes? What makes it your favorite? Solve this problem: If ten apples cost $2.00, how much do three apples cost? Create unusual but appropriate titles for the drawings shown in Figure 9-1 (for example, "giant egg on a baseball diamond" for 9-1(a)). In this chapter, we will examine descriptions and explanations for the mental work you have just done. How did you accomplish the tasks? What processes did you use? We will look at a number of different thinking tasks and discuss what makes thinking either easy or hard.

Thinking is a broad term. Psychologists who study thinking often study what look like very different tasks. Defining *thinking* turns out to be a tough job, and one that itself requires thought. *Thinking* has been defined as "going beyond the information given" (Bruner, 1957); "a complex and high-level skill" that "fill[s] up gaps in the evidence" (Bartlett, 1958, p. 20); a process of searching through a problem space (Newell & Simon, 1972); and as what we do "when we are in doubt about how to act, what to believe, or what to desire" (Baron, 1988, p. 3).

Clearly, the term *thinking* is used to refer to more than one specific activity. This suggests that there may be different types of thinking. One distinction that may prove useful is between *focused* and *unfocused* thinking. Focused thinking is that which begins with a clear starting point and has a specific goal. (We will see examples of focused thinking in this chapter, as well as in much of the material to be covered in Chapters 10 and 11.) Unfocused thinking has the character of daydreaming, or unintentionally calling

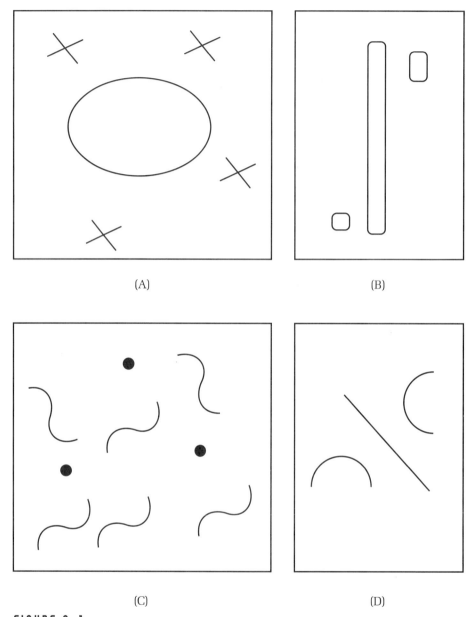

(A)

(B)

(C)

(D)

FIGURE 9-1.   Ambiguous drawings

to mind a number of different and loosely related ideas. We will primarily explore focused thinking, especially in the first section of the chapter, in the discussion on problem solving. We will next turn our attention to creative thinking, which some have described as including aspects of unfocused thinking. Finally, we will examine how people evaluate the products of their thinking. In particular, we will look at the ways in which they assess their ideas, reflect on the implications of their conclusions, and guard against bias or impulsivity.

You might wonder why psychologists study thinking through the use of problems and puzzles, which appear *not* to mirror the kind of thinking that occurs in everyday life (such as when you think about what shirt to wear, or what to order in a restaurant, or what route to take to get to work). One reason stems from the intuition that everyday thinking often occurs so rapidly and automatically that it would be hard to study. Moreover, it is likely that people bring much of their background knowledge to bear in their everyday thinking. You choose what to wear for the day, presumably, based on your expectations of what you will be doing and perhaps on external standards or expectations there might be regarding dress. Because people have varying background knowledge, then, it would be nearly impossible to devise a problem equal in difficulty for multiple subjects. By presenting standardized sets of problems, investigators have more control over the information subjects have available and how it is given to them.

Various problems will be presented throughout the chapter to give you an opportunity to experience the phenomena of thinking firsthand. I suggest that to maximize the value of these undertakings, you rely on a time-honored method of observation in experimental psychology: **introspection.** Introspection is the detailed, concurrent, and nonjudgmental observation of the contents of your consciousness as you work a problem. Although introspection has problems and critics (see Ericsson & Simon, 1984, for a detailed summary), it can at the very least provide the basis for hypotheses and tests using more objective measures. The key to the proper use of this technique is to avoid doing more than is asked for: don't explain or justify what you're thinking about, just report it. Box 9-1 provides instructions on how to introspect. Before you read further, obtain paper and a writing utensil for note taking or, preferably, a tape recorder into which you can dictate your thoughts as you work the problems. Work in the privacy of your room or other quiet place. You won't be showing your notes or tapes to anyone else, so don't censor or try to control your thoughts—just be a careful observer. You can then compare your notes with descriptions of theories to be presented, to assess how well the theories describe your performance.

The problems presented below are similar in at least one respect: they fall into the class of problems called *well-defined.* Well-defined problems have a clear goal (you know immediately if you've reached the solution), present a small set of information to start from, and often (but not always) present a set of rules or guidelines to abide by while working toward a solution. In contrast, *ill-defined* problems don't have their goals, starting information, or steps very clearly spelled out.

The difference between well- and ill-defined problems can be illustrated. Consider the problem of figuring the sales tax on a purchase, given that you know the price of the item you are buying, whether it is taxable, the rate of taxation, and basic rules of multiplication. Armed with this background information, it should be relatively easy for you, a college student, to arrive at the tax. Contrast this with another problem often encountered: composing a letter that articulately and sensitively conveys a difficult message (for example, a "Dear John" or "Dear Joan" letter to someone you're still fond of, or a letter to your boss asking for a promotion). It's not clear in any of these cases of ill-defined problems what information you should start from (how much of your education and how many of your qualifications and past year's accomplishments do you tell your boss about?). It's not clear when you've reached the goal (is the current draft good enough, or can it be made better?) or what rules (if any) apply.

Psychologists have focused on well-defined problems for several reasons: they are easy to present, they don't take weeks or months to solve, they are easy to score, and they are easy to change. It is assumed that problem solving for ill-defined problems works in similar ways to problem solving for well-defined problems, although the assumption has not been tested (Galotti, 1989).

B O X 9 - 1   Instructions for Introspecting

1. Say whatever's on your mind. Don't hold back hunches, guesses, wild ideas, images, intentions.
2. Speak as continuously as possible. Say something at least once every five seconds, even if only, "I'm drawing a blank."
3. Speak audibly. Watch out for your voice dropping as you become involved.
4. Speak as telegraphically as you please. Don't worry about complete sentences and eloquence.
5. Don't overexplain or justify. Analyze no more than you would normally.
6. Don't elaborate past events. Get into the pattern of saying what you're thinking now, not of thinking for a while and then describing your thoughts.

SOURCE: *Reprinted by permission of the publishers from THE MIND'S BEST WORK by D. N. Perkins, Cambridge, Mass.: Harvard University Press, Copyright © 1981 by D. N. Perkins.*

Psychologists studying problem solving typically focus on well-defined problems, such as those encountered in playing chess.

Classic Problems and General Methods of Solution

The way to solve a problem depends, to a great extent, on the problem. For instance, if your problem is to fly to Los Angeles, you might call various airlines or travel agents. On the other hand, if your problem is to balance your checkbook, you normally would not ask for assistance from travel agents, but you might from a banker. Nonetheless, certain techniques that are not *domain-specific* (as the technique of calling a travel agent is) exist and will be reviewed here. These methods are stated at a general enough level so that, in principle, they can be used with a wide variety of problems, not just with problems of a certain type or domain.

Generate-and-Test

Here is the first problem for you to try. Think of ten words that begin with the letter *c* that are things to eat or drink. Write down all of the things that occur to you, even if they end up not meeting the criteria. How are you solving this problem?

My husband and I faced a real-life problem somewhat like this several years ago. We were in Minnesota and had to get 100 Swiss francs within a week to a hotel in Bern, Switzerland, to hold a room reservation. I went to the post office to get an international money order but discovered it would take about a month for the order to make its way to the hotel. My husband and I deliberated over how to solve the problem. We came up with a number of ideas. We could call people at American Express, and see if they could help. We could see if by chance any of our friends would be traveling to Bern in the next week. We could call Western Union and wire the money. We could get a cashier's check from a bank. We could go to our automobile club, purchase a traveler's check in Swiss francs, and mail it. The first four options, as it turned out, wouldn't work or were much too expensive. The fifth one met our criteria of being possible, working within a week's time, and being (relatively) affordable.

The process we used in solving this problem is a good example of the **generate-and-test** technique. As the name suggests, it consists of generating possible solutions (for example, "Let's call people at American Express, and see if they can help") and then testing them (for example, "Hello, American Express? I have the following problem. . . ."). The tests didn't work for the first four possibilities but did for the fifth (it would work, the cost was reasonable, the money would get there in time).

You may have used generate-and-test in the problem of generating names of things to eat or drink that begin with *c*. When I worked on this problem, some names came to mind that sound like they start with *c* but don't (for example, "ketchup," [unless you spell it "catsup"] or "sarsaparilla"), and some with *c* but aren't edible or drinkable ("cable," "canoe"). Again, the process used was thinking of possible solutions (generating) and then seeing if those possibilities met all the criteria (testing).

Generate-and-test is a technique that loses its effectiveness very rapidly when there are many possibilities and no particular guidance over the generation process. If you forget the combination to your locker, for instance, the technique will eventually work, but your frustration level by that time might exceed your willingness to persevere with the task. Moreover, if you do not have a means of keeping track of the possibilities you have tried, along with the ones you have yet to try, you might be in real trouble. There's a joke in the movie *UHF*, in which a blind man, working on a Rubik's cube puzzle sits next to a sighted man. The blind man twists the Rubik's cube into a particular pattern, thrusts it in front of the sighted man and asks, "Is this it [the correct pattern]?" "No," says the latter. The interchange is repeated, rapidly, several times. The joke is that this method of problem solving is all but doomed to failure, given the large number of possible configurations and the lack of any systematic way of trying them.

On the other hand, generate-and-test can be useful when there aren't a lot of possibilities to keep track of. If you've lost your keys somewhere between the cafeteria and your room, and you made intermediate stops in a classroom, the snack bar, and the bookstore, you can use the technique to help you search.

Means-Ends Analysis

Suppose that I want to visit my mother, who lives in Gloucester, Massachusetts. How can I get there from my home in Northfield, Minnesota? There are several possible means of transportation: walking, bicycling, taking a taxi, taking a bus, taking a train, driving my car, taking a plane or helicopter. The most practical means for me is to fly on a commercial airline; it's the fastest and fits my budget. However, before I can board my flight, I have to be at the Minneapolis-St. Paul airport, 40 miles to the north. Again, I could walk, bicycle, take a taxi, and so on. The most efficient and cost-effective means is to drive my car. However, my car is parked in the garage, not where I am sitting. So, I will have to get to the car. I would probably choose to walk.

The technique of problem solving described here is called **means-ends analysis.** It involves comparing the goal (Gloucester) with the starting point (Northfield), thinking of possible ways of overcoming the difference (walking, bicycling, taking a taxi, and so on), and choosing the best one. The selected option (taking a plane) may have certain prerequisite conditions (for example, being at the airport, with a ticket). If the preconditions aren't met, then a *subgoal* is created (for example, "How can I get to the airport?").

Newell and Simon (1972) and their associates studied means-ends analysis while solving certain crypt arithmetic problems, such as that shown here:

```
  DONALD
+ GERALD
  ROBERT
```

Given that D = 5, determine the values for the other letters.

They created a computer program, called GPS, or General Problem Solver, which solves problems in crypt arithmetic and in logic using means-ends analysis.

GPS uses the following basic strategy. First, it looks at the object it is given (such as the above crypt arithmetic problem, with letters) and compares it with the desired object (an arithmetic problem with numbers in place of all letters, where the solution is actually the addition of the two numbers above the line). GPS detects any differences between the actual and the desired object. Next, GPS considers the operations it has available to change objects. (In the example, the available operations include those that replace certain letters with certain digits, for example, D = 5). The operations used are chosen with the aim of reducing differences between actual and desired objects. In cases where none of the available operations applies to the actual object, GPS tries to modify the actual object so that operations could apply. GPS also tries to keep track of different kinds of differences between desired and actual objects, and to work on the most difficult differences first. Thus, if several possible operations are found, all of which could apply to an actual object, GPS has some means of prioritizing the different operations such that certain ones are used first.

Newell and Simon (1972) gave several problems in logic and in crypt arithmetic to both human subjects and GPS, and compared the "thinking" of both. (Human subjects generated verbal protocols, much like the ones you have been asked to generate as you have read this chapter; GPS gave a printout of its goals, subgoals, and operations it applied as it worked.) Comparing the protocols generated, Newell and Simon concluded that there were many similarities between the performance of GPS and the performance of the Yale students who served as subjects.

Notice that means-ends analysis, the general **heuristic,** or rule-of-thumb strategy used by GPS, is a more focused method of solution than generate-and-test: it guides the problem solver more in choosing what next step to take. Means-ends analysis also forces the problem solver to analyze aspects of the problem before starting to work on it, and to generate a plan to solve it. Often, this requires establishing subgoals. Notice here that the problem solver is acting less "blindly," and only after some thought.

Means-ends analysis is not always the optimal way to reach a solution, however, because sometimes the way involves taking a temporary step backward or further from the goal. For example, imagine that you live in an eastern suburb of Los Angeles but want to take a flight from Los Angeles to New York City. To do so, you have to move, temporarily, a greater distance from your goal than your current distance. Means-ends analysis can make it more difficult to see that the most efficient path toward a goal isn't always the one that is most direct.

Working Backward

Another general problem-solving technique is called *working backward*. Its user analyzes the goal to determine the last step needed to achieve it, then the next-to-last-step, and so on. For instance, in the problem of getting to my mother's apartment, the very last step is to walk from outside her front door into the apartment. The problem in getting to her front door can be solved by taking a cab to her apartment. I can get a cab at Logan airport, and

FIGURE 9-2.   The Towers of Hanoi problem. Determine a sequence of moves to transfer the three disks from the first to the third peg, moving only one disk at a time and never placing a bigger disk on top of a smaller one.

so on. Working backward often involves establishing subgoals, intermediate points at which certain subsidiary goals need to be achieved.

Working backward is a very important technique for solving many problems, including the famous Towers of Hanoi problem, depicted in Figure 9-2. A successful episode of problem solving might be something like the following: "First I have to get the bottom disk moved over. But to do that I have to move the top two disks. I can do that if I move the second disk to the spare peg, but to do that I have to move the top disk out of the way. I could do that by temporarily moving it to the goal peg, then move the second disk to the spare peg, then move the top disk back to the spare peg, then move the bottom disk over." Notice that the solution process usually does not start with the problem solver's making a move and seeing what happens. Instead, even after only a little practice, the usual pattern is to plan moves in advance, setting up many intermediate goals along the way (Egan & Greeno, 1974).

Backtracking

Try this next problem: Imagine there are five women, Cathy, Debbie, Judy, Linda, and Sonya. The five women each own a different breed of dog (either a Bernese mountain dog, a golden retriever, a Labrador retriever, an Irish setter, or a Shetland sheepdog), and they each have different occupations (clerk, executive, lawyer, surgeon, teacher). They also each have different numbers of children (0, 1, 2, 3, or 4). Given the information in Box 9-2, figure out how many children the person who owns the Shetland Sheepdog has.

In solving a problem you often need to make certain provisional assumptions. Sometimes, they turn out to be wrong and need to be "unmade." In those instances, it is useful to have some means of keeping track of when and which assumptions were made, in order to back up to certain choice points and start over. The women, dogs, children, and jobs problem in Box 9-2 is a case in point. Many people solve such problems by setting up a chart like the one shown in Figure 9-3. The chart is incomplete, and corresponds to the chart of someone who has read only the first 11 lines of Box 9-2. At this point, a problem solver can determine that the golden retriever's owner, who is an executive with four children, is either Debbie or Linda. He might temporarily assume that it's Debbie, only to find out when he reads the 12th line that Debbie owns the Bernese mountain dog. He would enter that information into his chart. But if the problem solver backs up to the point at which he made the incorrect assumption (that is, where he knows that either Debbie or Linda is the golden retreiver–owning, mother-

---

BOX 9 - 2   The Women, Dogs, Children, and Jobs Problem

From the following information, determine how many children the owner of the Shetland sheepdog has.

There are five women: Cathy, Debbie, Judy, Linda, and Sonya.
There are five occupations: clerk, executive, lawyer, teacher, and surgeon.
Everyone has a different number of children: 0, 1, 2, 3, or 4.
Cathy owns the Irish setter.
The teacher has no children.
The owner of the Labrador retriever is a surgeon.
Linda does not own the Shetland sheepdog.
Sonya is a lawyer.
The owner of the Shetland sheepdog does not have three children.
The owner of the golden retriever has four children.
Judy has one child.
The executive owns a golden retriever.
Debbie owns the Bernese mountain dog.
Cathy is a clerk.

	Cathy	Debbie	Judy	Linda	Sonya
Woman	Cathy	Debbie	Judy	Linda	Sonya
Dog	Irish Setter				
Number of Children			1		
Occupation					Lawyer

Golden Retriever	Laborador Retriever	Shetland Sheepdog	
4		≠3	0
Executive	Surgeon		Teacher

FIGURE 9-3.   Partial solution to the women, dogs, children, and jobs problem

of-four executive), he would know now that it is Linda, and this information will be necessary to solve the rest of the problem.

Reasoning by Analogy

The next problem is famous in the literature and is known as the tumor problem:

> Given a human being with an inoperable stomach tumor, and rays that destroy organic tissue at sufficient intensity, by what procedure can one free him of the tumor by these rays and at the same time avoid destroying the healthy tissue that surrounds it?

Originally posed to subjects by Duncker (1945, p. 1), the problem is often a difficult challenge. Duncker argued from studying the performance of several subjects (Box 9-3 presents an example protocol) that problem solving is not a matter of blind trial and error; rather, it involves a deep understanding of the elements of the problem and their relationships. To find a solution, the solver must grasp the "principle, the functional value of the solution," first and then arrange the specific details. The solution to the tumor problem is to send weak rays of radiation (weak enough so that no individual ray will inflict damage) from several angles, such that all rays converge at the site of the tumor. Although the radiation from any one ray will not be strong enough to destroy the tumor (or the healthy tissue in its path), the convergence of rays will.

Gick and Holyoak (1980) presented subjects with Duncker's tumor problem, after each subject had read a story such as that shown in Box 9-4.

B O X   9 - 3   Protocol from One of Duncker's (1945) Subjects

1. Send rays through the esophagus.
2. Desensitize the healthy tissues by means of a chemical injection.
3. Expose the tumor by operating.
4. One ought to decrease the intensity of the rays on their way; for example— would this work?—turn the rays on at full strength only after the tumor has been reached. (Experimenter: False analogy; no injection is in question.)
5. One should swallow something inorganic (which would not allow passage of the rays) to protect the healthy stomach-walls. (E: It is not merely the stomach walls which are to be protected.)
6. Either the rays must enter the body or the tumor must come out. Perhaps one could alter the location of the tumor—but how? Through pressure? No.
7. Introduce a cannula.—(E: What, in general, does one do when, with any agent, one wishes to produce in a specific place an effect which he wishes to avoid on the way to that place?)
8. (Reply:) One neutralizes the effect on the way. But that is what I have been attempting all the time.
9. Move the tumor around to the exterior. (Compare 6.) (The E repeats the problem and emphasizes ". . . which destroy *at sufficient intensity*.")
10. The intensity ought to be variable. (Compare 4.)
11. Adaptation of the healthy tissues by previous weak application of the rays. (E: How can it be brought about that the rays destroy only the region of the tumor?)
12. (Reply:) I see no more than two possibilities: either to protect the body or to make the rays harmless. (E: How could one decrease the intensity of the rays en route? [Compare 4.])
13. (Reply:) Somehow divert . . . diffuse rays . . . disperse . . . stop! Send a broad and weak bundle of rays through a lens in such a way that the tumor lies at the focal point and thus receives intensive radiation. (Total duration about half an hour.)

SOURCE: From "On Problem Solving," by K. Duncker, 1945, Psychological Monographs, 58, 2–3. Copyright © 1945 by the American Psychological Association.

Although the story appeared very dissimilar to the tumor problem, the underlying method of solution was the same. Gick and Holyoak found that subjects who had read the story of the general and were told that it contained a relevant hint were more likely to solve the tumor problem.

The tumor problem and the problem of the general differ in their surface features but share an underlying structure. The components of one correspond at least roughly with the components of the other: the army is analogous to the rays; the capturing of enemy forces to the destruction of the tumor; the convergence of soldiers at the fortress to the convergence of rays at the site of the tumor. To make use of the analogy, subjects have to engage in the "principle-finding" analysis described by Duncker: to move beyond the details and focus on the relevant structures of the problem. Gick and Holyoak (1980) refer to this process as the induction of an abstract *schema* (using the term in the ways defined in Chapter 5). They present evidence that subjects who construct such a representation are more likely to benefit from work on analogous problems.

It is interesting that subjects often had to be explicitly told to use the story of the general to solve the tumor problem. Only 30% of subjects spontaneously noticed the analogy, although 75% could solve the problem

---

BOX 9-4   The Story of the General

A small country was ruled from a strong fortress by a dictator. The fortress was situated in the middle of the country, surrounded by farms and villages. Many roads led to the fortress through the countryside. A rebel general vowed to capture the fortress. The general knew that an attack by his entire army would capture the fortress. He gathered his army at the head of one of the roads, ready to launch a full-scale direct attack. However, the general then learned that the dictator had planted mines on each of the roads. The mines were set so that small bodies of men could pass over them safely, since the dictator needed to move his troops and workers to and from the fortress. However, any large force would detonate the mines. Not only would this blow up the road, but it would also destroy many neighboring villages. It therefore seemed impossible to capture the fortress.

However, the general devised a simple plan. He divided his army into small groups and dispatched each group to the head of a different road. When all was ready he gave the signal and each group marched down a different road. Each group continued down its road to the fortress so that the entire army arrived together at the fortress at the same time. In this way, the general captured the fortress and overthrew the dictator.

SOURCE: *From "Analogical Problem Solving," by M. L. Gick and K. J. Holyoak, 1980,* Cognitive Psychology, 12, *351–353. Copyright © 1980 by Academic Press. Reprinted by permission.*

if told that the story of the general would be useful in constructing the solution (for comparison, only about 10% solved the problem without the story). This is similar to a finding reported by Reed, Ernst, and Banerji (1974): subjects' performance was facilitated by their previous work on an analogous problem, but only if the analogy was pointed out to them.

In later work, Gick and Holyoak (1983) found that they could do away with explicit hints *if* they gave two analogous stories rather than one. Subjects read the story of the general and a story about a fire chief's putting out a fire by having a circle of firefighters surround it, each one throwing buckets of water at once. Subjects were told that the experiment was about story comprehension, and were asked to write summaries of each story and a comparison of the two before being given the tumor problem to solve. The authors argued that providing multiple examples helps subjects to form an abstract schema (in this case, what the authors call a "convergence" schema), which they later apply to new, analogous problems. Catrambone and Holyoak (1989) further argued that unless subjects were explicitly asked to compare stories, they did not form the necessary schema with which to solve the problem.

Blocks to Problem Solving

A problem, by definition, is something that can't be solved in a single, obvious step. For instance, we don't count combing our hair as an instance of problem solving because the step of using a comb does not require much thought, and there are no particular obstacles that need to be overcome. Problem solving, in contrast, carries the meaning of a goal with some barriers or constraints to reaching it. Sometimes, the barriers and constraints are so strong that they prevent, or at least seriously interfere with, successful solution. In this section, we will review some factors that apparently make problem solving on a variety of problems more difficult.

Mental Set

Figure 9-4 presents a number of problems all having to do with the same theme: obtaining an exact amount of water, given three different-size measuring jugs. Before reading on, work on each of the problems in the order given, and write the time it takes you to complete each one. Also record any thoughts about the relative difficulty of the problems.

What you probably found if you actually worked the problems was the following: the first one took a relatively long time, but you were faster and faster at solving the subsequent problems, given the number of problems you previously worked. You also probably noticed a common pattern to the problems: all could be solved by the formula $B - A - 2C$. Did you use this formula to solve the second-to-last problem? If you did, that is

Problem	Capacity of Jar A	Capacity of Jar B	Capacity of Jar C	Desired Amount
1	21	127	3	100
2	14	163	25	99
3	18	43	10	5
4	9	42	6	21
5	20	59	4	31
6	23	49	3	20
7	18	48	4	22
8	14	36	8	6

FIGURE 9-4. The water jar problem. SOURCE: From "Mechanization in Problem Solving: The Effect of *Einstellung*," by A. S. Luchins, 1942, *Psychological Monographs, 54*, 1. Copyright © 1942 by the American Psychological Association.

interesting because an apparently more direct solution would be $A + C$. The last problem is also interesting, in that it does not fit the first formula at all, but is easily solved with a very easy one, $A - C$. Did it take you some time to realize this? If so, your performance might be characterized as being constrained by **mental set.**

Mental set is the tendency to adopt a certain framework, strategy, or procedure, or more generally to see things in a certain way instead of in other, equally plausible ways. Mental set is analogous to perceptual set, which was discussed in Chapter 2. Recall that perceptual set is the tendency to perceive an object or pattern in a certain way based on your immediate perceptual experience. Like perceptual set, mental set seems to be induced by even short amounts of practice. Working on several water jug problems in a row that follow a common pattern makes it easy to apply the formula but harder to see new relationships among the three terms.

Luchins (1942) reports on experiments where problems such as those in Figure 9-4 were given to university students. After solving the first four problems using the formula $B - A - 2C$, all of them solved the fifth problem using this method, instead of the more direct $A + C$ method available.

Mental set often causes people to make certain unwarranted assumptions, without being aware of making them. Figure 9-5(a) gives an example. Most people, when asked to solve the famous nine-dot problem

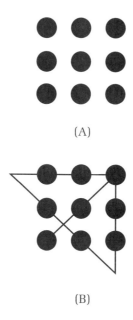

(A)

(B)

FIGURE 9-5.   The nine-dot problem and its solution. Connect all nine dots using four straight lines, without lifting your pen or pencil as you draw them.

make the assumption that the four lines must stay within the "borders" of the dots. This constraint makes it impossible to come up with the solution, shown in Figure 9-5(b).

Another problem relevant to mental set is borrowed from Perkins (1981). I will describe a situation, and you determine what the situation is:

> There is a man at home. That man is wearing a mask. There is a man coming home. What is happening?

Because I can't interact with you, I'll report on the questions (constrained to be of the yes/no type) that my students ask when I present this. Is the man at home at his own home? (Yes.) Does the man at home know the other man? (Yes.) Does the man at home expect the other man? (Yes.) Is the mask a disguise? (No.) Is the man at home in a living room? (No.) Is the man at home in the kitchen? (No.)

Part of where my students start to go wrong is in making assumptions about the home in the situation. Many equate "home" with "house," although the answer to the problem is a baseball game. Perkins (1981) would argue that the assumptions that people make in interpreting the problem are a kind of mental set, and that this mental set hurts problem solving.

Another example of mental set is illustrated in Figure 9-6, which depicts another famous problem in the literature, known as the two-string

FIGURE 9-6.   The two-string problem

problem (Maier, 1930, 1931). A person is shown to a room that has two strings attached to the ceiling. The strings are spaced far enough apart that the person can't hold onto both at the same time. Her task is to tie these strings together somehow. All she has in the room with her are a chair, an umbrella, a pair of pliers, and a bowl. What can she do?

The solution, which many subjects have difficulty discovering, is to use the pliers as a weight to make one of the strings into a pendulum. Swing this string, walk to the other string and grab it, wait for the pendulum to swing toward you, grab it, and tie the two strings together. Fewer than 40% of Maier's subjects solved this without a hint. One source of difficulty seemed to be the subjects' unwillingness to think of other functions for a pair of pliers; they failed to notice that the pliers could be used as a weight as well as for its intended function. This phenomenon is called **functional fixedness.** It appears to be an instance of mental set, in that a person subject to functional fixedness has apparently adopted a rigid mental set toward an object.

Using Incomplete or Incorrect Representations

A related difficulty in problem solving has to do with the initial interpretation of the problem. If the problem is misunderstood, or if the wrong information is focused on, the solver will be at a disadvantage. The checkerboard problem well illustrates this block to problem solving.

The problem is depicted in Figure 9-7, which shows a standard checkerboard with two diagonally opposite corner squares cut off. Next to the checkerboard are a number of dominoes of such dimensions that each takes up exactly two checkerboard squares. Intact checkerboards, you'll recall, have 64 squares. This one has 62. Is there a way to arrange 31 dominoes such that every checkerboard square is covered by a domino?

The key to the solution is to realize that whatever the arrangement, each domino will cover exactly one black square and one red square, given the way checkerboards are arranged. But now notice that the two excised squares are the same color. Because a domino must cover two differently colored squares, there is no way to arrange 31 dominos to cover the muti-

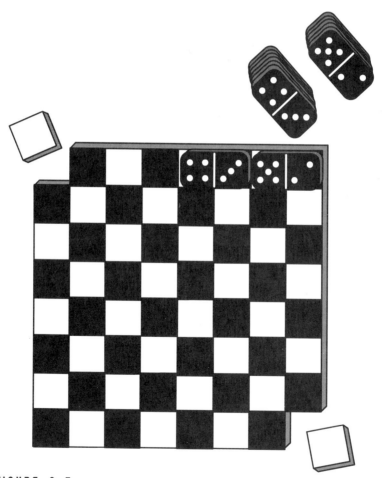

FIGURE 9-7.   The mutilated checkerboard problem. Can 31 dominoes be arranged to cover the remaining checkerboard squares? Each domino covers two squares.

lated checkerboard. The difficulty most people have with this problem is that they fail to include these two pieces of crucial information in their initial representation of the problem. Thus, the representation is incomplete.

Similarly, in the baseball game (man at home) problem given earlier, representing the problem in terms of a person sitting in a house would be sure to lead you down the wrong path. It would be a case of using an incorrect representation—one that included information that was not presented in the problem, and in fact that was not correct.

The choice of representation can often make a great deal of difference. Schwartz (1971), studying problems like the women-dogs-children-jobs problem of Box 9-2, found that people who constructed charts like the one in Figure 9-3 were much more successful in solving the problems relative to those who merely wrote down names, dogs, jobs, and so forth, with arrows or lines connecting them (for example, Cathy—Irish setter; golden retriever—four children).

Lack of Problem-Specific Knowledge or Expertise

Until now, we have been discussing general problem-solving abilities, with problems that have a puzzle-like character to them. The assumption is that most of these problems are about equally unfamiliar to everyone, and that people basically go about solving them in the same way. Other kinds of problems—for example, those in chess or other skilled games; textbook problems in physics, geometry, or electronics; computer programming; and problems in diagnosis—seem to be different in kind from the puzzles we have been talking about. In particular, most such problems are approached differently by experts and novices (Chi, Glaser, & Farr, 1988).

We saw in Chapter 2 that experts and novices differed in their perceptual abilities, with experts better able to "pick up on" more perceptual information than a novice would. Effects of expertise are not limited to perceptual abilities, however. Familiarity with a domain of knowledge seems to change the way one solves problems within that frame of reference. A good example is to compare the ability of undergraduate psychology majors and their professors to design experiments. Typically, the professor is much better at solving the problems connected to the task. Her experience in designing experiments allows her to sort out the relevant from the irrelevant information and to call to mind various situations that need to be attended to. It also provides her with a number of rules of thumb to be used in estimating the number of subjects to be used, the kinds of statistical analyses that can be performed, the duration of the experiment, and so on. Problem solvers who come to a problem with a limited knowledge base are clearly at a disadvantage.

Lesgold, Rubinson, Feltovich, Glaser, Klopfer, and Wang (1988) compared the performance of five expert radiologists with that of first- and second-, and third- and fourth-year medical residents as they diagnosed

X-ray pictures. They found that the experts noted more specific properties of the X-ray films, hypothesized more causes and more effects, and clustered more symptoms together than did either of the two nonexpert groups of medical residents.

Glaser and Chi (1988) reviewing this and other studies of expert/novice differences, describe several qualitative distinctions between the two groups. First, experts excel in their own domains—that is, their knowledge is domain-specific. A grand master chess player, for example, would not be expected to solve chemistry problems as well as a chemist would. We have already noted in Chapter 2 that experts perceive larger meaningful patterns in their domain of expertise than novices do. Experts are faster than novices at performing skills in their domain of expertise, and they show greater memorial abilities for information within that domain.

In problem solving, experts see and represent a problem in their domain at a deeper and more principled level than do novices, who tend to represent information superficially (Chi, Feltovich, and Glaser, 1981). For example, when solving physics problems, experts tend to organize the problems in terms of principles of physics, such as Newton's first law of motion; novices instead tend to focus on the objects mentioned in the problem, such as an inclined plane or a frictionless surface. Experts also spend proportionately more time on qualitatively analyzing a problem, trying to grasp or understand it, relative to novices, who are more likely to plunge in and start looking for solutions. Finally, throughout the process of problem solving, experts are more likely to check for errors in their thinking.

The Problem Space Hypothesis

Researchers studying problem solving often think about the processes in terms of mentally searching a **problem space** (Baron, 1988; Lesgold, 1988; Newell, 1980; Newell & Simon, 1972). The idea here is that every possible state of affairs within a problem corresponds to a node in a mental graph. The entire set of nodes occupies some mental area, and this area, together with the graph, is the problem space. Figure 9-8 shows a problem space for the Towers of Hanoi problem. Alan Lesgold compares a problem space to a "maze of mental activity through which we must wander, searching for a solution" (1988, p. 190).

If it is possible to move from one state to another by means of some operation, it can be depicted in any paper-and-pencil representation of the problem space by a line connecting the two nodes. Any sequence of "mental moves" is depicted as a sequence of moves from one node to another. Any sequence of moves beginning at the initial state and ending at the final goal state constitutes a path through the problem space.

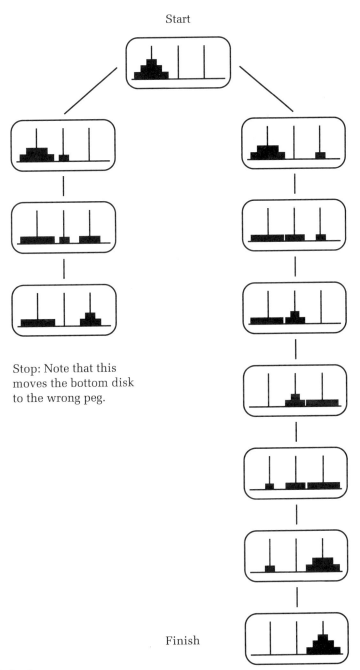

Stop: Note that this moves the bottom disk to the wrong peg.

FIGURE 9-8.   A part of the problem space for the Towers of Hanoi problem, showing the solution

Good problem solving is argued to be the creation of efficient paths: ones that are as short as possible and take as few detours as possible between the initial state and the goal state. It is assumed that the best paths are found through searching—with thorough searches being more likely to turn up solutions. Presumably, the acquisition of expertise allows people to develop better hunches about which areas of the problem space will be the most useful ones to explore, and in what order. Searches that fail to explore parts of the space (because of mental set, for example) can block problem solving when the solution lies in a part of the space that isn't searched. Incomplete or incorrect representations are likely to result in the construction of an incomplete or incorrect problem space, which in turn also harms problem solving.

Newell (1980) argues that problem spaces are the fundamental organizational unit of not only problem solving but reasoning and decision making as well (these topics will be covered in Chapters 10 and 11, respectively): "The [problem space] hypothesis is common ground for all symbolic cognition. Analysis of a cognitive task involves first specifying the problem space and then specifying the search control knowledge [the order in which various parts of the space will be considered] used within that problem space" (p. 712).

Finding Creative Solutions

Many of the problems psychologists ask people to solve require *insight,* a change in frame of reference or in the way elements of the problem are interpreted and organized. The process by which insight occurs is not well understood. Whatever it is, it appears to play a vital role in what is commonly called *creativity.* Although the term is a difficult one to define precisely, many psychologists agree that creativity has to do with appropriate novelty, that is, originality that suits some purpose (Hennessey & Amabile, 1988). Appropriate ideas that lack novelty are mundane; conversely, original ideas that do not address some problem in a useful way are bizarre.

Great moments of artistic, musical, scientific, or other types of discovery often seem to share a critical moment, in which the discoverer has a mental "Eureka" experience—when the proverbial "light bulb" is turned on. Many biographies of composers, artists, scientists, and other eminent experts begin with "Eureka" stories (Perkins, 1981, presents a review of some of these). Such stories lead to the notion that creative people have something that less creative people don't have, or that their cognitive processes work in very different ways (at least while they are being creative) than those of less creative people. In this section, we will focus on two types of explanations for creative insight: one that describes creativity as special cognitive processing, and one that describes creativity as the result of normal, everyday cognition.

Unconscious Processing and Incubation

As a college junior, I took courses in calculus, which, although extremely useful, were often extremely frustrating to me. I would work on the homework assignment, only to find one of the problems absolutely unworkable. The problem would nag at me, and I'd try every technique I could think of. In frustration, I would put the problem aside and go on to other things. Late that night, sometimes waking from sleep, I would see the problem in a whole new light. Often, I had discovered the correct solution. On occasions when I'd hit upon another incorrect solution, the feelings of frustration were renewed.

The experience I am describing is a "textbook case" of unconscious processing, or *incubation*. The idea is that while my mind was busy running other cognitive processes, some other sort of processing was happening in the background. (Those of you who like computer metaphors might describe this as "batch" processing, as opposed to "interactive processing.") The unconscious processing churned away, even as I slept, until the answer was found, then the answer announced itself all at once, even if it had to wake me from a sound sleep. Those who believe in incubation typically believe in the existence of an unconscious layer of the mind that is able to process information without giving rise to conscious awareness.

Smith and Blakenship (1989) offered one empirical demonstration of incubation effects by means of picture-word puzzles called *rebuses*. After their subjects had solved 15 rebuses, they were presented with the 16th, which had a misleading cue that caused fixation on an incorrect interpretation. Subjects were later given this critical rebus a second time, without the cue, and were again asked to solve the puzzle and also to recall the cue. Control subjects saw the second presentation of the rebus immediately, but experimental subjects received either a five- or fifteen-minute "break" from the puzzle, during which they either did nothing or were asked to complete a demanding music-perception task (to prevent them from continuing to work on the rebus). The authors predicted that subjects who were given longer "filled" intervals (that is, intervals during which the music task was presented) would be more likely to forget the misleading cue, and thus to solve the rebus. In fact, this pattern of results is just the one they report.

Most empirical studies, however, fail to find positive effects of incubation: subjects who take physical and mental breaks during problem solving, and therefore have more opportunity for incubation, rarely show any increased ability to solve problems more thoroughly or more quickly relative to subjects who work steadily at the problem (Olton, 1979). Moreover, subjects in another study on incubation effects reported that during the "break" periods they thought aloud about the problem surreptitiously. In fact, subjects in another experimental condition who were prevented from this covert thinking about the problem (by having them memorize a text passage) during the break showed very few effects of incubation (Browne & Cruse, 1988).

Designing critical tests of the incubation hypothesis is also very difficult: experimenters must make sure that subjects really do cease thinking about the problem during the incubation interval, a challenging task for anyone who cannot read minds!

Everyday Mechanisms

Does creative insight depend on special cognitive processes, such as incubation? An alternative view asserts that it results from ordinary cognitive processes that virtually every person uses in the normal course of life (Perkins, 1981). Perkins's ideas provide a coherent overview of this approach to the study of creativity, and will be reviewed in detail here. Other authors offer slightly different proposals, sharing with Perkins the idea that the processes that lead to creativity are not extraordinary (Langley & Jones, 1988; Sternberg, 1988a; Weisberg, 1988).

Perkins (1981) describes examples of cognitive processes that underlie normal, everyday functioning, as well as creative invention. One such process is *directed remembering.* This is the ability to channel your memory in order to bring to consciousness past experience or knowledge that meets various constraints. The first task in this chapter, asking you to think of foods and drinks whose names begin with *c* is a directed-remembering task. Perkins argues that the same process goes on in creative invention. Darwin's construction of the theory of evolution, for instance, had to provide an explanation that was consistent with existing scientific knowledge. That knowledge acted as a constraint on the types of explanations he could invent.

A second relevant cognitive process is *noticing.* An important part of creation, artists and scientists assert, is revising drafts. In revising, one needs to notice where the problems are. Noticing also plays a role in many "Eureka" experiences, according to Perkins, when creators notice a similarity between one problem and another.

Contrary recognition, or the ability to recognize objects not for what they are but as something else, is another important creative process. Seeing a cloud as a castle is a familiar example. This ability obviously relates to analogical thinking, in that it requires the creator to move beyond the bounds of reality and of what is and to imagine reality in other ways.

This approach to creativity, then, assumes that creative individuals use the same cognitive processes that so-called noncreative people do. Reported episodes of "flashes of insight," are then argued to have occurred in a more progressive, step-by-step fashion. Incubation, following this line of argument, has to do with making a fresh start on the solution process, forgetting old approaches that did not work. Note that this

Perkins argues that creative people rely on ordinary cognitive processes when they create.

description is quite similar to descriptions of what it means to break mental set.

Indeed, the relationship between problem solving and the contrary-recognition approach to creativity is strong. Both include the idea of mental search for possibilities that are novel and that meet various requirements or constraints. A person's creativity has to do with her willingness to search harder and longer for solutions that meet multiple constraints. What makes for creativity, then, are a creator's own values for original, useful results; her ability to withstand potentially long periods without success; and her plans and abilities.

Many of the proposed accounts of creativity remain, for the most part, untested empirically. Thus, the question of whether acts of creativity use special-purpose or regular cognitive processes remains open. These proposals, then, should be seen as ideas that can guide future investigations rather than as well-developed theories that have survived rigorous testing.

Finding Productive Solutions

Many proposals for creativity hinge on people's abilities to generate a number of ideas that might at first seem "off the wall" or "out of touch." Once a novel idea is generated, however, it must be evaluated and assessed in terms of its appropriateness. Does the proposed solution really meet all the objectives and constraints? Are there hidden or subtle flaws in the idea? What are the proposal's implications?

A person asking these kinds of questions can be described as exercising what psychologists, philosophers, and educators call **critical thinking.** Many definitions of critical thinking exist. Dewey (1933), who called it "reflective thinking," defined it as "active, persistent, and careful consideration of any belief or supposed form of knowledge in the light of the grounds that support it and the further conclusions to which it tends" (p. 9). Dewey distinguishes between reflective thought and other kinds: random ideas, rote recall, beliefs that a person does not have evidence for.

Wertheimer (1945) a Gestalt psychologist, presents several examples that illustrate critical thinking quite well. One concerns learning how to find the area of a parallelogram. One way to teach someone to do this is to teach him a formula, such as the familiar one from high school geometry: Area = Base × Altitude. (Figure 9-9(a) presents an example parallelogram, with the base and altitude labeled.) If the student memorizes this formula carefully, he will have a "rote" or what Wertheimer called a "mechanically repetitive" means of solving the problem.

One problem with rote solutions, however, is that if a student forgets the formula, he may be at a complete loss. A better approach, Wertheimer argued, was to try to teach the student to grasp the "essential structure" of the problem—to identify and understand the fundamental issues.

Consider next the parallelogram in Figure 9-9(b), noting the shaded area. Suppose this area were to be cut off the parallelogram but added to the other side, as shown in Figure 9-9(c). The transformation of the object creates a familiar and simple geometric object, that of a rectangle. The formula for finding the area of a rectangle is well known (Base × Altitude). Note that the transformation has added exactly the same area to the right side of the figure as was subtracted from the left. As a result, the total area has not been changed. Instead, a more "regular" geometric figure, with exactly the same area, has been created.

What is the advantage of teaching this method of solution? For one thing, it is more generalizable. The method applies not just to parallelograms but to many geometrically irregular figures, such as the one depicted in Figure 9-9(d). For another, the solution shows a deeper understanding of *why* the formula works. In this instance, the formula is not simply blindly applied to the problem but, rather, grows out of the student's understanding of the nature of a parallelogram as a geometric object.

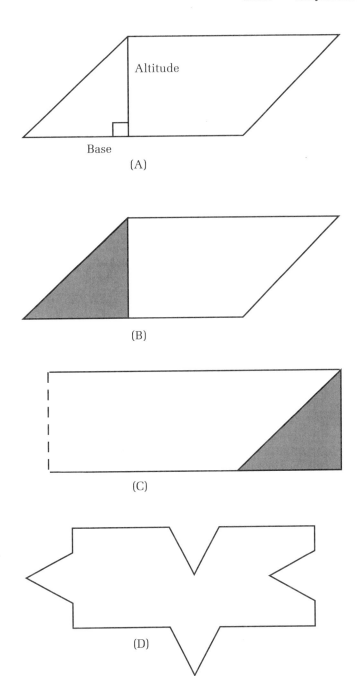

FIGURE 9-9.   Parallelograms and another geometric figure

In a more recent study of critical thinking, David Perkins and his colleagues (Perkins, Allen, & Hafner, 1983) presented students and adults of various levels of educational background with various controversial issues. Subjects were asked to reason aloud about each issue. One example was "Would a law requiring a five-cent deposit on bottles and cans reduce litter?" (Perkins, Allen, & Hafner, 1983, p. 178). The authors measured critical thinking by looking at the number of times a subject raised objections or challenges to his own thinking. An example of what they would consider good critical thinking is the following:

> The law wants people to return the bottles for the five cents, instead of littering them. But I don't think five cents is enough nowadays to get people to bother. But wait, it isn't just five cents at a blow, because people can accumulate cases of bottles or bags of cans in their basements and take them back all at once, so probably they would do that. Still, those probably aren't the bottles and cans that get littered anyway; it's the people out on picnics or kids hanging around the street and parks that litter bottles and cans, and they wouldn't bother to return them for a nickel. But someone else might. (p. 178)

Notice the structure of the thinking here: each sentence in some way presents an objection to the previous one.

According to Perkins, good thinking requires a large knowledge base and some means of using it efficiently. Good thinking also requires the kind of objection raising illustrated above, showing the thinker actively trying to question himself, and to construct examples and counterexamples to his conclusions. What often hampers critical thinking is a kind of mental laziness—stopping thinking whenever you get any answer at all. A noncritical thinker might reason about the bottle bill as follows: "Well, it'd be nice to try to reduce litter, but five cents won't motivate people, so it won't work." Notice that in this case the person constructs one mental scenario, then stops, without questioning any of the assumptions or trying to think of any other possibilities. Perkins and his associates (1983) urge people to overcome this tendency to think about an issue only until things make superficial sense and, instead, to search harder and look longer for other possibilities and interpretations.

Summary

Thinking, the manipulation of information, occurs for a wide range of what appear to be very different tasks. Psychologists draw distinctions among types of problems, for example, between well-defined and ill-defined ones, and among types of thinking, for example, focused versus unfocused. It is not yet clear, however, whether the cognitive processes used for different tasks are themselves really different in kind. An alternative possibility is that what looks like different kinds of thinking really stems from different combinations of the very same cognitive processes. This issue is quite an open one in the field.

Some psychologists studying problem solving have discovered general strategies (for example, generate-and-test; means-ends analysis; reasoning by analogy) that they believe people use in a wide variety of situations, and different blocks to problem solving (mental set, functional fixedness, incorrect or incomplete problem representations). Others argue for the importance of domain-specific knowledge and strategies as a better predictor of whether or not a given person will have success solving a given problem. These investigators point out that problem-solving strategies often vary with the expertise, or background knowledge, of the problem solver.

Similarities among kinds of thinking can also be identified. Some psychologists argue that the similarities can be explained by a common framework. The idea that all sorts of instances of thinking (including episodes of problem solving, inventing, and even reasoning and decision making, covered in Chapters 9 and 10) are all a kind of mental search (Baron, 1988). This proposal accepts the problem space hypothesis, or something close to it, as a good account of how people mentally manipulate information. Recall that the problem space hypothesis views thinking as finding a path through a "mental graph" of possibilities (the mental graph being the problem space). Sometimes, the search for a path is very focused and constrained; other times (for example, during episodes of daydreaming) it meanders without a definite goal.

It is interesting that some psychologists have argued that the factors that seem to promote good performance on one type of thinking task also seem to help on the others. Included in the list of these factors are adopting the values and strategies to remain open minded, to explore unusual possibilities, to question the first conclusion you come to, to try to avoid bias, to try to find new and fresh approaches. Although no one would argue that thinking skills can substitute for a broad and deep knowledge base, what is suggested is that good thinking skills help you get the most out of the knowledge you have. This suggestion, based largely on anecdotal proposals from educators, philosophers, and psychologists, awaits future research on the processes used in all kinds of thinking.

Recommended Readings

Classic works on thinking and problem solving are Dewey (1933), Luchins, (1942), Duncker (1945), Wertheimer (1945), and Newell and Simon (1972). Guilford (1950) and Koestler (1964) are early and influential works on creativity. General reviews of topics relating to thinking, creativity, and problem solving are contained in a volume edited by Sternberg and Smith (1988), and in textbooks such as Baron (1988) and Mayer (1992).

Greeno and Simon (1988) present a comprehensive and recent review of the literature on problem solving. Kotovsky, Hayes, and Simon (1985) explore problem solving on different versions of the Towers of Hanoi problem. Catrambone and Holyoak (1990) describe experiments investigating techniques of teaching people to identify subgoals in solving problems in probability. Hayes's (1989) text describes research and applications of the literature on problem solving. Students who enjoy problem solving might enjoy a book of problems and solutions by Gardner (1978) entitled, appropriately, *aha! Insight*. Recent work by Cummins (1992) explores cognitive processes by which people can develop expertise in problem solving.

Sternberg (1988b) edited a volume in which a number of authors present different views on creativity. Sternberg and Lubart (1991) also present a theory of creativity outlining the necessary elements and how they interact. A series of experiments by Yaniv and Meyer (1987) explores possible links between incubation effects and memory-retrieval phenomena, and Smith and Blakenship (1991) report five experiments suggesting that incubation effects depend on initial induction of fixation on misleading information.

Nickerson, Perkins, and Smith (1985) present an overview of works on critical thinking; Baron and Sternberg (1987) edited a volume containing essays by a number of investigators of this topic.

REVIEW QUESTIONS

1. Compare and contrast the generate-and-test, the means-ends analysis, and the reasoning by analogy approaches to problem solving.

2. In what ways is *mental set* a phenomenon similar to *perceptual set* (described in Chapter 2)? In what ways are the two phenomena dissimilar?

3. Describe some of the expert/novice differences in problem solving.

4. Discuss the *problem space hypothesis.* How might it account for and explain the various blocks to problem solving reviewed in the chapter?

5. What kinds of cognitive processes have been proposed to account for creativity? How might an experimental psychologist test the role of any one of these processes?

6. Explore the connections and differences among problem solving, creativity, and critical thinking.

CHAPTER 10

Reasoning

It is six o'clock, and you've been waiting for more than an hour for your friend to arrive for dinner. She's almost always on time, and she's the kind of person who would call if she knew she'd be late. You remember her telling you that she would be driving her car to get to your place.

Putting all of this information together, you conclude that, more than likely, she's caught in traffic. Psychologists use the term **reasoning** to describe these and other cognitive processes "that . . . [transform] given information (called the set of *premises*) in order to reach conclusions" (Galotti, 1989, p. 333).

The term *reasoning* is often used interchangeably with the term *thinking,* and you may therefore notice a great deal of overlap in the topics covered in this chapter and those covered in Chapter 9 ("Thinking and Problem Solving"). The psychologists who do make a distinction between reasoning and thinking see the first as a special case of the second. Specifically, when cognitive psychologists speak of reasoning, they have in mind a specific kind of thinking: the thinking that is done in solving certain kinds of puzzles or mysteries. Often, reasoning involves the use of certain principles of logic. At other times, the term is used more broadly, to cover instances of thinking, in which people take certain information as input and by making various inferences, either create new information or make implicit information explicit.

When reasoning, we have one or more particular goals in mind—our thinking is focused. Reasoning involves inferences or conclusions drawn from other information. Some of the conclusions we draw involve new information; however, many are mundane, so much so that we may not even notice that we have done any mental work to draw them. For instance, a friend says to you, "Last night at softball, I managed to catch a pop fly." From this, you almost automatically infer that your friend in fact tried to catch that ball. Her word "managed" presupposes effort on the part of the subject, and this presupposition cues your inference. All of this happens rather quickly and so automatically that you would probably not even notice that you had drawn an inference. In fact, you took your friend's statement (the premise), and drew the conclusion you did based on your understanding of the words in the premise and their presuppositions.

Psychologists studying reasoning often give people logical puzzles to solve. One of my favorite examples (based on the *Alice in Wonderland* stories) is shown in Box 10-1. Try to solve this one on your own, before comparing your thinking with the solution, which is laid out at the end of the chapter. In these kinds of tasks, the inferences that people draw often follow principles of logic. This has led some cognitive psychologists to develop a "psychologic," or a set of logical principles they believe people rely on to draw inferences. We will see examples of such systems below.

Other psychologists have noted, however, that some situations that require inferences do not have logical principles that apply. For example, consider the following *analogical reasoning* task: *Washington* is to *one* as *Jefferson* is to *what?* It seems unlikely that any general rule will apply to this problem, and likely that drawing the correct inference depends on your knowledge of U.S. presidents and either their serial order of office (Washington was the first president; Jefferson the third) or their appearance on U.S. paper currency (Washington on the dollar bill, Jefferson on the two-dollar bill).

We will examine a variety of reasoning tasks in the upcoming sections. To review people's performance, we will first need to understand something about logical principles and arguments and kinds of reasoning tasks. These will be reviewed in the next section. We will also examine some factors that seem to hinder reasoning performance and cause people either to draw erroneous conclusions or to overlook counterexamples and exceptions to the conclusions they draw. Finally, we will examine three general frameworks that attempt to explain the mental processes we use when we draw inferences and conclusions.

Types of Reasoning

Cognitive psychologists, along with philosophers, draw many distinctions between kinds of reasoning. One common distinction divides reasoning into two types: *deductive* and *inductive*. There are several ways to explain this distinction. One way of thinking about the difference is to say that deductive reasoning goes from the general to the specific or particular (for example, "All college students like pizza. Terry is a college student. Therefore, Terry likes pizza."). Inductive reasoning goes from the specific to the general (for example, "Brian is a college student. Brian lives in a dormitory. Therefore, all college students live in dormitories."). Another way to describe the difference between the two types of reasoning is to say that in deductive reasoning, no new information is added; any conclusion drawn represents information that was already implicit in the premises. Inductive reasoning, on the other hand, can result in conclusions that contain new information.

B O X 1 0 - 1   A Logic Puzzle

'How about making us some nice tarts?' the King of Hearts asked the Queen of Hearts one cool summer day.

'What's the sense of making tarts without jam?' said the Queen furiously. 'The jam is the best part!'

'Then use jam,' said the King.

'I can't!' shouted the Queen. 'My jam has been stolen!'

'Really!' said the King. 'This is quite serious! Who stole it?'

'How do you expect *me* to know who stole it? If I knew, I would have had it back long ago and the miscreant's head in the bargain!'

Well, the King had his soldiers scout around for the missing jam, and it was found in the house of the March Hare, the Mad Hatter, and the Dormouse. All three were promptly arrested and tried.

'Now, now!' exclaimed the King at the trial. 'I want to get to the bottom of this! I don't like people coming into my kitchen and stealing my jam!' . . .

'Did *you* by any chance steal the jam?' the King asked the March Hare.

'I never stole the jam!' pleaded the March Hare. . . .

'What about *you*?' the King roared to the Hatter, who was trembling like a leaf. 'Are you by any chance the culprit?'

The Hatter was unable to utter a word; he just stood there gasping and sipping his tea.

'If he has nothing to say, that only proves his guilt,' said the Queen, 'so off with his head immediately!'

'No, no!' pleaded the Hatter. 'One of us stole it, but it wasn't me!' . . .

'And what about *you*?' continued the King to the Dormouse. 'What do you have to say about all of this? Did the March Hare and the Hatter both tell the truth?'

'At least one of them did,' replied the Dormouse, who then fell asleep for the rest of the trial.

As subsequent investigation revealed, the March Hare and the Dormouse were not both speaking the truth.

Who stole the jam?

SOURCE: *From* Alice in Puzzleland, *by R. M. Smullyan. Copyright © 1982 Raymond M. Smullyan. Reprinted by permission of William C. Morrow & Company, Inc.*

A third, related way of talking about the differences between deductive and inductive reasoning has to do with the claims that can be made for the kinds of conclusions drawn. Deductive reasoning, if performed correctly, results in conclusions that are said to have **deductive validity** (Skyrms, 1975). An argument is deductively valid if and only if it is impossible for the premises to be true and the conclusion (or conclusions) to be false. Deductive validity thus provides the reasoner with a nice guarantee: start with true premises, reason according to logical principles, and the conclusion you come to cannot be false. The argument about Terry and the pizza is a deductive argument: if it is true that all college students like pizza and that Terry is a college student, then we know that Terry likes pizza.

It would be very nice, in many ways, if all kinds of reasoning resulted in guaranteed conclusions. However, deductive validity is a property that holds only for deductive reasoning. Many kinds of reasoning are inductive rather than deductive, and in these cases, we cannot be certain of our conclusions; we can have only stronger or weaker beliefs in them. Take the argument about Brian's living in a dormitory. *Even* if Brian is a college student and lives in a dormitory, that does not in any way guarantee the conclusion that all college students live in dormitories. In general, inductive reasoning deals with *probable truth,* not guaranteed truth. Assuming that inductive reasoning has begun with true premises and followed acceptable principles, it has the property of **inductive strength.** An argument has inductive strength if it is improbable (but not impossible) for the premises to be true and the conclusion false (Skyrms, 1975).

In the next two sections, we will review examples of specific deductive and inductive reasoning tasks. These examples should help to clarify the distinction between the two types of reasoning.

Deductive Reasoning

Deductive reasoning has been of interest to psychologists, philosophers, and logicians, since at least Aristotle (Adams, 1984). Various systems of logic were devised to set a standard to evaluate human reasoning. Although there are several kinds of deductive reasoning, we will examine only two: propositional and syllogistic reasoning. Before examining people's performance on these reasoning tasks, it will first be necessary for us to review the tasks themselves. To do so, a brief review of some logical terms will be necessary.

Propositional Reasoning

Propositional reasoning involves drawing conclusions from premises that are in the form of propositions. A *proposition* can be thought of as an assertion—for example, "John likes chocolate cake," "The population of Northfield, MN, is around 12,000," "Today is Friday." Propositions are either true or false. For the sake of convenience, they may be abbreviated to single letters—or example, letting p stand for the proposition "Mary is a philosophy major."

Simple propositions, such as the ones above, can be hooked together into more complicated (compound) propositions, by use of certain *connectives*. These connectives include *&,* which functions somewhat as the English word *and* does (for example, "John likes chocolate cake & Mary likes root beer."); *v,* which functions somewhat as the English word *or* does, only less so (for example, "George lives in Omaha or my skirt is made of cotton."); ¬, the negation operator, akin to *not* (for example, "It is not the case that the moon is made of green cheese."); and → called the material implication connective, which works roughly like the English construction "if . . . then . . . " (for example, "It is after five o'clock → I should go home.").

In the above definitions, I said that each logical symbol functions somewhat as an English word does. What do I mean by this? The differences between the way logical connectives work and the meaning of the English words is that the connectives are defined *truth-functionally.* That means, the truth or falsity of a compound proposition such as p & q depends only on the truth or falsity of p and the truth or falsity of q (Suppes, 1957). Notice that truth-functionality works differently than the way English is typically interpreted to work. Consider two sentences: "John got dressed and John left the house." "John left the house and John got dressed." We tend to interpret these two sentences differently, seeing the first as a typical day in the life of John and the second as a possibly bizarre episode. However, if we let p = "John got dressed," and q = "John left the house," then p & q has exactly the same interpretation as q & p. We call these two compound propositions *logically equivalent.* The expression p & q is given the truth value "true" if and only if p is true and q is true.

The connective **v** matches up even less well to the English *or.* The English term is typically used in the exclusive sense, as in "You can have a cookie or a candy bar" (implying that you can't have both). In contrast, **v** is used in the inclusive sense. Thus, a person who heard the above sentence and interpreted it in a strictly logical fashion could get more to eat than a person who interpreted the sentence in the typical way. The expression p **v** q is true if and only if p is true, q is true, or both are true. Said another way, p **v** q is false if and only if p is false and q is false.

Next, let's consider the connective →. In logical terms, p → q is equivalent (carries the same truth value) as ¬p **v** q (read: not-p or q). The equivalence is not at all intuitive but results from the way that → is defined. We call p in the expression p → q the **antecedent,** and q the **consequent,** and say that p → q is true whenever the antecedent is false or the consequent is true. Alternatively, we could say that p → q is false only when p is true and q is false. Thus, the sentence "If my maternal grandmother lived to be 569 years old, then my car is a Mercedes-Benz" is automatically true (even though I own a Honda Accord and a Plymouth Voyager and no other cars), because the antecedent ("My maternal grandmother lived to be 569 years old") is false. Notice that no cause-and-effect relationship has to be present, or is even implied, in logic. This contrasts with English because we normally expect the antecedent to be related to the cause of the consequent when we use the expression "If . . . then. . . ."

Also, when using the English expression, we consider "If p then q" to be false if p is false and q true (unlike in logic, where it would be considered true). An example would be the following: I say, "If you don't stop practicing your tuba playing, I'll scream." In response, you cease your irritating playing. I scream anyway. I have behaved perfectly reasonably according to logic, even though I've violated your expectations. To see why, remember that the logical interpretation of "If p then q" is equivalent to the logical interpretation of "Not-p or q." Substituting for p and q with our example, then, "If you don't stop practicing your tuba playing (then) I'll scream" is the same thing (in logic) as "You [will] stop practicing your tuba playing [or] I'll scream [or both]."

Table 10-1 presents **truth tables** for the four connectives mentioned above. A truth table (Suppes, 1957) is a means of showing when compound expressions are true and when they are false. Note that the final truth values of any compound expression depend on only the truth values of the individual propositions. A truth table can be thought of as a systematic way to consider all possibilities. In a truth table, you list every possible combination of truth values of individual propositions, and follow the definitions of the connectives to fill in the overall truth value of the final expression.

Truth tables can also be used to establish the truth values of very complicated expressions, as Table 10-2 shows. This method of solution is algorithmic, in the sense that it's guaranteed to reveal whether a compound proposition is always true (in which case it's called a **tautology**), sometimes true, or always false (in which case it's called a **contradiction**). One big problem with truth tables, however, is that they grow at a very fast rate as the number of individual propositions increases. If there are n simple propositions in an expression, the truth table for that expression will be 2^n lines long.

TABLE 10-1.   Truth tables for different logical connectives

p	q	$p \mathbin{\&} q$	$p \lor q$	$p \to q$	$\neg p$	$\neg q$
T	T	T	T	T	F	F
T	F	F	T	F	F	T
F	T	F	T	T	T	F
F	F	F	F	T	T	T

T means that a proposition is true; F, false. The first two columns show truth values for the individual propositions p and q. The remaining columns show truth values for propositions containing p and q, and joined by logical connectives. Truth values provide a systematic way of listing every possible combination of truth values for all propositions.

TABLE 10-2.   Truth tables with complicated expressions

p	q	r	s	$[(p\&q) \to r]v \neg s$
T	T	T	T	T
T	T	T	F	T
T	T	F	T	F
T	T	F	F	T
T	F	T	T	T
T	F	T	F	T
T	F	F	T	T
T	F	F	F	T
F	T	T	T	T
F	T	T	F	T
F	T	F	T	T
F	T	F	F	T
F	F	T	T	T
F	F	T	F	T
F	F	F	T	T
F	F	F	F	T

The complicated expression on the right is true in all cases but one.

For this reason, various "shortcut" methods have been developed, many of them in the form of rules of inference. Two well-known rules are *modus ponens* and *modus tollens.* Box 10-2 presents examples of valid rules of inference. To say that a rule is valid is to say that if the premises are true and the rules are followed, the conclusions will also be true.

Also in Box 10-2 are two other "rules" that turn out not to be valid—that is, they can produce conclusions that are false even if the premises are true. "Rules" of this sort are called **fallacies.** Let's work through examples of why these rules are fallacies. Consider "Affirming the

BOX 10-2 Examples of Inferences Rules and Fallacies

Symbols above the lines are premises; symbols below the lines are conclusions.

Modus Ponens (valid)	Modus Tollens (valid)	Denying the Antecedent (fallacy)	Affirming the Consequent (fallacy)
$p \to q$	$p \to q$	$p \to q$	$p \to q$
p	$\neg q$	$\neg p$	q
---	---	---	---
q	$\neg p$	$\neg q$	p

Consequent (A. C.)," as it applies to the following example: If a man wears a tie, then he's a Republican. John is a Republican. Therefore, he wears a tie." Notice that the first premise ("If a man wears a tie, then he's a Republican") is *not* equivalent to the converse ("If a man is a Republican, then he wears a tie.") In fact, the first premise allows for the possibility of T-shirt–clad Republicans, which contradicts the conclusion.

The second fallacy, "Denying the Antecedent," is exemplified in the argument $p \rightarrow q$; $\neg p$, therefore $\neg q$. Using our example above, these propositions would be instantiated as "If a man wears a tie, then he's a Republican. John does not wear a tie. Therefore, he is not a Republican." For the reason given above (namely, the possible existence of T-shirt–wearing Republicans), this argument is also false.

Now that we have discussed the nature of propositional reasoning, it is time to examine psychological investigations of how people actually perform on such tasks. Wason (1968, 1969, 1983; Wason & Johnson-Laird, 1970) has studied people's propositional reasoning in a task he invented called the selection task, or the four-card task. Figure 10-1 presents an example. Subjects see four cards, two with a letter and two with a digit. They are told that all four cards have a letter on one side, and a digit on the other. They are given a rule such as "If a card has a vowel on one side, then it has an even number on the other side."

We can restate this rule in propositional terms by letting p = "a card has a vowel on one side" and q = "a card has an even number on the other side." Then the rule can be written as $p \rightarrow q$. The four cards presented to subjects might be something like "A" (exemplifying p), "D" (exemplifying $\neg p$), "4" (exemplifying q), and "7" (exemplifying $\neg q$). The subject is asked to turn over all and only the cards that would allow her to see if the rule is true. Write down the one or more cards you would turn over before reading on. Also, write down the reasons for your selections.

This is a task on which people make many errors. The correct answer is to select "A" and "7." To see why, refer to Box 10-2. Card "A" is relevant because together with the rule ("If a card has a vowel on one side, then it has an even number on the other side") it forms an instance of *modus ponens*: $p \rightarrow q$, and p. Card "7" is similarly relevant because together with the rule it forms an instance of *modus tollens*. The "D" card is irrelevant, because it exemplifies $\neg p$, and so would be an instance of denying the antecedent. And choosing the "4" card is equivalent to committing

FIGURE 10-1.   Depiction of the Wason (1968) selection task.

the fallacy of affirming the consequent. Generally, most people know to select "A" but neglect to select "7," or mistakenly select "4." We will discuss some general explanations for this pattern of performance below.

The puzzle given in Box 10-1 is also an instance of propositional reasoning. This puzzle is an example of a class of puzzles often called "truar/liar" or "knight/knave" puzzles, where the task is to determine which speakers are telling the truth and which are lying, assuming that every speaker is either a truar (knight) or a liar (knave) and that truars always tell the truth, and liars always lie (Rips, 1989). Once again, we can translate the "stolen-jam" story into propositions, letting p stand for "The March Hare is telling the truth," q stand for "The Hatter is telling the truth," and r stand for "The Dormouse is telling the truth." (Notice then that $\neg p$ would be "The March Hare is not telling the truth," and so on).

Syllogistic Reasoning

Another type of puzzle or problem commonly used to study reasoning is called a *syllogism.* This problem presents two or more premises, and asks the reasoner either to draw a conclusion or to evaluate a conclusion that the problem supplies, to see if the conclusion *must be* true whenever the premises are true. Although logicians recognize different types of syllogisms, we'll deal only with what are called *categorical syllogisms.* Box 10-3 presents examples. As you look at these, try to solve them, making notes on which ones are hard, which ones are easy, and why.

Categorical syllogisms present premises that deal with classes of entities. As a result, the premises have words called *quantifiers* in them. Quantifiers provide information about how many members of a class are

---

BOX 10-3   Examples of Categorical Syllogisms

Premises are above the lines; valid conclusions, if they exist, are below the lines.

All red books are astronomy books.
All astronomy books are large.
All red books are large.

Some pilots are magicians.
All magicians are Pisces.
Some pilots are Pisces.

No liberals are Republicans.
Some wealthy people are not Republicans.
Nothing follows.

Some documents are not paper.
Some documents are not legal.
Nothing follows.

All psychology majors are curious.
No tennis players are curious.
No tennis players are psychology majors.

No union members are fearful.
No children are fearful.
Nothing follows.

under consideration: all, none, or some. All of the following are examples of quantified premises: "All Gordon setters are dogs," "No polar bears are inanimate objects," "Some flowers are blue," and "Some ballerinas are not tall." As you might expect by now, the words *all* and *some* are being used in ways that differ slightly from normal English usage. *All* here means "every single"; *some* means "at least one, and perhaps all." (It is important to note that, logically speaking, the proposition "Some *X* are *Y*" does *not* mean that "Some *X* are not *Y*," even though this inference seems a natural one to draw.)

Certain rules can be used to draw valid conclusions from categorical syllogisms (Damer, 1980). For example, a categorical syllogism with two negative premises (for example, "No *X* or *Y*" or "Some *X* are not *Y*") has no conclusion that necessarily follows. Similarly, a categorical syllogism where both premises are quantified by "some" has no valid conclusion. In fact, the majority of categorical syllogisms do not have valid (always true in every case) conclusions. With practice, people seem to develop their own "shortcut rules" of solving syllogisms. A research participant in a syllogistic reasoning study articulated such a rule after working on several syllogisms: "I thought about it a lot . . . and I realized that, when there's a "some" and a "some," nothing ever follows" (Galotti, Baron, & Sabini, 1986, p. 19).

People's performance with many categorical syllogisms is error-prone (Ceraso & Provitera, 1971; Woodworth & Sells, 1935). In general, people often judge invalid conclusions to be valid, are slower and make more errors when one or more premises are quantified by "some" or when one or more of the premises are negative. So, for example, when presented with syllogisms such as "Some businessmen are Republicans. Some Republicans are conservative," most people erroneously conclude that it must be true that "Some businessmen are conservative." (To see why this is not the case, notice that the first premise allows for the possibility that there exist some Republicans who are not businessmen. Maybe they are all lawyers. It might be that it is only these Republican lawyers who are the conservatives.)

The way that premises are presented also affects the difficulty of syllogistic reasoning. Johnson-Laird and his colleagues (Johnson-Laird & Steedman, 1978; Johnson-Laird & Bara, 1984) describe the *figural effect:* syllogisms that present terms in an order such as *B-A*; *C-B* or *A-B*; or *C-B* are much harder to work with than are syllogisms with terms in the order *A-B*; *B-C*. We will examine proposed explanations of this effect later.

Inductive Reasoning

Inductive reasoning, or reasoning about conclusions that are *likely* (but not guaranteed) to be true, probably occurs several times in the course of an ordinary day. Although inductive conclusions aren't guaranteed to be true, they may be more useful to us because they actually add new information to our thinking. In general, it is easier to think of real-life examples of inductive reasoning than it is to think of real-life examples of deductive reasoning. Holyoak and Nisbett (1988) provide several examples of ordinary induction:

> A child who has never heard verbs rendered incorrectly into the past tense exclaims, "I goed to bed." A stock analyst, observing that for several years market prices for petroleum stocks have risen steadily in the final two months of the year and then dropped in January, urges her clients to buy petroleum stocks this year at the end of October and sell in late December. A physicist, observing the patterns formed by light as it undergoes refraction and diffraction, hypothesizes that light is propagated as waves. (p. 50)

These authors define induction as "inferential processes that expand knowledge in the face of uncertainty" (p. 1). They note that induction often involves categorization and the formation of rules or hypotheses. Thus, you'll probably observe a great deal of overlap among induction, categorization (covered in Chapter 6), and thinking (covered in Chapter 9). There are a number of different inductive reasoning tasks, but I'll focus here on two: analogical reasoning and hypothesis testing.

Analogical Reasoning

Figure 10-2 presents an example of both verbal and pictorial analogies. You may be familiar with this type of problem from standardized tests such as the SAT or ACT. The format of such a problem is A is to B as C is to ———. The general idea is that the first two terms (A and B) suggest some relationship; the third term (C) provides a partial description of another relationship. The job of the reasoner is to figure out what the fourth term (the one that goes in the blank) should be such that its relationship to the third term is the same (or nearly so) as the relationship between the first and the second terms. Analogies can also be extended into what are called series completion and matrix problems. Figure 10-3 gives an example. Although these problems include more terms, the same general mental processes used in analogies are probably used to solve them (Sternberg & Gardner, 1983).

The ease of reasoning about an analogy depends on the complexity of the problem. Complexity, in turn, depends on a number of things, among them the following: How complicated to comprehend are the individual terms? How knowledgeable is the reasoner about the terms? How easy is it to find a relationship between the first two terms? How many possibilities are there for the blank term, and how easy are they to call to mind? (Pellegrino & Glaser, 1980; Sternberg, 1977a).

You have probably noted here a specific link to a topic we covered in Chapter 9, namely, reasoning by analogy as a problem-solving technique. The general idea is that analogical reasoning is so common in our experience that we use it in all sorts of tasks: just as we try to find relations between terms in an analogy problem, so we try to find relationships between apparently dissimilar problems (for example, between the tumor

Dog : Cocker Spaniel : : Cat :

a. Sennenhund   b. Persian   c. Arabian

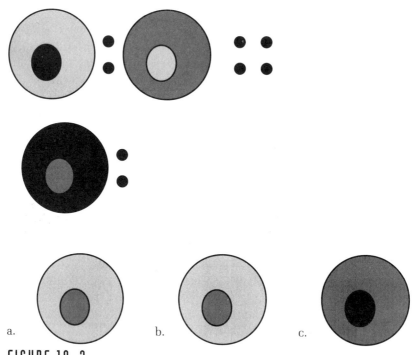

FIGURE 10-2.   Examples of verbal and pictorial analogies

problem and the problem of the general). In both cases, we try to apply the relationship found to determine the solution.

Hypothesis Testing

Another example of inductive reasoning also was developed by Peter Wason (1960, 1977). The task is as follows: You are given the numbers 2, 4, and 6, and told that this triplet of numbers follows a rule. Your job is to determine what the rule is, but to do so you need to observe certain guide-

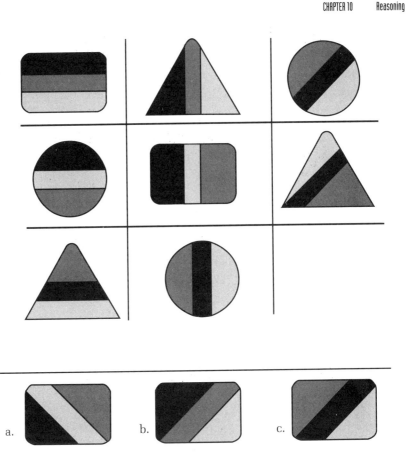

FIGURE 10-3.   Example of a matrix completion problem

lines. You may not ask direct questions about the rule. Instead, you have to offer your own examples of triplets, and for each one you give, you'll be told whether or not it follows the rule. Also, you should try not to guess—announce a rule only when you are confident that you know what it is.

Of the 29 original subjects, only six discovered the correct rule without first making incorrect guesses. Thirteen others made one wrong guess, nine reached two or more incorrect conclusions, and one reached no conclusion at all (Wason, 1960). These results suggest, first of all, that this task is deceptively difficult. The manner in which most people go wrong seems to be as follows: they develop a general idea of the rule, then construct examples that follow that rule. What they fail to do is to test their rule by constructing a counterexample—a triplet that, if their rule is correct, won't receive a "yes" answer from the experimenter. Wason calls this approach "confirmation bias" because the subjects appear to be trying to *confirm* that their rule is true rather than trying to test their rule.

To explain why this approach is problematic, Wason points out a feature of the task that mirrors the situation facing any scientist testing other scientific hypotheses: an infinite number of hypotheses can be constructed that are consistent with any set of data (in this case, the triplets that are judged by the experimenter to follow the rule). For instance, suppose at a certain point in the experiment, you've found out that all of the following triplets follow the rule (whatever it is): 2, 4, 6; 8, 10, 12; 20, 22, 24; 100, 102, 104. What rules are consistent with this set? Here are just a few: "Any three even numbers that increase by two"; "Any three even numbers that increase by two but the last number is not greater than 500"; "Any three even numbers where the second is the arithmetic average of the first and third"; "Any three even numbers where the second is the arithmetic average of the first and third, but the last number is not greater than 500"; "Any three even numbers that increase"; "Any three increasing numbers"; "Any three numbers." The above list suggests that it's very easy, with a little thought, to generate hundreds of rules for any given set of numbers.

What this means is that no rule can be "proven" to be true, just as no scientific hypothesis can be proven true. To see this latter point, pretend that you are a scientist with a hypothesis that predicts certain experimental results. You think to yourself, "If my hypothesis is true [p] then I'll obtain this pattern of results [q]." You then run the experiment, and as luck or nature would have it, do in fact obtain that pattern of results. Can you, based on your rule ($p \rightarrow q$) and your obtained pattern of results (q), conclude that your hypothesis is proven true (p)? No, for if you did, you would be committing the fallacy of affirming the consequent.

There simply is no pattern of results (even from hundreds of experiments) that can *prove* a theory true, just as no rule about three numbers can be proven true, even by a large number of examples that apparently follow it. Instead, the best one can do is to try to disprove as many incorrect rules (or, if you are a scientist, as many alternative hypotheses) as possible. So, if you think the correct rule is "Any three increasing even numbers," you are better off testing the rule with a triplet that is a counterexample to the rule (for example, 3, 5, 7). Why? If this triplet follows the rule, then you know immediately that your hypothesis is wrong. Suppose you instead generate another example of the rule (for example, 14, 16, 18). If you're told that it does follow the rule, you won't be able to use it to prove your hypothesis true (because no hypothesis can ever be proven true), and you haven't managed to rule anything out.

Everyday Reasoning

All of the reasoning tasks presented so far are typical of tasks psychologists use in experiments, or teachers might use in classes. These kinds of tasks have been grouped together under the label *formal reasoning tasks* (Galotti, 1989). The assumption that philosophers, psychologists, and educators make is that these kinds of tasks are at the heart of all kinds of reasoning, even the kind of reasoning we do in everyday life. Consider the following everyday example, for instance. You're in the middle of preparing dinner, and the recipe you are following calls for mozzarella cheese. You search your refrigerator but can't find any. You conclude that you don't have any mozzarella cheese, and that you'll need to go to the grocery store.

We can analyze the inferences you drew as follows. The inference that you had no mozzarella cheese might be seen as an instance of deductive reasoning, more specifically as an instantiation of *modus tollens* (for example, "If I had mozzarella cheese, it would be in the refrigerator. There is no mozzarella cheese in the refrigerator. Therefore, I have no mozzarella cheese."). Your inference that you need to go to the grocery store might be seen as an inductive inference (for example, "The grocery store usually stocks mozzarella cheese. Therefore, it will have mozzarella cheese in stock today."). These analyses assume that the mental processes you use in making inferences about mozzarella cheese are the same ones you would use in laboratory investigations of reasoning, such as knight/knave, categorical syllogism, or pictorial analogies tasks. The mozzarella cheese example can be regarded as a more familiar variant of some of these tasks.

There is some reason to question, however, how similar the reasoning we use in everyday life is to the reasoning we use in laboratory tasks (Galotti & Komatsu, 1993). Collins and Michalski (1989), for example, have identified certain kinds of inferences people draw in everyday reasoning that do not seem to occur on formal reasoning tasks. For example, two people (identified as Q, the questioner, and R, the respondent) are having the following dialogue about geography:

> **Q:** Is Uruguay in the Andes Mountains?
>
> **R:** I get mixed up on a lot of South American countries (pause). I'm not even sure. I forget where Uruguay is in South America. It's a good guess to say that it's in the Andes Mountains because a lot of the countries are. (Collins & Michalski, 1989, p. 4)

In this example, the respondent first expresses doubt, then draws an (incorrect, as it turns out) inference—because many South American countries include a part of the Andes range within their territories and because Uruguay is a typical South American country, the respondent concludes that it, too, includes some of the Andes Mountains. Collins and Michalski (1989) label this as a kind of "plausible deduction" (in our terminology, it might be better to call it a plausible induction because the conclusion is *not* guaranteed to be true).

TABLE 10-3.   Formal and everyday reasoning tasks compared

Formal	Everyday
All premises are supplied.	Some premises are implicit, and some are not supplied at all.
Problems are self-contained.	Problems are not self-contained.
There is typically one correct answer.	There are typically several possible answers that vary in quality.
Established methods of inference that apply to the problem often exist.	There rarely exist established procedures for solving the problem.
It is typically unambiguous when the problem is solved.	It is often unclear whether the current "best" solution is good enough.
The content of the problem is often of limited, academic interest.	The content of the problem typically has potential personal relevance.
Problems are solved for their own sake.	Problems are often solved as a means of achieving other goals.

SOURCE: From "Approaches to Studying Formal and Everyday Reasoning," by K. M. Galotti, 1989, *Psychological Bulletin, 105*, 335. Copyright © 1989 by the American Psychological Association. Reprinted by permission.

Distinctions between everyday reasoning tasks and formal reasoning tasks have been offered (see Table 10-3). The differences may necessitate that cognitive psychologists studying reasoning reevaluate the usefulness of laboratory reasoning tasks as a model of real-life reasoning performance. Research on people's everyday reasoning is beginning, and we will need to await more findings before assessing the fit between everyday and formal reasoning.

Patterns of Reasoning Performance

We have just reviewed examples of different reasoning tasks. We have seen that all of them can be quite demanding, and that people who are untrained in logic often struggle with them. We have also seen that people can draw erroneous conclusions and be quite confident about them (even though they are wrong!). In this section, we will look at some patterns of performance across these different reasoning tasks, trying to identify some reasons that people's reasoning can sometimes go astray. We will also review explanations psychologists have offered for the mental processes people use in reasoning.

Effects of Premise Phrasing

One general source of difficulty in reasoning, many psychologists assert, lies in the way the premises are phrased. Premises that have negatives (the words *no* or *not* in them) are generally more difficult to work with, result in more errors, and take people longer to comprehend than premises that don't have negatives in them (Evans, 1972). Similarly, quantifiers such as *all* or *no* are easier for most people to deal with than quantifiers such as *some* (Neimark & Chapman, 1975). In addition, the order in which information is presented can be important. As mentioned above, a syllogism presented in the order *A-B*; *B-C* is much easier to work with than one presented in the order *A-B*; *C-B* or *B-A*; *B-C* (Johnson-Laird, 1975).

More generally, it appears that the way information is stated can make a reasoning task easy or hard. Presumably, part of the explanation is that syntactically complex statements require more processing resources for the reasoner to comprehend, encode, represent, and store in working memory. Hence, there are fewer mental resources available to tackle other reasoning processes necessary to draw conclusions or to check for validity.

Alteration of Premise Meaning

A second general finding is that people often misinterpret premises (despite the efforts of experimenters to get them to do otherwise). That is, people often make assumptions or alter the meanings of certain terms, such that their interpretations of what the premises mean do not correspond very well with what the problem actually states. For example, when told "All daxes are wugs," (daxes and wugs being mythical amoeba-like creatures), people often automatically assume that daxes and wugs are the same thing, and/or that all wugs are daxes. In fact, the exact statement above allows for two possibilities: every single dax is a wug, and every single wug is a dax (the common interpretation) *or* every single dax is a wug, and there are other wugs that are not daxes. Figure 10-4 provides an illustration.

The quantifier "some" in a premise compounds the difficulties. To say "Some bers are sabs" (bers and sabs are different amoebalike things) is to say *only* the following: "At least one ber is a sab, but there may or may not be other bers that aren't sabs, and there may or may not be other sabs that aren't bers." Figure 10-5 provides an illustration of all the possibilities. Generally, people wrongly interpret the statement as if it meant only the first possibility of Figure 10-5: that some bers are sabs, and some bers aren't sabs. People make a similar mistake with if-then statements. The statement "If *A* then *B*" does *not* mean the same thing as "If *B* then *A*," but this confusion is common. As in the case with "some," people overlook possible interpretations of the premise.

It has been argued that many errors in drawing deductively valid conclusions can be traced to misinterpretations of premises (Revlis, 1975). It has also been shown that the problem persists even when people are given detailed definitions, as well as a fair amount of practice in applying these definitions (Galotti, Baron, & Sabini, 1986). It may be that the usual everyday understandings of words such as *all, some,* and *if-then* are so

Dax = Creature with a pointed head
Wug = Creature with sneakerlike feet

All daxes are wugs.
(And all wugs are daxes.)

All daxes are wugs.
(And there are other wugs
who aren't daxes.)

FIGURE 10-4.   Illustration of possible meanings of "All daxes are wugs."

powerful that people have difficulty ignoring the fact that in reasoning tasks, these terms are defined slightly differently.

Failure to Consider All Possibilities

The discussion above implies that when people interpret premises, they often fail to think of all possible meanings. Similarly, when combining

Ber = Creature with a square body
Sab = Creature with antennae

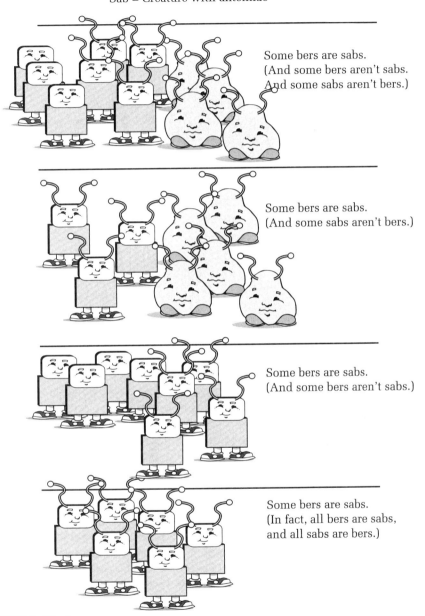

Some bers are sabs.
(And some bers aren't sabs.
And some sabs aren't bers.)

Some bers are sabs.
(And some sabs aren't bers.)

Some bers are sabs.
(And some bers aren't sabs.)

Some bers are sabs.
(In fact, all bers are sabs,
and all sabs are bers.)

FIGURE 10-5.   Illustrations of possible meanings of "Some bers are sabs."

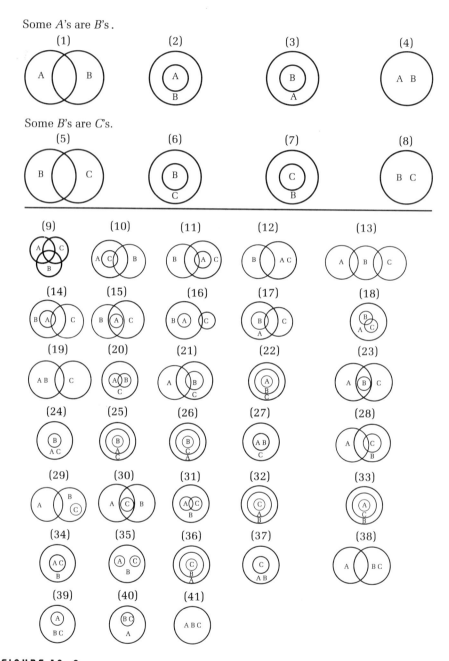

FIGURE 10-6.   Illustration of combinations of the premises "Some *A*'s are *B*'s," and "Some *B*'s are *C*'s." SOURCE: From COGNITIVE PSYCHOLOGY AND ITS IMPLI-CATIONS, by John R. Anderson. Copyright © 1980 by W. H. Freeman and Company. Reprinted by permission.

premise information, people often fail to think of many possibilities (Erickson, 1978). Here's an example: Refer to Figure 10-5, which shows all the possible meanings of a premise quantified by "Some." Now, using the same kinds of diagrams, draw all the possible combinations of the *A, B,* and *C* terms for the following syllogism: "Some *A*'s are *B*'s. Some *B*'s are *C*'s." Try to generate them all, and when you think you have finished, look at Figure 10-6, which presents all the possibilities. How many are in your drawing?

A similar phenomenon is found with the Wason 2-4-6 task. People tend to think of only one (or very few) of the many possible rules that describe these triplets. As a consequence, the kinds of triplets they generate themselves are not as informative as they could be. If people realized the vast number of possible rules that could describe any set of triplets, they would probably test more of their own triplets before announcing a rule.

Content and Believability Effects

Two people reasoning with exactly the same kind of premises will perform differently, depending on what the premises are "about." This is called a *content effect.* Recall the Wason card task, where four cards are laid in front of you, labeled "A," "D," "4," and "7." Your task is to turn over all and only the cards that could test the rule "If a card has a vowel on one side, it has an even number on the other." It turns out that performance improves dramatically if the four cards contain different information: On one side, information on a person's age, and on the other, information about what a person is drinking. Then, the four cards shown say "Drinking a beer," "Drinking a Coke," "16 years of age," and "22 years of age." The rule to be investigated is "If a person is drinking a beer, then the person must be over 19 years of age." This experiment was conducted by Griggs and Cox (1982, Experiment 3), who found that about three-quarters of their college-student subjects solved the problem correctly when it was about drinking age, but none could solve the equivalent problem about letters and numbers.

What explains this effect? Griggs (1983) offers what he calls a "memory-cueing" explanation. The idea is that certain contents of the problem cue, or call to mind, personal experiences that are relevant to the rule. College-student subjects of Griggs and Cox (1982) did well on the drinking-age version of the problem, it is argued, because their own experience with drinking-age laws (and perhaps with violations of those laws) allowed them to think of what kinds of combinations of ages and beverages would violate the rule. The same subjects had no comparable relevant experience to draw on when they reasoned about vowels and numbers in the other version of the task.

Related to content effects are *believability effects.* People are likely to judge as valid any conclusion that reinforces their initial assumptions, regardless of whether the conclusion follows from the premises (Evans, Barston, & Pollard, 1983). Consider this syllogism: "Some college professors are intellectuals. Some intellectuals are liberals." The correct response to this syllogism (as you now know) is that no particular conclusion follows from it. Generally, though, most people (who haven't just read a chapter on reasoning) tend to conclude that these premises lead inevitably to the conclusion "Some college professors are liberals." This conclusion agrees with their previous beliefs and stereotypes about college professors—professors are absent-minded and theoretical, they are intelligent but sometimes impractical, they are unconcerned about money but are concerned about social justice. Notice that a change in content of this syllogism makes it much clearer why the above conclusion isn't always true: "Some men are teachers. Some teachers are women." This syllogism calls to mind a different mental picture. Our world knowledge lets us filter out the suggested conclusion, "Some men are women," because we know this to be false in the world.

Biases

A **bias** in thinking is defined as a tendency to perform in a certain way regardless of the information presented. You might think of it as an error that frequently distorts thinking in a particular way. For example, a person might be biased toward coming to the most general conclusions possible, and might then erroneously decide that broad generalizations necessarily follow from any set of premises. Relative to another person who lacks this bias, the first person might be shown to draw all sorts of false conclusions, for example, from the premise "I like vanilla ice cream," she might conclude, "Everyone likes vanilla ice cream."

Investigators have identified some biases relevant to reasoning. One, mentioned above with regard to the Wason 2-4-6 task, is called **confirmation bias.** Confirmation bias is the tendency to look *only* for information that supports your existing beliefs. So, for example, if you believe that all college professors are liberal, you might try to "test" your conclusion but fail to do so adequately because you seek out only college professors who are liberal to interview, somehow overlooking or forgetting about conservative college professors. In general, people have been shown to be much less likely to think of counterexamples to their own tentative conclusions (Baron, 1985, 1988). Thus, when assessing their own reasoning or other performance, people typically find it much easier to think of or gather information consistent with their predictions than to think of or gather information that goes against their predictions.

There exist several other examples of biases in thinking, many of which are more relevant to decision making. We will therefore defer an extended discussion of biases in thinking to Chapter 11. The important point for our present purposes is to note that people often appear to exhibit thinking that is distorted in the direction of making it seem that their thinking or reasoning has been more careful or thorough than it actually has been.

Three Approaches to the Study of Reasoning

So far, we've looked at a number of different reasoning tasks, and offered several descriptions of the way people approach these tasks. In this section, I'll outline three of the major approaches to the study of reasoning—frameworks that attempt to explain a wide variety of reasoning, not just the reasoning that occurs on a specific task. I have labeled the approaches the componential, the rules/heuristics, and the mental-models approaches (Galotti, 1989).

The Componential Approach

The componential approach studies reasoning by analyzing a task into its component cognitive processes. A computer metaphor may be useful here. Those of you who have programmed computers know that programs can be built from subroutines, where each subroutine performs a very specific function (for example, sorting a list of numbers; adding a list of numbers). To understand how reasoning works, we need to figure out if analogous mental subroutines of reasoning exist, and if so what they are, when and for how long each is executed, and the chances of each one's running without error.

To illustrate, let's return to the example analogy given at the beginning of the chapter: Washington is to one as Jefferson is to what? Robert Sternberg (1977a, 1977b, 1986a, 1986b) has studied people's performance on such problems extensively. He argues that to fill in the blank, we must perform several mental subroutines or, put more formally, execute a number of *component* cognitive processes. First, we must *encode* each of the terms. That is, we must read the words "Washington," "one," and "Jefferson." We then must recognize these terms, retrieving from memory the meanings of each term and mentally representing these meanings. Next, we must *infer* the relationship between the first two terms (often called the A and the B terms), in this case, "Washington" and "one." One relationship that comes immediately to mind is that Washington was the first president of the United States. The next step is to *map* the A term and the C term (here, "Jefferson"), that is, to find a relationship between them. Jefferson was also a president of the United States. In the next step, we *apply* the relationship previously found between A and the B terms onto the C term, remembering (if we recall our U.S. history) that Jefferson was the third president. Thus, our answer to the analogy would be three.

Sometimes, analogies are provided in multiple-choice format, and in those cases, the answers don't always fit. Suppose the above analogy had been presented in this form: Washington is to one as Jefferson is to (a) two, (b) ten, (c) sixteen. Which answer would you choose? It might take a bit of reorganizing and a look through your wallet (or a trip to your local Federal Reserve Bank), but after awhile, the answers presented might cue you that the first relationship you thought of between Washington and one was not a good one for this problem. In that case, you might think of other possibilities: Washington is pictured on the one-dollar bill, for instance. Here, the answer (a) fits neatly. In the case where none of the provided answers fits perfectly, you may need to engage in a process of *justification,* to provide reasons that the answer you choose, though imperfect, is better than the others.

In Sternberg's theory, each component has associated with it several *parameters* that determine, for instance, the probability that it will be used, the amount of time it will take to execute, the difficulty of executing it. Sternberg's method of estimating these parameters is quite clever. He presented subjects with a number of different verbal and pictorial analogies (Sternberg, 1977a) on a tachistoscope, and each trial consisted of two parts: precueing, and presentation of the full analogy. Figure 10-7 presents examples.

During precueing, subjects saw either a blank field (no cues), the A term of the analogy only, the A and the B terms of the analogy only, or the A, B, and C terms of the analogy. Sternberg (1977a) compared the amounts of time it took subjects to decide if the full analogy was true or false on tri-

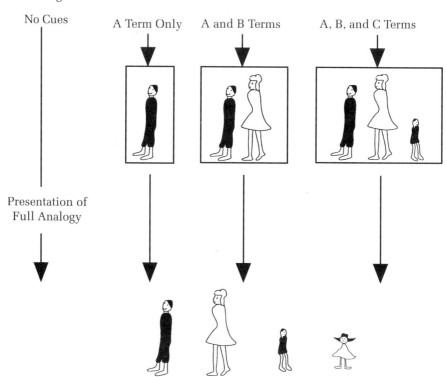

FIGURE 10-7.   Examples of stimuli and experimental design. SOURCE: From "Component Processes in Analogical Reasoning," by R. J. Sternberg, 1977, *Psychological Review, 84,* 361. Copyright © 1977 by the American Psychological Association. Reprinted by permission.

als with no cues to the amounts of time on trials where cues had first appeared. For example, when subjects had been precued with the A term, Sternberg reasoned that they had been able to encode this term. Thus, the subjects should be (and were) faster to respond to the full analogy. Let's say it took subjects, on average, 2 seconds to respond to the full analogy but only 1.8 seconds when the A term was precued. That .2-second difference presumably reflects the time it takes to encode the A term. Similarly, if subjects were precued with the A and B terms, and then took only 1 second to respond to the full analogy, we infer that the other 1 second is the time it takes to encode the A term, encode the B term, and infer a relationship between them.

Sternberg and his colleagues (Sternberg & Gardner, 1983; Sternberg & Turner, 1981) have studied other inductive reasoning tasks, and have presented "componential" models of each. Each componential model identifies the mental processes (such as encoding or comparing) that are used in each task. From these studies, Sternberg argues that the componential approach to studying reasoning will reveal important insights into what reasoning is and how it can be improved (Sternberg, 1986a).

In later work, Sternberg (1983, 1984) distinguished among three kinds of components used in reasoning. Components that consist of individual cognitive processes are called *performance components,* and include those given above. *Metacomponents* are "executive" processes, used in the planning and monitoring of a task. For example, metacomponents select which performance components will be used and in what order. *Knowledge-acquisition components* are used whenever we acquire new information. These include things such as selective encoding (sifting relevant from irrelevant information), selective combination of previously encoded information, and selective comparison.

Consider some concrete examples of each type of component. We have already seen examples of performance components, including such things as encoding (mentally representing stimuli), comparing, applying a rule, and so on in the discussion of Sternberg's studies of analogies. Metacomponents have to do with planning and monitoring of performance. You would use metacomponents when confronted with a reasoning task and you step back to think about how you would go about solving it. Any time you plan a strategy for a task or question your performance on that task ("Let's see. I should probably be on guard for confirmation bias. Is there any way I've overlooked evidence contrary to my beliefs?"), you are making use of metacomponents.

Knowledge-acquisition components have to do with how we learn or pick up new information. Sternberg (1986a) argues that people differ in the ways in which they learn: given the same exposure to the same novel situation, two people might acquire different kinds and amounts, of information from it. The mental processes we use in learning are knowledge-acquisition components.

Sternberg's (1986a) book gives advice and examples to provide practice with performance components, metacomponents, and knowledge—acquisition components. One important source of errors in reasoning tasks appears to stem from problems in encoding (a performance component). Many of the problems in reasoning noted above (for example, problems with premise interpretations, alteration of premise meanings, failure to consider all possibilities) come about because reasoners fail to encode enough relevant information. Moreover, complicated syntactic expressions (those with many terms, those with negatives) presumably take more processing resources to encode, thus leaving fewer resources available for other components of reasoning. Other problems in reasoning could be described in terms of differences in using metacomponents. A reasoner who plans her approach to a problem ("Let's see. Before I start let me be sure I understand what terms like "some" and "all" mean—the people who wrote the problem might mean something different than I do with these terms") and monitors her performance ("OK, wait a minute. Have I checked to be sure I've covered all possibilities?") is less likely to be biased or to make other kinds of errors.

The Rules/Heuristics Approach

Sternberg's componential approach treats reasoning as just another mental activity, similar in kind to tasks such as problem solving or making decisions. Other philosophers and psychologists have seen reasoning as a special mental process, one for which people rely on special-purpose mental rules to draw conclusions.

One idea is that the rules of logic are the same rules we use to draw conclusions (this position was articulated by the philosophers Kant and Mill; see Henle, 1971 for details). Most modern psychologists reject the strong version of this idea but agree that there are "mental logics" or systems of inference rules that people use to draw conclusions (Braine, 1978, 1990; Braine, Reiser, & Rumain, 1984; Osherson, 1975; Rips, 1984, 1988, 1990). These researchers make an analogy between mental logics and grammars: both are systems of rules to which we have only *implicit* access. That means that you can't be expected to state what all of the rules you follow to draw conclusions are—you might not even know that you do follow rules! However, the researchers argue that if we carefully observe your behavior while you reason, we will find regularities in the way you draw conclusions that are most easily explained by assuming you have followed—probably without being conscious of it—a set of rules. (You might review our discussion in Chapter 8 of people's implicit awareness of grammatical rules to get a better idea of how this might work.)

Different researchers describe slightly different sets of inference rules. Generally, rules take the form: (premises) → (conclusion). Here's a specific example (from Braine, 1978): p or q; not p → q. The idea is that when given information, people try to match it to one of these rules, and use the rules to draw appropriate conclusions. Imagine being told, for instance, that either Jesse "The Body" Ventura or Hulk Hogan won a wrestling match, and that Jesse "The Body" did not win. You would match this information to the rule given above, and easily conclude that the victor must have been Hulk Hogan. Braine considers the use of inference rules to be automatic, and typically, errorless.

The key issue for the rules explanation of reasoning is how people figure out when and what rules apply. Braine (1990) proposes the existence of abstract rules that we use in all situations. Patricia Cheng and her colleagues (Cheng & Holyoak, 1985; Cheng, Holyoak, Nisbett, & Oliver, 1986; Nisbett, Fong, Lehman, & Cheng, 1987) reject the idea of abstract rules, instead proposing sets of rules that are sensitive to the context. The idea here is that different rules are called to mind in different situations.

One example is the permission schema, which is made up of the four rules shown below:

Rule 1. If the action is to be taken, then the precondition must be satisfied.

Rule 2. If the action is not to be taken, then the precondition need not be satisfied.

Rule 3. If the precondition is satisfied, then the action may be taken.

Rule 4. If the precondition is not satisfied, then the action must not be taken.[1]

The permission schema would be activated in certain contexts but not others. For instance, the problem "One may consume alcoholic beverages only if born before July 12, 1968. Andrea's birthday is June 6, 1966. May Andrea drink a beer?" would evoke the permission schema. Presumably, people's familiarity with age restrictions on drinking help them to construe the problem in terms of permission: Does Andrea, given her age, have legal permission to consume an alcoholic beverage? A problem similar in abstract form, "All employees use Midnight Airlines whenever they travel to New England. Sara, an executive, is flying to San Francisco. Will Sara necessarily fly Midnight?" would not necessarily evoke the permission schema because nothing in the problem makes the reasoner construe it as a problem about permission.

Notice the difference between the proposals of Braine (1990) and Cheng (Cheng et al., 1986). Cheng's idea is that in reasoning, people interpret problems based on what they are about (for example, drinking), and based on this analysis, use different schemata. In her view, two problems that have the same abstract logical structure (that is, can be expressed the same way symbolically) may be treated very differently, depending on how people interpret the problems. Braine, instead, argues that people can and do use the same set of abstract rules in all situations.

These proposals are not the only ones that view reasoning in terms of mental rules. Work by philosophers on *practical logic* also follows a rules approach. The goal of practical logic is to teach people to avoid falla-

[1]From "Pragmatic Reasoning Schemas," by P. W. Cheng and K. J. Holyoak, 1985, *Cognitive Psychology, 17,* 397. Copyright © 1989 by Academic Press. Reprinted by permission.

cies or errors that occur in real-life arguments. Box 10-4 presents some common fallacies. Rules for avoiding fallacies could take the form "If (this particular fallacy occurs), then the argument is not a good one." Thus, the strategy of practical logic, as it is typically taught, is to compare real-world arguments against a list of fallacies. If no matches are found, and if the list is complete, the argument is considered a good one.

We saw above that the componential approach locates the source of errors in reasoning in people's inability to use certain performance components or metacomponents effectively. The rules approach to reasoning offers a different interpretation: a common source of error in reasoning is the failure to interpret a problem in terms of the appropriate rules—in other words, a failure to see which rules are relevant in a particular instance. People may fail to make any mental match to an appropriate rule or may make use of inference rules that do not apply to a given situation. It may also be that inference rules do not exist for many kinds of reasoning; in such cases, people are assumed to use some other kinds of strategies, and these may be prone to error.

The rules approach to reasoning is particularly effective at explaining content effects in reasoning. The explanation goes as follows: presumably, different contents "cue" different sets of rules, although exactly how this process works is not well understood. It may be that personal experience facilitates this cueing, so that people are more likely to reason cor-

---

BOX 10-4   Examples of Fallacies in Reasoning

- *Equivocation.* Using a word in two ways, while appearing to use the same meaning throughout. Example: "Scientific authorities believe that smoking causes cancer, but I know a lot of scientists who don't even control their own kids very well, so what kind of authorities are they?"
- *Illicit contrast.* Leading a listener to draw an inappropriate inference by placing unusual emphasis upon certain words or phrases. Example: "I'm glad I'm a Democrat. *Democrats* aren't crooks."
- *Argument by innuendo.* Directing the listener to a particular conclusion by a careful choice of words or arrangement of sentences. Example: "Is Jeff a good guy? Well, we've never caught him doing anything illegal."
- *Loaded question.* Using language that presupposes a certain conclusion. Example: "When are you going to stop cheating on your income taxes?"
- *Fallacy of the continuum.* Assuming that small differences are always unimportant. Example: "I know that our monthly payments are already very high, but what's another $40 a month?"
- *Fallacy of composition.* Assuming that what is true of the parts is true of the whole. Example: "Anna has a good head on her shoulders, and Scott's good with people, so their success as business partners is guaranteed."

SOURCE: *After Damer, 1980; his book describes many other fallacies and examples.*

rectly with premises about drinking ages simply because their own experiences cause them to interpret the situation in terms of a permission rule.

Cheng and colleagues (1986) have reported success in teaching people to recognize and use pragmatic reasoning rules correctly after only brief periods of practice. This suggests that people quickly learn to use inference rules as a guide to processing information on certain tasks. Similarly, the existence of logic courses in colleges and universities suggests that rules of logic can be taught. The hope is, of course, that people who learn to use a set of inference rules in one situation will transfer their understanding of the rules to new circumstances.

The Mental-Models Approach

Proponents of the mental-models approach deny that reasoning consists of using special-purpose rules of inference, and that reasoning involves special-purpose cognitive processes. Philip Johnson-Laird, a major spokesperson for the models approach, argues that the processes we use to draw conclusions are also the ones we use to comprehend language (1982, 1983). Reasoning, for Johnson-Laird, consists of constructing mental models to depict the premises. Effective reasoning occurs when the reasoner checks to be sure that his first idea of what the conclusion might be is assessed by trying to construct alternative models that are consistent with the premises but inconsistent with the hypothesized conclusion.

To illustrate Johnson-Laird's approach, consider the following syllogism: "Some of the scientists are parents. All of the parents are drivers." Box 10-5 offers one interpretation of how these premises might be mentally

---

BOX 10-5   Model Representation of an Easy Categorical Syllogism

The *o* before the elements indicates optional individuals who may or may not be present.

```
o scientist o parent = driver
o scientist o parent = driver
  scientist = parent = driver
  scientist = parent = driver
                      o driver
                      o driver
```

Syllogism depicted: Some of the scientists are parents. All of the parents are drivers.

SOURCE: *From "Believability and Syllogistic Reasoning," by J. Oakhill, P. N. Johnson-Laird, and A. Garnham, 1989,* Cognition, 31, *117–140. Copyright © 1989 by Elsevier Science Publishers BV. Reprinted by permission.*

modeled for this relatively easy-to-solve reasoning problem. Figures connected by an equal sign indicate that both refer to the same individual. Figures preceded by *o* indicate "optional" individuals who may or may not exist; in this instance, scientists who are not parents, parents who are not scientists, and drivers who are not parents. The diagram indicates that there are some scientists who are drivers, but (possibly) some other scientists who aren't drivers and, also possibly, some drivers who aren't parents. Notice that the two scientists in the bottom of the diagram (the ones who aren't "optional") are drivers, leading to the necessarily true conclusion, "Some of the scientists are drivers."

How do people construct these mental models? The fact that people understand stories or conversations, Johnson-Laird argues, makes them expert mental-model constructors. Whenever we read a story, for instance, we build some sort of mental picture of the text in order to comprehend it. Similar mental processes occur when we take part in or even observe a conversation. These processes are also the ones we use when we encode a premise such as "Some of the scientists are parents."

What, then, distinguishes language comprehension from reasoning? In the case of language comprehension, we usually stop constructing models once we construct one that both represents the essential information and makes sense. Reasoning requires one more thing: the ability and willingness to try to construct alternative models that represent all of the possibilities. Consider another of Johnson-Laird's syllogisms, this one a more difficult one to work with: "All of the beekeepers are artists. None of the chemists are beekeepers." You might try this one yourself before reading on. Box 10-6(a) depicts the model that most people generate first. The solid line indicates that no individual is both a chemist and a beekeeper. Notice that the solid line also separates the chemists from the artists, which would lead one to the conclusion "None of the chemists are artists." However, if they keep at it, people might discover that there are other possible depictions, such as the one shown in Box 10-6(b), where one artist is a chemist. This depiction means that the above conclusion cannot be true. At this point, a reasoner who had constructed both models might conclude, "Some of the chemists are not artists." Again, however, another possibility exists, the one depicted in Box 10-6(c). Here, all of the chemists are artists, so the last conclusion cannot be valid, either. Is there no valid conclusion, then? In fact, there is. The one statement true of all three models is "Some of the artists are not chemists." In particular, the beekeeper-artists, necessarily depicted in each model, are not chemists.

One problem with the mental-models framework is specifying what information models contain, and what information is omitted. Notice, for instance, that in Boxes 10-5 and 10-6 we did not specify any physical, ethnic, or philosophical information about the individuals depicted. How much information the reasoner chooses to represent and how this decision affects performance are issues that remain to be investigated.

The construction of a mental model can be considered a creative act. Perkins (1985b) argues that—contrary to stereotype—model building (and therefore, good reasoning) relies on imagination. The more imaginative the process, the more likely a reasoner is to generate potential counterexamples and avoid drawing hasty conclusions. It is interesting that this view links reasoning with other kinds of thinking, helping to explain the apparent links between reasoning, problem solving, and decision making.

In the mental-models approach, errors in reasoning derive from several possible sources. One is the failure to construct relevant models. If the premises are not presented in an optimal order (for example, in a syllogism, in the order *A-B*, *B-C*), it is harder to construct an integrated representation of both premises that accurately depicts all of the relevant information. If there is a great deal of extraneous information in the premises, mental resources may be diverted from the processes needed to selectively represent the essential information. A second source of error is the failure to assess the implications of all the models found. For instance, in the previ-

---

BOX 10-6 Model Representation of an Easy Categorical Syllogism

The *o* before the elements indicate optional individuals who may or may not be present.

(A)   beekeeper = artist
      beekeeper = artist
                 o artist
      _____
      chemist
      chemist

(B)   beekeeper = artist
      beekeeper = artist
                 o artist

      _____
      chemist = artist
      chemist

(C)   beekeeper = artist
      beekeeper = artist
                 o artist

      _____
      chemist = artist
      chemist = artist

Syllogism depicted: All of the beekeepers are artists. None of the chemists are beekeepers.

SOURCE: *From "Believability and Syllogistic Reasoning," by J. Oakhill, P. N. Johnson-Laird, and A. Garnham, 1989,* Cognition, 31, *117–140. Copyright © 1989 by Elsevier Science Publishers BV. Reprinted by permission.*

TABLE 10-4.   Three approaches to reasoning compared

Point of Comparison	Componential	Rules/Heuristics	Models/Search
• Nature of the fundamental unit	• Component (information-processing routine)	• Inference rule (rule)	• Mental model (representation)
• Definition of reasoning	• Using one or more particular assemblies of component processes to encode, find, map, or apply a relationship	• Following (implicitly or explicitly) a rule, heuristic, or schema to make inferences	• Constructing one or more representations consistent with given information to reach and test conclusions
• Range of existing reasoning tasks applied to so far	• Analogies; series completions; conditional, categorical, and linear syllogisms; mathematical and verbal induction; detective-story problems	• Conditional, categorical, and linear syllogisms; probabalistic and statistical reasoning problems	• Conditional, categorical, and linear syllogisms; open-ended reasoning about social and political issues
• Major findings easily explained	• Difficulty with negative and marked premise terms; problems in encoding on formal reasoning tasks	• Content effects; intrusion of background knowledge	• Failure to consider all possible interpretations or consequences of premises; intrusion of background knowledge
• Other strengths	• Great deal of empirical data that tests theory	• Good amount of empirical data that tests theory; has attracted investigators from several fields (philosophy, psychology, artificial intelligence, linguistics)	• Specifically designed to be extendable to everyday reasoning
• Major shortcomings	• Lack of analysis of which components are used in everyday reasoning; lack of definition of the term *component*	• Lack of specificity over when and how rules are used; lack of definition of the term *rule*	• Lack of empirical data, especially training studies; lack of definition of the terms *model* and *search*

SOURCE: From "Approaches to Studying Formal and Everyday Reasoning," by K. M. Galotti, 1989, *Psychological Bulletin, 105*, 346. Copyright © 1989 by the American Psychological Association. Reprinted by permission.

ous example, one might have decided that no conclusion relating artists and chemists was valid, overlooking the one relation that was shown in all three models. A final and important source of error is the failure to search for and construct enough models. This accounts for the findings described earlier—namely, that people often fail to consider enough of the possibilities allowed by any set of premises.

Having now reviewed the three approaches to reasoning, you are probably trying to determine which one fits the data best. Table 10-4 provides a comparison of the three, and shows that each one has particular strengths and weaknesses. The three approaches also differ with respect to the level of investigation toward which each approach is aimed. The componential approach seeks to explain the individual cognitive processes used in each episode of reasoning. The rules approach focuses on a more general issue, the patterns involved in thinking. The mental-models approach has a different goal, to explain reasoning performance at a general level of mental strategy. Each one of these approaches is a necessary one if we are eventually to understand all of the significant reasoning phenomena.

Summary

We first reviewed a classification of reasoning tasks, separating deductive from inductive reasoning, and then separating both of these (called formal reasoning) from everyday reasoning tasks. We have examined several reasoning tasks in some detail, pausing to master the terminology of logic, which is useful in deriving conclusions.

Because psychologists seek general principles of human experience, we tried to avoid theories that apply only to one limited reasoning task. Instead, we examined some findings from the reasoning literature that seem to hold true of people's performance on a variety of reasoning tasks. Among these are the fact that the way premises are phrased can have a large influence on performance, the fact that people often misinterpret what premises mean or overlook possible interpretations of the premises' meanings. We also discussed the existence of content and believability effects in reasoning, noting that people can perform very differently with different versions of the same problem, depending on the content of the problem.

We have seen that theoretical approaches to the study of reasoning vary, and depend heavily on whether reasoning is considered a very separate process from other kinds of mental activity. Those who consider reasoning to be very distinct study very self-contained problems of the type discussed throughout this chapter, often emphasizing special-purpose rules of inference as the mechanisms for drawing conclusions. Others see reasoning as an extension of different aspects of mental life, for example, language comprehension or thinking. In this view, the way to understand reasoning is not to search for special-purpose cognitive processes or rules but to examine general aspects of mental performance—why people fail to consider enough of the relevant evidence or to imagine enough of the possibilities.

Recommended Readings

Two good texts on logic and probability are Suppes (1957) and Skyrms (1975). General works on the psychology of reasoning are Evans (1982, 1983); Falmagne (1975); Wason and Johnson-Laird (1972); Johnson-Laird and Byrne (1991), who concentrate on deductive reasoning; and Holland,

Holyoak, Nisbett, and Thagard (1986), who review work on inductive reasoning. Recent reviews of the literature can be found in Galotti (1989) and Rips (1990).

Sternberg (1984), Braine (1990), and Johnson-Laird (1983) provide good overviews of the componential, rules, and mental-models approaches, respectively. A recent paper by Smith, Langston, and Nisbett (1992) explores in greater depth what it means for people to follow rules in reasoning, and suggests criteria investigators can use in designing and evaluating reasoning experiments. Nisbett (1993) has recently edited a collection of papers by investigators who all adopt a rules approach. Gentner and Clement (1988) describe investigations into the ways mapping of analogies works.

Recent work on content effects in reasoning has been reported by Markovits and Nantel (1989) and Oakhill, Johnson-Laird, and Garnham (1989). Collins and Michalski (1989) present a theory of everyday reasoning that combines aspects of the mental-models and the rules frameworks. Klayman and Ha (1987) report investigations into hypothesis-testing strategies on the Wason 2-4-6 task.

Smullyan (1982) presents a number of reasoning problems from *Alice in Wonderland*. Sternberg (1986a) and Nisbett et al. (1987) suggest different ways of improving reasoning performance.

Solution to the "Who Stole the Jam" problem [from Smullyan, 1982, p. 140]

The Hatter said, in effect, that either the March Hare or the Dormouse stole it. If the Hatter lied, then neither the March Hare nor the Dormouse stole it, which means that the March Hare didn't steal it, hence was speaking the truth. Therefore, if the Hatter lied, then the March Hare didn't lie, so it is impossible that the Hatter and the March Hare both lied. Therefore, the Dormouse spoke the truth when he said that the Hatter and March Hare didn't both lie. So we know that the Dormouse spoke the truth. But we are given that the Dormouse and the March Hare didn't both speak the truth. Then, since the Dormouse did, the March Hare didn't. This means that the March Hare lied, so his statement was false, which means that the March Hare stole the jam.

REVIEW QUESTIONS

1. Describe the similarities and differences between inductive and deductive reasoning.
2. Describe and contrast two methods by which people can derive conclusions in propositional reasoning tasks.
3. Distinguish between formal and everyday reasoning. How might the former be relevant to the latter?
4. (Challenging): Consider factors that hinder people's reasoning. In what ways are these factors present for other kinds of thinking and problem-solving tasks (hint: review Chapter 9). What does your answer imply about the relationship between thinking and reasoning?
5. Describe and give a new example of confirmation bias.
6. Describe the componential, rules, and mental-models approaches to studying reasoning. What are the differences and similarities among them?
7. In what ways are inference rules (for example, *modus ponens*) similar to, and different from, syntactic rules we discussed in Chapter 8?

CHAPTER 11

Making Decisions

You've arrived at your sophomore year of college and realize that you must soon declare a major—and perhaps a minor. What cognitive processes do you use to consider the options, evaluate your priorities, and make a choice? Cognitive psychologists use the term "decision making" to refer to the mental activities that take place in choosing among alternatives.

In the above instance, the decision about an undergraduate major often is part of a larger set of decisions about a career and future life. Typically, decisions are made in the face of some amount of *uncertainty*. It is not 100% certain, say, how well you will do in the courses required for various majors, or how well you will like them, or how much various majors will help you obtain a good job after graduation. You will not know for sure if you will enjoy the faculty who teach the courses you have not yet taken, or if the topics will be interesting or useful, or if they will be relevant to your long-term goals and aspirations. Nonetheless, at some point, you have to decide.

Students at the college where I teach who seek my advice in choosing a major often appear in my office showing unmistakable signs of agitation, nervousness, and confusion. They know that they need to make a decision but do not know how to do it. They wish the uncertainty over, but they don't want to close off options prematurely. They are aware that a lot of information relevant to the decision exists but don't know quite how to collect, organize, and use it all in the time allotted. They know there are no guarantees, but don't want to make an unfortunate choice.

The dilemma is familiar to anyone who has had to make a

significant and difficult life choice. The degree of uncertainty is vexatious. So, too, the number of conflicting goals and objectives. The sophomore student typically wants not only a major that is interesting but also one in which she shows some aptitude, enjoys the faculty and other majoring students, and sees some relevance to a future job, and some flexibility for future career paths. The number of options available also comes into play. Many schools have more than 25 majors available (some of them, many more). There are also options to double major, declare minors, participate in off-campus study programs, and so on, adding complications. The amount of information that is potentially relevant can quickly grow to be staggering, in which case the decision maker needs some help in organizing it all.

Because decisions are often made under conditions of uncertainty, some do not yield the hoped-for results, even if made carefully and after thorough, unbiased consideration of the evidence. Psychologists generally argue that "goodness" of decision making cannot be measured by the success of individual decisions—luck, for instance, often plays too great a role.

Real-life decisions, like buying a home, are often difficult because of the number of criteria and alternatives available.

Instead, the yardstick of success is often taken to be the **rationality** of the decision. Many people define this term differently, but a typical definition comes from von Winterfeldt and Edwards (1986a, p. 2): rational decision making "has to do with selecting ways of thinking and acting to serve your ends or goals or moral imperatives, whatever they may be, as well as the environment permits." In other words, to be rational means to consider all of your relevant goals and principles, not just the first ones to come to mind. It also involves gathering information as painstakingly and fairly as possible under the circumstances. Rational decision making, then, requires that we look at not only evidence that supports our initial inclinations but also evidence that does not.

Many psychologists see decision making, reasoning, and problem solving as aspects of thinking. Not surprisingly, they propose models of decision making and planning that are quite similar to models of reasoning and problem solving (for example, Newell, 1980). In this chapter, however, we will concentrate on models specific to the task of making decisions.

We will look at descriptions of how people gather and use information in making decisions. Many of these descriptions will show how decision making falls short of optimality. Psychologists have argued that the lack of optimality stems, in large part, from *cognitive overload*—when the information available overwhelms the cognitive processing available. Strategies for coping with information overload, though often useful, can lead to error and irrationality. Next, we will examine what people do after they have gathered the evidence, how all the pieces are put together. Finally, we will look briefly at ways of improving decision making.

Basic Concepts of Probability

As mentioned above, most difficult decisions and plans are made under conditions of uncertainty. After all, it would be no problem to decide which major to declare if you knew how your life would turn out in consequence of each available option. In this ideal case, you would simply look over all the outcomes and choose the option that led to the outcome you most preferred. Because we are rarely, if ever, in these circumstances, most real-life decisions involve estimating the chances or odds of different outcomes and events. To understand how we do this, it is necessary to first understand some concepts relevant to probability and uncertainty.

Although there are other competing interpretations (see Baron, 1988) **probability** can be generally thought of as a measurement of a degree of uncertainty (von Winterfeldt & Edwards, 1986a). Probabilities are numbers between zero and one, where zero represents complete certainty that an event will not happen, and one represents complete certainty that it will. Intermediate values can be thought of as corresponding to intermediate levels of confidence that an event will occur. Someone who asserts the probability of an event to be .90 is saying that he is very sure (though not certain) that the event will take place.

Generally, people untrained in probability theory have little trouble with probabilities of either zero or one; they are less adept at using intermediate values of probability in a coherent way. Their use of intermediate numbers departs in significant ways from probability theory, and it is not hard to see why. What does it mean to say that you are 30% sure of something, and how is that different from 40% sure? It is not at all intuitive what these numbers "mean" in the context of a real-life decision.

Probability theory treats differences in intermediate values of probability as corresponding to different gambles or lotteries. Consider a lottery in which there are ten tickets, and you have purchased three. If the winning ticket is *randomly selected* (meaning that each of the ten tickets has a completely equal chance to be chosen), then the probability of your winning is .3. If you were to buy another of the remaining seven tickets, the probability would rise to .4. The difference between the probabilities of .4 and .3 corresponds to one lottery ticket in this example.

Probability theory provides rules for combining probabilities of different events. For example, the probability of an event's *not* occurring is equal to 1 minus the probability that it will. If you own three of ten lottery tickets, the probability that you *won't* win is .7 (1 minus the probability that you *will* win, which is .3).

A second rule of probability theory states that if two events are *mutually exclusive,* meaning that they cannot both be true at the same time, then the probability of one or the other's occurring is equal to the sum of the individual probabilities. In the lottery example above, if you own three (of the ten) tickets and your roommate owns two other ones, and only one winning number will be drawn, then the probability that one or the other of you will win is .5 (that is, .3 + .2). In this case, the event of your owning the winning ticket and your roommate's owning the winning ticket are mutually exclusive—only one of you owns each ticket.

A third rule of probability also involves combining events. It concerns events that are *independent,* meaning that the probability of one event's occurring has no influence on the probability of the other event's occurring. Consider the lottery example above, but this time assume that the person who chooses the winning number will also flip a fair (that is, balanced) coin. Because the outcome of the lottery should neither affect nor be affected by the outcome of the coin toss, we would expect the two events—(1) your winning, given that you have three of the ten tickets, and (2) heads coming up—to be independent. This rule of probability says that the probability of two independent events co-occurring is equal to the product of the two individual probabilities multiplied. Thus, if the probability of heads is .5, and the probability of your winning is .3, and the two events are independent, then the probability of heads *and* your winning is .15.

A fourth rule of probability theory is used when we want to know the probability that an event, A, is true, given that we know another event, B, is true. For example, you might want to know the probability of a thunderstorm's occurring soon (A), given that it is cloudy outside (B). We calculate this probability as the ratio of two things: (1) the probability that B is true, given that A is true, divided by (2) the overall probability of B's being true. A formula originally given by Bayes (1958/1764) expresses this relationship:

(1)
$$p(A/B) = \frac{p(B/A) \cdot p(A)}{p(B)}.$$

In this formula, $p(A/B)$ is read as "the probability of A given B," and is called the conditional probability of A given B. (Space constraints prevent me from deriving this formula, but Baron [1988] gives a readable explanation.)

People's intuitions regarding the rules of probability theory are often "way off the mark." Baron (1988) offered the following illustrative example. (Do it intuitively first, then compare it to the calculations): A 30-year-old woman discovers a lump in her breast and goes to her physician. The physician knows that only about five in a hundred women of the patient's age and health have breast cancer. A mammogram (breast X ray) is taken. It indicates cancer 80% of the time in women who have breast cancer but falsely indicates cancer in healthy patients 20% of the time. The mammogram comes out positive. What is the probability that the patient has cancer? (Stop here and give your estimate.)

Although your intuitive estimate may be as high as 50% or 80%, application of the formula above results in an answer of .17. To see why, look at formula 2a and 2b, which "plug in" the values given in the problem to formula 1, above.

(2a)
$$p(C/M) = \frac{p(M/C) \cdot p(C)}{p(M)}$$

Note: $p(C)$ is the probability of cancer; $p(M)$ is the probability of a positive mammogram; $p(C/M)$ is the probability of cancer given a positive mammogram; and $p(M/C)$ is the probability of a positive mammogram given the existence of cancer. Numerical values for these symbols are given in the problem above. Plugging into equation 1, we have

(2b)
$$p(C/M) = \frac{(.80)(.05)}{(.80)(.05) + (.20)(.95)} = .17.$$

Note: $p(M)$ (the overall probability of a positive mammogram) = the probability of a positive mammogram in patients with cancer + the probability of a positive mammogram in patients without cancer.

How does this value compare with your estimate? Most people find that their own intuitive estimates are much higher (sometimes four or five times higher) than the actual value. But even though the .17 value is nonintuitive, we can explain how it comes about. Take a random sample of 100 women of this age and health status. Five should be expected to have cancer. Four should be expected to show a positive test. That leaves 95 women who should be expected not to have cancer, of whom 19 should be expected to have a positive test result. So, 4 of the 23 people with a positive test result actually have cancer. Dividing 23 into 4 yields .17.

We have now reviewed some basic probability theory and seen that it is not always a good model of how people intuitively use information. In the next section, we will examine the ways in which people collect, organize, and use information in decision making.

Cognitive Illusions in Decision Making

How do people gather the information they will use to make a decision? Often, the information comes from their own memories. Students choosing a major, for instance, often think back to their experiences in different courses or to things they have heard older students say about their experiences in different majors. Once information is gathered, the decision maker has to decide on the importance and/or relevance of each piece of information. If you don't care about becoming a biologist, for instance, the information on the biology department's course offerings may not seem very important to you. The way people gather and assess the relevance of different pieces of information is the topic of this section.

Research on people's decision-making skills and styles has consistently demonstrated the existence of certain systematic and common biases. Typically, the biases are understandable and often justifiable ways of thinking under most conditions but can lead to error when misapplied. These systematic biases have been labeled "cognitive illusions" (von Winterfeldt & Edwards, 1986b). The term itself is meant to invoke the analogy to perceptual illusions: errors of cognition that come about for understandable reasons and that provide information relevant to understanding normal functioning. Consider, for example, any of the illusions described in Chapter 2. We can and do consider these illusions "errors," in the sense that one's percept does not correspond with what's really there. On the other hand, these illusions are not used as evidence that the whole perceptual system is faulty and unreliable. Rather, illusions (perceptions under certain specific conditions) tell us something about the way the perceptual system works generally—what cues are attended to, how they are interpreted, and so forth.

In a similar way, errors in decision making tell us something about the ways in which people gather, sort, and integrate the information that goes into making a choice. The cognitive illusions described below also give us information describing when unaided human decision making is likely to be optimal and when it is not. Finally, these descriptions can help us design and implement educational programs or interventions to improve the quality of the decisions and plans that people make.

Just what is a cognitive illusion? Von Winterfeldt and Edwards (1986b) specify that something counts as a cognitive illusion only if there is a "correct" way of answering a question or making a decision and also an intuitive estimate or decision, and a discrepancy between the two that always goes in the same direction. Answers that randomly fluctuate around the correct value, then, do not count as illusions.

We will examine a number of specific illusions below, but this list of illusions is far from complete. The recommended readings at the end of the chapter can point the interested reader in relevant directions.

Availability

Consider the problems in Box 11-1, and give your first intuitive response to each before reading further. Tversky and Kahneman (1973) presented problems such as these to undergraduate students. The general findings were that people's intuitions were systematically wrong. In Problem 1, for instance, the letter *L* occurs more frequently in the third than in the initial position. In Problems 2 and 3, the A and B options have the same number (of committees, in the former case, and of paths, in the latter).

What accounts for the errors? Tversky and Kahneman (1973) argue that when faced with the task of estimating probability, frequency, or numerosity, people rely on shortcuts or rules of thumb, known as **heuristics,** to help make these judgments easier. One such heuristic is known as the **availability heuristic**—"assessing the ease with which the relevant mental operation of retrieval, construction, or association can be carried out" (p. 208). In other words, instances (for example, particular words, or particular committees, or particular paths) that are more easily thought of, remembered, or computed stand out more in one's mind. Those instances are particularly salient, and hence are deemed to be more frequent or probable.

In Problem 1, it turns out to be easier to think of words that begin with L (for example, *lawn, leftover, licorice,* . . .) than it is to think of words that have L as the third letter (*bell, wall, ill,* . . .). The reason for this may have to do with the way our lexicons, or "mental dictionaries," are organized or with how we learn or practice words—alphabetically by the first letter. As with paper or electronic dictionaries, it's relatively easy to search for words by initial letter than by "interior" letters.

In Problem 2, the appropriate formula for determining the number of distinct committees that can be formed is $10!/(x!)(10-x!)$, where x is the size of the committee. Notice that for $x = 2$, $10 - x = 8$, and that for $x = 8$, $10 - x = 2$, implying that there should be an equal number of 2-person committees and 8-person committees (namely, 45). Tversky and Kahneman

(1973) argue that 2-person committees are more distinct. There are five 2-person committees, with no overlap in membership, but any two 8-person committees will have at least some overlap. Distinctiveness makes different committees easier to think of. Therefore, 2-person committees are more available (because they are more distinctive), and hence deemed to be more numerous. You can easily see, however, that 2-person and 8-person committees have to be equally numerous. Consider the fact that every 2-person committee defines an 8-person noncommittee, and vice versa.

The same kind of analysis applies to Problem 3. The number of paths in either structure is given by the formula x^y, where x is the number of x's in a row, and y is the number of rows. The number of paths in struc-

---

BOX 11-1   Problems Demonstrating Availability

1. Consider the letter *L*. In the English language, is this letter more likely to appear in the first position of a word or the third position of a word? Give your intuition or "gut reaction."

2. Ten students from a nearby college have indicated a willingness to serve on a curriculum committee. Their names are Ann, Bob, Dan, Elizabeth, Gary, Heidi, Jennifer, Laura, Terri, and Valerie.
   a. The dean wants to form a two-person committee. What is your estimate of the number of distinct committees that could be formed? (Don't use formulas; just respond intuitively.)
   b. The dean wants to form an eight-person committee. What is your estimate of the number of distinct committees that could be formed? (Don't use formulas; just respond intuitively.)

3. Consider the two structures shown below:

A	B
x x x x x x x x	x x
x x x x x x x x	x x
x x x x x x x x	x x
	x x
	x x
	x x
	x x
	x x
	x x

   A *path* in a structure is a line that connects one "x" from each row, starting with the top row and finishing at the bottom row. How many paths do you think each structure has? (Again, give an intuitive estimate.)

   SOURCE: *From "Availability: A Heuristic for Judging Frequency and Probability," by A. Tversky and D. Kahneman, 1973,* Cognitive Psychology, 5, *212–213. Copyright © 1973 by Academic Press. Reprinted by permission.*

ture A, then, is $8^3 = 512$. The number of paths in structure B is 2^9, also equal to 512. Again though, it is easier to see more nonoverlapping paths in A than in B; different paths in A are less confusable than different paths in B. Paths in A are shorter and therefore easier to visualize than those in B. The ease of visualization makes paths more available, and hence deemed more numerous in A than in B.

Everyday analogs that involve the use of the availability heuristic have also been reported. Ross and Sicoly (1979), for instance, surveyed 37 married couples (husbands and wives separately and independently) about the estimated extent of their responsibility for various household activities, such as making breakfast, shopping for groceries, caring for children. Husbands and wives both were more likely to say that they had greater responsibility than did their spouse for 16 of the 20 activities. Moreover, when asked to give examples of their own and their spouse's contributions to each activity, each spouse listed more of her or his own activities than activities of her or his spouse.

Ross and Sicoly (1979) explain these findings in terms of the availability heuristic. Our own efforts and behaviors are more apparent and available to us than are the efforts and behaviors of others. After all, we are certain to be present when we perform an action, but may or may not be when a friend or spouse does. Our own thoughts and plans are important to us, and we may be formulating them just at the time when other people do or say something, thus distracting us from their contributions. In general, what we do, think, say, or intend is more accessible to us than to anyone else, and also more accessible than anyone else's deeds, thoughts, words, or intentions. Small wonder, then, that in joint ventures, it is often the case that each partner feels that she or he shoulders a greater share of the burden.

Availability is not always a bad heuristic to use. If we can be sure that ease of constructing or calling instances to mind is unbiased, then it may be the best, or even only, tool to use when judging frequency or probability. If you are trying to decide which course you typically do more papers for, psychology or philosophy, it probably is fair to judge the frequency of papers by trying to recall specific paper assignments for each course. In this case, there is probably no particular reason to believe that psychology papers are more memorable than philosophy papers. If there were (for example, you took philosophy three years ago but psychology this semester), then the comparison is probably not a fair one.

However, if you are trying to decide which occurs more often, hours you spend working on a group project or hours someone else spends working on the same project, using availability to judge may not be fair. You have been there whenever you have worked, but you may not have been there all the times when other group members have worked. Thus, examples of your own work are likely to be more memorable and more available to you than examples of anyone else's work.

The point of demonstrating the availability heuristic, then, is not to warn you away from its use. Instead, as with all other heuristics, the idea is to suggest that you think carefully first about whether the range of examples you are drawing from is equally accessible.

Representativeness

Two students, Linda and Joe, are having a boring Saturday afternoon in the student union. For lack of something better to do, they each begin flipping a quarter, keeping track of the way it lands over time. Then, they compare results. Linda reports that her sequence of coin flips was heads, heads, heads, tails, tails, tails. Joe obtained the following results: tails, tails, heads, tails, heads, heads. Which of the two students obtained a more statistically probable series of results?

Most people who respond to this question intuitively believe that Joe did. After all, his sequence of responses are less patterned, and more "random looking." In fact, however, both outcomes are equally likely. The problem is that people generally expect that a random *process,* such as a coin flip, will always produce results that are random looking. That is, they expect the results to be representative of the process that generated them. People who make judgments this way are said to be using the **representativeness heuristic.**

Kahneman and Tversky (1973) demonstrated people's use of the representativeness heuristic in a series of studies. In one study, undergraduate subjects were assigned to three conditions. *Base-rate*-condition subjects were instructed, "Consider all first-year graduate students in the United States today. Please write down your best guesses about the percentage now enrolled in each of the following nine fields of specialization." The nine fields are shown in Box 11-2. *Similarity*-condition subjects were presented with the personality sketch shown in Box 11-2(a), and asked to rank the nine fields in terms of "how similar is Tom W. to the typical graduate student in each of the following nine fields of graduate specialization." *Prediction*-condition subjects were also given the personality sketch but told that it was written several years ago, during Tom W.'s senior year of high school, based on his response to projective tests (for example, a Rorschach test). They were then asked to predict the likelihood for each field that Tom W. was currently a graduate student in it.

Box 11-2(b) shows that the mean similarity rankings are very similar to the mean likelihood rankings, and independent of the mean judged base rate, again suggesting the use of the representativeness heuristic. Subjects asked to estimate the likelihood that Tom W. is a graduate student in field X do so, apparently, by comparing his personality description to their beliefs about what typical graduate students in field X are like, ignoring base rates. Base rates are important information, however. Just as in the mammogram example given earlier, the failure to include base rate information in your estimates of probability can lead to answers that are in error, often by an order of magnitude or more.

A related error in judgment is called **gambler's fallacy.** Imagine yourself standing beside a roulette wheel in Atlantic City. You watch the wheel come up red on eight successive trials. Assuming you are still willing to believe that the wheel is equally likely to come up black as it is to come up red, where would you place a bet for the next spin? Many people would want to bet on black, reasoning that if black and red are equally likely, that the previous outcomes have tilted the process a bit out of balance, and that it is "black's turn." However, the chances of black on the next trial are exactly the same as the chances of red on the next trial. The wheel is not

---

BOX 11-2   Data from a Prediction Study

Tom W. is of high intelligence, although lacking in true creativity. He has a need for order and clarity, and for neat and tidy systems in which every detail finds its appropriate place. His writing is rather dull and mechanical, occasionally enlivened by somewhat corny puns and by flashes of imagination of the sci-fi type. He has a strong drive for competence. He seems to have little feel and little sympathy for other people and does not enjoy interacting with others. Self-centered, he nonetheless has a deep moral sense.

(A)

Graduate Specialization Area	Mean Judged Base Rate (in %)	Mean Similarity Rank	Mean Likelihood Rank
Business administration	15	3.9	4.3
Computer science	7	2.1	2.5
Engineering	9	2.9	2.6
Humanities and education	20	7.2	7.6
Law	9	5.9	5.2
Library science	3	4.2	4.7
Medicine	8	5.9	5.8
Physical and life sciences	12	4.5	4.3
Social science and social work	17	8.2	8.0

(B)

(A) Personality sketch of Tom W.
(B) Estimated base rates of nine areas of graduate specialization, and summary of similarity and prediction data for Tom W.

SOURCE: *From "On the Psychology of Prediction," by D. Kahneman and A. Tversky, 1973,* Psychological Review, 80, *237–251. Copyright © 1973 by American Psychological Association. Reprinted by permission.*

Gambler's fallacy can cause people to make biased decisions.

"keeping track" in any way of past results, and so, is not going to "correct" or "make up for" past results. Although *in the long run* the number of times black comes up should equal the number of times red comes up, this does not mean that in the short run that the proportions will be even. This explanation applies also to the coin-flipping example given earlier. A random process (such as a coin flip or a roulette-wheel spin) will not always produce results that look random, especially in the short run.

Tversky and Kahneman (1971) describe people's (mistaken) belief in *the law of small numbers.* The idea is that people expect small samples (of people, of coin flips, of trials in an experiment) to resemble in every respect the populations from which they are drawn. In actuality, small samples are much more likely to deviate from the population and are therefore a less reliable basis from which to draw a conclusion. The gambler's fallacy problem, above, can be thought of as an instance of belief in the law of small numbers. People expect that a small sample of roulette-wheel spins (for example, 8) will show the same proportion of reds as will a very large sample (for example, 100,000). However, the chances of finding large deviations from the expected proportion are much larger with a small sample. Said another way, only very large samples can be expected to be representative of the population from which they come.

"Man-who" arguments are another example of the misuse of the representativeness heuristic. The term was coined by Nisbett and Ross

(1980). A "man-who" argument is usually advanced by someone who has just confronted, for instance, a statistical summary of a number of cases reporting that lung cancer rates are significantly higher among smokers than nonsmokers. The reply, "I know a *man who* smoked three packs a day and lived to be 110" is a particularly vivid example of ignoring base-rate information, and instead paying as much attention to small sample sizes (the individual man who was known; $N = 1$) as to large ones (those cases summarized, where N may be 10,000).

Framing Effects

Driving on the road, you notice your car is running low on gasoline, and you see two service stations, both of which are advertising gasoline. Station A's price is $1.00 per gallon; Station B's, $0.95. Station A's sign also announces: "5 cents/gallon discount for cash!" Station B's sign announces "5 cents/gallon surcharge for credit cards." All other factors being equal (for example, cleanliness of the stations, whether you like the brand of gasoline carried, number of cars waiting at each), to which station would you choose to go? Many people report a preference for Station A, the one that offers a cash discount (Thaler, 1980). It is interesting that people have this preference because both stations are actually offering the same deal: a price of $.95 per gallon if you use cash, and $1.00 per gallon if you use credit cards.

Tversky & Kahneman (1981) provide an explanation of this phenomenon in terms of *framing effects*: people evaluate outcomes as changes from a reference point, their current state. Depending on how their current state is described, they perceive certain outcomes as gains or losses. The description is therefore said to "frame" the decision, or to provide a certain context for it. We have already seen in previous cognitive topics (for example, perception, thinking, reasoning) that context effects can play a large role in affecting cognitive performance. Framing effects, in essence, can be thought of as context effects in decision making.

What appears to be going on in the gas station example is this. When described as a "cash discount," the price seems to you to be a bargain—you assume that you are starting from a reference point of a dollar a gallon, and then saving or gaining a nickel. In the case of Station B, however, you describe the situation to yourself as follows. "OK, so they're charging ninety-five cents. Sounds good. But hey, wait a minute. If I want to use my card, they'll jack up the price to a dollar. Hey, I'd lose a nickel a gallon that way. What rip-off artists they are! Heck, I'll just go to Station A."

Kahneman and Tversky (1979) argue that we treat losses more seriously than we treat gains of an equivalent amount (whether it be of money or some other measure of satisfaction). That is, we care more about losing a dollar than we do about gaining a dollar; or more about losing a nickel than gaining a nickel. The problem is that simply changing the *description* of a situation can cause us to adopt different reference points, and therefore to see the same outcome as a gain in one situation and a loss in the other. That in turn might cause us to change our decision making, not because anything in the problem has changed but simply because the way we describe the situation to ourselves has.

Illusory Correlation

You and a friend, both students of (if not majors in) psychology, observe fellow students around campus and discover a behavioral pattern you call "hair twisting": the subject pinches a strand of hair between thumb and forefinger, and proceeds to twist it around the forefinger. You believe that this behavior is especially likely to be found in people undergoing a great deal of stress. In need of a research paper for your psychology class, you undertake a study with your friend. You observe a random sample of 150 students for a day, categorizing them as hair twisters or not hair twisters. (Assume you and the friend make your observations independently, and that your interrater reliability, the agreement of categorization between the two of you, is high.) Later, each of the subjects is given a battery of psychological tests to decide whether they are under significant amounts of stress. The results are shown in Box 11-3. Given these data, give your intuitive estimate of the relationship between stress and hair pulling. If you have had a course in statistics, you can try estimating the correlation coefficient; if not, try to put into words your belief about how strong the relationship is.

I posed this question to 30 students taking a cognitive psychology course. Most of them believed that there was at least a weak relationship between the two variables. In fact, there is absolutely no relationship. Notice that the proportion of hair twisters is .25 (20/80 and 10/40) for both the subjects under stress and the subjects not under stress. Nevertheless, my students' intuitions are typical: people report seeing associations in data that seem plausible even when associations are not present. In this example, hair twisting and stress are plausibly related because hair twisting

---

BOX 11-3   Example of Illusory Correlation

	Under Stress	Not Under Stress
Hair twister	20	10
Non–hair twister	80	40

Given the data above, give your intuitive estimate of the correlation between the two variables (from 0 to 1).

sounds like a nervous behavior, and nervous behaviors are likely to be produced under conditions of anxiety.

The phenomenon of seeing relationships that are not present is called *illusory correlation.* Notice that in the above example, it occurs even under ideal conditions (all of the data are summarized and presented in a table, and so you do not need to recall all the relevant cases from memory). There is no ambiguity over where individual cases fall (everyone is classified as being a hair twister or not, and under stress or not), and there is no reason to expect personal biases on your part to interfere with your estimate. The data are dichotomous (that is, "yes" or "no") for both variables, and therefore, easy to work with.

Chapman and Chapman (1967a, 1967b, 1969) presented an even more compelling demonstration of the phenomenon of illusory correlation. The authors were puzzled by a controversy within the field of clinical psychology over the use of the draw-a-person test. This is a psychodiagnostic test in which the client is asked to "draw a person," and the drawings are scored according to a number of dimensions (for example, whether the figure drawn is muscular, has atypical eyes, is childlike, is fat). Clinicians had reported strong correlations between some of the features of drawings and particular symptoms and behavioral characteristics (for example, atypical eyes are drawn by suspicious clients; big heads are drawn by intelligent clients). However, these reports were never confirmed by researchers studying the test itself.

In one study, Chapman and Chapman (1967a) gave undergraduates who were unfamiliar with the draw-a-person test a series of 45 drawings that they randomly paired with symptoms allegedly displayed by the people who drew them. These undergraduates "discovered" the same correlations that clinicians had been reporting. Because the drawings and symptoms were randomly paired, it appeared that the undergraduates shared with the clinicians a preexisting bias as to what relationships would be found in the data. That is, they "discovered" relationships they expected to find, even when those relationships really were not there.

Variables that tend to be falsely associated are typically ones that seem to have some prior association in the minds of people (Chapman & Chapman, 1967b). On the surface, it seems to make sense that suspicious clients might draw wide-eyed figures—the wide eyes might be an artistic or symbolic representation of their suspiciousness. The point here is that the associations we bring to a situation often color our judgment to the point where we see them even if they are not there.

Hindsight Bias

Consider the following decision: You need to choose between declaring a psychology major and an economics major. You consult your own performance, goals, likes, and dislikes, and have long discussions with faculty in both departments, majors in both departments, teachers from both areas who have instructed you, friends, parents, and relevant others. You finally decide to become an economics major, primarily because of the interest you have in the topics in your classes, and also because you like the economics faculty so much.

A few months later you start to discover that you like your economics classes less and less, and you find your psychology courses more interesting than you previously had. You reopen the decision about your major, spend another couple of weeks rethinking your goals and interests, and decide to switch majors to psychology. When you announce this decision to your best friend, she says, "Well, I knew this was going to happen. It was pretty much inevitable. You don't seem to be the type to fit in with the other majors in that department, and also, given the stuff you said about last term's assignments, I knew you wouldn't like it for long." Other friends of yours also express little surprise at your latest decision, confiding that they "knew all along" that your change of major would happen.

How is it that you yourself didn't foresee this inevitable change in majors? How is it that your friends really could see into your future and you could not? In fact, one likely answer is that your friends are in error, and that they are suffering from something called **hindsight bias.** Fischhoff (1982a) describes this bias as a tendency to "consistently exaggerate what could have been anticipated in foresight" when looking back (in hindsight) on an event (p. 341). The idea is that once you know how a decision has turned out, you look back on the events leading up to the outcome as being more inevitable than they really were.

Fischhoff demonstrated hindsight bias experimentally in the following way. Subjects were asked to read a passage similar to the one shown in Box 11-4. Passages described either historical events (as does the one in Box 11-4) or clinical case descriptions of people. All subjects were asked to rate the likelihood of a number of possible outcomes of the event. Some subjects were additionally told that one of the outcomes had actually occurred, and asked to estimate (in hindsight) the probabilities of all of the possible outcomes. Results showed that subjects who were told what the outcome actually was gave higher estimates of the probability that it would have happened, given the description in the passage, than did subjects who were not told what outcome had occurred. Surprisingly, subjects saw the outcome that they were told had happened as inevitable, regardless of which outcome it was. Subjects told that the British won saw British victory "all along" in the passage; subjects told that the Gurkas won saw that outcome as inevitable. Subjects told that the clash ended in a military stalemate also said that they saw that outcome coming.

How does hindsight bias apply to your friends in the hypothetical dilemma described above? Recall that in the dilemma, they told you that they "knew all along" that your decision to major in economics would not turn out well. It is likely, however, that your friends are looking back in hindsight, knowing how your original decision turned out and therefore more able to think of reasons that your decision turned out this way. Their ability to predict, in foresight, how your decision would turn out is probably far weaker. In short, to quote an old maxim, "Hindsight is always 20-20."

Overconfidence

Consider the questions in Box 11-5, and choose from the two possible answers. After answering, give a rating of your confidence. If you have absolutely no idea of what the answer is, you should choose the value .5, to

---

B O X 1 1 - 4   Example of Hindsight Bias

Read the following passage, then answer the question below:

[1] For some years after the arrival of Hastings as governor-general of India, the consolidation of British power involved serious war. [2] The first of these wars took place on the northern frontier of Bengal where the British were faced by the plundering raids of the Gurkas of Nepal. [3] Attempts had been made to stop the raids by an exchange of lands, but the Gurkas would not give up their claims to country under British control, [4] and Hastings decided to deal with them once and for all. [5] The campaign began in November, 1814. It was not glorious. [6] The Gurkas were only some 12,000 strong; [7] but they were brave fighters, fighting in territory well-suited to their raiding tactics. [8] The older British commanders were used to war in the plains where the enemy ran away from a resolute attack. [9] In the mountains of Nepal it was not easy even to find the enemy. [10] The troops and transport animals suffered from the extremes of heat and cold, [11] and the officers learned caution only after sharp reverses. [12] Major-General Sir D. Octerlony was the one commander to escape from these minor defeats.

In light of the information appearing in the passage, what was the probability of occurrence of each of the four possible outcomes listed below? (The probabilities should sum to 100%.)

———British victory
———Gurka victory
———Military stalemate with no peace settlement
———Military stalemate with a peace settlement

SOURCE: *From "Hindsight/Foresight: The Effect of Outcome Knowledge of Judgment Under Certainty," by B. Fischhoff (1975),* Journal of Experimental Psychology: Human Perception and Performance, 1, *288–299. Copyright © 1975 by the American Psychological Association. Reprinted by permission. The passage was taken from Woodward (1938, pp. 383-384).*

indicate that you think that the odds that you are right are 50-50. (Any number lower than .5 would indicate that you think you are more likely to be wrong than right, so you should have chosen the other answer.) A rating of 1.00 means that you are 100% certain that your answer is correct. Values between .5 and 1.00 indicate intermediate levels of confidence, with higher numbers reflecting higher confidence.

It matters very little how accurate your answers are for the purposes of this discussion. What matters here is the relationship between your accuracy and your confidence rating. In several studies (reviewed by Lichtenstein, Fischhoff, & Phillips, 1982), subjects were given a long list of questions similar to the ones in Box 11-5. After the subjects answered all questions and gave confidence ratings, a plot of their accuracy as a function of their confidence ratings was made. For example, the experimenters looked at all of the questions for which a subject rated his confidence as .6, and calculated the proportion of those questions he answered correctly. Typical findings are shown in Figure 11-1. Notice that the 45-degree line would indicate that confidence and accuracy were perfectly synchronized: questions for which a subject had a confidence rating of .6 would actually be answered accurately 60% of the time. This kind of finding is rarely if ever found. Instead, typical curves are "bowed" out from the 45-degree line, as shown in the figure.

This kind of curve—plotting confidence against accuracy—is called a **calibration curve.** The closer the curve is to the 45-degree line, the better the calibration, or "fit," between confidence and accuracy. Deviations from the curve below this line are said to indicate **overconfidence,** where confidence ratings are higher than actual accuracy. Deviations above the line would indicate *underconfidence,* a phenomenon that almost never

---

BOX 11-5   Some Trivia Questions

Choose one answer for each question, and rate your confidence in your answer on a scale from .5 (just guessing) to 1.0 (completely certain).

Which magazine had the largest circulation in 1978?
    a. *Time*   b. *Reader's Digest*
Which city had the larger population in 1953?
    a. St. Paul, MN   b. New Orleans, LA
Who was the 21st president of the United States?
    a. Arthur   b. Cleveland
Which Union ironclad ship fought the Confederate ironclad ship *Merrimack?*
    a. Monitor   b. Andover
Who began the profession of nursing?
    a. Nightingale   b. Barton

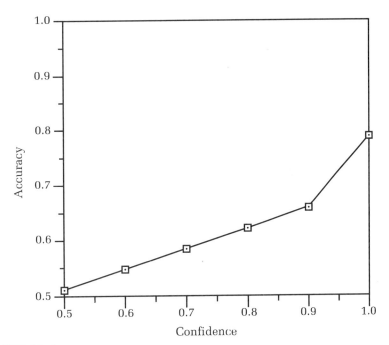

FIGURE 11-1.   Example of a calibration curve

occurs. The general idea is this: for all of the questions that subjects give a .8 confidence rating to (presumably, meaning that they estimate the probability of their answering correctly as .8), they are correct only about 60% of the time. Further, when subjects say they are 100% certain of the answer, they are correct only about 75–80% of the time. Said another way, people's impressions of their own accuracy are inflated.

Overconfidence is a real impediment to good decision making. If your confidence in your judgment is inappropriately high, you probably will spurn any offers of help in making decisions because you will fail to see the need for it. Even when good decision aids are available to help you overcome other biases and errors of judgment, overconfidence will make you weigh your own intuitions more heavily than any objective information that might be available. Overconfidence, then, can be thought of as arrogance in decision making.

We have reviewed a (very incomplete) list of heuristics and biases in decision making and planning in this section. Again, the point here is not that these ways of gathering and assessing information are always wrong or bad. Instead, the above examples point out places where decision making does not go as smoothly as it could. The existence of these biases also tells us something about how human beings "naturally" cope with information, particularly when information is in abundance. Documentation of such errors can be the first step to setting up effective remedial programs.

Utility Models of Decision Making

The above section described errors and patterns of thinking people use when gathering information. Another issue, though, is how people sift through all the information that has been gathered in order to reach a decision. In this section, we will review two models that describe, or purport to describe, exactly what people are doing when they choose from alternatives. There are many other models of decision making that will not be covered, but the recommended readings at the chapter's end should be helpful to the interested reader.

It will be useful first to describe in a more general way the kinds of models of decision making (and thinking) that exist. **Normative models** define ideal performance under ideal circumstances. **Prescriptive models** tell us how we "ought" to make decisions. They take into account the fact that circumstances in which decisions are made will rarely be ideal and provide guidance about how to do the best that one can. Teachers try to get students to follow prescriptive models. **Descriptive models,** in contrast, simply detail what it is that people actually do when they make decisions. These are not necessarily endorsements of good ways of thinking; rather, they describe actual performance. The distinctions among normative, prescriptive, and descriptive models will be important as we consider various specific theories.

Expected Utility Theory

Making a decision such as choosing a major can be compared to a gamble. In most gambles, you win (or lose) particular amounts of money depending on certain outcomes. Probability theory tells us (assuming fair coins, decks of cards, and the like), what the odds are of any outcome. The dollar amount won or lost tells us the monetary worth of each outcome.

It would be nice if we could somehow combine information about probabilities and amounts that can be won or lost. In fact, one way of doing so is to calculate the *expected value* of each outcome. By multiplying the probability of each outcome by the amount of money won or lost for that outcome, and summing these values over all possible outcomes, we can determine the expected value of the gamble. Presumably, then, if we were offered a choice between two gambles, we could choose the better one by calculating the expected value of each, and choosing the gamble with the higher value.

This idea of expected value can be expressed in the form of an equation,

(3)
$$EV = \Sigma_i[p(i) \cdot v(i)],$$

where *EV* stands for "expected value" of the gamble, $p(i)$ is the probability of the ith outcome, and $v(i)$ is the monetary value of that outcome.

As an example, imagine a lottery with ten tickets, numbered 1 through 10. If the ticket drawn is numbered 1, you win $10. If the ticket drawn is numbered 2, 3, or 4, you win $5. Any other numbers drawn are worth nothing. The expected value of this lottery, then, is

$.1 \cdot \$10 + .3 \cdot \$5, + .6 \cdot \$0 = \$1.60.$

What good does it do you to calculate the expected value? For one thing, it provides you with a guide to how much money (if any) you should be willing to spend to buy a lottery ticket. If you are making rational decisions, you should not spend more for the ticket than the expected value of the lottery. (In some lotteries for charity, of course, you may want to donate more money simply to support the cause. In that case, you would need to add the expected value of the lottery and the amount of money you are willing to donate.)

Not every decision involves monetary outcomes. We often care about other aspects of possible outcomes: our chances for happiness, success, or fulfillment of goals. Psychologists, economists, and others use the term **utility** to capture ideas of happiness, pleasure, and the satisfaction that comes from achieving one or more personal goals. A choice that fulfills one goal will have less utility than a choice that fulfills that same goal plus another. For these decisions, we can use the kind of equation given above, using utility instead of monetary value. Equation 3 now becomes

(4) $EU = \Sigma_i \, [p(i) \cdot u(i)],$

where EU stands for the expected utility of a decision, and $u(i)$ is the utility of the ith outcome. The summation is again over all the possible outcomes.

Let's translate our original example of choosing a major into the expected utility model. Imagine that you have listed all possible majors, estimated the probability of success in each, and determined your overall utility for success or failure. Table 11-1 provides an example. You estimate that you have a good chance of success in some majors (for example, sociology). You do not think that you have much chance of success in others (perhaps, physics). At the same time, you place different values on success in various majors. In this example, you value psychology the most, followed by chemistry and biology. Your utility for failure also differs among the possible majors. For some, your overall utility even for failure is positive (for example, biology, mathematics). For others, your overall utility for failure is strongly negative (for example, psychology, sociology). The last column gives the overall expected utility for each major. It suggests that the best decision, given the estimates of probability and utility, is a chemistry major, with psychology and biology as second and third choices, respectively.

You might be wondering how utility is measured in this example. It turns out that the measurement of utilities is fairly straightforward. If you select one outcome and assign it the value of zero, then you can assign other values using this as the reference point. It does not matter which outcome is chosen as the zero point because the final decision depends on differences in expected utilities, not on the absolute value of the utilities (see Baron, 1988, for more on this process).

Expected utility theory is a normative model of decision making. It can be shown (see Baron, 1988) that if you always choose so as to maximize expected utility, then over a sufficiently large number of decisions, your own satisfaction will be highest. In other words, there is no better way of choosing among options that in the long run will increase overall satisfaction than using expected utility.

Multiattribute Utility Theory

Like many others, you may be feeling that using expected utility theory to choose a major oversimplifies the decision. Specifically, you may find it hard to quantify your utility for success or for failure of any specific major. You may care about several goals, and find it hard to figure out how they all fit together.

In one study (Galotti & Kozberg, 1987), undergraduates were asked to list the factors they had thought of (or, in the case of freshmen and

TABLE 11-1.   An example of expected utility calculations for the decision to major in selected subjects

Major	Probability of Success	Utility		Expected Utility
		For Success	For Failure	
Art	.75	10	0	7.50
Asian studies	.50	0	−5	−2.50
Biology	.30	25	5	11.00
Chemistry	.45	30	4	15.70
Economics	.15	5	−10	−7.75
English	.25	5	0	1.25
French	.60	0	−5	−2.00
German	.50	0	−5	−2.50
History	.25	8	0	2.00
Mathematics	.05	10	5	5.25
Philosophy	.10	0	−5	−4.50
Physics	.01	0	0	0.00
Psychology	.60	35	−20	13.00
Religion	.50	5	−5	0.00
Sociology	.80	5	−25	−1.00

NOTE: The probability of each outcome (success and failure) is multiplied by the utility for each outcome, and summed across both, giving the overall expected utility of choosing that major. Probabilities and utilities come from the individual making the decision and are subjective estimates.

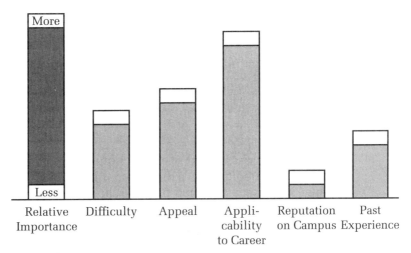

FIGURE 11-2.   Weightings of five dimensions in the decision "choosing a major"

sophomores, that they were thinking of) when they chose a major. Respondents listed a number of things, among them, the difficulty and appeal of the major; the applicability of the major to their future careers; the reputation of the department and instructors on campus; and their past experience in courses in the major.

One principal source of difficulty in making this decision appeared to involve how the various factors and goals were integrated. Calculation of expected utility, using Equation 4, might be difficult because information about several aspects of the decision must be integrated. Fortunately, there is a model that provides a means of integrating different dimensions and goals of a complex decision. It is called multiattribute utility theory (MAUT).

MAUT involves six steps: (1) breaking a decision into independent dimensions (such as the five listed above for choosing a major); (2) determining the relative weights of each dimension; (3) listing all of the alternatives (for example, possible majors); (4) ranking the alternatives along the five dimensions; (5) multiplying the ranking by the weighting of each alternative to determine its final value; and (6) choosing the alternative with the highest value.

Figures 11-2 through 11-5 provide an example of MAUT applied to the decision of choosing a major, created with the computer program Decision Map (Kopp & Slayter, 1984). Look first at Figure 11-2, the first two steps in MAUT. It shows the five dimensions described above, along with weightings that might be given by a particular student. (Again, weightings indicate how important a given aspect of the decision is to the decision

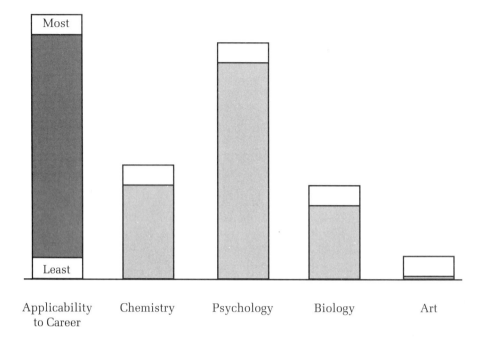

FIGURE 11-3.   Assessment of four possible majors on one dimension in the decision "choosing a major"

maker.) For this student, the most important goal is choosing a major that is relevant to future career goals. Notice that in the graph, the goal or dimension "applicability to career" has the highest value, and hence the most weight. The next most important goals, for this student, are the difficulty and appeal of the major, and the student's past record of success in its courses. The goal "reputation on campus" has been given very little weight by this student, indicating that it is of relatively little importance. Of significance here is that these weights are subjective, and would change for different students. Your own weightings could be very dissimilar to the ones given in this example.

After weighting all of the dimensions, the decision maker must consider all of the alternatives, and assess them on all of the dimensions described in the previous paragraph. Figure 11-3 depicts part of this process, the ranking of various majors on the dimension "applicability to career." To simplify the example, only the top four potential majors from Table 11-1 are shown here: chemistry, psychology, biology, and art. The subject would need to rate each of these alternatives on each of the dimensions identified in the first two steps. There would thus be five graphs of this kind, one for each dimension identified in Figure 11-2.

Figure 11-4 depicts the fifth step in the MAUT process: the putting together of the assessments of alternatives on all the dimensions, together with the weights of those dimensions. It shows that psychology is the best alternative, according to the rankings and weightings given earlier. Figure 11-5 provides an analysis of why this is so: psychology far outranks other alternatives on the dimension "applicability to career" and is not very far below other alternatives on the other dimensions.

To use MAUT in decision making, it is critical that the dimensions listed be independent of one another. For instance, the possible dimensions "difficulty of courses" and "past grades in course" are presumably related. Thus, the decision maker has to be careful to choose each dimension carefully. Second, the decision maker has to be willing to make trade-offs among the various dimensions. Although it may be true that the decision maker in our example cares most about future career goals, MAUT assumes that the person would be willing to choose an alternative that was not highest on this dimension *if* its relative position on other dimensions was enough to compensate.

MAUT can also be shown to be a normative model of decision making. That is to say, if people follow MAUT, they will maximize their own utility in a way that is best for achieving all of their goals. Unfortunately, little is known about whether MAUT is ever used spontaneously by people when making important decisions, especially if the information relevant to making the decision is extensive.

A study by Payne (1976) suggests that people do not always spontaneously use MAUT. Payne examined how people chose apartments when

FIGURE 11-4.   Final choice of a major

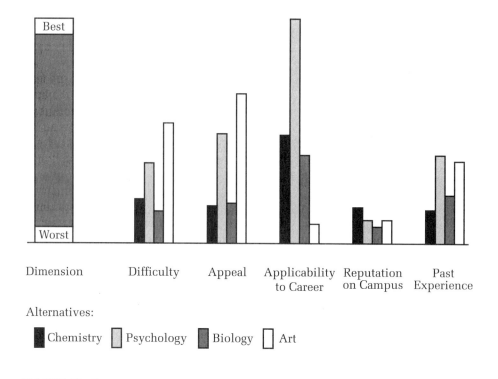

FIGURE 11-5.   An analysis of the decision "Choosing a major"

given different amounts of information about different numbers of alternatives. Subjects were presented with an "information board" carrying a number of cards. Each card represented a different one-bedroom furnished apartment and carried the name of a factor, for example, "noise level," "rent," or "closet space." The back of the card gave the value of that dimension for that apartment; possible values for the rent factor for example, were $110, $140, or $170.

Subjects could examine one piece of information at a time (for example, the rent for apartment number 1), and could examine as many or as few pieces of information as they needed to make a decision. The experimenter kept track of which pieces of information were examined. Two factors were varied in the experiment: the number of alternatives (that is, apartments) presented, 2, 6, or 12; and the number of factors of information available per alternative, 4, 8, or 12.

When choosing between only two apartments, subjects examined the same number of factors for each. That is, if they asked about rent, closet space, parking, and laundry facilities for one, they asked about rent, closet space, parking, and laundry facilities for the other. Subjects were willing to make trade-offs in this decision, letting a desirable value of one factor (for example, low rent) trade off against a less desirable value of another (for example, little closet space).

When subjects had to decide among 6 or 12 apartments, however, they used another strategy. In these cases, subjects eliminated some alternatives on the basis of only one or a few dimensions. For instance, subjects looked first at rent, and immediately eliminated all apartments with high rents, without considering trade-offs with other factors. This strategy has been called *elimination by aspects* (Tversky, 1972). It works as follows: First, a factor is selected, say, rent. All the alternatives that exceed a threshold value for this factor (for example, more than $140) are eliminated. Next, another factor is selected, say, noise level, and any alternatives found to exceed a threshold value on that dimension (for example, very noisy) are eliminated. This process continues until only one alternative is left. Payne (1976) believes that when decision makers have too much information to deal with, they reduce "cognitive strain" by resorting to such nonoptimal heuristics as elimination by aspects.

MAUT is a normative model; elimination by aspects is a descriptive model. It provides a picture of what people actually do. Whether elimination by aspects is the best one can do, with limited time or memory, to make a decision is an open question. In some cases, it may be entirely rational. If an apartment seeker simply cannot afford a rent above a certain amount, then it makes no sense to expend energy considering apartments that cost more than that, regardless of how well they rate on other dimensions. In other cases, it may be important for decision makers to take the time and trouble to engage in a MAUT analysis of a decision. Various kinds of decision aids (including computer-assisted ones) exist, and may prove useful.

Improving Decision Making

We have reviewed evidence suggesting that two major components of decision making—the gathering and the integration of information—are typically performed less than optimally. These studies therefore raise the question "How can these activities be improved?" In this section, we will look at the major reasons that decision making goes awry and suggest some ways of eliminating the problems or at least reducing their impact.

One of the major obstacles to improving the ways in which people gather and integrate information is overconfidence. People who believe that their decision making is already close to optimal simply will not see the need for any assistance, even if it is available and offered. Such people may not even seek or look at evidence regarding their performance. Overconfidence, then, is a twofold problem because of its effects in particular decisions and because it inflates people's view of their own decision making and planning capabilities.

In general, simply telling people about biases in decision making and planning (including overconfidence) results in little or no improvement (Arkes, 1986; Fischhoff, 1982b). Real improvement in reducing bias seems to require extensive practice with the task, individual feedback about one's performance, and some means of making the statistical and/or probabilistic aspects of the decisions clearer. Under some of these conditions, substantial reductions in bias have been reported (Arkes, 1986; Nisbett, Krantz, Jepson, & Kunda, 1983).

Nisbett and his collaborators (1983) found, for instance, that making certain aspects of a situation more salient increases people's tendency to reason statistically. In one study, they presented subjects with one of two versions of a problem (shown in Box 11-6) about a high school senior making college decisions. Version 2 was intended to highlight the fact that what David L. saw during his campus visit was simply a subset, or sample, of all of the things he could have possibly seen, and thus depended to some degree on chance. Subjects reading Version 2 apparently took account of the role of chance in David L.'s visit because they were significantly less likely to say that he should go to the Ivy League university (and thus ignore his friends' advice, which is presumably based on a much larger sample of information than the sample David received from his own visit) than were subjects who read Version 1. The implication here is that making the role of chance in a situation more obvious encourages people to weight information in ways that reduce bias and error. In other studies (reviewed by Nisbett, Fong, Lehman, & Cheng, 1987), Nisbett and his collaborators found that even relatively brief, 30-minute training sessions in statistical reasoning can improve people's ability to apply statistical principles to everyday life. Apparently, then, certain kinds of training can improve at least some aspects of decision making.

A second obstacle to improving decision making has to do with people's feelings and expectations about how decisions ought to be made. Our cultural expectations lead many of us to trust our intuitions (or at least the intuitions of experts) over any kind of judgment made with equations, computer programs, mathematical models, or the like. This preference is especially evident with very important decisions. We want to be sure that decisions concerning, say, job or graduate school applicants, medical diagnoses and treatments, or even mortgage loans, are made humanely—taking all relevant evidence into account and not just looking at numbers.

Meehl (1954, 1965) confronted this issue some years ago. He examined the relative effectiveness of holistic, clinical impressions with judgments made by statistical models of data. A good example of this would be to compare an admissions counselor's prediction of an applicant's chances for success at a given college with the prediction of a statistical model that weighted SAT scores, high school GPA, degree of involvement in extracurricular activities, strength of letters of recommendation (however measured), and whatever other variables were established to be relevant to predicting success at that college. Numerous studies of this kind have been conducted, and they overwhelmingly support the use of the nonhuman model (Dawes & Corrigan, 1974; Dawes, 1982). Thus, contrary to our (strong) intuitions, it *is* often better, fairer, more rational, and in the long run more humane to use decision aids rather than to rely exclusively on human impressions or intuitions (Kleinmuntz, 1990).

Does this mean that all decisions should be made by computer? To the contrary, people will always be needed to select and judge the relevance of the information that is to be used in a decision. Dawes (1982) argues that

---

BOX 11-6   Sample Stimuli from Nisbett et al. (1983)

Version 1

David L. was a senior in high school on the East Coast who was planning to go to college. He had compiled an excellent record in high school and had been admitted to his two top choices: a small liberal arts college and an Ivy League university. David had several older friends who were attending the liberal arts college and several who were attending the Ivy League university. They were all excellent students like himself and had interests similar to his. The friends at the liberal arts college all reported that they liked the place very much and that they found it very stimulating. The friends at the Ivy League university reported that they had many complaints on both personal and social grounds and on educational grounds.

David initially thought that he would go to the smaller college. However, he decided to visit both schools himself for a day.

He did not like what he saw at the private liberal arts college: Several people whom he met seemed cold and unpleasant; a professor he met with briefly seemed abrupt and uninterested in him; and he did not like the "feel" of the campus. He did like what he saw at the Ivy League university: Several of the people he met seemed like vital, enthusiastic, pleasant people; he met with two different professors who took a personal interest in him; and he came away with a very pleasant feeling about the campus.

Version 2 (Same as Version 1, with the following material added after the second paragraph)

He proceeded systematically to draw up a long list, for both colleges, of all the classes which might interest him and all the places and activities on campus that he wanted to see. From each list, he randomly selected several classes and activities to visit, and several spots to look at (by blindly dropping a pencil on each list of alternatives and seeing where the point landed).

SOURCE: *From "The Use of Statistical Heuristics in Everyday Inductive Reasoning," by R. E. Nisbett, D. H. Krantz, C. Jepson, and Z. Kunda (1983),* Psychological Review, 90, *339–363. Copyright © 1983 by the American Psychological Association. Reprinted by permission.*

people are quite proficient at figuring out *which* variables are good predictors. Human shortcomings show up when people try to figure out how to integrate all of the information that is relevant to a decision. Linear models (such as the one used in Figures 11-2 through 11-5), on the other hand, are good at integrating the information that human judges have selected as relevant. Decision analysis (Keeney, 1982; von Winterfeldt & Edwards, 1986b) is a newly emerging technology that helps people to gather and integrate information in a way similar to that used in the MAUT analysis of choosing a major, above. It makes use of human judges' feelings, beliefs, and judgments of relevance but helps to ensure that integration of information is carried out in an unbiased way.

Summary

We have seen that decision making is a task that requires gathering, organizing, combining, and evaluating information. Because real-life decisions are often made under conditions of uncertainty, many of the decisions we face require that we make some sort of probability estimates, even if only vague and intuitive ones.

Because decision making can be so complex, it is perhaps unsurprising that it is capable of going wrong or being suboptimal in a number of ways. People's intuitions about uncertainty and probability, their activities to acquire or remember relevant information, and the processes they use to integrate different pieces of information can easily be shown to be error prone. One can think of at least some of the biases and errors in decision making as cognitive illusions: they arise for understandable reasons, and may actually be quite useful in some circumstances. For example, using availability to estimate the relative frequence of occurrence of something may work perfectly well, as long as you can be sure that the examples have been collected in an unbiased fashion.

One of the most general biases people typically exhibit is overconfidence in their own judgment. Several demonstrations make the point that people often feel much more sure of their thinking and their predictions for the future than they may have a right to (based on their track records, for instance). Overconfidence can also play a role in more specific biases, such as hindsight bias or illusory correlation. In general, overconfidence might prevent people from critically examining their own thinking, or from admitting of possibilities other than their favored one.

We also examined specific models of decision making. Some, normative, models purport to show how people *should* make decisions under ideal circumstances. One example is multiattribute utility theory (MAUT), which describes how information about the probability and the utility of various possible outcomes can be combined and compared. Other, descriptive, models describe how people *actually* make decisions. One such model, elimination by aspects, assumes that the amount of information people seek depends upon the number of alternative possibilities under consideration.

Despite all the literature documenting people's errors in judgment and decision making, people do make decisions every day. It is therefore worth remembering that any good theory of decision making must explain how people have survived thus far, and where the sources of people's competence lie. At the same time, it is probably safe to conclude that complex and important decisions can usually be made more carefully. Decision analysis, a collection of techniques to help people consider all relevant options and trade-offs, can improve the quality of decision making.

Decision making is a relatively new addition to cognitive psychology. Therefore, we can expect to learn a great deal more about it in the years to come. This kind of research will not only produce better models of the ways in which people process and use information but, it is hoped, help in the long run to improve these skills.

Recommended Readings

"Classic" works on decision making and planning include Edwards (1954), Janis and Mann (1977), and Simon (1956). Recent literature reviews are provided by Pitz and Sachs (1984), Slovic, Lichtenstein, and Fischhoff (1988), and Payne, Bettman, and Johnson (1992). The last two describe a number of recent theoretical challenges and modifications of utility theory.

Arkes (1991) offers an analysis of the costs and benefits of different errors and biases in decision making. Kleinmuntz (1990) discusses the use of intuition versus formal decision-making models, and describes conditions under which each can complement the other.

Two edited volumes containing a number of articles reporting on recent research in the area of decision making are Arkes and Hammond (1986), and Kahneman, Slovic, and Tversky (1982). A recent volume edited by Edwards (1992) includes research on utility theory. Textbooks focusing on this area of cognition include Baron (1988), Rachlin (1989), and Plous (1993). Baron (1985) discusses rationality of thinking and decision making in more detail. Decision analysis is described in von Winterfeldt and Edwards, (1986a). Nelson-Jones (1990) provides advice for making better personal decisions.

REVIEW QUESTIONS

1. Why do some psychologists regard heuristics and biases in decision making as "cognitive illusions"? Evaluate this theoretical assertion.

2. Give two examples of the use of the availability heuristic in everyday life—one where it would be appropriate, and another where it might not. Show why your examples are illustrative of availability.

3. Give an explanation for the illusory-correlation phenomenon. Discuss the implications of your explanation.

4. Discuss the relationship of hindsight bias and overconfidence.

5. What is a *calibration curve?* Illustrate your answer with a diagram and text explaining the relevant features.

6. Explain the distinctions among normative models, prescriptive models, and descriptive models of thinking.

7. What is expected utility theory, and how does it relate to decision making?

8. What do studies of clinical impressions and intuitions imply about decision making. Do you accept these implications? Why or why not?

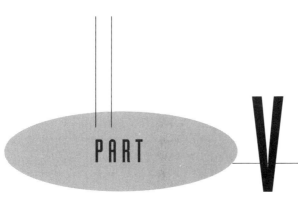

V

Individual and Situational Differences in Cognition

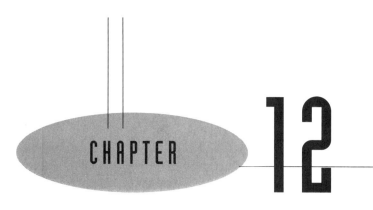

CHAPTER 12

Cognitive Development Through Adolescence

So far, we've looked at cognition in adults. The capacities, skills, and strategies used in cognitive tasks have all been described in terms of a person who has presumably mastered or acquired most, or even all, of the requisite skills considered necessary for a fully functioning cognitive being. It can be argued, however, that our understanding of adult cognition is fundamentally incomplete unless we understand its development.

The reasons that an adult uses her memory, reaches one conclusion rather than another, or perceives something in a certain way may have a great deal to do with her previous experience with cognitive tasks, as well as with her current ability to understand the demands of the task in front of her.

In this chapter, we will pause to consider how cognitive capacities, skills, and strategies come to be—when and how they are acquired or mastered, and what sorts of influences affect their growth. We will examine how infants and children at different points in their development cope with different cognitive tasks.

Our review of cognitive development will necessarily be quite selective. There simply isn't room in one chapter to consider the development of performance on all of the cognitive tasks we have previously discussed. Instead, we will first look at broad theoretical approaches to cognitive development, considering the general question "How do cognitive abilities change and grow as an infant matures through adolescence?" To do this, we will focus on two major kinds of theoretical approaches: stage theories, such as that of Piaget; and nonstage theories, such as information-processing models.

Stage theories are so named because they describe development as consisting of a series of qualitatively different periods, called *stages.* Each stage consists of a different way of making sense of the world. Stage theories view children as fundamentally and qualitatively different from adults in one or more respects, by virtue of their being in different developmental stages. Stage theories assume children go through stages in a fixed or stable order, never skipping stages or going backward. Presumably, the cognitive abilities and capacities gained in one stage make the child ready to acquire the abilities and capacities of the next stage. In this sense, stages build on one another. Most stage theorists also claim *universality* for their stages, seeing them as applicable to children from a wide variety of cultures and environments.

Nonstage theories do not see qualitative changes at different developmental periods. Instead, these theories view development as the gradual acquisition of one or more things—for example, mental associations, memory capacity, perceptual discrimination, attentional focus, knowledge, or strategies. Generally speaking, nonstage theories view children as quantitatively but not qualitatively different from adults.

After reviewing these two theoretical approaches in greater detail, we will examine cognitive development on selective specific cognitive tasks. In doing so, we will review several proposals for what children acquire and master in the course of their development. We will see that there currently exist a number of distinct, although not mutually exclusive answers to the question "What is it that develops?" (Siegler, 1978).

Theoretical Descriptions of Cognitive Development

Developmental theories, Miller (1989) tells us, "have saved developmental psychology from drowning in a sea of data on children" (p. 2). Developmental theories, like other theories, are organized ways of explaining phenomena. They include assumptions and hypothetical constructs that can be translated into testable hypotheses. In particular, developmental theories try to explain how and why certain changes occur in children's behavior and performance at different periods. Further, developmental theories focus mainly on long-lasting changes. Miller describes three specific goals of developmental theories: (1) to describe changes within one or several areas of behavior, (2) to describe changes in the relationships among several areas of behavior, and (3) to explain the course of development that has been described (p. 5).

There are hundreds of developmental theories in psychology. Most have a narrow focus, describing only one aspect of development (for example, memory, perception), and many focus on only one developmental period (for example, infancy, adolescence). Here, we will first consider one very broad developmental approach that set out to describe and explain many aspects of cognitive development over a broad time span. This approach, Piagetian theory, is arguably the single most important theory in the field of cognitive development. Next we will consider alternatives to Piagetian theory. There is not one opposing theory here but, rather, a collection of proposals from different researchers. Each of these usually focuses on a more limited aspect of cognitive development.

Piagetian Theory

Jean Piaget (1896–1980) was fascinated by the question of how intelligence and cognitive functions come to be. He quickly rejected the idea that intelligence consists of the passive acquisition, storage, and organization of knowledge from the environment. Neither did he accept the view that intelligence arises solely as a function of physical maturation. Instead, he saw intelligence as something that adapts to its environment over time, through the active participation of both the child and her environment (Piaget, 1970/1988). We will review a few general principles of Piagetian theory before turning to look at descriptions of specific cognitive stages of development.

General Principles

Piaget's long-standing interest in the development of children's thinking actually began, in a way, in his own childhood, as he studied and wrote about birds, fossils, and mollusks. In adolescence, he added the study of philosophy to his ever-widening circle of interests. His knowledge of natural history and science led him to think about psychological concepts, such as thinking and intelligence, in very ethological terms. Specifically, Piaget saw how an organism adapts to its environment as sharing many similarities to how children's intelligence develops. Both processes involve a sort of adaptation. Intelligence, Piaget believed, represented an adaptation of mental structures to the physical, social, and intellectual environment (Ginsburg & Opper, 1988).

Piaget saw children as active participants in their own development. He rejected the idea that cognitive structures somehow slowly emerge or unfold, or that they are thrust upon an unsuspecting and passive child by a parent, teacher, or other aspect of the environment. Instead, Piaget believed that children construct their own *mental structures,* the building blocks of cognition and intelligence, through a constant and active series of interactions with their environment.

Construction of mental structures begins shortly after birth. The infant comes into the world with very little cognitive "equipment." Indeed, about all the neonate has is a set of reflexes, including such things as sucking and grasping. These reflexes (the precursors to mental structures) encounter the environment, and the interaction of the two results in the gradual growth and change of the original reflexes. Throughout the process, the infant (and later, the child, and still later, the adolescent) actively participates through practice, experimentation, and accidental discovery. In

According to Piaget, the sucking scheme demonstrated by this infant will undergo assimilation and accommodation.

Piaget's words: "[Mental] structures . . . are not given in the objects, since they are dependent on action, nor in the subject [child], since the subject must learn how to coordinate his actions which are not generally hereditarily programmed" (1970/1988, p. 5).

Piaget saw the major mechanism of development as the *adaptation* of mental structures. Adaptation consisted of two distinct but interrelated processes: *assimilation* and *accommodation*. Piaget defined *assimilation* as the "integration of external elements into evolving or completed structures" (1970/1988, p. 7). The idea here is that mental structures are applied to new objects in the world. An infant who has a structure (Piaget called it a *scheme*) for sucking at first may suckle only at the mother's breast. However, when new objects are placed within easy reach of his mouth, the infant may apply that structure to the new object, say, a bent finger. We say that the finger has been assimilated to the sucking scheme.

Accommodation, by contrast, involves the changing of the structures to fit new objects. A finger has a different shape and texture from a breast, and has to be sucked in a slightly different way. Each time the infant sucks on a new object, he changes, even if ever so slightly, the sucking scheme. That internal change in the structure is known as accommodation.

Assimilation and accommodation are always present, to at least some degree, in every act of adaptation because it is impossible for one to exist in the absence of the other. Optimally, the two are balanced, or in equilibrium.

Piaget assumed that all cognitive functioning is organized in a particular manner at every level of development. By "organized," Piaget meant to suggest that the various mental structures have some relationships to one another. With development, these relationships become more complex, more numerous, and more systematic. Although some organization among mental structures always exists, the specific interrelationships of mental structures changes in different developmental stages. As a result, the ways in which the child understands the world also changes with development. According to Piaget, this is because knowledge is always acquired and interpreted through whatever mental structures currently exist.

Stages of Development

Piaget describes four major periods (we will refer to them here as *stages*) of development. Some of these stages can be divided into a series of substages. For our purposes, we will concentrate on the four main stages, but interested students can learn more about the substages by consulting other sources (for example, Ginsburg & Opper, 1988; Miller, 1989).

The Sensorimotor Stage   The first stage is the *sensorimotor*, beginning at birth and lasting roughly eighteen months. The stage is so named because Piaget believed that an infant in this phase of development experienced the world almost entirely through sensory and motor experiences. According to Piaget, knowledge gained during this stage is acquired through, and is often equivalent to, sensation or action. The infant is described as lacking the capacity for mental representation. Thus, all experience must happen in the here and now, and must be centered on things that are present.

The implications of this description are profound. They suggest that infants experience the world in ways completely different from those of older children or adults. Older children can have thoughts, conscious recollections of past experiences, and ideas about the past and future. All of these abilities, however, require the capacity for mental representation. The infant, lacking the capacity for mental representation, cannot have any of these things. For the infant, thought *is* action or sensation, because there is no means of representing thought except through action or sensation.

Piaget saw all of cognitive development as beginning with the infant's biological heritage: a simple set of reflexes, such as sucking, rooting (moving the head in the direction of a touch on the cheek), and others. This primitive "mental equipment" slowly changes and evolves as the infant matures and acquires many experiences in the world. Sucking, for instance, will be applied to many different objects—fingers, toys, keys, strands of hair—thus demonstrating assimilation of new objects to the sucking scheme. Each of these objects has a different shape, size, and texture, and so the way the infant sucks on each one will be slightly different, forcing accommodation of the sucking scheme. Gradually, over the period of eighteen months, the schemes grows more complex, will be executed more smoothly and more efficiently, and will become integrated with other developing schemes. At first, for example, an infant may suck only on objects placed near his mouth. Later in infancy, he will learn how to grasp objects in front of him. As these two schemes—sucking and grasping—develop, they can also be coordinated so that the older infant can reach out for an interesting novel object, pull it toward her, and place it in her mouth as a new thing to suck on.

One of the important developments in the sensorimotor stage is the acquisition of the *object concept*. Figure 12-1 depicts a task showing this development in a young (for example, 4-month-old) infant. An adult holds

(A)

(B)

FIGURE 12-1.   Drawing of 5-month-old infant in an object permanence demonstration a novel and interesting toy in front of a seated infant, attracting her attention. As she reaches for the toy, however, the adult frustrates her attempts to grab it by first moving it out of reach, then blocking the infant's view by placing a screen between the infant and the toy. The reaction of the 4-month-old infant is quite surprising: A few seconds after the toy disappears from sight, the infant looks away and shows no inclination to search for it. Piaget interpreted this reaction as follows: having no capacity for mental representation, the infant experiences objects only when they are present in the here and now. Quite literally, objects out of sight are also objects out of mind.

An older infant (say, around 8 months) will demonstrate more, if not complete, understanding of the idea that objects continue to exist even when they are not immediately in view. An infant at roughly this age will continue to search for objects that are partly hidden. A slightly older infant (10–12 months) will even search for completely hidden objects. However, this infant still shows incomplete understanding of how objects function. The infant watches an adult hide an object in one location and then successfully retrieves it from its hiding place a few times. Next, the adult (with the infant observing) hides the object in a new location. The infant immediately searches for the object in the old location. According to Piaget, this error (called the "A, not B error," with letters referring to the old and new locations, respectively) occurs because the infant still does not fully understand that objects are independent of her actions. If one action, say, looking in location A, has previously resulted in the object's reappearing there, the infant continues to use that action even after having seen the object hidden in location B. It is not until about 18 months that a typical infant will show complete mastery over the object concept.

Another important developmental achievement of the sensorimotor period is the increasing intentionality and understanding of causality. Piaget's description of this aspect of development (as well as other aspects) involves the concept of *circular reactions*—behaviors that are repeated over and over. At first, young infants (1–4 months) display *primary circular reactions*—behaviors that are set off by chance, are centered on the infant's own body, lead to an interesting (from the infant's point of view) result, and are then continued. Thumb sucking is an example. Young infants' thumbs find their way into mouths almost at random. Once a thumb is properly situated, however, most infants will keep it there and continue to suck on it.

Secondary circular reactions emerge at roughly 4–8 months. These are oriented to objects outside the infant's body, and might include such things as shaking a rattle to produce a noise, or banging the side of a crib to make a mobile attached to the crib move. At around 18 months, *tertiary circular reactions* appear. Piaget compares the infant's tertiary circular reactions to scientific experiments. Here, the infant begins with a goal in mind to produce an interesting result. For example, he might drop a toy over the side of his high chair and watch it fall. This interesting result leads the infant to experiment, varying different aspects of the situation. Different toys are dropped, from varying heights, on different sides. Other things—

bottles, cups of juice, and bowls of food—can also be dropped, to the infant's glee and the caretaker's frustration.

The sensorimotor period ends after approximately 18 to 24 months. Having begun her cognitive life with little more than reflexes, the infant now has a new understanding of objects and their existence independent of her actions, a better sense of her own ability to affect things in the world, and most important, the ability mentally to represent objects, events, and people. Older infants show some recall of past events. For example, one of Piaget's daughters, Jacqueline, was able at about 14 months to recreate many of the features of a temper tantrum she had seen a little boy produce 12 hours before (Miller, 1989). This event displays a number of cognitive abilities—the ability to store and recall information, and the ability to imitate these behaviors at a later time *(deferred imitation),* all of which require the existence of mental representation. All of these achievements are necessary for the cognitive tasks to be confronted in the next period of development.

The Preoperational Stage   The next stage of development, lasting from roughly age 18 months to roughly age 7 years, is known as the *preoperational stage* of cognitive development. Armed with the capacity for mental representation, the preoperational child now understands the world in new and more complex ways than the infant or toddler. In particular, the preoperational child has acquired the *semiotic function,* the ability to use one thing to represent or stand for another. The child now shows a great deal of symbolic functioning: pretending to drink from an empty cup; cradling a doll or stuffed toy as if it were a baby; "riding" on a "pretend horse" made of a stick.

A second, and related, ability is the use of language. Children at this age are busy rapidly acquiring a vocabulary of words that "stand for" real objects or events in the world. In this sense, language requires symbolic-thought capacities. Piaget saw children's language development as a reflection, rather than a cause, of their intellectual structures.

The child's capacity for representational thought now allows a greater variety of cognitive activities and, thus, a greater range of exploration. Children can now play in more complex ways than ever before, including elements of fantasy and reenactment. They can talk with others about their experiences, those in the present and those that have previously happened. They can also talk about and begin to plan for future events, such as a trip to the store after nap time.

At the same time, as the name of the stage suggests, there are important gaps in children's thinking. In fact, the name "preoperational" suggests a contrast with the later period of concrete operations. Preoperational children are typically described as lacking mental operations that older children have (such as those to be described below; Gelman, 1978) and, consequently, as having significant limits on their thinking.

Piaget described the preoperational child as *egocentric* in her thinking. This term refers to the fact that children of this age apparently have a difficult time taking into account any viewpoint other than their own. For example, a 4-year-old coming home from nursery school might tell her mother that "Ted did it," failing to explain who Ted is or what it is he did. According to Piaget, this egocentric language results from her inability to take her mother's perspective, to understand that her mother might not know who Ted is. The 4-year-old assumes that everyone knows what she knows, sees things as she does, and remembers what she remembers.

An experimental demonstration of egocentrism came from the work of Piaget and Inhelder (1967). They presented children with a three-dimensional model of three mountains. Arranged around the mountains were different objects, such as a small house and a cross, that were visible from some angles but not others. Preschool children were asked to describe whether an observer (a small wooden doll) on the other side of the table could see particular objects (see Figure 12-2). Children typically responded that the observer could see everything the child could see, failing to take into account the observer's different vantage point.

Preoperational children's thinking has also been described as *centered* on their perceptions of the world. This means that the children attend to, or focus on, only a limited amount of the information available at any given point (Ginsburg & Opper, 1988). Moreover, the thought of preoperational children is said to be *static,* focusing on states rather than transformations or changes. Finally, preoperational children are described as lacking a concept of *reversibility,* the ability to "mentally reverse" an action. One

FIGURE 12-2.   Example of the stimulus apparatus for the three-mountain task

well-known illustration of these aspects of preoperational thinking comes from Piagetian number *conservation* tasks. They work as follows: The experimenter sets two rows of checkers in front of the child, one black and one red, each containing five checkers. Initially, checkers in each row are set out in one-to-one correspondence (that is, each black checker is lined up with a red checker), and the child judges both rows of checkers to be equal in number. Next, the experimenter spreads out one of the rows of checkers (see Figure 12-3), and asks the child which row has more, or if the two rows

Initial Display

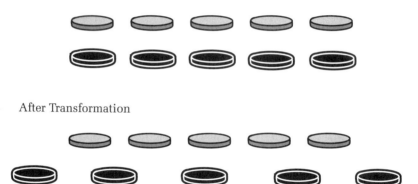

After Transformation

(A) Conservation of Number

Initial Display

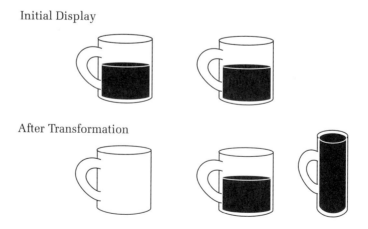

After Transformation

(B) Conservation of Liquid

FIGURE 12-3.   Depiction of conservation of number and conservation-of-liquid tasks

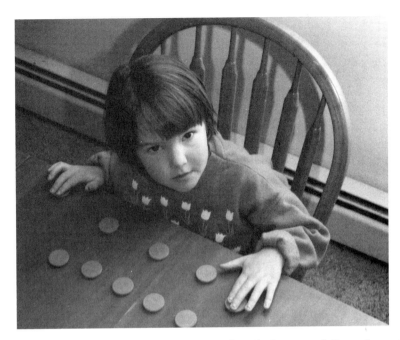

To a preoperational child, it might seem as though the row of discs closer to her contains more than the row farther away.

still have the same number of checkers. The typical 4-year-old responds that the longer row has more checkers than the shorter row. He has failed to appreciate the fact that operations such as moving checkers around the table are number-irrelevant: they do not affect the numerosity of the rows.

What has happened here? One explanation for this puzzling response is that the child is overwhelmed by what the two rows of checkers look like. One row does indeed look "bigger" (longer) and perhaps therefore more numerous. The child has centered on the length of the rows, and ignored the density (the space between checkers) or the numerosity. The child has paid attention to what the rows of checkers now look like (the static stimulus display) and ignored the fact that the transformation involved did not add or subtract any checkers, and thus could not affect the number of checkers in either row. Finally, the child has failed to reverse mentally the action of spreading out one row of checkers, to see that he can mentally push the less dense row into its original formation, in which the two rows of checkers are numerically equal. According to Piaget, the things that the preoperational child lacks—the ability to decenter, to focus on transformations, to reverse actions—all leave him with little to rely on other than his perceptual experience.

Another aspect of young children's thinking is called *animism*.

Briefly, this term refers to the tendency to attribute qualities of being alive to inanimate objects—for example, believing that the sun shines when it is happy, that the moon follows people around, that dolls and stuffed animals have feelings, that clouds move when they want to. The child, in effect, credits the sun and the moon with human abilities and characteristics (Ginsburg & Opper, 1988). Again, this way of thinking is foreign to both older children and adults, who almost always divide the world into animate (living) and inanimate kinds of things (although we often talk to young children in animistic terms, for example, "Can you see Mr. Moon?").

The Concrete-Operations Stage   Children's thinking changes, again dramatically, when they move into the next stage of development, the period of *concrete operations,* around the age of 7 until about the age of 11 or 12. At this point, the child is able to attend to much more information than before, and therefore is able to take into account more than one aspect of a situation. Piaget described this aspect of children's thought as *decentered,* to draw a contrast with the centered nature of preoperational thought. Concrete-operational children are also able to pay attention to transformations, and not just to initial and final states.

The conservation task provides a familiar example. The child who conserves number or liquid (see Figure 12-3) moves beyond her perception, recognizing that certain changes (for example, in number or in the amount of liquid) result only from certain transformations, such as adding or taking away, and not from others, such as spreading out or changing shape. This child's thought is said by Piaget to exhibit *reversibility.* A concrete operational child can construct (as the preoperational child cannot) a mental representation of the transformation, and of the "reverse" of the transformation (in this case, pouring the liquid back into the original container), and can use this knowledge to judge correctly the relative amounts of liquid.

Another ability that matures during the stage of concrete operations is *classification.* The younger, preoperational child has a great deal of trouble in consistently sorting a group of objects into categories (for example, all of the round things, all of the square things; or all of the blue things, all of the red things). The preoperational child has difficulty maintaining a consistent basis of classification. He may start out sorting wooden blocks on the basis of shape but midway through the task start sorting on the basis of color. The groups he ends up with will include blocks that vary in both shape and color. The older, concrete-operational child is much more consistent and hence better able to keep track of the task.

Indeed, the concrete-operational child is much more flexible in his thinking in a variety of contexts, as Ginsburg and Opper (1988) note:

> As the child grows older and comes into contact with opposing points of view and varied social institutions, his thought goes through a process of decentration. In speech, he considers both what he wants to express and the listener's needs. In games, he considers the other's interests as well as

his own and is, therefore, willing to follow and modify the rules. In moral judgment, he considers both the outcomes of a person's behavior and its intent. (p. 111)

The typical concrete-operational child seems like a very mature thinker when compared with a younger child; however, there are still areas of limitation in this period of development. In particular, the child has difficulty thinking in abstract terms. Her thinking is limited to actual or imagined concrete things. And, when compared with an older adolescent, her thinking is seen to be less systematic.

The Formal-Operations Stage   The final stage of cognitive development, that begins around puberty, is that of *formal operations*. The adolescent shows much more systematic thinking. For instance, when given a number of beakers containing different liquids and asked to determine how they can be mixed together to produce a liquid of a certain color, the adolescent does a number of things that the younger child does not. First, he is able to

According to Piaget, hypothetical and deductive reasoning typical of that required for scientific experimentation awaits the development of formal operations.

generate all of the possible combinations of liquids, and often does so in a systematic way. He tests one combination at a time, and keeps track of the results of each one. He is better able to isolate and hold constant all factors except one, and to report on his results accurately.

The formal-operational thinker is also able to think more abstractly than the concrete-operational thinker. The adolescent now sees reality as one of several possibilities, and can imagine other kinds of realities. This new liberation of thought has been described as one of the sources of adolescent idealism and political awakening. Her awareness of different possibilities opens up for her many different possible paths to the future because she is able to "think beyond old limits" (Keating, 1980). Piaget describes adolescent thought poetically: "Formal operations provide thinking with an entirely new ability that detaches and liberates thinking from concrete reality and permits it to build its own reflections and theories. With the advent of formal intelligence, thinking takes wings" (1968, p. 63).

Typically, adolescents are also more adept at logical thinking. In part, this has to do with their ability to think abstractly and to reason from arbitrary propositions such as "If all of the X's are Y's, and none of the Y's are Z's, then at least some of the X's are not Z's." Adolescents, unlike younger children, are able to understand the idea of *logical necessity* in reasoning. This is the notion that for some arguments, if the premises are true, then the conclusion is guaranteed to be true as well (Moshman & Timmons, 1982).

Logical thinking also derives from a newly emerging ability Piaget called *reflective abstraction* (Piaget, 1968). The adolescent can, for the first time, acquire new knowledge and understanding simply from thinking about her own thoughts and abstracting from these reflections. By doing so, she may begin to notice inconsistencies in her beliefs. Reflective abstraction is also useful in other realms of thinking, notably those of social and moral thinking. The adolescent is now quite capable of taking the points of view of others, and trying to think about issues as they would.

There is much debate over whether all adolescents ever reach the period of formal operations, although Piaget (1972) maintained that they do. However, Piaget did not mean to suggest that even those who do would always display their highest competence. Instead, his idea was that adolescents who acquired formal operations had the ability to think abstractly, systematically, and logically, even if they do not always do so.

Piaget's theory of cognitive development thus describes how thought evolves from simple reflexes to an organized, flexible, logical system of internal mental structures that allow thinking about a wide variety of objects, events, and abstractions. A child at each stage of development has a remarkable set of abilities but often (especially in stages before formal operations) faces several limitations in thinking. The mental structures that allow and organize thought develop slowly through the child's active exploration of the world.

Reactions to Piaget's Theory

Piaget's major writings date from the 1920s, although his fame in the United States was not really established until the early 1960s. Halford (1989) describes the 1960s as a period of intense optimism about Piagetian theory in this country as many psychologists and educators sought ways of applying it to problems of designing appropriate educational curricula for children and adolescents of varying ages. However, beginning around the 1970s, enthusiasm for Piaget's ideas began to fade, when a number of studies appeared to disconfirm some of the theory's predictions (see Gelman & Baillargeon, 1983, and Halford, 1989, for reviews).

Many researchers were concerned about methodological problems in Piaget's studies. His reports of sensorimotor cognitive development, for example, were based on the observation of only three infants, all Piaget's own children (Miller, 1989). Accordingly, it is hard to know how free from bias or overinterpretation Piaget's observations were, although later research has replicated nearly all of the phenomena that he reported (Ginsburg & Opper, 1988). In work with older children and adults, Piaget again employed the *clinical method,* often modifying the tasks or questions for each child in response to her performance or explanation. Although this approach allows for a great deal of flexibility, it also opens the door to various threats to validity, especially the possibility that the experimenter will unconsciously and subtly provide the child with cues or leading questions. Ginsburg and Opper (1988) provide an excellent discussion of the strengths and limitations of the clinical method.

Siegel and Hodkin (1982) point out other methodological problems in the tasks Piaget developed. Many of them seem to require much more than simply the understanding of the concept under investigation. Children in a conservation task, for instance, must not only observe the materials undergoing different transformations and make the correct judgments but also explain their answers carefully and, in some cases, must resist counter-suggestions from the experimenter. Siegel and Hodkin argue that

> when a child is asked the same question several times, to assess the particular cognitive ability with different stimuli, the child may change the answer because he or she believes the adult is asking the question again because the first answer was wrong. Usually adults do not repeat a question when the answer is correct, but only when it is wrong. [The child's] response vacillation may be interpreted as a sign of unstable cognitive structures, but it may also reflect children's eagerness to provide the answers they think the adult is seeking. (p. 59)

Other investigators and theorists have raised problems with parts of Piaget's theory. Many have agreed that the evidence for the existence of distinct stages of cognitive development is not strong (Brainerd, 1978; Miller, 1989). Others have concluded that there is a lack of evidence for the existence of the specific cognitive structures Piaget described as underlying the different stages (Halford, 1989). Further, a variety of empirical studies have demonstrated a great deal of competence and knowledge among young children that Piaget's theory has difficulty accounting for. Baillargeon (1987), for instance, has shown that 4- to 6-month-old infants, at least in some circumstances, expect that objects that have disappeared from view continue to exist. Rochel Gelman, studying preschoolers' understanding of numerical concepts, has demonstrated that young children can be taught to conserve numbers rather easily (1969, 1972), and that they actually know a great deal more about counting and numerosity than Piaget's theory grants them (Gelman & Gallistel, 1978).

Nonetheless, even his sharpest critics acknowledge a tremendous debt to Piaget. Siegel and Hodkin (1982), for example, note that he has "generated the most significant theory in the field of cognitive development [which has] provided a framework and a stimulus to much of the research in cognitive development" (p. 78). Most investigators share an admiration for the wide-ranging scope of the theory, and for the cleverness Piaget has shown in devising tasks to reveal important aspects of children's thinking at different periods in development.

Non-Piagetian Approaches to Cognitive Development

Many psychologists who study cognitive development appreciate the keen observations that Piaget reported but do not accept his interpretation of their underlying causes. In particular, many believe that cognitive development does not proceed through a series of qualitatively different stages or periods, and that qualitatively different intellectual structures underlie cognition at different periods. Instead, these investigators assert that cognitive skills and abilities emerge or are acquired gradually.

Many of these psychologists use adult models of cognitive processes as a framework from which to understand the way children process information. Many take information-processing models, such as those described in earlier chapters, as the starting point for a model of cognitive development. The basic strategy is to discover the ways in which information-processing models of adult cognition have to be modified in order to describe and explain the performance of children at different ages and abilities.

As with models of adult cognition, information-processing models of children's cognition use the digital computer as a metaphor for the child's mind. Information presented to the child (either explicitly or implicitly) can be regarded as input. Just as computers have various storage devices (buffers, disks), so children are assumed to have one or more distinct memory stores. Just as computers retrieve information from their stores, so too are children assumed to be able to access (at least some of) their information, and to use it in a number of cognitive tasks, including calculation, classification, identification, integration, and so on. Finally, just as computers write information on disks or on printers or terminal screens, so too do children often produce output of one sort or another: a verbal response, a drawing, a gesture, or some other behavior.

Other psychologists focus on physiological (particularly neurological) and other innate factors that contribute to cognitive development. These psychologists begin with the premise that young infants do not have "blank slates" for minds but instead bring to their cognitive life certain mental structures that are present from birth. Not surprisingly, these psychologists investigate the cognitive competencies of young infants and toddlers, who presumably have had relatively little opportunity for learning cognitive skills.

In this section, we will review a few examples of work that departs from the Piagetian tradition. The examples span a range of types of cognitive tasks, as well as different periods of development. Although they represent only a minute proportion of the possible examples of important research on cognitive development, they provide a sense of the kinds of questions cognitive developmental psychologists ask and the ways in which they seek answers.

Selected Examples

We saw in Chapter 2 ("Perception and Pattern Recognition") that our perceptual activities are crucial to our acquiring information from and about the world around us. It behooves a cognitive psychologist interested in perception, then, to understand how perceptual abilities, skills, and capacities develop.

Perceptual Development in Infancy

Elizabeth Spelke (1976) investigated young infants' abilities to explore their world perceptually. Specifically, Spelke is interested in how well infants are able to put together information acquired from different sensory domains, for instance, visual and auditory. To investigate this question, she adapted a methodological paradigm known as the *preference method*. Four-month-old infants were seated in infant seats in front of a translucent movie screen. Projected onto the screen, side by side, were two short ($2\frac{1}{2}$-minute) films: one of a woman continually playing "peekaboo," using her hands to cover and uncover her face; the other of a hand holding a wooden baton and striking a wooden block and tambourine repeatedly and rhythmically. The sound track of one of the films was played through a speaker placed slightly behind the center of the movie screen. The question was "Would infants coordinate their looking with their hearing, that is, spend more time looking at the film coordinated with the sound track?"

The answer was yes. Observers who surreptitiously watched the infants recorded which side of the movie screen they were looking at, and found that infants looked longer at the film that best went along with the sound track being played (Spelke, 1976). Apparently, then, infants by 4 months of age are able to coordinate what they see with what they hear, thus demonstrating *intermodal perception.* This ability allows them to direct their visual attention to the object or event that they are hearing. Note that unifying the visual and auditory information was made fairly difficult in this task; the physical location of the sound did not coincide with the physical location of the film to which it belonged. Spelke's results suggest that from quite a young age, infants' different perceptual systems cooperate in picking up and integrating information (Rose & Ruff, 1987).

Spelke and her colleagues have also investigated young infants' knowledge of Gestalt principles of perception (see Chapter 2 to review these). One principle that these investigators have focused on is the *principle of good continuation.* In a typical experiment (Kellman & Spelke, 1983), 4-month-old infants were shown a stimulus display such as that in the top left of Figure 12-4, which, to adults, appears as a rod partially hidden ("occluded") by another square object. Other groups of same-aged infants, serving as control groups, were shown the other displays in the top of Figure 12-4. Next, all infants were shown the test displays in the bottom of Figure 12-4.

Infants in the control groups preferred to look at the test display showing the rod that was different from the one they had initially seen. Thus, infants in the complete-rod control group preferred to look at the test display on the lower right; infants in the broken-rod control group, the test display on the lower left. This *dishabituation* is thought to reflect the fact that infants like to look at new things when given a choice.

Infants in the experimental ("rod-occlusion") group showed no looking preferences. Their performance suggests that they did not perceive a "broken" rod when the occluding object had been removed. These 4-month-old infants, then, showed little evidence of honoring the principle of good continuation that adults routinely do. However, *if* during the presentation of the first display the experimenters caused the rod to move back and forth behind the occluding block, then infants did show "surprise" in the form of looking longer at the test display on the right. That is, the experience of seeing the moving display appears to suggest to the infants that the rod behind the block is actually one object. Apparently, infants are particularly sensitive to information coming from moving objects. With stimulus displays in motion, infants show the same kinds of perceptual performance that older children and adults do. It appears, then, that some of the developing perceptual abilities have to do with interpreting information from static, nonmoving, displays.

Unfortunately, as Small (1990) points out, much of this research has not been developmental because it usually includes only one age group of infants. Thus, we don't know whether these abilities develop rapidly over the first four months of life or instead are present at birth. What we do know, however, is that some important perceptual abilities exist from at least a very young age.

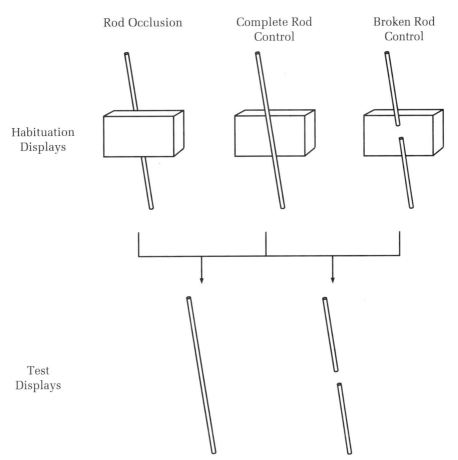

Rod Occlusion   Complete Rod Control   Broken Rod Control

Habituation Displays

Test Displays

FIGURE 12-4.   Stimuli from Kellman and Spelke (1983). SOURCE: From "Perception of Partially Occluded Objects in Infancy," by P. J. Kellman and E. S. Spelke, 1983, *Cognitive Psychology, 15,* 483–524. Copyright © 1983 by Academic Press. Reprinted by permission.

Toddlers' Acquisition of Syntax   In Chapter 8 ("Language") we discussed several aspects of language abilities and usage. Each of the aspects shows interesting developmental changes. Most psychologists and linguists who study language development agree on a proposition that at first might seem startling: children do not *learn* syntax (Chomsky, 1959). That is, the way in which syntax develops from infancy through adolescence is difficult to account for in terms of simple learning mechanisms. One reason is the fact that syntactic development typically occurs in a very short time frame—in only a few years. Further, children undergoing language development hear many different utterances of a language—from parents, siblings, teachers, and others. However, what children appear to acquire are not specific sentences or utterances but, rather, the underlying rules that govern a particular language. As I hope Chapter 8 convinced you, the rules that govern a language are complex and very difficult to articulate. Thus, it is quite unlikely that parents and other adults are teaching these syntactic rules.

Moreover, studies of parents interacting with their children demonstrate that parents rarely correct syntactic errors of children's speech (for instance, "Yesterday I goed to the playground"), responding instead to the content of what is said (for example, "No, honey, yesterday we went to the *zoo.*") (Ingram, 1989). These and other arguments cause developmental psychologists to speak of *language acquisition* rather than *language learning.*

Many developmental psychologists studying language acquisition agree with Chomsky's (1957, 1959) assertions that people are born with *language universals,* that is, they are biologically prepared to acquire a human language (as opposed to a computer or other kind of artificial language). The actual language that a child acquires almost certainly is subject to environmental influences—children born to English speakers invariably acquire English; those born to parents who speak Hungarian unfailingly acquire that language. Chomsky believes that people have a *language acquisition device* (LAD), an inborn set of mechanisms and knowledge that requires only an environmental trigger to be set in motion. The environment controls *which* language(s) is(are) acquired, but the capacity to acquire a human language is regarded as innate.

Although children typically begin to use recognizable words at around a year of age, it is usually not until their second year that they begin producing utterances of more than one word. It is not possible to speak of *syntax* in a toddler's language until he produces multiword utterances, simply because it is not possible to structure a one-word utterance in different ways.

If children's two-word utterances had absolutely no structure, then what we should observe are random pairings of words in a child's vocabulary. In fact, what we observe is quite the opposite: children's two-word utterances display a considerable amount of regularity. Consider Box 12-1, which presents a number of two-word utterances spoken by my niece, Brandi Lee, when she was about 18 months old. You'll note that certain words or phrases, such as "Rockabye" or "Oh deah" always occur initially in the utterance; that other words or phrases, such as "down" or "didit" always occur at the end of the utterance; and that certain other words, such as "Dassie," "Mummy," and "Santa," occur either initially or at the end of the utterance.

Braine (1963) hypothesized a *pivot grammar* to account for these regularities. Braine argued that children begin to form two-word utterances by first somehow selecting a small set of frequently occurring words in the language they hear. These words are called "pivots." Children's knowledge about pivots includes not only the pronunciation and something about the word's meaning but where in an utterance the pivot should appear. Other words that the child uses are called "open" words. Braine argued from data much like that in Box 12-1 that toddlers form "syntactic" rules of the following sort: "Pivot$_1$ + Open" or Open + Pivot$_2$," where Pivot$_1$ includes all sentence-initial pivots (for example, "Oh deah," "Rockabye"), and Pivot$_2$ includes all sentence-final pivots (for example, "didit," "down").

Braine's (1963) pivot grammar accounts for some of the regularities apparent in the speech of some children. However, work by other investigators (Bowerman, 1973; Brown, 1973) soon showed that it failed to account for the utterances of all children. Although current consensus is that the grammar is at best incomplete and in many cases incorrect, some investigators have argued that it might provide some useful ideas about how children begin to construct a grammar from the language they hear around them (Ingram, 1989).

Roger Brown (1973) took a different tack in accounting for regularities in children's two-word utterances. Brown asserted that children at the two-word stage are constructing their utterances *not* by following rules of syntax but by using a small set of semantic relations. Table 12-1 presents the semantic relations he proposed are used. Brown argued that this particular set of relations is an outgrowth of the knowledge about the world toddlers of this age should have. He believed that children at this point in development focus on actions, agents, and objects, and are concerned with issues such as where objects are located and when and how they can disappear and reappear. As such, Brown's proposals fit nicely with the Piagetian view of sensorimotor development (Ingram, 1989).

One problem with Brown's approach is that it requires an adult to interpret what the child intended to communicate at the time of the utterance. It makes adults interpret children's language in terms of adult

---

B O X   12 - 1   Sample Two-Word Utterances

Dassie (her word for "Kathie") down. (meaning "Kathie, sit on the floor.")
Oyd (her word for "Lloyd") down. (meaning, "Lloyd, sit on the floor.")
Mummy down.
Rockabye baby.
Rockabye turkey.
Rockabye Santa.
Oh deah (dear) Santa.
Oh deah Dassie.
Oh deah Mummy.
Oh deah turtle.
Mummy didit. ("didit" meant, roughly, to have performed an action.)
Dassie didit.
Brannie (her word for "Brandi") didit.

TABLE 12-1.   Proposed semantic relations for early grammars

Relation	Definition and Examples
1. Nomination	The naming of a referent, without pointing, usually in response to the question 'What's that?' Often indicated with words such as 'this', 'that', 'here', 'there'. (Also see Demonstrative and Entity below.)
2. Recurrence	The reappearance of a referent already seen, of a new instance of a referent class already seen, or an additional quantity of some mass already seen, e.g. 'more' or 'another' X.
3. Non-existence	The disappearance of something which was in the visual field, e.g. 'no hat', 'allgone egg'.
	Semantic Functions
4. Agent + Action	The agent is 'someone or something, usually but not necessarily animate, which is perceived to have its own motivating force and to cause an action of process' (p. 193), e.g. 'Adam go', 'car go', 'Susan off'.
5. Action + Object	The object is 'someone or something (usually something, or inanimate)either suffering a change of state or simply receiving the force of an action' (p. 193).
6. Agent + Object	A relation which uses the two definitions above. It can be considered a direction relation without an intervening action.
7. Action + Location	'the place or locus of an action' (p. 194), as in 'Tom sat in the chair.' Often marked by forms like 'here' and 'there'.
8. Entity + Locative	The specification of the location of an entity, i.e. any being or thing with a separate existence. These take a copula in adult English, e.g. 'lady home' meaning 'the lady is home'.
9. Possessor + Possession	The specification of objects belonging to one person or another, e.g. 'mommy chair'.
10. Entity + Attribute	The specification of 'some attribute of an entity which could not be known from the class characteristics of the entity alone' (p. 197), e.g. 'yellow block', 'little dog'.
11. Demonstrative and Entity	The same as Nomination except that the child points and uses a demonstrative.

source: From *First Language Acquisition: Method, Description, and Explanation,* by D. Ingram. Copyright © 1989 by Cambridge University Press. Reprinted by permission.

assumptions and beliefs, and it assumes that adults and children use language to refer to events and objects in the world in similar ways. Ingram (1989) points out that this assumption can be erroneous.

Much of the work since the 1970s has attempted to avoid problems in both syntactic and semantic approaches. The complexity and specificity of many of the existing models preclude their discussion here. However, there is agreement that even from the early days of language use, children's utterances show many regularities. Because many of the regularities observed come from children of very different cultures and language communities, it is further hypothesized that children's language acquisition cannot be the simple result of learning.

The Use of Memorial Strategies by Preschoolers
Another important cognitive capacity is memory, as we saw in Chapter 4 ("Memory"). As for previous topics, the literature on memory development from infancy through

adolescence is vast (Brown, Bransford, Ferrara, & Campione, 1983, provide a review), and our look at the topic here will be quite brief and selective.

Many differences in memorial abilities between younger and older children and adults have been reported. Dempster (1981) reviewed the literature and found that in a digit-span task (where subjects are presented with a string of digits to remember), college students can retain about seven digits, but 3-year-olds can remember only about three. This suggests that working-memory capacity is something that develops over time. Recall from Chapter 4 that working memory is hypothesized to have (at least) two important functions: maintaining information for immediate use (for example, in reasoning or comprehension tasks) and transferring information to a more permanent, long-term store. Thus, having less working memory capacity may in turn limit other cognitive abilities and the performance of more complicated cognitive tasks.

Many researchers who study the development of memory in children have been struck by the different approaches to memory tasks adopted by younger and older children. A particularly striking difference concerns the use of memorial *strategies,* defined as "deliberate plans and routines called into service for remembering" (Brown et al., 1983, p. 85). One important memorial strategy is **rehearsal** of the to-be-remembered material. Rehearsal can involve silent or out-loud repetition, and is thought to maintain information in working memory, thereby making it more likely to be stored for longer periods of time (Ornstein & Naus, 1978).

A number of studies (reviewed by Ornstein & Naus, 1978) have repeatedly demonstrated two things. One, younger children (that is, preschoolers and younger elementary-school-aged children) are less likely to rehearse material than are older children (that is, older elementary-school-aged children and middle-school-aged children). The other, when children who do not spontaneously rehearse can be induced to do so, their memory performance often rises to the level of similar-aged children who do rehearse spontaneously.

A classic study by Flavell, Beach, and Chinsky (1966) demonstrates the first of these points. The authors worked with children in kindergarten (K) and second and fifth grades. Each child was shown two sets of seven pictures, and asked to point to the pictures in the same order that the experimenter did. In one condition, the wait was 15 seconds between the time the experimenter finished pointing and when the child was asked to recreate the order. The children wore special "space helmets" that prevented them from looking at the pictures or seeing the experimenter but allowed the experimenter to observe whether or not they were verbalizing the items they had to remember (one of the experimenters, trained in lip reading, spent each session watching and listening for such verbalizations). Results were dramatic: very few of the kindergarten subjects showed evidence of rehearsal; a little more than half of the second graders and almost all of the fifth graders did so.

A later study (Keeney, Cannizzo, & Flavell, 1967), using a similar procedure, illustrates the second point. These researchers found that 6- and 7-year-old "rehearsers" performed significantly better in recalling information than same-aged "nonrehearsers." When the nonrehearsers were later trained to rehearse, their performance became indistinguishable from that of the initial "rehearsers." However, when left to their own devices, the initial "nonrehearsers" abandoned the rehearsal strategy. Brown and colleagues (1983) believe that the use of rehearsal during early childhood is fragile, disappears easily, and occurs under only very limited circumstances (p. 94).

Other research on memory development has shown that children's performance on a memory task is often a function of their preexisting knowledge of, and expertise with, the materials of the memory task. Michelene Chi (1978) demonstrated this in a study with children (in grades three through eight) with chess-tournament experience and adults with casual experience with chess. When given standard digit-span tasks, the adults tended to outperform the children. However, when the memory task involved the recall of positions of chess pieces on boards, the children outperformed the adults. One possible explanation could be that their knowledge allowed the chess-experienced children to notice more relationships between chess pieces (for example, "the king's rook is attacking the queen"), thus facilitating more retrieval cues than were available to the less-experienced adults. Chi concluded that

> the amount of knowledge a person possesses about a specific content area can determine to a large extent how well he or she can perform in . . . memory . . . tasks. The implication is that the sources of some of the age differences we often observe in developmental studies must be attributable to knowledge about the stimuli. (p. 94)

Conceptual Development in Early Childhood   The subject of how children acquire and structure knowledge is the focus of researchers studying conceptual development. Susan Gelman and her colleagues (Gelman & Markman, 1986; Gelman, 1988) have centered their investigations on the questions of how children make inferences about different kinds of things, given that they have some information about the category membership of those things.

Let's examine a specific example. Most of us know that although whales share a number of similarities with various kinds of fish (they swim; they live in water; they are often found in aquariums; they have an overall shape that is fishlike), they are in fact mammals (they are warm-blooded; they bear live young). As adults, we know that the categorization of a whale has to be on the basis of something other than perceptual features. The question is "Do children know this too?" Notice that the Piagetian view would predict that preschool children, being "perceptually bound," would probably perform the classification solely on the basis of how the thing to be classified appears.

In a series of studies, Gelman and Markman (1986) showed children sets of three pictures like the one shown in Figure 12-5. Each set was carefully constructed so that the third picture *looked* like one of the first two pictures but was really in the same category as the one that it did not resemble. Note, for example, that in Figure 12-5 the owl looks more like the bat but is really (to a knowledgeable adult) in the same category as the flamingo. Children were given information about the first two pictures in a set (for example, "This bird's heart has a right aortic arch only" [as the experimenter points to a picture of the flamingo]; "This bat's heart has a left aortic arch only" [as the experimenter points to a picture of the bat]). While looking at the third picture (for example, an owl shaped like the bat), the child was asked to predict what would be true of the owl's heart. Contrary to Piagetian predictions, 4-year-old children based their inferences on category membership rather than on physical appearance (when the two were in conflict) approximately 68% of the time.

In further work, Gelman (1988) investigated the constraints on children's inferences based on category membership. Preschoolers and second graders first learned presumably new facts about objects (for example, "This apple has pectin inside") and then were asked whether these facts were true of other items of varying similarity (for example, other apples, a banana, a stereo). Gelman used two kinds of categories: natural kinds (naturally occurring objects, such as animals, plants, fruits, and other things not constructed by humans) and artifacts, (objects constructed by people usually to perform a certain function, such as chairs, tools, computers). Recall from Chapter 6 that adults treat these two kinds of concepts differently. The question was "Do children also treat these two kinds of concepts differently, and if they do, at what age do they start to make the distinction?"

Gelman (1988) found that children (preschoolers and second graders) consistently drew the inference that items in the same category shared the new property they had just learned about. For example, upon being told that "apples have pectin," all of the children were also likely to infer that a banana had pectin, too. They were much less likely, however, to infer that a stereo had pectin. Apparently, then, even preschoolers use their knowledge of category membership to make inferences about what kinds of

FIGURE 12-5.   Stimuli from Gelman and Markman (1986). SOURCE: From "Categories and Inductions in Young Children," by S. A. Gelman and E. M. Markman, 1986, *Cognition, 23,* 183–209. Copyright © 1986 by Elsevier Science Publishers. Reprinted by permission.

properties different things might have. It is interesting that second graders were sensitive to the natural kind/artifact distinction, and drew more inferences with natural-kind concepts. Preschoolers, on the other hand, appeared to be relatively insensitive to the distinction. Gelman believed this insensitivity resulted from their relative lack of deep knowledge about the objects being talked about.

The Development of Reasoning Abilities in Middle and Late Childhood   The final set of examples illustrating information-processing models of cognitive development describes the development of reasoning abilities. A classic study by Osherson and Markman (1975) showed that first, second, and third graders had apparent difficulty distinguishing between statements that were empirically true or false (that is, true in fact) from those that were logically true or false (that is, true by necessity or definition). The experimenter showed children, adolescents, and adults small plastic poker chips in assorted solid colors. Children were told that the experimenter would be saying some things about the chips, and that the children should indicate after each statement that it was true, false, or they "couldn't tell."

Some of the statements were made about chips held visibly in the experimenter's open hand. Other, similar statements were made about chips held nonvisibly in the experimenter's closed hand. Among the statements used were logical **tautologies** (statements true by definition), for example, "Either the chip in my hand is yellow or it is not yellow"; logical **contradictions** (statements false by definition), for example, "The chip in my hand is white and it is not white"; and statements that were neither true nor false by definition but depended on the color of the chip being referred to.

First, second, third, and even sixth graders did not respond correctly to tautologies and contradictions, especially in the nonvisible condition. They tended to believe, for example, that a statement such as "Either the chip in my hand is blue or it is not blue" cannot be assessed unless the chip in question is visible. Tenth graders and adults, in contrast, were much more likely to respond that even when the chip couldn't be seen, the statement about it could be evaluated on the basis of form if the statement was a tautology or contradiction. These results were consistent with Piaget's assertion that logical reasoning, particularly abstract, hypothetical reasoning, awaits the attainment of formal operations, in adolescence.

A later study by Hawkins, Pea, Glick, and Scribner (1984) has painted a different picture. They gave 4- and 5-year-olds a number of verbal syllogisms, such as "Pogs wear blue boots. Tom is a pog. Does Tom wear blue boots?" The syllogisms required logical reasoning. Contrary to expectation, the preschool subjects could correctly answer many of the syllogisms and provide appropriate justifications for their answers, especially if the problems were about make-believe animals, as in the example above. The authors believe that these problems in particular prevented the children from using their preexisting knowledge of animals (they had probably not had previous knowledge of, or experience with, a pog).

With other syllogisms that were about real animals or objects, the children performed noticeably worse, especially when the premises in the problem were incongruent with the children's preexisting world knowledge (for example, "Glasses bounce when they fall. Everything that bounces is made of rubber. Are glasses made of rubber?"). This result implies that, although some ability to reason logically might begin in early childhood, much of it is undeveloped or unreliable, at least until early adolescence, and maybe all through adulthood (see the discussion on adults' reasoning abilities in Chapter 10).

Another study, by Moshman and Franks (1986), supports this view. They gave children (fourth and seventh graders) a more stringent test of logical reasoning competence. The children were presented with sets of three cards. On each card was typed an argument that was either empirically true or false, or logically *valid* (the conclusion followed necessarily from the premises; see Chapter 10) or not. Subjects were asked to sort the cards in as many ways as they could. In some of the studies, subjects were given definitions of the concepts of validity, and prompted to sort on this basis. However, even when specifically asked to do so, fourth graders had difficulty sorting on the basis of validity (as opposed, say, to truth of the conclusion, or to format of the argument). Moshman and Franks interpret these results as indications that even when children can draw logically valid conclusions, they lack a full appreciation of the idea of validity before the age of 12 or so.

Our examination of recent work in the non-Piagetian traditions of cognitive development has yielded narrower and more specific descriptions of what actually develops. Typically, instead of focusing on general and widespread cognitive achievements, researchers in these traditions offer accounts that are more specific to the particular tasks being used. Thus, an account of how reasoning ability develops may show little resemblance to an account of how children acquire and organize new information into concepts. Researchers such as those whose work is described above, however, see this narrowness of scope as positive. By attending to specific tasks and domains, they believe that a clearer and more accurate picture of what children know and can do will emerge.

Some Answers to the Question "What Develops?"

Recall from our discussion earlier that Piagetian theory describes cognitive development as the acquisition of progressively more sophisticated mental structures. Researchers in other traditions do not necessarily believe that children at different ages possess qualitatively different mental structures. These researchers instead provide a variety of answers to the question "How do children develop cognitively?" Here, we will review some of the most common answers given.

Neurological Maturation   One factor that cognitive and cognitive developmental psychologists are paying increasing attention to is that of neurological, or brain, development. Although many of the neurons or nerve cells in the brain emerge during gestation, the brain continues to grow and develop after birth, especially in the first four years (Nowakowski, 1987). Early exposure to stimuli helps to develop a normal level of interconnections among neurons, such that a more complex network of nerve cells is formed. The network allows for the efficient transmission of a great deal of information.

Do neurological developments bear directly on cognitive developments? Goldman-Rakic (1987) describes research with monkeys that suggests that the age at which infant monkeys can perform certain cognitive tasks (such as a Piagetian object-permanence task) coincide with the peak of the development of neuronal connections in an area of the brain known as the prefrontal cortex.

The issue of neurological underpinnings of cognitive performance is one that is at the cutting edge of research at the moment. Whether certain cognitive tasks require a certain level of neurological development, and the role environmental experience plays in neurological functioning and development are matters that will surely be addressed in the coming decade.

Working-Memory Capacity and Processing Speed
Our review of memory in Chapter 4 suggested that working memory is an essential ingredient of many cognitive tasks. Recall that working memory is the system in which currently active information is stored and manipulated. It stands to reason, then, that the larger the working-memory capacity, the more complex the cognitive tasks a person is capable of. Researchers such as Pascual-Leone (1970) have attempted to measure the amount of "mental space" children seem to have available to perform cognitive tasks, and report increases in this capacity with age. Some of the research has involved estimation of *memory span,* done by giving children lists of items, such as numbers, letters, or words, and asking the children to repeat them. The memory span is thus the number of items a child of a particular age can reliably reproduce. Figure 12-6 displays data from several studies suggesting that the memory span increases with age.

Other researchers have argued that what develops is not working-memory capacity per se but the speed and/or efficiency with which information is processed (Case, 1978; Dempster, 1981). For example, children at different ages have been shown to differ widely in the speed with which they can name items presented to them, rotate mental images, or search through a visual display (Kail, 1986; 1988). Adults and older children typically perform all of these tasks faster than younger children.

Presumably, all of these tasks are carried out in working memory. When one task takes longer to carry out than another, it may reflect the expenditure of more "mental effort." If mental effort is limited, as information-processing theories typically assume, then tasks that require more mental effort will leave fewer cognitive resources available for other processing. This in turn could explain the generally poorer cognitive performance of younger children relative to older children and adults—the younger the processor, the more mental effort is required for a given task.

FIGURE 12-6.   Developmental differences in digit span, word span, and letter span. From Dempster (1981). SOURCE: From "Memory Span: Sources of Individual and Developmental Differences," by F. N. Dempster (1981), *Psychological Bulletin, 89,* 66–68. Copyright © 1981 by the American Psychological Association. Reprinted by permission.

The question of how working memory capacity and efficiency change with development is still a current research question.

Attention and Perceptual Encoding   Ask any parent or teacher: younger children have shorter attention spans than older ones. Because of this, they often spend less time exploring the information available to them from the environment. Preschoolers, in particular, often respond to complex cognitive tasks *impulsively,* that is, quickly and with many errors (Kogan, 1983). Perhaps relatedly, younger children are less likely than older children to make as many discriminations between similar objects (Gibson & Spelke, 1983). A good example of this phenomenon can be observed if you obtain the comics sections of many Sunday newspapers. Some run a puzzle activity that calls for the child to examine two very similar pictures and to find ten things that are different between them. The two pictures are usually visually complex, with a great number of objects and/or people, and a great deal of detail and elaboration of each object. The differences tend to be in the details. For example, one picture might depict a girl with a spotted bow in her hair; another shows the same girl, in the same pose, with the same clothes except for a striped bow. Preschoolers and children in early elementary school typically find these puzzles much more challenging than do older children or adolescents. In part, this has to do with the amount of time they spend looking back and forth between the two pictures. Another part of the explanation, predicted by perceptual learning theory (Gibson, 1969), seems to be that younger children notice fewer differences in the first place.

Kemler (1983) has extended this idea, arguing that with development, children shift from a *holistic* approach to processing information to a more *analytic* one. Kemler means by these terms that younger children approach information globally, and pay attention to the overall similarities between and among objects. For example, given a red triangle, an orange diamond, and a green triangle, and asked to "put together the items that belong together," younger children would tend to sort the red triangle and orange diamond together, because overall, these two objects are more similar to each other than either is to the green triangle. In contrast, older children and adults pay attention to particular parts or aspects of information. Given the same sorting task, adults would be likely to classify the red and the green triangles together, because they both share the dimension of shape.

Children have also been shown to have difficulty focusing their attention. In one study, Strutt, Anderson, and Well (1975) asked children and adults to sort a deck of cards showing various geometric figures as quickly as possible. Some cards showed figures that differed only in the relevant dimension, for example, only circles and squares when the child was asked to sort on the basis of shape. Other cards included figures that differed on both the relevant dimension and other, irrelevant dimensions (for example, the presence of a line or star either above or below the picture). The presence of irrelevant information did not affect the speed of sorting of adults. However, it did slow down the sorting for 6-year-olds, 9-year-olds, and 12-year-olds; the younger the child, the greater the interference.

This answer to the question "What develops?" implies that younger children approach cognitive tasks differently than older children both perceptually and attentionally. Younger children encode and pay attention to different aspects of information than older children and adults do. As a consequence, their information processing differs because it begins with different input.

The Knowledge Base and Knowledge Structures   Some developmental psychologists working in the information-processing tradition regard the acquisition of general knowledge and expertise as a crucial aspect of cognitive development. It is known from studies of adults that people differ in some cognitive processes as a function of level of expertise with the materials used in the task. For example, Chase and Simon (1973) showed a chess master (a certified "expert"), an experienced chess player, and a chess novice different chess boards with the pieces arranged in various ways. The task was to look at a particular board for 5 seconds; then after the board was removed from view, to reconstruct the placement of the pieces on a second, empty chess board.

The investigators found that when the first chess boards depicted actual games (that is, the pieces were arranged in ways that might actually occur during a game), the master and experienced player performed much better than the novice in the number of pieces they could correctly place. However, when the pieces were displayed in random configurations, the chess master performed no better than the novice or the experienced player. Chase and Simon concluded that experts extract more information than novices do when the information being presented is one for which their expertise is relevant. Said another way, expertise helps a person to acquire and organize information much more efficiently, thus leading to better over-all performance when the information pertains to her area of expertise. Notice that this explanation fits well with the findings of Chi with child chess experts, discussed earlier.

A related study was carried out by Chi and Koeske (1983) with a single $4^1/_2$-year-old dinosaur fancier. The investigators first queried the child about his familiarity and knowledge about different kinds of dinosaurs, and divided 40 of these into two groups: those that the child knew relatively more about, and those that the child knew relatively less about. The child was then presented on three different occasions with each list of 20 dinosaurs, at the rate of 1 dinosaur name every three seconds, and then asked to recall the list. The child recalled significantly more of the "familiar" dinosaurs (about 9 out of 20) than the "unfamiliar" ones (about 4 out of 20).

Chi and Koeske argue from these and other results that part of the reason children may typically perform so poorly on memory (or presumably other cognitive) tasks is because of their relative lack of knowledge or expertise with the information used in the tasks. When given the opportunity to perform the same tasks with materials they know well, their performance improves dramatically. Presumably, familiar materials require less cognitive effort to encode, retrieve relevant information about, notice novel features of, and so on.

Other work, by Katherine Nelson and her colleagues, has looked in a slightly different way at how children store and organize knowledge, particularly knowledge about events (Nelson, 1986). The primary method here is to ask children to describe their knowledge of familiar routines, such as "What happens when you go to day care?" or "Tell me what happens when you make cookies." In response to the latter request, Nelson and Gruendel (1981) obtained a variety of responses from children of different ages, ranging from "Well, you bake them and eat them" (a 3-year-old) to

First you need a bowl, a bowl, and you need about two eggs and chocolate chips and an egg beater! And then you gotta crack the egg open and put it in a bowl and ya gotta get the chips and mix it together. And put it in a stove for about 5 or 10 minutes, and then you have cookies. Then ya eat them! (a child of 8 years, 8 months). (p. 135)

It should be evident, first, that even 3-year-olds have some knowledge of this event. Nelson describes the organization of this knowledge in terms of *scripts,* or *generalized event representations* (GERs). If you recall our discussion of scripts from Chapter 6, you'll remember that scripts contain information organized temporally, that is, by the time in which each thing occurs in an event. Notice how the children use temporal links from one step to another, for example, "*First* you do X, *then* Y, and *after that* you do Z."

One trend that appears with development is that the scripts become longer and more elaborate. Fivush and Slackman (1986) also showed that as children become more familiar with an event (for example, if the event is "going to kindergarten" and children are tested repeatedly as the school year goes on), their scripts also become more complex, with specification of

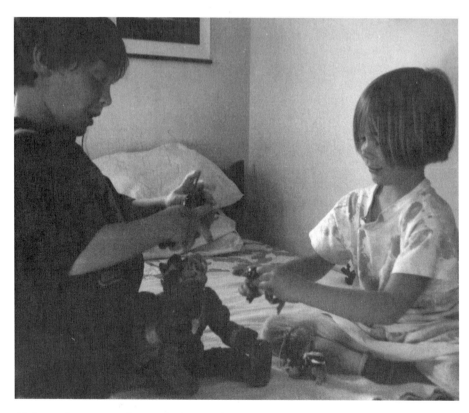

Chi's work suggests that in domains where children have expertise, such as knowledge of toys, children demonstrate better memorial ability.

more conditional information, such as "If it's raining, we play indoors" and the like. Children's organization becomes more hierarchical as they specify more options or choices for different activities (for example, "I can play house, or I can draw, or I can read a book, until circle time."). Their organization also becomes more abstract, and they mention fewer details specific to a certain day's activity when describing their script.

Nelson (1986) argues that scripts help to support many cognitive activities, including comprehension, memory, and conversation. Scripts and GERs are said to provide the child with a "cognitive context" with which to interpret actions, events, and people in a situation. Especially because younger children appear to perform at their cognitive best only in certain contexts, it is important to learn which aspects of the context help or hinder them. Nelson believes that "the observed difference between situations where children perform well or poorly is that between those for which children have established a relevant GER and those for which they have not" (p. 16).

Strategies   When confronted with a complex cognitive task, adults often develop certain systematic approaches to it that help them to manage the task requirements more efficiently. Such approaches are called **strategies.** For example, when studying for an upcoming examination, many college students review their lecture notes, develop outlines of each course reading, and consult with the instructor about material they find unclear. All of these are strategies.

The role of strategies in cognitive development has already been alluded to, in the discussion of Flavell's classic work on rehearsal strategies (Flavell et al., 1966; Keeney et al., 1967). Recall that their work showed that younger children were less likely spontaneously to adopt a rehearsal strategy in a memory task but could be taught to use one. However, when not required to use the strategy, most of the younger children abandoned it. Keeney and colleagues (1967) argued that nonrehearsers suffer from a *production deficiency,* that is, a tendency not to produce the appropriate strategy for a given task. Although the children were capable of using the rehearsal strategy, they did not do so spontaneously and did not use it when given the option not to. This raises the question "Why?" Some have argued that strategies require mental effort, and that younger children may simply find it much harder to use a strategy than older children (Howe & O'Sullivan, 1990). Perhaps with increasing cognitive development (for example, greater neurological maturation, more working-memory capacity, larger knowledge bases or some other factor or combination of factors), the mental effort required to execute a strategy declines, making it a more useful addition to the cognitive repertoire.

This explanation is consistent with other research findings on strategy use, where older children have been shown to be more flexible and better able to tailor their choice of which strategy to use on a task that allowed for several different strategies (Miller, Haynes, DeMarie-Dreblow, & Woody-Ramsey, 1986). Siegler and Jenkins (1989), reviewing work on children's arithmetic strategies, also point out that although children and adults at almost any age usually have a variety of strategies they could use, with age and experience comes the likelihood of using more sophisticated strategies (that presumably demand more mental effort for execution). In any case, it is clear that strategies facilitate the processing of information, and that people who use better strategies (for whatever reason) often have better cognitive performance. Younger children do not show the same use of strategies that older children and adults do, and thus, are at a disadvantage on many cognitive tasks.

Metacognition   Given the same cognitive task to perform, older children are usually better than younger children at evaluating its complexity and monitoring their own performance. For example, in a memory study conducted by Flavell, Friedrichs, and Hoyt (1970), preschool and elementary school children were given a set of items to study until they were sure they could remember them. Older children were better able to judge when they had studied adequately, and to predict how many items they would be able to recall.

Flavell (1985) describes this as one aspect of **metacognition,** defined broadly as "any knowledge or cognitive activity that takes as its object, or regulates, any aspect of any cognitive enterprise" (p. 104). The general idea is that metacognition consists of "cognition about one's own cognition." It includes *metacognitive knowledge,* that is, knowledge about one's own cognitive abilities and limitations. You are probably pretty accurate, for example, at describing your memorial abilities, your attention span, and the relative depth and breadth of your knowledge of a particular domain (for example, football, cognitive psychology, trivia). You know your own areas of strength and weakness, you know what strategies work best for you, and you know when to use them. Younger children are less knowledgeable about their own abilities, and are typically much too optimistic about how well, how easily, or how fast they can perform on most cognitive tasks.

Metacognition also includes *metacognitive experiences,* things that happen to you that pertain to your knowledge or understanding of your own cognitive processes. For example, experiences of uncertainty or doubt, and periods of deep reflection over your performance, decision making, or values are all examples of metacognitive experiences. Flavell's (1985) idea is that older children and adults are better able to recognize, and realize the significance of, different metacognitive experiences.

Metacognitive knowledge and regulation are obviously important in many cognitive tasks. It may be that part of the reason younger children perform more poorly on cognitive tasks is that they do not have the metacognitive knowledge about what the tasks demand. That is, they do not know how to judge the difficulty of the task, and thus do not approach it with the necessary procedures or other tools.

It may also be that younger children have less metacognitive control over their processing of information (Brown et al., 1983). Markman (1979), for instance, showed that third graders were less able than sixth graders to report inconsistencies or contradictions in passages that they read, even when prompted to read the passages aloud. In a later study (Markman and Gorin, 1981), 8- and 10-year-old children who were explicitly told to look for inconsistencies in passages were able to do so. The general conclusion from these studies is that children do not spontaneously monitor their cognitive performance while reading but can be induced to do so. However, unless the conditions are optimal, children, especially younger children, may fail to notice when cognitive processing goes awry.

Cognitive developmental psychologists have recently turned their attention to a related area of investigation: that of children's theories of mind (for example, Butterworth, Harris, Leslie, & Wellman, 1991). The term *theory of mind* is meant to capture the intuition that adults treat one another as cognitive beings, making certain assumptions about one another's perceptual, attentional, memorial, language, and thinking skills, as well as their desires and intentions—in other words, their mental states. This set of assumptions is collectively referred to as a theory of mind. How a child comes to make such assumptions and whether the assumptions change with age are the questions cognitive developmental psychologists hope to address.

Summary

We have reviewed a great deal of material on cognitive development. Yet, given the number of active investigators in the field, we have barely scratched the surface of all the important available information. Summarizing this field is a tough challenge. Here, I will remind you of a few major points.

The first is that cognitive performance varies for children of different ages. In other words, children do not perform in the same way as adults on many cognitive tasks, including tasks of perception, memory, categorization, problem solving, or reasoning. Generally speaking, the younger the child, the more the difference between his performance and that of a typical adult. Because children do differ from adults, it takes cleverness and care to design informative studies that can help to explain how cognitive development occurs and can be facilitated.

A second important point is that the description of how children differ from adults or how younger and older children differ from one another is still a matter of debate. Some psychologists, especially those working in a Piagetian tradition, believe that the best description of cognitive development is one that emphasizes qualitative differences among people at various developmental levels and underlying intellectual structures.

Researchers working within a non-Piagetian tradition focus on changes in the basic cognitive capacities (for example, memory capacity, attention span, knowledge base) and in the ways in which information is organized. They consider genetic and maturational underpinnings of cognitive functioning and also the developmental changes that affect the approaches children of different ages take toward cognitive tasks. Unlike Piagetian researchers, however, many non-Piagetian theorists reject the idea of different qualitative stages of cognitive development. Instead, they regard cognitive development as the gradual acquisition and organization of capacities, strategies, and knowledge that allow for more efficient cognitive performance.

Cognitive developmental psychologists are also challenged by the question "What causes development?" In particular, there is ongoing and lively debate over how much of cognitive development is due to physical factors, such as genetics or maturation, and how much can be attributed to environmental forces, such as schooling or the opportunity for practice. A current focus within the field is to identify the factors that cause, hinder, or facilitate cognitive development.

Because this chapter focuses on infants, children, and adolescents, you might be left with the impression that cognition in adulthood does not change and/or is the same for all adults. This impression is a false one, as we will see in Chapter 13. Adults, as well as children, differ in their amount of expertise, as well as in the ways they characteristically carry out cognitive tasks. Moreover, recent work in cognition and aging (to be reviewed in the next chapter) also suggests that changes in cognition as a function of age do not cease at puberty.

Recommended Readings

Good, general introductions to the topics of cognitive development are texts by Bjorklund (1989), Small (1990), and Richardson and Sheldon (1988).

A good reference work on Piagetian theory that includes much of Piaget's own writing is edited by Gruber and Vonèche (1977). Flavell (1963) and Ginsburg and Opper (1988) provide more introductory treatments. Recent critiques of the theory can be found in a volume edited by Modgil and Modgil (1982). A very recent volume, edited by Beilin and Pufall (1992), explores recent directions in Piagetian theory.

Examples of research in the non-Piagetian tradition, in addition to those given in the text, are chapters in a volume edited by Flavell and Markman (1983). In particular, Gibson and Spelke (1983) review perceptual development; Brown and colleagues (1983) describe the development of memory and learning; Braine and Rumain (1983) review the development of reasoning ability; and Clark (1983) provides a review of conceptual development. Chapters from a recent advanced developmental textbook, including those of Bornstein (1992), Kuhn (1992), Klahr (1992), and de Villiers and de Villiers (1992), review recent theoretical and empirical developments in perception, neo-Piagetian theory, information-processing theory, and language acquisition.

Sternberg (1984) edited a volume in which psychologists discussed different proposals for the underlying causes of cognitive development. A recent edited volume (Gibson & Petersen, 1991) presents work on neurological underpinnings of cognitive development. Siegler and Jenkins (1989) describe some of their empirical work on strategy development.

REVIEW QUESTIONS

1. What are the major assumptions of stage theories of development?
2. Explain how, in Piagetian theories, cognitive structures adapt during the course of development.
3. Piaget asserts that children at different stages of development differ from one another cognitively in qualitatively different ways. Illustrate the assertion with some specific examples.
4. Describe the major features of preoperational thought, according to Piaget.
5. Evaluate the implications of Spelke's research on perceptual development in infancy.
6. Why do most cognitive developmental psychologists distinguish between the terms *language learning* and *language acquisition?* What sorts of arguments are used in support of this distinction?
7. In what ways does research on the development of reasoning abilities in middle and late childhood support or run counter to Piagetian predictions?
8. Contrast two mechanisms that have been proposed to account for cognitive development.

CHAPTER 13

Individual and Gender Differences in Cognition

So far, we have been assuming that cognitive development proceeds in pretty much the same way for everyone. In the previous chapter, of course, we saw that children often don't approach cognitive tasks exactly the way adults do, but we made the assumption that with time, maturity, and perhaps education, they come to do so. In effect, we've been ignoring what psychologists call individual differences, stable patterns of performance that differ qualitatively and/or quantitatively across individuals.

In Chapter 14, we will consider differences in cognition as a function of one's culture. Here, we will consider some other sources of **individual differences**—differences in cognitive abilities, concentrating on intelligence, and differences in cognitive styles of approaching particular tasks. We will also consider *gender differences* in cognition: stable differences in cognition or cognitive processing of information that vary as a function of one's biological sex and psychological attitudes associated with one's sex.

Why are cognitive psychologists interested in either individual or gender differences in cognition? Simply stated, if people vary systematically in the way they approach cognitive tasks, then psychologists cannot speak of "the" way cognition works. To present only one approach, if in fact there are several, is to ignore human diversity, and to assume there exists only one way of carrying out a task. Researchers interested in individual and gender differences try to explain why some people seem consistently to outperform others on cognitive tasks, and why some people feel more comfortable with certain cognitive tasks rather than others.

Individual Differences in Cognition

The term *individual difference* is meant to capture the intuition that different people can approach the same task in different ways. Psychologists who study personality traits are among those most likely to be interested in individual differences. The general individual differences that are of interest to cognitive psychologists are of two distinct types: individual differences in *abilities,* that is, the capacities to carry out cognitive tasks, and individual differences in *style,* that is, the characteristic manner in which one approaches cognitive tasks.

Ability Differences

Many psychologists equate cognitive abilities with intelligence. Hunt (1986) for example, has stated that "'intelligence' is solely a shorthand term for the variation in competence on cognitive tasks that is statistically associated with personal variables. . . . Intelligence is used as a collective term for 'demonstrated individual differences in mental competence'" (p. 102). Other psychologists do not make this equation, but most agree that people do vary in their intellectual (as well as several other important) abilities. Psychologists disagree over whether the best way to describe this variation is in terms of one general mental ability (called intelligence) or in terms of more numerous and varied intellectual abilities (Sternberg & Detterman, 1986).

Even among psychologists who accept the idea of a general mental ability called intelligence, there is debate over just what the ability is. Some see it in terms of a capacity to learn efficiently; others, a capacity to adapt to the environment. Other conceptions of intelligence include viewing it as mental speed, mental energy, or mental organization (Sternberg, 1986a).

Many psychologists who study intelligence have looked at stable individual differences among various cognitive capacities to describe more general differences in people's performance on broader intellectual tasks. Although there are many lively and ongoing debates over what the set of cognitive capacities are, one representative list, described by Horn (1989), appears below.

- Verbal comprehension (understand words, sentences, paragraphs)
- Sensitivity to problems (suggest ways to solve problems)
- Syllogistic reasoning (draw conclusions from premises)
- Number facility (compute arithmetic operations)
- Induction (indicate a principle of relations)

- General reasoning (find solutions for algebraic problems)
- Associative memory (recall associated element when given another element)
- Span memory (immediately recall a set of elements after one presentation)
- Associational fluency (produce words similar in meaning to a given word)
- Expressional fluency (produce different ways of saying the same thing)
- Spontaneous flexibility (produce diverse functions and classifications for an object)
- Perceptual speed (find instances of a pattern under speeded conditions)
- Visualization (mentally manipulate forms to visualize how they would look)
- Spatial orientation (visually imagine parts out of place and put them in place)
- Length estimation (estimate lengths or distances between points)

The topic of intelligence, its nature, testing, and improvement, would take us too far afield for our purposes, although references at the end of the chapter can guide you to the literature. The important point to think about is the idea that people (both adults and children) can vary in many ways. Just as we all vary in athletic prowess, musical talent, or sense of humor, so too can we vary in intellectual or cognitive ways: in terms of memory capacity, attention span, concentration, and so on. These differences, in turn, can cause differences in the ways in which we approach and perform cognitive tasks.

A study by Keating and Bobbitt (1978) illustrates this point. These investigators conducted three experiments with both high-mental-ability and average-mental-ability third-, seventh-, and eleventh-graders. The experiments were all based on cognitive tasks previously used with adults, including the memory-scanning experiments described in Chapter 4. The authors found that when they controlled for the effects of age (and presumably, therefore, for developmental level), ability differences still were apparent, especially on the more complicated cognitive tasks. Figure 13-1, for instance, shows results of the memory-scanning task as a function of set size, age, and ability level. Note that older children have faster reaction times than younger children, and that within each age group, high-ability subjects are faster than average-ability subjects. Keating and Bobbitt believe that both age and ability differences result from the efficiency with which basic cognitive processes (for example, encoding, memory scanning) are carried out. They assert that high-ability children (and adults) simply acquire, store, and manipulate basic information more rapidly and efficiently than do their same-age, normal ability peers. The same kinds of speed and efficiency differences also occur between older and younger children.

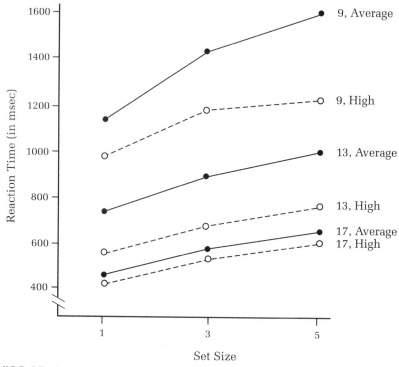

FIGURE 13-1.   Mean reaction time (RT) for children of different ages and abilities. SOURCE: From "Individual and Developmental Differences in Cognitive-Processing Components of Mental Ability," by D. P. Keating and B. L. Bobbit, 1978, *Child Development, 49,* 155–167. Copyright © 1978 by The Society for Research in Child Development, Inc. Reprinted by permission.

A related, and classic, study by Hunt, Lunneborg, and Lewis (1975) examines a specific hypothesized component of intelligence, verbal ability. These authors examined two groups of undergraduate subjects: those with relatively high scores on a verbal subtest of a standardized test similar to the Scholastic Aptitude Test (SAT) and those with relatively low scores on the same test. (The authors point out that the latter group had scores that would be considered "average" in the general population.) The aim of the study was to investigate whether differences in verbal ability, as reflected in standardized scores, might be explained by differences in basic cognitive skills.

One of the many cognitive tasks they assigned to subjects was based on a perceptual matching task created by Posner, Boies, Eichelman, and Taylor (1969). In this task, subjects are presented with two letters, for example, A and B, or A and a, or A and A. They are to decide, as quickly as possible, whether the two letters presented are the same. In one condition (called "physical match") subjects are instructed to respond yes only when the two stimuli match exactly—"A A" or "a a," for example, but not "A a."

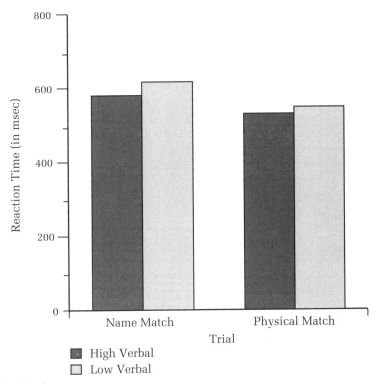

FIGURE 13-2.   Mean reaction time (RT) for high- and low-verbal subjects in a perceptual matching task. SOURCE: Adapted from Hunt et al. (1975).

In another condition (called "name match") subjects are instructed to respond yes if the two stimuli refer to the same letter, so that "*A A*," "*a a*," and "*A a*" should all receive yes responses.

Hunt and colleagues (1975) designed their experiment according to the following logic: a person's being highly verbal ought to imply "an ability to interpret arbitrary stimuli" and, in particular, an ability to translate "from an arbitrary visual code to its name" (p. 200). Thus, they expected their high-verbal subjects to be especially adept at the name-match condition, relative to the low-verbal subjects. Indeed, as Figure 13-2 indicates, this is what they found. Both groups of subjects were approximately equally fast at the physical-match condition (the high-verbal group was in fact a little faster here, too); the high-verbal group's superiority really became evident only when the task became a little more complex. The authors explained that high-verbal ability stems at least in part from an ability to make a conversion rapidly between a physical stimulus and a conceptual meaning, in this case, recognition of the particular letters.

Cognitive Styles

One way that individuals may differ from one another cognitively, as we have just seen, is in terms of their set of abilities, their capacities, and the efficiency with which they use their capacities. Another way in which individuals may differ from one another is in terms of their **cognitive style,** their habitual and preferred means of approaching cognitive tasks (Globerson & Zelnicker, 1989; Tyler, 1974). The term *cognitive style* is meant to imply certain personality and motivational factors that influence the way in which a person approaches a cognitive task (Kogan, 1983).

One example of a type of cognitive style is FDI, an acronym for "field dependence versus independence," a term coined by psychologists who studied perceptual processing (Witkin, Dyk, Faterson, Goodenough, & Karp, 1962; Witkin & Goodenough, 1981). The term refers to several phenomena, one of which is that some people find it much easier to identify parts of a figure as separate from a whole than other people do. An example of a task of field independence is shown in Figure 13-3. Field-dependent individuals would have a more difficult time finding the embedded picture in the larger picture (they are less able perceptually to divorce the embedded picture from its context), whereas field-independent individuals would find this task relatively easy.

Witkin and his associates see this style of cognition as related to issues broader than perception of figures. According to the theory, the FDI style refers to "the degree to which the person relies primarily on internal [field-independent] or external [field-dependent] referents in processing information from the self and the surrounding field" (Kogan, 1983, p. 663). Later conceptualizations broadened the definition of the style still more,

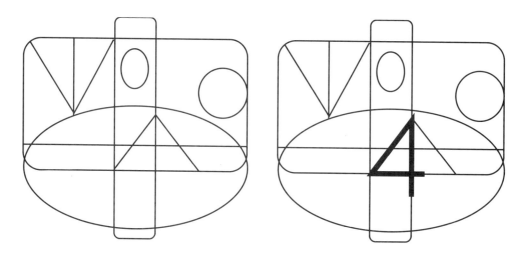

Item: Find the "4" in the figure above.   Correct Response

FIGURE 13-3.   Example of an FDI test item

FIGURE 13-4. Example of an MFFT item. SOURCE: From "Information Processing in the Child: Significance of Analytic and Reflective Attitudes," by J. Kagan, B. L. Rosman, D. Day, J. Albert, and W. Phillips, 1964, *Psychological Monographs, 78,* 1–37. Copyright © 1964 by the American Psychological Association. Reprinted by permission.

associating the FI style with a generally autonomous manner in interpersonal relationships, whereas FD individuals are seen as more likely to rely on others, especially in ambiguous situations.

A second example of different types of cognitive styles has been called *cognitive tempo,* or *reflectivity-impulsivity.* Kogan (1983) defines this style as "the extent to which a child delays response in the course of searching for the correct alternative in a context of response uncertainty" (p. 672). This can be illustrated with reference to Figure 13-4, depicting an item from the *Matching Familiar Figures Test* (MFFT), developed by Kagan and his associates to assess cognitive tempo (Kagan, Rosman, Day, Albert, & Phillips, 1964). The task posed to respondents is to find the item that exactly matches the item shown at the top. As you look at the other six pictures, you will notice that each is very similar to the top item, and that it requires your careful attention to find the one that matches exactly.

Children vary in the way they respond to items on the MFFT. Some respond very quickly; others, more slowly. Some make very few errors, even on difficult items; others make a number of errors, even on easy items. Many children fall into two categories: those who respond rapidly and make many errors (called an *impulsive* style), and those who respond slowly, with relatively few errors (demonstrating a *reflective* style) (Tyler, 1974).

Originally, cognitive styles were thought of as optional, modifiable manners or problem-solving approaches that were independent of both intelligence and age. Recent research has challenged these assumptions. Cognitive styles do not appear to be easily modified through training. Moreover, cognitive styles show developmental differences; younger children are more likely to display impulsive and field-dependent styles, and older children, more reflective and field-independent styles (Zelnicker, 1989).

Zelnicker (1989) also argues that reflectivity-impulsivity and FDI are not completely independent styles, and that each relates to three underlying dimensions: selective attention, in particular the tendency to respond to whole stimuli or to their parts; attentional control, the focusing and shifting of attention; and stimulus organization, mental transformation of stimulus input (for example, in mental-rotation tasks such as those described in Chapter 7). Zelnicker asserts that an individual's cognitive style "determine[s] the quality of stimulus information accessible for further processing in solving . . . problems" (p. 187).

Expert/Novice Differences

Throughout earlier chapters, we have seen that people with expertise in a certain realm often approach a cognitive task differently than do novices. We first encountered this topic in Chapter 2 ("Perception and Pattern Recognition"), when we discussed perceptual learning. If you recall, the point made there was that experts and novices having equal exposure to information will acquire or "pick up on" different amounts of it. In general, experts will perceive more distinctions, especially subtle ones, than novices will. This point is illustrated in an example of an art historian and a layperson unfamiliar with art standing before a Picasso painting. The layperson (novice) "sees" less information than the art historian (expert), who might be rather effortlessly picking up information about brushstrokes or composition that the novice simply cannot perceive.

We saw next in Chapter 6 that experts and novices differ in their conceptual representations of information. Novices in a given domain, for example, tend to classify objects or instances together, based on superficial or perceptual similarities; experts often use their knowledge to form deeper principles with which to classify. For example, if given a number of paintings, a novice might categorize on the basis of the subject of the picture (landscapes, still lifes, portraits). An art expert would be far more likely to categorize on the basis of artist, historical period, composition, or the like—aspects of a painting that require a certain degree of knowledge.

Work by de Groot (1965) and Chase and Simon (1973) on chess experts and chess novices has suggested other relevant cognitive-processing differences between the two groups. For example, when shown a chess board arranged in a midgame configuration (that is the pieces arranged in such a way as to represent a game in process), an expert chess player could reconstruct the positions of approximately 16 (out of 25) pieces after only a 5-second glance. A chess beginner, given the same board and the same exposure, could reconstruct only about 5 of the pieces. It is interesting that the authors showed that it was *not* simply that the experts had better memories. Indeed, when shown chess boards with 25 chess pieces randomly arranged on them, the expert and the beginner showed equivalent performance, being able to reconstruct the positions of only two or three pieces. Instead, Chase and Simon argued that the chess expert used chess knowledge to group or "chunk" chess pieces into meaningful configurations. As Chapter 4 suggests, chunking is a process that can increase the amount of information held in working memory.

The findings on expert/novice differences do sound a common theme: one's level of knowledge in a domain affects one's cognition within that domain. Many cognitive processes, including perception and recognition, encoding, classification and categorization, and problem solving and reasoning about information within the domain of expertise appear to be affected.

The Effects of Aging on Cognition

We saw in the previous chapter that cognitive skills and abilities *develop*, which is to say that children of different ages and levels of development can approach the same cognitive task in different ways. Age-related changes in cognitive processing do not cease in adolescence. In fact, researchers looking at adult development and aging have found a number of differences in cognitive processing between younger and older adults. Once again, this topic is a broad one, and we have space to mention only a few illustrative examples.

Relative to younger adults (those in their 20s and 30s), older adults (those in their 60s and older) show several differences in cognitive abilities and skills. For example, older adults have been shown to perform less well on tasks of divided attention (such as those discussed in Chapter 3; McDowd & Craik, 1988), to show age-related decrements in speech recognition and speech discrimination (Corso, 1981), and to show declines in memory performance on a variety of memory tasks (Cavanaugh, 1993).

One example of the latter findings has to do with performance on working memory tasks. Salthouse and Babcock (1991) studied the performance of adults aged 18 to 87 on various working-memory tasks, such as digit span, sentence comprehension, and mental arithmetic. The authors found, first, that older subjects had shorter spans than younger subjects. They hypothesized, after extensive statistical analyses of their data that the major factor accounting for this decline in span length was a decline in *processing efficiency*, or the speed with which various elementary cognitive operations (such as performing a simple addition, comprehending a simple sentence) could be carried out.

Campbell and Charness (1990) found similar age-related declines in working memory. They gave three groups of adults (20-, 40-, and 60-year-olds) a task in which they learned an algorithm for squaring two-digit numbers. Subjects worked for six sessions lasting an hour or two each. The authors report two significant findings. First, practice with the algorithm improved performance, in that errors declined over sessions. However, adults in the oldest group made more errors than the "middle-aged" adults, who in turn made more errors than the youngest adults. Even with practice, these age differences remained.

It is important to keep in mind, however, that differences in cognitive processing as a function of aging are still subject to individual differences from other sources. Such factors as intelligence, health, years of formal education, expertise, and cognitive style all continue to play important roles. The topic of the effects of aging on cognition, still in its relative scholarly infancy, will no doubt continue to support the idea that any individual's level of cognitive functioning depends on many factors, including factors specific to the individual, such as those just described, as well as those of the task and the overall context (Lerner, 1990).

This brief look at individual differences in cognitive abilities was intended to stress an important point: not all people approach cognitive tasks in exactly the same way. Age or ability differences among people can affect their efficiency in acquiring or processing information, leading to differences in how much information is picked up or how thoroughly it is processed. These differences in turn could have large effects on how well a complicated cognitive task is performed. Age and ability differences are not the only ways in which people differ, however. Recent work on cognitive styles suggests that other motivational or personality differences can affect the assumptions and goals different people bring to different cognitive tasks. We will also examine whether or not men and women adopt different cognitive styles in their approaches to cognitive tasks.

Gender Differences in Cognition

The possible existence of gender differences can be fascinating. This fascination is especially pronounced in our culture, as psychologist Carol Nagy Jacklin (1989) notes:

> Speculation about differences between females and males is a national preoccupation. In our culture, people care whether there are fundamental differences between girls and boys, and we place more emphasis on the possibility of such differences than on other kinds of distinctions that could be made. For example, we rarely wonder whether blue-eyed and brown-eyed or short and tall children differ from one another in intellectual abilities or personality. (p. 127)

Some cautions are in order before we examine the evidence regarding gender differences in cognition, especially because of the sensitive nature of the topic. One of the most important cautions regards the term *gender difference.* To say that there is a gender difference in performance on task X can mean a number of very different things, as illustrated in Figure 13-5. One possible meaning is that the scores from subjects of one sex are higher than the scores from subjects of another sex, a possibility illustrated in Figure 13-5(a). Notice that the lowest-scoring member of one sex (the distribution to the right) still outperforms the very best member of the lower-scoring sex. Although many people interpret statements about gender (or other group) differences in these terms, reality is almost never this simple.

More realistic depictions of gender differences in performance are given in Figure 13-5(b), 13-5(c), and 13-5(d). The first illustrates no gender difference. The last two illustrate real gender differences in the mean level of performance, with different degrees of overlap in scores between people of different genders. In each case, although females, on average, score more highly than males, there are some males who score more highly than some females. In both of these cases, then, it would be impossible to predict how any individual (for example, Sally Smith or Jack Jones) would score. All we can say is that given large numbers of men and women, the average score for women will be higher than the average score for men.

A second caution has to do with built-in biases in the research literature. Scientific journals are simply much more likely to publish research that reports significant differences between or among groups of people than they are to include research that does not find differences. In part, this is because journal space is limited, and studies that find differences tend to be more interesting than those that don't (Tavris & Wade, 1984). In part, this is also because of difficulties in interpretation: Researchers who find no group differences cannot conclude that there are no differences, for this would amount to accepting the null hypothesis. The logic scientists use in testing hypotheses forbids this, and Halpern (1992) offers a concrete example of why:

> Suppose you formulate the null hypothesis that no one has more than or less than one head. You could collect a large sample of people, count the number of heads per person, and presumably find that each has only one. However, you have not *proved* the null hypothesis, because only one exception, that is only one person with more or less than one head, can disprove it, and it is possible that you failed to include this person in your sample. Similarly, even large amounts of negative evidence cannot be used to prove that sex differences do not exist. (p. 33)

Another set of problems in interpreting research on gender differences has to do with **experimenter expectancy effects,** the tendency for researchers unintentionally to influence the responses or behavior of research participants in the direction of the experimenter's hypothesis (Rosenthal & Rosnow, 1984). In many psychological studies, experimenters can avoid or minimize these effects by remaining "blind" to which condi-

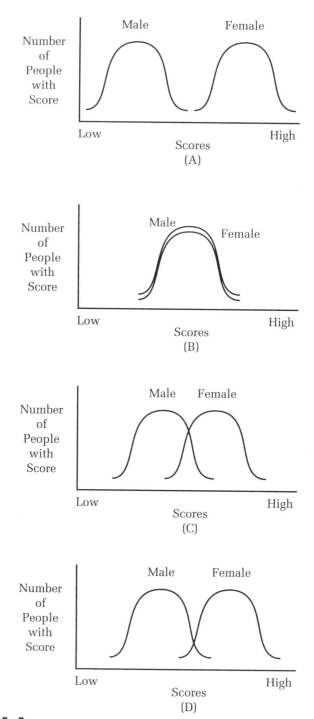

FIGURE 13-5. Examples of hypothetical gender distributions. Each curve depicts a hypothetical distribution of scores on some test for persons of one gender.

tion a subject is in. For example, in a memory study, one experimenter could randomly assign subjects to the experimental and control groups, and a second experimenter, who did not know which subjects came from which groups, could administer the tests.

With gender-differences research, however, it is a different story. Whenever participants are observed or interviewed, it is almost impossible for the observer or interviewer to remain blind to the participant's gender. Thus, the observer or interviewer runs a risk of unintentionally and subtly "leading" the participant to behave in ways consistent with either the study's hypotheses, the cultural stereotypes, or both. For example, an interviewer who expects women to be more "verbal" or more "emotionally expressive" may unconsciously reinforce this behavior in women, perhaps by smiling more, thereby allowing or encouraging more responses in the predicted direction. Some studies can avoid these problems by having participants respond in writing (and then having their responses typed and scored by raters who do not know the gender of the writer), but this limits

In a face-to-face interview, it is impossible to keep the respondent's gender hidden from the experimenter. This can lead the interviewer to guide the discussion, or subtly reinforce certain responses, as a function of her gender-based expectations of the respondent.

the kinds of observations and data that can be collected. For these reasons it will be important to keep in mind throughout our discussion that there can be significant problems of bias in studies of gender differences particularly.

Gender Differences in Skills and Abilities

Is there an overall difference in cognitive ability between women and men? Many people in our culture have different and strongly held opinions on this question (for example, "Everyone knows men are smarter" or "Women are smart enough to let men think that they [the men] are more talented"). But a cognitive psychologist needs more than opinion, however loudly voiced. Asked this question, she must first begin by defining what it means to have greater overall cognitive ability, and then translate this definition into specific behaviors or patterns of responses on specific tasks (this is called *operationalizing* the question). Finally, she must recruit appropriate samples of men and women and administer the tasks that have been chosen.

One kind of task the psychologist might choose to use is an intelligence test. However, a problem with this approach stems from the way intelligence tests are constructed. As Halpern (1992) points out, constructors of intelligence tests work hard to ensure that no overall differences exist between the scores of men and women. That is, many test constructors exclude from intelligence tests any items that show a reliable gender difference in responses. However, this does not mean that men and women never show any differences in cognitive performance. In an early classic—but later heavily criticized—review of the sex-differences literature, Maccoby and Jacklin (1974) identified three kinds of cognitive abilities that appeared to show reliable gender differences: verbal abilities, visual-spatial abilities, and quantitative abilities. In this section, we will look at each of these in turn.

Before going any further, we need first to consider methodological techniques used by psychologists while reviewing existing literature. Three major kinds of techniques have been used. The first, *narrative review,* involves the reviewer's locating and reading as many sources as she can, then writing up her conclusions. Although such summaries can be of use, Hyde and Linn (1988) point out that the narrative review has several shortcomings: "It is nonquantitative, unsystematic, and subjective, and the task of reviewing 100 or more studies simply exceeds the information-processing capacities of the human mind" (p. 54).

A second technique, the one used by Maccoby and Jacklin (1974), is called *vote counting.* As the name implies, it involves listing each study, and counting the number of studies of the total that demonstrate a particular effect. In essence, each study then receives one "vote" in the final tally. Studies that do demonstrate a gender difference "vote" for the idea that gender differences really exist; studies that do not find a gender difference "vote" for the opposite proposition. Although an advance over the narrative review, vote counting still suffers from a number of problems. The most important is that each study is given equal weight, although many studies differ in overall quality, sample sizes, precision of the instruments used, and statistical power (Block, 1976; Hedges & Olkin, 1985; Hyde & Linn, 1988).

Recently, a new technique has been developed. The technique is called **meta-analysis,** and involves the use of statistical methods in integrating the findings from different studies (Hedges & Olkin, 1985). This approach is gaining widespread popularity among psychologists. It allows the investigator to compare different studies quantitatively. A measure commonly used in meta-analysis is d, defined as the difference in mean scores between two groups, divided by the average standard deviation for the two groups. This measure is known as the **effect size.**

To take a concrete example of effect sizes, consider the following example: Suppose that women outperform men on a specific verbal task. If the mean score for women is 100, and the mean score for men is 50, but on average, the standard deviation for the two groups is 75, the effect size of the study would be [100-50]/75 = .67. Cohen (1969) provides rules of thumb for interpreting this value: Effect sizes of .20 are considered small; of .50, medium, and of .80, large. So, our hypothesized value of .67 would count as a medium-to-large effect.

Verbal Abilities

What kinds of abilities count as "verbal abilities"? Different authors provide different definitions, of course, but a typical description would include breadth of vocabulary, speech fluency, grammar, spelling, reading comprehension, oral comprehension, and the ability to solve language puzzles such as verbal analogies or anagrams (Halpern, 1992; Williams, 1983). In a classic review, Maccoby and Jacklin (1974) concluded that the bulk of studies conducted up until that time suggested that although girls and boys showed approximately the same pattern of verbal abilities, after about age 11 and continuing through high school and beyond, females outperformed males on a variety of verbal tasks, including language comprehension and production, creative writing, verbal analogies, and verbal fluency.

A recent review (Hyde & Linn, 1988) challenges Maccoby and Jacklin's conclusion. Using meta-analysis, the authors surveyed 165 studies (both published and unpublished) that met the following criteria: subjects were from the United States and Canada; were over 3 years of age; were free from language deficits (for example, dyslexia); the studies reported original data; and the authors provided enough information for the calculation of effect sizes. The types of verbal abilities examined included vocabulary, analogies, reading comprehension, oral communication, essay writing, general ability (a mixture of other measures), SAT verbal scores, and anagrams.

Of the studies surveyed, roughly a quarter showed superior male performance; three-quarters showed superior female performance. However, when assessed in terms of statistical significance, only 27% of the studies found statistically significant higher female performance, 66% found no statistically significant gender differences, and 7% found statisti-

Early work suggested that females had greater verbal abilities than males. Recent analyses, however, have disputed this claim. The gender differences, if they exist, are small at best.

cally significant higher male performance. When the types of verbal tasks were taken into account, the only tasks to show reliable female superiority were those for anagrams, speech production, and general ability. The average d measure for these tasks was .22, .20, and .33, respectively, suggesting that even the significant gender differences were rather small. Analyzing gender differences as a function of age, the authors also found little variation in d measures whether the subjects were preschoolers, elementary school–aged, adolescents, or adults. Interestingly, studies published before 1973 showed a significantly larger gender difference (mean $d = .23$) than did more recent studies (those published after 1973; mean $d = .10$).

Hyde and Linn (1988) concluded:

> We are prepared to assert that there are no gender differences in verbal ability, at least at this time, in American culture, in the standard ways that verbal ability has been measured. We feel that we can reach this conclusion with some confidence, having surveyed 165 studies that represent the testing of 1,418,899 subjects . . . and averaged 119 values of d to obtain a mean value of $+0.11$. A gender difference of one tenth of a standard deviation is

scarcely one that deserves continued attention in theory, research, or textbooks. Surely we have larger effects to pursue. (p. 62)

Visual-Spatial Abilities

The term *visual-spatial abilities* is awkward and hard to define, as previous authors have noted (Halpern, 1992; McGee, 1979; Williams, 1983). Typically, it refers to one's performance on tasks such as the mental rotation, or mental transformation of different objects, shapes, or drawings, similar to those described in Chapter 7 ("Visual Imagery"). Maccoby and Jacklin (1974) reported gender differences in visual-spatial abilities as extremely reliable, asserting that boys "excel" in them, once childhood is over. They reported a *d* measure of up to .40.

Other investigators have some quarrel with this number and with this conclusion. Caplan, MacPherson, and Tobin (1985), for example, argued that much of the research had not defined *spatial ability* very clearly, and that the information available did not warrant the conclusion that gender differences in this ability existed.

Different studies in the literature have used different tasks as purported measures of spatial ability. One of the most widely used is the rod-and-frame test, depicted in Figure 13-6. In this test, subjects see a tilted square frame enclosing a rod, and are asked to move the rod to be horizontal. Supposedly, the test measures the ability to ignore, or be independent from, the tilted square frame, and subjects who are able to do this successfully are thought to have better spatial skills. In general, the test has shown large gender differences (Harris, 1978).

FIGURE 13-6.   Depiction of the rod-and-frame task. Subjects see a tilted frame (in black), and are asked to position the rod inside the frame so that the rod is horizontal (perpendicular to the floor), ignoring the frame.

Caplan and associates (1985) offer two arguments regarding the use of this test. First, the test seems not to be a pure measure of spatial abilities but, rather, to be influenced by other variables, such as assertiveness or fear (the test is often given in dark rooms to individual subjects). Second, results on this particular test are greatly influenced by what subjects are told about the test. If told that the test measures empathy, female performance improves; if shown a human figure rather than a rod, the gender difference disappears. The authors also offer additional arguments about other tests of spatial abilities, concluding that the term itself has been poorly defined. Therefore, they believe, it is probably most accurate to believe that gender differences in spatial abilities have not been documented and, indeed, that until the term is more well defined, investigation of gender differences in spatial abilities is premature.

Linn and Petersen (1985) conducted a meta-analysis of studies on sex differences in spatial ability. They first delineated three types of spatial ability: *spatial perception,* the ability to determine "spatial relationships with respect to the orientation of their own bodies" (for example, to perform well on the rod-and-frame test, mentioned earlier), *mental rotation,* and *spatial visualization,* for example, the ability to find specific shapes in larger, more complex figures, or to imagine how a three-dimensional paper object would look if unfolded. Figure 13-7 presents examples of tasks of each type.

The meta-analysis they completed showed values of d ranging from .13 on the spatial-visualization tasks, to .73 on mental rotation tasks, to .44 on spatial-perception tasks. However, the last two types of spatial-ability tasks yielded different values of $d,$ depending on either the age of subjects or the specific type of test used. In general, effect sizes on spatial perception tasks were much larger for older subjects, meaning that gender differences were less apparent for younger subjects. This trend might be due to biological changes with age or to differences in the populations sampled. For example, older female subjects might have less experience with spatial tasks (due to differences in toys or curriculum experienced during childhood) than younger subjects.

For mental rotation, the size of the gender difference differed as a function of the specific task but remained constant over all ages studied. Generally speaking, the more rapid processing of symbolic information required, the larger the gender difference. Some mental rotation tasks that involved complex three-dimensional items generally showed larger gender differences than did mental rotation tasks with more simple, two-dimensional items. Linn and Petersen (1985) offer a number of possible reasons for the gender difference: females may rotate items more slowly, may use different strategies, or simply may display more caution and less trust in their responses (thereby going back and double-checking more often) than males.

Another reason may have to do with neurological findings on male and female brains. In a recent review, Levy and Heller (1992) note that, in

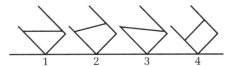

A spatial perception item. Respondents are asked to indicate which tilted bottle has a horizontal water line.

(A)

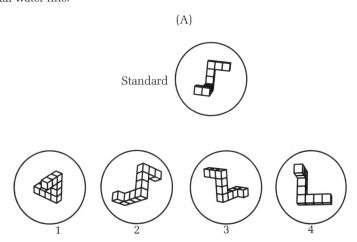

A mental rotation item. Respondents are asked to identify the two responses that show the standard in a different orientation.

(B)

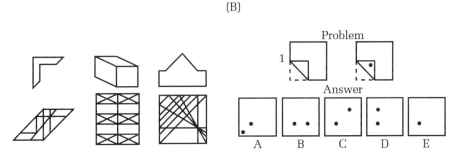

Spatial visualization items. Left, Embedded Figures: respondents are asked to find the simple shape on the top in the complex shape shown on the bottom. Right, Paper Folding: respondents are asked to indicate how the paper would look when unfolded.

(C)

FIGURE 13-7.   Examples of three spatial-ability tasks. SOURCE: From "Emergence and Characterization of Sex Differences in Spatial Ability: A Meta-Analysis," by M. C. Linn and A. C. Peterson, 1985, *Child Development, 59,* 1479–1498. Copyright © 1985 by The Society for Research in Child Development, Inc. Reprinted by permission.

One task that appears to show reliable gender differences is that of mental rotation. On average, males perform better than females. However, many individual females can outperform many individual males, even on this task.

general, females tend to have cerebral hemispheres of the brain that are less **lateralized,** or specialized in function, than are the cerebral hemispheres of males. It has long been known in psychology that the cerebral hemispheres have slightly different roles to play in our cognitive lives. For most of us (especially right-handed people), verbal fluency, verbal reasoning, and other types of analytical reasoning seem to be governed by left-hemisphere functioning. The right hemisphere, in contrast, seems to be specialized for understanding spatial relations as well as interpreting emotional information.

To say that males are more lateralized than females is to say that males show greater asymmetries in the functioning of their two cerebral hemispheres. Females, for example, appear to have language functions represented in both hemispheres, at least to some degree. Relatedly, women who suffer left-hemisphere damage often show better recovery of language functioning than do men with the same type of damage (Levy & Heller, 1992).

What might it mean to have greater asymmetries in functioning? It probably implies greater specialization in functioning; the more specialization, the more resources one has to perform a task. Overall, males' greater lateralization may equip them with more resources to devote to specific spatial tasks, such as mental rotation. Of course, this conclusion must be interpreted carefully. Although a gender difference in lateralization is well documented, this does not imply that *every* male shows greater lateralization than *every* female. Moreover, the tasks on which gender differences in spatial ability have been found are restricted to a narrow set. Linn and Petersen (1985) concluded that "results . . . suggest (a) that sex differences arise on some types of spatial ability but not others, (b) that large sex differences are found only on measures of mental rotation, (c) that smaller sex differences are found on measures of spatial perception, and (d) that, when sex differences are found, they can be detected across the life span" (p. 1479).

Quantitative and Reasoning Abilities

The term *quantitative abilities* covers a variety of skills, including arithmetic knowledge and skill as well as understanding of quantitative concepts (for example, fractions or proportions, inverses). As with the terms *verbal abilities* and *visual-spatial abilities,* the term *quantitative abilities* has meant slightly different things to different investigators.

Maccoby and Jacklin (1974) believed that boys and girls showed similar levels and patterns of mathematical ability through elementary school. Beginning at age 12 or 13, however, boys' achievement and skill began to increase faster than girls'. Hyde (1981), conducting a meta-analysis of the studies originally cited by Maccoby and Jacklin, concluded that the median *d* score for all the studies was .43, showing that, on average, boys tend to outperform girls by about a half a standard deviation.

Studies by Benbow and Stanley (1980, 1983) provided more evidence in support of gender differences in mathematical ability. The investigators used data collected by the Study of Mathematically Precocious Youth (SMPY), a talent search used to identify extremely able junior high school students. The logic here is that until junior high, male and female students are exposed to the same math classes in schools. By using junior high school subjects, the role of differential exposure to mathematics that might occur in high school, when males often enroll in more math classes than females, is reduced.

In the SMPY studies, seventh and eighth graders took the College Board's Scholastic Aptitude Test (SAT), a familiar test for high school juniors and seniors. Table 13-1 presents some of the results. Benbow and Stanley (1980) found that the score for males on the mathematical section of the SAT was approximately 30 points higher than that for females, although both groups performed equally well on the verbal section. Moreover, the higher the score, the higher the ratio of men to women who have that score. For example, considering SAT scores of 700 and above (only 1 in 10,000 students scores this highly), the ratio of men to women is 13 to 1 (Benbow &

TABLE 13-1. Mean SAT scores of mathematically precocious youths

Test Date	Grade	Number		SAT-V Score[*] $\overline{X} \pm S.D.$		SAT-M Scores[†] $\overline{X} \pm S.D.$		Highest Score		Percentage Scoring above 600 on SAT-M	
		Boys	Girls	Boys	Girls	Boys	Girls	Boys	Girls	Boys	Girls
March 1972	7	90	77			460 ± 104	423 ± 75	740	590	7 .8	0
	8+	133	96			528 ± 105	458 ± 88	790	600	27.1	0
February 1973	7	135	88	385 ± 71	374 ± 74	495 ± 85	440 ± 66	800	620	8.1	1.1
	8+	286	158	431 ± 89	442 ± 83	551 ± 85	511 ± 63	800	650	22.7	8.2
January 1974	7	372	222			473 ± 85	440 ± 68	760	630	6.5	1.8
	8+	556	369			540 ± 82	503 ± 72	750	700	21.6	7.9
December 1976	7	495	356	370 ± 73	368 ± 70	455 ± 84	421 ± 64	780	610	5.5	0.6
	8‡	12	10	487 ± 129	390 ± 61	598 ± 126	482 ± 83	750	600	58.3	0
January 1978	7 and 8‡	1549	1249	375 ± 80	372 ± 78	448 ± 87	413 ± 71	790	760	5.3	0.8
January 1979	7 and 8‡	2046	1628	370 ± 76	370 ± 77	436 ± 87	404 ± 77	790	760	3.2	0.9

$N = 9,927$

*Mean score for a random sample of high school juniors and seniors was 368 for males and females (8).

† Mean for juniors and seniors: males, 416; females, 390.

‡These rare 8th graders were accelerated at least 1 year in school grade placement.

SOURCE: From "Sex Differences in Mathematical Ability: Fact or Artifact," by C. P. Benbow and J. C. Stanley, 1980, *Science, 210,* 1262–1264. Copyright © 1980 by the AAAS. Reprinted by permission.

Stanley, 1983). There is some evidence, however, that gender differences occurred only on specific items, usually ones having to do with algebra rather than with those having to do with geometry or arithmetic (Deaux, 1985).

Anita Meehan (1984) examined gender differences in other, related tasks, specifically Piagetian tasks of formal operations. Recall from Chapter 12 that formal-operational tasks include such things as logical reasoning, the ability to think systematically, and the ability to consider all possibilities. Meehan examined three kinds of formal-operational tasks: propositional-logic tasks, combinatorial-reasoning tasks, and proportional-reasoning tasks. Performing meta-analyses on a total of 53 studies, Meehan discovered small and statistically nonsignificant values of d for the first two tasks, .22 and .10, respectively. The third task, a more explicitly quantitative task (having to do with ratios), showed an average d of .48.

We have seen so far that gender differences in some cognitive tasks—namely, some visual-spatial and some quantitative tasks—seem to be well established. However, Hyde (1981) makes an important point: A statistically reliable effect (that is, with relatively large values of d) need not necessarily be a large effect. One way to measure the magnitude of an effect is to compute a quantity known to psychologists as the percentage of variance accounted for. In laypersons' terms, this measure reflects how much of the difference among scores is explained by a variable of interest. Hyde computed various measures of this magnitude and found that even for the highly reliable gender differences, the percentage of variance accounted for by gender was between only 1% and 5%. That is to say, knowing that a person is male or female can improve your guess about how well he or she might perform on a specific cognitive task (for example, visual-spatial or quantitative) by at most only 5%. Thus, generalizations such as "women should avoid engineering" or "men make more 'natural' mathematicians" are wholly unwarranted from the existing data.

Gender Differences in Learning and Cognitive Styles

So far, the evidence reviewed suggests that gender differences in cognition occur for only a few very specific tasks, and even then the magnitude of the gender differences is often small. This in turn suggests that we have yet to find evidence that men and women have different basic cognitive capacities, skills, or abilities, except perhaps for certain specific spatial and quantitative tasks.

On the other hand, women and men, as well as girls and boys, certainly often appear to teachers and instructors to have differential aptitudes or preferences. More women than men exhibit a "fear of mathematics" and avoid quantitative or analytical courses (for example, mathematics, science, logic) when given a choice, beginning in high school

(Oakes, 1990). Certainly, it seems to teachers and others who work with students that cognitive gender differences abound. What accounts for the discrepancy between this anecdotal information and the studies reviewed earlier?

One possibility is that gender differences arise not so much in basic cognitive resources (capacities, abilities, and the like) but, rather, in how these resources are used. Recall our earlier discussion of cognitive styles. Recall that a "cognitive style" is a habitual and preferred way of approaching cognitive tasks. Perhaps it is in such approaches that women and men differ. In this section, we will review two different but related proposals relevant to this idea.

Motivation for Cognitive Tasks

Research by psychologist Carol Dweck and her associates (Dweck & Bush, 1976; Dweck, Davidson, Nelson, & Enna, 1978; Dweck, Goetz, & Strauss, 1980) has shown that even in elementary school, boys and girls show differential patterns of *achievement motivation.* This term refers to the ways in which people define and set goals, particularly the goals that are presumed to

The work of Dweck and others suggests that teachers and other adults who work with children might provide different patterns of feedback to boys and girls about their intellectual abilities.

relate to their own competence (Dweck, 1986). Two major patterns of behavior that appear to affect the ways people approach a broad range of tasks have been identified: a *mastery-oriented* and a *helpless* pattern (Dweck & Leggett, 1988).

Children and adults who adopt a mastery-oriented approach set goals to challenge themselves, and therefore to increase their competence, understanding, or mastery of something new. These individuals persist when they encounter obstacles or difficulty. Often, they also appear to enjoy putting in more effort when it is called for. In contrast, individuals with a helpless approach fail to set challenging goals, and give up rather easily when "the going gets tough."

In a number of studies, Dweck and her colleagues have given older elementary school–aged children a number of puzzles or similar problem-solving tasks. Often, the tasks are set up to be insoluble, and children are given "failure feedback"—information that they have failed to complete a particular task correctly. In one study (Dweck & Bush, 1976), children received failure feedback from either a male or female adult or peer. When the evaluator was an adult, and especially when the adult was female, girls tended to adopt a "helpless" strategy, attributing the cause of their failure to their own inability or lack of competence. Boys, in contrast, were likely in the same circumstances to attribute the failure to the evaluator's "fussiness." It is interesting that when peers administered the failure feedback, boys were much more likely to become helpless, and girls much more likely to attribute problems to their own efforts.

Dweck and colleagues (1978) reported other findings that might explain why adults' feedback has such different effects on girls and boys. They examined the kind of feedback given to fourth- and fifth-grade girls and boys by classroom teachers. Every instance of feedback to children by the teacher was coded. The experimenters found that when looking at just the positive feedback given, over 90% of it related to the intellectual quality of work for boys, but the corresponding figure for girls was less than 80%. The discrepancy for negative feedback was even stronger: for boys, only about a third of the feedback concerned intellectual quality (the rest tended to be about conduct, effort, neatness, or other such things) but well over two-thirds of the negative feedback girls received had to do with work-related aspects of their performance.

Dweck and Goetz (1978) concluded that girls, perhaps because of their greater compliance with adult demands, are seen by teachers (as well as by themselves) as expending maximum effort and motivation. Therefore, they come to believe that failure can be attributed only to lack of ability. Boys, in contrast, are more often seen by teachers as lacking in conduct or effort. Thus, when their performance falls short of expectation, teachers are more likely (in fact, eight times more likely) to attribute the problem to a lack of motivation rather than to a lack of ability. As a consequence, boys may be inadvertently taught both to be less devastated by criticism (because they receive so much), and to take it less personally (because so much of it has to do with nonintellectual aspects of work, and so much is directed to a perceived lack of motivation). Girls, receiving less criticism, have less opportunity to learn how to handle it. Further, adult criticism of girls' work tends to focus on a perceived lack of competence or ability. In short, girls get the message that failure signals lack of ability (something there is little remedy for); boys, that failure signals a lack of effort (for which the remedy is obvious).

Dweck and her colleagues (1978) tested these ideas in a follow-up study. In it, they had children work on anagram puzzles, and a male experimenter provided failure feedback. Sometimes, the feedback was of the sort given by teachers to boys ("You didn't do very well that time—it wasn't neat enough") and sometimes, of the sort typically given by teachers to girls ("You didn't do very well that time—you didn't get the word right"). Following these experiences, all children were given another puzzle and again given negative feedback, and asked the following question: "If the man told you that you did not do very well on this puzzle, why do you think that was?" The following choices were provided: "(a) I did not try hard enough. (b) The man was too fussy. (c) I am not very good at it." Children (both girls and boys) in the teacher-girl condition were more than twice as likely to attribute failure to choice (c), a perceived lack of ability. Children (again, both girls and boys) in the teacher-boy condition were far more likely to attribute failure to choice (a), a perceived lack of effort, or choice (b) the "fussiness" of the evaluator.

This research supports the idea that "evaluative feedback given to boys and girls . . . can result directly in girls' greater tendency to view failure feedback as indicative of their level of ability" (Dweck et al., 1978, p. 274). Whether and when these patterns of attribution become stable and generalized is an open question, but one that can bode poorly for women's self-assessment, particularly for tasks perceived to be difficult.

Connected Learning

Recent feminist critiques of psychology (Belenky, Clinchy, Goldberger, & Tarule, 1986; Gilligan, 1982) make even stronger claims about the different ways in which men and women approach cognitive tasks. Belenky and collaborators believe that today's predominant culture, historically dominated by males, has come to prize rationality and objectivity over other, equally legitimate, ways of learning and understanding. These ways of understanding may be more common among women:

> It is likely that the commonly accepted stereotype of women's thinking as emotional, intuitive, and personalized has contributed to the devaluation of women's minds and contributions, particularly in Western technologically oriented cultures, which value rationalism and objectivity. . . . It is generally assumed that intuitive knowledge is more primitive, therefore less valuable, than so-called objective modes of knowing. (p. 6)

Belenky and collaborators (1986) obtained their data from interviews of 135 women, some of whom were college students or alumnae, others of whom were members of what the authors called the "invisible colleges"—human service agencies supporting women while they parented their children. Women are described by the investigators as seeking *connected knowing,* in which one discovers "truth" through a conscious process of trying to understand. The kind of understanding sought involves discovery of a personal connection between the individual and the thing, event, person, or concept under consideration. It entails an acceptance and an appreciation for the thing, event, person, or concept on its own terms, within its own framework.

Another style of knowing that these authors describe, termed *separate knowing,* is perhaps more typical of males, and also of women who are socialized and successful in traditional male environments. This kind of knowing strives for objectivity and rigor, for the learner to "stand apart from" the thing, event, person, or concept being learned or understood. The orientation is toward impersonal rules or standards, and learning involves "mastery of" rather than "engagement with" the information to be learned.

Separate knowing, according to Belenky and collaborators (1986) involves a different intellectual style:

> Separate knowers are tough-minded. They are like doormen at exclusive clubs. They don't want to let anything in unless they are pretty sure it is good. . . . Presented with a proposition, separate knowers immediately look for something wrong—a loophole, factual error, a logical contradiction, the omission of contrary evidence. (p. 104)

Connected knowing, on the other hand,

> builds on the [learner's] conviction that the most trustworthy knowledge comes from personal experience rather than the pronouncements of authorities. . . . At the heart of these procedures is the capacity for empathy. (pp. 112–113)

If men and women do indeed have different styles of learning and understanding, then perhaps certain ways of processing information will also differ in ease or familiarity. For example, mathematics or logic, each with an emphasis on rigor and proof, might seem more attractive to someone with a "separate" way of knowing; more interpretive cognitive tasks, such as understanding a poem or seeking out alternative perceptions, might come more easily to a "connected knower." If styles of knowing vary by gender, then, this could influence the kinds of cognitive tasks men and women find most easy or most appealing.

Little work has been done to assess the degree to which the different responses articulated by Belenky and collaborators' (1986) female subjects are a function of gender, socioeconomic status, level of education, or other factors. Moreover, it is not yet clear whether the different "ways of knowing" they describe actually do differ as a function of gender in that only female subjects were interviewed. Because Belenky and collaborators draw primarily from interview data, it is hard to assess whether their findings reflect subtle experimenter (interviewer) effects. Further, and equally important, it is not yet clear whether different ways of knowing would actually predict different kinds of cognitive performance on actual tasks. It remains for future research to examine these important issues.

Summary

We have paused in this chapter to consider the possibility that cognition does not always operate the same way for all people. Here, we have examined different potential sources of variation in the way people approach the cognitive tasks in their lives.

We began by examining individual differences in cognitive abilities, in cognitive styles, in expertise, and with aging. We saw first that individuals apparently differ in their cognitive abilities, especially in such things as mental speed, storage capacity, attention span, and so on. We noted that some psychologists equate these cognitive abilities with intelligence. Other cognitive psychologists do not make this equation but see cognitive abilities as a part of intelligence. Still other psychologists reject the idea that there is one single thing called intelligence.

We also saw that people can have different cognitive approaches to, or styles in regard to, different tasks. Two of the most investigated cognitive stylistic dimensions are field dependence/independence, and reflectivity/impulsivity. Whether the two dimensions are unrelated and the degree to which cognitive styles are modifiable are two important questions for future research. We also noted that peoples' expertise can affect the ways in which they approach a cognitive task within their domain of expertise. Finally, we observed that age-related changes in cognitive processing do not disappear in adolescence; adults of different ages show some systematic differences in cognitive performance.

We next turned to the question of gender differences in cognition. Gender-differences research is very much in an active stage, and therefore any conclusions we can draw must of necessity be tentative. At present, it seems safe to say that with regard to questions of ability, the overall patterns of performance of men and women, boys and girls, are far more similar than they are different. Many descriptions of cognitive gender differences (for example, in verbal ability) have on close inspection proven to be either false or at best greatly exaggerated. Other, more well established cognitive gender differences (for example, on mental rotation tasks, or on certain mathematical tasks, especially ones of an algebraic nature) are often dependent on the age and educational backgrounds of the subjects surveyed and on the particular items used. Even for very well established differences, the magnitude of the difference between the average performance for males and the average performance for females is often quite small, accounting for up to only 5% of the total variance.

As of now, it is hard to conclude that there is much evidence for widespread gender differences in specific cognitive processes. Of course, the verbal, spatial, and quantitative tasks studied represent a small fraction of all possible cognitive tasks. Thus, it remains a possibility that other kinds of cognitive tasks might show large and reliable gender differences. However, very few have yet been demonstrated.

A final set of questions has to do with gender differences in cognitive style or approach. The issue here is whether females and males adopt different strategies in the ways in which they gather, process, or evaluate information. Carol Dweck's work does suggest that boys and girls adopt different approaches to cognitive tasks, with girls tending to adopt a more "helpless" outlook, especially in the face of failure. It is not yet clear how girls and boys come to adopt different strategies, although Dweck's work implicates the typical patterns of feedback that boys and girls receive from teachers. We can speculate that these kinds of feedback may also come from other agents of socialization—parents, siblings, peers, and others—but the evidence on this question remains to be gathered.

Recent interesting proposals from feminist research suggests that cognitive gender differences might not occur on very specific tasks but, rather, in broad approaches to cognition itself. Future work must establish how different the "ways of knowing" are for people of different genders, and must investigate how these differences in approach might translate into performance on specific cognitive tasks. It will also be important to assess the effect of gender, independent of other demographic variables, such as socioeconomic status, level of education, or racial and ethnic heritage.

Recommended Readings

Sternberg and Detterman (1986) explore different views on the nature of intelligence. Sternberg (1986a) provides an application of his theory of intelligence to education, arguing that with certain kinds of practice and training, the component processes of intelligence can be increased. Carpenter, Just, and Shell (1990) report on research analyzing the cognitive processes involved in performance on the Raven Progressive Matrices Test, a widely used nonverbal intelligence test.

Recent research on cognitive styles is reported in a volume edited by Globerson and Zelnicker (1989). An edited volume by Chi, Glaser, and Farr (1988) on expertise contains a number of studies describing cognitive changes with practice and experience. Tanaka and Taylor (1991) report on their studies of dog and bird experts and how their expertise affects categorization. A basic review of cognitive changes in aging can be found in Cavanaugh (1993).

Two general works exploring the issue of gender differences in cognition are Deaux (1985) and Halpern (1992); the latter is especially recommended as an introductory work. Tavris and Wade (1984) discuss the issue of gender differences more broadly and from a variety of perspectives. Review articles using meta-analyses of different cognitive skills include Hyde and Linn (1988), Linn and Petersen (1985), and Meehan (1984). Feingold (1988) presents recent data from standardized tests, showing that average gender differences (initially favoring boys in mathematical and spatial items, and girls in verbal items) have shown large declines over the years from 1947 to 1983. Hedges and Olkin (1985) present an overview of how meta-analyses can be conducted and interpreted.

The book by Belenky and colleagues (1986) spells out in some detail their study and the assumptions behind the idea that women and men come to learn and to understand in different ways.

REVIEW QUESTIONS

1. Discuss the reasons that cognitive psychologists need to know about stable individual and/or gender differences in cognition.

2. What does it mean to assert that there exist stable individual differences in cognitive capacities? Is the assertion synonymous with the belief that there exist stable individual differences in intelligence?

3. Discuss the idea of *cognitive styles.* How does this concept differ from the concepts of intelligence or cognitive abilities?

4. What cautions must be given in interpreting findings in gender differences (or for that matter, any group-related individual differences) in cognition?

5. Explain the logic of a meta-analysis.

6. Discuss the implications of the major findings regarding gender differences in cognitive abilities.

7. How might the work of Dweck and colleagues and Belenky and colleagues bear on the research on gender differences in cognition?

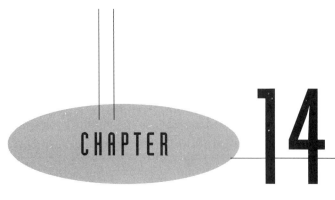

CHAPTER 14

Cognition in Cross-Cultural Perspective

Much of the literature covered so far has described the cognitive capacities and processes of people (usually adults, but in some cases, children), in the United States or Europe. The implicit assumption has been that the models and theories of cognition developed from such samples are universal—they apply to and can describe the performance and behavior of people throughout the world. However, research conducted with people from other cultures has often shown this assumption to be problematic, if not in error.

In this chapter, we will examine some of this research, and consider its implications for the study of cognition.

A number of issues must be discussed in order to consider cross-cultural research. First and foremost, we must come to terms with what makes for a *culture*. Certainly, most would agree that people in rural India live in a different culture from people in downtown Baltimore. However, do people in rural New Hampshire experience a culture different from that experienced by people living in Los Angeles?

Psychologists, anthropologists, sociologists, and others have debated the issue of what defines a culture and come to no widespread and clear-cut resolution to date. Cole and Scribner (1974) note some of the ingredients of a culture: a distinct language; distinct customs, habits, modes of dress; distinct beliefs and philosophies. More recently, psychologists performing cross-cultural research have also examined factors such as ethnicity and social class in relation to performances on different types of tasks or to attitudes and beliefs (Kagitçibasi & Berry, 1989; Segall, 1986). In fact, Segall (1984) has made the argument that the concept of culture is nothing more than a collection of independent variables such as language, customs, and so on, although others (for example, Rohner, 1984) disagree.

The general issue is this: the term *culture* connotes so much, that simply finding differences among individuals from one culture to another and attributing those differences to "culture" is a fairly empty statement. Instead, the goal is to "unpack" the term *culture,* and to try to determine which aspects or dimensions of a culture contribute to the differences found. For example, might differences in counting skill be attributed to different uses of number within a culture? Might differences in perception have to do with the typical landscapes encountered by participants of different cultures? What, specifically, is it within the culture that affects the ways in which people acquire, store, and process information?

Bovet's (1974) research comparing the performance of Algerian and Genevan children and adults on Piagetian tasks of cognitive development provides an example of research addressing these questions. Bovet found some unusual patterns of results among her Algerian subjects, which she was able to relate to specific features of the Algerian culture. For example, Algerian children had a difficult time with the conservation of quantities. Bovet speculated that some of their difficulty reflected their everyday environment and customs:

> A further point to be mentioned is that eating and cooking utensils (bowls, glasses, plates) of the particular environment studied were of all shapes and sizes, which makes it somewhat difficult to make any comparisons of dimensions. Furthermore, the way of serving food at table was for each person to help from a communal dish, rather than for one person to share it out amongst those present; no comparison of the size of the portions takes place. Finally, the attitude of the mother who does not use any measuring instrument, but "knows" how much to use by means of intuitive approximations and estimations, may have some influence on the child's attitude. Thus, adult modes of thought can influence the development of notions of conservation of quantity in the child by means of familiar types of activities, in which the child participates, even if only as spectator. (p. 331)

Bovet's (1974) assertion is that aspects of the culture, physical (the shapes and dimensions of eating utensils) as well as behavioral (the practices surrounding the serving of food), guide and constrain the assumptions and questions children naturally have about quantities. Contrast her description of Algerian culture with your impressions of middle-class American culture: Dinner tables are set such that everyone has the same kind of glasses, spoons, plates, and so on. A parent serves each child with roughly the same serving size (perhaps affected by the age or size of the child). Disputes about who "got more" (of say, an appealing dessert) are common. All of these factors might help, in subtle ways, to focus attention on quantities and how quantities relate to such things as container shape

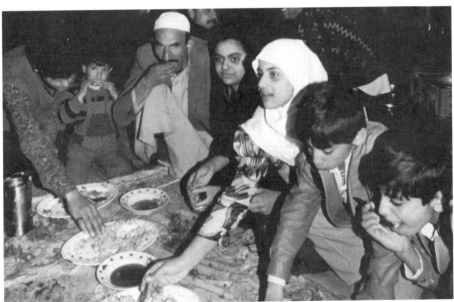

According to Bovet, even an ordinary setting, such as the dinner table, can affect certain cognitive processing, such as concepts of measurement.

and perceptual appearance. This focus, in turn, may help performance on later tests of conservation. Of course, these assertions warrant more rigorous testing before we can accept them. It may be that other aspects of the culture produce the effect; without empirical testing, we can't be sure.

A fundamental question raised by cross-cultural research is the degree to which practices, beliefs, competences, and capacities are **cultur-**

ally relative or **culturally universal.** To assert that a cognitive process is culturally relative is to assert that the process is specific to a particular culture or set of cultures (Poortinga & Malpass, 1986). For example, the ability to form hierarchically organized categories (for example, poodles are dogs, which are mammals, which are animals, which are living things) may be something that is much more relevant to people in some cultures than in others. *Cultural universality,* by contrast, refers to phenomena that are believed to be common to humankind, such as the use of language.

This question has profound effects upon the way research questions are framed. If, for instance, a process, capacity, or strategy is assumed to be universal, the cross-cultural questions about it are likely to ask how cultural factors influence and shape it. The assumption here is that the process, capacity, or strategy exists in all cultures, but that culture (or some aspect of culture) can facilitate, hinder, or otherwise alter the way in which it is expressed.

In contrast, those who hold a position of culture relativism, or especially radical cultural relativism (Berry, 1981, 1984), would not assume that the process, capacity, or strategy necessarily is present in all cultures. Moreover, they would be less likely to view culture as the sum of several independent factors. Instead, these researchers believe that culture is a kind of Gestalt that cannot be broken into pieces. Certain concepts, processes, capacities, and the like will be relevant to, and therefore found in, only certain cultures. Thus, the kinds of theories and explanations of cognition offered will necessarily be different for each (or at least many) cultures.

Cross-cultural researchers face many methodological challenges that do not play as large a role in the research programs of researchers who operate strictly within a culture (for example, most of the work described in Chapters 2 through 13). You may recall from introductory psychology that a true experiment involves (1) random assignment of subjects to experimental conditions, (2) control over experimental treatments (that is, manipulation of independent variables), and (3) control over other confounding factors or events. Any experimenter has a difficult (if not impossible) task in achieving such control, but a cross-cultural researcher, in principle, can never achieve the first criterion (people cannot be randomly assigned to a culture either practically or ethically) and can probably never in reality ever achieve the second or third. After all, especially if certain tasks are more relevant to some cultures than others, it will be nearly impossible to chose experimental tasks (for example, memory tests, problem-solving tests) that are equally difficult and familiar, and equally a good measure of the aspect of behavior or ability under study for people from different cultures (Malpass & Poortinga, 1986). People from cultures where the task is more familiar might outperform people from cultures where the task is less familiar for a variety of reasons unrelated to cognitive abilities. It may be simply because people from the former culture have had more practice with the task, or feel more comfortable with the task, or enjoy the task more. We will see specific illustrations of this point in the examples to come. By the way, you might have noticed that the inability to assign people to cultures at random is a problem equivalent to the one faced by researchers studying gender or developmental differences. So-called subject variables, such as age, gender, culture, and ethnic origin, are variables that a researcher cannot assign; this makes the interpretation of experimental results all the more tricky.

In the last section of the chapter, we will examine research in the cross-cultural tradition carried out in the United States. Specifically, we will look at how people's performance on everyday (that is, nonlaboratory, and often nonschool) cognitive tasks works. One important question will serve as our focus: How well do theories and models of cognition, such as those described in earlier chapters, account for cognition "in the real world"? Much of the work to be reviewed in this chapter will demonstrate that peoples' performance often displays *context sensitivity;* that is, it varies according to the task, the instructions, or other features of the environment.

Examples of Studies of Cross-Cultural Cognition

In this section, we will review a selection of cross-cultural cognition studies. As was the case in the two previous chapters, it will be impossible to examine each facet of human cognition cross-culturally. Instead, we will examine a very small sample of studies of cognitive capacities and processes from a cross-cultural point of view. Readings at the chapter's end will direct the interested student to other studies of cognition from a cross-cultural framework.

Cross-Cultural Studies of Perception

You may recall from Chapter 2 that the term *perception* refers to the interpretation of sensory stimuli, for example, using the information from your retinal image to see an object against a background, or recognizing the furry creature meandering toward you as your cat. Because our perceptions typically occur quickly and effortlessly, it is tempting (but wrong, for reasons we reviewed in Chapter 2) to conclude that perception is a built-in, hardwired consequence of the way our sensory systems work. However, some landmark studies from cross-cultural psychology have directly challenged this assumption, showing that quite literally people from different cultures often "see things" quite differently.

Picture Perception

Studies by Hudson (1960, 1967) demonstrate that people from different cultures frequently do not see eye to eye. Hudson began with the intuition that Bantu workers in South African mines and factories seemed to have difficulty interpreting posters and films. To investigate why, he presented a variety of South Africans (both black and white, schooled and unschooled) with pictures such as those shown in Figure 14-1. Notice that all of the pictures depict an elephant, an antelope, a tree, and a man holding a spear. The cards differ in the depth cues presented. Card 1 uses object size (farther away objects are rendered smaller in size). Cards 2 and 3 also use superposition (nearer objects partially occlude farther objects). Card 4 uses all of these cues, and in addition, some cues of linear perspective (lines that are parallel appear to meet in the distance; other outlines or contours are scaled to fit in this framework).

Results showed that subjects attending school typically came to a three-dimensional interpretation of the pictures (for example, seeing the man aiming the spear at the antelope, and not the elephant; seeing the elephant as far away rather than very small). However, the nonliterate workers, both black and white, typically "saw" the pictures two-dimensionally. Hudson (1960) argued that schooling per se is not the cause of perceiving pictures three-dimensionally but, rather, informal instruction and habitual exposure to pictures. He believed that such factors as exposure to pictures, photographs, and other illustrations in books and magazines available in the home provide a great deal of crucial, informal practice in "pictorial literacy." His speculation was based on the observation that schools provide little formal instruction in the interpretation of pictures, coupled with the observation that even the schooled black workers had greater difficulty coming to three-dimensional pictorial interpretations.

Deregowski (1968), studying children and adult workers in Zambia,

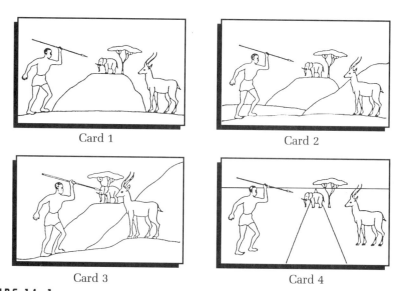

Card 1

Card 2

Card 3

Card 4

FIGURE 14-1.   Stimuli from Hudson (1960). SOURCE: *Journal of Social Psychology, 52,* 183–208, 1960. Reprinted with permission of the Helen Dwight Reid Educational Foundation. Published by Heldref Publications, 1319 Eighteenth St., N.W., Washington, D.C. 20036-1802. Copyright © 1960.

Central Africa, considered a different possibility. He wondered whether cross-cultural differences in pictorial perception really existed or whether some feature of Hudson's tasks caused subjects to respond as if they couldn't interpret the pictures three-dimensionally. In one study, he gave his subjects two tasks: a version of the Hudson task and a task requiring them to make models from pictured depictions (such as those shown in Figure 14-2) out of sticks. Deregowski found that although upward of 80% of his subjects failed to perceive the Hudson pictures three-dimensionally, more than half of them did construct three- rather than two-dimensional models. Deregowski (1980) argued, among other things, that perhaps his task and Hudson's differed in difficulty, Hudson's requiring a more demanding response. It could be, for instance, that the building task provides more guidance for the visual inspection of the picture, thus providing more cues to subjects as to the "correct" interpretations.

Cole and Scribner (1974) conclude from these and other studies that it is too simplistic to conclude that people either can or cannot perceive pictures three-dimensionally. The issue, they argue, is when and how people come to interpret a two-dimensional stimulus as having depth. Perhaps the content of the pictures (depictions of people and animals, and depictions of abstract geometric forms) also influences perception. Perhaps the mode of response (answering a question, building a model) influences the way people perceive pictures. Whatever the reasons, this work argues that the ways in which people view and interpret two-dimensional pictures depicting three-dimensional scenes is not necessarily or exactly the same from culture to culture.

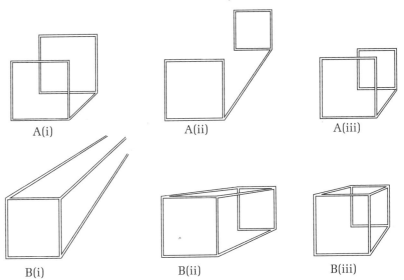

A(i)   A(ii)   A(iii)

B(i)   B(ii)   B(iii)

FIGURE 14-2.   Stimuli from Deregowski (1968). SOURCE: From "Difficulties in Pictorial Depth Perception in Africa," by J. B. Deregowski, 1968, *British Journal of Psychology, 59,* 195–204. Copyright © 1968 by the British Psychological Society. Reprinted by permission.

Visual Illusions

Other cross-cultural studies of perception have centered on visual illusions, such as those depicted in Figure 14-3. Rivers (1905) studied aspects of visual perception of people from the Torres Straits (Papuans from New Guinea) along with the Todas, people from southern India. Rivers reported that relative to Western samples, the subjects he worked with were more prone to the horizontal-vertical illusion, but less prone to the Müller-Lyer illusion.

Segall, Campbell, and Herskovits (1966) followed up on this observation, conducting a now-classic study. In it, they used the Müller-Lyer and the horizontal-vertical illusion (refer to Figure 14-3), and worked with approximately 2,000 people from 14 African and Philippine locations and the United States. The investigators' hypothesis was that people's previous

(A) The Horizontal-Vertical Illusion
(The horizontal line appears to be longer than the vertical line)

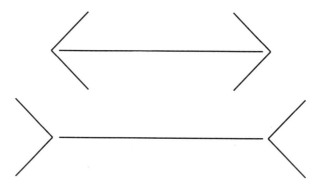

(B) The Müller-Lyer Illusion
(The bottom line appears to be longer than the top line.)

FIGURE 14-3.   Some visual illusions studied cross-culturally experience would affect their susceptibility to the illusions. In particular, Segall and colleagues believed that people who came from *carpentered* environments, in which pieces of wood or other materials exist consisting of straight lines, rectangular shapes, and other such geometric relationships, would be relatively more susceptible to the Müller-Lyer illusion. The idea here was that carpentered environments provide the people who live in them with a great deal of practice seeing rectangular shapes (boards, houses, windows) and therefore certain angles and junctions. The Müller-Lyer illusion taps into this experience as follows:

> [A]mong persons raised in a carpentered world there would be a tendency to perceive the Müller-Lyer figure . . . as a representation of three-dimensional objects extended in space. In this instance the two main parts of the drawing represent two objects. On the [top of Figure 14-3], for example, if the horizontal segment were perceived as the representation of the edge of a box, it would be a *front edge;* while on the [bottom], if the horizontal segment were perceived as the edge of another box, it would be the *back edge* along the inside of the box. Hence, the [top] horizontal would "have to be" shorter than the drawing makes it out, and the left-hand horizontal would "have to be" longer. (pp. 85-86)

This argument is based on one offered by the psychologist Egon Brunswik (1956): People interpret cues in any situation according to the ways in which they have interpreted such cues in the past. People do this because in the past they have typically been correct in the way they have interpreted these cues. However, in certain situations, cues can be misleading, and can cause people to make false interpretations.

Using analogous reasoning, Segall and colleagues (1966) predicted that people from cultures where the horizon was a part of the everyday landscape (for example, desert or plains dwellers) would be more susceptible to the horizontal-vertical illusion than people from cultures where the environment did not afford opportunities to view vast distances (for example, jungle dwellers).

Segall and colleagues (1966) explained the task carefully to all subjects, took many methodological precautions to make sure subjects understood each task and had opportunities to respond to several versions of each illusion. On each trial, subjects were presented with a stimulus pair containing two lines (sometimes consisting of illusions, sometimes consisting of other pairs of lines that produce no illusion), and had to indicate which line was longer. In general, the results confirmed the predictions described above, although both illusions were present in all cultures, to a greater or a lesser degree.

Despite some later disagreements over the findings by other investigators (see Deregowski, 1980 and 1989, for reviews), Segall (1979) still argued that

> people perceive in ways that are shaped by the inferences they have learned to make in order to function most effectively in the particular ecological settings in which they live. The generalization that we can

Segall and colleagues predicted that people from cultures in which the horizon figures in the landscape will show increased susceptibility to the horizontal-vertical illusion.

derive . . . is that we learn to perceive in the ways that we need to perceive. In that sense, environment and culture shape our perceptual habits. (p. 93)

Cross-Cultural Studies of Memory

Like perception, memory is widely regarded as a process central to almost every other form of cognition. It seems self-evident that all people need a means of storing some of the information they may encounter at one time for possible later use. Thus, it seems reasonable to believe that memory should show many commonalities across cultures. In this section, we will examine some of the work on memory carried out with people of non-Western cultures.

Free Recall

Given the assumptions just stated, results from studies carried out with the Kpelle people of Liberia, Africa (Cole, Gay, Glick, & Sharp, 1971), were surprising. As one part of a long series of studies on Kpelle cognition, Cole and associates administered a free-recall task. They read subjects a list of nouns (that were all demonstrated to refer to familiar objects). One set of lists (see Table 14-1) consisted of items that "clustered" into different categories (for example, tools, articles of clothing); another set consisted of the same number and types of items but in which there were no apparent clusters. Previous work using educated American subjects had shown that people's free recall performance is enhanced when given clustered lists, relative to nonclustered lists, especially when the items are presented in blocks, with all items from the same category presented together (Bousfield, 1953; Cofer, 1967).

Kpelle children (ranging in age from 6 to 14) and adults participated. Of the children, some were in school (first through fourth grades) and some were not; none of the adults was schooled. The performance of the subjects was compared with that of white, middle-class children from southern California. Cole and colleagues found large age differences in their American sample, with older children recalling far more of the words on each list than younger children. Kpelle subjects, however, showed only slight age differences. Moreover, the schooled Kpelles did not outperform the nonschooled Kpelles by much of a margin. Although the clusterable lists were easier for all Kpelle and American samples, only the American

TABLE 14-1.   Stimuli used by Cole and colleagues (1971)

Clusterable	Nonclusterable
Plate	Bottle
Calabash	Nickle
Pot	Chicken feather
Pan	Box
Cup	Battery
	Animal horn
Potato	Stone
Onion	Book
Banana	Candle
Orange	Cotton
Coconut	Hard mat
	Rope
Cutlass	Nail
Hoe	Cigarette
Knife	Stick
File	Grass
Hammer	Pot
	Knife
Trousers	Orange
Singlet	Shirt
Headtie	
Shirt	
Hat	

SOURCE: From *Culture and Thought: A Psychological Introduction,* by Michael Cole and Sylvia Scribner. Copyright © 1974 by John Wiley & Sons, Inc. Reprinted by permission.

subjects displayed much clustering in their free recall. That is, regardless of how the items from the clusterable lists were presented, American children, especially those 10 years and older, were more likely to recall all the tools, then all the foods, and so on. The Kpelle subjects, by contrast, were quite unlikely to do so.

It appeared, at first, as though the Kpelle have memory systems that work in different ways from those of Americans. However, Cole and colleagues followed up this work by testing a number of rival hypotheses. Perhaps, for example, the Kpelle did not understand the task. Perhaps they were not very interested in the task, and therefore did not try very hard. Perhaps the cues provided weren't clear enough. In a number of studies, the investigators gathered evidence against each of these.

In one series of studies, Cole and colleagues (1971) demonstrated that when the Kpelle were cued to recall items by category (for example, at the time of recall only, the experimenter said something like, "Tell me all the *clothing* you remember. [S. responds]. Okay, now tell me all the *tools* you remember. . . ."), their performance improved dramatically. This result (along with several others we don't have space to review) suggested to Cole and Scribner (1974) that although the Kpelle may perform differently on a memory task, there is little evidence to support the view that memory systems function in ways that differ qualitatively from the ways in which American or Western European people's memory systems do. In particular, Cole and Scribner argue:

> It appears that the cultural difference in memory performance tapped in the free-recall studies rests upon the fact that the more sophisticated (highly educated) subjects respond to the task by searching for and imposing a structure upon which to base their recall. Noneducated subjects are not likely to engage in such structure-imposing activity. When they do, or when the task itself gives structure to the material, cultural differences in performance are greatly reduced or eliminated. (p. 139)

We will return to the issue of the effects of education, particularly in Western-type schools, below.

Visual-Spatial Memory

One criticism often raised when traditional, laboratory-based experiments are "exported" to other cultures is that the tasks themselves vary in familiarity, importance, and general level of interest to people therein. If the charge is true, it raises serious problems for any cross-cultural research comparing performance of people from different cultures on the same task. If experimental tasks are not closely derived from tasks people normally engage in during their daily lives, people's performance will not be particularly informative with regard to their real abilities.

Many investigators, taking the criticism seriously, have tried to design studies that closely model real-life tasks. In one such study, Kearins (1981), studying visual-spatial memory in desert Australian Aboriginal children and adolescents, presented subjects with tasks wherein they viewed arrays of objects for 30 seconds, then, after the objects were scrambled, reconstructed the arrays.

Kearins's (1981) rationale was this: Traditional desert living requires a great deal of movement among widely spaced sites, many of which are "visually unremarkable." For various reasons having to do with unpredictable rainfall and the requirements of hunting and other food gathering, the routes between sites are rarely exactly duplicated. Presumably, this requires kinds of spatial knowledge other than route knowledge. One possibility is greater ability to remember spatial relationships:

> Memory for a single environmental feature would be unlikely to have been a reliable identifier of any particular spot, both because outstanding features are rare in this region of many recurring features, and because of the need for approach for any direction. But particular spatial relationships between several features could uniquely specify a location, more or less regardless of orientation. Accurate memory for such relationships is thus likely to have been of considerable value both in movement between water sources and in daily foraging movements from a base camp. (p. 438)

Kearins (1981) presented both Aboriginal and white Australian children with four conditions. In each one, they saw a collection of 20 familiar objects. In two of the conditions, the objects were person-made artifacts (for example, knife, thimble); in two, naturally-occurring objects (for example, feather, rock). In two of the conditions, all of the objects were of the same type (for example, all rocks or all bottles), in two, of different types (for example, a knife, an eraser, a thimble). Testing took place on benches in playgrounds or under trees, and care was taken to minimize the "test-like" nature of the task. Children viewed each array for 30 seconds, then closed their eyes while the objects were jumbled in a heap, then were asked to reconstruct the array with no time limit.

Results, shown in Figure 14-4, revealed that Aboriginal adolescents outperformed their white agemates in every condition. Kearins commented that the task seemed almost too easy for Aboriginal subjects, a significant portion (ranging from 14 to 54% in different conditions, compared to an average of 4.5% for white subjects) made no errors.

Observation of the subjects revealed that Aboriginal subjects tended to sit very still while viewing arrays, and did not show any evidence of rehearsal. White children and adolescents were much more likely to move around in their seats, to pick up objects, and to "mutter." In the reconstruction phase, Aboriginal subjects placed objects at a steady, deliberate pace, and made few changes as they worked. White Australian subjects began the reconstruction phase "in great haste" and subsequently made many changes in where the objects were placed. Kearins believed that Aboriginal subjects were using a visual strategy; white subjects, a verbal strategy. When asked how they were performing the task, Aboriginal subjects tended to shrug or to say they remembered the "look" of the array; white Australians tended to describe verbal rehearsal strategies at length.

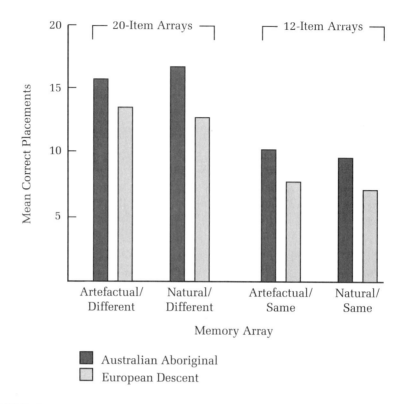

FIGURE 14-4.   Results from Kearins (1981). SOURCE: From "Visual Spatial Memory in Australian Aboriginal Children of Desert Regions," by J. M. Kearins, 1981, *Cognitive Psychology, 13,* 434–460. Copyright © 1981 by Academic Press. Reprinted by Permission.

Kearins (1981) took the data from this and other experiments as supporting her idea that culture can impose "environmental pressure" selectively to enhance certain cognitive skills, in this case, visual rehearsal strategies. She further believed that once a certain skill is established, individuals will be more likely to practice it, thus possibly enhancing it. Moreover, cognitive (and other) skills and habits useful within a culture are likely to be encouraged by parents and other adults from a child's early years. As a result, certain cognitive abilities will become more prevalent and better performed.

Cross-Cultural Studies of Categorization

Imagine walking into a room and seeing a number of blocks of various sizes. On one side of each is painted a small, medium, or large circle, square, or triangle that is red, yellow, or red and yellow striped. Imagine being asked to "put the ones together that go together," a vague instruction that asks you to classify. You can see immediately, I hope, that there are several ways of sorting the blocks: by painted shape, by block size, or by marking. We could observe your performance, and we could ask two questions about it: What basis do you use to classify the blocks, and how consistent are you in using this basis?

According to psychologist Jerome Bruner (Bruner et al., 1966), the way we carry out classification tasks changes with development. At first, we tend to use perceptual bases for classification, especially color (Olver & Hornsby, 1966). Later, the basis of our sorting (when more meaningful objects, as opposed to blocks, are used) becomes less perceptual and more "deep," as we start to group objects together on the basis of function rather than form. So, while a young child might group a carrot and a stick in one set, and a tomato and a ball in another (paying attention to shape), an older child might be expected to group the two foods and the two artifacts. Moreover, children's ability to sort objects *consistently,* using whatever basis they choose, also increases with development.

Patricia Greenfield, a collaborator of Bruner's, carried out similar studies with unschooled Wolof children in rural Senegal, West Africa (Greenfield, Reich, & Olver, 1966). Children (aged 6 to 16) saw ten familiar objects, four of which were red, four of which were items of clothing, and four of which were round (some objects had two or more of these properties). They were told to choose the objects that were "alike," and then to say how they were alike. The question was "Did children use any of these bases in a systematic way, selecting all and only the red objects, all and only the round objects, or all and only the articles of clothing?"

Most of the Wolof children (typically over 65%) selected items on the basis of color, but there was a great improvement with age in their ability to do so systematically. At ages 6 or 7, only about 10% systematically selected all and only the four red objects; at age 9, about 30%; by age 15, close to 100%.

In a second study with schooled and unschooled Wolof children (aged 6 to 13) and unschooled adults, Greenfield and her associates (1966) presented sets of three pictured objects. Within each set, two objects shared a color; two, a shape; and two, a function. Figure 14-5 provides some examples. Subjects were asked to show which two of the three objects in each set were "most alike" and to explain why. Greenfield examined the bases children and adults used to group items. Schooling was found to have a very powerful effect. First, unschooled subjects had more trouble interpreting the pictures and recognizing the depicted objects, a finding consistent with those reported by Hudson (1960), discussed earlier. Second, children who had attended school were much less likely to use color as a classification basis, and the decrease in preference for color was associated with years of schooling. Conversely, sorting on the basis of form and of function both rose with years of schooling. In fact, the use of either form or function as a basis for sorting was "virtually nonexistent" for unschooled subjects (p. 295). In general, the authors concluded that "schooling appears to be the

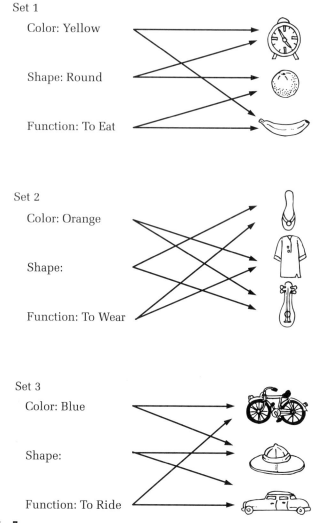

Set 1

Color: Yellow

Shape: Round

Function: To Eat

Set 2

Color: Orange

Shape:

Function: To Wear

Set 3

Color: Blue

Shape:

Function: To Ride

FIGURE 14-5.   Stimuli used by Bruner et al. (1966). SOURCE: From *Studies in Cognitive Growth: A Collaboration at the Center for Cognitive Studies,* by J. S. Bruner, R. Olver, and P. Greenfield. Copyright © 1966 by John Wiley & Sons, Inc. Reprinted by permission.

single most powerful factor we have found in the stimulation of abstraction" (p. 315).

Sharp and Cole, working with Mayan people in Yucatan, Mexico, wondered whether a preference for grouping by color necessarily precluded other bases for grouping (Cole & Scribner, 1974). They presented subjects (children in first, third, and sixth grade, and adolescents with three or fewer years of school) with cards depicting various geometric figures that varied in color, shape, and number (for example, one circle, two circles). After the subjects had sorted the cards, the experimenters asked them to *re-sort* the cards on another dimension. The results showed, first, that the percentage of subjects able to sort consistently on the basis of color, shape, or number rose dramatically with years of schooling. Second, the ability to reclassify also depended on schooling: first graders were almost completely unable to reclassify, and fewer than half of the third graders and adolescents (with three or fewer years of schooling) could reclassify. Sixty percent of the sixth graders were able to re-sort, using a dimension different from that used in the first sort.

Irwin and McLaughlin (1970) found another variable that affected performance on this task. They performed a similar experiment, using stimuli like those employed by Sharp and Cole, and, in another condition, stimuli consisting of eight bowls of rice. Rice was a very familiar quantity to the Mano rice farmers in central Liberia, who were the subjects. The bowls of rice differed in type of bowl (large or small), type of rice (polished or not polished). Results showed that although unschooled adults were not very able to *re-sort* either the cards or the bowls, everyone, including the adults, was much more able to sort the rice than the cards quickly.

In a later study, Irwin and associates (Irwin, Schafer, & Feiden, 1974) worked with Mano farmers and American undergraduates. Both groups were given geometric shapes on cards (in one condition) and rice (in another condition) to sort. As expected, the Mano had trouble with the shapes but sorted the rice quite easily. Conversely, the Americans did quite well sorting and re-sorting the shapes but were less adept at noticing all the possible bases for sorting the rice.

Apparently, then, using familiar materials helps to uncover cognitive competence, a principle we discussed originally in Chapter 12. Once again, the results described in this section provide reasons for caution in interpreting cognitive abilities, especially cross-culturally. There is a tendency to believe that there is only one (or only one correct) way of processing information in a cognitive task. The results from Greenfield, Sharp, and Cole, and Irwin and associates remind us that there may be considerably more flexibility in our cognitive processing, and that the ways in which we approach a task depend on the context, the instructions, and even the stimulus materials.

Cross-Cultural Studies of Reasoning

We saw in Chapter 10 that formal reasoning involves drawing conclusions based solely on the given information, or premises. Many psychologists and philosophers have assumed that such processing underlies the kinds of reasoning and thinking that occurs more frequently, the idea being that problems such as

All men are mortal.
Socrates is a man.
(Therefore) Socrates is mortal.
are basic and therefore rather easy to deal with.

A. R. Luria (1976), a student of the Soviet psychologist Lev Vygotsky, examined how farming residents of Central Asia, some of whom were literate and some of whom were not, approached such verbal syllogisms. Some of the syllogisms had familiar, practical content but required application of a familiar principle to a new environment, for example, "Cotton grows where it is hot and humid. England is cold and damp. Can cotton grow there or not?" or "In the Far North, where there is snow, all bears are white. Novaya Zemlya is in the Far North. What color are the bears there?"

The responses to these syllogisms depended on the background of the farmers. Those with no schooling simply refused to deal with the problem, typically responding something like "I don't know; I've seen a black bear, I've never seen any others. . . . Each locality has its own animals; if it's white, they will be white; if it's yellow; they will be yellow," or "How should I know?" (Luria, 1976, pp. 109–110). One subject, a nonliterate thirty-seven-year-old resident of a remote village, summed up the problem: "We always speak only of what we see; we don't talk about what we haven't seen." [Experimenter: "But what do my words imply?" The syllogism is repeated.] "Well, it's like this: our tsar isn't like yours, and yours isn't like ours. Your words can be answered only by someone who was there, and if a person wasn't there he can't say anything on the basis of your words" (p. 109).

Nonliterate subjects faced three limitations, according to Luria (1976). First, they had difficulty accepting (even for the sake of argument) initial premises that contradicted their own experience. Often, such premises were dismissed and forgotten. Second, nonliterate subjects refused to treat general premises (for example, in the Far North, all bears are white) as truly general. Instead, they treated these statements as descriptions particular to one person's experience, and again often ignored the premise in their reasoning. Third, subjects lacking literacy tended not to see the various premises as parts of a single problem but, rather, treated all the premises as independent pieces of information. The farmers who had participated in a literacy program, by contrast, accepted the fact that conclusions could be drawn not just from their own knowledge but from the problem (premises) itself, and drew the correct conclusion.

Cole and Scribner (1974) report similar results with reasoning tasks given to Kpelle tribespeople from Liberia. The following is an example:

> **Experimenter (local Kpelle man):** At one time spider went to a feast. He was told to answer this question before he could eat any of the food. The question is: Spider and black deer always eat together. Spider is eating. Is black deer eating?
>
> **Subject (village elder):** Were they in the bush?
>
> **Experimenter:** Yes.
>
> **Subject:** Were they eating together?
>
> **Experimenter:** Spider and black deer always eat together. Spider is eating. Is black deer eating?
>
> **Subject:** But I was not there. How can I answer such a question?

> **Experimenter:** Can't you answer it? Even if you were not there, you can answer it. (*Repeats question*)
> **Subject:** Oh, oh, black deer is eating.
> **Experimenter:** What is your reason for saying that black deer is eating?
> **Subject:** The reason is that black deer always walks about all day eating green leaves in the bush. Then he rests for a while and gets up again to eat. (p. 162)*

Notice here a few things. First, the subject avoids answering the question, asserting that his lack of personal knowledge or experience prevents him from knowing the answer. His assumption is that questions can be answered based on only personal, firsthand knowledge. When pressed by the experimenter, the subject comes up with a response, but again gives reasons that are based in his knowledge rather than in the premises of the syllogism itself. In Henle's (1962) terms, the subject has "failed to accept the logical task," refusing to draw conclusions based on (or based on only) the premises supplied by the experimenter.

Other subjects in this study showed different ways of avoiding the task set for them by the experimenter. Some introduced new premises, usually ones that incorporated the subject's personal knowledge, so that a conclusion could be drawn and justified based on this knowledge. Research by Sylvia Scribner suggested that subjects appeared to distort the syllogisms in memory, forgetting some premises, and altering others, as this example shows:

> **Problem:** The chief's brother either gave him a goat or he gave him a chicken. The chief's brother did not give him a goat. Did he give him a chicken?
> **Subject:** Yes. I know he gave it to him.
> (*Subject is then asked to recall the problem*): The chief's brother will give him a goat. If he does not give him a goat, he will give him a chicken.
> **Experimenter:** What question did I ask?
> **Subject:** You asked me, is the chief's brother going to give him a goat?
> **Experimenter:** (*Reads problem again*)
> (*Subject is asked to recall the problem*): Yes. That is what you told me. The chief's brother will give him a goat. If he does not give him a goat, he will give him a chicken.
> **Experimenter:** What question did I ask you?
> **Subject:** You asked me, the chief's brother will give him a goat. If he does not give him a goat, will he give him a chicken? (Cole & Scribner, 1974, p. 165)

Notice here that the subject does not reproduce all the premises in the problem. On each recall, he omits the second premise, that the chief's brother did not give him a goat. Without this premise, the question cannot be answered, perhaps accounting for the fact that the subject continually has difficulty keeping in mind the question asked.

Apparently, then, one difficulty with syllogistic reasoning with non-literate people is their ability or willingness to "remain within problem boundaries" (Cole & Scribner, 1974, p. 168). Instead, people tend to omit, add, or alter premises so that conclusions can be drawn from personal knowledge.

It is worth pointing out that such errors are not unique to people from nonliterate cultures. As we saw in Chapter 12, young children have difficulty staying "within bounds" when working on a reasoning task. In addition, the tendency to alter, omit, or add premises to a syllogism occurs with adults in the United States as well, especially on difficult problems, as Henle (1962) argues. This in turn suggests that the reasoning of people from other cultures does seem similar in terms of basic processes, and that what is difficult for one culture seems also to be difficult for others. There is a suggestion in the data that schooling or literacy helps people's formal reasoning abilities, something we will explore in greater depth below.

Cross-Cultural Studies of Counting

One of the most fascinating lines of cross-cultural cognitive research centers on the development of mathematical (usually arithmetical) knowledge and problem solving. If you think about it, the development and use of an arithmetical system is critical for many kinds of everyday activities in almost all cultures: buying, selling, making change, keeping inventories, determining relative amounts, and the like. It is of great interest to note that not all cultures have developed the same systems, and to examine the ways in which the systems that exist have evolved.

Let us first examine the arithmetical skill of counting. Work by Rochel Gelman and Randy Gallistel (1978) with preschoolers in the United States demonstrated that even very young children in the United States know a great deal about counting. With small numbers (that is, less than about 5), even 2- and 3-year-olds can count the number of items in a set. But what does it mean to count? Gelman and Gallistel offer this surprisingly complicated definition: Counting "involves the coordinated use of several components: noticing the items in an array one after another; pairing each noticed item with a number name; using a conventional list of number names in the conventional order; and recognizing that the last name used represents the numerosity of the array" (p. 73).

Gelman and her colleagues observed the counting behavior of preschoolers, and were able to identify several distinct "principles" of counting. These are described in the following list:

- The One-One Principle. Each item in a to-be-counted array is "ticked" in such a way that one and only one distinct "tick" is assigned to each item.

- The Stable-Order Principle. The tags (count words) assigned to each item must be chosen in a repeatable order.
- The Cardinal Principle. When counting an array, the final tag represents the number of items in the set.
- The Abstraction Principle. Any group of items, whether physical or not, whether of the same type or not, can be counted.
- The Order-Irrelevance Principle. The order of enumeration (that is, which item is tagged "one," and which "two," and so on) of items in a set does not affect the number of items in the set or the counting procedure.*

A child might have some but not all of these principles at any stage of development. Nonetheless, even if her "counting" behavior doesn't exactly match that of an adult, she can be properly described as "counting" if her behavior shows evidence of honoring at least some of the principles. For example, a child aged 2 years and 6 months counted a plate containing three toy mice as follows: "One, two, six!" Asked by the experimenter to count the mice once again, the child happily complied: "Ya, one, two, six!" (Gelman & Gallistel, 1978, p. 91). This child shows clear evidence of respecting the one-one and the stable-order principles, and therefore really *is* counting, even though she uses a different count-word sequence than adults do.

Cross-cultural work by Geoffrey Saxe (1981; Saxe & Posner, 1983) provides evidence that counting systems also vary in different cultures. Saxe reported studies of children in a remote Oksapmin village in Papua New Guinea. Unlike the base-10 system of numbers used in our culture, Saxe found that the Oksapmin developed a body-part counting system with no base structure. Instead, the Oksapmin label 27 distinct body parts on the hands, arms, shoulders, neck, and head. Just as we count on our fingers, the Oksapmin count fingers, as well as arm, shoulder, neck, and head locations, looping back and adding prefixes when they need a number larger than 27. Figure 14-6 illustrates the Oksapmin counting system.

One question that arose for Saxe and others was whether or not the existence of a "baseless" numeration system, as in the one used by the Oksapmin, would change the understanding of certain numerical relations. For example, is a Piagetian number conservation task (see Chapter 12 if you need a review) much harder for Oksapmin children than for U.S. children? Saxe (1981) found that although Oksapmin children generally developed counting and conservation concepts at later ages, their developmental pattern is quite similar to that of children from the United States. It is interesting that Oksapmin who participate frequently in a newly introduced money economy, which requires more arithmetic computation than does more traditional Oksapmin life, are changing and reorganizing their body-part numeration systems to make computation easier.

These studies suggest, once again, that different cultures have

*Reprinted by permission of the publisher from THE CHILD'S UNDERSTANDING OF NUMBER by Rochel Gelman and C. R. Gallistel, Cambridge, Mass.: Harvard University Press, Copyright © 1978 by the President and Fellows of Harvard College.

FIGURE 14-6.   The Oksapmin counting system. The conventional sequence of body parts used by the Oksapmin, in order of occurrence: (1) tip^na, (2) tipnarip, (3) bumrip, (4) h^tdip, (5) h^th^ta, (6) dopa, (7) besa, (8) kir, (9) tow^t, (10) kata, (11) gwer, (12) nata, (13) kina, (14) aruma, (15) tan-kina, (16) tan-nata, (17) tan-gwer, (18) tan-kata, (19) tan-tow^t, (20) tan-kir, (21) tan-besa, (22) tan-dopa, (23) tan-tip^na, (24) tan-tipnarip, (25) tan-bumrip, (26) tan-h^tdip, (27) tan-h^th^ta. SOURCE: From "Body Parts as Numerals: A Developmental Analysis of Numeration Among the Oksapmin in Papua New Guinea," by G. B. Saxe, 1981, *Child Development, 52,* 306–316. Copyright © 1981 by the Society for Research in Child Development, Inc. Reprinted by permission.

numeration systems that differ, sometimes greatly. The systems may affect the ease with which certain numerical concepts are acquired, but the evidence suggests that the relationships between numeration systems and mathematical thinking are complex ones, and therefore predictions are not always easy to make.

Throughout this section, we have seen examples of the ways in which cognitive tasks and performance can differ across different cultures. We have also seen that one important variable affecting a number of different cognitive tasks is schooling. In the next section, we will examine the effects of this variable more closely, trying to isolate just what aspects of schooling produce the effect.

Effects of Schooling and Literacy

What is it about schooling that apparently produces such widespread changes in cognition? Is there something about the curriculum specifically,

Schooling has been shown in many studies to affect performance on a variety of cognitive tasks.

or do the changes result from a more global aspect in the context of going to school? These are questions just beginning to be addressed in the cross-cultural study of cognition.

One candidate for the source of schooling effects is literacy, the ability to read and write. Among many psychological, linguistic, and anthropological scholars is a belief that literacy has profound effects on society (Scribner & Cole, 1981). One assertion to be reviewed is that literacy changes thought in fundamental ways because it allows the mind to expand and to grow. For example, scholars dating back to Plato and Socrates wondered whether written language promoted logical and abstract thinking in a way that oral language does not and cannot (Scribner & Cole, 1981). Goody and Watt (1968) argued, for instance, that disciplines such as history and logic are impossible without written language. Writing a text offers a permanency that oral language does not. This permanency allows people to carry on certain processes that might be impossible otherwise—for example, comparing two sentences, looking for implications or inconsistencies; examining the internal structure or syntax of a sentence.

Lev Vygotsky, a noted Marxist psychologist, argued, as Marx had, that a human being's "nature" was actually the product of his or her interaction with the environment (Vygotsky, 1986). Thus, cognitive processes and capabilities are not simply the result of our biological heritage but, rather, the result of human-environmental interaction, which changes and shapes not only the environment but the nature of our cognition (Scribner & Cole, 1981).

At any given time, the tools available for a task change the ways in which a task is carried out. For example, the invention and availability of word-processing software has changed the ways in which many professors and college students write papers. Vygotsky thought that the same principle applied to the existence of written language: it significantly transformed intellectual processes.

The Laboratory of Comparative Human Cognition (1983) described Vygotskian principles of how cultures affect cognition and cognitive development (p. 335). First, cultures "arrange for the occurrence or non-occurrence" of particular problems and problem-solving environments. For example, whether or not one needs to learn to memorize prayers or pledges depends on whether or not the culture presents tasks or occasions for which they are recited from memory. If the culture does not require such memorization, then people within that culture have less need to develop strategies and approaches to this task.

Second, the culture determines the frequency with which problems and practices occur. Does recitation take place daily? Weekly? Monthly? Frequency will no doubt have an effect on how often practice with the tasks occurs. Third, cultures determine which events go together. Does memorization occur with other tasks, such as reading or measuring? It seems likely that the co-occurrence of two tasks provides a different context for each, and might therefore affect the way each is carried out.

Last, cultures "regulate the level of difficulty" of tasks within contexts (Laboratory of Comparative Human Cognition, 1983, p. 335). Cultures determine how younger members might approach the memorization task, for example, and figure out ways of establishing a graded series of tasks that culminate in final mastery. A 4-year-old, for example, might start out learning simple rhymes and gradually work up to long prayers or epic poems. The culture determines the path from first to final achievement.

Recall discussion of the work of Alexander Luria (a Vygotsky student), who worked with farmers in Uzbekistan, a remote part of the former Soviet Union, during the 1930s (Luria, 1976). During that time, collectivization of farming and industrialization were being introduced, and the region experienced profound socioeconomic changes. As part of this social and economic revolution, some of the residents attended literacy programs. Luria compared the performance of people who had and had not participated in a literacy program on a variety of perceptual, reasoning, and classification tasks. He found consistent group differences: nonliterate people were most likely to respond to tasks in a concrete, perceptual, and context-bound manner; the schooled group showed greater ability or propensity to deal with materials more abstractly and conceptually. Schooled subjects could reason from premises, and draw inferences based on something other than their own experience.

One problem in interpreting Luria's (1976) findings is that two related but conceptually independent factors were confounded: literacy and schooling. As Scribner and Cole (1981) note, schooling and literacy are often related but are not synonymous. In Luria's research, the subjects who were literate were also those who had attended schools; the nonliterate subjects were also unschooled.

What effects might schooling have on cognition? First of all, it is worth noting the somewhat bizarre demands school itself places on students. School is one of the few places one encounters where one person (the teacher) asks questions of other people (the students) that she or he already knows the answer to. Think how incongruous this situation would be in other contexts. Imagine someone walking up to you to ask directions to the library. Being a local resident, you know the way and provide a set of directions, for example, "Go up two blocks to the light, take a right, then take your first left, go halfway down the block, and you'll see it." Next, your conversation partner tells you that your directions are faulty, that there is a simpler way to go. Would you feel this conversation was "normal" or "typical"? Only in school-like situations can a teacher pose questions for the purpose of assessing students' knowledge rather than of obtaining information. This makes the school context somewhat removed from everyday life.

School differs from everyday contexts in a number of other respects. The subjects taught often make little contact with everyday life; students learning about, say, geography or history may never have the chance to experience the phenomenon being discussed. Some of the subjects taught are abstract (for example, arithmetic and geometry) and make little direct appearance in day-to-day living. The motivation to complete a task, for example, learning a spelling list, are not intrinsic to the task itself in a way that the motivation for an everyday task, for example, learning to ride a bike, is. In the latter case, you learn because the task itself is important to you; in the former case, students often learn because the teacher or parent tells them to do so. Bruner (1966) has argued that because of this, schooling provides practice in thinking about abstract topics in a *decontextualized* way, that is, removed from the present context of here and now: "[T]he important thing about the school . . . is that it *is* removed from immediate context of socially relevant action. This very disengagement makes learning an act in itself. . . . *Verbal* understanding, the ability to *say* it and to enumerate instances becomes the criterion of learning" (pp. 62–63).

Scribner and Cole (1981) carried out a series of studies to disentangle the effects of literacy from the effects of schooling. They worked with the Vai people in Liberia, West Africa, during the 1970s. The Vai are an interesting people to study because they invented their own writing system, called *Vai script,* that they use for many commercial and personal transactions. Vai script is taught not in school but in the home. Although only about 7% of the entire population was literate in Vai script at the time of the study, it was the most common written language known by adult males (20% were literate in Vai script; 16% in Arabic [acquired mostly in the context of learning the Qur'an]; and 6% in English, the official language of schools and government).

Interviews were held with 650 people, all aged 15 or older. In addition to a lengthy autobiographical questionnaire (regarding demographic information, schooling and literacy status, family schooling and literacy status, occupation, and the like), all respondents participated in an hour-long session in which various cognitive tasks were administered (Scribner & Cole, 1981). Included in these were sorting tasks (stimuli used included both geometric figures and familiar objects), memory tasks (for example, recalling the names of objects used in the sorting tasks), a logic task (presenting syllogisms, such as those described earlier), and a task of linguistic awareness (for example, asking whether the names of the objects "sun" and "moon" could be switched, and what the consequences of such a switch would be). For some of the tasks, subjects were asked to provide verbal explanations, which were later scored.

Scribner and Cole divided their subjects into seven groups. The first six included only men 15 and older: nonliterate men; men who were literate with Vai script only; men literate in Arabic only; men literate in both Arabic and Vai; men who had attended some school and were literate in English, Arabic, and Vai; and men who had attended ten years or more of school. The seventh group consisted of nonliterate women 15 and older (the data from eleven literate Vai women were not reported, presumably because the women were quite atypical in their literacy).

The general design called for comparisons of nonliterates, Vai script literates, and schooled groups. The results, some of which are summarized in Table 14-2, were quite surprising. For most of the cognitive tasks, there were only scattered and small effects of literacy per se. The authors concluded that unschooled literacy (for example, acquisition of Vai script literacy in the home) does not produce the general cognitive effects previously reported by Luria (1976) and others.

Schooling, on the other hand, did produce a number of effects. Most evidently, schooling, especially that with English instruction, increased the ability to provide verbal explanations and justifications. The subjects who had attended school were much better able to provide coherent explanations of their answers than the subjects who hadn't attended school. The group differences in explanations were sometimes evident even when the schooled and unschooled groups did not differ in performance. In other words, schooling affected not so much which responses were chosen but, rather, the skill with which the respondent could explain and justify his choice.

There were some specific tasks on which Scribner and Cole did discover literacy effects, however. Most of these had to do with knowledge of language in one form or another. For example, literate subjects were more likely to give good explanations of what makes for grammaticality of sentences in Vai. They also found it easier to learn to "read" other scripts, modeled after children's rebus puzzles (see Figure 14-7 for an example of a rebus puzzle). Scribner and Cole used these principles to invent Vai

TABLE 14-2.   Results of Scribner and Cole (1981)

Tasks and Measures	Nonliterate men	Vai-Script Mono literate	Arabic Mono literate	Vai-Arabic Biliterate	English Schooled	Grade 10+	Nonliterate Women
Geometric sorting (number dimensions sorted out of 3)	1.6	2.0	2.0	1.9	1.7	1.9	1.7
Verbal explanation (max score = 12)	5.3	5.1	5.8	5.6	5.6	9.3	4.9
Classification (max score = 6)	3.4	3.5	3.0	3.5	3.8	3.9	3.4
Verbal explanation (max score = 42)	31.5	31.2	29.0	29.5	32.5	34.6	30.5
Memory (number recalled, max = 24)	16.2	16.0	16.2	16.2	17.1	14.9	16.5
Logic number correct max = 6)	1.6	1.3	1.7	1.5	3.0	3.9	1.7
Theoretic explanations (max = 10)	6.1	5.7	6.2	5.7	7.6	7.9	6.2
Language objectivity (max = 3)	.7	.5	.9	1.2	1.3	1.3	.7

SOURCE: Reprinted and adapted with permission of the publishers from THE PSYCHOLOGY OF LITERACY by Sylvia Scribner and Michael Cole, Cambridge, Mass.: Harvard University Press, Copyright © 1981 by the President and Fellows of Harvard College.

rebuses, and taught these puzzles to both Vai-literate (unschooled) and non-literate villagers. Literate subjects learned the task much more easily, and significantly outperformed the nonliterate subjects.

What can we make of Scribner and Cole's (1981) findings? Contrary to some conventional wisdom, their studies do not support the idea that either literacy or schooling has profound effects on the ways in which cognitive processes operate. Although it is true that on some tasks, schooled and/or literate subjects outperformed unschooled, nonliterate subjects, it is also true that the latter group often performed just as well, or only slightly worse, than the former groups. However, both literacy and schooling do apparently affect the ways in which some cognitive tasks are carried out, at least in some circumstances. So, apparently, both schooling and literacy make a difference to cognition, at least sometimes.

Reviewing all of their findings, Scribner and Cole (1981) developed a "practice account of literacy" as a framework for understanding the exper-

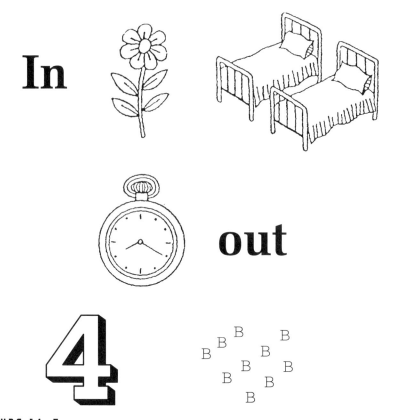

FIGURE 14-7.   Example of a rebus puzzle. Translation: In flower beds, watch out for bees. SOURCE: Reprinted and adapted with permission of the publishers from THE PSYCHOLOGY OF LITERACY by Sylvia Scribner and Michael Cole, Cambridge, Mass.: Harvard University Press, Copyright © 1981 by the President and Fellows of Harvard College.

imental results. By "practice," they refer to "a recurrent, goal-directed sequence of activities using a particular technology and particular systems of knowledge." These authors examine the knowledge and skills required for literacy, and the knowledge and skills that the practice of literacy enables. What one does to become literate, and what one does when one practices his or her literacy (say, by reading or writing a letter) strengthen some very specific skills. Scribner and Cole assert that literacy does not promote broad, general, cognitive changes but, rather, more localized and task-specific, contextualized ones.

The same kind of argument might account for the effects of schooling. Recall that schooled Vai outperformed unschooled Vai only on tasks requiring verbal explanations. Scribner and Cole (1981) point to the "practice" of schooling, particularly English schooling, as a potent cause. Schools are places in which a premium is placed on the ability to offer an articulate set of reasons for one's responses, and to figure out ways to approach and master tasks removed from practical experience (Bruner, 1966). No wonder, then, that those with the most experience in this setting show the best ability to apply the specific skills this setting promotes in other circumstances.

To summarize, Scribner and Cole (1981) argue that cognitive skills are often context-bound. From their perspective, it seems unlikely that there exist many broad cognitive abilities or skills such as "thinking" or "categorization" that can be affected or improved by one or a few manipulations. Instead, these authors would argue that cognition is *situated,* or intimately bound, to the conditions in which it naturally occurs. One's culture and one's everyday surroundings and tasks set both boundaries and possibilities for the cognitive tasks that are practiced and therefore strengthened. Context and culture affect, and are affected by, cognition.

Situated Cognition in Everyday Settings

Situated cognition is not simply a phenomenon that occurs in foreign, distant cultures. Sylvia Scribner's recent work before her death included field studies in the United States at an industrial milk-processing plant (a "dairy"), investigating on-the-job cognition, or what she called "working intelligence" (Scribner, 1984, p. 9). In particular, she drew a distinction between practical and theoretical thought (1986). The latter is the kind of thinking demanded in many school activities: thinking divorced from a meaningful context, carried out on a task of perhaps limited interest, performed for its own sake. Practical thought, by contrast, is more familiar, and involves thinking "embedded in the larger purposive activities of daily life . . . [that] functions to achieve the goals of those activities" (p. 15). Examples include figuring out a supermarket "best buy" or diagnosing the cause of malfunctioning machinery.

The site of Scribner's (1984) field studies employed 300 people in both white- and blue-collar positions. Certain blue-collar tasks were selected for study. These included product assembly (a warehouse job), inventory, and pricing delivery tickets. Scribner and associates began by observing people performing these jobs under normal working conditions, then constructing and presenting workers with experimental simulations of these tasks.

From her earlier cross-cultural research, Scribner (1984) believed that cognitive skills are dependent upon "socially organized experiences" (p. 10). That means that the way in which a cognitive task is approached varies according to the environment and the context. She found the same sorts of patterns emerging in the dairy: even as apparently so basic a task as mental calculation was accomplished in different ways by the same people in different circumstances.

The product assemblers (or preloaders, as they are sometimes called) provide a concrete example. Their job consists mainly of putting together specified quantities of various products and getting them ready to be loaded onto trucks. Scribner describes the working conditions in more detail:

> Product assembly is a warehouse job. It is classified as unskilled manual labor and is one of the lowest paying jobs in the dairy. The perishable nature of dairy products requires that warehouse temperature be maintained at 38 degrees Fahrenheit; accordingly, the warehouse is, and is refered to as, an icebox. During the day, thousands of cases of milk products (e.g. skim milk, chocolate milk) and fruit drinks are moved on conveyor belts from the plant filling machines into the icebox, where they are stacked in designated areas along with many other dairy products (e.g. yogurt, cottage cheese). Preloaders arrive at the icebox at 6 p.m. Awaiting them is a sheaf of route delivery orders, called load-out order forms. Each form lists the products and their amounts that a wholesale driver has ordered for his next day's delivery. The preloader's task is to locate each product. Using a long metal "hook," he pulls the required number of cases and partial cases of that product and transports them to a common assembly area near a moving track that circles the icebox. When all the items of a given truck order are assembled, they are pulled onto the track and carried past a checkpoint to the loading platform. (pp. 18–19)

Scribner noticed an interesting problem that preloaders faced in their jobs. Truck drivers wrote orders that expressed quantities of items in terms of one set of units (for example, quarts of milk, half-pints of chocolate milk), but fluid products in the warehouse were stored in cases, not in units. Cases of all products were the same size, but contained a different number of units, depending on the product. So, a full case could contain 4 gallon units, 9 half-gallon units, 16 quart units, 32 pint units, or 48 half-pint units.

Load-out forms were created by computer by converting drivers' orders into cases. So, a request for 4 gallons of fruit juice by a particular driver would be translated into one case. Often, a driver's request did not divide evenly into number of cases. For example, if a driver requested 5 gallons of milk, that would translate into 1 case + 1 unit. The load-out forms followed the following convention: If the number of "leftover" units was equal to half a case or less, the order was expressed as the number of cases + the number of units (as in the 5-gallon example). If the number of "leftover" units was more than half a case, the number was expressed as the number of cases minus the number of units. So, in the case of quarts (which come 16 to a case), if a driver ordered 30 quarts of chocolate milk, the load-out form would read 1 (case = 16 quarts) + 1 case − 2 (quarts), that is, 16 + 14. (Warning: this system is not intuitive, so work through this example carefully yourself.)

Scribner's question was how preloaders dealt with mixed numbers, such as 3 + 1, or 7 − 5, in assembling orders. You might think that such a question is easily answered in a fairly obvious way: A preloader with an order for 1 − 6 would simply grab one case, and remove 6 units from it. It is interesting that this is not what happened. In fact, the preloaders handled the very same problem (that is, 1 − 6) in several different ways. Sometimes they filled the order in the "obvious" way just described. Other times, they mentally "rewrote" the order, and used nearby partially filled cases to reduce the actual number of units that had to be moved. For example, when a nearby partially filled case of quarts (remember, 16 quarts to the case) contained 14 quarts, the preloader simply removed 4 (1 case − 6 quarts = 10 quarts; 14 quarts − 4 quarts = 10 quarts). In another situation, a partially filled case contained 8 quarts, and the preloader simply added two more.

Scribner (1984, 1986) found that although the same problem was solved in different ways, the solution always honored the following rule: satisfy the order with the least number of moves, that is, the least number of transfers of product units. Even when the "saving" of labor was small (for example, saving one transfer in an order totaling 500 units), experienced preloaders rapidly and almost automatically calculated and followed the most efficient solution. The mental calculations required are impressive because of both the rapidity and the accuracy of calculation. Errors were rarely made. And, most of the time the workers were assembling a group of orders at the same time, thus most certainly increasing the cognitive demands.

It also turned out that on-the-job training was necessary to develop this cognitive flexibility. "Novice" preloaders, that is, other workers in the dairy and a comparison group of ninth graders, were much less efficient and skilled, relative to the preloaders, at finding the optimal solution. Scribner (1984) constructed a simulation task with various orders and administered it to other dairy workers and to a group of ninth-grade students. When the optimal solution required some mental transformation of the order, preloaders found it about 72% of the time; inventory people (many of whom had some experience working as a preloader), 65%; clerks at the dairy (with little if any product assembly experience), 47%; and ninth graders, 25%. Students in particular tended to be very "algorithmic" and "literal" in their approaches to problems, solving each problem in the same way and in the way specified on the load-out form even when much easier strategies (that required some mental transformations) were available.

Scribner found similar examples of cognitive flexibility in other experienced workers working at other jobs. She concludes that although formal problem solving, such as that required in school, on tests, and in many cognitive-psychology experiments, requires or encourages set approaches and fixed rules, practical thinking does not. Instead, practical thinking "frequently hinges on an apt formulation or redefinition of the initial problem" (1986, p. 21). Practical problem solving is flexible and requires different approaches to the "same" problem, with each approach tailored to the immediate context. Note the difference between this kind of thinking and "academic" thinking, typically requiring or at least encouraging all instances of a problem to be solved in the same way.

Similar findings were reported in another kind of "work" setting, a grocery store (Lave, Murtaugh, & de la Rocha, 1984). Although not generally thought of as part of a paying job, grocery shopping is a frequent activity that must be completed to maintain a family. Lave and associates studied

25 grocery shoppers. Participants represented a range of socioeconomic statuses and had varying educational backgrounds. Researchers accompanied shoppers throughout shopping trips, and recorded conversations they had with shoppers.

Typical supermarkets contain around 7,000 distinct items, and typical shoppers purchase about 50 weekly (Lave et al., 1984). Obviously, then, the number of potential decisions to be made is quite large. How does the typical shopper manage to complete the chore in about an hour?

Again, the answer has to do with cognitive flexibility, and adapting solutions to specific features of the problem. One shopper, for example, found a package of cheese marked with a price the shopper found to be surprisingly high. To determine whether the price was correct, he found another package of cheese in the bin that weighed approximately the same amount. He then compared the prices on the two packages and found them to be indeed discrepant. Which one had the error? To find out, he compared these two packages to others in the bin, determining that the first one was, in fact, priced incorrectly. Notice here a "saving" in amount of mental effort: although he could have calculated the price per ounce of each package, such calculations are mentally demanding and subject to error. Instead, he found an alternate way of solving the problem that is both more easily accomplished, and less likely to be inaccurate.

Lave and his associates have used the grocery store as a setting for studies of cognitive processing in everyday life.

Lave and his associates (1984) were specifically interested in the arithmetic people used in grocery stores. They found that people's in-store arithmetic was virtually flawless—accuracy was 98%, compared with an average accuracy of 59% that the same people had on "school-like" arithmetic tests. Why the discrepancy? In part, people often invented ways of circumventing the traditional calculations, as in the example above. Again, we see that the skills learned in school may be used outside the classroom but in ways that can be much more creative, flexible, and effective.

Summary

Our brief look at cross-cultural cognitive research has yielded a number of important points. First, the ways in which a cognitive task is approached and executed need not be exactly the same for all people at all times. Some tasks, by virtue of their familiarity, are easier to do, at least in the way expected by a cognitive psychologist from our culture. As Wober (1969) puts it, too often the blind adoption of cognitive tasks developed in one culture to study the cognition of people from another culture simply measures "How well can *they* do *our* tricks?" People from the second culture may perform poorly on the test but still have the cognitive capacities the test was designed to measure.

Cross-cultural research has shown us that people from different cultures find ways of solving the cognitive (and other) challenges that confront them. A given environment, including a cultural one, strengthens certain skills, strategies, and approaches at the expense of others. This in turn makes certain tasks easier and more "natural" and others harder.

Our examination has also reinforced another point made earlier: cognition is often quite flexible. Practice with any task will typically speed execution and enable greater accuracy. This point raises another one, however: practice often affects the way a task is done. This suggests that researchers need assess not only the familiarity of a task to a person from a given culture but also the person's specific level of practice with that (or a similar) task.

We have also seen that formal schooling changes some, although certainly not all, important aspects of cognitive processing. In particular, schooling affects one's ability to deal with more "abstract" materials, to rely less heavily on contextual, immediate cues from the surrounding environment, and to explain one's responses and thinking more clearly. Schooling also helps people figure out how to approach novel tasks, especially in planning and structuring. All in all, schooling apparently helps people "step back" from their everyday routine, and also promotes their thinking from different points of view. And, as the Laboratory of Comparative Human Cognition (1983) points out, school prepares people especially well to participate in cognitive-psychology experiments!

Interestingly, basic academic skills turn out not to be entirely optimal in the cognitive challenges that confront people in their everyday lives. Practice with a specific task, whether grocery shopping or conducting inventory, apparently leads to the invention of clever shortcuts that serve the function of reducing the effort (mental or physical) required and of increasing accuracy. Although schools might insist that students approach all calculation problems in similar ways, research is beginning to suggest that in the "real world," the approaches taken to a problem vary with the immediate context.

A general and important point made throughout the chapter is this: models of a cognitive process often presume, implicitly, that the task in question is universally important and familiar, an assumption this chapter has questioned. Relatedly, existing cognitive models often assume that the same cognitive procedures are used the same way for all versions of a problem, although new research challenges this belief. Dropping these assumptions will no doubt make the job of cognitive researchers much more difficult. In the long run, however, the new models built will be more accurate and more complete.

Recommended Readings

Two excellent introductions to cross-cultural cognitive research come from the same authors: Cole and Scribner (1974) and Scribner and Cole (1981). The former is a more dated but more introductory treatment of relevant issues; the latter details a specific project investigating the consequences of literacy among the Vai in Liberia.

An edited volume by Berry and Dasen (1974) contains a number of classic studies; Irvine and Berry (1988) present a series of more recent and more theoretical papers, as do Berry, Irvine, and Hunt (1988). Recent review articles are those of the Laboratory of Comparative Human Cognition (1983), Kagitçibasi and Berry (1989), and Segall (1986). These describe cross-cultural research more generally but include a number of references to recent studies. Lonner and Berry (1986) have edited a book about research methods in cross-cultural work, and the points they raise bear on the topics discussed here in important ways. A four-volume work edited by Triandis and Lonner (1980) also reviews almost all aspects of cross-cultural research.

Deregowski (1989) presents an extensive review of cross-cultural studies of perception, particularly pictorial and space perception. Miller and Stigler (1987) present an interesting analysis of counting in Chinese, while Stevenson and colleagues (1990) analyze how attitudes toward mathematics among Americans and Chinese may be affecting mathematics achievement in the two cultures. Gallistel and Gelman (1992) describe a preverbal system of counting they believe to be the source of the principles used in verbal counting.

David Olson (1986, 1987) discusses the psychological consequences of literacy. Ceci (1991) offers a controversial argument that schooling influences the cognitive processes that in turn underlie performance on IQ tests.

A number of articles on everyday cognition are included in two volumes, one edited by Rogoff and Lave (1984), the other by Sternberg and Wagner (1986). Jean Lave (1988) gives a report on a number of studies of the uses of arithmetic in nonschool settings. Geoffrey Saxe (1992) presents an updated view of the role of cultural practices and educational activities in children's learning.

Finally, Markus and Kitayama (1991) discuss cross-cultural differences in how people perceive and think about themselves, and the implications of these differences on cognition, emotion, and motivation.

REVIEW QUESTIONS

1. What does it mean to assert that a particular cognitive capacity or skill is culturally relative or culturally universal? How do the assertions differ?
2. Describe Hudson's studies of pictorial perception and discuss their implications.
3. Kearins concluded that culture can impose "environmental pressure" on certain cognitive skills. Discuss this conclusion with respect to empirical findings (either those of Kearins or others).
4. Schooling appears to help cognitive performance, especially on tasks such as formal reasoning. Explain why this might be so.
5. Schooling and literacy are distinct factors that appear to affect cognitive performance differently. Describe one or two of the differences and speculate on reasons for the difference.
6. How are Scribner's studies of dairy workers consistent with, and inconsistent with, cross-cultural studies of cognition?

Glossary

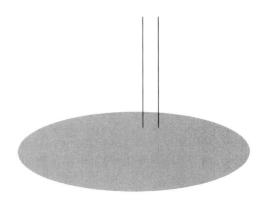

Affordance A term associated with Gibsonian theories of perception, referring to the things an object or event offers to the organism perceiving it. Gibson makes a controversial assertion that affordances are directly perceived.

Amnesia A loss of memory, usually memory for either recent events or memory for past events.

Analytic processing of information Attending to particular parts or aspects of a situation in processing information about it.

Artificial intelligence A branch of computer science in which ways of making computers perform tasks that are thought to require "intelligence," "problem-solving," or other kinds of cognition when performed by human beings are studied.

Association A connection or link between two units or elements.

Attention Cognitive resources, mental effort, or concentration devoted to a cognitive process.

Attention, divided The ways in which a cognitive processor allocates cognitive resources to two or more tasks that are carried out simultaneously.

Attention, selective The focusing of cognitive resources on one or a small number of tasks to the exclusion of others.

Automatic processing The carrying out of a cognitive task with minimal resources. Typically, automatic processing is that which occurs without intention, interferes minimally with other cognitive tasks, and may not involve conscious awareness.

Availability heuristic A strategy in which one estimates the frequency or probability of an event by the ease with which mental operations such as retrieval of examples or construction of examples can be carried out.

Behaviorism A school of psychology that seeks to define psychological research in terms of observable measures, emphasizing the scientific study of behavior.

Between-subjects design A research paradigm in which different experimental subjects participate in different experimental conditions.

Bias A tendency to think in a certain way or to follow certain procedures regardless of the facts of the matter.

Bottom-up processes Cognitive (usually perceptual) processes that are guided by environmental input. Also called "data-driven" processes.

Calibration curve A plot of accuracy against confidence judgments. The more the curve approaches a 45-degree line, the better the "calibration" or "fit" between the two.

Capacity The sum total of cognitive resources available at any given time.

Categorization The organization of information into coherent, meaningful groups.

Category A grouping of items sharing one or more similarities.

Chunking The formation of individual units of information into larger units. This is often used as a means of overcoming short-term memory limitations.

Clinical interview A research paradigm in which an investigator begins by asking a series of open-ended questions of participants but follows up on the responses with specific questions that have been prepared in advance.

Coding The form in which information is mentally or internally represented.

Cognitive economy A principle of hierarchical semantic networks such that properties and facts about a node are stored at the highest level possible. For example, the fact "is alive" would be stored with the node for "animal" rather than stored with each node under animal, such as "dog," "cat," and the like.

Cognitive neuropsychology A school of psychology that investigates the cognitive abilities and deficits of people with damaged or otherwise unusual brain structures.

Cognitive science An interdisciplinary field drawing on research from cognitive psychology, computer science, philosophy, linguistics, neuroscience, and anthropology. The central issues addressed involve the nature of mind and cognition, how information is acquired, stored, and represented.

Cognitive style A habitual and/or preferred means of approaching cognitive tasks.

Competence (versus performance) Underlying knowledge that allows a cognitive processor to engage in a particular cognitive activity, independent of behavior expressing that knowledge.

Concept A mental representation of a category.

Confirmation bias A tendency to seek only information consistent with one's hypothesis.

Connectionism A newly developed approach to cognition emphasizing parallel processing of information through immense networks of interconnected nodes. Models developed in the con-

nectionist tradition are sometimes declared to share certain similarities with the way collections of neurons operate in the brain; hence, some connectionist models are referred to as *neural networks*.

Context effects The effects on a cognitive process (for example, perception) of the information surrounding the target object or event. Sometimes called "expectation effects" because the context is thought to set up certain expectations in the mind of the cognitive processor.

Contradiction A statement that is false by definition of its form (for example, "*A* and not-*A* are both true").

Controlled observation A research paradigm in which an observer standardizes the conditions of observation for all participants, often introducing specific manipulations and recording responses.

Controlled processing The carrying out of a cognitive task with a deliberate allocation of cognitive resources. Typically, controlled processing is that which occurs on difficult and/or unfamiliar tasks requiring attention, and is under conscious control.

Creativity Cognitive processes that employ appropriate novelty; originality that suits some purpose.

Critical thinking A type of thinking that involves careful examination of assumptions and evidence, and that is purposeful and deliberate.

Cultural relativism A belief that cognitive practices, beliefs, competences, and capacities differ from culture to culture, depending on the tasks and contexts specific to a culture.

Cultural universality A belief that cognitive practices, beliefs, competences, and capacities do not differ from culture to culture but are common to humankind.

Data-driven processes See **Bottom-up processes.**

Decay A hypothesized process of forgetting in which material is thought to erode, break apart, or otherwise disintegrate or fade.

Decision analysis A technology that helps people to gather and integrate information in an optimal way.

Decision making The process(es) by which a processor selects one course of action from among alternatives.

Declarative memory A memory system thought to contain knowledge, facts, information, ideas, or anything that can be recalled and described in words, pictures, or symbols.

Deductive validity A property of some logical arguments such that it is impossible for the premises to be true and the conclusion(s) to be false.

Demand characteristics A property of certain tasks such that an experimental subject's behavior or responses are "cued" by the task itself.

Descriptive models of thinking Models that depict the processes people actually use in making decisions or solving problems.

Dichotic listening task A task in which a person hears two or more different, specially recorded messages over earphones and is asked to attend to one of them.

Direct perception A theory of perception by James J. Gibson that holds that information in the world is "picked up on" by the cognitive processor without much construction of internal representations or inferences. The emphasis is on the direct acquisition of information.

Dual-coding hypothesis Paivio's assertion that long-term memory can code information in two distinct ways, verbally and visually, and that items coded both ways (for example, pictures or concrete words) are more easily recalled than items coded in only one way (for example, abstract words).

Ecological approach An approach to the study of cognition emphasizing the natural contexts or settings in which cognitive activities occur, and the influences such settings have in the ways in which cognitive activities are acquired, practiced, and executed.

Ecological validity A property of research such that the focus of study is something that occurs naturally outside an experimental laboratory.

Effect size (*d*) A measure used in meta-analysis that is defined as the difference in mean scores between two groups, divided by the average standard deviation for the two groups.

Empiricism A philosophical doctrine emphasizing the role of experience in the acquisition of knowledge.

Encoding The cognitive process(es) by which information is translated into a mental or internal representation and stored.

Encoding specificity A principle of retrieval asserted by Tulving: at the time material is first put into long-term memory, it is encoded in a particular way, depending on the context present at the time; at the time of recall, the person is at a great advantage if the same information available at encoding is once again available.

Episodic memory A memory system proposed by Tulving that is thought to hold memories of specific events with which the cognitive processor had direct experience.

Expected utility theory A normative model of decision making in which the decision maker weights the personal importance and the probabilities of different outcomes in choosing among alternatives in order to maximize overall satisfaction of personal goals.

Experimental control A property of research such that the causes of different behaviors or other phenomena can be isolated and tested. Typically, this involves manipulating independent variables and holding all factors but the one(s) of interest constant.

Experimenter expectancy effects The influences on the performance of experimental subjects generated by an experimenter's beliefs or hypotheses, which somehow get subtly translated to the subjects.

Explicit memory Memory that is consciously recalled or recollected.

Fallacy An erroneous argument.

Family resemblance A structure of categories in which each member shares different features with different members. Few, if any, features are shared by every single member of the category.

Featural analysis   A model of perception emphasizing the analysis of a stimulus into parts, called features.

Feature   A component, or part, of an object, event, or representation.

Feature, characteristic   A feature that is typically, though not always, a part of an object or concept.

Feature, defining   A feature that is necessarily a part of an object or concept. Also called a *necessary feature*.

Filter theory   A theory of attention that proposes that information that exceeds the capacity of a processor to process at any given time is blocked from further processing.

Flashbulb memory   A phenomenon in which people recall their personal circumstances (for example, where they were, whom they were with, what they were doing) at the time they heard of or witnessed an unexpected and very significant event (for example, an assassination, a natural disaster).

Forgetting   The processes that prevent information from being retrieved from a memory store.

Functional fixedness   A problem-solving phenomenon in which people have difficulty seeing alternate uses for common objects.

Functionalism   A school of psychology emphasizing questions such as why the mind or a particular cognitive process works the way(s) in which it does.

Gambler's fallacy   An erroneous belief that a random process (for example, a coin flip or a spin of a roulette wheel) will automatically keep track of the outcomes in order to make the overall rate of an outcome in the short run equal to the overall rate of that outcome in the long run.

Generate-and-test   A problem-solving strategy in which the solver enumerates (generates) possible solutions and then tries each one to see if it constitutes a solution.

Genetic epistemology   A Piagetian approach to the study of cognitive development that emphasizes the intellectual structures underlying cognitive experience at different developmental points, and the ways in which the structures adapt to environmental experience.

Gestalt principles of perceptual organization   Laws that explain the regularities in the way people come to the perceptual interpretations of stimuli. The emphasis is on the apprehension of whole structures rather than the detection and assembly of parts of structures. The principles include those of closure, common fate, good continuation, Pragnanz, proximity, and similarity.

Gestalt psychology   A school of psychology emphasizing the study of whole entities rather than simple elements. Gestalt psychologists concentrated on problems of perception and problem solving, and argued that people's cognitive experience was not reducible to their experience of simple elements (for example, sensations) but, rather, to the overall structure(s) of their experience.

Grammar   A system of rules that produces well-formed, or "legal," entities, such as sentences of a language.

Heuristic   A rule of thumb, or shortcut method, used in thinking, reasoning, and/or decision making.

Hindsight bias   A tendency to exaggerate the certainty of what could have been anticipated ahead of time.

Holistic processing of information   Attending to global aspects of a situation in processing information about it.

Human factors engineering   An applied area of research that focuses on the design of equipment and technology that are well suited to people's cognitive capabilities.

Ill-defined problem   A problem that does not have the goals, starting information, and/or legal steps stated explicitly.

Implicit memory   Memory that is not deliberate or conscious but exhibits evidence of prior experience.

Incidental learning   The retention of information even when it is not required of, or even intended by, the processor.

Individual differences Stable patterns of performance that differ qualitatively and/or quantitatively across individuals.

Inductive strength A property of some logical arguments such that it is improbable (but not impossible) for the premises to be true and the conclusion false.

Inference rules Hypothesized special-purpose rules used in reasoning to draw conclusions. Reasoning is sometimes defined in terms of the use of these special-purpose rules.

Information-processing An approach to cognition that makes use of a computer metaphor in its explanations. Information-processing equates cognition with the acquisition, storage, and manipulation of information (for example, what we see, hear, read about, think about) through a system consisting of various storage places and systems of exchange.

Intelligence Postulated by some psychologists to represent the sum total of a person's cognitive abilities and resources.

Interference A hypothesized process of forgetting in which material is thought to be buried or otherwise displaced by other information but still exists somewhere in a memory store.

Introspection A methodological technique in which trained observers are asked to reflect upon, and report on, their conscious experience while performing cognitive tasks.

Knowledge representation The mental depiction, storage, and organization of information.

Language A system of communication that is governed by a system of rules (a grammar) and can express an infinite number of propositions.

Language acquisition The process(es) by which a cognitive processor comes to develop linguistic competence and performance.

Lateralization Specialization of function of the two cerebral hemispheres.

Levels of processing An alternative to the modal view of memory, proposed by Craik and Lockhart, that postulates that memory depends *not* on a particular memory store but on the initial processing done to the information at the time of acquisition. "Shallow" or superficial levels of processing (for example, processing at the level of visual shape or acoustic sound) are thought to lead to less retention than "deeper" levels of processing (for example, processing done on the meaning of the information).

Lexical decision task A task in which an experimental subject is presented with letter strings and asked to judge, as quickly as possible, if the strings form words.

Lexicon A mental store thought to hold a cognitive processor's knowledge of words, including their spelling, pronunciation, definition, part of speech, and so on.

Limited-capacity processor A system that acquires, stores, manipulates, and/or transmits information but has fixed limits on the amount or rate of processing that it can accomplish.

Linguistics A field of study focusing on the structure, use, and acquisition of language.

Logical connectives Symbols used in logical arguments used to form compound propositions. Examples: $\&, v$.

Long-term memory A memory store thought to have a large, possibly infinite capacity that holds onto incoming information for long periods of time, perhaps permanently. Also called "secondary memory."

Means-ends analysis A problem-solving strategy in which the solver compares the goal to the current state, then chooses a step to reduce maximally the difference between them.

Memory The cognitive processes underlying the storage, retention, and retrieval of information.

Memory system A kind of memory (for example, episodic memory, semantic memory) that operates on distinct principles and stores a distinct kind of information.

Memory trace The mental representation of stored information.

Mental representation An internal depiction of information.

Mental rotation   A type of visual imagery task in which subjects are asked to form an image of a stimulus and then to imagine how it would look as it rotates around a horizontal or vertical axis.

Mental set   The tendency to adopt a certain framework, strategy, or procedure based on immediate experience or context.

Meta-analysis   A technique to review findings in the literature involving the use of specific statistical methods in integrating the findings from different empirical studies.

Metacognition   Awareness or knowledge of one's own cognitive processes and systems.

Mnemonics   Strategies to facilitate retention and later retrieval of information.

Modal approach to memory   A theoretical approach to the study of memory that emphasizes the existence of different memory stores, for example, sensory memory, short-term memory, long-term memory.

Modularity hypothesis   Fodor's proposal that some cognitive processes, in particular language and perception, operate on only certain kinds of inputs and operate independent of the beliefs and other information available to the cognitive processor or other cognitive processes.

Morpheme   The smallest meaningful unit of language.

Multiattribute utility theory (MAUT)   A normative model of decision making that provides a means of integrating different dimensions and goals of a complex decision. It involves six steps: (1) breaking a decision down into independent dimensions; (2) determining the relative weights of each of those dimensions; (3) listing all of the alternatives; (4) ranking all of the alternatives along the dimensions; (5) multiplying the rankings by the weightings to determine a final value for each alternative; and (6) choosing the alternative with the highest value.

Nativism   A philosophical doctrine emphasizing the role of innate factors in the acquisition of knowledge.

Naturalistic observation   A research paradigm in which an observer observes participants in familiar, everyday contexts while ideally remaining as unobtrusive as possible.

Neural network   See **Connectionism.**

Normative models of thinking   Models that define ideal performance under ideal circumstances in making decisions or solving problems.

Overconfidence   An overly positive judgment of one's own decision-making abilities and performance.

Paired associate learning   A memory task in which experimental subjects are first presented with a list of pairs of words (for example, flag-spoon) and later asked to recall the second word in a pair (for example, spoon) when presented with the first (for example, flag).

Paradigm   A body of knowledge that selects and highlights certain issues for study. It includes assumptions about how a particular phenomenon ought to be studied and the kinds of experimental methods and measures that are appropriate to use.

Pattern recognition   The classification of a stimulus into a category.

Percept   The outcome of a perceptual process; the meaningful interpretation of incoming information.

Perception   The interpretation of sensory information to yield a meaningful description or understanding.

Perceptual learning   The changes in perception that occur as a function of practice or experience with the stimuli.

Perceptual set   The tendency to perceive an object or pattern in a certain way based on one's immediate perceptual experience.

Performance (versus competence)   The behavior or responses actually produced by a cognitive processor engaged in a particular cognitive activity.

Phoneme   The smallest unit of sound that makes a meaningful difference in a given language.

Phonetics   The study of speech sounds.

Phonology   The study of the ways in which speech sounds are combined and altered in language.

Pragmatics   The rules governing the social aspects of language.

Prescriptive models of thinking   Models that tell us how we "ought" to make decisions or solve problems but that take into account actual circumstances.

Primacy effect   The improvement in retention of information learned at the beginning of a task.

Priming   The facilitation in responding to one stimulus as a function of prior exposure to another stimulus.

Proactive interference   A phenomenon in which earlier learned material disrupts the learning of subsequent material.

Probability   Measurement of a degree of uncertainty, expressed as a number between 0 and 1.

Problem solving   The cognitive process(es) used in transforming starting information into a goal state, using specified means of solution.

Problem-space hypothesis   The idea that problem solving is isomorphic to a search through a mental graph, with nodes corresponding to every possible state of affairs of a problem and connections corresponding to legal moves.

Procedural memory   A memory system thought to contain information concerning action and sequences of actions—for example, one's knowledge of how to ride a bicycle or swing a golf club.

Prototype   An abstract representation of an idealized member of a class of objects or events.

Quasi-experiment   An empirical study that appears to involve some, but incomplete, experimental control—for example, through nonrandom assignment of subjects to conditions.

Rationality   A property of thinking or decision making such that the processes used are selected with the processor's overall goals and principles in mind.

Reasoning   Cognitive process(es) used in transforming given information, called premises, into conclusions. Reasoning is often seen as a special kind of thinking.

Recall   The retrieval of information in which the processor must generate most of the information without aids. See also **Recognition**.

Recency effect   The improvement in retention of information learned at the end of a task.

Recognition   The retrieval of information in which the processor must decide whether the information presented has been previously presented. See also **Recall**.

Rehearsal   A mnemonic strategy of repeating information (either aloud or silently) to facilitate retention and later retrieval.

Representativeness heuristic   A belief that outcomes will always reflect characteristics of the process that generated them—for example, an expectation that the outcome of a series of coin flips will always look random.

Retinal image   A proximal stimulus for vision, consisting of the projection of light waves reflected from stimuli and projected to a surface at the back of the eye.

Retrieval   The processes by which stored information is brought back to conscious awareness.

Retroactive interference   A phenomenon in which subsequently learned material lowers the probability of recall of earlier learned material.

Schema   An organized framework for representing knowledge that typically includes characters, plots, and settings, and incorporates both general knowledge about the world and information about particular events.

Script   A schema for routine events.

Search, exhaustive   A search for information in which each item in a set is examined, even after the target is found.

Search, parallel   A search for information in which several stores or slots of information are simultaneously examined to match to the target.

Search, self-terminating   A search for information that stops when a target is found.

Search, serial   A search for information in which several stores or slots of information are sequentially examined to match to the target.

Semantic memory   A memory system proposed by Tulving that is thought to hold memories of general knowledge.

Semantic network   A depiction of semantic memory consisting of nodes (which roughly correspond to words or concepts) and connections between nodes.

Semantics   The study of meaning.

Sensory memory   A memory store thought to hold onto incoming sensory information for very brief periods of time. A different sensory memory store is hypothesized for each sensory system, for example, the *icon* for visual sensory memory, the *echo* for auditory sensory memory.

Short-term memory   A memory store thought to hold onto incoming information for up to 20–30 seconds. Also called "primary memory." It is thought to have a small capacity (up to 7 plus or minus 2 "slots").

Situated cognition   A belief that one's culture and one's everyday surroundings and tasks set both boundaries and possibilities for the cognitive tasks that are practiced and therefore strengthened in the normal course of daily living.

Size constancy   The phenomenon that one's perception of an object remains constant even as the retinal image of the object changes size, for example, because the object has moved closer or farther away from the perceiver.

Spacing effect   A phenomenon in which recall of material that is presented repeatedly is superior when the presentations are some time apart rather than immediately following one another.

Spreading activation   The excitation of one node in a semantic network by the excitation of another node to which it is connected; the excitation is said to flow across the connections.

Stage theories   Theories of development that postulate qualitatively different periods (stages).

State-dependent learning   The phenomenon that material is easier to retrieve when the learner is experiencing the same state or context (for example, physical location, physiological state) that she or he was at the time of encoding. See also **Encoding specificity.**

Story grammar   A structure people are thought to use to comprehend large, integrated pieces of text. See also **Schema** and **Script.**

Strategies   Deliberate plans or routines used to carry out particular cognitive tasks.

Stroop task   A task invented by J. R. Stroop in which a subject sees a list of words (color terms) printed in an ink color that differs from the word named (for example, *green* printed in blue ink). The subject is asked to name the ink colors of the words in the list and demonstrates great difficulty in doing so, relative to a condition in which noncolor words form the stimuli.

Structuralism   One of the earliest schools of cognitive psychology. It focused on the search for the simplest possible mental elements and the laws governing the ways in which they could be combined.

Syntax   The arrangement of words within sentences; the structure of sentences.

Tachistiscope   An experimental apparatus that allows experimenters to present displays for a controlled and brief amount of time (for example, milliseconds). Sometimes called a "t-scope."

Tacit knowledge   People's underlying and implicit beliefs about a task or event.

Tautology   A statement that is true by definition of its form (for example, "*A* is either true or it is false.")

Template   A stored pattern or model to which incoming information is matched in order to be recognized and classified.

Top-down processes   Cognitive (usually perceptual) processes that are directed by expectations (derived from context, past learning, or both) to form a larger percept, concept, or interpretation. Also called "conceptually driven" or "theory-driven" processes.

Truth tables   A method of showing when compound logical expressions are true and when they are false by considering every possible assignment of truth values to propositions.

Typicality effect   The phenomenon in which experimental subjects are faster to respond to typical instances of a concept (for example, "robin" for the concept "bird") than they are to atypical instances (for example, "penguin").

Utility   A measure of a person's happiness, pleasure, or satisfaction with a particular outcome.

Visual images   A mental representation of a stimulus thought to share at least some properties with a pictorial or spatial depiction of the stimulus.

Visual search task   A task in which subjects are asked to detect the presence of a particular target against an array of similar stimuli.

Well-defined problem   A problem that has the goals, starting information, and legal steps stated explicitly.

Within-subjects design   A research paradigm in which the same experimental subjects participate in different experimental conditions.

Word-superiority effect   The phenomenon that single letters are more quickly identified in the context of words than they are when presented alone or in the context of random letters.

Working memory   A memory structure proposed by Baddeley, described as consisting of a limited-capacity work space that can be allocated, somewhat flexibly, into storage space and control processing. It is thought to consist of three components: a central executive, a phonological loop, and a visual-spatial scratch pad.

References

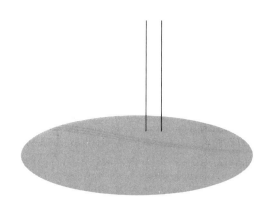

ADAMS, M. J. (1984). Aristotle's logic. In G. H. Bower (Ed.), *The psychology of learning and motivation* (Vol. 18, pp. 255–311). Orlando: Academic Press.

ALTMANN, G. (1987). Modularity and interaction in sentence processing. In J. L. Garfield (Ed.), *Modularity in knowledge representation and natural language understanding* (pp. 249–257). Cambridge: MIT Press.

ALTMANN, G., & STEEDMAN, M. (1988). Interaction with context during human sentence processing. *Cognition, 30,* 191–238.

AMSEL, A. (1989). *Behaviorism, neobehaviorism, and cognitivism in learning theory: Historical and contemporary perspectives.* Hillsdale, NJ: Erlbaum.

ANDERSON, J. R. (1976). *Language, memory, and thought.* Hillsdale, NJ: Erlbaum.

ANDERSON, J. R. (1978). Arguments concerning representations for mental imagery. *Psychological Review, 85,* 249–277.

ANDERSON, J. R. (1980). *Cognitive psychology and its implications.* San Francisco, CA: W. H. Freeman.

ANDERSON, J. R. (1983). *The architecture of cognition.* Cambridge: Harvard University Press.

ANDERSON, J. R., & BOWER, G. H. (1973). *Human associative memory.* New York: Wiley.

ARKES, H. R. (1986). Impediments to accurate clinical judgment and possible ways to minimize their impact. In H. R. Arkes & K. R. Hammond (Eds.), *Judgment and decision making* (pp. 582–592). Cambridge: Cambridge University Press.

ARKES, H. R. (1991). Costs and benefits of judgment errors: Implications for debiasing. *Psychological Bulletin, 110,* 486–498.

ARKES, H. R., & HAMMOND, K. R. (Eds.). (1986). *Judgment and decision making.* Cambridge: Cambridge University Press.

ARMSTRONG, S. L., GLEITMAN, L. R., & GLEITMAN, H. (1983). What some concepts might not be. *Cognition, 13,* 263–308.

ARNHEIM, R. (1986). The two faces of Gestalt psychology. *American Psychologist, 41,* 820–824.

ASHCRAFT, M. H. (1978). Property norms for typical and atypical items from 17 categories: A description and discussion. *Memory & Cognition, 6,* 227–232.

ATKINSON, R. C., & SHIFFRIN, R. M. (1968). Human memory: A proposed system and its control processes. In K. W. Spence & J. T. Spence (Eds.), *The psychology of learning and motivation: Advances in research and theory* (Vol. *2,* pp. 89–195). New York: Academic Press.

AU, T. K. (1983). Chinese and English counterfactuals: The Sapir-Whorf hypothesis revisited. *Cognition, 15,* 155–187.

AU, T. K. (1984). Counterfactuals: In reply to Alfred Bloom. *Cognition, 17,* 289–302.

AVERBACH, E., & CORIELL, A. S. (1961). Short-term memory in vision. *Bell System Technical Journal, 40,* 309–328.

BADDELEY, A. D. (1966a). Short-term memory for word sequences as a function of acoustic, semantic, and formal similarity. *Quarterly Journal of Experimental Psychology, 18,* 362–365.

BADDELEY, A. D. (1966b). The influence of acoustic and semantic similarity on long-term memory for word sequences. *Quarterly Journal of Experimental Psychology, 18,* 302–309.

BADDELEY, A. D. (1976). *The psychology of memory.* New York: Basic Books.

BADDELEY, A. D. (1978). The trouble with levels: A reexamination of Craik and Lockhart's framework for memory research. *Psychological Review, 85,* 139–152.

BADDELEY, A. D. (1981). The concept of working memory: A view of its current state and probable future development. *Cognition, 10,* 17–23.

BADDELEY, A. D. (1984). Neuropsychological evidence and the semantic/episodic distinction. *Behavioral and Brain Sciences, 7,* 238–239.

BADDELEY, A. D. (1986). *Working memory.* New York: Oxford University Press.

BADDELEY, A. D. (1990). *Human memory: Theory and practice.* Boston: Allyn & Bacon.

BADDELEY, A. D., & HITCH, G. J. (1974). Working memory. In

G. A. Bower (Ed.), *The psychology of learning and motivation* (Vol. 8, pp. 47–90). New York: Academic Press.

BAHRICK, H. P. (1983). The cognitive map of a city: Fifty years of learning and memory. In G. H. Bower (Ed.), *The psychology of learning and motivation* (Vol. 17, pp. 125–163). New York: Academic Press.

BAHRICK, H. P. (1984). Semantic memory content in permastore: Fifty years of memory for Spanish learned in school. *Journal of Experimental Psychology: General, 113,* 1–29.

BAILLARGEON, R. (1987). Object permanence in 3 1/2- and 4 1/2-month-old infants. *Developmental Psychology, 23,* 655–664.

BANAJI, M. R., & CROWDER, R. G. (1989). The bankruptcy of everyday memory. *American Psychologist, 44,* 1185–1193.

BANKS, W. P. (1981). Assessing relations between imagery and perception. *Journal of Experimental Psychology: Human Perception and Performance, 7,* 844–847.

BANKS, W. P., & KRAJICEK, D. (1991). Perception. *Annual Review of Psychology, 42,* 305–331.

BARNES, J. M., & UNDERWOOD, B. J. (1959). "Fate" of first-list associations in transfer theory. *Journal of Experimental Psychology, 58,* 97–105.

BARON, J. (1985). *Rationality and intelligence.* Cambridge: Cambridge University Press.

BARON, J. (1988). *Thinking and deciding.* Cambridge: Cambridge University Press.

BARON, J. B., & STERNBERG, R. J. (Eds.). (1987). *Teaching thinking skills: Theory and practice.* New York: W. H. Freeman.

BARSALOU, L. W. (1983). Ad hoc categories. *Memory & Cognition, 11,* 211–227.

BARSALOU, L. W. (1985). Ideals, central tendency, and frequency of instantiation as determinants of graded structure in categories. *Journal of Experimental Psychology: Learning, Memory, and Cognition, 11,* 629–654.

BARSALOU, L. W. (1987). The instability of graded structure: Implications for the nature of concepts. In U. Neisser (Ed.), *Concepts and conceptual development* (pp. 101–140). New York: Cambridge University Press.

BARTLETT, F. C. (1932). *Remembering: A study in experimental and social psychology.* Cambridge: Cambridge University Press.

BARTLETT, F. (1958). *Thinking: An experimental and social study.* New York: Basic Books.

BARTON, M. E., & KOMATSU, L. K. (1989). Defining features of natural kinds and artifacts. *Journal of Psycholinguistic Research, 18,* 433–447.

BAYES, T. (1958). An essay towards solving a problem in the doctrine of chances. *Biometrika, 45,* 293–315. (Original work published in 1764.)

BECK, J. (Ed.). (1982). *Organization and representation in perception.* Hillsdale, NJ: Erlbaum.

BEILIN, H., & PUFALL, P. B., (Eds.), (1992). *Piaget's theory: Prospects and possibilities.* Hillsdale, NJ: Erlbaum.

BELENKY, M. F., CLINCHY, B. M., GOLDBERGER, N. R., TARULE, J. M. (1986). *Women's ways of knowing: The development of self, voice, and mind.* New York: Basic Books.

BENBOW, C. P., & STANLEY, J. C. (1980). Sex differences in mathematical ability: Fact or artifact? *Science, 210,* 1262–1264.

BENBOW, C. P., & STANLEY, J. C. (1983). Sex differences in mathematical reasoning: More facts. *Science, 222,* 1029–1031.

BERLIN, B., & KAY, P. (1969). *Basic color terms: Their universality and evolution.* Berkeley: University of California Press.

BERRY, J. W. (1981). Cultural systems and cognitive styles. In M. P. Friedman, J. P. Das, & N. O'Connor (Eds.), *Intelligence and learning* (pp. 395–406). New York: Plenum.

BERRY, J. W. (1984). Towards a universal psychology of cognitive competence. *International Journal of Psychology, 19,* 335–361.

BERRY, J. W., & DASEN, P. R. (Eds.). (1974). *Culture and cognition: Readings in cross-cultural psychology.* London: Methuen.

BERRY, J. W., IRVINE, S. H., & HUNT, E. G. (Eds.). (1988). *Indigenous cognition: Functioning in cultural context.* Boston: Martinus Nijhoff.

BIEDERMAN, I. (1987). Recognition-by-components: A theory of human image understanding. *Psychological Review, 94,* 115–147.

BIEDERMAN, I., GLASS, A. L., & STACY, E. W., JR. (1973). Searching for objects in real-world scenes. *Journal of Experimental Psychology, 97,* 22–27.

BIERWISCH, M. (1970). Semantics. In J. Lyons (Ed.), *New horizons in linguistics* (pp. 166–184). Baltimore: Penguin Books.

BJORKLUND, D. F. (1989). *Children's thinking: Developmental functions and individual differences.* Pacific Grove, CA: Brooks/Cole.

BLOCK, J. H. (1976). Issues, problems, and pitfalls in assessing sex differences: A critical review of the *Psychology of Sex Differences. Merrill-Palmer Quarterly, 22,* 283–308.

BLOCK, N. (Ed.). (1981). *Imagery.* Cambridge: MIT Press.

BLOOM, A. H. (1981). *The linguistic shaping of thought: A study in the impact of language on thinking in China and the West.* Hillsdale, NJ: Erlbaum.

BLOOM, A. H. (1984). Caution—the words you use may affect what you say: A response to Au. *Cognition, 17,* 275–287.

BOBROW, D. G., & COLLINS, A. (Eds.). (1975). *Representation and understanding: Studies in cognitive science.* New York: Academic Press.

BOCK, J. K. (1986). Syntactic persistence in language production. *Cognitive Psychology, 18,* 355–387.

BONHANNON, J. N., III (1988). Flashbulb memories for the Space Shuttle disaster: A tale of two theories. *Cognition, 29,* 179–196.

BORNSTEIN, M. H. (1992). Perception across the life span. In M. H. Bornstein & M. E. Lamb (Eds.), *Developmental psychology: An advanced textbook* (3rd ed., pp. 155–209). Hillsdale, NJ: Erlbaum.

BOURNE, L. E., JR. (1970). Knowing and using concepts. *Psychological Review, 77,* 546–556.

BOURNE, L. E., JR., & EKSTRAND, B. R. (1985). *Psychology: Its principles and meanings* (5th ed.). New York: Holt, Rinehart & Winston.

BOUSFIELD, W. A. (1953). The occurrence of clustering in recall of randomly arranged associates. *Journal of General Psychology, 49,* 229–240.

BOVET, M. C. (1974). Cognitive processes among illiterate children and adults (S. Opper, Trans.). In J. W. Berry & P. R. Dasen (Eds.), *Culture and cognition: Readings in cross-cultural psychology* (pp. 311–334). London: Methuen.

BOWER, G. H. (1970a). Analysis of a mnemonic device. *American Scientist, 58,* 496–510.

BOWER, G. H. (1970b). Imagery as a relational organizer in associative learning. *Journal of Verbal Learning and Verbal Behavior, 9,* 529–533.

BOWER, G. H. (1981). Mood and memory. *American Psychologist, 36,* 129–148.

BOWER, G. H., BLACK, J. B., & TURNER, T. J. (1979). Scripts in memory for text. *Cognitive Psychology, 11,* 177–220.

BOWER, G. H., & KARLIN, M. B. (1974). Depth of processing pictures of faces and recognition memory. *Journal of Experimental Psychology, 103,* 751–757.

BOWERMAN, M. (1973). *Early syntactic development: A cross-linguistic study with special reference to Finnish.* Cambridge: Cambridge University Press.

BRAINE, M. D. S. (1963). The ontogeny of English phrase structure: The first phase. *Language, 39,* 1–13.

BRAINE, M. D. S. (1978). On the relation between the natural logic of reasoning and standard logic. *Psychological Review, 85,* 1–21.

BRAINE, M. D. S. (1990). The "natural logic" approach to reasoning. In W. F. Overton (Ed.), *Reasoning, necessity, and logic: Developmental perspectives* (pp. 133–157). Hillsdale, NJ: Erlbaum.

BRAINE, M. D. S., REISER, B., & RUMAIN, B. (1984). Some empirical justification for a theory of natural propositional logic. In G. H. Bower (Ed.), *The psychology of learning and motivation* (Vol. 18, pp. 313–371). Orlando: Academic Press.

BRAINE, M. D. S., & RUMAIN, B. (1983). Logical reasoning. In J. H. Flavell & E. M. Markman (Eds.), P. H. Mussen (Series Ed.), *Handbook of child psychology: Vol. 3 Cognitive development* (pp. 263–340). New York: Wiley

BRAINERD, C. J. (1978). The stage question in cognitive-developmental theory. *The Behavioral and Brain Sciences, 2,* 173–213.

BRANSFORD, J. D., & FRANKS, J. J. (1971). Sentence memory: A constructive versus interpretive approach. *Cognitive Psychology, 3,* 331–350.

BRANSFORD, J. D., & JOHNSON, M. K. (1972). Contextual prerequisites for understanding: Some investigations of comprehension and recall. *Journal of Verbal Learning and Verbal Behavior, 11,* 717–726.

BRIAND, K. A., & KLEIN, R. M. (1989). Has feature integration theory come unglued? A reply to Tsal. *Journal of Experimental Psychology: Human Perception and Performance, 15,* 401–406.

BRIGGS, G. E. (1954). Acquisition, extinction, and recovery functions in retroactive inhibition. *Journal of Experimental Psychology, 47,* 285–293.

BROADBENT, D. E. (1958). *Perception and communication.* Oxford: Pergamon Press.

BROADBENT, D. E. (1982). Task combination and selective intake of information. *Acta Psychologica, 50,* 253–290.

BROOKS, L. R. (1968). Spatial and verbal components of the act of recall. *Canadian Journal of Psychology, 22,* 349–368.

BROOKS, L. R. (1978). Nonanalytic concept formation and memory for instances. In E. Rosch & B. B. Lloyd (Eds.), *Cognition and categorization* (pp. 169–211). Hillsdale, NJ: Erlbaum.

BROOKS, L. R. (1987). Decentralized control of categorization: The role of prior processing episodes. In U. Neisser (Ed.), *Concepts and conceptual development: Ecological and intellectual factors in categorization* (pp. 141–174). Cambridge: Cambridge University Press.

BROOKS, L. R., NORMAN, G. R., & ALLEN, S. W. (1991). Role of specific similarity in a medical diagnostic task. *Journal of Experimental Psychology: General, 120,* 278–287.

BROWN, A. L., BRANSFORD, J. D., FERRARA, R. A., & CAMPIONE, J. C. (1983). Learning, remembering, and understanding. In P. Mussen (Series Ed.), J. H. Flavell & E. M. Markman (Vol. Eds.), *Handbook of child psychology: Vol. 3. Cognitive development* (pp. 77–166). New York: Wiley.

BROWN, E. L., & DEFFENBACHER, K. (1979). *Perception and the senses.* New York: Oxford University Press.

BROWN, J. (1958). Some tests of the decay theory of immediate memory. *Quarterly Journal of Experimental Psychology, 10,* 12–21.

BROWN, R., & HANLON, C. (1970). Derivational complexity and order of acquisition in child speech. In J. R. Hayes (Ed.), *Cognition and the development of language* (pp. 11–53). New York: Wiley.

BROWN, R., & KULIK, J. (1977). Flashbulb memories. *Cognition, 5,* 73–99.

BROWN, R. W. (1973). *A first language: The early stages.* Cambridge: Harvard University Press.

BROWNE, B. A., & CRUSE, D. F. (1988). The incubation effect: Illusion or illumination? *Human Performance, 1,* 177–185.

BRUNER, J. S. (1957). Going beyond the information given. In Colorado University Psychology Department (Eds.), *Contemporary approaches to cognition* (pp. 41–69). Cambridge: Harvard University Press.

BRUNER, J. S. (1966). On cognitive growth: II. In J. S. Bruner, R. Olver, P. Greenfield, J. R. Hornsby, H. J. Kenney, M. Maccoby, N. Modiano, F. A. Mosher, D. R. Olson, M. C. Potter, L. C. Reich, & A. M. Sonstroem (Eds.), *Studies in cognitive growth: A collaboration at the Center for Cognitive Studies* (pp. 30–67). New York: Wiley.

BRUNER, J. S., GOODNOW, J. J., & AUSTIN, G. A. (1956). *A study of thinking.* New York: Wiley.

BRUNER, J. S., OLVER, R., GREENFIELD, P., HORNSBY, J. R., KENNEY, H. J., MACCOBY, M., MODIANO, N., MOSHER, F. A., OLSON, D. R., POTTER, M. C., REICH, L. C., & SONSTROEM, A. M. (Eds.). (1966).

Studies in cognitive growth: A collaboration at the Center for Cognitive Studies. New York: Wiley.

BRUNSWIK, E. (1956). *Perception and the representative design of psychological experiments* (2nd ed.). Berkeley: University of California Press.

BRYAN, W. L., & HARTER, N. (1899). Studies on the telegraphic language: The acquisition of a hierarchy of habits. *Psychological Review, 6,* 345–375.

BUGELSKI, B. R., KIDD, E., & SEGMEN, J. (1968). Image as a mediator in one-trial paired associate learning. *Journal of Experimental Psychology, 76,* 69–73.

BUTTERWORTH, G. E., HARRIS, P. L., LESLIE, A. M., & WELLMAN, H. M. (Eds.). (1991). *Perspectives on the child's theory of mind.* Oxford: Oxford University Press.

CAMPBELL, D. T., & STANLEY, J. C. (1963). *Experimental and quasi-experimental designs for research.* Chicago: Rand McNally.

CAMPBELL, J. I. D., & CHARNESS, N. (1990). Age-related declines in working memory skills: Evidence from a complex calculation task. *Developmental Psychology, 26,* 879–888.

CANTOR, N., MISCHEL, W., & SCHWARTZ, J. C. (1982). A prototype analysis of psychological situations. *Cognitive Psychology, 14,* 45–77.

CAPLAN, P. J., MACPHERSON, G. M., & TOBIN, P. (1985). Do sex-related differences in spatial ability exist? *American Psychologist, 40,* 786–799.

CARLSON, L., ZIMMER, J. W., & GLOVER, J. A. (1981). First-letter mnemonics: DAM (Don't Aid Memory). *Journal of General Psychology, 104,* 287–292.

CARMICHAEL, L., HOGAN, H. P., & WALTER, A. A. (1932). An experimental study of the effect of language on the reproduction of visually perceived form. *Journal of Experimental Psychology, 15,* 73–86.

CARPENTER, P. A., & JUST, M. A. (1983). What your eyes do while your mind is reading. In K. Rayner (Ed.), *Eye movements in reading: Perceptual and language processes* (pp. 275–307). New York: Academic Press.

CARPENTER, P. A., JUST, M. A., & SHELL, P. (1990). What one intelligence test measures: A theoretical account of the processing in the Raven Progressive Matrices Test. *Psychological Review, 97,* 404–431.

CARROLL, D. W. (1986). *Psychology of language.* Monterey, CA: Brooks/Cole.

CASE, R. (1978). Intellectual development from birth to adulthood: A neo-Piagetian interpretation. In R. S. Siegler, (Ed.), *Children's thinking: What develops?* (pp. 37–71). Hillsdale, NJ: Erlbaum.

CATRAMBONE, R., & HOLYOAK, K. J. (1989). Overcoming contextual limitations on problem-solving transfer. *Journal of Experimental Psychology: Learning, Memory, and Cognition, 15,* 1147–1156.

CATRAMBONE, R., & HOLYOAK, K. J. (1990). Learning subgoals and methods for solving probability problems. *Memory & Cognition, 18,* 593–603.

CAVANAUGH, J. C. (1993). *Adult development and aging* (2nd ed.). Pacific Grove, CA: Brooks/Cole.

CAVE, K. R., & WOLFE, J. M. (1990). Modeling the role of parallel processing in visual search. *Cognitive Psychology, 22,* 225–271.

CECI, S. J. (1991). How much does schooling influence general intelligence and its cognitive components? A reassessment of the evidence. *Developmental Psychology, 27,* 703–722.

CERASO, J., & PROVITERA, A. (1971). Sources of error in syllogistic reasoning. *Cognitive Psychology, 2,* 400–410.

CHANG, T. M. (1986). Semantic memory: Facts and models. *Psychological Bulletin, 99,* 199–220.

CHAPMAN, L. J., & CHAPMAN, J. P. (1967a). Genesis of popular but erroneous psychodiagnostic observations. *Journal of Abnormal Psychology, 72,* 193–204.

CHAPMAN, L. J., & CHAPMAN, J. P. (1967b). Illusory correlation in observational report. *Journal of Verbal Learning and Verbal Behavior, 6,* 151–155.

CHAPMAN, L. J., & CHAPMAN, J. P. (1969). Illusory correlation as an obstacle to the use of valid psychodiagnostic signs. *Journal of Abnormal Psychology, 74,* 271–280.

CHARNIAK, E., & MCDERMOTT, D. (1985). *Introduction to artificial intelligence.* Reading, MA: Addison-Wesley.

CHASE, W. G., & SIMON, H. A. (1973). Perception in chess. *Cognitive Psychology, 4,* 55–81.

CHEN, H.-C., & HO, C. (1986). Development of Stroop interference in Chinese-English bilinguals. *Journal of Experimental Psychology: Learning, Memory and Cognition, 12,* 397–401.

CHENG, P. W., & HOLYOAK, K. J. (1985). Pragmatic reasoning schemas. *Cognitive Psychology, 17,* 391–416.

CHENG, P. W., HOLYOAK, K. J., NISBETT, R. E., & OLIVER, L. M. (1986). Pragmatic versus syntactic approaches to training deductive reasoning. *Cognitive Psychology, 18,* 293–328.

CHERRY, E. C. (1953). Some experiments on the recognition of speech, with one and two ears. *Journal of the Acoustical Society of America, 25,* 975–979.

CHI, M. T. H. (1978). Knowledge structures and memory development. In R. S. Siegler, (Ed.), *Children's thinking: What develops?* (pp. 73–96). Hillsdale, NJ: Erlbaum.

CHI, M. T. H., FELTOVICH, P. J., & GLASER, R. (1981). Categorization and representation of physics problems by experts and novices. *Cognitive Science, 5,* 121–125.

CHI, M. T. H., GLASER, R., & FARR, M. (Eds.). (1988). *The nature of expertise.* Hillsdale, NJ: Erlbaum.

CHI, M. T. H., & KOESKE, R. D. (1983). Network representation of a child's dinosaur knowledge. *Developmental Psychology, 19,* 29–39.

CHOMSKY, N. (1957). *Syntactic structures.* The Hague: Mouton.

CHOMSKY, N. (1959). A review of Skinner's *Verbal Behavior. Language, 35,* 26–58.

CHOMSKY, N. (1965). *Aspects of the theory of syntax.* Cambridge: MIT Press.

CHOMSKY, N. (1972). *Language and mind* (enlarged ed.). New York: Harcourt Brace Jovanovich.

CLARK, E. V. (1983). Meanings and concepts. In J. H. Flavell & E. M. Markman (Eds.), P. H. Mussen (Series Ed.), *Handbook of child psychology: Vol. 3. Cognitive development* (pp. 787–840). New York: Wiley.

CLARK, H. H., & CLARK, E. V. (1977). *Psychology and language.* New York: Harcourt Brace Jovanovich.

COFER, C. (1967). Does conceptual clustering influence the amount retained in immediate free recall? In B. Kleinmuntz (Ed.), *Concepts and the structure of memory* (pp. 181–214). New York: Wiley.

COHEN, J. (1969). *Statistical power analysis for the behavioral sciences.* New York: Academic Press.

COHEN, J., DUNBAR, K., & MCCLELLAND, J. L. (1990). On the control of automatic processes: A parallel distributed processing account of the Stroop effect. *Psychological Review, 97,* 332–361.

COHEN, N. J., MCCLOSKEY, M., & WIBLE, C. G. (1990). Flashbulb memories and underlying cognitive mechanisms: Reply to Pillemer. *Journal of Experimental Psychology: General, 119,* 97–100.

COLE, M., GAY, J., GLICK, J., & SHARP, D. W. (1971). *The cultural context of learning and thinking: An exploration in experimental anthropology.* New York: Basic Books.

COLE, M., & SCRIBNER, S. (1974). *Culture and thought: A psychological introduction.* New York: Wiley.

COLLINS, A. M., & LOFTUS, E. F. (1975). A spreading-activation theory of semantic processing. *Psychological Review, 82,* 407–428.

COLLINS, A., & MICHALSKI, R. (1989). The logic of plausible reasoning: A core theory. *Cognitive Science, 13,* 1–49.

COLLINS, A. M., & QUILLIAN, M. R. (1969). Retrieval time from semantic memory. *Journal of Verbal Learning and Verbal Behavior, 8,* 240–247.

COLTHEART, M. (1980). Iconic memory and visible persistence. *Perception & Psychophysics, 27,* 183–228.

CONRAD, C. (1972). Cognitive economy in semantic memory. *Journal of Experimental Psychology, 92,* 149–154.

CONRAD, R. (1964). Acoustic confusion in immediate memory. *British Journal of Psychology, 55,* 75–84.

COOPER, L. A. (1975). Mental rotation of random two-dimensional shapes. *Cognitive Psychology, 7,* 20–43.

COOPER, L. A. (1976). Demonstration of a mental analog of an external rotation. *Perception & Psychophysics, 19,* 296–302.

COOPER, L. A., & SHEPARD, R. N. (1973). The time required to prepare for a rotated stimulus. *Memory & Cognition, 1,* 246–250.

COOPER, L. A., & SHEPARD, R. N. (1975). Mental transformations in the identification of left and right hands. *Journal of Experimental Psychology: Human Perception and Performance, 1,* 48–56.

CORSO, J. F. (1981). *Aging sensory systems and perception.* New York: Praeger.

COWAN, N. (1988). Evolving conceptions of memory storage, selective attention, and their mutual constraints within the human information processing system. *Psychological Bulletin, 104,* 163–191.

COWPER, E. A. (1992). *A concise introduction to syntactic theory: The government binding approach.* Chicago: University of Chicago Press.

CRAIK, F. I. M., & LOCKHART, R. S. (1972). Levels of processing: A framework for memory research. *Journal of Verbal Learning and Verbal Behavior, 11,* 671–684.

CRAIK, F. I. M., & TULVING, E. (1975). Depth of processing and retention of words in episodic memory. *Journal of Experimental Psychology: General, 104,* 268–294.

CROWDER, R. G. (1976). *Principles of learning and memory.* Hillsdale, NJ: Erlbaum.

CUMMINS, D. D. (1992). Role of analogical reasoning in the induction of problem categories. *Journal of Experimental Psychology: Learning, Memory, and Cognition, 18,* 1103–1124.

CUTTING, J. E. (1987). Perception and information. *Annual Review of Psychology, 38,* 61–90.

DAMER, T. E. (1980). *Attacking faulty reasoning* (2nd ed.). Belmont, CA: Wadsworth.

DARWIN, C. T., TURVEY, M. T., & CROWDER, R. G. (1972). An auditory analogue of the Sperling partial report procedure: Evidence for brief auditory storage. *Cognitive Psychology, 3,* 255–267.

DAWES, R. M. (1982). The robust beauty of improper linear models in decision making. In D. Kahneman, P. Slovic, & A. Tversky (Eds.), *Judgment under uncertainty: Heuristics and biases* (pp. 391–407). Cambridge: Cambridge University Press.

DAWES, R. M., & CORRIGAN, B. (1974). Linear models in decision making. *Psychological Bulletin, 81,* 95–106.

DEAUX, K. (1985). Sex and gender. *Annual Review of Psychology, 36,* 49–81.

DE GROOT, A. D. (1965). *Thought and choice in chess.* The Hague: Mouton.

DEMERS, R. A. (1988). Linguistics and animal communication. In F. J. Newmeyer (Ed.), *Linguistics: The Cambridge survey: Vol. 3. Language: Psychological and biological aspects* (pp. 314–335). Cambridge: Cambridge University Press.

DEMPSTER, F. N. (1981). Memory span: Sources of individual and developmental differences. *Psychological Bulletin, 89,* 63–100.

DEREGOWSKI, J. B. (1968). Difficulties in pictorial depth perception in Africa. *British Journal of Psychology, 59,* 195–204.

DEREGOWSKI, J. B. (1980). Perception. In H. C. Triandis & W. Lonner (Eds.), *Handbook of cross-cultural psychology: Vol. 3. Basic processes* (pp. 21–115). Boston: Allyn & Bacon.

DEREGOWSKI, J. B. (1989). Real space and represented space: Cross-cultural perspectives. *Behavioral and Brain Sciences, 12,* 51–119.

DE ROSA, D. V., & TKACZ, D. (1976). Memory scanning of organized visual material. *Journal of Experimental Psychology: Human Learning and Memory, 2,* 688–694.

DEUTSCH, J. A., & DEUTSCH, D. (1963). Attention: Some theoretical considerations. *Psychological Review, 70,* 80–90.

DE VILLIERS, P. A., & DE VILLIERS, J. G. (1992). Language development. In M. H. Bornstein & M. E. Lamb (Eds.), *Developmental psychology: An advanced textbook* (3rd ed., pp. 337–418). Hillsdale, NJ: Erlbaum.

DEWEY, J. (1933). *How we think.* Boston: D. C. Heath.

DIEHL, R. L. (1981). Feature detectors for speech: A critical reappraisal. *Psychological Bulletin, 89,* 1–18.

DUNCKER, K. (1945). On problem-solving. *Psychological Monographs, 58* (Whole No. 270).

DWECK, C. S. (1986). Motivational processes affecting learning. *American Psychologist, 41,* 1040–1048.

DWECK, C. S., & BUSH, E. S. (1976). Sex differences in learned helplessness: I. Differential debilitation with peer and adult evaluators. *Developmental Psychology, 12,* 147–156.

DWECK, C. S., DAVIDSON, W., NELSON, S., & ENNA, B. (1978). Sex differences in learned helplessness: II. The contingencies of evaluative feedback in the classroom, and III. An experimental analysis. *Developmental Psychology, 14,* 268–276.

DWECK, C. S., & GOETZ, T. E. (1978). Attributions and learned helplessness. In J. H. Harvey, W. J. Ickes, & R. F. Kidd (Eds.), *New directions in attribution research* (Vol. 2, pp. 157–179). Hillsdale, NJ: Erlbaum.

DWECK, C. S., GOETZ, T. E., & STRAUSS, N. L. (1980). Sex differences in learned helplessness: IV. An experimental and naturalistic study of failure generalization and its mediators. *Journal of Personality and Social Psychology, 38,* 441–452.

DWECK, C. S., & LEGGETT, E. L. (1988). A social-cognitive approach to motivation and personality. *Psychological Review, 95,* 256–273.

EBBINGHAUS, H. (1885/1913). *Memory: A contribution to experimental psychology* (H. A. Ruger & C. E. Bussenius, Trans.). New York: Columbia University, Teacher's College. 1964 Edition: New York: Dover Press.

EDWARDS, W. (1954). The theory of decision making. *Psychological Bulletin, 51,* 380–417.

EDWARDS, W. (Ed.). (1992). Utility theories: Measurements and applications. Norwell, MA: Kluver Academic Publishers.

EGAN, D. E., & GREENO, J. G. (1974). Theory of rule induction: Knowledge acquired in concept learning, serial pattern learning, and problem solving. In L. W. Gregg (Ed.), *Knowledge and cognition* (pp. 43–103). Potomac, MD: Erlbaum.

EICH, J. E. (1980). The cue-dependent nature of state-dependent retention. *Memory & Cognition, 8,* 157–173.

ELLIS, A. W., & YOUNG, A. W. (1988). *Human cognitive neuropsychology.* London: Erlbaum.

ELLIS, H. C., & HUNT, R. R. (1993). *Fundamentals of cognitive psychology* (5th ed.). Madison, WI: Brown & Benchmark.

ERICKSON, J. R. (1978). Research on syllogistic reasoning. In R. Revlin & R. E. Mayer (Eds.), *Human reasoning* (pp. 39–50). Washington, DC: V. H. Winston.

ERICSSON, K. A., & SIMON, H. A. (1984). *Protocol analysis: Verbal reports as data.* Cambridge: MIT Press/Bradford.

ESTES, W. (1980). Is human memory obsolete? *American Scientist, 68,* 62–69.

ESTES, W. (1988). Human learning and memory. In R. C. Atkinson (Ed.), *Stevens' handbook of experimental psychology: Vol. 2. Learning and cognition* (2nd ed., pp. 351–415). New York: Wiley.

EVANS, J. ST. B. T. (1972). Reasoning with negatives. *British Journal of Psychology, 63,* 213–219.

EVANS, J. ST. B. T. (1982). *The psychology of deductive reasoning.* London: Routledge & Kegan Paul.

EVANS, J. ST. B. T. (Ed.). (1983). *Thinking and reasoning: Psychological approaches.* London: Routledge & Kegan Paul.

EVANS, J. ST. B. T., BARSTON, J., & POLLARD, P. (1983). On the conflict between logic and belief in syllogistic reasoning. *Memory & Cognition, 11,* 295–306.

FALMAGNE, R. J. (Ed.). (1975). *Reasoning: Representation and process.* Hillsdale, NJ: Erlbaum.

FANCHER, R. E. (1979). *Pioneers of psychology.* New York: Norton.

FARAH, M. J. (1985). Psychophysical evidence for a shared representational medium for mental images and percepts. *Journal of Experimental Psychology: General, 114,* 91–103.

FARAH, M. J. (1988). Is visual imagery really visual? Overlooked evidence from neuropsychology. *Psychological Review, 95,* 307–317.

FARAH, M. J., HAMMOND, K. M., LEVINE, D. N., & CALVANIO, R. (1988). Visual and spatial mental imagery: Dissociable systems of representation. *Cognitive Psychology, 20,* 439–462.

FARAH, M. J., PÉRONNET, F., GONON, M. A., & GIARD, M. H. (1988). Electrophysiological evidence for a shared representational medium for visual images and visual percepts. *Journal of Experimental Psychology: General, 117,* 248–257.

FEHR, B. (1988). Prototype analysis of the concepts of love and commitment. *Journal of Personality and Social Psychology, 55,* 557–579.

FEINGOLD, A. (1988). Cognitive gender differences are disappearing. *American Psychologist, 43,* 95–103.

FELDMAN, J. A., & BALLARD, D. H. (1982). Connectionist models and their properties. *Cognitive Science, 6,* 205–254.

FERREIRA, F., & CLIFTON, C., JR. (1986). The independence of syntactic processing. *Journal of Memory and Language, 25,* 348–368.

FINKE, R. A. (1989). *Principles of mental imagery.* Cambridge: MIT Press.

FISCHHOFF, B. (1975). Hindsight≠foresight: The effect of outcome knowledge on judgment under uncertainty. *Journal of Experimental Psychology: Human Perception and Performance, 1,* 288–299.

FISCHHOFF, B. (1982a). For those condemned to study the past: Heuristics and biases in hindsight. In D. Kahneman, P. Slovic, & A. Tversky (Eds.), *Judgment under uncertainty: Heuristics and biases* (pp. 335–351). Cambridge: Cambridge University Press.

FISCHHOFF, B. (1982b). Debiasing. In D. Kahneman, P. Slovic, & A. Tversky (Eds.), *Judgment under uncertainty: Heuristics and biases* (pp. 422–444). Cambridge: Cambridge University Press.

FISHER, D. L. (1984). Central capacity limits in consistent mapping, visual search tasks: Four channels or more? *Cognitive Psychology, 16,* 449–484.

FIVUSH, R., & SLACKMAN, E. A. (1986). The acquisition and development of scripts. In K. Nelson (Ed.), *Event knowledge: Structure and function in development* (pp. 71–96). Hillsdale, NJ: Erlbaum.

FLAVELL, J. H. (1963). *The developmental psychology of Jean Piaget.* New York: Van Nostrand.

FLAVELL, J. H. (1985). *Cognitive development* (2nd ed.). Englewood Cliffs, NJ: Prentice Hall.

FLAVELL, J. H., BEACH, D. R., & CHINSKY, J. M. (1966). Spontaneous verbal rehearsal in memory task as a function of age. *Child Development, 37,* 283–299.

FLAVELL, J. H., FRIEDRICHS, A. G., & HOYT, J. D. (1970). Developmental changes in memorization processes. *Cognitive Psychology, 1,* 324–340.

FLAVELL, J. H., & MARKHAM, E. M. (Eds.). (1983). P. H. Mussen (Series Ed.), *Handbook of child psychology: Vol. 3. Cognitive development*. New York: Wiley.

FODOR, J. A. (1983). *The modularity of mind: An essay on faculty psychology*. Cambridge: MIT Press.

FODOR, J. A. (1985). Précis of *The modularity of mind*. *Behavioral and Brain Sciences, 8,* 1–42.

FODOR, J. A., & PYLYSHYN, Z. W. (1981). How direct is visual perception? Some reflections on Gibson's "Ecological Approach." *Cognition, 2,* 139–196.

FROMKIN, V., & RODMAN, R. (1974). *An introduction to language*. New York: Holt, Rinehart & Winston.

GALLISTEL, C. R., & GELMAN, R. (1992). Preverbal and verbal counting and computation. *Cognition, 44,* 43–74.

GALOTTI, K. M. (1989). Approaches to studying formal and everyday reasoning. *Psychological Bulletin, 105,* 331–351.

GALOTTI, K. M., BARON, J., & SABINI, J. P. (1986). Individual differences in syllogistic reasoning: Deduction rules or mental models? *Journal of Experimental Psychology: General, 115,* 16–25.

GALOTTI, K. M., & GANONG, W. F., III (1985). What non-programmers know about programming: Natural language procedure specification. *International Journal of Man-Machine Studies, 22,* 1–10.

GALOTTI, K. M., & KOMATSU, L. K. (1993). Why study deduction? *Behavioral and Brain Sciences, 16,* 350.

GALOTTI, K. M., & KOZBERG, S. F. (1987). Older adolescents' thinking about academic/vocational and interpersonal commitments. *Journal of Youth and Adolescence, 16,* 313–330.

GALTON, F. (1907/1883). *Inquiries into human faculty and its development*. London: J. M. Dent & Sons.

GARDNER, B. T., & GARDNER, R. A. (1971). Two-way communication with an infant chimpanzee. In A. M. Schrier & F. Stollnitz (Eds.), *Behavior of nonhuman primates* (Vol. 4, pp. 117–184). New York: Academic Press.

GARDNER, H. (1985). *The mind's new science: A history of the cognitive revolution*. New York: Basic Books.

GARDNER, M. (1978). *aha! Insight*. New York: Scientific American.

GARFIELD, J. L. (Ed.). (1987). *Modularity in knowledge representation and natural language understanding*. Cambridge: MIT Press.

GARRETT, M. F. (1988). Processes in language production. In F. J. Newmeyer (Ed.), *Linguistics: The Cambridge survey: Vol. 3. Language: Psychological and biological aspects* (pp. 69–96). Cambridge: Cambridge University Press.

GARRETT, M. F. (1990). Sentence processing. In D. N. Osherson & H. Lasnik (Eds.), *An invitation to cognitive science: Vol. 1. Language* (pp. 133–175). Cambridge: MIT Press.

GELMAN, R. (1969). Conservation acquisition: A problem of learning to attend to relevant attributes. *Journal of Experimental Child Psychology, 7,* 167–187.

GELMAN, R. (1972). Logical capacity of very young children: Number invariance rules. *Child Development, 43,* 75–90.

GELMAN, R. (1978). Preschool thought. *American Psychologist, 34,* 900–905.

GELMAN, R., & BAILLARGEON, R. (1983). A review of some Piagetian concepts. In P. Mussen (Series Ed.), J. H. Flavell & E. M. Markman (Vol. Eds.), *Handbook of child psychology: Vol. 3. Cognitive development* (pp. 167–230). New York: Wiley.

GELMAN, R., & GALLISTEL, C. R. (1978). *The child's understanding of number*. Cambridge: Harvard University Press.

GELMAN, S. A. (1988). The development of induction within natural kind and artifact categories. *Cognitive Psychology, 20,* 65–95.

GELMAN, S. A., & MARKMAN, E. M. (1986). Categories and inductions in young children. *Cognition, 23,* 183–209.

GENTNER, D., & CLEMENT, C. (1988). Evidence for relational selectivity in the interpretation of analogy and metaphor. In G. H. Bower (Ed.), *The psychology of learning and motivation* (Vol. 22, pp. 307–358). San Diego: Academic Press.

GIBBS, R. W., JR. (1986). What makes some indirect speech acts conventional? *Journal of Memory and Language, 25,* 181–196.

GIBSON, E. J. (1969). *Principles of perceptual learning and development*. New York: Meredith.

GIBSON, E. J. (1982). Contrasting emphases in Gestalt theory, information processing, and the ecological approach to perception. In J. Beck (Ed.), *Organization and representation in perception* (pp. 159–165). Hillsdale, NJ: Erlbaum.

GIBSON, E. J., & SPELKE, E. S. (1983). The development of perception. In P. Mussen (Series Ed.), J. H. Flavell & E. M. Markman (Vol. Eds.), *Handbook of child psychology: Vol. 3. Cognitive development* (pp. 1–76). New York: Wiley.

GIBSON, J. J. (1950). *The perception of the visual world*. Boston: Houghton Mifflin.

GIBSON, J. J. (1979). *The ecological approach to visual perception*. Boston: Houghton Mifflin.

GIBSON, J. J. (1982). What is involved in surface perception? In J. Beck (Ed.), *Organization and representation in perception* (pp. 151–157). Hillsdale, NJ: Erlbaum.

GIBSON, J. J., & GIBSON, E. J. (1955). Perceptual learning: Differentiation or enrichment? *Psychological Review, 62,* 32–41.

GIBSON, K. R., & PETERSEN, A. C. (Eds.). (1991). *Brain maturation and cognitive development: Comparative and cross-cultural perspectives*. New York: Aldine de Gruyter.

GICK, M. L., & HOLYOAK, K. J. (1980). Analogical problem solving. *Cognitive Psychology, 12,* 306–355.

GICK, M. L., & HOLYOAK, K. J. (1983). Schema induction and analogical transfer. *Cognitive Psychology, 15,* 1–38.

GILLIGAN, C. (1982). *In a different voice: Psychological theory and women's development.* Cambridge: Harvard University Press.

GINSBURG, H. P., & OPPER, S. (1988). *Piaget's theory of intellectual development* (3rd ed.). Englewood Cliffs, NJ: Prentice Hall.

GLASER, R., & CHI, M. T. H. (1988). Overview. In M. T. H. Chi, R. Glaser, & M. J. Farr (Eds.), *The nature of expertise* (pp. xv–xxviii). Hillsdale, NJ: Erlbaum.

GLENBERG, A. M. (1977). Influences of retrieval process on the spacing effect in free recall. *Journal of Experimental Psychology: Human Learning and Memory, 3,* 282–294.

GLOBERSON, T., & ZELNICKER, T. (Eds.). (1989). *Human Development: Vol. 3. Cognitive style and cognitive development.* Norwood, NJ: Ablex.

GODDEN, D. R., & BADDELEY, A. D. (1975). Context-dependent memory in two natural environments: On land and underwater. *British Journal of Psychology, 66,* 325–332.

GODDEN, D. R., & BADDELEY, A. D. (1980). When does context influence recognition memory? *British Journal of Psychology, 71,* 99–104.

GOLDMAN-RAKIC, P. S. (1987). Development of cortical circuitry and cognitive function. *Child Development, 58,* 601–622.

GOODY, J., & WATT, I. (1968). The consequences of literacy. In J. Goody (Ed.), *Literacy in traditional societies* (pp. 27–68). Cambridge: Cambridge University Press.

GORDON, I. E. (1989). *Theories of visual perception.* Chichester, Great Britain: Wiley.

GREENFIELD, P. M., REICH, L. C., & OLVER, R. R. (1966). On culture and equivalence: II. In J. S. Bruner, R. Olver, P. Greenfield, et al. (Eds.), *Studies in cognitive growth* (pp. 270–318). New York: Wiley.

GREENO, J. G., & SIMON, H. A. (1988). Problem solving and reasoning. In R. C. Atkinson, R. J. Herrnstein, G. Lindzey, & R. D. Luce (Eds.), *Stevens' handbook of experimental psychology: Vol. 2. Learning and cognition* (2nd ed., pp. 589–672). New York: Wiley.

GREGORY, R. L. (1972). Cognitive contours. *Nature, 238,* 51–52.

GRICE, H. P. (1975). Logic and conversation. In P. Cole & J. L. Morgan (Eds.), *Syntax and semantics: Vol. 3. Speech acts* (pp. 41–58). New York: Seminar Press.

GRIGGS, R. A. (1983). The role of problem content in the selection task and in the THOG problem. In J. St. B. T. Evans (Ed.), *Thinking and reasoning: Psychological approaches* (pp. 16–43). London: Routledge & Kegan Paul.

GRIGGS, R. A., & COX, J. R. (1982). The elusive thematic-materials effect in Wason's selection task. *British Journal of Psychology, 73,* 407–420.

GRUBER, H. E., & VONECHE, J. J. (Eds.). (1977). *The essential Piaget: An interpretive and reference guide.* New York: Basic Books.

GUILFORD, J. P. (1950). Creativity. *American Psychologist, 5,* 444–454.

HABER, R. N. (1983). The impending demise of the icon: A critique of the concept of iconic storage in visual information processing. *Behavioral and Brain Sciences, 6,* 1–54.

HALFORD, G. S. (1989). Reflections on 25 years of Piagetian cognitive developmental psychology, 1963–1988. *Human Development, 32,* 325–357.

HALLE, M. (1990). Phonology. In D. N. Osherson & H. Lasnik (Eds.), *An invitation to cognitive science: Vol. 1. Language* (pp. 43–68). Cambridge: MIT Press.

HALPERN, D. F. (1992). *Sex differences in cognitive abilities* (2d ed.). Hillsdale, NJ: Erlbaum.

HARNAD, S. (Ed.). (1987). *Categorical perception.* Cambridge: Cambridge University Press.

HARRIS, L. J. (1978). Sex differences in spatial ability: Possible environmental, genetic, and neurological factors. In M. Kinsbourne (Ed.), *Asymmetrical function of the brain* (pp. 405–522). New York: Cambridge University Press.

HASHER, L., & ZACKS, R. T. (1984). Automatic processing of fundamental information. *American Psychologist, 39,* 1372–1388.

HAVILAND, S. E., & CLARK, H. H. (1974). What's new? Acquiring new information as a process in comprehension. *Journal of Verbal Learning and Verbal Behavior, 13,* 512–521.

HAWKINS, J., PEA, R. D., GLICK, J., & SCRIBNER, S. (1984). "Merds that laugh don't like mushrooms": Evidence for deductive reasoning by preschoolers. *Developmental Psychology, 20,* 584–594.

HAYES, J. R. (1989). *The complete problem solver* (2nd ed.). Hillsdale, NJ: Erlbaum.

HAYES-ROTH, B., & HAYES-ROTH, F. (1977). Concept learning and the recognition and classification of examples. *Journal of Verbal Learning and Verbal Behavior, 16,* 321–338.

HAYES-ROTH, F. (1979). Distinguishing theories of representation: A critique of Anderson's "Arguments concerning mental imagery." *Psychological Review, 86,* 376–382.

HEDGES, L. V., & OLKIN, I. (1985). *Statistical methods for meta-analysis.* New York: Academic Press.

HEIDBREDER, E. (1933). *Seven psychologies.* New York: Century.

HEIDER, E. R. (1972). Universals in color naming and memory. *Journal of Experimental Psychology, 93,* 10–20.

HENLE, M. (1962). On the relation between logic and thinking. *Psychological Review, 69,* 366–378.

HENLE, M. (1971). Of the scholler of nature. *Social Research, 38,* 93–107.

HENNESSEY, B. A., & AMABILE, T. M. (1988). The conditions of creativity. In R. J. Sternberg (Ed.), *The nature of creativity* (pp. 11–35). Cambridge: Cambridge University Press.

HERRMANN, D. (Ed.). (1992). *Memory improve: Implications for memory theory.* New York: Springer-Verlag.

HILLNER, K. P. (1984). *History and systems of modern psychology: A conceptual approach.* New York: Gardner Press

HIRST, W., & KALMAR, D. (1987). Characterizing attentional resources. *Journal of Experimental Psychology: General, 116,* 68–81.

HIRST, W., SPELKE, E. S., REAVES, C. C., CAHARACK, G., & NEISSER, U. (1980). Dividing attention without alternation or automaticity. *Journal of Experimental Psychology: General, 109,* 98–117.

HOCHBERG, J. E. (1978). *Perception* (2nd ed.). Englewood Cliffs, NJ: Prentice Hall.

HOCHBERG, J. (1988). Visual perception. In R. C. Atkinson (Ed.), *Stevens' handbook of experimental psychology: Vol. 1. Perception and motivation* (2nd ed., pp. 195–276). New York: Wiley.

HOCKETT, C. F. (1960). The origin of speech. *Scientific American, 203*(3), 88–96.

HOFFMAN, R. R., BAMBERG, M., BRINGMANN, W., & KLEIN, R. (1987). Some historical observations on Ebbinghaus. In D. S. Gorfein & R. R. Hoffman (Eds.), *Memory and learning: The Ebbinghaus Centennial Conference* (pp. 57–76). Hillsdale, NJ: Erlbaum.

HOLLAND, J. H., HOLYOAK, K. J., NISBETT, R. E., & THAGARD, P. R. (1986). *Induction.* Cambridge: MIT Press.

HOLYOAK, K. J., & NISBETT, R. E. (1988). Induction. In R. J. Sternberg & E. E. Smith (Eds.), *The psychology of human thought* (pp. 50–91). Cambridge: Cambridge University Press.

HOMA, D., STERLING, S., & TREPEL, L. (1981). Limitations of exemplar-based generalization and the abstraction of categorical information. *Journal of Experimental Psychology: Human Learning and Memory, 7,* 418–439.

HORN, J. L. (1989). Cognitive diversity: A framework of learning. In P. L. Ackerman, R. J. Sternberg, and R. Glaser (Eds.), *Learning and individual differences: Advances in theory and research* (pp. 61–116). New York: W. H. Freeman.

HORTON, D. L., & MILLS, C. B. (1984). Human learning and memory. *Annual Review of Psychology, 35,* 361–394.

HOWE, M. L. & O'SULLIVAN, J. T. (1990). The development of strategic memory: Coordinating knowledge, metamemory, and resources. In D. F. Bjorklund (Ed.), *Children's strategies: Contemporary views of cognitive development* (pp. 129–155). Hillsdale, NJ: Erlbaum.

HUBEL, D. H., & WIESEL, T. N. (1962). Receptive fields, binocular interaction, and functional architecture in the cat's visual cortex. *Journal of Physiology, 166,* 106–154.

HUBEL, D. H., & WIESEL, T. N. (1968). Receptive fields and functional architecture of the monkey striate cortex. *Journal of Physiology, 195,* 215–243.

HUDSON, W. (1960). Pictorial depth perception in sub-cultural groups in Africa. *Journal of Social Psychology, 52,* 183–208.

HUDSON, W. (1967). The study of the problem of pictorial perception among unacculturated groups. *International Journal of Psychology, 2,* 89–107.

HUNT, E. B. (1978). Mechanics of verbal ability. *Psychological Review, 85,* 109–130.

HUNT, E. (1986). The heffalump of intelligence. In R. J. Sternberg and D. K. Detterman (Eds.), *What is intelligence? Contemporary viewpoints on its nature and definition* (pp. 101–107). Norwood, NJ: Ablex.

HUNT, E., & AGNOLI, F. (1991). The Whorfian hypothesis: A cognitive psychology perspective. *Psychological Review, 98,* 377–389.

HUNT, E., LUNNEBORG, C., & LEWIS, J. (1975). What does it mean to be highly verbal? *Cognitive Psychology, 7,* 194–227.

HUPET, M., & TILMANT, B. (1986). What are clefts good for? Some consequences for comprehension. *Journal of Memory and Language, 25,* 419–430.

HYDE, J. S. (1981). How large are cognitive gender differences? *American Psychologist, 36,* 892–901.

HYDE, J. S., & LINN, M. C. (1988). Gender differences in verbal ability: A meta-analysis. *Psychological Bulletin, 104,* 53–69.

INGRAM, D. (1989). *First language acquisition: Method, description, and explanation.* Cambridge: Cambridge University Press.

INTONS-PETERSON, M. J. (1983). Imagery paradigms: How vulnerable are they to experimenters' expectations? *Journal of Experimental Psychology: Human Perception and Performance, 9,* 394–412.

INTONS-PETERSON, M. J., & ROSKOS-EWOLDSEN, B. B. (1989). Sensory-perceptual qualities of images. *Journal of Experimental Psychology: Learning, Memory, and Cognition, 15,* 188–199.

IRVINE, S. H., & BERRY, J. W. (Eds.). (1988). *Human abilities in cultural context.* Cambridge: Cambridge University Press.

IRWIN, M. H., & MCLAUGHLIN, D. H. (1970). Ability and preference in category sorting by Mano schoolchildren and adults. *Journal of Social Psychology, 82,* 15–24.

IRWIN, M. H., SCHAFER, G. N., & FEIDEN, C. P. (1974). Emic and unfamiliar category sorting of Mano farmers and U. S. undergraduates. *Journal of Cross-Cultural Psychology, 5,* 407–423.

ISAACS, E. A., & CLARK, H. H. (1987). References in conversation between experts and novices. *Journal of Experimental Psychology: General, 116,* 26–37.

JACKLIN, C. N. (1989). Female and male: Issues of gender. *American Psychologist, 44,* 127–133.

JAMES, W. (1983). *The principles of psychology.* Cambridge: Harvard University Press. (Original work published 1890.)

JANIS, I. L., & MANN, L. (1977). *Decision making.* New York: Free Press.

JARVELLA, R. J. (1971). Syntactic processing of connected speech. *Journal of Verbal Learning and Verbal Behavior, 10,* 409–416.

JOHANSSON, G. (1973). Visual perception of biological motion and a model for its analysis. *Perception and Psychophysics, 14,* 201–211.

JOHNSON, M. K., & HASHER, L. (1987). Human learning and memory. *Annual Review of Psychology, 38,* 631–668.

JOHNSON-LAIRD, P. N. (1975). Models of deduction. In R. J. Falmagne (Ed.), *Reasoning: Representation and process* (pp. 7–54). Hillsdale, NJ: Erlbaum.

JOHNSON-LAIRD, P. N. (1982). Ninth Bartlett memorial lecture. Thinking as a skill. *Quarterly Journal of Experimental Psychology, 34A,* 1–29.

JOHNSON-LAIRD, P. N. (1983). *Mental models.* Cambridge: Harvard University Press.

JOHNSON-LAIRD, P. N., & BARA, B. G. (1984). Syllogistic inference. *Cognition, 16,* 1–61.

JOHNSON-LAIRD, P. N., & BYRNE, M. J. (1991). *Deduction.* Hillsdale, NJ: Erlbaum.

JOHNSON-LAIRD, P. N., HERRMANN, D. J., & CHAFFIN, R. (1984). Only connections: A critique of semantic networks. *Psychological Bulletin, 96,* 292–315.

JOHNSON-LAIRD, P. N., & STEEDMAN, M. (1978). The psychology of syllogisms. *Cognitive Psychology, 10,* 64–99.

JOHNSTON, W. A., & HEINZ, S. P. (1978). Flexibility and capacity demands of attention. *Journal of Experimental Psychology: General, 107,* 420–435.

JUST, M. A., & CARPENTER, P. A. (1980). A theory of reading: From eye fixations to comprehension. *Psychological Review, 87,* 329–354.

JUST, M. A., & CARPENTER, P. A. (1987). *The psychology of reading and language comprehension.* Boston, MA: Allyn & Bacon.

KAGAN, J., ROSMAN, B. L., DAY, D., ALBERT, J., & PHILLIPS, W. (1964). Information processing in the child: Significance of analytic and reflective attitudes. *Psychological Monographs, 78* (1, Whole No. 578).

KAGITÇIBASI, C., & BERRY, J. W. (1989). Cross-cultural psychology: Current research and trends. *Annual Review of Psychology, 40,* 493–531.

KAHNEMAN, D. (1973). *Attention and effort.* Englewood Cliffs, NJ: Prentice Hall.

KAHNEMAN, D., SLOVIC, P., & TVERSKY, A. (1982). *Judgment under uncertainty: Heuristics and biases.* Cambridge: Cambridge University Press.

KAHNEMAN, D., & TVERSKY, A. (1973). On the psychology of prediction. *Psychological Review, 80,* 237–251.

KAHNEMAN, D., & TVERSKY, A. (1979). Prospect theory: An analysis of decisions under risk. *Econometrica, 47,* 263–291.

KAIL, R. (1986). Sources of age differences in speed of processing. *Child Development, 57,* 969–987.

KAIL, R. (1988). Developmental functions for speeds of cognitive processes. *Journal of Experimental Child Psychology, 45,* 339–364.

KANIZA, G., & GERBINO, W. (1982). Amodal completion: Seeing or thinking? In J. Beck (Ed.), *Organization and representation in perception* (pp. 167–190). Hillsdale, NJ: Erlbaum.

KASSIN, S. M., ELLSWORTH, P. C., & SMITH, V. L. (1989). The "general acceptance" of psychological research on eyewitness testimony. *American Psychologist, 44,* 1089–1098.

KATZ, J. J. (1972). *Semantic theory.* New York: Harper & Row.

KAYE, J. (1989). *Phonology: A cognitive view.* Hillsdale, NJ: Erlbaum.

KEARINS, J. M. (1981). Visual spatial memory in Australian Aboriginal children of desert regions. *Cognitive Psychology, 13,* 434–460.

KEATING, D. P. (1980). Thinking processes in adolescence. In J. Adelson (Ed.), *Handbook of adolescent psychology* (pp. 211–246). New York: Wiley.

KEATING, D. P., & BOBBITT, B. L. (1978). Individual and developmental differences in cognitive-processing components of mental ability. *Child Development, 49,* 155–167.

KEENEY, R. L. (1982). Decision analysis: An overview. *Operations Research, 30,* 803–838.

KEENEY, T. J., CANNIZZO, S. R., & FLAVELL, J. H. (1967). Spontaneous and induced verbal rehearsal in a recall task. *Child Development, 38,* 953–966.

KEIL, F. C. (1989). *Concepts, kinds, and cognitive development.* Cambridge: MIT Press.

KELLMAN, P. J., & SPELKE, E. S. (1983). Perception of partially occluded objects in infancy. *Cognitive Psychology, 15,* 483–524.

KEMLER, D. G. (1983). Holistic and analytic modes in perceptual and cognitive development. In T. J. Tighe & B. E. Shepp (Eds.), *Perception, cognition, and development: Interactional analyses* (pp. 77–102). Hillsdale, NJ: Erlbaum.

KEMLER NELSON, D. K. (1984). The effect of intention on what concepts are acquired. *Journal of Verbal Learning and Verbal Behavior, 23,* 734–759.

KEMLER NELSON, D. K. (1990). When experimental findings conflict with everyday observations: Reflections on children's category learning. *Child Development, 61,* 606–610.

KEPPEL, G., & UNDERWOOD, B. J. (1962). Proactive inhibition in short-term retention of single items. *Journal of Verbal Learning and Verbal Behavior, 1,* 153–161.

KERLINGER, F. N. (1986). *Foundations of behavioral research* (3rd ed.). New York: Holt, Rinehart & Winston.

KERR, N. H. (1983). The role of vision in "visual imagery" experiments: Evidence from the congenitally blind. *Journal of Experimental Psychology: General, 112,* 265–277.

KINTSCH, W., & KEENAN, J. (1973). Reading rate and retention as a function of the number of propositions in the base structure of sentences. *Cognitive Psychology, 5,* 257–274.

KIRKPATRICK, E. A. (1894). An experimental study of memory. *Psychological Review, 1,* 602–609.

KLAHR, D. (1992). Information-processing approaches to cognitive development. In M. H. Bornstein & M. E. Lamb (Eds.), *Developmental psychology: An advanced textbook* (3rd. ed., pp. 273–335). Hillsdale, NJ: Erlbaum.

KLATZKY, R. L. (1980). *Human memory: Structures and processes* (2nd ed.). San Francisco: W. H. Freeman.

KLAYMAN, J., & HA, Y. W. (1987). Confirmation, disconfirmation, and information in hypothesis testing. *Psychological Review, 94,* 211–228.

KLEINMUNTZ, B. (1990). Why we still use our heads instead of formulas: Toward an integrative approach. *Psychological Bulletin, 107,* 296–310.

KOESTLER, A. (1964). *The act of creation.* New York: Dell.

KOFFKA, K. (1935). *Principles of Gestalt psychology.* New York: Harcourt Brace & Company.

KOGAN, N. (1983). Stylistic variation in childhood and adolescence: Creativity, metaphor, and cognitive styles. In J. H. Flavell & E. M. Markman (Eds.), *Handbook of child psychology: Vol. 3. Cognitive development* (pp. 630–706). New York: Wiley.

KÖHLER, W. (1929/1947). *Gestalt psychology: An introduction to new concepts in modern psychology.* New York: Liveright.

KOMATSU, L. K. (1992). Recent views of conceptual structure. *Psychological Bulletin, 112,* 500–526.

KOPP, J., & SLAYTER, C. (1984). *DecisionMap* (software for Apple Macintosh). Honolulu: SoftStyle.

KOSLOWSKI, L. T., & CUTTING, J. E. (1977). Recognizing the sex of a walker from a dynamic point-light display. *Perception and Psychophysics, 21,* 575–580.

KOSSLYN, S. M. (1973). Scanning visual images: Some structural implications. *Perception & Psychophysics, 14,* 90–94.

KOSSLYN, S. M. (1976). Can imagery be distinguished from other forms of internal representation? Evidence from studies of information retrieval times. *Memory & Cognition, 4,* 291–297.

KOSSLYN, S. M. (1980). *Image and mind.* Cambridge: Harvard University Press.

KOSSLYN, S. M., BALL, T. M., & REISER, B. J. (1978). Visual images preserve metric spatial information: Evidence from studies of image scanning. *Journal of Experimental Psychology: Human Perception and Performance, 4,* 47–60.

KOSSLYN, S. M., CAVE, C. B., PROVOST, D. A., & VON GIERKE, S. M. (1988). Sequential processes in image generation. *Cognition, 20,* 319–343.

KOSSLYN, S. M., REISER, B. J., FARAH, M. J., & FLIEGEL, S. L. (1983). Generating visual images: Units and relations. *Journal of Experimental Psychology: General, 112,* 278–303.

KOTOVSKY, K., HAYES, J. R., & SIMON, H. A. (1985). Why are some problems hard? Evidence from Tower of Hanoi. *Cognitive Psychology, 17,* 248–294.

KUBOVY, M., & POMERANTZ, J. R. (Eds.). (1981). *Perceptual organization.* Hillsdale, NJ: Erlbaum.

KUHN, D. (1992). Cognitive development. In M. H. Bornstein & M. E. Lamb (Eds.), *Developmental psychology: An advanced textbook* (3rd. ed., pp. 211–272). Hillsdale, NJ: Erlbaum.

LABORATORY OF COMPARATIVE HUMAN COGNITION (1983). Culture and cognitive development. In W. Kessen (Ed.), *Handbook of child psychology* (4th ed., Vol. 1, pp. 295–356). New York: Wiley.

LACHMAN, R., LACHMAN, J. L., & BUTTERFIELD, E. C. (1979). *Cognitive psychology and information processing: An introduction.* Hillsdale, NJ: Erlbaum.

LADEFOGED, P. (1975). *A course in phonetics.* New York: Harcourt Brace Jovanovich.

LAKOFF, G. (1987). Cognitive models and prototype theory. In U. Neisser (Ed.), *Concepts and conceptual development: Ecological and intellectual factors in categorization* (pp. 63–100). Cambridge: Cambridge University Press.

LANDAU, B. (1982). Will the real grandmother please stand up? The psychological reality of dual meaning representations. *Journal of Psycholinguistic Research, 11,* 47–62.

LANDAUER, T. K., & MEYER, D. E. (1972). Category size and semantic-memory retrieval. *Journal of Verbal Learning and Verbal Behavior, 11,* 539–549.

LANGLEY, P., & JONES, R. (1988). A computational model of scientific insight. In R. J. Sternberg (Ed.), *The nature of creativity: Contemporary psychological perspectives* (pp. 177–201). Cambridge: Cambridge University Press.

LARSON, R. K. (1990). Semantics. In D. N. Osherson & H. Lasnik (Eds.), *An invitation to cognitive science: Vol. 1. Language* (pp. 23–42). Cambridge: MIT Press.

LAUGHLIN, P. R., LANGE, R., & ADAMOPOULOS, J. (1982). Selection strategies for "Mastermind" problems. *Journal of Experimental Psychology: Learning, Memory, and Cognition, 8,* 475–483.

LAVE, J. (1988). *Cognition in practice.* Cambridge: Cambridge University Press.

LAVE, J., MURTAUGH, M., & DE LA ROCHA, O. (1984). The dialectic of arithmetic in grocery shopping. In B. Rogoff & J. Lave (Eds.), *Everyday cognition: Its development in social context* (pp. 67–94). Cambridge: Harvard University Press.

LEA, G. (1975). Chronometric analysis of the method of loci. *Journal of Experimental Psychology: Human Perception and Performance, 1,* 95–104.

LERNER, R. M. (1990). Plasticity, person-context relations, and cognitive training in the aged years: A developmental contextual perspective. *Developmental Psychology, 26,* 911–915.

LESGOLD, A. (1988). Problem solving. In R. J. Sternberg & E. E. Smith (Eds.), *The psychology of human thought* (pp. 188–213). Cambridge: Cambridge University Press.

LESGOLD, A. M., & PERFETTI, C. A. (Eds.). (1981). *Interactive processes in reading.* Hillsdale, NJ: Erlbaum.

LESGOLD, A., RUBINSON, H., FELTOVICH, P., GLASER, R., KLOPFER, K., & WANG, Y. (1988). Expertise in a complex skill: Diagnosing x-ray pictures. In M. T. H. Chi, R. Glaser, & M. J. Farr (Eds.), *The nature of expertise* (pp. 311–342). Hillsdale, NJ: Erlbaum.

LETTVIN, J. Y., MATURANA, H. R., McCULLOGH, W. S., & PITTS, W. H. (1959). What the frog's eye tells the frog's brain. *Proceedings of the Institute of Radio Engineering, 47,* 1940–1941.

LEVY, J., & HELLER, W. (1992). Gender differences in human neuropsychological function. In A. A. Gerall, H. Moltz, & I. L. Ward (Eds.), *Handbook of behavioral neurobiology* (Vol. 11, pp. 245–274). New York: Plenum.

LICHTENSTEIN, S., FISCHHOFF, B., & PHILLIPS, D. (1982). Calibration of probabilities: The state of the art to 1980. In D. Kahneman, P. Slovic, & A. Tversky (Eds.), *Judgment under uncertainty: Heuristics and biases* (pp. 306–334). Cambridge: Cambridge University Press.

LINN, M. C., & PETERSEN, A. C. (1985). Emergence and characterization of sex differences in spatial ability: A meta-analysis. *Child Development, 56,* 1479–1498.

LISKER, L., & ABRAMSON, A. (1970). The voicing dimension: Some experiments in comparative phonetics. *Proceedings of the Sixth International Congress of Phonetic Sciences, Prague, 1967* (pp. 563–567). Prague, Czechoslovakia: Academia.

LIU, L. G. (1985). Reasoning counterfactually in Chinese: Are there any obstacles? *Cognition, 21,* 239–270.

LOCKE, J. (1964/1690). *An essay concerning human understanding* (A. D. Woozley, Ed.). New York: New American Library.

LOFTUS, E. F. (1975). Leading questions and the eyewitness report. *Cognitive Psychology, 7,* 560–572.

LOFTUS, E. F. (1979). *Eyewitness testimony.* Cambridge: Harvard University Press.

LOFTUS, E. F. (1983). Silence is not golden. *American Psychologist, 38,* 564–572.

LOFTUS, E. F., MILLER, D. G., & BURNS, H. J. (1978). Semantic integration of verbal information into a visual memory. *Journal of Experimental Psychology: Human Learning and Memory, 4,* 19–31.

LONNER, W. J., & BERRY, J. W. (Eds.). (1986). *Field methods in cross-cultural research.* Beverly Hills: Sage Publications.

LUCHINS, A. S. (1942). Mechanization in problem solving: The effect of *Einstellung. Psychological Monographs, 54* (Whole No. 248).

LUCY, J. A., & SCHWEDER, R. A. (1979). Whorf and his critics: Linguistic and nonlinguistic influences on color memory. *American Anthropologist, 81,* 581–615.

LURIA, A. R. (1968). *The mind of a mnemonist.* (L. Solotaroff, Trans.). New York: Basic Books.

LURIA, A. R. (1976). *Cognitive development: Its cultural and social foundations.* (M. Cole, Ed., M. Lopez-Morillas & L. Solotaroff, Trans.). Cambridge: Harvard University Press.

MACCOBY, E. E., & JACKLIN, C. N. (1974). *The psychology of sex differences.* Stanford: Stanford University Press.

MACKAY, D. G. (1973). Aspects of the theory of comprehension, memory, and attention. *Quarterly Journal of Experimental Psychology, 25,* 22–40.

MACLEOD, C. M. (1991). Half a century of research on the Stroop Effect: An integrative review. *Psychological Bulletin, 109,* 163–203.

MAIER, N. R. F. (1930). Reasoning in humans. I. On direction. *Journal of Comparative Physiological Psychology, 10,* 115–143.

MAIER, N. R. F. (1931). Reasoning in humans. II. The solution of a problem and its appearance in consciousness. *Journal of Comparative Physiological Psychology, 12,* 181–194.

MALPASS, R. S., & POORTINGA, Y. H. (1986). Strategies for design and analysis. In W. J. Lonner & J. W. Berry (Eds.), *Field methods in cross-cultural research* (pp. 47–83). Beverly Hills: Sage.

MANDLER, G. (1967). Organization and memory. In K. W. Spence and J. T. Spence (Eds.), *The psychology of learning and motivation* (Vol. 1, pp. 327–372). New York: Academic Press.

MANDLER, G. (1980). Recognizing: The judgment of previous occurrence. *Psychological Review, 87,* 252–271.

MANDLER, J. M., & JOHNSON, N. S. (1977). Remembrance of things parsed: Story structure and recall. *Cognitive Psychology, 9,* 111–151.

MARKMAN, E. M. (1979). Realizing that you don't understand: Elementary school children's awareness of inconsistencies. *Child Development, 50,* 643–655.

MARKMAN, E. M., & GORIN, L. (1981). Children's ability to adjust their standards for evaluating comprehension. *Journal of Educational Psychology, 73,* 320–325.

MARKOVITS, H., & NANTEL, G. (1989). The belief-bias effect in the production and evaluation of logical conclusions. *Memory & Cognition, 17,* 11–17.

MARKUS, H. R., & KITAYAMA, S. (1991). Culture and the self: Implications for cognition, emotion, and motivation. *Psychological Review, 98,* 224–253.

MARR, D. (1982). *Vision.* San Francisco: W. H. Freeman.

MARSLEN-WILSON, W., & WELSH, A. (1978). Processing interactions and lexical access during word recognition in continuous speech. *Cognitive Psychology, 10,* 29–63.

MARTIN, D. W. (1991). *Doing psychology experiments* (3rd ed.). Pacific Grove, CA: Brooks/Cole.

MASSARO, D. (1979). Letter information and orthographic context in word perception. *Journal of Experimental Psychology: Human Perception and Performance, 5,* 595–609.

MASSARO, D. W., & COHEN, M. M. (1983). Evaluation and integration of visual and auditory information in speech perception. *Journal of Experimental Psychology: Human Perception and Performance, 9,* 753–771.

MATLIN, M. W. (1988). *Sensation and perception* (2nd ed.). Boston: Allyn & Bacon.

MAYER, R. E. (1992). *Thinking, problem solving, cognition* (2nd ed.). New York: W. H. Freeman.

MCCLELLAND, J. L. (1988). Connectionist models and psychological evidence. *Journal of Memory and Language, 27,* 107–123.

MCCLELLAND, J. L., & RUMELHART, D. E. (1981). An interactive activation model of context effects in letter perception: Part 1. An account of basic findings. *Psychological Review, 88,* 375–407.

MCCLELLAND, J. L., & RUMELHART, D. E. (Eds.). (1986). *Parallel distributed processing: Volume 2. Psychological and biological models.* Cambridge: MIT Press.

MCCLOSKEY, M., & EGETH, H. E. (1983). Eyewitness identification: What can a psychologist tell a jury? *American Psychologist, 38,* 550–563.

MCCLOSKEY, M. E., & GLUCKSBERG, S. (1978). Natural categories: Well defined or fuzzy sets? *Memory & Cognition, 6,* 462–472.

MCCLOSKEY, M., & GLUCKSBERG, S. (1979). Decision processes in verifying category membership statements: Implications for models of semantic memory. *Cognitive Psychology, 11,* 1–37.

MCCLOSKEY, M., WIBLE, C. G., & COHEN, N. J. (1988). Is there a special flashbulb-memory mechanism? *Journal of Experimental Psychology: General, 117,* 336–338.

MCDOWD, J. M., & CRAIK, F. I. M. (1988). Effects of aging and task difficulty on divided attention performance. *Journal of Experimental Psychology: Human Perception and Performance, 14,* 267–280.

MCGEE, M. G. (1979). Human spatial abilities: Psychometric studies and environmental, genetic, hormonal, and neurological influences. *Psychological Bulletin, 86,* 889–918.

MCGEOCH, J. A. (1932). Forgetting and the law of disuse. *Psychological Review, 39,* 352–370.

MCKOON, G., RATCLIFF, R., & DELL, G. S. (1986). A critical evaluation of the semantic-episodic distinction. *Journal of Experimental Psychology: Learning, Memory, and Cognition, 12,* 295–306.

MCNEILL, D. (1966). Developmental psycholinguistics. In F. Smith & G. A. Miller (Eds.), *The genesis of language: A psycholinguistic approach* (pp. 15–84). Cambridge: MIT Press.

MEDIN, D. L. (1989). Concepts and conceptual structure. *American Psychologist, 44,* 1469–1481.

MEDIN, D. L., ALTOM, M. W., EDELSON, S. M., & FREKO, D. (1982). Correlated symptoms and simulated medical classification. *Journal of Experimental Psychology: Learning, Memory, and Cognition, 8,* 37–50.

MEDIN, D. L., & SMITH, E. E. (1984). Concepts and concept formation. *Annual Review of Psychology, 35,* 113–138.

MEDIN, D. L., WATTENMAKER, W. D., & HAMPSON, S. E. (1987). Family resemblance, conceptual cohesiveness, and category construction. *Cognitive Psychology, 19,* 242–279.

MEEHAN, A. M. (1984). A meta-analysis of sex differences in formal operational thought. *Child Development, 55,* 1110–1124.

MEEHL, P. E. (1954). *Clinical versus statistical prediction: A theoretical analysis and a review of the evidence.* Minneapolis: University of Minnesota Press.

MEEHL, P. E. (1965). Seer over sign: The first good example. *Journal of Experimental Research in Personality, 1,* 27–32.

MELTON, A. W. (1963). Implications of short-term memory for a general theory of memory. *Journal of Verbal Learning and Verbal Behavior, 2,* 1–21.

MERVIS, C. B. (1980). Category structure and the development of categorization. In R. Spiro, B. C. Bruce, W. F. Brewer (Eds.), *Theoretical issues in reading comprehension* (pp. 279–307). Hillsdale, NJ: Erlbaum.

MERVIS, C. B., CATLIN, J., & ROSCH, E. (1976). Relationships among goodness-of-example, category norms, and word frequency. *Bulletin of the Psychonomic Society, 7,* 283–284.

MERVIS, C. B., & ROSCH, E. (1981). Categorization of natural objects. *Annual Review of Psychology, 32,* 89–115.

MEYER, D. E. (1970). On the representation and retrieval of stored semantic information. *Cognitive Psychology, 1,* 242–300.

MEYER, D. E., & SCHVANEVELDT, R. W. (1971). Facilitation in recognizing pairs of words: Evidence of a dependence between retrieval operations. *Journal of Experimental Psychology, 90,* 227–234.

MICHAELS, C. F., & CARELLO, C. (1981). *Direct perception.* Englewood Cliffs, NJ: Prentice Hall.

MILLER, G. A. (1956). The magical number seven, plus or minus two: Some limits on our capacity for processing information. *Psychological Review, 63,* 81–97.

MILLER, G. A., & GLUCKSBERG, S. (1988). Psycholinguistic aspects of pragmatics and semantics. In R. C. Atkinson (Ed.), *Stevens' handbook of experimental psychology: Vol. 2. Learning and cognition* (2nd ed., pp. 417–472). New York: Wiley.

MILLER, G. A., & JOHNSON-LAIRD, P. N. (1976). *Language and perception.* Cambridge: Harvard University Press.

MILLER, G. A., & NICELY, P. (1955). An analysis of perceptual confusions among some English consonants. *Journal of the Acoustical Society of America, 27,* 338–352.

MILLER, J. L. (1990). Speech perception. In D. N. Osherson & H. Lasnik (Eds.), *An invitation to cognitive science: Vol. 1. Language* (pp. 69–93). Cambridge: MIT Press.

MILLER, K. F., & STIGLER, J. W. (1987). Counting in Chinese: Cultural variation in a basic cognitive skill. *Cognitive Development, 2,* 279–305.

MILLER, P. H. (1989). *Theories of developmental psychology* (2nd ed.). New York: W. H. Freeman.

MILLER, P. H., HAYNES, V. F., DEMARIE-DREBLOW, D., & WOODY-RAMSEY, J. (1986). Children's strategies for gathering information in three tasks. *Child Development, 57,* 1429–1439.

MODGIL, S., & MODGIL, C. (Eds.). (1982). *Jean Piaget: Consensus and controversy.* New York: Praeger.

MORAY, N. (1959). Attention in dichotic listening: Affective cues and the influence of instructions. *Quarterly Journal of Experimental Psychology, 11,* 56–60.

MORAY, N., BATES, A., & BARNETT, T. (1965). Experiments on the four-eared man. *Journal of the Acoustical Society of America, 38,* 196–201.

MOSHMAN, D., & FRANKS, B. A. (1986). Development of the concept of inferential validity. *Child Development, 57,* 153–165.

MOSHMAN, D., & TIMMONS, M. (1982). The construction of logical necessity. *Human Development, 25,* 309–323.

MOYER, R. S. (1973). Comparing objects in memory: Evidence suggesting an internal psychophysics. *Perception & Psychophysics, 13,* 180–184.

MURDOCK, B. B. (1962). The serial position effect of free recall. *Journal of Experimental Psychology, 62,* 482–488.

MURPHY, G. L., & MEDIN, D. L. (1985). The role of theories in conceptual coherence. *Psychological Review, 92,* 289–316.

MURRAY, D. J. (1988). *A history of western psychology* (2nd ed.) Englewood Cliffs, NJ: Prentice Hall.

MURTAUGH, M. (1985). The practice of arithmetic by American grocery shoppers. *Anthropology and Education Quarterly, 16,* 186–192.

NAVON, D., & GOPHER, D. (1979). On the economy of the human-processing system. *Psychological Review, 86,* 214–255.

NAVON, D., & MILLER, J. (1987). Role of outcome conflict in dual-task interference. *Journal of Experimental Psychology: Human Perception and Performance, 13,* 435–448.

NEELY, J. H. (1990). Semantic priming effects in visual word recognition: A selective review of current findings and theories. In D. Besner & G. Humphreys (Eds.), *Basic processes in reading: Visual word recognition.* Hillsdale, NJ: Erlbaum.

NEIMARK, E. D., & CHAPMAN, R. H. (1975). Development of the comprehension of logical quantifiers. In R. J. Falmagne (Ed.), *Reasoning: Representation and process* (pp. 135–151). Hillsdale, NJ: Erlbaum.

NEISSER, U. (1963). Decision-time without reaction-time: Experiments in visual scanning. *American Journal of Psychology, 76,* 376–385.

NEISSER, U. (1967). *Cognitive psychology.* New York: Appleton-Century-Crofts.

NEISSER, U. (1976). *Cognition and reality: Principles and implications of cognitive psychology.* San Francisco: W. H. Freeman.

NEISSER, U. (1982a). Memory: What are the important questions? In U. Neisser (Ed.), *Memory observed: Remembering in natural contexts* (pp. 3–19). San Francisco: W. H. Freeman.

NEISSER, U. (1982b). Snapshots or benchmarks? In U. Neisser (Ed.), *Memory observed: Remembering in natural contexts* (pp. 43–48). San Francisco: W. H. Freeman.

NEISSER, U. (1983). The rise and fall of the sensory register. *Behavioral and Brain Sciences, 6,* 34.

NEISSER, U. (1987a). Introduction: The ecological and intellectual bases of categorization. In U. Neisser (Ed.), *Concepts and conceptual development: Ecological and intellectual factors in categorization* (pp. 1–10). Cambridge: Cambridge University Press.

NEISSER, U. (Ed.). (1987b). *Concepts and conceptual development: Ecological and intellectual factors in categorization.* Cambridge: Cambridge University Press.

NEISSER, U. (1991). A case of misplaced nostalgia. *American Psychologist, 46,* 34–36.

NEISSER, U., & BECKLEN, R. (1975). Selective looking: Attending to visually specified events. *Cognitive Psychology, 7,* 480–494.

NEISSER, U., WINOGRAD, E., & WELDON, M. S. (1991). Remembering the earthquake: "What I experienced" versus "How I heard the news." Paper presented at the 32nd Annual Meeting of the Psychonomic Society, San Francisco.

NELSON, K. (1986). Event knowledge and cognitive development. In K. Nelson (Ed.), *Event knowledge: Structure and function in development* (pp. 1–20). Hillsdale, NJ: Erlbaum.

NELSON, K., & GRUENDEL, J. M. (1981). Generalized event representation: Basic building blocks of cognitive development. In A. Brown & M. Lamb (Eds.), *Advances in developmental psychology* (Vol. 1, pp. 131–158). Hillsdale, NJ: Erlbaum.

NELSON-JONES, R. (1990). *Thinking skills: Managing and preventing personal problems.* Pacific Grove, CA: Brooks/Cole.

NEWELL, A. (1980). Reasoning, problem solving, and decision processes: The problem space as a fundamental category. In R. S. Nickerson (Ed.), *Attention and performance, VIII* (pp. 693–718). Hillsdale, NJ: Erlbaum.

NEWELL, A., & SIMON, H. A. (1972). *Human problem-solving.* Englewood Cliffs, NJ: Prentice Hall.

NEWMEYER, F. J. (Ed.). (1988). *Linguistics: The Cambridge survey: Vol. 3. Language: Psychological and biological aspects.* Cambridge: Cambridge University Press.

NICKERSON, R. S., & ADAMS, M. J. (1979). Long-term memory for a common object. *Cognitive Psychology, 11,* 287–307.

NICKERSON, R. S., PERKINS, D. N., & SMITH, E. E. (1985). *The teaching of thinking.* Hillsdale, NJ: Erlbaum.

NISBETT, R. E. (Ed.). (1993). *Rules for reasoning.* Hillsdale, NJ: Erlbaum.

NISBETT, R., & ROSS, L. (1980). *Human inference: Strategies and shortcomings.* Englewood Cliffs, NJ: Prentice Hall.

NISBETT, R. E., FONG, G. T., LEHMAN, D. R., & CHENG, P. W. (1987). Teaching reasoning. *Science, 238,* 625–631.

NISBETT, R. E., KRANTZ, D. H., JEPSON, C., & KUNDA, Z. (1983). The use of statistical heuristics in everyday inductive reasoning. *Psychological Review, 90,* 339–363.

NORMAN, D. A. (1968). Toward a theory of memory and attention. *Psychological Review, 75,* 522–536.

NORMAN, D. A., & BOBROW, D. G. (1975). On data-limited and resource-limited processes. *Cognitive Psychology, 7,* 44–64.

NOWAKOWSKI, R. S. (1987). Basic concepts of CNS development. *Child Development, 58,* 568–595.

OAKES, J. (1990). Lost talent: The underparticipation of women, minorities, and disabled persons in science. (Report R-3774-NSF/RC). Santa Monica, CA: Rand.

OAKHILL, J., JOHNSON-LAIRD, P. N., & GARNHAM, A. (1989). Believability and syllogistic reasoning. *Cognition, 31,* 117–140.

OLSON, D. R. (1986). The cognitive consequences of literacy. *Canadian Psychology, 27,* 107–121.

OLSON, D. R. (1987). An introduction to understanding literacy. *Interchange, 18,* 1–8.

OLTON, R. M. (1979). Experimental studies of incubation: Searching for the elusive. *Journal of Creative Behavior, 13,* 9–22.

OLVER, R. R., & HORNSBY, J. R. (1966). On equivalence. In J. S. Bruner, R. R. Olver, P. M. Greenfield, J. R. Hornsby, H. J. Kenney, M. Maccoby, N. Modiano, F. A. Mosher, D. R. Olson, M. C. Potter, L. C. Reich, & A. M. Sonstroem (Eds.), *Studies in cognitive growth: A collaboration at the Center for Cognitive Studies* (pp. 68–85). New York: Wiley.

ORNE, M. T. (1962). On the social psychology of the psychology experiment: With particular reference to demand characteristics and their implication. *American Psychologist, 17,* 776–783.

ORNSTEIN, P. A., & NAUS, M. J. (1978). Rehearsal processes in children's memory. In P. A. Ornstein (Ed.), *Children's memory* (pp. 69–99). Hillsdale, NJ: Erlbaum.

OSHERSON, D. (1975). Logic and models of logical thinking. In R. J. Falmagne (Ed.), *Reasoning: Representation and process* (pp. 81–91). Hillsdale, NJ: Erlbaum.

OSHERSON, D. N., KOSSLYN, S. M., & HOLLERBACH, J. M. (Eds.). (1990). *An invitation to cognitive science: Vol. 2. Visual cognition and action.* Cambridge: MIT Press.

OSHERSON, D. N., & LASNIK, H. (Eds.). (1990). *An invitation to cognitive science: Vol. 1. Language.* Cambridge: MIT Press.

OSHERSON, D. N., & MARKMAN, E. (1975). Language and the ability to evaluate contradictions and tautologies. *Cognition, 3,* 213–226.

OSHERSON, D. N., & SMITH, E. E. (1981). On the adequacy of prototype theory as a theory of concepts. *Cognition, 9,* 35–58.

OSHERSON, D. N., & SMITH, E. E. (Eds.). (1990). *An invitation to cognitive science: Vol. 3. Thinking.* Cambridge: MIT Press.

OWENS, J., BOWER, G. H., & BLACK, J. B. (1979). The "soap opera" effect in story recall. *Memory & Cognition, 7,* 185–191.

PAIVIO, A. (1965). Abstractness, imagery, and meaningfulness in paired-associate learning. *Journal of Verbal Learning and Verbal Behavior, 4,* 32–38.

PAIVIO, A. (1969). Mental imagery in associative learning and memory. *Psychological Review, 76,* 241–263.

PAIVIO, A. (1971). *Imagery and verbal processes.* New York: Holt, Rinehart & Winston.

PAIVIO, A. (1975). Perceptual comparisons through the mind's eye. *Memory & Cognition, 3,* 635–647.

PAIVIO, A. (1983). The empirical case for dual coding. In J. C. Yuille (Ed.), *Imagery, memory and cognition* (pp. 307–332). Hillsdale, NJ: Erlbaum.

PALMER, S. E. (1975). The effects of contextual scenes on the identification of objects. *Memory & Cognition, 3,* 519–526.

PAPP, K. R., NEWSOME, S. L., MCDONALD, J. E., & SCHVANEVELDT, R. W. (1982). An activation-verification model for letter and word recognition: The word-superiority effect. *Psychological Review, 89,* 573–594.

PASCUAL-LEONE, J. (1970). A mathematical model for the transition rule in Piaget's developmental stages. *Acta Psychologica, 63,* 301–345.

PATTERSON, R. D. (1990). Auditory warning sounds in the work environment. In D. E. Broadbent, J. Reason, & A. Baddeley (Eds.), *Human factors in hazardous situations* (pp. 37–44). Oxford: Clarendon Press.

PAYNE, J. W. (1976). Task complexity and contingent processing in decision making: An information search and protocol analysis. *Organizational Behavior and Human Performance, 16,* 366–387.

PAYNE, J. W., BETTMAN, J. R., & JOHNSON, E. J. (1992). Behavioral decision research: A constructive processing perspective. *Annual Review of Psychology, 43,* 87–131.

PELLEGRINO, J. W., & GLASER, R. (1980). Components of inductive reasoning. In R. E. Snow, P. A. Federico, & W. E. Montague (Eds.), *Aptitude, learning, and instruction: Cognitive process analyses of aptitude* (pp. 177–217). Hillsdale, NJ: Erlbaum.

PERKINS, D. N. (1981). *The mind's best work.* Cambridge: Harvard University Press.

PERKINS, D. N. (1985a). Postprimary education has little impact on informal reasoning. *Journal of Educational Psychology, 77,* 562–571.

PERKINS, D. N. (1985b). Reasoning as imagination. *Interchange, 16,* 14–26.

PERKINS, D. N., ALLEN, R., & HAFNER, J. (1983). Difficulties in everyday reasoning. In W. Maxwell (Ed.), *Thinking: The expanding frontier* (pp. 177–189). Philadelphia: Franklin Institute.

PERKY, C. W. (1910). An experimental study of imagination. *American Journal of Psychology, 21,* 422–452.

PETERSON, L. R., & PETERSON, M. J. (1959). Short-term retention of individual items. *Journal of Experimental Psychology, 58,* 193–198.

PHAF, R. H., VAN DER HEIJEN, A. H. C., & HUDSON, P. T. W. (1990). SLAM: A connectionist model for attention in visual selection tasks. *Cognitive Psychology, 22,* 273–341.

PIAGET, J. (1965). *The child's conception of number.* New York: Norton.

PIAGET, J. (1968). *Six psychological studies.* (D. Elkind & A. Tenzer, Trans.; D. Elkind, Ed.). New York: Vintage Books. (Original work published 1964).

PIAGET, J. (1970/1988). Piaget's theory. In P. H. Mussen (Ed.), *Manual of child psychology,* (3rd ed., pp. 703–732). London: John Wiley and Sons. Reprinted (extract) in K. Richardson & S. Sheldon (Eds.), *Cognitive development to adolescence* (pp. 3–18). East Sussex: Erlbaum.

PIAGET, J. (1972). Intellectual evolution from adolescence to adulthood. *Human Development, 15,* 1–12.

PIAGET, J., & INHELDER, B. (1967). *The child's conception of space.* (F. J. Langdon & J. C. Lunzer, Trans.). (Originally published in 1948.) New York: Norton.

PILLEMER, D. (1984). Flashbulb memories of the assassination attempt on President Reagan. *Cognition, 16,* 63–80.

PILLEMER, D. (1990). Clarifying the flashbulb memory concept: Comment on McCloskey, Wible, & Cohen (1988). *Journal of Experimental Psychology: General, 119,* 92–96.

PINKER, S. (1980). Mental imagery and the third dimension. *Journal of Experimental Psychology: General, 109,* 354–371.

PINKER, S. (1984). Visual cognition: An introduction. *Cognition, 18,* 1–63.

PITZ, G. F., & SACHS, N. J. (1984). Judgment and decision: Theory and application. *Annual Review of Psychology, 35,* 139–163.

PLOUS, S. (1993). *The psychology of judgment and decision making.* New York: McGraw-Hill.

POMERANTZ, J. R., & KUBOVY, M. (1981). Perceptual organization: An overview. In M. Kubovy and J. R. Pomerantz (Eds.), *Perceptual organization* (pp. 423–456). Hillsdale, NJ: Erlbaum.

POORTINGA, Y. H., & MALPASS, R. S. (1986). Making inferences from cross-cultural data. In W. J. Lonner & J. W. Berry (Eds.), *Field methods in cross-cultural research* (pp. 17–46). Beverly Hills: Sage.

POSNER, M. I., BOIES, S. J., EICHELMAN, W. H., & TAYLOR, R. L. (1969). Retention of visual and name codes of single letters [Monograph]. *Journal of Experimental Psychology, 79,* 1–16.

POSNER, M. I., GOLDSMITH, R., & WELTON, K. E., JR. (1967). Perceived distance and the classification of distorted patterns. *Journal of Experimental Psychology, 73,* 28–38.

POSNER, M. I., & KEELE, S. W. (1968). On the genesis of abstract ideas. *Journal of Experimental Psychology, 77,* 353–363.

POSNER, M. I., & SNYDER, C. R. R. (1975). Attention and cognitive control. In R. L. Solso (Ed.), *Information processing and cognition: The Loyola Symposium* (pp. 55–85). Hillsdale, NJ: Erlbaum.

POSTMAN, L., & PHILLIPS, L. (1965). Short-term temporal changes in free recall. *Quarterly Journal of Experimental Psychology, 17,* 132–138.

POSTMAN, L., & STARK, K. (1969). Role of response availability in transfer and interference. *Journal of Experimental Psychology, 79,* 168–177.

PREMACK, D. (1976). *Language and intelligence in ape and man.* Hillsdale, NJ: Erlbaum.

PULLUM, G. K. (1991). *The great Eskimo vocabulary hoax and other irreverent essays on the study of language.* Chicago: University of Chicago Press.

PUTNAM, H. (1975). The meaning of 'meaning.' In H. Putnam (Ed.), *Philosophical papers: Vol. 2. Mind, language and reality* (pp. 215–271). New York: Cambridge University Press.

PYLYSHYN, Z. W. (1973). What the mind's eye tells the mind's brain: A critique of mental imagery. *Psychological Bulletin, 80,* 1–24.

PYLYSHYN, Z. W. (1979a). The rate of "mental rotation" of images: A test of a holistic analogue hypothesis. *Memory & Cognition, 7,* 19–28.

PYLYSHYN, Z. W. (1979b). Validating computational models: A critique of Anderson's indeterminancy of representation claim. *Psychological Review, 86,* 383–394.

PYLYSHYN, Z. W. (1981). The imagery debate: Analogue media versus tacit knowledge. *Psychological Review, 88,* 16–45.

RACHLIN, H. (1989). *Judgment, decision, and choice.* New York: W. H. Freeman.

RADFORD, A. (1988). *Transformational grammar.* Cambridge: Cambridge University Press.

REBER, A. S. (1967). Implicit learning of artificial grammars. *Journal of Verbal Learning and Verbal Behavior, 6,* 855–863.

REBER, A. S. (1969). Transfer of syntactic structure in synthetic languages. *Journal of Experimental Psychology, 81,* 115–119.

REBER, A. S. (1976). Implicit learning of synthetic languages: The role of instructional set. *Journal of Experimental Psychology: Human Learning and Memory, 2,* 88–94.

REBER, A. S. (1989). Implicit learning and tacit knowledge. *Journal of Experimental Psychology: General, 118,* 219–235.

REED, S. K. (1972). Pattern recognition and categorization. *Cognitive Psychology, 3,* 382–407.

REED, S. K., ERNST, G. W., & BANERJI, R. (1974). The role of analogy in transfer between similar problem states. *Cognitive Psychology, 6,* 436–450.

REIBER, R. W. (Ed.). (1980). *Wilhelm Wundt and the making of a scientific psychology.* New York: Plenum.

REICHER, G. M. (1969). Perceptual recognition as a function of meaningfulness of stimulus material. *Journal of Experimental Psychology, 81,* 275–280.

REISBERG, D., RAPPAPORT, I., & O'SHAUGHNESSY, M. (1984). Limits of working memory: The digit digit-span. *Journal of Experimental Psychology: Learning, Memory and Cognition, 10,* 203–221.

REITMAN, J. S. (1971). Mechanisms of forgetting in short-term memory. *Cognitive Psychology, 2,* 185–195.

REITMAN, J. S. (1974). Without surreptitious rehersal, information in short-term memory decays. *Journal of Verbal Learning and Verbal Behavior, 13,* 365–377.

REVLIS, R. (1975). Syllogistic reasoning: Logical decisions from a complex data base. In R. J. Falmagne (Ed.), *Reasoning: Representation and process* (pp. 93–133). Hillsdale, NJ: Erlbaum.

RICHARDSON, K., & SHELDON, S. (Eds.). (1988). *Cognitive development to adolescence.* East Sussex, UK: Erlbaum.

RIPS, L. J. (1975). Quantification and semantic memory. *Cognitive Psychology, 7,* 307–340.

RIPS, L. J. (1984). Reasoning as a central intellective ability. In R. J. Sternberg (Ed.), *Advances in the psychology of human intelligence* (Vol. 2, pp. 105–147). Hillsdale, NJ: Erlbaum.

RIPS, L. J. (1988). Deduction. In R. J. Sternberg & E. E. Smith (Eds.), *The psychology of human thought* (pp. 116–152). Cambridge: Cambridge University Press.

RIPS, L. J. (1989). The psychology of knights and knaves. *Cognition, 31,* 85–116.

RIPS, L. J. (1990). Reasoning. *Annual Review of Psychology, 41,* 321–353.

RIPS, L. J., SHOBEN, E. J., & SMITH, E. E. (1973). Semantic distance and the verification of semantic relations. *Journal of Verbal Learning and Verbal Behavior, 12,* 1–20.

RIVERS, W. H. R. (1905). Observations on the senses of the Todas. *British Journal of Psychology, 1,* 321–396.

ROBERTSON, L. C., & LAMB, M. R. (1991). Neuropsychological contributions to theories of part/whole organization. *Cognitive Psychology, 23,* 299–330.

ROCK, I. (1983). *The logic of perception.* Cambridge: MIT Press.

ROEDIGER, H. L., III. (1990). Implicit memory: Retention without remembering. *American Psychologist, 45,* 1043–1056.

ROGOFF, B. (1990). *Apprenticeship in thinking: Cognitive development in social context.* New York: Oxford University Press.

ROGOFF, B., & LAVE, J. (Eds.). (1984). *Everyday cognition: Its development in social context.* Cambridge: Harvard University Press.

ROHNER, R. (1984). Toward a conception of culture for cross-cultural psychology. *Journal of Cross-Cultural Psychology, 15,* 111–138.

ROLAND, P. E., & FRIBERG, L. (1985). Localization of cortical areas activated by thinking. *Journal of Neurophysiology, 53,* 1219–1243.

ROSCH, E. H. (1973). On the internal structure of perceptual and semantic categories. In T. E. Moore (Ed.), *Cognitive development and the acquisition of language* (pp. 111–144). New York: Academic Press.

ROSCH, E. (1975). Cognitive representations of semantic categories. *Journal of Experimental Psychology: General, 104,* 192–233.

ROSCH, E. (1978). Principles of categorization. In E. Rosch & B. B. Lloyd (Eds.), *Cognition and categorization* (pp. 27–48). Hillsdale, NJ: Erlbaum.

ROSCH, E. (1983). Prototype classification and logical classi-cation: The two systems. In E. K. Scholnick (Ed.), *New trends in conceptual representation: Challenges to Piaget's theory?* (pp. 73–86). Hillsdale, NJ: Erlbaum.

ROSCH, E., & LLOYD, B. B. (Eds.). (1978). Cognition and categorization. Hillsdale, NJ: Erlbaum.

ROSCH, E., & MERVIS, C. B. (1975). Family resemblances: Studies in the internal structure of categories. *Cognitive Psychology, 7,* 573–605.

ROSCH, E., MERVIS, C. B., GRAY, W. D., JOHNSON, D. M., & BOYES-BRAEM, P. (1976). Basic objects in natural categories. *Cognitive Psychology, 8,* 382–439.

ROSCH, E., SIMPSON, C., & MILLER, R. S. (1976). Structural bases of typicality effects. *Journal of Experimental Psychology: Human Perception and Performance, 2,* 491–502.

ROSE, S. A., & RUFF, H. A. (1987). Cross-modal abilities in human infants. In J. D. Osofsky (Ed.), *Handbook of infant development* (pp. 318–362). New York: Wiley.

ROSENTHAL, R., & ROSNOW, R. L. (1984). *Essentials of behavioral research: Methods and data analysis.* New York: McGraw-Hill.

ROSS, B. H., & LANDAUER, T. K. (1978). Memory for at least one of two items: Test and failure of several theories of spacing effects. *Journal of Verbal Learning and Verbal Behavior, 17,* 669–680.

ROSS, J., & LAWRENCE, K. A. (1968). Some observations on memory artifice. *Psychonomic Science, 13,* 107–108.

ROSS, M., & SICOLY, F. (1979). Egocentric biases in availability and attribution. *Journal of Personality and Social Psychology, 37,* 322–336.

ROTH, E. M., & SHOBEN, E. J. (1983). The effect of context on the structure of categories. *Cognitive Psychology, 15,* 346–378.

ROTH, J. D., & KOSSLYN, S. M. (1988). Construction of the third dimension in imagery. *Cognitive Psychology, 20,* 344–361.

RUMELHART, D. E. (1989). The architecture of mind: A connectionist approach. In M. I. Posner (Ed.), *Foundations of cognitive science* (pp. 133–159). Cambridge: Bradford Books.

RUMELHART, D. E., & MCCLELLAND, J. L. (1982). An interactive activation model of context effects in letter perception: Part 2. The contextual enhancement effect and some tests and extensions of the model. *Psychological Review, 89,* 60–94.

RUMELHART, D. E., & MCCLELLAND, J. L. (Eds.). (1986). *Parallel distributed processing: Vol. 1. Foundations.* Cambridge: MIT Press.

RUMELHART, D. E., & NORMAN, D. A. (1988). Representation in memory. In R. C. Atkinson (Ed.), *Stevens' handbook of experimental psychology: Vol. 2. Learning and cognition* (2nd ed., pp. 511–587). New York: Wiley.

RUMELHART, D. E., & ORTONY, A. (1977). The representation of knowledge in memory. In R. C. Anderson, R. J. Spiro, & W. E. Montague (Eds.), *Schooling and the acquisition of knowledge* (pp. 99–135). Hillsdale, NJ: Erlbaum.

SACHS, J. S. (1967). Recognition memory for syntactic and semantic aspects of connected discourse. *Perception & Psychophysics, 2,* 437–442.

SALTHOUSE, T. A., & BABCOCK, R. L. (1991). Decomposing adult age differences in working memory. *Developmental Psychology, 27,* 763–776.

SAMUEL, A. G. (1981). Phonemic restoration: Insights from a new methodology. *Journal of Experimental Psychology: General, 110,* 474–494.

SAVAGE-RUMBAUGH, S., MCDONALD, K., SEVCIK, R. A., HOPKINS, W. D., & RUBERT, E. (1986). Spontaneous symbol acquisition and communicative use by pygmy chimpanzees *(Pan paniscus). Journal of Experimental Psychology: General, 115,* 211–235.

SAXE, G. B. (1981). Body parts as numerals: A developmental analysis of numeration among the Oksapmin in Papua New Guinea. *Child Development, 52,* 306–316.

SAXE, G. B. (1992). Studying children's learning in context: Problems and prospects. *Journal of the Learning Sciences, 2,* 215–234.

SAXE, G. B., & POSNER, J. (1983). The development of numerical cognition: Cross-cultural perspectives. In H. P. Ginsburg (Ed.), *The development of mathematical thinking* (pp. 291–317). New York: Academic Press.

SCHACTER, D. L. (1987). Implicit memory: History and current status. *Journal of Experimental Psychology: Learning, Memory and Cognition, 13,* 501–518.

SCHACTER, D. L. (1989). On the relation between memory and consciousness: Dissociable interactions and conscious experience. In H. L. Roediger III & F. I. M. Craik (Eds.), *Varieties of memory and consciousness* (pp. 355–389). Hillsdale, NJ: Erlbaum.

SCHANK, R. C., & ABELSON, R. P. (1977). *Scripts, plans, goals, and understanding: An inquiry into human knowledge structures.* Hillsdale, NJ: Erlbaum.

SCHANK, R. C., COLLINS, G. C., & HUNTER, L. E. (1986). Transcending inductive category formation in learning. *Behavioral and Brain Sciences, 9,* 639–686.

SCHNEIDER, W., & FISK, A. D. (1982). Concurrent automatic and controlled visual search: Can processing occur without resource cost? *Journal of Experimental Psychology: Learning, Memory and Cognition, 8,* 261–278.

SCHNEIDER, W., & SHIFFRIN, R. M. (1977). Controlled and automatic human information processing: I. Detection, search, and attention. *Psychological Review, 84,* 1–66.

SCHWARTZ, S. H. (1971). Modes of representation and problem solving: Well evolved is half solved. *Journal of Experimental Psychology, 91,* 347–350.

SCHWARTZ, S. P. (1978). Putnam on artifacts. *Philosophical Review, 87,* 566–574.

SCHWARTZ, S. P. (1979). Natural kind terms. *Cognition, 7,* 301–319.

SCHWARTZ, S. P. (1980). Natural kinds and nominal kinds. *Mind, 89,* 182–195.

SCRIBNER, S. (1984). Studying working intelligence. In B. Rogoff & J. Lave (Eds.), *Everyday cognition: Its development in social context* (pp. 9–40). Cambridge: Harvard University Press.

SCRIBNER, S. (1986). Thinking in action: Some characteristics of practical thought. In R. J. Sternberg & R. K. Wagner (Eds.), *Practical intelligence: Nature and origins of competence in the everyday world* (pp. 13–30). Cambridge: Cambridge University Press.

SCRIBNER, S., & COLE, M. (1981). *The psychology of literacy.* Cambridge: Harvard University Press.

SEARLE, J. R. (1979). *Expression and meaning: Studies in the theory of speech acts.* Cambridge, England: Cambridge University Press.

SEGALL, M. H. (1979). *Cross-cultural psychology: Human behavior in global perspective.* Pacific Grove, CA: Brooks/Cole.

SEGALL, M. H. (1984). More than we need to know about culture but are afraid not to ask. *Journal of Cross-Cultural Psychology, 15,* 153–162.

SEGALL, M. H. (1986). Culture and behavior: Psychology in global perspective. *Annual Review of Psychology, 37,* 523–564.

SEGALL, M. H., CAMPBELL, D. T., & HERSKOVITS, M. J. (1966). *The influence of culture on visual perception.* Indianapolis: Bobbs-Merrill.

SELFRIDGE, O. G. (1959). Pandemonium: A paradigm for learning. In *Symposium on the mechanization of thought processes* (pp. 513–526). London: HM Stationery Office.

SHEPARD, R. N. (1966). Learning and recall as organization and search. *Journal of Verbal Learning and Verbal Behavior, 5,* 201–204.

SHEPARD, R. N. (1967). Recognition memory for words, sentences, and pictures. *Journal of Verbal Learning and Verbal Behavior, 6,* 156–163.

SHEPARD, R. N., & COOPER, L. A. (Eds.). (1982). *Mental images and their transformations.* Cambridge: MIT Press.

SHEPARD, R. N., & METZLER, J. (1971). Mental rotation of three-dimensional objects. *Science, 171,* 701–703.

SHIFFRIN, R. M. (1988). Attention. In R. C. Atkinson, R. J. Herrnstein, G. Lindzey, & R. D. Luce (Eds.), *Steven's handbook of experimental psychology: Vol. 2. Learning and cognition* (2nd ed., pp. 739–811). New York: Wiley.

SHIFFRIN, R. M., & SCHNEIDER, W. (1977). Controlled and automatic human information processing: II. Perceptual learning, automatic attending, and a general theory. *Psychological Review, 84,* 127–190.

SHIMURA, A. P. (1986). Priming effects in amnesia: Evidence for a dissociable memory function. *Quarterly Journal of Experimental Psychology, 38A,* 619–644.

SIEGEL, L. S., & HODKIN, B. (1982). The garden path to the understanding of cognitive development: Has Piaget led us into the poison ivy? In S. Modgil & C. Modgil (Eds.), *Jean Piaget: Consensus and controversy* (pp. 57–82). New York: Praeger.

SIEGLER, R. S. (Ed.). (1978). *Children's thinking: What develops?* Hillsdale, NJ: Erlbaum.

SIEGLER, R. S., & JENKINS, E. (1989). *How children discover new strategies.* Hillsdale, NJ: Erlbaum.

SIMON, H. A. (1956). Rational choice and the structure of the environment. *Psychological Review, 63,* 129–138.

SIMON, H. A. (1992). What is an "explanation" of behavior? *Psychological Science, 3,* 150–161.

SKINNER, B. F. (1984/1963). Behaviorism at fifty. *Behavioral and Brain Sciences, 7,* 615–667.

SKYRMS, B. (1975). *Choice and chance: An introduction to inductive logic* (2nd ed.). Encino, CA: Dickenson.

SLOVIC, P., LICHTENSTEIN, S., & FISCHHOFF, B. (1988). Decision making. In R. C. Atkinson, R. J. Herrnstein, G. Lindzey, & R. D. Luce (Eds.), *Steven's handbook of experimental psychology: Vol. 2. Learning and cognition* (2nd ed., pp. 673–738). New York: Wiley.

SMALL, M. Y. (1990). *Cognitive development.* San Diego, CA: Harcourt, Brace, Jovanovitch.

SMITH, E. E. (1990). Categorization. In D. N. Osherson & E. E. Smith (Eds.), *Thinking: An invitation to cognitive science* (Vol. 3, pp. 33–53). Cambridge: MIT Press.

SMITH, E. E., LANGSTON, C., & NISBETT, R. E. (1992). The case for rules in reasoning. *Cognitive Science, 16,* 1–40.

SMITH, E. E., & MEDIN, D. L. (1981). *Categories and concepts.* Cambridge: Harvard University Press.

SMITH, E. E., SHOBEN, E. J., & RIPS, L. J. (1974). Structure and process in semantic memory: A featural model for semantic decisions. *Psychological Review, 81,* 214–241.

SMITH, J. D., & KEMLER, D. G. (1984). Overall similarity in adults' classification: The child in all of us. *Journal of Experimental Psychology: General, 113,* 137–159.

SMITH, J. D., & SHAPIRO, J. H. (1989). The occurrence of holistic categorization. *Journal of Memory and Language, 28,* 386–399.

SMITH, S. M., & BLAKENSHIP, S. E. (1989). Incubation effects. *Bulletin of the Psychonomic Society, 27,* 311–314.

SMITH, S. M., & BLAKENSHIP, S. E. (1991). Incubation and the persistence of fixation in problem solving. *American Journal of Psychology, 104,* 61–87.

SMITH, S. M., BROWN, H. O., TOMAN, J. E. P., & GOODMAN, L. S. (1947). The lack of cerebral effects of d-Tubercurarine. *Anesthesiology, 8,* 1–14.

SMULLYAN, R. (1982). *Alice in puzzle-land.* New York: Penguin Books.

SOLSO, R. L. (1991). *Cognitive psychology* (3rd ed.). Boston: Allyn & Bacon.

SOLSO, R. L., & MCCARTHY, J. E. (1981). Prototype formation of faces: A case of pseudomemory. *British Journal of Psychology, 72,* 499–503.

SPELKE, E. (1976). Infants' intermodal perception of events. *Cognitive Psychology, 8,* 553–560.

SPELKE, E., HIRST, W., & NEISSER, U. (1976). Skills of divided attention. *Cognition, 4,* 215–230.

SPERLING, G. (1960). The information available in brief visual presentations. *Psychological Monographs, 74* (Whole number 498).

SQUIRE, L. R. (1989). On the course of forgetting in very long-term memory. *Journal of Experimental Psychology: Learning, Memory and Cognition, 15,* 241–245.

STEIN, B. S., & BRANSFORD, J. D. (1979). Constraints on effective elaboration: Effects of precision and subject generation. *Journal of Verbal Learning and Verbal Behavior, 18,* 769–777.

STERNBERG, R. J. (1977a). Component processes in analogical reasoning. *Psychological Review, 84,* 353–378.

STERNBERG, R. J. (1977b). *Intelligence, information-processing, and analogical reasoning: The componential analysis of human abilities.* Hillsdale, NJ: Erlbaum.

STERNBERG, R. J. (1983). Components of human intelligence. *Cognition, 15,* 1–48.

STERNBERG, R. J. (1984). Toward a triarchic theory of human intelligence. *Behavioral and Brain Sciences, 7,* 269–315.

STERNBERG, R. J. (1986a). *Intelligence applied: Understanding and increasing your intellectual skills.* San Diego: Harcourt Brace Jovanovich.

STERNBERG, R. J. (1986b). Toward a unified theory of human reasoning. *Intelligence, 10,* 281–314.

STERNBERG, R. J. (1988a). A three-facet model of creativity. In R. J. Sternberg (Ed.), *The nature of creativity: Contemporary psychological perspectives* (pp. 125–147). Cambridge: Cambridge University Press.

STERNBERG, R. J. (Ed.). (1988b). *The nature of creativity: Contemporary psychological perspectives.* Cambridge: Cambridge University Press.

STERNBERG, R. J., & DETTERMAN, D. K. (Eds.). (1986). *What is intelligence? Contemporary viewpoints on its nature and definition.* Norwood, NJ: Ablex.

STERNBERG, R. J., & GARDNER, M. K. (1983). Unities in inductive reasoning. *Journal of Experimental Psychology: General, 112,* 80–116.

STERNBERG, R. J., & LUBART, T. I. (1991). An investment theory of creativity and its development. *Human Development, 34,* 1–31.

STERNBERG, R. J., & SMITH, E. E. (Eds.). (1988). *The psychology of human thought.* Cambridge: Cambridge University Press.

STERNBERG, R. J., & TURNER, M. E. (1981). Components of syllogistic reasoning. *Acta Psychologica, 47,* 245–265.

STERNBERG, R. J., & WAGNER, R. K. (Eds.). (1986). *Practical intelligence: Nature and origins of competence in the everyday world.* Cambridge: Cambridge University Press.

STERNBERG, S. (1966). High-speed scanning in human memory. *Science, 153,* 652–654.

STERNBERG, S. (1969). Memory-scanning: Mental processes revealed by reaction-time experiments. *American Scientist, 57,* 421–457.

STEVENSON, H. W., LEE, S., CHEN, C., LUMMIS, M., STIGLER, J., FAN, L., & GE, F. (1990). Mathematics achievement of children in China and the United States. *Child Development, 61,* 1053–1066.

STROOP, J. R. (1935). Studies of interferences in serial verbal reactions. *Journal of Experimental Psychology, 18,* 643–662.

STRUTT, G. F., ANDERSON, D. R., & WELL, A. D. (1975). A developmental study of the effects or irrelevant information on speeded classification. *Journal of Experimental Child Psychology, 20,* 127–135.

SUPPES, P. (1957). *Introduction to logic.* Princeton: Van Nostrand.

SWINNEY, D. A. (1979). Lexical access during sentence comprehension: (Re)consideration of context effects. *Journal of Verbal Learning and Verbal Behavior, 18,* 645–659.

TAKANO, Y. (1989). Methodological problems in cross-cultural studies of linguistic relativity. *Cognition, 31,* 141–162.

TANAKA, J. W., & TAYLOR, M. (1991). Object categories and expertise: Is the basic level in the eye of the beholder? *Cognitive Psychology, 23,* 457–482.

TAVRIS, C., & WADE, C. (1984). *The longest war: Sex differences in perspective* (2nd ed.). San Diego: Harcourt Brace Jovanovich.

TERRACE, H. S. (1979). *Nim.* New York: Knopf.

THALER, R. H. (1980). Toward a positive theory of consumer choice. *Journal of Economic Behavior and Organization, 1,* 39–60.

THOMPSON, R. F., DONEGAN, N. H., & LAVOND, D. G. (1988). The psychobiology of learning and memory. In R. C. Atkinson (Ed.), *Stevens' handbook of experimental psychology: Vol. 2. Learning and cognition* (2nd ed., pp. 245–347). New York: Wiley.

THOMSON, D. M., & TULVING, E. (1970). Associative encoding and retrieval: Weak and strong cues. *Journal of Experimental Psychology, 86,* 255–262.

THORNDYKE, P. W. (1977). Cognitive structures in comprehension and memory of narrative discourse. *Cognitive Psychology, 9,* 77–110.

TIPPETT, L. J. (1992). The generation of visual images: A review of neuropsychological research and theory. *Psychological Bulletin, 112,* 415–432.

TOLMAN, E. C. (1932). *Purposive behavior in animals and men.* New York: Century.

TREISMAN, A. M. (1960). Contextual cues in selective listening. *Quarterly Journal of Experimental Psychology, 12,* 242–248.

TREISMAN, A. M. (1964). Verbal cues, language, and meaning in selective attention. *American Journal of Psychology, 77,* 206–219.

TREISMAN, A. M. (1986). Features and objects in visual processing. *Scientific American, 255* (5), 114B–125.

TREISMAN, A. M., & GELADE, G. (1980). A feature-integration theory of attention. *Cognitive Psychology, 12,* 97–136.

TREISMAN, A. M., & SCHMIDT, H. (1982). Illusory conjunctions in the perception of objects. *Cognitive Psychology, 14,* 107–141.

TRIANDIS, H. C., & LONNER, W. (Eds.). (1980). *Handbook of cross-cultural psychology* (4 vols.). Boston: Allyn & Bacon.

TSAL, Y. (1989a). Do illusory conjunctions support the feature integration theory? A critical review of theory and findings. *Journal of Experimental Psychology: Human Perception and Performance, 15,* 394–400.

TSAL, Y. (1989b). Further comments on feature integration: A reply to Briand and Klein. *Journal of Experimental Psychology: Human Perception and Performance, 15,* 407–410.

TULVING, E. (1972). Episodic and semantic memory. In E. Tulving and W. Donaldson (Eds.), *Organization of memory* (pp. 381–403). New York: Academic Press.

TULVING, E. (1983). *Elements of episodic memory.* New York: Oxford University Press.

TULVING, E. (1984). Précis of *Elements of Episodic Memory* (and following commentaries). *Behavioral and Brain Sciences, 7,* 223–268.

TULVING, E. (1986). What kind of a hypothesis is the distinction between episodic and semantic memory? *Journal of Experimental Psychology: Learning, Memory, and Cognition, 12,* 307–311.

TULVING, E., & DONALDSON, W. (Eds.). (1972). *Organization of Memory.* New York: Academic Press.

TULVING, E., & THOMSON, D. M. (1973). Encoding specificity and retrieval processes in episodic memory. *Psychological Review, 80,* 352–373.

TURING, A. M. (1936). On computable numbers, with an application to the Entscheidungsproblem. *Proceedings of the London Mathematical Society* (Series 2), *42,* 230–265.

TURVEY, M. T., SHAW, R. E., REED, E. S., & MACE, W. M. (1981). Ecological laws of perceiving and acting: In reply to Fodor and Pylyshyn (1981). *Cognition, 9,* 237–304.

TVERSKY, A. (1972). Elimination by aspects: A theory of choice. *Psychological Review, 79,* 281–299.

TVERSKY, A., & KAHNEMAN, D. (1971). Belief in the law of small numbers. *Psychological Bulletin, 2,* 105–110.

TVERSKY, A., & KAHNEMAN, D. (1973). Availability: A heuristic for judging frequency and probability. *Cognitive Psychology, 4,* 207–232.

TVERSKY, A., & KAHNEMAN, D. (1981). The framing of decisions and the psychology of choice. *Science, 211,* 453–458.

TYLER, L. E. (1974). *Individual differences: Abilities and motivational directions.* Englewood Cliffs, NJ: Prentice Hall.

VON WINTERFELDT, D., & EDWARDS, W. (1986a). *Decision analysis and behavioral research.* Cambridge: Cambridge University Press.

VON WINTERFELDT, D., & EDWARDS, W. (1986b). On cognitive illusions and their implications. In H. R. Arkes & K. R. Hammond (Eds.), *Judgment and decision making: An interdisciplinary reader* (pp. 642–679). Cambridge: Cambridge University Press.

VOSNIADOU, S., & ORTONY, A. (Eds.). (1989). *Similarity and analogical reasoning.* Cambridge: Cambridge University Press.

VYGOTSKY, L. S. (1986). *Thought and language* (A. Kozulin, Trans.). Cambridge: MIT Press.

WARD, T. B. (1990). Further comments on the attribute availability hypothesis of children's category learning. *Child Development, 61,* 611–613.

WARD, T. B., & SCOTT, J. (1987). Analytic and holistic modes of learning family-resemblance concepts. *Memory & Cognition, 15,* 42–54.

WARD, T. B., VELA, E., & HASS, S. D. (1990). Children and adults learn family-resemblance categories analytically. *Child Development, 61,* 593–605.

WARREN, R. M. (1970). Perceptual restoration of missing speech sounds. *Science, 167,* 392–393.

WARREN, R. M., & OBUSEK, C. J. (1971). Speech perception and phonemic restorations. *Perception and Psychophysics, 9,* 358–362.

WARREN, R. M., & WARREN, R. P. (1970). Auditory illusions and confusions. *Scientific American, 223,* 30–36.

WARRINGTON, E. K., & WEISKRANTZ, L. (1968). New method of testing long-term retention with special reference to amnesic patients. *Nature, 217,* 972–974.

WARRINGTON, E. K., & WEISKRANTZ, L. (1970). Amnesic syndrome: Consolidation or retrieval? *Nature, 228,* 628–630.

WARRINGTON, E. K., & WEISKRANTZ, L. (1982). Amnesia: A disconnection syndrome? *Neuropsychologia, 20,* 233–248.

WASON, P. C. (1960). On the failure to eliminate hypotheses in a conceptual task. *Quarterly Journal of Experimental Psychology, 12,* 129–140.

WASON, P. C. (1968). Reasoning about a rule. *Quarterly Journal of Experimental Psychology, 20,* 273–281.

WASON, P. C. (1969). Regression in reasoning? *British Journal of Psychology, 60,* 471–480.

WASON, P. C. (1977). 'On the failure to eliminate hypotheses . . .'—a second look. In P. N. Johnson-Laird and P. C. Wason (Eds.), *Thinking: Readings in cognitive science* (pp. 307–314). Cambridge: Cambridge University Press.

WASON, P. C. (1983). Realism and rationality in the selection task. In J. St. B. T. Evans (Ed.), *Thinking and reasoning: Psychological approaches* (pp. 44–75). Boston: Routledge & Kegal Paul.

WASON, P. C., & JOHNSON-LAIRD, P. N. (1970). A conflict between selecting and evaluating information in an inferential task. *British Journal of Psychology, 61,* 509–515.

WASON, P. C., & JOHNSON-LAIRD, P. N. (1972). *Psychology of reasoning: Structure and content.* Cambridge: Harvard University Press.

WATKINS, O. C., & WATKINS, M. J. (1980). The modality effect and visual persistence. *Journal of Experimental Psychology: General, 109,* 251–278.

WATSON, J. (1930). *Behaviorism.* New York: Norton.

WATSON, J. B. (1913). Psychology as the behaviorist views it. *Psychological Review, 20,* 158–177.

WAUGH, N. C., & NORMAN, D. A. (1965). Primary memory. *Psychological Review, 72,* 89–104.

WEISBERG, R. W. (1988). Problem solving and creativity. In R. J. Sternberg (Ed.), *The nature of creativity* (pp. 148 –176). Cambridge: Cambridge University Press.

WERTHEIMER, M. (1945). *Productive thinking.* New York: Harper & Brothers.

WHORF, B. L. (1956). *Language, thought, and reality.* Cambridge: MIT Press.

WICKENS, C. D. (1987). Attention. In P. A. Hancock (Ed.), *Human factors psychology* (pp. 29–80). Amsterdam: North Holland.

WICKENS, D. D., BORN, D. G., & ALLEN, C. K. (1963). Proactive inhibition and item similarity in short-term memory. *Journal of Verbal Learning and Verbal Behavior, 2,* 440–445.

WILENSKY, R. (1983). Story grammars versus story points. *Behavioral and Brain Sciences, 6,* 579–623.

WILLIAMS, J. H. (1983). *Psychology of women: Behavior in a biosocial context* (2nd ed.). New York: Norton.

WITKIN, H. A., DYK, R. B., FATERSON, H. F., GOOD ENOUGH, D. R., & KARP, S. A. (1962). *Psychological differentiation: Studies of development.* New York: Wiley.

WITKIN, H. A., & GOODENOUGH, D. R. (1981). *Cognitive styles: Essence and origins.* New York: International Universities Press.

WITTGENSTEIN, L. (1953). *Philosophical investigations.* New York: Macmillan.

WOBER, M. (1969). Distinguishing centri-cultural from cross-cultural tests and research. *Perceptual and Motor Skills, 28,* 488.

WOODWARD, E. L. (1938). *Age of reform.* London: Oxford University Press.

WOODWORTH, R. S., & SELLS, S. B. (1935). An atmosphere effect in formal syllogistic reasoning. *Journal of Experimental Psychology, 18,* 451–460.

WOODY, C. D. (1986). Understanding the cellular basis of memory and learning. *Annual Review of Psychology, 37,* 433–493.

YANIV, I., & MEYER, D. E. (1987). Activation and metacognition of inaccessible stored information: Potential bases for incubation effects in problem solving. *Journal of Experimental Psychology: Learning, Memory, and Cognition, 13,* 187–205.

YATES, F. A. (1966). *The art of memory.* London: Routledge & Kegan Paul.

YUILLE, J. C. (Ed.). (1983). *Imagery, memory and cognition.* Hillsdale, NJ: Erlbaum.

ZELNICKER, T. (1989). Cognitive style and dimensions of information processing. In T. Globerson & T. Zelnicker (Eds.), *Human Development: Vol. 3. Cognitive style and cognitive development* (pp. 172–191). Norwood, NJ: Ablex.

NAME INDEX

SUBJECT INDEX

Accommodation of mental structures, 374–375
ACT* model, 156–157
Adaptation of mental structures, 373, 374
Affordance, 64–65
Ambiguity
  lexical, 246–247
  syntactic, 246–247
Amnesia, 100, 157–160, 162
Analytic processing of information, 400–401
Animism, 381–382
Artifacts
  as a kind of concept, 189, 395, 453
  in experiments, 264
Artificial intelligence, 17, 67, 227, 255
Assimilation of mental structures, 374–375
Association, 7, 221
Attention, 3, 67, 71–97, 230, 399–400, 416
  divided, 90–95, 417
  selective, 74–83
Attenuation theory, 77–79
Automatic encoding, 127
Automaticity. *See* Automatic processing
Automatic processing, 73, 83–89, 93, 160
Availability heuristic, 343–346, 366

Backtracking, 278–279
Basic level (of concepts), 171–172
Bayes's theorem, 341
Behaviorism, 9–11, 12, 16, 19, 29, 30, 196

Believability effect, 321–322, 333
Between-subjects design, 21
Bias, 322, 342, 355, 363, 366
Bottom-up processes, 37, 38, 49, 51, 56, 67
Brown-Peterson task, 107–108, 110

Calibration curve, 354–355
Capacity, 23–24, 371–372, 393, 398, 405–406, 410
  attentional, 80, 81, 83
  of memory systems, 106, 115, 123
Capacity theory, 81–82
Categorization, 36, 120, 165–192, 199, 237, 311, 382, 394, 405, 416–417, 444, 454–457
Category, 166, 395
Category size effect, 151, 154, 156
Characteristic feature, 152–154, 170
Chunking, 106–107, 124, 417
Circular reaction, 377
Classical view of concepts, 167–169, 186, 190, 191
Classification. *See* Categorization
Closure, Gestalt principle of, 60
Cocktail party effect, 75–76
Coding, 107, 114, 115, 122, 124, 199–200, 219, 221
Cognitive architecture, 157
Cognitive economy, principle of, 145, 149, 156, 190
Cognitive illusions, 342–355, 366
Cognitive neuropsychology, 18, 19, 26, 30, 67, 135

Photo Credits

Chapter 1: 4, Nancy J. Ashmore; **28**, Nancy J. Ashmore; **Chapter 2: 50**, Nancy J. Ashmore; **51**, Nancy J. Ashmore; **53**, Courtesy of Dominique Davis, American Kennel Club GAZETTE; **Chapter 3: 73**, Elvis Upitis/The Image Bank; **84**, Nancy J. Ashmore; **Chapter 4: 116**, St. Olaf College; **131**, Elizabeth Loftus; **Chapter 5: 146**, Nancy J. Ashmore; **Chapter 7: 205**, Courtesy Spectrum Holobyte, photo by Nancy J. Ashmore; **217**, Nancy J. Ashmore; **Chapter 8: 228**, Richard Wrangham/Anthro-Photo; **249**, Nancy J. Ashmore; **257**, Nancy J. Ashmore; **Chapter 9: 273**, Jami Anson, U.S. Chess Federation, New Windsor, NY; **293**, Nancy J. Ashmore; **Chapter 11: 338**, Nancy J. Ashmore; **348**, R. Campoluongo/The Image Bank; **Chapter 12: 374**, Nancy J. Ashmore; **381**, Nancy J. Ashmore; **383**, Nancy J. Ashmore; **402**, Nancy J. Ashmore; **Chapter 13: 424**, Nancy J. Ashmore; **427**, Nancy J. Ashmore; **431**, Nancy J. Ashmore; **436**, Elizabeth Crews; **Chapter 14: 447**, top: © Myrleen Ferguson/PhotoEdit; **447**, bottom: Reuters/Bettman; **454**, Nancy J. Ashmore; **467**, Lou Jones/ The Image Bank; **476**, Nancy J. Ashmore.

TO THE OWNER OF THIS BOOK:

We hope that you have found *Cognitive Psychology In and Out of the Laboratory* useful. So that this book can be improved in a future edition, would you take the time to complete this sheet and return it? Thank you.

School and address: _____

Department: _____

Instructor's name: _____

_____

1. What I like most about this book is: _____

_____

2. What I like least about this book is: _____

_____

_____

3. My general reaction to this book is: _____

_____

4. The name of the course in which I used this book is: _____

_____

5. Were all of the chapters of the book assigned for you to read? _____

   If not, which ones weren't? _____

6. In the space below, or on a separate sheet of paper, please write specific suggestions for improving this book and anything else you'd care to share about your experience in using the book.

_____

_____

_____

_____

_____

_____

_____

Optional:

Your name: ___*Piya*___ Date: ___*12/11/97*___

May Brooks/Cole quote you, either in promotion for *Cognitive Psychology In and Out of the Laboratory*, or in future publishing ventures?

Yes: ___✓___ No: _____

Sincerely,

Kathleen M. Galotti

FOLD HERE

||||||

BUSINESS REPLY MAIL

FIRST CLASS   PERMIT NO. 358   PACIFIC GROVE, CA

POSTAGE WILL BE PAID BY ADDRESSEE

ATT: ___*Kathleen M. Galotti*___

Brooks/Cole Publishing Company
511 Forest Lodge Road
Pacific Grove, California 93950-9968

FOLD HERE